ALCOHOLISM AND SUBSTANCE ABUSE

Strategies for Clinical Intervention

Thomas E. Bratter
Gary G. Forrest

THE FREE PRESS
A Division of Macmillan, Inc.
NEW YORK

Collier Macmillan Publishers
LONDON

The Free Press
A Division of Macmillan, Inc.
866 Third Avenue, New York, N. Y. 10022

Collier Macmillan Canada, Inc.

Printed in the United States of America

printing number

6 7 8 9 10

Library of Congress Cataloging in Publication Data

Main entry under title:

Alcoholism and substance abuse.

Includes index.
1. Alcoholism. 2. Substance abuse. I. Bratter, Thomas Edward. II. Forrest, Gary G.
RC565.A44554 1985 616.86'1 84–24725
ISBN 0–02–904260–7

To Carole and Sandy

Ch.
2, 4, 5
7, 9, 10

Contents

About the Contributors

Helen M. Annis, Ph.D., C. Psych.
Head of Health Care Systems Research
Addiction Research Foundation Clinical Institute
Associate Professor of Health Administration
Faculty of Medicine
University of Toronto
Toronto, Canada

Sheila B. Blume, M.D.
Medical Director
National Council on Alcoholism
New York, N.Y.

Thomas Edward Bratter, Ed.D.
Founder–President
The John Dewey Academy
Great Barrington, Mass.
Independent Practice of Psychotherapy
Scarsdale, N.Y.

Milton Earl Burgess, M.D., M.P.H., M.Div., M.S.
Consulting Psychiatrist
North Charles Institute for the Addictions
Instructor in Psychiatry
Department of Psychiatry
Harvard Medical School
Boston, Mass.

Ernest A. Collabolletta, Psy.D. (cand.)
Faculty
Scarsdale High School
Scarsdale, N.Y.

Gary G. Forrest, Ed.D., Ph.D.
Executive Director
Psychotherapy Associates, P.C.
and
The Institute for Addictive Behavioral Change
Colorado Springs, Colo.

Allen J. Fossbender, Ed.D.
State Director
Guidance and Counseling Services
Department of Education
State of Connecticut
Hartford, Conn.

Herbert J. Freudenberger, Ph.D., P.C.
Psychologist–Psychoanalyst
Independent Practice
New York, N.Y.

DeAnne C. Gauya, M.A. (cand.)
Teachers College
Columbia University
New York, N.Y.

Frederick B. Glaser, M.D., F.R.C.P.(C)
Head of Psychiatry
Addiction Research Foundation
Clinical Institute
Professor of Psychiatry
Faculty of Medicine
University of Toronto
Toronto, Canada

Florence Kaslow, Ph.D.
Kaslow Associates
West Palm Beach, Fla.

Janice Kay Kaufman, R.N., M.P.H.
Director
North Charles Institute for the Addictions
Lecturer on Psychiatry
Department of Psychiatry
Harvard Medical School
Boston, Mass.

Edward Kaufman, M.D.
Director of Residency Training, Medical Student Education and Family Therapy Section
Department of Psychiatry and Human Behavior
University of California, Irvine Medical Center
Editor-in-Chief
American Journal of Drug and Alcohol Abuse
Irvine, Calif.

Robert C. Kolodny, M.D.
Medical Director
Behavioral Medicine Institute
New Canaan, Conn.

Gillian Leigh, Ph.D.
Scientist
Health Care Development Research
Addiction Research Foundation
Clinical Institute
Toronto, Canada

Ernest Matuschka, Ph.D.
Professor
Department of Psychology
Kearney State College
Kearney, Neb.

Paul R. Matuschka, R. ph., Pharm. D.
Clinical Pharmacist
Jewish Hospital
Louisville, Ky.

Robert A. Mines, Ph.D.
Assistant Professor
Department of Counseling Psychologist
University of Denver
Denver, Colo.

Thomas C. Mountz, Psy.D.
Clinical Psychologist
United States Navy
Virginia Beach, Va.

Alan C. Ogborne, Ph.D., C. Psych.
Senior Scientist
Community Programs Evaluation Centre
Addiction Research Foundation
Associate Professor of Psychology
Faculty of Letters and Science
University of Western Ontario
Ontario, Canada

Shelly Pearlman, Ph.D.
Associate Director
Addiction Research Foundation Clinical Institute
Assistant Professor of Social Work
Faculty of Social Work
University of Toronto
Toronto, Canada

Matthew A. Pennacchia, B.A.
Director
Westchester Outreach Center
Daytop Village, Inc.,
Hartsdale, N.Y.

Arnold W. Rachman, Ph.D., F.A.G.P.
Independent Practice of Psychoanalysis
Faculty and Group Training Analyst
Postgraduate Center for Mental Health
New York, N.Y.

Richard R. Raubolt, Ph.D.
Psychology Associates, P.C.
Adjunct Faculty
Aquinas College
Grand Rapids, Mich.

John R. Rubel, Psy.D.
Staff Psychologist
Federal Bureau of Prisons
Federal Correctional Institute
El Reno, Okla.

Ruth L. Segal, Ph.D. [deceased]
[Late] *Head, Pharmacy Department and Discipline*
Addiction Research Foundation Clinical Institute
Assistant Professor of Pharmacy
University of Toronto
Toronto, Canada

Howard Shaffer, Ph.D.
Chief Psychologist
North Charles Institute for the Addictions
Assistant Professor
Department of Psychiatry
Harvard Medical School
Boston, Mass.

Barry V. Sisson, M.D.
Head of Medical Screening Programme
Addiction Research Foundation Clinical Institute
Lecturer, Family and Community Medicine
Faculty of Medicine
University of Toronto
Toronto, Canada

Harvey A. Skinner, Ph.D.
Senior Scientist, Head Care Systems Research
Addiction Research Foundation Clinical Institute
Associate Professor of Preventive Medicine and Biostatistics
Faculty of Medicine
University of Toronto
Toronto, Canada

M. Duncan Stanton, Ph.D.
Director of the Division of Family Programs
Professor
Department of Psychiatry
University of Rochester School of Medicine
Rochester, N.Y.

J. Kelly Yost, M.Ed., Ph.D. (cand.)
Institute for Family and Personal Development
Colorado Springs, Colo.

Introduction

Substance abuse and alcoholism cause major health and social problems throughout the world. Many behavioral scientists believe that alcohol addiction is the number one health problem facing America. There are several million addicts in this country. Millions of Americans are also consistent abusers of alcohol and various other addictive chemicals. Substance abusers and addicts have an impact on all of our lives in many ways. Thousands of addicts die each year as a direct result of their addictions. Each year drunk drivers kill thousands of innocent victims on our highways. Substance abuse and alcoholism destroy millions of families. Addiction and drug abuse cost industry and the American collective billions of dollars each year. Suicide and divorce, as well as homicide, rape, child abuse, and a diversity of other criminal behaviors, are associated with substance abuse and alcoholism. Indeed, for over two decades addictive substances have consistently resulted in the emotional and physical destruction of hundreds of thousands of Americans.

This book is written for behavioral scientists and clinicians who work with substance abusers and alcoholics. The first section presents several etiological factors in the development of substance abuse and alcoholism. The second part addresses the issue of clinical assessment of the substance abuser and alcoholic. This section also includes treatment outcome assessment techniques, medical-biological aspects of addictive substances, and an evaluation of Alcoholics Anonymous. Part Three offers an in-depth exploration of various treatment modalities. Strategies of individual, group, family, self-help, somatic, and systems treatment are included in this section. The final section is devoted to special clinical issues: ethical and legal considerations in the treatment of alcoholics and substance abusers, sexual problems of substance abusers, and alcoholism and psychotropic medications.

Clinicians and therapists will find this book to be very helpful in their efforts to treat and do research on substance abusers and alcoholics. The contributors to this book are preeminent therapists and researchers within the addictions field. Each chapter includes data and clinical perspectives that are filled with information, and are creative and pragmatic: Most importantly, this book is useful to the psychotherapist in his or her direct clinical work with alcoholics and substance abusers. Thus, physicians and psychiatrists, psychologists, social workers, alcoholism and substance abuse counselors, vocational rehabilitation counselors, school guidance personnel, educators in the health science professions, family and marriage therapists, nurses, and behavioral science researchers will find this text beneficial in their professional work.

The overall depth and scope of the treatment-oriented material presented in this book will prove interesting and heuristic for clinicians who have spent several years treating alcoholics and substance abusers. Indeed, this book presents a basic, as well as advanced, understanding of the most important clinical issues in the field.

Many people have contributed directly or indirectly to the completion of this book. First of all, we must thank our wives and families for their support and patience throughout the difficult process of finalizing hundreds of pages of manuscript. Without the efforts of each author, this text would not have become a reality. Finally, we want to thank the hundreds of clients we have worked with in psychotherapy over the past fifteen years. They have taught us what we think we know!

Thomas E. Bratter
Gary G. Forrest

Part One

ETIOLOGICAL FACTORS IN THE DEVELOPMENT OF SUBSTANCE ABUSE AND ALCOHOLISM

THE INITIAL CHAPTER in this part (Chapter 1) explores the various psychosocial factors in the etiology of substance abuse. Gillian Leigh indicates that several broad categories of psychosocial factors influence a person's decisions to drink alcohol or take drugs. This chapter considers only those psychosocial factors which have been found through research to be associated with both the development and maintenance of drug and alcohol use.

Paul Matuschka explores the psychopharmacology of addiction in the second chapter of this part. After defining drug use, drug abuse, and addiction, the chapter examines the acute and long-term effects, the pharmacology (chemistry, action, and uses), and the pharmacokinetics of alcohol, sedative-hypnotics, opiates, minor tranquilizers, and marijuana.

The final chapter in this unit (Chapter 3) elucidates the various relationships between stress, stressors, and alcoholism. J. Kelley Yost and Robert A. Mines define stress and explore the effects of stress on humans. These authors also delineate a number of cognitive-behavioral strategies of stress-reduction for alcoholics—an area that has not received adequate research attention.

1

Psychosocial Factors in the Etiology of Substance Abuse

Gillian Leigh

Many factors influence the decision to drink alcohol or take drugs. These range from the availability of the product and the means to buy it to the more complex issues of family, social, and personality interactions. At present no single theory or model can adequately account for either the development or the maintenance of this problem.

Psychosocial factors may be grouped into the categories of cultural, environmental, interpersonal, and intrapersonal influences. All these influences will affect the person's decision to drink or ingest drugs at some point during the process of initiation to the substance or its later continuation of use. To these factors must be added those biological influences of genetic, biochemical, and physiological differences between people which affect the predisposition to take the substance.

In order to set out the various influences affecting drug and alcohol consumption in a more systematic way, Figure 1–1 shows the different categories which have been associated with drug use. Within each category are to be found factors which are most closely related to that particular category, although this does not mean that these factors will not also affect other areas of life functioning. For example, affect, which is included in this figure as an intrapersonal factor, most likely will have an effect on interpersonal relationships and be deter-

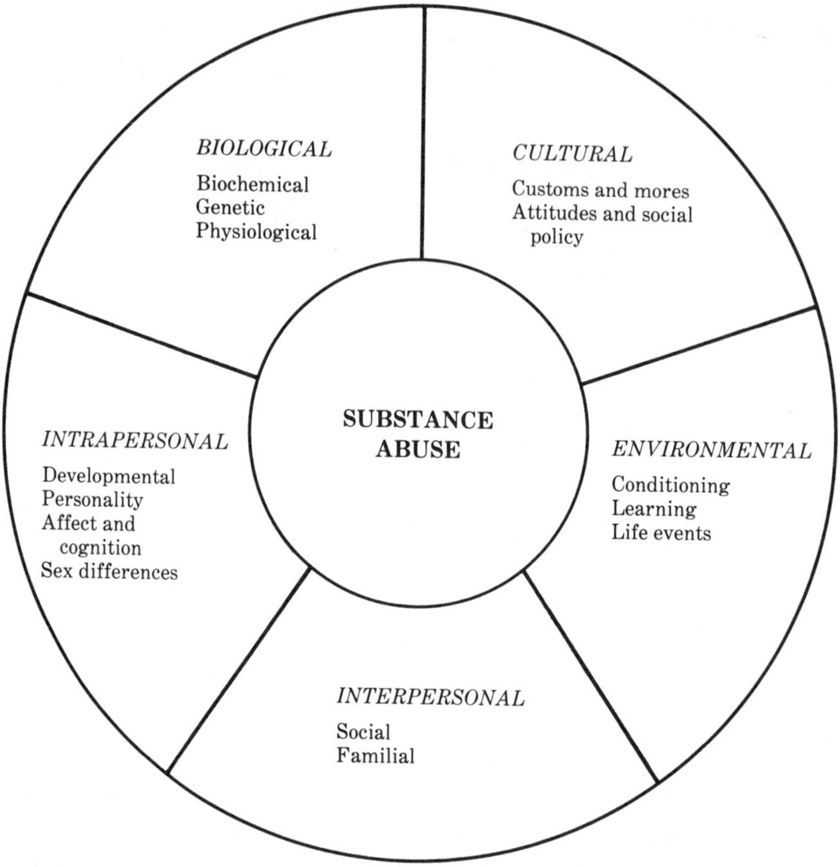

BIOLOGICAL
Biochemical
Genetic
Physiological

CULTURAL
Customs and mores
Attitudes and social policy

SUBSTANCE ABUSE

INTRAPERSONAL
Developmental
Personality
Affect and cognition
Sex differences

ENVIRONMENTAL
Conditioning
Learning
Life events

INTERPERSONAL
Social
Familial

Figure 1–1. Categorized factors influencing substance abuse.

mined by the person's physiological constitution. However, the intrapersonal domain seems the most appropriate category for consideration of affect in the present text, since it will be discussed mainly in relation to tension reduction and the mood-altering properties of drugs.

These categories may also be thought of as varying in scope and influence at certain stages of drug use. For example, cultural factors—which include the customs and mores of a society in relation to drug use, as well as the policies and sanctions associated with certain drugs—shape in a general way the amount and frequency of use. In contrast, intrapersonal factors are more likely to determine the specific choice and use of a drug by an individual responding to particular life events and stresses. Broader factors are likely to operate through *predisposing* a person toward use of a particular substance, while the more specific, or narrower, factors may precipitate actual use, or work toward maintaining heavier use after initiation.

One of the categories set out in Figure 1–1 is biological influence, which includes genetic, biochemical, and physiological factors. While it is recognized that these factors at times may play a reasonably important part in predisposition toward substance abuse, they are considered outside of this present chapter. This chapter considers only those psychosocial factors which have been found, through research, to be associated with both the development and maintenance of drug and alcohol use.

Factors may be combined into models, which are then used to test particular theories. However, theories may derive from very different conceptual standpoints while using similar factors. For example, peer pressure may be agreed upon as an important factor within a learning theory framework and also by those who propose a psychodynamic theory. At the same time the different proponents will disagree over the theoretical basis of its origin and influence in developing drug use. It seems, therefore, most appropriate to give the reader factual information, together with an outline of the possibilities for incorporating some of these findings into an approach to treatment.

Cultural Factors

Customs and Mores

Studies of various cultures have illustrated how certain drugs, especially alcohol, have been integrated into the traditional practices of a society so that eventually the drugs become part of larger patterns of social behavior. Each society reflects its own attitudes and feelings about the use of particular substances within its culture. One of the earliest examples of this specificity was shown in a study conducted by Ruth Bunzel in 1940. Bunzel showed how two societies within a single cultural area reflected a very different attitude concerning alcohol, which determined how the alcohol would be used within each society. One society used alcohol as a way of dealing with anxieties arising from pressures engendered by surrounding cultures. In the other society drinking performed the function of lubricating social relations, to the extent that dialogue with another person was not initiated until a drink was shared. Similar examples of alcohol use by specific societies have been reported for the Bolivian Camba (Heath, 1958), the Peruvian Quechua (Mangin, 1957), and the Society Islanders of Oceania (Lemert, 1964).

For American Indians, drinking patterns are affected by tribal membership. Public drinking as a group is encouraged by Navaho Indians, and the deviant drinker is one who drinks alone and will not share his liquor. Navahos keep group control by allowing a drinking member to retain his community supports until he is able to stop drinking (Kunitz and Levy, 1974). Drinking style is in the form of group "binges," separated by months of sobriety. For the Hopi Indians, in comparison, drinking is more likely to be a solitary affair, and an individual may drink steadily and alone for a long period. If this practice becomes disruptive for the village, the drinker is driven out and forced to move to an area which is relatively free from surveillance where drinking can continue unimpeded. American Indian university students with a history of familial alcoholism, describe their drinking practices in terms of an attempt to deal with the dilemma of conforming to a dominant white society while retaining their own cultural identity. This may be a potent predisposing force to excessive drinking for the American Indian who has left his own culture (Jones-Saumty et al. 1983).

Societies that have incorporated drinking into the social behavior of the group for religious ceremonies and rituals (Galanter, 1983) and for social gatherings have given to alcohol and other drugs a positive social meaning. The term "integrated drinking" has been used in relation to societies which show generalized approval of and widespread participation in drinking, often with a high rate of alcohol consumption. The association between integrated drinking and a high rate of consumption indicates that heavy alcohol use is not always considered disruptive of social life. In fact, tribal societies which emphasize integrated drinking have often shown general approval of drunkenness. However, there appears to be no relationship between integrated drinking and actual drunkenness (Bacon, 1973).

Examples of integrated drinking are not restricted to tribal societies. In European countries, drinking often is associated with social custom. In Sweden, for example, drinking has been used primarily in connection with visiting friends. In France and in Italy, for centuries wine has been considered an essential part of the family meal. Heavy drinking in France has been regarded as a sign of virility. The Finns and Irish have used the hard drinking of liquor for the release of aggression. The English "pub" is known for its attraction as a social meeting place (Ahlström-Laakso, 1976).

An idea associated with integrated drinking is that alcohol used within a social context can reduce the incidence of alcoholism. This is questionable, however, and such drinking may provoke a steady deterioration through liver cirrhosis or other physical ailments without overt signs of drunkenness being apparent. A distinction should be made between the acute effects of alcohol, which result in periods of drunkenness, and the chronic effects of lifelong alcohol consumption, where few behavioral effects may be seen. This can be exemplified by different practices of the American Indians. The Navahos, because of their custom of infrequent but heavy alcohol "binges," are likely to be the target of greater disapproval than the Hopis, who probably drink more alcohol over longer periods, but the latter probably incur more direct alcohol-related physical damage (Kunitz and Levy, 1974).

Many societies have developed protective safeguards for use of a drug which has been integrated into social or religious custom. For example, peyote, which contains the hallucinogen mescaline, has been used in large quantities by the Native American Church for several decades. The peyote is used in a sacramental manner during an all-night ritual which also contains the Christian element of hymns, baptism, confession, and a ritual breakfast (Lidz and Rothenberg, 1968). Safeguards against a bad reaction to the drug are built into the ceremony. Those who attend are required to stay until the service ends, and individuals are prevented from going off into the night alone; considerable effort is made to help participants return to an awareness of other people should they become excessively withdrawn. In this way, only the more positive effects of the drug are apparent (Bergman, 1971).

In general, the excessive use of recreational drugs is subject to disapproval by middle-class American adult society. This has led to the development of specific subcultures in response to the prevailing attitudes of the culture in general. These subcultures have their own norms and values, which often conflict with those held by the society in which the subculture developed. Johnson (1980) identified four distinct subcultures within North American society, each of which centered around a particular drug or class of drugs. Those identified were concerned with (1) alcohol abuse, (2) cannabis, (3) multiple drugs, and (4) heroin injection. The alcohol abuse subculture (Forrest, 1983) stressed using alcohol to get "high," "ripped," or "smashed"—that is, the aim of drinking was to get drunk. This provided a set of behavioral norms reflecting different attitudes toward alcohol from those held by the general North American drinking population. The cannabis subculture promoted the sharing of marijuana joints and hashish on a weekly basis, with informal peer pressure to buy and share in a social atmosphere among group members. The multiple drug subculture appeared to develop from the cannabis subculture and was distinguished by the use of many other substances in conjunction with cannabis, all aimed at achieving euphoria. These substances included sedatives, stimulants, inhalants, and hallucinogens. They could all be tried within a week or even on one day, and, as in the case of the cannabis subculture, members were expected to share. The heroin subculture promoted the use of heroin by injection, and there was less emphasis on sharing the actual drug than on providing it, with the obligation to return the favor by providing heroin for the other members at a later date.

Customs and mores, whether they be for the larger society or for a smaller group or subculture, set the tone and feeling regarding use of a drug or alcohol, and this stance will have a broad influence on consumption levels. This factor must be considered, therefore, in relation to etiology, although it does not explain individual abuse within a particular society.

Attitudes and Social Policy

Drug subcultures are shaped by availability and current social attitudes. They undergo frequent modification through the changing conduct norms of the group, which develop in response to a larger society's broad definitions of adult expectations concerning youth.

Adult attitudes toward both drinking and drug-taking have changed considerably over the past century in North America. Substances such as marijuana, opium, tobacco, cocaine, caffeine, and alcohol were brought to the continent by traders from such various parts of the globe as China, India, Europe, South America, and Mexico. Many substances were originally welcomed for their medicinal purposes and used with considerable freedom. It was only when the drugs were marketed and used for recreational purposes in the late nineteenth and early twentieth centuries that attitudes toward them changed. For example, in the nineteenth century opium was legally available, and it was smoked frequently in "opium dens" by both men and women. In the 1920s marijuana "tea pads" were established where a "high" from smoking cannabis could be obtained at a very low price (Brecher, 1972).

The Harrison Narcotic Act of 1914 and the Eighteenth (Prohibition) Amendment against alcohol, passed in 1917, introduced legal sanctions in the United States against the use of many substances. For a variety of reasons Prohibition did not last, but it fostered, in middle-class culture, the development of the attitude that alcohol is an evil influence. Today there still remains an ambiguity about the use of alcohol, with its possibility of instigating both merrymaking and destruction (Levine, 1980). This ambiguity is reflected in present social policy. There are those who believe that integration of alcohol into social life by education and advocacy of moderate use will reduce the incidence of alcoholism. There are those who believe that the only way to prevent alcohol problems is to reduce availability by imposing sanctions, increasing prices, and restricting accessibility. Research on the distribution of consumption does show a positive relationship between average level of consumption in a population and the incidence of alcohol-related damage, such as death by cirrhosis of the liver (de Lint and Schmidt, 1971). Similar connections are suggested for other drugs and the incidence of related problems (Whitehead, 1974; Whitehead, Smart, and La Forest, 1972), indicating that the most effective way to reduce drug problems is to effect a lowering of average consumption by some kind of social policy or education.

A study by Whitehead and Harvey (1974) illustrated the positive relation between alcohol-related problems and the general level of consumption within a society. These authors also found no support for the idea that the rate of alcoholism will be low in societies which accept integrated drinking. Societies with high levels of alcohol-related problems also had high levels of consumption. Moreover, the frequency of integrated drinking, and the degree of approval of drinking and approval of drunkenness, explained at least some of the variances in the number of alcohol-related problems. This tends not to support the thesis that integrated drinking benefits society as a whole.

Cultural factors clearly influence the individual's decision to take a particular drug, since they mold attitudes toward taking psychoactive substances, influence the practices imposed by the person's group or subculture, and help determine a drug's availability. With the blending of many different cultures from Europe and elsewhere during the evolution of modern North America, there has been an increase in emphasis on individual factors in both the development and later maintenance and abuse of drugs and alcohol. Essentially, treatment evolving from cultural factors will be manifested mainly in terms of prevention, through either education or policy controls. There is little evidence that either education or the imposition of sanctions has been effective in reducing consumption levels, particularly of alcohol. Prohibition, in fact, may lead to the development of illegal consumption and, concomitantly, the more hazardous effects of homemade beverages, drugs of unknown origin that are not subject to government-imposed safeguards, and the use of any product that will produce an "altered state" experience (Brecher, 1972).

Environmental Factors

Conditioning

Another influence to consider in the etiology of substance abuse is the effect of the environment in encouraging the use of many of the drugs. One important factor is the effect of the drugs themselves. Many are pleasant to take, or produce a "high," which encourages the user to repeat the experience. Thus, the intrinsically reinforcing properties of addictive drugs are reinforced by various environmental factors. A potentially reinforcing interactive effect always exists between the drug user and his or her drug-taking environment.

In this area of research, much useful work has been done with animals in an attempt to establish the importance of the pharmacological properties of many drugs in their action as reinforcers. An informative review of this area is given by Pickens, Meisch, and Thompson (1978). The studies give an indication of the inherent attractiveness of some of the drugs. For instance, if a rat has unlimited access to cocaine, the result is a rapid increase in self-administration until the animal dies. When cocaine is available for only six hours daily, the rat responds by self-administering regularly and shows no sign of abstention. Rats will self-administer opiates by gradually increasing intake over a period of three to four months. Sedatives such as pentobarbital are initiated and maintained by rats or monkeys with a gradual increase from the first day of administration. Alcohol intake first must be established by conditioning procedures, after which the rat self-administers the solution in an initial burst of activity, followed by shorter sprees during the rest of the drinking session. In spite of the unpleasant effects of withdrawal, rats will abstain from alcohol for short periods (two to four days), followed by a resumption of periodic bursts of activity.

Not all drugs appear immediately attractive when they are presented to animals, and many drugs, including alcohol, first must be established as the correct response by conditioning procedures before an animal will start to increase the dosage by itself. The animal initially must learn to acquire a preference for a particular drug. Some drugs such as mescaline, nalorphine, acetylsalicylic acid, and fenfluramine will not be increased by self-administration even after conditioning has occurred. This suggests that any abuse of these substances would depend upon factors other than their pharmacological properties.

In substance abuse, reinforcing factors (Natlan, 1983) may be described as those which become associated with a favorable outcome of drinking or drug use, such that the event is more likely to be repeated on future occasions. The reinforcement process is called "conditioning." The direct effects of a drug on behavior are limited to the metabolic life of the drug. The functional effects continue beyond the metabolic life and are affected by environmental influences. For instance, reacquisition of morphine dependence is more rapid in a rat if it occurs in the same environment in which the original acquisition took place (Jones and Prada, 1973). If the rat is given a shock or an unpleasant experience, it is likely to increase its intake of alcohol or a sedative drug (Mello and Mendelson, 1964). If a rat is given a drug as a reward every time it presses a bar, it will have a higher rate of daily drug intake than if it is given the drug only after pressing the bar several times. This means that if the rat has to work harder for each measure of the drug it receives, it will have a lower overall intake. If, for example, the rat has to press the bar five times instead of once for each measure of alcohol, it will halve its intake of alcohol. However, rats have been trained to work up to pressing the bar 256 times to obtain only one measure of alcohol (Meisch and Thompson, 1973).

These studies show that increased intake of a substance may be affected by (1) similar or different environments, (2) encountering unpleasant environments, and (3) ease of obtaining the substance. However, both the positive and negative effects of taking the drug itself should be considered (Solomon, 1980). The aversive consequences of taking a drug may be equally as reinforcing as the pleasurable effects under some environmental conditions. Thus addiction may be seen as an acquired motivation, learned through affective contrast. Affective contrast describes progression through the stages of baseline state ⟶ state A ⟶ state B ⟶ baseline state. If state A is pleasurable, state B will be painful in contrast. If state A contains elements of fear or pain, state B will be one of euphoria or relaxation. In the case of alcohol and other drugs, the more immediately pleasurable effects of the substance are contrasted with the subsequent painful effects of withdrawal—an affective contrast in which the subject is motivated to seek state A again to relieve the painful event. Alternatively, the euphoria produced after an unpleasant sensation, event, or task is thought to result in motivation to seek and endure the event in order to acquire the later experience of euphoria.

The idea of returning to a drug in order to relieve the effects of withdrawal is not new. The proposition that the pleasurable aftereffects of state B may actually be induced by the negative effect of state A suggests other factors which were previously not considered. Animal studies have suggested that the pleasurable aftereffects may be more enduring than the initial aversive experience. A similar pattern has been observed in human subjects. Inexperienced military parachutists have exhibited physiological and behavioral signs of fear just before jumping out of the plane, but have experienced euphoria afterward. After many jumps the preceding fear became less noticeable. The excitement and euphoria remained, and was if anything increased (Epstein, 1967).

Laboratory findings have also identified variables influencing the development of this opponent process. The acquired response to the B state is increased by use or exercise, and decreased by disuse, there being no response after a certain length of delay between presentations of the stimuli, or A state, and the effect of the response (Starr, 1978). Rats will eat a greater amount if the presentation of the food is immediately preceded by an aversive stimulus or shock (La Barbera and Caul, 1976). This kind of finding may be important when considering the frequency, quality, and size of the drug dose in relation to the response, which in human substance abuse represents the decision to take another dose or drink. Both habituation to the drug and the intensity and length of the withdrawal effects appear to be determined by variables such as these (Overmier et al., 1979).

If these factors are considered in the development of substance abuse, it becomes clear that not only the event itself but the aftereffects of the event are important variables. Those who have researched the question "Why do people drink?" report that alcohol is taken both for the pleasurable psychological change it induces in one and for the removal of discomfort (Conger, 1956). Therefore, both the aftereffect of the pleasure and the development of withdrawal—the relief of which is pleasurable—may increase the probability that the drug will be taken again. The emphasis on the aftereffect of an event which will influence consequent behavior, rather than the event itself, has implications for both an understanding of the development of abuse and for its treatment.

Excessive alcohol intake has also been researched in animals by observing the conditions under which "adjunctive" drinking occurs. This type of drinking was first observed by Falk (1961), who found that rats, given food pellets on an intermittent schedule of an average of once a minute, increased their water consumption rate to 3.43 times the usual daily intake. This excessive drinking has been given the name "schedule-induced polydipsia," and it has been found to produce increased alcohol intake (Lester, 1961; McMillan, Leander, and Ellis, 1974) as well as excessive intake of narcotic analgesic solutions (Leander and McMillan, 1975). Other excessive activities during intermittent schedules have also been observed, such as undue aggression, overeating, tail gnawing, air licking, and wheel running (Falk, 1972). Schedule induction of a particular excessive behavior appears to be a function of the immediate environmental situation, so that any particular response could be replaced by another activity if the surrounding conditions changed. The activity chosen is usually not a new behavior, but an excessive production of those which already exist in response to the present situation (Falk and Samson, 1975).

The transition to human substance abuse from these animal behavior patterns, which have developed in response to specific laboratory situations, may appear to be rather contrived. However, the fact that such behavior patterns do exist and can be reliably demonstrated in animals suggests that an examination of the environmental influences surrounding excessive substance use in people is important. In human alcohol consumption, drinking as a learned response to particular situations could increase in the face of certain environmental stimuli. The identification of some of these stimuli might therefore be an important step in defining appropriate treatment strategies for a particular individual. For example, drinking rates in chronic alcoholics can be substantially reduced by making a period of physical and social isolation the consequence of each drink of alcohol (Bigelow, Liebson, and Griffiths, 1974). The withdrawal of social interaction and alternate sources of reinforcement, such as watching television, has also been found to function in a similar way (Griffiths, Bigelow, and Liebson, 1974).

Learning Factors

Perhaps it is a combination of the effects of the drug itself and the presence of others using the substance which motivates young people to learn to drink or take drugs. Surveys demonstrate that the majority of men and women learn to drink by the time they reach eighteen years of age, and some by then have already established drinking patterns (Albrecht, 1973; Liban and Smart, 1980). Whether or not an adolescent may have the first drink at home with parents or relatives, or with peers at parties, in cars, or on dates depends upon the principal agent of socialization in the young person's life (Albrecht, 1973). Stumphauser (1980) has emphasized the importance of peers exerting influence by serving as models (who have had prior drinking experience) and by being present when the novice takes the first drink.

The effects of modeling, imitation, and identification on behavior change can be seen from early childhood onward (Bandura and Walters, 1963). In relation to drug consumption, the family appears to be an important influence. For example, Ahlgren et al. (1982) found that adolescents were more likely to begin smoking if they had parents providing a smoking model.

In general, parental use of a drug is moderately related to use by their children (Fawzy, Coombs, and Gerber, 1983). Annis (1974) conducted a study of a large number of families of adolescents in which each family member was questioned separately about drug practices. There was a tendency for family members to use the same drugs and also a tendency toward multiple drug use by each family member. Distinct patterns emerged in the use of similar drugs by a mother and daughter, or a father and son, which indicated that adolescents followed parental example in learning how to use specific drugs.

For alcohol consumption, the presence of a heavy-drinking partner has been found to increase both the amount and rate at which alcohol is consumed (Lied and Marlatt, 1979). Similar results in the number and rate of cigarettes smoked have been obtained from smokers exposed to a high-rate smoking confederate as opposed to a low-rate model (Antonuccio and Lichtenstein, 1980). With each particular substance used, the extent of perceived use in the peer group, self-reported use by peers, and perceived tolerance by peers for drug use all appear to be important predictors for a young person's initiation to a particular drug (Kandel, 1978). This is especially true for marijuana (Kandel, Kessler, and Margulies, 1978). For the use of prescription drugs such as tranquilizers and sedatives, parental use as a model appears to be important. Adolescents are more likely to use any of these drugs if they are being used by their parents. They are also more likely to use marijuana, LSD, or other illicit drugs than are adolescents whose parents do not use any psychoactive substances (Annis, 1975).

Modeling may continue to be an important factor once the young person enters the work force. Cosper (1979) has proposed that conformity may be important in accounting for the large differences that have been observed among the various occupations in the amount of alcohol drunk by employees. People have been found to drink to relieve the stress of a job, or to have chosen a job which provides a certain amount of opportunity or even allows considerable freedom to drink on the job. However, Cosper (1979) has found that the incidence of drinking is increased in occupations where (1) plenty of leisure time with coworkers is provided; (2) drinking is highly valued as part of the occupation's subculture; and (3) drinking can be used to express solidarity or group identity.

Adolescent and occupational research both suggest that drinking is a learned behavior, and that it is learned from those who have the most social influence. To be part of certain subcultures, it is necessary to drink. For the majority of people, however, drinking does not develop into excessive use, and it is important to ask how environmental influences can encourage such heavy use that drinking becomes a problem which interferes with other areas of functioning.

A person who later develops drinking problems is likely to have started using alcohol at an earlier age than is typical for the general population (Cahalan, 1970). Heavy or problem drinkers also appear less able to estimate their own blood alcohol level by using internal cues, when compared with moderate social drinkers. Silverstein, Nathan, and Taylor (1974) found alcoholics to be quite inaccurate in estimating blood alcohol levels unless some external cues were given them, even after training sessions. By comparison, male social drinkers can use internal and external cues, giving equally accurate estimates, after some training has been given (Huber, Karlin, and Nathan, 1976; Lansky, Nathan, and Lawson, 1978). While heavy social drinkers have also been found to drink more heavily in the company of a heavy-drinking confederate model, light social drinkers do not increase their drinking to any great extent in the company of such a confederate, although the modeling effects are still seen. Lied and Marlatt (1979) found this effect most marked for males exposed to a male drinking model, and suggested that under these conditions the model acts as a signal for these drinkers, indicating to them that a higher drinking rate is appropriate or desirable in a particular situation or context.

Life Events

The association between significant life events (e.g., marriage, divorce, a jail term, a change in work status, the death of a friend) and the onset of illness has received much attention in the past two decades (Rahe et al., 1964; Rahe and Arthur, 1968; Myers et al., 1972; Dohrenwend, 1973; Rabkin and Struening, 1976). A positive association has been found between stressful life events and severe neurotic and suicidal symptoms (Harder et al., 1980), onset of depression, (Lloyd, 1980), and poor general mental status (Myers et al., 1972).

Although abuse appears to be associated with a large number of stressful life events, together with a lower perception of the stressful nature of those events which are usually described as being so by the general population (Mules, Hague, and Dudley, 1977). Alcoholics also appear to be less perceptive of the impact that significant changes have in their life (Dudley et al., 1974) and experience proportionately less control over both internal and external pressures when compared with nonalcoholics (Donovan and O'Leary, 1975; Wright and Obtiz, 1984). There is also some indication that alcoholics in treatments may regress when faced with significant life events (Hore, 1971), and a similar finding for heroin abusers on a methadone maintenance programme confirms the detrimental effect of stressful life events on this group (Krueger, 1981). Although heroin abusers and alcoholics both have a high number of stressful life events compared with the general population, the former appear to have a heightened perception of life change and severity of disease in contrast to the lowered perception of alcoholics (Dudley et al., 1974).

It appears that life events may be mediating factors in the development of psychiatric illness in general, and drug abuse in particular. However, the fact that similar events can occur in the general population without such undue effects suggests that the development of illness depends upon the characteristics of the stressful situation, the individual's biological and psychological attributes, and the availability of a social support system for the individual (Rabkin and Struening, 1976). The multidimensional nature of these events must also be considered, since not all life events will have the same effect on various individuals or contribute in the same way to the development of particular illnesses. Rahe (1975) has suggested six categories of life events, based upon the Recent Life Changes Questionnaire: (1) family, (2) personal, (3) work, (4) financial, (5) health, and (6) marriage. Skinner and Lei (1980) have identified similar categories using the Schedule of Recent Events, developed by Holmes and Rahe (1967). These categories may provide a fruitful way of determining more precisely which types of life events are the most stressful for different populations or individuals, and they could be used both in prognosis and treatment.

Environmental factors appear to exert a fairly broad influence on a person's decision to drink or take drugs. In adolescence, peer pressure is considered powerful in requiring conformity with the expectations of a group which considers membership to involve taking a particular drug. With heavy-drinking peers, the pressure is increased to keep pace with the standard that is set. Such conformity seems prevalent within many occupations, and may even encourage drinking where no particular predisposition originally existed. An environment of encouragement and positive association with drinking or taking a particular drug should, therefore, be considered as creating an atmosphere in which drinking could increase. On the other hand, the phenomenon of adjunctive or excessive drinking may be encouraged where a monotonous or uncertain situation exists. Therefore, when looking at the development of substance abuse in an individual, the context within which the person has grown up will probably influence the amount, frequency, and choice of substance used. Details of this context would be a necessary precondition to understanding the etiology of the abuse and providing a basis for treatment.

Interpersonal Factors

Social Influences

In modern industrial societies, less emphasis is placed upon the group, and behavior in general has become more individualized. Cultural patterns are less clearly defined. Through the media, a general attitude of acceptance of alcohol as part of adult status clearly exists (Cafiso et al., 1982), and there is evidence to suggest that advertising stimulates consumption levels in the general population (Atkin, Neuendorf, and McDermott, 1983).

It is not surprising, therefore, that the onset of drinking in junior and high school students was found by Jessor and Jessor (1975) to be related to that phase of adolescent development which was directed toward achieving adult status. Those students who did not drink throughout the four years of this particular study placed a greater emphasis on school achievement, were more conforming and religious, and lived in a home environment which provided little opportunity to drink.

For many teenagers, the adoption of drinking appears to signify the dissolution of adolescent status and the adoption of an adult life-style (Maddox and McCall, 1964). The association of alcohol with "deviance," suggested by Jessor and Jessor (1975), may simply reflect a tendency for young people to start drinking before it is legally sanctioned by adult practice. Indeed, these authors have found that the majority of those teenagers who were classified as problem drinkers did not continue with problem drinking in young adulthood (Donovan, Jessor, and Jessor, 1983). However, more consistent evidence of delinquency has been found in literature concerning initiation and continuation of other illegal drug use (Kandel, Kessler, and Margulies, 1978; Hundleby, 1979). Involvement in delinquent activities has been found to progress with continued use of an illegal substance, determined in part by its cost and availability (Jessor, Jessor, and Finney, 1973).

There appears to be a fairly consistent progression of young people's involvement with substances of abuse, beginning with beer or wine, followed by cigarettes and/or hard liquor, marijuana, and finally other illicit drugs (Kandel, 1978). Use of adult legal substances appears to be a necessary intermediary between complete nonuse and illicit drug use. Many substance abusers continue the use of their first drug as they try a second or third one, which, incidentally, helps to explain the development of multiple drug use (Hochhauser, 1977).

Kandel, Kessler, and Margulies (1978) observed a progression through the various substance categories but found different influences affecting initiation to each new substance. Four groups of variables were associated with initiation in general, with a different emphasis on the relative importance of the variables for each substance tried. These variables were parental influence, peer influence, adolescent belief and values, and involvement in minor delinquent activities such as cutting classes (resulting in lower school grades) and becoming involved in delinquent behaviors. For hard liquor, initiation depended upon both the frequency of use by parents and the students' perceptions of their peers who were already drinking liquor; for marijuana use, the critical variables were peer use and approval. In starting to use other illegal drugs, a lack of influence by parents who were attempting to keep strict control over their sons and daughters appeared to be the most relevant factor. Other social factors connected with alcohol abuse by high school students are a lack of social integration, negative relations with parents, peer group influences, heavy cigarette and cannabis consumption, and lower social status of the father (Sieber, 1979). Vicary and Lerner (1983) have suggested that these early maladjustment problems may begin before high school. Using data from a longitudinal study, these authors concluded that young children, seen by parents and teachers to have emotional and/or behavioral problems, were at greater risk for earlier and higher levels of substance abuse.

A more general factor, which can best be described as "nonconformity," is often found among university students who use drugs. With these students, the ease of obtaining a drug and the number of friends who use it are important influences (Somekh, 1978).

There is, therefore, little doubt that peer pressure (Forrest, 1983) exerts a strong influence on initial drug or alcohol use. Peer influence reduces the possibility that negative aspects of the drug will be considered. The expected probability of positive aspects of taking the drug is related to the number of friends who use it, and provides the groundwork for the development of a set of forms which favor its use (Orcutt, 1978). It is also interesting that students who approve of excessive drinking tend to believe that peer group reaction and opinions have no influence on their own decision to drink (Alsikafi, Globetti, and Christy, 1979). This belief reveals a tendency to enhance the positive aspects of drinking or drug taking, which will encourage its use among people who wish to feel part of their peer group. Peer influence in students and adolescents also cuts across levels of socioeconomic status (SES) and other groupings that affect patterns of consumption in adults. There is a higher incidence of problem alcohol use among adults of lower SES who live in urban areas (Cahalan, Cisin, and Crossley, 1969), but in young people these factors appear to be overridden by both peer and parental influence (Alexander and Campbell, 1968; Forslund and Gustafson, 1970).

In adults, the social expectations of the reinforcing value of alcohol show that people expect alcohol to reduce tension; enhance social and physical pleasure and sexual performance and experience; and increase a sense of power and aggression as well as actual social assertiveness (Brown et al., 1980). When questioned, social drinkers reported that they "felt good" immediately after drinking, placing less importance on the later more unpleasant effects (Stumphauser, 1980). In this context, it is interesting to note that heavy drinkers have been found to believe more strongly than light drinkers that drinking heavily results in enjoyable experiences, and does not produce unpleasant experiences (McCarty, Morrison, and Mills, 1983). Perhaps this is indeed the case for heavy drinkers.

Familial Factors

Environmental factors and cultural attitudes contribute largely to initial use of a drug or alcohol. However, further explanation is needed as to why a small proportion of the population persists with drug abuse or develops heavy alcohol use with all the consequent social and personal problems.

It is thought by some researchers that excessive alcohol use may have adaptive consequences for the couple or family. Steinglass, Weiner, and Mendelson (1971) observed familial pairs before, during, and after a period of heavy drinking. Role reversal, "caretaking" functions, and dramatic changes in behavior after intoxication suggested that the couples were keeping to a well-practiced set of rules. From their observations, the authors suggested two possible reasons for heavy drinking by the pairs: (1) drinking might appear as a sign of stress, and (2) it might serve to satisfy unconscious needs or cement a clearcut role differentiation between two people. These conclusions were reached after observing how one member usually started drinking after a period of tension between the couple. This action often provided the possibility for a change of roles in which one could dominate or care for the other in a manner not tolerated when the couple was sober.

Both of these notions suppose that alcohol acts as a tension reducer for the couple, first by relieving the tensions arising from conflicts between them, and secondly by reducing the perceptions of ambiguity about roles or power relationships. Thus, alcohol can be used to reduce tension. However, at a more general level, the idea is that alcohol serves a function within the family or marriage to keep the system intact. It suggests that the maintenance of heavy drinking is encouraged by the other family members, and if drinking ceased, other more functional supports would need to be substituted in order to keep the family unit intact.

In studying the interaction between heavy-drinking fathers and their heavy-drinking sons, Weiner et al. (1971) observed differences between the personalities of the two men when they were drunk and when they were sober. The pairs appeared to switch roles when the one drinking would become drunk and childlike, and the other would remain sober and caretaking. When drinking ceased the pair quickly returned to their predrinking interactional pattern. The authors suggested that drinking provided an opportunity for role reversal and also served as a signal of stress in the system. This last conclusion receives some support from Burton and Kaplan (1968), who found that the fewer the problems reported by marriage partners, the more likely it was that drinking episodes would be decreased or abstinence maintained after treatment. However, this particular study did not have an independent control group, and these ideas have received only moderate support by other researchers using more rigorous controls (Paolino and McCrady, 1977). It has also been suggested that other marriage adjustment problems and those related to drinking are relatively independent (Cohen and Krause, 1971), but Orford (1975) has questioned this approach and suggests a more generalized viewpoint in which alcoholism is dealt with as one of the general problems within a marriage.

Although marriage and family-related explanations often do not clarify why people start to drink in the first place, it does seem that maladaptive patterns can be observed in the family or marriage where one or several members indulge in episodes of heavy drinking (Steinglass, 1976). The question then arises as to the relative contribution of genetic and physiological factors, on the one hand, and maladaptive behavioral patterns within the family or social system, on the other hand. For example, adoptee studies have shown that a larger proportion of adoptees raised apart from biologic parents develop drinking problems compared with a control group (Goodwin et al., 1974; Cadoret, Cain, and Grove, 1980); and concordance among monozygotic twins is also greater both for the amount of alcohol consumed and for alcohol elimination rate (Goodwin, 1980). Alcoholics with a family history of alcoholism differ in the age of first intoxication, in psychosocial skills, and in general immaturity. Tarter and Alterman (1984) have suggested that there may be differential susceptibility to brain damage from drinking in these alcoholics, which might account for later development of the problem.

These studies suggest that some genetic component in the development of alcoholism may exist, and Goodwin (1980) has suggested diagnosis in terms of familial and nonfamilial alcoholism. However, only 30 percent of persons with alcohol-related problems have even a single parent with alcoholism (Cotton, 1979), and the high incidence of alcoholism within the families of alcoholics reporting for treatment is probably due in part to environmental and social factors. For example, the presence of a parent who drinks heavily may create unusual situations for the family members. Children of such parents experience inconsistency and distorted role models, which may later lead to such negative expressions as overt aggression, distrust, hostility, depression, or anxiety (Woititz, 1978). In interviewing twenty-five families with alcohol problems, Wolin et al. (1980) found that the children were more likely to become alcoholics if the times a family typically spent together (for example, during dinner, on holidays and weekends, or receiving visitors) were disrupted by heavy parental drinking. In general, there is modest support for the view that children of alcoholics develop significant difficulties in psychological, social, and family functioning (Jacob et al., 1978).

Heavy drinkers who report a family history of alcoholism appear to differ from those who do not on many demographic and behavioral variables. In a large group of military personnel, for example, those men who had at least one alcoholic relative entered the service with worse academic and social records from school, had less stable employment histories, showed more antisocial behavior, and exhibited more severe physical symptoms related to heavy use of alcohol (Frances, Timm, and Buckley, 1980).

Studies on the development of drug abuse (especially heroin abuse) within the family system have attempted to find a distinct interaction pattern which is centered around the taking of the drug itself. From observational studies, Stanton et al. (1978) have described the heroin addiction cycle as part of a complex family pattern, in which maintenance of the addiction in one of its members provides a paradoxical resolution to the problem of maintaining or dissolving the family unit. One effect of taking the drug appears to be that of keeping the addicted person in a childlike and dependent state, yet at a distance, and through the drug cycle of addiction and withdrawal the family becomes engaged in a symbolic leaving and returning of its members. Stanton (1979) has also found that the drug abuser's family characteristically contains one parent who is intensely involved with the abuser, while the other is more punitive and distant, and/or is frequently absent. The abusing offspring may function as a source of distraction from the parents' own problems, or the drug may be used to assume a childlike position in the family in order to gain attention. The pattern of drug abuse within the family may involve both of the parents and the abusing offspring, while other family members contrive to keep the abuser in a dependent role.

Stanton (1980) has compared drug abuse with other psychiatric disorders for evidence of dysfunctional differences in the family system. From his observations, the following differences are to be found: In drug abuse families there is (1) a higher frequency of multigenerational chemical dependency, together with a tendency for other addictive behaviors such as gambling and watching television excessively; (2) a tendency for a greater expression of conflict, especially from the parent excessively involved with the individual on drugs; (3) no sign of schizophrenia in the parents; (4) a peer group to which the abuser can turn in times of family conflict; (5) a longer period of symbiotic connection between mother and offspring; (6) an emphasis on death themes together with the premature or untimely deaths of family members; and (7) evidence of close ties with all or several family members remaining in adulthood, despite the profession of independence by the abuser.

The factors of death, separation, and loss have also been found to be significant precursors of heroin abuse. In studying the family histories of twenty-five addicts, Coleman (1980) found that sudden death or a life-threatening illness had occurred in a larger number of cases than normally expected, and this observation was supported by clinical impressions of death-related issues which figured frequently in therapy. According to Coleman (1980) these events form part of an integral pattern of homeostasis within the family, in which the abuser stays at home. Within the complex set of feedback mechanisms involved in the drug-taking process lies an overall sense of family hopelessness and lack of purpose or meaning in life for every family member. It appears that family separations or losses have not been effectively resolved, and drug-taking behavior serves to reinforce this sense of helplessness.

From the findings in the literature, it does appear that familial factors are important in fostering the development and maintenance of substance abuse. As mentioned previously, the specific drug chosen may depend upon its use by the parents or other family members (Annis, 1974).

Intrapersonal Factors

These factors pertain to individual differences and may contribute in a more specific way to the development and maintenance of substance abuse in a particular person.

Development Influences

The psychodynamic approach to the etiology of substance abuse is often postulated to be based on a need to compensate for fixation at the oral stage of psychosexual development. An inordinate need for oral gratification is viewed as resulting from dependency conflicts which arise from developmental difficulties. Drug and alcohol abuse, among other behavior, is viewed as providing such gratification.

Psychodynamic theories are notoriously difficult to substantiate. Accurate reports on child rearing are difficult to obtain in retrospect, and other socialization effects on the developing child are not usually considered. Nevertheless, some cultural studies have found that societies with a high frequency of drinking tend also to be less indulgent of the dependency needs of their children. This characteristic is thought to induce oral frustration. Conversely, societies with a low consumption of alcohol or infrequent drunkenness typically (1) take care of the physical and emotional needs of infants; (2) use permissive rather than punitive methods of socialization; (3) do not stress overachievement and independence; (4) tolerance dependent behavior in adulthood; (5) engage in communal eating; and (6) relate folktales which describe the world as essentially kind and friendly (Bacon, 1973).

In reviewing a large number of studies of alcoholics, Blane and Barry (1973) have observed that heavy alcohol users are often the last born of the family. These authors have suggested that the pressure to remain dependent in a society which stresses adult self-reliance may result in a dependency conflict that could last beyond the one which is usually experienced in childhood. The high incidence of disruptive conditions in early life—including broken homes—frequently found among alcoholics does not provide the opportunity for such dependency conflicts to be resolved.

Many personality studies have confirmed that alcohol abusers show a lack of maturity, impulsivity, antisocial behavior, or evidence of an inability to cope with life events (Khantzian, Mack, and Schatzberg, 1974; Milkman and Frosch, 1980; Hill, 1980). However, a careful study by Vaillant (1980), which followed up college freshman when they had reached the age of fifty, has revealed no association between childhood environment and the later development of alcohol abuse. Vaillant estimated the number of each person's oral-dependent traits, such as pessimism, passivity, dependence, fear of sex, self-doubt, and suggestability, by collecting observed vignettes of the person's adult life. Although these "oral" vignettes were found to be associated with a conflicted childhood, personality instability in college, and adult evidence of personality disorder, they were not found to be antecedents of alcohol abuse. However, "oral" vignettes and alcohol abuse were both correlated with other kinds of drug use, and with each other, with the indication that those who had developed alcohol problems became depressed and unable to cope as a consequence of their inability to control alcohol consumption, rather than as a cause in the development of the problem. Using the same data base, Vaillant (1983) proposed a similar explanation for the association between sociopathy and alcoholism. Although many sociopaths later abuse alcohol as part of their antisocial behavior, most alcoholics are not premorbidly antisocial, but they violate enough social practices while drinking to become eventually to be viewed as sociopaths. These findings question those developmental factors which have been proposed in etiology such as weak ego development. For example, Khantzian (1980) suggests that drug-dependent individuals are predisposed to use and become dependent upon their substances mainly because of severe ego impairment and disturbances in the sense of self. This involves difficulties with drive and affects defense, self-care, dependency, and need satisfaction. Khantzian believes that preference for and selection of the appropriate drug involve its distinct pharmacologic effects interacting with the individual's unique personality organization and reactive pattern. Milkman and Frosch (1980) have proposed similar antecedents: Having once experienced the gratification of a supportive, drug-induced pattern of ego functioning, users attempt to repeat this satisfying experience as a solution to their own conflicts.

Personality Factors

Much effort has been invested in trying to identify an alcoholic personality. To do this, it would be necessary to show that a certain set of personality characteristics predispose a person to become an alcoholic; that such a set did not arise as a later consequence of the problem; and that such a set could discriminate between all other groups and those people who later became alcohol abusers. Such a distinct set of personality characteristics has not been identified, and it is now more generally accepted that alcohol abusers form a heterogeneous group. A recent review of the literature has suggested that there is no clear evidence of a simple personality type, but that certain personality traits may play an important part in both the development and maintenance of alcohol dependence (Barnes, 1979).

One way of classifying the personality factors thought to be relevant in the development of alcohol abuse is in the form of subtypes. Barnes (1980) has identified two such subtypes: "prealcoholic personality" and "clinical alcoholic personality." The former refers to the pattern of characteristics occurring before the onset of heavy drinking, some of which may be different from those identified in the second subtype. Main characteristics of this prealcoholic personality are impulsivity, poor self-esteem, low ego strength, and low social conformity. These characteristics have been identified in longitudinal research studies on people who later developed alcohol problems (Loper, Kammeier, and Hoffman, 1973; McCord, 1972; Kammeier, Hoffman, and Loper, 1973).

The clinical alcoholic personality can be recognized by the pattern of personality characteristics which are evident at the time of treatment. Barnes (1979) identified four attributes which occur with consistency in the literature. These are neuroticism, a weak ego, stimulus augmentation, and field dependence. The neuroticism factor is supported mainly by the finding that alcoholics often score higher than normal on anxiety, using the Minnesota Multiphasic Personality Inventory (MMPI), Cattel's 16 Personality Factors, and Eysenck's neuroticism scale. Depression also seems a fairly common factor among alcoholics, especially women (Hoffman, 1970; Richman, Teichman, and Fine, 1980; Steer, McElroy and Beck, 1983), and is one of the triad of neuroticism factors on the MMPI scale, together with hypochondriasis and hysteria. There is also evidence for weaker ego-strength, as defined by Barnes in terms of impulsivity, hostility, antisocial behavior, low masculinity, display of negative self-concepts, difficulty in establishing relationships and need for short-term gratification (Kassebaum, Couch and Slater, 1959; Williams, McCourt, and Schneider, 1971; Laudeman, 1977). There is, however, less support for the attribute of stimulus augmentation (heightened intensity in experiencing environmental stimulation), since this trait has been found less related to alcoholism per se than to the fact that the alcoholics tested were in general older than the comparison group (Barnes, 1980). However, a weak relationship exists between stimulus augmentation and introversion, which does lend some support to this characteristic. Alcoholics and other drug (cocaine and opiate) users have been found to be more introverted than nonusers (Tarnai and Young, 1983; Spotts and Shontz, 1984). Field dependence, which measures the ability to separate out the different elements in a perceptual field from the context of the ground, may be related to the alcoholic's experience of being within a treatment setting or to the effects of alcohol, rather than being a predisposing factor (Goldstein and Chotlos, 1966; McWilliams, Brown, and Minard, 1975).

Many of the personality traits identifying alcoholics are also common to other psychiatric groups. Skinner, Jackson, and Hoffman (1974) identified eight subtypes of alcoholics from among a large number of patients who presented for treatment. Using cluster analytic techniques, the five clearest bipolar typal dimensions which emerged were acute anxiety vs. blunted affect, antisocial attitudes vs. hypochondriasis, hostile–hallucinative vs. neurotic depression, neurotic disorganization vs. hostile–paranoid, and emotional instability vs. interpersonal conflict and depression. In a later study, Skinner, Reed, and Jackson (1976) found that four bipolar subtypes (denial, general anxiety, character disorder, and hypochondriasis) were common among such diverse groups as alcoholics, college students, psychiatric patients, and prison inmates. There is a difficulty, therefore, in using these subtypes to describe an alcohol personality as distinct from other populations. The identification of such attributes is more useful for considering treatment implications than for an understanding of etiological factors, since it follows that identified subtypes should receive a form of treatment appropriate to their particular needs (Nerviano and Gross, 1983). Some studies have examined the effect of matching subtypes with different treatments (Edwards et al., 1977; McLachlan, 1974; Finney and Moos, 1979), but careful matching and evaluation is necessary for positive results (Glaser, 1980; Skinner, 1981). McLachlan (1974), for example, matched clients according to their conceptual level (degree of structuring) with types of treatment which differed in structural content. A greater proportion of those matched for conceptual level both in therapy and aftercare recovered, compared with those who were not matched. Potentially, there are a number of ways in which matches could be achieved (Glaser, 1980): (1) by matching attributes of clients to attributes of therapists; (2) by matching attributes of clients to treatment goals; and (3) by matching the problems of clients to the specific capabilities of treatments.

Psychopathic and depressive response styles have also been associated with alcohol problems. The psychopathic style may be defined as an inability to anticipate (and therefore avoid) the aversive consequences of behavior. In relation to alcohol, this would be an inability to anticipate consequences of overdrinking (such as hangovers and inability to drive safely), the level of consumption varying with the amount of anticipatory deficit. The depressive style is characterized by a subjective discomfort of negative affect, and one theory is that this would lead to a pattern of more sustained alcohol intake, in which the physiological effect of alcohol would temporarily relieve such affect (Gorenstein, 1980).

The response styles of depression and psychopathy may relate to the concept of reactive and essential dimensions of alcohol dependence proposed by Jacobson (1976, 1980). The essential alcoholic, a category which was originally proposed by Knight (1937), is similar to the antisocial personality as defined by the psychopathic deviate (Pd) subscale on the MMPI, while the reactive alcoholic may demonstrate depressive characteristics. In many cases, however, it is difficult to determine whether onset of depression precedes alcohol dependence or is caused by alcohol abuse. Depression is also common to many other psychiatric problems. The question of change in affect after alcohol use will be discussed in another section.

As with the attempt to find distinct personality factors for alcoholism, there has been equally little success regarding drug abuse. Adolescent drug use is associated with such concepts as deviancy, rebelliousness, alienation, and adolescent behavior problems (Hundleby, 1979), and drug use appears to be encouraged by any disruption of the normal child–parent relationships, a lack of involvement in organized groups, or involvement with drug-using peers. Preadolescents who begin to smoke are more likely to be low in self-esteem, dislike school, and fear failure (Ahlgren et al., 1982). Motives for beginning heroin use have been identified as pleasure, curiosity, and peer pressure. These motives have been found to change after use, to physiological addiction, pleasure seeking, and a way of dealing with such unpleasant emotional states as depression, boredom, tension, and loneliness (Fulmer and Lapidus, 1980).

A sensation-seeking factor, or experience-seeking, appears to be the most discriminating characteristic for drug use among adolescents (Segal, Huba, and Singer, 1980). A recent study of college students who were using marijuana revealed a group of people more concerned with internal sensation and novelty-seeking than the general population of students (Eisenman, Grossman, and Goldstein, 1980). Their work supports an earlier study by Kohn and Annis (1977), who found that an internal sensation–seeking measure was related to the use of alcohol, tobacco, and marijuana, but not to analgesics. Sensation-seeking variables of boredom susceptibility and disinhibition have also been found to discriminate between aging alcoholics (over 55 years), and a control group from the same medical center (Kilpatrick et al., 1982).

Carlin and Stauss (1977) have identified three categories of drug users as (1) the basic self-medicator, (2) the streetwise self-medicator, and (3) the streetwise recreational user. The basic self-medicator appeared better-educated and less deviant, and reported more depressive affect, than the other two groups, and acquired the drugs through prescriptions. The main influence for this group may be through observation of parental drug use, by which the adolescent has an expectation of deriving more positive results from the drugs than he or she in fact receives (Gorsuch and Butler, 1976). The streetwise recreational user appeared less disordered than the streetwise self-medicator, although both groups obtained their drugs from similar street sources (Carlin and Stauss, 1977).

In conclusion, there is clearly no evidence for either an alcoholic or a drug-abusing personality per se. It is also difficult to determine whether some of the characteristics reported are inherent characteristics of a person prior to using a particular substance or whether these characteristics have developed through the pharmacological effect of the substance itself, or through the social conditions surrounding heavy drug use. Studies which have identified subtypes by cluster analysis and other classification techniques, and those individual characteristics which appear fairly consistently across subjects, may help to define appropriate treatment for different groups of substance abusers. The problem of identifying and correctly assigning differential treatment appropriate for subgroups of alcoholics has received more attention in recent years, although there remains much work to be done with this approach in future (Pattison, 1979; Ogborne and Glaser, 1985). It has also been suggested that for recreational drug use, there is a need to find alternative means of satisfying the desire for new experiences to replace those sought in using drugs. These should be tailored to the characteristics of the individual, and might include yoga, biofeedback, and transcendental meditation (Kohn et al., 1979).

Affect and Cognition

It has long been suggested that drugs are used for the relief of depression (Rado, 1933); and for alcohol abuse, especially, the question of whether alcohol really acts as a tension reducer has been the subject of much debate (Conger, 1956; Cappell and Herman, 1972). Farber, Khavari, and Douglass (1980) have found that among the heavy drinkers in a large population sample, 93 percent preferred to describe themselves as "escape" drinkers, for the relief of negative affect, rather than as "social" drinkers seeking positive reinforcement. However, it has been pointed out that heavy consumption of alcohol leads to dysphoria, anxiety, and affective discomfort, which is likely to increase, rather than decrease, as drinking continues (Mello and Mendelson, 1978). It is, therefore, possible that in the later stages of alcohol abuse, at least, the cognitive appraisal of alcohol acting as a tension reducer may be a more important inducement to drinking than the actual pharmacological effects.

There has been an increasing awareness of the importance of cognitive factors such as beliefs and expectations in influencing the development and maintenance of heavy drug or alcohol use. Not only is expectancy of outcome important in deciding whether an action will be repeated, but also the belief there will be a temporary relief from the unpleasant situation which becomes a powerful predictor of whether a response will occur. (Bandura, 1977; Meichenbaum, 1977). Although expectation alone cannot produce the desired performance of the potent effect of alcohol without the ability to execute it, expectation can create favorable conditions for its production. For example, Marlatt (1978) has suggested that people with low expectation of their own efficacy in influencing or changing a situation are more likely to relapse into heavy drinking after a period of abstinence, in order to avert further distress.

Social expectations of the effects of alcohol include the idea that alcohol will help to reduce tension or discomfort, increase euphoria, provide a sense of personal power, and enhance social interaction.

However, while low quantities of alcohol do appear to induce the sought-after euphoric state, increasing blood alcohol levels lead to dysphoria or negative affect changes. Since the immediate pleasurable effects of the initial phase appear to have the most influence on shaping the individual's expectations regarding the effects of alcohol on mood (Donovan and Marlatt, 1980), it has been suggested that a drinker will continue to drink through this second phase of negative affect in order to try and regain the euphoria experienced at a lower blood alcohol level.

There may be a difference between the expectations of the average social drinker and those who become heavy drinkers concerning the effects of alcohol on both mood and performance. Heavy drinkers have been found to rate their first and later drinking experiences as more pleasant and euphoric, with fewer negative consequences than a comparable group of social drinkers (Senter et al., 1979; McCarty, Morrison, and Mills, 1983. At an earlier stage of problem development, those adolescents who expected alcohol to improve their cognitive and motor functioning experienced problem drinking. In contrast, social drinking adolescents expected alcohol to enhance social behavior. Both of these expectancies proved to be good predictors of actual drinking behavior (Christiansen and Goldman, 1983).

Both heavy and social drinkers have been found to drink more at a taste-rating session when they were told that the beverages they were tasting were alcohol rather than tonic water, regardless of whether they did in fact receive alcohol (Marlatt, Demming, and Reid, 1973). This experiment is an example of the balanced placebo design which has been used to try and separate the actual effects of alcohol from those which are expected. In this design, half of the subjects are told they will receive alcohol and the other half are told they will receive a placebo; half of each group are then given alcohol, while the other half of each group are given placebo. Under these conditions, those who expect alcohol and receive it have been found more likely (than those who received alcohol but did not expect it) to report an increase in euphoric effects (Pliner and Cappell, 1974), higher levels of positive affect (McCollam et al., 1980), a decrease in anxiety in response to stress (Polivy, Schueneman, and Carlson, 1976), and a decrease in amount of social anxiety shown in physiological measures (Abrams and Wilson, 1979). However, some measures are not as greatly influenced by expectancies, such as, for example, assertiveness (Parker, Gilbert, and Speltz, 1981) and psychomotor behaviour (Vuchinich and Sobell, 1978). In this kind of research, much depends upon how well the taste of the alcohol can be disguised, and whether the subject accepts the information that he is given on beverage content. When larger quantities of alcohol are given, the deception becomes more difficult, but the pharmacological effects of the alcohol are clearer (Levenson et al., 1980).

The results do demonstrate the importance of cognitive set and expectancy in influencing the type of response made in the drinking situation, and also the amount consumed (Marlatt, Demming, and Reid, 1973; Berg et al., 1981). A direct measurement of subjective expectancy is difficult, and for this purpose an attempt has been made to design situational questionnaires focusing on the probability that a drink will be consumed when the respondent is faced with experiencing certain events or conditions (Deardorff et al., 1975; Marlatt, 1976). Research on the effects of expectancy, together with situational analyses of the conditions under which the probability of drinking alcohol is increased, has shown that individuals who drink heavily appear to be at least partially motivated by their expectations of the positive reinforcement they will receive. One conclusion that may be drawn from this is that drinking is an overlearned behavior used to cope with a variety of situations.

Affective change may be an important factor in the decision to take many of the psychoactive substances. For instance, McAuliffe and Gordon (1974) have found chronic heroin addicts to state that euphoria is an important goal in addiction maintenance. The drug gives immediate, unlearned gratification (Ausubel, 1980). Since a large proportion of heroin addicts report that euphoria remains an important aspect of drug-taking, despite the development of tolerance, it may not be merely the release from withdrawal effects which prompts the repetition of the drug injection. Relief from withdrawal has often been thought to be the main reason for continuity of use (Wickler, 1980).

Sex Differences

A realization that etiological factors may differ for men and women has only recently developed, and many earlier studies, especially on alcohol abuse, have either controlled for sexual differences by excluding women or have not reported the data separately for the two sexes. However, much of the information needed to compare sex differences is obtainable from these studies if they are reevaluated, and the first major review volume on this subject has recently been published (Kalant, 1980).

Reviewing genetic and familial factors involved in the development of alcohol abuse, Swinson (1980) concluded that genetic factors appear to be a strong etiological influence in men, whereas environmental factors may play a larger part in the etiology of alcoholism in women. Midanik (1983) found women with drinking problems reported in a national survey to have more alcoholic first-degree relatives than men. McKenna and Pickens (1983) add support to this latter finding. In a survey of patients admitted to a treatment center for substance abuse, they found women were more likely than men to report alcoholism in their mothers but not their fathers, and they reported alcoholism in both parents more than twice as often as did men. However, very few twin or adoption studies have made male–female comparisons, and genetic factors may not have been sufficiently investigated for women.

Although maladjustment problems appear frequently in the early histories of both men and women, the expression of this maladjustment is liable to be different. Psychopathology is more common among men with substance abuse, and there appears to be a greater tendency toward neuroticism and depression among women. Women are more likely to have had depressive episodes before the onset of alcohol abuse (Schuckit, 1973) and many more women alcoholics than men report suicidal thoughts and delusions. Women who have experienced broken homes before the age of ten are also more likely to become heavy drinkers than men with the same life history, and women also have a greater tendency to relate the onset of heavy drinking to an identified stressful event or situation (Boothroyd, 1980).

It has been found that men use illicit drugs and licit drugs nonmedically at significantly higher rates than women, but that women use licit drugs medically at higher rates than men. An interesting question is whether in fact women use sedatives and tranquilizers and men use alcohol for their similar pharmacological properties, indicating an underlying need for drugs common to both men and women. Cross-addiction occurs to barbiturates and alcohol in both men and women (Kalant, 1980).

Although narcotic addiction is less common among women than men, there are relatively few personality differences to distinguish them. Both men and women show evidence of antisocial and other behavioral problems, and an equal proportion (about 20 percent) of men and women indicate that they began taking an addictive drug for medical reasons (Martin and Martin, 1980).

Sufficient evidence has accumulated to make it clear that additional well-controlled studies are needed to evaluate the different factors in men and women leading to the development of drug abuse. This is important not only for understanding causative factors but also for planning treatment. A comparison of early histories of men and women may also help to determine the relative importance of genetic and familial factors in the etiology of both alcohol and other drug dependence. The latter question has been sadly neglected, especially in the area of dependence on drugs other than alcohol.

Etiological Factors and Treatment Implications

When it is considered that cultural and social attitudes toward drugs in general, and particularly alcohol, are mainly positive, it is not surprising that a proportion of the population will consume them to excess. It is apparent that death from liver cirrhosis increases proportionately with the amount of alcohol consumed per capita by a society (de Lint and Schmidt, 1968). Similar trends may be found in the incidence of disease in smokers, and those who combine heavy smoking with drinking are at an even greater risk than users of either drug alone (Rothman and Keller, 1972). It is, therefore, anomalous in Western societies that these substances are not only approved of in moderate doses but consumption is actively encouraged through the media and at social gatherings. This occurs in the face of enormous costs to employment potential, and to the physical and psychological health of a great many individuals.

Given these prevailing attitudes, it is also not surprising that sporadic efforts at temperance or policies of increased taxation have not had much effect. Primary prevention or intervention in the development of substance abuse would appear to be an important form of treatment to advocate, but there is to date little evidence that educational programs, which are aimed at increasing knowledge in the general population, are effective. School-based education programs for example, can improve students' knowledge about alcohol, but they appear to have little effect upon attitude (Goodstadt, Sheppard, and Chan, 1982).

Physicians and health care providers must learn to identify those people at high risk for substance abuse as early as possible in the sequence of events leading to heavy use. Many people with heavy alcohol or drug use present at hospital or medical clinics for a whole range of symptoms, from psychological problems such as depression and anxiety to physical ailments such as burns, bruising, and broken limbs. There is evidence to suggest that treatment is most successful in patients who have not yet reached the more advanced stages of physiological damage due to excessive consumption (Ogborne, 1974), and attempts are now being made to develop composite biomedical and psychosocial indicators which may alert treatment personnel to those people at high risk for developing serious abuse problems (Holt, Skinner, and Israel; 1981; Skinner, Holt, and Israel, 1981). However, this is a relatively new area for research, and the effectiveness of using these indicators for early detection of cases needs systematic investigation.

It is possible that in some cases the identification of etiological factors may help to determine the most appropriate treatment, but it should be remembered that the presenting symptoms do not necessarily indicate the causes of substance abuse, nor does the fact that a treatment is effective necessarily help to understand etiology. A consideration of etiological factors may, however, be made with treatment implications in mind. The finding of factors common to many forms of substance abuse may, for example, have treatment implications for dealing with problems of excessive behavior in general rather than excessive use of particular substances. Studies of environmental and social causes have highlighted three of these common factors: the reinforcing effect of drugs; the modeling of drug-taking behavior; and the expectation of positive drug effects. These elements will also interact with the availability of a particular substance and the prevailing attitudinal tolerance toward drug use in the individual's culture. They will also be affected by the individual's past experience of using the drug and a belief in his own personal adequacy.

There appears to be an increased tendency to use and abuse multiple drugs, which also suggests that substance abuse should be looked at as a more general problem. Student surveys reveal that multiple drug use may now be more common than the use of one drug alone. Hochhauser (1977), for instance, has found that tobacco, alcohol, and marijuana are the primary drugs taken in combination with each other or with secondary drugs. In this study, alcohol was usually the first drug of choice; when another was introduced, it was taken concurrently with alcohol. As each new drug was tried, it was incorporated into the existing pattern of usage. As noted earlier with high school students, a predictable progression of drug use has been found, beginning with beer and tobacco and progressing to illicit drug use, with no indication that the earlier drugs that were tried were then discarded (Kandel, Kessler, and Margulies, 1978).

Most drug abusers appear to have a preferred drug, but when deprived of it they tend to turn to other substances. Heavy narcotic users often have a prior history of marijuana use; those in methadone maintenance programs, when deprived of heroin, may turn to barbiturates, alcohol, amphetamines, or benzodiazepines (Ausubel, 1980). The incidence of heavy cigarette smoking among heavy alcohol consumers is high (Maletsky and Klotter, 1974; Miller, 1976), and cigarette smokers often have a high caffeine intake (Friedman, Siegelaub, and Seltzer, 1974).

The inability to find a specific drug or alcoholic personality, or characteristics within a person which consistently relate to a tendency to take one particular drug, also points to a broader consideration of the person prone to excessive behavior in general. Gilbert (1976) suggests that the relevant questions to be asked concerning etiology should be: (1) Why is this person behaving to excess? (2) Why is alcohol drinking (or abuse of source other substance) the excessive behavior? Perhaps it might be appropriate to ask this second question first, since many cultural and social factors have been identified which prompt a person to take up a particular substance. These include such factors as peer pressure, availability of the substance, and modeling influences, which have already been considered. However, beyond this question is the first asked by Gilbert, namely, why is this person behaving to excess?

The literature on schedule-induced adjunctive behavior suggests that excessive substance use has much in common initially with compulsive behavior in general, since animals appear to produce to excess those behaviors already learned and most available to them in the present environment. It is also probable that the psychological and pharmacological effects of drugs help to maintain their use, once begun, especially where the withdrawal effects are severe. The tendency for a person to maintain a hedonic balance between positive and negative states may also contribute to maintenance. Beyond this, taste preference, the reinforcing effects of intoxication, and the general tendency to increase frequency and size of overlearned responses in all probability contribute to an escalating problem for the individual. Such a passage of events may go unchecked until physiological and social systems begin to break down and treatment becomes imperative.

Some treatment programs are now individually tailored to specific problem areas within a person's life, and there is also a tendency to broaden the definition of "success" in treatment beyond the confines of abstinence (Sobell and Sobell, 1978; Pattison, 1979). Research into etiological factors has emphasized the multidimensional nature of the problem, since both alcoholism and other types of substance abuse appear to derive from many areas of functioning within a person's life. Broader categories or distinct subsets of people with excessive use of one or several substances in relation to life functioning may suggest new and alternative treatment programs (Hart and Stueland, 1979).

Alterman and McLellan (1981) have suggested developing a classificatory model which distinguishes between five subgroups of substance abusers on the basis of psychological effects and the number of drugs used. These subgroups are (1) single-substance abusers of psychodepressants (alcohol, narcotics), (2) single-substance abusers of psychostimulants, (3) multiple similar-substance abusers of psychodepressants, (4) multiple similar-substance abusers of psychostimulants, and (5) multiple dissimilar-substance abusers. This type of classification is based upon the theory that substance abusers may take a particular class of drugs to satisfy distinctive physiological and behavioral needs. As yet, this type of approach has not been evaluated in terms of treatment efficacy, and it focuses on only a few of the factors which have been identified as causative. Huba, Wingard, and Bentler (1980) have attempted to classify all of the intraindividual and extraindividual factors which are thought to contribute to drug use and abuse. These include biological, interpersonal, intrapersonal, and sociocultural factors, involving genetics, organismic and psychological status, socioeconomic resources, behavioral styles, expectations, stresses, and product availability, to name a few of the variables. These authors found five independent patterns of drug use when the principal substances are categorized as (1) marijuana and hashish, (2) beer, wine, and liquor, (3) cocaine, tranquilizers, and drugstore medication, (4) tobacco, and (5) inhalants (Huba, Wingard, and Bentler, 1979).

The identification of the numerous factors thought to contribute to the excessive use of a substance creates a dilemma for those who are planning treatment. An overinclusion of variables may provide too little specific information to identify a basis for therapeutic action, whereas focusing on too few variables may ignore other potentially important factors. At present, there is room for treatment to be planned from both perspectives until the most salient variables have been determined, and this determination can be facilitated by an investigation of both the causative factors and by the presenting symptoms. The present trend is toward a realization that substance abuse is part of a larger life health problem, the type of substance abused depending on availability, social policy, and general attitudes as well as the nature of the substance itself and its effect on the individual. This broadening concept of substance abuse may help us to understand a little more clearly why a proportion of the population does take such substances to excess.

References

Abrams, D. B., and Wilson, G. T. Effects of alcohol on social anxiety in women: cognitive vs. physiological processes. *Journal of Abnormal Psychology,* 1979, *88,* 161–173.

Ahlgren, A., Norem, A. A., Hochhauser, M., and Garvin, J. Antecedents of smoking among pre-adolescents. *Journal of Drug Education,* 1982, *12,* 325–340.

Ahlström-Laakso, S. European drinking habits: a review of research and some suggestions for conceptual integration of findings. In M. W. Everett, J. O. Waddell, and D. B. Heath (eds.), *Cross-cultural Approaches to the Study of Alcohol: An Interdisciplinary Perspective.* The Hague: Mouton, 1976.

Albrecht, G. L. The alcoholism process: a social learning viewpoint. In P. G. Bourne, and R. Fox (eds.), *Alcoholism: Progress in Research and Treatment.* New York: Academic Press, 1973.

Alexander, C. N., Jr., and Campbell, E. Q. Peer influences on adolescent drinking. *Quarterly Journal of Studies on Alcohol,* 1968, *28,* 444–453.

Alsikafi, M., Globetti, G., and Christy, E. G. Abusive alcohol drinking: a study of social attitudes of youth in a military community. *Drug Forum,* 1979, *7,* 317–329.

Alterman, A. I., and McLellan, A. T. A framework for refining the diagnostic categorization of substance abusers. *Addictive Behaviors,* 1981, *6,* 23–27.

Annis, H. M. Patterns of intra-familial drug use. *British Journal of Addictions,* 1974, *69,* 359–367.

———. Adolescent drug use: the role of peer groups and parental example. *The Ontario Psychologist,* 1975, *7*(*4*), 7–9.

Antonuccio, D. O., and Lichtenstein, E. Peer modeling influences on smoking behavior of heavy and light smokers. *Addictive Behaviors,* 1980, *5,* 299–306.

Atkin, C. K., Neuendorf, K. & McDermott, S. The role of alcohol advertising in excessive and hazardous drinking. *Journal of Drug Education,* 1983, *4,* 313–325.

Ausubel, D. P. An interactional approach to narcotic addiction. In D. J. Lettieri, M. Sayers, and H. W. Pearson (eds.), *Theories on Drug Abuse: Selected Contemporary Perspectives.* National Institute on Drug Abuse Research Monograph no. 30. Rockville, Md.: National Institute on Alcohol Abuse and Alcoholism, 1980.

Bacon, M. K. Cross-cultural studies of drinking. In P. G. Bourne, and R. Fox (eds.), *Alcoholism: Progress in Research and Treatment.* New York: Academic Press, 1973.

Bandura, A. Self-efficacy: toward a unifying theory of behavior change. *Psychological Review,* 1977, *84,* 191–215.

———, and Walters, R. H. *Social Learning and Personality Development.* New York: Holt, Reinhart & Winston, 1963.

Barnes, G. E. The alcoholic personality: a reanalysis of the literature. *Journal of Studies on Alcohol,* 1979, *40,* 571–634.

———. Characteristics of the clinical alcoholic personality. *Journal of Studies on Alcohol,* 1980, *41,* 894–910.

Berg, G., Laberg, J. C., Skutle, A., and Öhman, A. Instructed versus pharmacological effects of alcohol in alcoholics and social drinkers. *Behavior, Research and Therapy,* 1981, *19,* 55–66.

Bergman, R. L. Navajo peyote use: its apparent safety. *American Journal of Psychiatry,* 1971, *128,* 695–699.

Bigelow, G., Liebson, I., and Griffiths, R. Alcoholic drinking: suppression by a brief time-out procedure. *Behaviour Research and Therapy,* 1974, *12,* 107–115.

Blane, H. T., and Barry, H. Birth order and alcoholism. *Quarterly Journal of Studies on Alcohol,* 1973, *34,* 837–852.

Boothroyd, W. E. Nature and development of alcoholism in women. In O. J. Kalant (ed.), *Alcohol and Drug Problems in Women.* New York: Plenum Press, 1980.

Brecher, G. M. *Licit and Illicit Drugs: The Consumers Union Report.* Toronto: Little, Brown & Co., 1972.

Brown, S. A., Goldman, M. S., Inn, A., and Anderson, L. R. Expectations of reinforcement from alcohol: their domain and relation to drinking patterns. *Journal of Consulting and Clinical Psychology,* 1980, *48,* 419–426.

Bunzel, R. The role of alcoholism in two Central American cultures. *Psychiatry,* 1940, *3,* 361–387.

Burton, G., and Kaplan, H. M. Group counselling in conflicted marriages where alcoholism is present: client's evaluation of effectiveness. *Journal of Marriage and the Family,* 1968, *30,* 74–79.

Cadoret, R. J., Cain, C. A., and Grove, W. M. Development of alcoholism in adoptees raised apart from alcoholic biologic relatives. *Archives of General Psychiatry,* 1980, *37,* 561–563.

Cafiso, J., Goodstadt, M. S., Garlington, W. K., and Sheppard, M. A. Television portrayal of alcohol and other beverages. *Journal of Studies on Alcohol,* 1982, *43,* 1232–1243.

Cahalan, D. *Problem Drinkers.* San Francisco: Jossey-Bass, 1970.

———, Cisin, I. H., and Crossley, H. M. *American Drinking Practices: A National Study of Drinking Behavior and Attitudes.* Monograph No. 6. New Brunswick, N.J.: Rutgers Center of Alcohol Studies, 1969.

Cappell, H., and Herman, C. P. Alcohol and tension reduction: a review. *Quarterly Journal of Studies on Alcohol,* 1972, *33,* 33–64.

Carlin, A. S., and Stauss, F. F. Descriptive and functional classifications of drug abusers. *Journal of Consulting and Clinical Psychology,* 1977, *45,* 222–227.

Christiansen, B. A., and Goldman, M. S. Alcohol related expectancies versus demographic/background variables in the prediction of adolescent drinking. *Journal of Consulting and Clinical Psychology,* 1983, *51,* 249–257.

Cohen, D. C., and Krause, M. S. *Case-Work with the Wives of Alcoholics.* New York: Family Service Association of America, 1971.

Coleman, S. B. Incomplete mourning and addict/family transactions: a theory for understanding heroin abuse. In D. J. Lettieri, M., Sayers, and H. W. Pearson (eds.), *Theories on Drug Abuse: Selected Contemporary Perspectives.* National Institute on Drug Abuse Research Monograph no. 30. Rockville, Md.: National Institute on Alcohol Abuse and Alcoholism, 1980.

Conger, J. J. Alcoholism: theory, problem and challenge. Part 2: Reinforcement theory and the diagnosis of alcoholism. *Quarterly Journal of Studies on Alcohol,* 1956, *17,* 296–305.

Cosper, R. Drinking as conformity; a critique of the sociological literature on occupational differences in drinking. *Journal of Studies on Alcohol,* 1979, *40,* 868–891.

Cotton, N. S. The familial incidence of alcoholism: a review. *Journal of Studies on Alcohol,* 1979, *40,* 89–116.

Deardorff, C. M., Melges, F. T., Hout, C. N., and Savage, D. J. Situations related to drinking alcohol: a factor analysis of questionnaire responses. *Journal of Studies on Alcohol,* 1975, *36,* 1184–1195.

de Lint, J., and Schmidt, W. Consumption averages and alcoholism prevalence: a brief review of epidemiological investigations. *British Journal of Addictions,* 1971, *66,* 97–107.

———. Distribution of alcohol consumption in Ontario. *Quarterly Journal of Studies on Alcohol,* 1968, *29,* 968–973.

Dohrenwend, B. S. Life events as stressors: a methodological inquiry. *Journal of Health and Social Behavior,* 1973, *14,* 167–175.

Donovan, D. M., and Marlatt, G. A. Assessment of expectancies and behaviours associated with alcohol consumption. *Journal of Studies on Alcohol,* 1980, *41,* 1153–1185.

Donovan, D. M., and O'Leary, M. R. Comparison of perceived and experienced control among alcoholics and nonalcoholics. *Journal of Abnormal Psychology,* 1975, *84,* 726–728.

Donovan, J. E., and Jessor, R. Problem drinking and the dimension of involvement with drugs: a Guttman scalogram analysis of adolescent drug use. *American Journal of Public Health,* 1983, *73,* 543–551.

———, and Jessor, L. Problem drinking in adolescence and young adulthood. *Journal of Studies on Alcohol,* 1983, *44,* 109–136.

Dudley, D. L., Roszell, D. K., Mules, J. E., and Hague, W. H. Heroin vs. alcohol addiction: quantifiable psychosocial similarities and differences. *Journal of Psychosomatic Research,* 1974, *18,* 327–335.

Edwards, G., Orford, J., Egert, S., Guthrie, S., Hawker, A., Hensman, C., Mitcheson, M., Oppenheimer, E., and Taylor, C. Alcoholism: a controlled trial of "treatment" and "advice." *Journal of Studies on Alcohol,* 1977, *38,* 1004–1031.

Eisenman, R., Grossman, J. C., and Goldstein, N. Undergraduate marijuana use as related to internal sensation, novelty seeking, and openness to experience. *Journal of Clinical Psychology,* 1980, *36,* 1013–1019.

Epstein, S. M. Toward a unified theory of anxiety. In B. A. Maher (ed.), *Progress in Experimental Personality Research,* vol. 4. New York: Academic Press, 1967.

Falk, J. L. Production of polydipsia in normal rats by an intermittent food schedule. *Science,* 1961, *133,* 195–196.

———. The nature and determinants of adjunctive behaviour. In R. M. Gilbert, and J. D. Keen (eds.), *Schedule Effects: Drugs, Drinking, and Aggression.* Toronto: University of Toronto Press, 1972.

———, and Samson, H. H. Schedule-induced physical dependence on ethanol. *Pharmacological Review,* 1975, *27,* 449–464.

Farber, P. D., Khavari, K. A., and Douglass, F. M. A factor-analytic study of reasons for drinking: empirical validation of positive and negative reinforcement dimensions. *Journal of Consulting and Clinical Psychology,* 1980, *48,* 780–781.

Fawzy, F. I., Coombs, R. H., and Gerber, B. Generational continuity in the use of substances: the impact of parental substance use on adolescent substance use. *Addictive Behaviors,* 1983, *8,* 109–114.

Finney, J. W., and Moos, R. H. Treatment and outcome for empirical subtypes of alcoholic patients. *Journal of Consulting and Clinical Psychology,* 1979, *47,* 25–38.

Forslund, M. A., and Gustafson, T. J. Influence of peers and parents and sex differences in drinking by high school students. *Quarterly Journal of Studies on Alcohol,* 1970, *31,* 868–875.

Frances, R. J., Timm, S., and Buckley, S. Studies of familial and non-familial alcoholism. *Archives of General Psychiatry,* 1980, *37,* 564–566.

Friedman, G. D., Siegelaub, A. B., and Selzer, C. C. Cigarettes, alcohol, coffee, and peptic ulcer. *New England Journal of Medicine,* 1974, *290,* 469–473.

Fulmer, R. H., and Lapidus, L. B. A study of professed reasons for beginning and continuing heroin use. *International Journal of Addiction,* 1980, *15,* 631–645.

Galanter, M. Religious influence and the etiology of substance abuse. In E. Gottheil, K. A. Druley, T. E. Skoloda, and H. M. Waxman (eds.), *Etiologic Aspects of Alcohol and Drug Abuse.* Springfield, Ill.: Charles C. Thomas, 1983.

Gilbert, R. M. Drug abuse as excessive behaviour. *Canadian Psychological Review,* 1976, *17,* 231–240.

Glaser, F. B. Anybody got a match? Treatment research and the matching hypothesis. In G. Edwards, and M. Grant (eds.), *Alcoholism Treatment in Transition.* Baltimore: Johns Hopkins University Press, 1980.

Goldstein, G., and Chotlos, J. W. Stability of field dependence in chronic alcoholic patients. *Journal of Abnormal Psychology,* 1966, *71,* 417–424.

Goodstadt, M. S., Sheppard, M. A., and Chan, G. C. An evaluation of two school based alcohol education programs. *Journal of Studies on Alcohol,* 1982, *43,* 352–369.

Goodwin, D. W. Genetic factors in alcoholism. In N. K. Mills (ed.), *Advances in Substance Abuse.* Greenwich, Conn.: JAI Press, 1980.

———, Schulsinger, F., Moller, N., Hermansen, L., Winokur, G., and Guze, S. B. Drinking problems in adopted and non-adopted sons of alcoholics. *Archives of General Psychiatry,* 1974, *31,* 164–169.

Gorenstein, E. E. Relationships of subclinical depression, psychopathy and hysteria to patterns of alcohol consumption and abuse in males and females. In M. Galanter (ed.), *Currents in Alcoholism: Recent Advances in Research and Treatment,* vol. 7. New York: Grune & Stratton, 1980.

Gorsuch, R. L., and Butler, M. C. Initial drug abuse: a review of predisposing social psychological factors. *Psychological Bulletin,* 1976, *83,* 120–137.

Griffiths, R., Bigelow, G., and Liebson, I. Suppression of ethanol self-administration in alcoholics by contingent time-out from social interactions. *Behaviour Research and Therapy,* 1974, *12,* 327–334.

Halsukami, D., Owen, P., Pyle, R., and Mitchell, J. Similarities and differences on the MMPI between women with bulimia and women with alcohol or drug abuse problems. *Addictive Behaviors,* 1982, *7,* 435–439.

Harder, D. W., Strauss, J. S., Kokes, R. F., Ritzler, B. A., and Gift, T. G. Life events and psychopathology severity among first psychiatric admissions. *Journal of Abnormal Psychology,* 1980, *89,* 165–180.

Hart, L. S., and Stueland, D. An application of the multidimensional model of alcoholism to program effectiveness. Rehabilitation status and outcome. *Journal of Studies on Alcohol,* 1979, *40,* 645–655.

Heath, D. B. Drinking patterns of the Bolivian Camba. *Quarterly Journal on Studies of Alcohol,* 1958, *19,* 491–508.

Hill, H. E. The social deviant and initial addiction to narcotics and alcohol. In D. J. Lettieri, M. Sayers, and H. W. Pearson (eds.), *Theories on Drug Abuse: Selected Contemporary Perspectives.* National Institute on Drug Abuse Research Monograph no. 30. Rockville, Md.: National Institute on Alcohol Abuse and Alcoholism, 1980.

Hochhauser, M. Alcohol and marijuana consumption among undergraduate polydrug users. *American Journal of Drug and Alcohol Abuse,* 1977, *4,* 65–76.

Hoffman, H. Depression and defensiveness in self-descriptive moods of alcoholics. *Psychological Reports,* 1970, *26,* 23–26.

Holmes, T. H., and Rahe, R. H. The social readjustment rating scale. *Journal of Psychosomatic Research,* 1967, *11,* 213–218.

Holt, S., Skinner, H. A., and Israel, Y. Early identification of alcohol abuse. Part 2: Clinical and laboratory indicators. *Canadian Medical Association Journal,* 1981, *124,* 1279–1295.

Hore, B. D. Life events and alcoholic relapse. *British Journal of Addictions,* 1971, *66,* 83–88.

Huba, G. J., Wingard, J. A., and Bentler, P. M. Beginning adolescent drug use and peer and adult interaction patterns. *Journal of Consulting and Clinical Psychology,* 1979, *47,* 265–276.

———. Framework for an interactive theory of drug use. In D. J. Lettieri, M. Sayers, and H. W. Pearson (eds.), *Theories on Drug Abuse: Selected Contemporary Perspectives.* National Institute on Drug Abuse Research Monograph no. 30. Rockville, Md.: National Institute on Alcohol Abuse and Alcoholism, 1980.

Huber, H., Karlin, R., and Nathan, P. G. Blood alcohol level discrimination by non-alcoholics: the role of internal and external cues. *Journal of Studies on Alcohol,* 1976, *37,* 27–39.

Hundleby, J. D. *Individual and environmental predictors and correlates of adolescent drug-related behaviour.* Report on Project 1212–5–126, Non-Medical Use of Drugs Directorate, Ottawa, Canada, 1979.

Jacob, T., Favorini, A., Meisel, S. S., and Anderson, C. M. The alcoholic's spouse, children, and family interactions. *Journal of Studies on Alcohol,* 1978, *39,* 1231–1251.

Jacobson, G. R. *The Alcoholisms: Detection, Diagnosis, and Assessment.* New York: Human Sciences Press, 1976.

———. An introduction to psychological factors in the etiology and treatment of alcoholism. In M. Galanter (ed.), *Currents in Alcoholism: Recent Advances in Research and Treatment,* vol. 7. New York: Grune & Stratton, 1980.

Jessor, R., and Jessor, S. L. Adolescent development and the onset of drinking: a longitudinal study. *Journal of Studies on Alcohol,* 1975, *36,* 27–51.

———, and Finney, J. A. A social psychology of marijuana use: longitudinal studies of high school and college youth. *Journal of Personality and Social Psychology,* 1973, *26,* 1–15.

Johnson, B. D. Toward a theory of drug subculture. In D. J. Lettieri, M. Sayers, and H. W. Pearson (eds.), *Theories of Drug Abuse: Selected Contemporary Perspectives.* National Institute on Drug Abuse Research Monograph no. 30. Rockville, Md.: National Institute on Alcohol Abuse and Alcoholism, 1980.

Jones, B. E., and Prada, J. A. Relapse to morphine use in dogs. *Psychopharmacologia,* 1973, *30,* 1–12.

Jones-Saumty, D., Hockhaus, L., Dru, R., and Zeiner, A. Psychological factors of familial alcoholism in American Indians and Caucasians. *Journal of Clinical Psychology,* 1983, *39,* 783–790.

Kalant, O. J., Alcohol and drug problems in women. In Y. Israel, F. B. Glaser, H. Kalant, R. E. Popham, W. Schmidt, and R. C. Smart (eds.), *Research Advances in Alcohol and Drug Problems.* Vol. 4. New York: Plenum Press, 1980.

Kammeier, M. L., Hoffman, H., and Loper, R. G. Personality characteristics of alcoholics as college freshmen and at time of treatment. *Quarterly Journal of Studies on Alcohol,* 1973, *34,* 390–399.

Kandel, D. B. (ed). *Longitudinal Research on Drug Use: Empirical Findings and Methodological Issues.* New York: Wiley, 1978.

———, Kessler, R. C., and Margulies, R. Z. Antecedents of adolescent initiation into stages of drug use. In D. B. Kandel (ed.), *Longitudinal Research on Drug Use: Empirical Findings and Methodological Issues.* New York: Wiley, 1978.

Kassebaum, C. G., Couch, A. S., and Slater, P. The factorial dimensions of the MMPI. *Journal of Consulting Psychology,* 1959, *23,* 226–236.

Khantzian, E. J. An ego/self theory of substance dependence: a contemporary psychoanalytic perspective. In D. J. Lettieri, M. Sayers, and H. W. Pearson (eds.), *Theories on Drug Abuse: Selected Contemporary Perspectives.* National Institute on Drug Abuse Research Monograph no. 30. Rockville, Md.: National Institute on Alcohol Abuse and Alcoholism, 1980.

———, Mack, J. E., and Schatzberg, A. F. Heroin use as an attempt to cope: clinical observations. *American Journal of Psychiatry,* 1974, *131,* 160–164.

Kilpatrick, D. G., McAlhany, D. A., McCurdy, R. L., Shaw, D. L., and Roitzsch, J. C. Aging, alcoholism, anxiety, and sensation seeking: an exploratory investigation. *Addictive Behaviors,* 1982, *7,* 97–100.

Knight, R. P. The dynamics and treatment of chronic alcohol addiction. *Bulletin of the Menninger Clinic,* 1937, *1,* 233–250.

Kohn, P. M., and Annis, H. M. Drug use and four kinds of novelty-seeking. *British Journal of Addictions,* 1977, *72,* 135–141.

Kohn, P. M., Fox, J., Barnes, G. E., Annis, H. M., Hoffman, F. M., and Eichental, B. Progressive development of a model of youthful marijuana use. *Representative Research in Social Psychology,* 1979, *9,* 122–139.

Krueger, D. W. Stressful life events and the return to heroin use. *Journal of Human Stress,* 1981, *7,* 3–8.

Kunitz, S. J., and Levy, J. E. Changing ideas of alcohol use among Navaho Indians. *Quarterly Journal of Studies on Alcohol,* 1974, *35,* 243–259.

La Barbera, J. D., and Caul, W. F. Decrement in distress to an aversive event during a conditioned opponent process. *Animal Learning and Behaviour,* 1976, *4,* 485–489.

Lansky, D., Nathan, P. E., and Lawson, D. M. Blood alcohol level discrimination by alcoholics: the role of internal and external cues. *Journal of Consulting and Clinical Psychology,* 1978, *46,* 953–960.

Laudeman, K. A. Personality, drinking patterns, and problem drinking among young adult offenders. *Journal of Drug Education,* 1977, *7,* 259–269.

Leander, J. D., and McMillan, D. E. Schedule-induced narcotic ingestion. *Pharmacology Review,* 1975, *27,* 475–487.

Lemert, E. M. Forms of pathology of drinking in three Polynesian societies. *American Anthropologist,* 1964, *66,* 361–374.

Lester, D. Self-maintenance of intoxication in the rat. *Quarterly Journal of Studies on Alcohol,* 1961, *22,* 223–231.

Levenson, R. W., Sher, K. J., Grossman, L. M., Newman, J., and Newlin, D. B. Alcohol and stress response dampening: pharmacological effects, expectancy, and tension reduction. *Journal of Abnormal Psychology,* 1980, *89,* 528–538.

Levine, H. G. Temperance and women in the nineteenth-century United States. In O. J. Kalant (ed.), *Alcohol and Drug Problems in Women.* Vol. 4 of *Research Advances in Alcohol and Drug Problems* (series eds. Y. Israel, F. B. Glaser, H. Kalant, R. E. Popham, W. Schmidt, and R. C. Smart). New York: Plenum Press, 1980.

Liban, C., and Smart, R. G. Generational and other differences between males and females in problem drinking and its treatment. *Drug and Alcohol Dependence,* 1980, *5,* 207–221.

Lidz, T., and Rothenberg, A. Psychedelism: Dionysius reborn. *Psychiatry,* 1968, *31,* 116–125.

Lied, E. R., and Marlatt, G. A. Modeling as a determinant of alcohol consumption: effect of subject sex and prior drinking history. *Addictive Behaviors,* 1979, *4,* 47–54.

Lindesmith, A. R. *Addictions and Opiates.* Chicago: Aldine Press, 1968.

Lloyd, C. Life events and depressive disorder reviewed. Part 2: Events as precipitating factors. *Archives of General Psychiatry,* 1980, *37,* 541–548.

Loper, R. C., Kammeier, M. L., and Hoffman, H. MMPI characteristics of college freshman males who later became alcoholics. *Journal of Abnormal Psychology,* 1973, *82,* 159–162.

MacAndrew, C. An examination of the relevance of the individual differences (A-Trait) formulation of the tension reduction theory to the etiology of alcohol abuse in young males. *Addictive Behaviors,* 1982, *7,* 39–45.

Maddox, G. L., and McCall, B. C. Drinking among teenagers: a sociological interpretation of alcohol use by high school students. New Brunswick, N.J.: Rutgers Center for Alcohol Studies, Monograph no. 4, 1964.

Maletzky, B. M., and Klotter, J. Smoking and alcoholism. *American Journal of Psychiatry,* 1974, *131,* 445–447.

Mangin, W. Drinking among the Andean Indians. *Quarterly Journal of Studies on Alcohol,* 1957, *18,* 55–66.

Marlatt, G. A. The drinking profile: a questionnaire for the behavioral assessment of alcoholism. In G. J. Mash and L. G. Terdal (eds.), *Behavior Therapy, Assessment, Diagnosis, Design, and Evaluation.* New York: Springer, 1976.

———. Craving for alcohol, loss of control, and relapse: a cognitive-behavioral analysis. In P. E. Nathan, G. A. Marlatt, and T. Løberg (eds.), *Alcoholism: New Directions in Behavioral Research and Treatment.* New York: Plenum Press, 1978.

———, Demming, B., and Reid, J. B. Loss of control drinking in alcoholics: an experimental analogue. *Journal of Abnormal Psychology,* 1973, *81,* 233–241.

Martin, C. A., and Martin, W. R. Opiate dependence in women. In O. J. Kalant (ed.), *Alcohol and Drug Problems in Women.* New York: Plenum Press, 1980.

McAuliffe, W. E., and Gordon, R. A. Issues in testing Lindesmith's theory. *American Journal of Sociology,* 1975, *81,* 154–163.

McCarty, D., Morrison, S., and Mills, K. C. Attitudes, belief and alcohol use. *Journal of Studies on Alcohol,* 1983, *44,* 328–340.

McCollam, J. B., Burish, T. G., Maisto, J. A., and Sobell, M. B. Alcohol's effects on physiological arousal and self-reported affect and sensations. *Journal of Abnormal Psychology,* 1980, *89,* 224–233.

McCord, J. Etiological factors in alcoholism: family and personal characteristics. *Quarterly Journal of Studies on Alcohol,* 1972, *33,* 1020–1027.

McKenna, T., and Pickens, R. Personality characteristics of alcoholic children of alcoholics. *Journal of Studies on Alcohol,* 1983, *44,* 688–700.

McLachlan, J. F. C. Therapy strategies, personality orientation, and recovery from alcoholism. *Canadian Psychiatric Association Journal,* 1974, *19,* 25–30.

McMillan, D. E., Leander, J. D., and Ellis, F. W. Consumption of ethanol and water under schedule-induced polydipsia (SIP). *Pharmacologist,* 1974, *16,* 637–646.

McWilliams, J., Brown, C. C., and Minard, J. C. Field dependence and self-actualization in alcoholics. *Journal of Studies on Alcohol,* 1975, *36,* 387–394.

Meichenbaum, D. *Cognitive Behavior Modification: An Integrative Approach.* New York: Plenum Press, 1977.

Meisch, R. A., and Thompson, T. Ethanol as a reinforcer: effects of fixed-ratio size and food deprivation. *Psychopharmacologia,* 1973, *28,* 171–183.

Mello, N. K., and Mendelson, J. H. Operant performance by rats for alcohol reinforcement. *Quarterly Journal of Studies on Alcohol,* 1964, *25,* 226.

———. Alcohol and human behavior. In L. L. Iversen, S. D. Iversen, and S. H. Snyder (eds.), *Handbook of Psychopharmacology.* New York: Plenum Press, 1978.

Midanik, L. Familial alcoholism and problem drinking in a national drinking practices survey. *Addictive Behaviors,* 1983, *8,* 133–141.

Milkman, H., and Frosch, W. Theory of drug use. In D. J. Lettieri, M. Sayers, and H. W. Pearson (eds.), *Theories on Drug Abuse: Selected Contemporary Perspectives.* National Institute on Drug Abuse Research Monograph no. 30. Rockville, Md.: National Institute on Alcohol Abuse and Alcoholism, 1980.

Miller, R. R. Effects of smoking on drug action. *Clinical Pharmacology and Therapeutics,* 1976, *22,* 749–756.

Mills, C. J., and Noyes, H. L. Patterns and correlates of initial and subsequent drug use among adolescents. *Journal of Consulting and Clinical Psychology,* 1984, *52,* 231–243.

Mules, J. E., Hague, W. H., and Dudley, D. L. Life change, its perception, and alcohol addiction. *Journal of Studies on Alcohol,* 1977, *38,* 487–493.

Myers, J. K., Lindenthal, J. J., Pepper, M. P., and Ostrander, D. R. Life events and mental status: a longitudinal study. *Journal of Health and Social Behavior,* 1972, *13,* 398–406.

Nerviano, V. J., and Gross, H. W. Personality types of alcoholics on objective inventories. *Journal of Studies on Alcohol,* 1983, *44,* 837–851.

Offord, J. Alcoholism and marriage: the argument against specialism. *Journal of Studies on Alcohol,* 1975, *36,* 1537–1563.

Ogborne, A. C. Patient characteristics as predictors of treatment outcomes for alcohol and drug abuses. In Y. Israel, F. B. Glaser, H. Kalant, R. E.

Popham, W. Schmidt, and R. C. Smart (eds.), *Research Advances in Alcohol and Drug Problems,* vol. 4. New York: Plenum Press, 1974.

———, and Glaser, F. B. Evaluating Alcoholics Anonymous. In T. E. Bratter and G. G. Forrest (eds.), *Alcoholism and Substance Abuse: Strategies for Clinical Intervention.* New York: The Free Press, 1985.

Orcutt, J. D. Normative definitions of intoxicated states: a test of several sociological theories. *Social Problems,* 1978, *25,* 385–396.

Overmier, J. B., Payne, R. J., Brachbill, R. M., Linder, B., and Lawry, J. A. On the mechanism of the post-asymptotic decrement phenomenon. *Acta Neurobiologiae Experimentalis,* 1979, *39,* 603–620.

Paolino, T. J., and McCrady, B. S. *The Alcoholic Marriage: Alternative Perspectives.* New York: Grune & Stratton, 1977.

Parker, J. C., Gilbert, G., and Speltz, M. L. Expectations regarding the effects of alcohol on assertiveness: a comparison of alcoholics and social drinkers. *Addictive Behaviors,* 1981, *6,* 29–33.

Pattison, E. M. The selection of treatment modalities for the alcohol patient. In J. H. Mendelson, and N. K. Mello (eds.), *The Diagnosis and Treatment of Alcoholism.* New York: McGraw-Hill, 1979.

Pickens, R., Meisch, R. A., and Thompson, T. Drug self-administration: an analysis of the reinforcing effects of drugs. In L. L. Iversen, S. D. Iversen, and S. H. Snyder (eds.), *Handbook of Psychopharmacology,* Vol. 12. New York: Plenum Press, 1978.

Pliner, P., and Cappell, H. Modification of affective consequences of alcohol: a comparison of social and solitary drinking. *Journal of Abnormal Psychology,* 1974, *83,* 418–425.

Polivy, J., Schueneman, A. L., and Carlson, K. Alcohol and tension reduction: cognitive and physiological effects. *Journal of Abnormal Psychology,* 1976, *85,* 595–600.

Rabkin, J. G., and Struening, E. L. Life events, stress, and illness. *Science,* 1976, *194,* 1013–1020.

Rado, S. The psychoanalysis of pharmacothymia (drug addiction). *Psychoanalytic Quarterly,* 1933, *2,* 1–23.

Rahe, R. H. Epidemiological studies of life change and illness. *International Journal of Psychiatric Medicine,* 1975, *6,* 133–146.

———, and Arthur, R. J. Life change patterns surrounding illness experience. *Journal of Psychosomatic Research,* 1968, *11,* 341–345.

Rahe, R. H., Meyer, M., Smith, M., Kjaer, G., and Holmes, T. H. Social stress and illness onset. *Journal of Psychosomatic Research,* 1964, *8,* 35–44.

Richman, S. A., Teichman, M., and Fine, E. W. Psychosocial differences between male and female alcoholics. In M. Galanter (ed.), *Currents in Alcoholism.* Vol. 7, *Recent Advances in Research and Treatment.* New York: Grune & Stratton, 1980.

Rothman, K., and Keller, A. The effect of joint exposure to alcohol and tobacco on risk of cancer of the mouth and pharynx. *Journal of Chronic Diseases,* 1972, *25,* 711–716.

Schuckit, M. A. Depression and alcoholism in women. *Proceedings, First Annual Alcoholism Conference of the NIAAA.* Washington, D.C.: U.S. Government Printing Office, 1971.

———, and Pitts, F. N. Two types of alcoholism in women. *Archives of General Psychiatry,* 1969, *20,* 301–306.

Segal, B., Huba, G. J., and Singer, J. L. Prediction of college drug use from personality and inner experience. *International Journal of Addictions,* 1980, *15,* 849–867.

Senter, R. J., Heintzelman, M., Dorfmueller, M., and Hinkle, H. A comparative look at ratings of the subjective effects of beverage alcohol. *Psychological Record,* 1979, *29,* 49–56.

Sieber, M. F. Social background, attitudes, and personality in a three-year follow-up study of alcohol consumers. *Drug and Alcohol Dependence,* 1979, *4,* 407–417.

Silverstein, S. J., Nathan, P. E., and Taylor, H. A. Blood alcohol level estimation and controlled drinking by chronic alcoholics. *Behavior Therapy,* 1974, *5,* 1–15.

Skinner, H. A. Different strokes for different folks: differential treatment for alcohol abuse. In R. E. Meyer, et al. (eds.), *Evaluation of the Alcoholic: Implications for Research, Theory and Treatment.* Rockville, Md.: National Institute on Alcohol Abuse and Alcoholism, 1981.

———, Holt, S., and Israel, Y. Early identification of alcohol abuse. Part 1: Critical issues and psychosocial indicators for a composite index. *Canadian Medical Association Journal,* 1981, *124,* 1141–1152.

Skinner, H. A., Jackson, D. N., and Hoffman, H. Alcoholic personality types: identification and correlates. *Journal of Abnormal Psychology,* 1974, *83,* 658–666.

Skinner, H. A., and Lei, H. The multidimensional assessment of stressful life events. *Journal of Nervous and Mental Disorders,* 1980, *168,* 535–541.

Skinner, H. A., Reed, P. L., and Jackson, D. N. Toward the objective diagnosis of psychopathology: generalizability of modal personality profiles. *Journal of Consulting and Clinical Psychology,* 1976, *44,* 111–117.

Sobell, M. B., and Sobell, L. C. *Behavioral Treatment of Alcohol Problems.* New York: Plenum Press, 1978.

Solomon, R. L. The opponent-process theory of acquired motivation: the costs of pleasure and the benefits of pain. *American Psychologist,* 1980, *35,* 691–712.

Somekh, D. Factors contributing to self-reported drug use among London undergraduates 1971–1972. *Drug and Alcohol Dependence,* 1978, *3,* 289–299.

Spotts, J. V., and Shontz, F. C. Drugs and personality: extraversion-introversion. *Journal of Clinical Psychology,* 1984, *40,* 624–628.

Stanton, M. D. Drugs and the family. *Marriage and Family Review,* 1979, *2,* 1–10.

———. A family theory of drug abuse. In D. J. Lettieri, M. Sayers, and H. W. Pearson (eds.), *Theories on Drug Abuse: Selected Contemporary Perspectives.* National Institute on Drug Abuse Research Monograph no. 30. Rockville, Md.: National Institute on Alcohol Abuse and Alcoholism, 1980.

———, Todd, T. C., Heard, D. B., Kirschner, S., Kleiman, J. I., Mowatt, D. T., Riley, P., Scott, S. M., and van Deusen, J. M. Heroin addiction as a family phenomenon: a new conceptual model. *American Journal of Drug and Alcohol Abuse,* 1978, *5,* 125–150.

Starr, M. D. An opponent-process theory of motivation. Part 6: Time and intensity variables in the development of separation-induced distress calling in ducklings. *Journal of Experimental Psychology: Animal Behavior Processes,* 1978, *4,* 338–355.

Steer, R. A., McElroy, M. G. and Beck, A. T. Correlates of self reported and clinically assessed depression in outpatient alcoholics. *Journal of Clinical Psychology,* 1983, *39,* 144–149.

Steinglass, P. Experimenting with family treatment approaches to alcoholism, 1950–1975: a review. *Family Process,* 1976, *15,* 97–123.

———, Weiner, S., and Mendelson, J. H. A systems approach to alcoholics: a model and its clinical application. *Archives of General Psychiatry,* 1971, *24,* 401–408.

Stumphauser, J. S. Learning to drink: adolescents and alcohol. *Addictive Behaviors,* 1980, *5,* 277–283.

Swinson, R. P. Sex differences in the inheritance of alcoholism. In O. J. Kalant (ed.), *Alcohol and Drug Problems in Women.* New York: Plenum Press, 1980.

Tarnai, J., and Young, F. A. Alcoholics' personalities: extravert or introvert? *Psychological Reports,* 1983, *53,* 123–127.

Tarter, R. E., and Alterman, A. I. Neuropsychological deficits in alcoholics: etiological considerations. *Journal of Studies on Alcohol,* 1984, *45,* 1–9.

Vaillant, G. E. Natural history of male psychosocial health. Part 7: Antecedents of alcoholism and "orality." *American Journal of Psychiatry,* 1980, *137,* 181–186.

Vaillant, G. E. Natural history of male alcoholism. Part V: Is alcoholism the cart or the horse to sociopathy? *British Journal of Addictions,* 1983, *78,* 317–326.

Vicary, J. R., and Lerner, J. V. Longitudinal perspectives on drug use: analyses from the New York longitudinal study. *Journal of Drug Education,* 1983, *13,* 275–285.

Vuchinich, R. E., and Sobell, M. B. Empirical separation of physiologic and expected effects of alcohol on complex perceptual motor performance. *Psychopharmacology,* 1978, *60,* 81–85.

Weiner, S., Tamerin, J. S., Steinglass, P., and Mendelson, J. H. Familial patterns in chronic alcoholism: a study of a father and son during experimental intoxication. *American Journal of Psychiatry,* 1971, *127,* 1646–1651.

Whitehead, P. C. Multidrug use: supplementary perspectives. *International Journal of the Addictions,* 1974, *9,* 185–204.

———, and Harvey, C. Explaining alcoholism: an empirical test and reformulation. *Journal of Health and Social Behavior,* 1974, *15,* 57–65.

Whitehead, P. C., Smart, R. G., and La Forest, L. Multiple drug use among marijuana smokers in Eastern Canada. *International Journal of the Addictions,* 1972, *7,* 179–190.

Wickler, A. A theory of opioid dependence. In D. J. Lettieri, M. Sayers, and H. W. Pearson (eds.), *Theories on Drug Abuse: Selected Contemporary Perspectives.* Rockville, Md.: National Institute on Alcohol Abuse and Alcoholism, 1980.

Williams, A. F., McCourt, W. F., and Schneider, L. Personality self-descriptions of alcoholics and heavy drinkers. *Quarterly Journal of Studies on Alcohol,* 1971, *32,* 310–317.

Woititz, J. G. Alcoholism and the family: a survey of the literature. *Journal of Alcohol and Drug Education,* 1978, *23,* 18–23.

Wolin, S. J., Bennett, L. A., Noonan, D. A., and Teitelbaum, M. A. Disrupted family rituals: a factor in the intergenerational transmission of alcoholism. *Journal of Studies on Alcohol,* 1980, *41,* 199–214.

Wright, M. H., and Obitz, F. W. Alcoholics and nonalcoholics' attributions of control of future life events. *Journal of Studies on Alcohol,* 1984, *45,* 138–143.

2

The Psychopharmacology of Addiction

PAUL R. MATUSCHKA

SINCE ANCIENT TIMES humanity has been occupied with the search for perfect bliss. The search continues to this day with chemical substances both old and new, and it sometimes leads to drug abuse and/or addiction.

People often resort to self-treatment to restore equilibrium to their lives. They may indulge in compulsive eating, smoking, or the use of various drugs such as alcohol, marijuana, sedative-hypnotic agents, or narcotics. The use and abuse of these drugs will be the primary focus of this chapter.

Drug use and drug abuse are two different things. Taking a sedative-hypnotic under medical supervision to induce sleep is considered "drug use," but taking the same amount of the drug to produce euphoria is considered "drug abuse." This is not to intimate that prescribed drugs are not abused. Drug abuse is an intricate psychological, social, biochemical, and, possibly, genetic problem (Denber, 1979). To date, this problem has evaded solution. The basic element of abuse is some psychological instability for which chemical substances may represent the so-called "therapeutic agent" needed for self-treatment.

Addiction can be defined as "a behavioral pattern of compulsive drug use, characterized by overwhelming involvement with the use of a drug [and] the securing of its supply and a high tendency to relapse after withdrawal" (Jaffe, 1975). Physical dependence can be defined as "an altered physiological state produced by the repeated administration of the drug, which necessitates the continued administration of the drug to prevent the appearance of a stereotyped syndrome, the withdrawal or abstinence syndrome, characteristic for the particular drug" (Jaffe 1975). This chapter will deal with the psychopharmacology of addiction, "psychopharmacology" meaning, quite simply, the use of drugs to influence affective and emotional states (*Stedman's Medical Dictionary,* 1977). We will examine the following substances: (1) alcohol, (2) sedative-hypnotics, (3) opiates, (4) minor tranquilizers, and (5) marijuana. In particular, the following aspects of these drugs will be covered: (1) their observed effects, both acute and long-term; (2) their pharmacology (chemistry, action, and uses) and pharmacokinetics (duration and metabolism); and (3) the treatment of abuse.

Alcohol

Ethyl alcohol, or ethanol (hereafter referred to as alcohol), found in alcoholic beverages, is derived by the fermentation of starch, sugar, or other carbohydrates. It has enjoyed use as a sedative and hypnotic for centuries. Alcohol is a central nervous system (CNS) depressant which produces an apparent stimulation preceding the depression (Daniels and Jorgensen, 1977).

A person is legally drunk if he or she has blood alcohol levels of at least 100 milligrams per 100 milliliters (100 mg. %). If blood alcohol levels are compared in adult nontolerant drinkers, effects appear in certain ranges. Acute alcohol intoxication, starting with blood concentrations in the 20–99 mg. % range, causes slight changes in mood and feelings, muscle incoordination, impaired sensory function, and personality or behavioral changes. With blood alcohol levels ranging from 100 to 199 mg. %, there is evidence of marked mental impairment, incoordination, clumsiness, unsteadiness in standing or walking, and prolonged reaction time. At levels of 200–299 mg. %, nausea, vomiting, diplopia, and marked ataxia are seen. At blood levels of 300–399 mg. %, hypothermia, severe dysarthria, amnesia, and first-stage anesthesia are manifested. At levels ranging from 400 to 700 mg. %, coma, respiratory failure, and death can occur.

Although all organ systems are affected by alcoholic consumption, the CNS is the major system affected. The areas of the brain associated with the most highly integrated functions are the first to be depressed, particularly the polysynaptic structures of the reticular activating system and certain cortical sites (Ritchie, 1975). The cortex then loses its integrating control, and the various thought processes occur in a disorganized manner. Mental processes dependent upon training and previous experience are affected first. Familiar or habitual tasks of a mechanical nature, involving less skill, thought, and attention, are affected to a much lesser degree. The effects of alcohol on the CNS are proportional to the alcoholic concentration in the blood. Since the brain has a rich blood supply, the central nervous system is affected rapidly. Alcohol acts on the area of the brain responsible for respiration, and in large quantities is a respiratory depressant. It causes vasodilatation primarily in cutaneous vessels, producing a warm and flushed skin. Alcohol does not affect the heart when taken in small amounts, but chronic use can cause cardiomyopathy. Moderate amounts increase heart rate and cardiac output, as well as pulse rate. Large doses of alcohol cause the central temperature-regulating mechanism to become depressed and the body temperature to fall.

Alcohol is an energy source and may improve circulation in skeletal muscle, but with moderate ingestion, the increase usually seen in performance is primarily due to a decreased appreciation of fatigue. Large doses of alcohol cause direct damage to skeletal muscle. This is substantiated by an increase in blood values indicative of muscle damage (serum creatine phosphokinase), as well as the structural changes in the muscle. Alcohol stimulates gastric secretions, which are highly acidic, and therefore alcohol consumption should be avoided in individuals with peptic ulcers. In large doses of high concentrations (40 percent and above), it produces an erosive gastritis. Approximately 30 percent of heavy drinkers suffer from chronic gastritis. Food in the stomach lessens this irritation, while aspirin increases it. Alcohol exerts a diuretic effect on the kidneys, which is further exaggerated by the large amounts of fluid consumed with the alcohol.

Alcoholics suffer from multiple nutritional deficiencies because alcohol depresses appetite and supplies calories without vitamins or amino acids necessary for protein production (Hurt et al. 1981). In small amounts, alcohol doesn't permanently damage the liver; however, cirrhosis of the liver is a common disorder seen in chronic alcoholics. The development of alcoholic liver disorders is related to both the amount and duration of alcohol intake (Boyer, 1978). Abstinence results in dramatic clinical improvement of the cirrhosis. There are four major factors which lead to alcoholic hematologic disorders: poor diet, blood loss, liver disease, and alcohol itself (Tong and Bernstein, 1979). Chronic alcoholics suffer from folic acid deficiency and the anemia associated with it.

Some neurological problems seen in alcoholics are polyneuropathy, a degenerative process of nerves presenting as subjective sensory disturbances and loss of reflexes and motor activity; Wernicke's disease, an organic and toxic psychosis, primarily caused from a thiamine (Vitamin B_1) deficiency, presenting with ocular disturbances and as diplopia, muscle weakness or paralysis, ataxia, disorientation, and confusion; Korsakoff's psychosis, with memory loss (recent memory being affected most), confusion and confabulation. During alcoholic inebriation there is an altered balance in intraneuronal sodium concentration. This abnormal electrolyte balance may be responsible for precipitating a biogenic amine dysfunction, since many of the enzyme systems involved in normal biogenic amine function are sodium-dependent. Biogenic amines are agents which produce a response similar to those produced by adrenergic nerve activity (e.g., epinephrine). There may be further impairment of certain diencephalic reinforcement mechanisms, so that psychomotor activity, appetite, sleep, and libido are altered (Coleman, 1978). Predominantly found in alcoholics is alcoholic cerebellar degeneration manifested by altered stance and gait, and this may indeed be related to Wernicke's disease. Also a cerebral atrophy has been found by computerized axial tomography (CAT) scan, with the most prominent convolutional atrophy seen in the frontal lobes. A disorder associated with the optic nerve (amblyopia) may occur, resulting in blurred vision. Other disorders seen with alcoholism include seborrhea, scabies, acne, pediculosis, eczema, and psoriasis. Alcoholics appear to be more prone to cancer of the mouth, pharynx, larynx, esophagus, and liver, particularly if they use tobacco. Alcohol may depress migration of leukocytes to inflamed areas of the body, as well as their production in bone marrow. This may be part of the reason that alcoholics have poor resistance to infection. If alcohol intake is chronic, infection can be rapidly fatal if unrecognized and not treated. Pulmonary infection is the most prevalent type (Greenblatt, and Shrader, 1978). Alcoholism is a factor which increases the risk of contracting tuberculosis (Young and Barriere, 1978).

Pregnant alcoholics subject their offspring to fetal alcohol syndrome (Victor and Adams, 1980). This syndrome is characterized by low birth weight. Affected infants may have cleft palate, dislocation of the hips, deformities in the fingers, limited range of motion of other joints, cardiac abnormalities, and numerous other abnormalities. These infants exhibit poor sucking and sleep responses; many are irritable and hyperactive, and suffer from persistent tremulousness.

Continual consumption of alcohol leads to an increased capacity to metabolize alcohol. Moreover, chronic use produces tolerance, and a higher blood alcohol concentration is required to produce intoxication. The lethal dose remains the same (400–700 mg. %). A constant concentration in the blood produces physical dependence, with a specific withdrawal or abstinence syndrome.

Alcohol is rapidly absorbed after ingestion, and its presence in the blood may be detected within five minutes. In the presence of milk or fatty foods the absorption of alcohol is slowed, while water enhances absorption. After entering the blood, alcohol enters all the different systems and the spinal fluid. It is metabolized (broken down) primarily in the liver at a constant rate. Therefore, to date there are no known ways in which to adequately speed up the sobering process of a drunk individual.

The rate of alcohol metabolism for the average person is about one ounce of 90-proof whiskey or 10 to 12 ounces of beer an hour (150 mg./kg. of blood/hour). It has been shown that alcohol is metabolized more than twice as rapidly in alcoholics who have recently been drinking as it is in nonalcoholics. This alteration of metabolic processes is a result of an increase in the concentration of the enzymes responsible for metabolism that has been termed "enzyme induction"). Other drugs may be affected by this enzyme induction. When first consumed, alcohol exerts a depressive effect on higher inhibitory control mechanisms in the brain, allowing other centers to show an increased activity, and thus accounting for the early stimulation often seen with consumption (Daniels and Jorgensen, 1977).

Mild to moderate stages of inebriation require no specific treatment. Blood-alcohol levels of over 300 mg. %, particularly if accompanied by other drugs, illnesses, or injury, may be fatal. In such a case, supportive treatment to maintain adequate respiration is necessary. Treatment for acute alcohol intoxication is anticipatory, dealing with various symptoms as they arise.

When the body's metabolic capacity to eliminate alcohol has been exceeded, dependency can occur within a few days of continual drinking. Withdrawal or abstinence syndromes usually show up within eight to seventy-two hours of total abstinence (Inaba and Katcher, 1978). These symptoms have been observed when there is a decrease in alcohol blood levels from 300 to 100 mg. % in alcoholics. The intensity of the symptoms is not directly related to the amount or duration of alcohol consumption.

There are four stages in the acute phase of the abstinence syndrome. The first stage is characterized by psychomotor agitation, tachycardia, hypertension, hyperhydrosis, anorexia, and insomnia. The next stage includes auditory, visual, and/or tactile hallucinations. The third stage includes delusions, disorientation, and delirium. In the fourth stage seizure activity is seen within twenty-four to forty-eight hours after withdrawal. The last two stages are commonly referred to as the "DTs" (delirium tremens). As the abstinence syndrome progresses, insight is lost, and the individual becomes weaker, more disoriented, confused, and agitated. The early or mild symptoms seen in withdrawal include anorexia, nausea, vomiting, abdominal discomfort and diarrhea, and muscle weakness and cramps, along with tremulousness, insomnia and nightmares, tachycardia, systolic hypertension, diaphoresis, and fever. The alcoholic becomes irritable, hostile, restless, and agitated, and has an exaggerated "startle" response. He has an inability to concentrate, is easily distracted, and has impaired memory, judgment, and other higher mental functions. As the syndrome progresses, there is a worsening of the above symptoms, along with delirium, disorientation to time and place, and hallucinations, which can be visual, auditory, or tactile, and can be threatening in nature. There are paranoid delusions, which are usually reinforced by the hallucinations, and seizures ("rum fits") may occur. These seizures are usually nonfocal and generalized. They can occur in the absence of prior seizure disorders and are usually self-limiting (Greenblatt and Shader, 1978). Alcoholics who are abstinent most commonly present in the emergency room with symptoms already in progress (Zimberg, 1982). If the individual presents with severe tremulousness or hallucinations, significant dehydration, fever (above 101 degrees Fahrenheit), a seizure in the absence of a seizure disorder, Wernicke's encephalopathy, or a previous history of serious DTs or major complications, he must be hospitalized.

In treatment the patient immediately receives a dose of thiamine, 100–200 mg. intramuscularly or intravenously, and the same dose is repeated, parenterally or orally, once a day for at least three consecutive days. If signs of Wernicke's disease are present, the thiamine can prevent irreversible brain damage. Since alcoholics are also deficient in folic acid, they should receive 1–5 mg. intramuscularly or orally, as well as a multivitamin supplement. Vitamin therapy should not be short-term.

In order to make the withdrawal experience less unpleasant, many clinicians administer sedatives or tranquilizers. This greatly lessens the severity of the situation. The benzodiazepines are the drugs of choice, since they are relatively safe and produce minimal respiratory or cardiovascular depression. Also, they allow REM (rapid eye movement) rebound, which is suppressed during alcohol intoxication. Of the benzodiazepines, chlordiazepoxide (Librium) and diazepam (Valium) are the drugs of choice. Both have a long duration of action and cumulative effects. Doses of chlordiazepoxide are 50–100 mg., given immediately and parenterally, then repeated every four hours or so as needed. (Some cases require drug administration every two to three hours and up to 1,600 mg. per day.) After this, the dosage is changed to oral, and one-fourth to one-half of the dose is given. Diazepam is very similar to chlordiazepoxide. The initial dose is 10–20 mg. parenterally as needed. Next the dose is changed to the oral form and 10 mg. are given every six to eight hours.

Diazepam is used to stop seizures in status epilepticus and to relax muscles: two functions that are beneficial in this instance. Since the benzodiazepines are poorly, slowly, and erratically absorbed upon intramuscular (IM) administration, the oral route is preferred.

In alcoholics with advanced liver disease (Wooddell, 1980), oxazepam (Serax), an active metabolite of diazepam, is the benzodiazepine of choice. A parenteral form has not been marketed yet, but the advantage is in a shorter half-life. (Half-life is the amount of time required for the body to remove half the absorbed dose of a particular compound.)

Benzodiazepines are metabolized in the liver. If an individual's liver function is compromised, the time it takes for the body to eliminate the drug increases. Oxazepam has an average half-life of seven hours. Diazepam, however, has a half-life of twenty to ninety hours. It is then metabolized to the active compound N-desmethyldiazepam, which has a half-life of forty-eight to ninety-six hours. Then N-desmethyldiazepam is metabolized to oxazepam (Hollister, 1978). In severe liver damage, the half-life of diazepam alone may be increased up to 105 hours. Heavy smoking will expedite the metabolism of the benzodiazepam. The benzodiazepines must be tapered off slowly, and care must be taken not to transfer the alcohol dependency to these drugs.

Other drugs used for alcohol withdrawal include chloral hydrate, the barbiturates, the antihistamine hydroxyzine, and the major tranquilizers such as chlorpromazine (Thorazine). The major tranquilizers make the individual more prone to develop grand mal seizures and may do more harm than good. Also, they cause serious and sometimes fatal hypotension. Since most alcoholics are cross-tolerant to barbiturates, they are of limited value here. In addition, they may further any respiratory depression.

Intravenous fluids should be given if necessary during treatment. This not only rehydrates an individual who may be dehydrated due to chronic vomiting and diarrhea, but provides a mechanism for repeated intravenous drug administration and an access for monitoring of blood values. Caution must be taken not to overload the patient with excess fluid. Attention should be paid to the blood glucose level, as hypoglycemia may develop in the post-withdrawal phase.

Complications such as infections, seizures, metabolic disturbances, hematological disorders, gastrointestinal bleeding, and trauma must be treated along with the withdrawal symptoms, and are an important part of the total treatment plan.

Successful treatment of the alcoholic depends upon total abstinence from alcohol (Forrest, 1984). The treatment of chronic alcoholism is very complex, and to date only one pharmacological agent has been able to assist in keeping the alcoholic dry. This drug is disulfiram

(Antabuse). Disulfiram is able to block the metabolism of alcohol. Alcohol is metabolized to acetaldehyde, and then further metabolized to carbon dioxide and water (Neuhaus and Orten, 1975). Disulfiram blocks the conversion of the acetaldehyde, resulting in a buildup of this compound in the body. While taking disulfiram, if the patient consumes alcohol, effects are seen in as few as thirty minutes. The effects are nausea, vomiting, facial flushing, headache, sweating, respiratory difficulty, chest pain, tachycardia, hypotension, dizziness, weakness, blurred vision, and confusion (*Modern Drug Encyclopedia,* 1977). In some instances a severe reaction including respiratory depression, cardiovascular collapse, arrythmias, coma, and convulsion may occur. These may be fatal. Reactions can occur when the blood alcohol levels are as low as 5–10 mg. %. But on the other hand, some alcoholics are able to consume alcohol while on average doses of disulfiram (250–500 mg. daily) and remain free from the adverse effects of this combination.

Serious problems are usually manifested when the blood alcohol of a person taking disulfiram reaches 150 mg. %. The adverse reactions last from thirty minutes to several hours, or as long as there is alcohol in the blood. Therefore, it is imperative the alcoholic have no alcohol in the blood before initiating disulfiram therapy. Dosing initially is up to 500 mg. a day for one to two weeks, and the maintenance dose ranges from 125 mg. to 500 mg. daily, with an average of 250 mg.

Since it requires very little alcohol to initiate the reaction, the individual must take care to avoid certain preparations containing alcohol. These include mouthwashes (5–25 percent alcohol), cough and cold preparations (10–25 percent alcohol), vitamins and tonics (12–20 percent alcohol), and various other medicinal formulations. If the person treated with disulfiram ingests alcohol and a severe reaction occurs, antidotal treatment is limited at best. Antihistamines, iron salts, and ascorbic acid (0.5 to 2.0 g. given intravenously) may reverse the reaction (Tong and Bernstein, 1979). Disulfiram is slowly eliminated, and one 500-mg. dose exerts effects for three or four days; one 1.5 g. dose exerts its effects for seven or eight days (*The Extra Pharmacopoeia,* 1978). Up to 20 percent of the drug remains in the body one week after cessation of therapy.

There are side-effects with disulfiram use. They are: occasional skin rashes, transient and mild drowsiness, impotence, headache, and a metallic aftertaste, but all of these are usually only experienced during the first two weeks of therapy. Also, cases of disulfiram-induced psychosis have been reported (Quail and Karelse, 1980).

If disulfiram is given in combination with oral anticoagulant (e.g., warfarin), an increase in the activity of the anticoagulant may occur via an inhibition of metabolism. A few patients have demonstrated a psychotic reaction including visual and auditory hallucinations when disulfiram therapy is combined with metronidazole (Flagyl). Simultaneous therapy of disulfiram and isoniazid causes coordination difficulties and changes in behavior via an alteration of brain catecholamines. This alteration consists of an increased metabolite such as norepinephrine. The barbiturates and the sedative-hypnotics show increased activity when given along with disulfiram.

Paraldehyde, once (now seldom) used in the treatment of alcohol withdrawal symptoms, depolymerizes to acetaldehyde, and since disulfiram blocks the metabolism of acetaldehyde, toxic levels may be produced. A suitable washout period should occur before starting disulfiram therapy if paraldehyde has been used. Also, the risks of anesthesia are increased with disulfiram therapy.

Depression sometimes accompanies alcoholism, and pharmacological treatment of the depression with the tricyclic antidepressants can be potentially lethal if drinking is resumed. Tricyclic antidepressants in combination with alcohol present as a severe CNS depression and coma (Martin, 1978). Disulfiram and phenytoin (Dilantin), given together, will result in a 100 to 500 percent increase in the phenytoin blood levels (James et al., 1978). Lithium, used in the treatment and prophylaxis of manic-depressive illness, has been used with some success, but more research is needed to assure the drug helps control the alcohol problem or an underlying behavioral problem.

Since alcoholics don't enjoy the disulfiram reaction, many tend to discontinue therapy on their own—thus the major failure in treatment. In Europe and Canada, disulfiram implants have been tried, but problems still abound (Becker, 1979; Wilson, 1979).

Sedative-Hypnotics

One class of drugs widely abused is the sedative-hypnotics. Their primary use is to produce drowsiness and/or sleep. Within the sedative-hypnotics are two groups: the barbiturates and the nonbarbiturates.

Barbiturates

There are several barbiturates on the market, but the more common ones include amobarbital (Amytal), pentobarbital (Nembutal), phenobarbital, secobarbital (Seconal), a combination of pentobarbital and secobarbital (Tuinal), thiopental (Pentothal), and methohexital (Brevital). These drugs are widely used and abused. Of the estimated 300 tons manufactured in the United States yearly, as much as half may enter the black market. Phenobarbital, thiopental, and methohexital are less commonly abused than the others.

The barbiturates depress activity of all tissue capable of depression (Harvey, 1975). The CNS is extremely sensitive; hence it is affected in doses small enough to produce very little effect on skeletal, cardiac, or smooth muscle. All degrees of CNS depression can be produced, from mild sedation to coma. In most cases barbiturate-induced sleep resembles physiological sleep with slightly less time spent in REM sleep. Although the produced drowsiness may last only a few hours, small alterations in mood, as well as impairment of judgment and fine motor skills, may last for several hours. Since small doses of the barbiturates actually increase reaction to painful stimuli, they are not classified as analgesics. They cannot be depended upon to reduce pain or produce sleep in the presence of severe pain. This is usually not a property of the nonbarbiturate sedative-hypnotics. The ultra-short-acting barbiturates may be used as anesthetics. However, anesthetic doses are often close to lethal doses. Laryngospasm is one of the major complications from this method of anesthesia. The effects are directly related to route of administration, dose, and degree of tolerance.

The cerebral cortex and the reticular activating system are the areas of the brain most sensitive to this class of drugs (Gold and Pottash, 1983). CNS effects seen with barbiturates include dizziness, confusion in the elderly, ataxia, slurred speech, sedation, and drowsiness (*Modern Drug Encyclopedia,* 1977). The barbiturates are respiratory depressants affecting all areas of respiratory drive (neurogenic, carbon dioxide tension, and hypoxic drive). Normal oral doses have little effect on the cardiovascular system other than a slight decrease in blood pressure. However, in higher doses or in combination with alcohol there may be a resulting cardiovascular collapse and death. An area of the brain that is particularly sensitive to the barbiturates is the medulla oblongata. This is where the respiratory center is located in the brain. In the event of acute overdose, apnea can also play a role in the immediate cause of death.

Regular doses do not alter normal liver function. However, the barbiturates do increase the rate of hepatic metabolism of many drugs, as well as their own. This may, in part, account for the buildup of tolerance to all barbiturates. This type of tolerance may begin after one or two doses.

Another mechanism of the development of barbiturate tolerance involves neurochemical adaption to a continual presence of the drug in the nervous tissue. Therefore, when the drugs are removed, the now-adapted brain tissue is chemically imbalanced and withdrawal symptoms may be manifested. Tolerance to these drugs develops swiftly, but it is completely reversible.

The chronic effects of barbiturate intoxication are similar to opioid or alcohol addiction. There is usually a cross-tolerance between these drugs. Slowed thought processes, great fluctuation of neurological signs, and cerebellar incoordination are evidence of chronic intoxication. Individuals who inject barbiturates intravenously may develop complications such as serum hepatitis, septicemia, pulmonary embolism, pneumonia, bacterial endocarditis, tetanus, abscesses, and allergic reactions (Khantzian and McKenna, 1979).

Withdrawal from barbiturates is considerably more dangerous than withdrawal from narcotics. Secobarbital has a normal oral sedating dose of 100 mg. With doses eight to twenty-two times that for thirty-five days, a physical dependency will occur. The same is true for pentobarbital, amobarbital, and the combination product of secobarbital and pentobarbital, Tuinal. Six to twelve hours after cessation of these drugs, withdrawal symptoms begin to occur. From two to five days are required for peak symptomatology to be evident. This withdrawal is related to the intensity of the preceding addiction (dose and duration of use).

Barbiturate overdose or acute intoxication is a grave yet common medical emergency. This class of drugs is the most commonly used in deliberate self-poisoning (Swonger and Constantine, 1976). Most cases of self-poisoning are attempted with either secobarbital or pentobarbital. Single doses of 2–3 g. can be fatal. Doses of 5 g. or more are required for phenobarbital.

Symptoms of acute intoxication are similar to all barbiturates. In the early stages, they include drowsiness, nystagmus, ataxia, dysarthria, and somnolence. Unless treated, the overdosed individual progresses into a more profound CNS depression consisting of muscle hypotonicity, hypotension, areflexia, deep coma, and apnea. Respiration becomes shallow, often with a Cheyne-Stokes rhythm (a cyclic breathing pattern with gradual increases in depth followed by gradual decreases resulting in apnea. Often the cycles are approximately thirty to sixty seconds long.) The individual develops a typical shock syndrome.

Treatment is usually limited to supportive care. Alkalinization of the urine, attained via intravenous administration of sodium bicarbonate, enhances the excretion of phenobarbital. Peritoneal dialysis is better for the removal of the phenobarbital because it happens quicker than other medications. However, hemodialysis may be the only alternative in severe cases, as it is more efficient than peritoneal dialysis. Still, hemodialysis will not remove large quantities of phenobarbital.

Administration of CNS stimulants should be avoided. When acute intoxication or overdose occurs in a barbiturate addict and the immediate crisis is overcome, abstinence symptoms usually follow.

Symptoms of a barbiturate abstinence syndrome occur in two general stages. Initially symptoms may include insomnia, anorexia, anxiety, diaphoresis, irritability, nausea, vomiting, abdominal cramping, confusion, tremors, hypotension, slurring of speech, and labile emotions. Unless the syndrome is treated, the latter phase ensues: a quasi-psychotic state, resembling delirium tremens, in which the patient is unable to sleep. This occurs in 60 percent of patients, between the second and third day and lasting up to eight days. Hyperpyrexia may appear, and if so, there is a poor prognosis for recovery. In the second or third day of the syndrome, convulsions of the grand mal type occur in 80 percent of patients. The convulsions may be seen as late as the eighth day, and they may last from three to fourteen days. The whole process may terminate in coma or death.

Before treatment of chronic intoxication ensues, the degree of addiction should be determined. This can be accomplished by giving the individual a 200-mg. test dose of pentobarbital, which will heavily sedate a nontolerant person but have no effect on an addict. In the chronic user, 500 mg. of pentobarbital will have only minimal effects. It may be necessary to give 800 mg. or more to alleviate the abstinence syndrome in a chronic addict. In order to establish a daily maintenance dose of a barbiturate for an addict before proceeding into detoxification, a 200-mg. test dose of pentobarbital is required. If this dose produces drowsiness, slurred speech, a coarse nystagmus, ataxia, and marked intoxication, there is definitely some degree of tolerance. This individual will require 400–600 mg. of pentobarbital every twenty-four hours as a stabilization dose before withdrawal proceedings are initiated. If after the test dose the individual is comfortable, and the only sign of intoxication is a fine lateral nystagmus, there is a marked degree of tolerance. The estimated twenty-four hour pentobarbital requirement is approximately 800 mg. In those instances where the test dose causes no signs of intoxication, and perhaps there are persisting signs of abstinence, the individual is extremely tolerant and the pentobarbital requirement is 1,000–1,200 mg. or more. Once the patient is symptom-free, a gradual reduction in dosage may be started. This should be only 5–10 percent daily. If the daily dosage requirement was above 1,200 mg., the reduction should be in smaller increments. Freedom from drug dependency is obtainable in fourteen to twenty-one days barring any complications. Haloperidol (Haldol), 4 mg. daily in divided doses, may be of benefit at this stage. If convulsions should occur, 100–150 mg. of phenobarbital should be given intravenously. Phenytoin is relatively ineffective for barbiturate-induced convulsions. At any time, if withdrawal symptoms recur, 100–200 mg. of phenobarbital should be given intramuscularly and the daily dosage should be increased.

Work is being done on an intravenous infusion loading dose of phenobarbital to prevent withdrawal symptoms at the beginning of therapy, but this method requires constant monitoring of the patient (Sellers, 1979). Also, oral doses of 120 mg. of phenobarbital every hour until the patient falls asleep are under trial for a loading dose. Robinson, Sellers, and Janecek (1981) prefer phenobarbital to pentobarbital in the management of withdrawal. They have found that it has several apparent advantages. Phenobarbital has a slow elimination rate (a half-life of eighty-six hours), which can be increased through acidification of the urine with ascorbic acid (500 mg.) every six hours. This drug provides a wider margin of safety between intoxication and dangerous CNS depression; also, it is less easily abused and has well-established anticonvulsant properties. A 30-mg. sedating dose of phenobarbital is approximately equivalent to 100 mg. of secobarbital, 100 mg. of pentobarbital, 65–100 mg. of amobarbital, and 50 mg. each of secobarbital and pentobarbital in combination (Tuinal).

Detoxification from barbiturates is impaired in individuals with severe liver disease. If the patient has a mixed addiction to both barbiturates and opiates, it is advisable to maintain the opiate dependency with methadone while gradually withdrawing the barbiturates; if barbiturate detoxification is successful, detoxification from opiates can be initiated. Clinical distinction between the withdrawal syndromes associated with opiates and barbiturates can be difficult, and the barbiturate syndrome is more dangerous.

At this time there is no barbiturate maintenance program other than complete withdrawal. Therefore, psychotherapy must be part of the total treatment plan.

Nonbarbiturates

The nonbarbiturate sedative-hypnotics associated with abuse include chloral hydrate (Noctec), ethchlorvynol (Placidyl), methaqualone (Quaalude), glutethimide (Doriden), and methyprylon (Noludar).

Chloral hydrate's therapeutic actions closely resemble those of the barbiturates. The oral dosing range for the relief of insomnia is from 500 mg. to 1 g. The dose and duration required to produce physical dependence are not exactly known; however, after consumption 12 g. daily for long periods of time, a dependency resembling alcoholism in physical findings has been observed. When chloral hydrate is combined with alcohol—a combination that has been termed a "Mickey

Finn" or "knockout drops" additive effects may sometimes be seen. The toxic oral dose of chloral hydrate is about 10 g; ranging from 4 to 30 g. Treatment for acute and chronic intoxication, abstinence syndrome, and withdrawal is similar to treatment for barbiturates. The sedation achieved from 250 mg. of chloral hydrate may be equated to 30 mg. of phenobarbital. Therefore, if an individual is dependent on 7 g. of chloral hydrate a day, the phenobarbital substitution dosage would be 840 mg. Once the individual is stabilized, a reduction in dosage of 5–10 percent should ensue until complete detoxification occurs.

One gram of ethchlorvynol produces CNS depression within fifteen to thirty minutes. Effects seen are similar to those of the barbiturates, and approximately 770 mg. are equal in sedating power to 100 mg. of secobarbital. Tolerance and dependency have been reported with this drug, and a typical dependency dose is at least 4 g. daily. Physical dependency may be produced upon ingestion of 1–1.5 g. for thirty days. After withdrawal, the onset of an abstinence syndrome will occur within six to twelve hours. Withdrawal symptoms are similar to delirium tremens and tend to mimic a schizophrenic reaction. A normal sedative dose of 200 mg. has a phenobarbital substitution dose equal to 30 mg. Treatment of dependency is comparable to that for the barbiturates.

Methaqualone possesses sedative-hypnotic, anticonvulsant, antispasmodic, local-anesthetic, and weak antihistaminic properties. Also, its antitussive properties (i.e., ability to depress the cough reflex) equal those of codeine. It lacks therapeutic analgesic properties. Normal doses are from 150 to 300 mg. per day. Doses of 2 g. taken for thirty days can produce physical dependency. When large doses are taken, cardiovascular and respiratory depression are not as severe as they are for the barbiturates; otherwise signs of intoxication are similar to those of the barbiturates. However, some abusers feel that the drug has aphrodisiac properties, and others have likened the effects to those of heroin. The lethal dose is approximately 8 g., and may in fact be lower if taken concurrently with alcoholic beverages. Withdrawal symptoms can be seen within six to twelve hours after cessation of the drug, and when the dependent individual takes large doses, grand mal convulsions may occur. A 75-mg. dose of methaqualone has a phenobarbital substitution dose of 30 mg. Treatment of dependency is similar to that for the barbiturates.

Glutethimide is a drug of questionable therapeutic capacity. It resembles the barbiturates, but is inferior in several respects. An overdose produces more severe cardiovascular and respiratory depression. The drug also possesses anticholinergic properties, which can be a problem. The lethal dose is 10–20 g. The normal sedative dose is 125 mg., which is equal to 30 mg. of phenobarbital. Doses of 1.5–3 g. for thirty days may produce dependency. The abstinence syndrome includes fever, tremors, nausea, tachycardia, tonic muscle spasms, and generalized convulsions. Treatment is the same as with the barbiturates.

Methyprylon resembles the barbiturates in pharmacology, dependency, and treatment of dependency. The normal sedative dose is 100 mg., which is equal to 30 mg. of phenobarbital. Dependency can occur after taking doses of 3 g. for thirty days, and the lethal dose may be as low as 6 g.

Opiates

Opiates are naturally occurring compounds found in opium, which is prepared from the sap of the poppy, *Papaver somniferum*. The drugs are acquired by making incisions on the plant's unripe seed capsule. This causes a milky exudate to form, and when it dries, it forms a brownish, gummy mass. Further drying and powdering yields the opium used to manufacture the various derivatives usually seen today. Approximately 10 percent of opium is morphine, a narcotic analgesic. Other compounds in this class include heroin, codeine, hydromorphone (Dilaudid), dihydrocodeinone (Hycodan), dihydroxycodeinone (Eucodal), oxymorphone (Numorphan), and oxycodone (Percodan). These are derived by modifications in the chemical structure of morphine. Another, similar chemical class of narcotic analgesics includes meperidine (Demerol) and its chemical derivatives: methadone (Dolophine), racemorphan (Dromoran), levorphan (Levo-Dromoran) propoxyphene (Darvon), alphaprodine (Nisentil), diphenoxylate (the main component in Lomotil), and phenazocine (Prinadol). Since members of each class exhibit similar actions, knowledge of the major compounds is sufficient for our purposes here.

The effects of morphine and its surrogates are primarily seen in the CNS and the bowel (Jaffe and Martin, 1975). Morphine produces analgesia without loss of consciousness, as well as drowsiness, changes in mood, and mental clouding in the CNS. With doses of 5 to 10 mg., the extremities seem to feel heavy, a warmth comes over the body, the face and particularly the nose may itch, and the mouth feels dry. Euphoria is commonly present, but dysphoria may result. The dysphoria may consist of mild anxiety, fear, nausea, vomiting, and mental clouding (drowsiness, inability to concentrate, apathy), as well as lessened physical activity and diminished visual acuity. The mental clouding is less pronounced in addicts. As the dose is increased, the effects become more advanced. The drowsiness leads to sleep, and the euphoria is increased, as is the analgesia. Analgesia is relatively selective, having little effect on sensations of touch, vibration, vision, and hearing. Pain can still be recognized, but it is not perceived as painful, thus rendering the individual more comfortable. Continual dull pain is more effectively relieved than intermittent sharp pain.

The action of analgesia is centered in the brain, as morphine neither alters the response of the nerve endings or conduction of the nerve impulses along the peripheral nerves. However, morphine does depress nociceptive reflexes in the spinal cord. At higher CNS levels, the effects of morphine become quite complex. A single dose will cause a shift toward increased voltage and lower frequencies in the electroencephalogram (EEG), as well as suppression of REM sleep. Morphine causes miosis due to a central action on the Edinger-Westphal nucleus of the oculomotor nerve. Miosis will occur even in total darkness. This is characteristic of opiate overdose. Morphine causes a reduction in the responsiveness of the respiratory centers located in the brain stem, as well as the pontine and medullary centers. This results in a depression of respiration, and is discernible after doses too small to produce sleep or alter consciousness have been given. Since the rhythm-regulating center has been affected, irregular breathing may be evident. The morphine compounds act on a cough center in the medulla, as is demonstrated by their antitussive properties. Nausea and vomiting seen upon administration of morphine involve direct stimulation of the chemoreceptor trigger zone (CTZ) in the postrema area of the medulla.

Therapeutic doses of morphine have no major effects on heart rate or rhythm, or blood pressure. Morphine does cause orthostatic hypotension, and this is mainly due to peripheral vasodilatation. The effects seen on the heart are insignificant.

For centuries opium has been used for the relief of diarrhea. Morphine will cause a decrease in hydrochloric acid secretion, as well as a decrease in the motility of the stomach. Digestion of food is delayed in the small intestine as a result of a decrease in biliary and pancreatic secretions, and propulsive contractions are also markedly decreased. In the large intestine, propulsive peristaltic waves are diminished or abolished. A ten- to fifteen-fold increase in the pressure of the biliary tract can be seen after a dose of 10 mg. of morphine, which may result in biliary colic.

All the morphine compounds are well absorbed following oral administration, and are well absorbed from nasal mucosa or the lungs. Injection is also a method of administration, rendering the drug readily available to the body. The duration of action for morphine is four to five hours; for heroin, three to four hours; and for codeine, four to six hours. The others all range from four to five hours in duration of action.

Meperidine and its surrogates, in therapeutic doses, produce analgesia, euphoria, sedation, respiratory depression, and the many CNS effects seen with morphine. Meperidine has a somewhat shorter duration of action (two to four hours) than morphine. Unlike morphine and its related compounds, meperidine is not useful in the treatment of cough or diarrhea.

More than any other drugs, narcotics are likely to cause tolerance, physical dependence, and even death from overdose. They are equaled in psychological dependence only by the stimulants (Swonger and Constantine, 1976).

Acutely overdosed individuals are commonly seen in emergency rooms. They overdose because they miscalculate how much to take, because a drug's potency may vary, or because they want to commit suicide. Also, because tolerance to a drug declines rapidly after withdrawal, a dose which was well tolerated prior to detoxification may now be too much. An overdosed individual presents clinically with varying degrees of unresponsiveness, shallow and slow respirations, miosis, bradycardia, and hypothermia. Unless the person is treated, the pupils dilate from severe brain hypoxia, the skin becomes cyanotic, and the circulation fails. Death is usually caused from respiratory depression and apnea.

Treatment is supportive, maintaining adequate circulatory and respiratory status. In severe cases narcotic antagonists are required. These are specific antidotes to the narcotics and include naloxone (Narcan), nalorphine (Nalline), levallorphan (Lorfan), naltrexone, and cyclazocine. These agents reduce or abolish most of the characteristic actions of narcotic compounds. Within a few seconds after intravenous administration, they produce a stimulation of respiration replacing the depressive effects produced by the narcotic. This action is due to a displacement of the narcotic from the receptor site of drug-tissue action, and the narcotic antagonists occupy the site with little or no effects of their own. They will not alter the respiratory-depressant effects produced by the barbiturates, alcohol, or other nonopioid CNS depressants. Narcotic antagonists have a shorter duration of action than narcotics. Therefore, repeated dosing is beneficial. These agents are known to initiate a withdrawal syndrome in addicts.

A characteristic feature of all the narcotics is the development of tolerance and dependence, both physical and psychological. Also, since euphoria is frequently encountered with use of these agents, abuse is quite prominent.

Chronic intoxication, or addiction, occurs in three phases. First is the episodic intoxication. This is followed by physical dependence, or addiction, and third there is the inclination to relapse after cure (Victor and Adams, 1980). Heroin is the major narcotic of addiction. One of the most important factors in the generation of addiction is the repeated self-administration of the drug. Here the individual experiences rapid development of tolerance and the need to increase the dosage in order to achieve the original effects. This leads to the development of a pharmacologically induced need for the drug, and the use of the drug then becomes self-perpetuating. The intensity of the dependency depends on the dose and duration of administration.

The chronic effects of habitual narcotic administration are numerous. They include decreased socialization and withdrawal from activity, diminished libido, and menstrual irregularities. The effects felt after an intravenous injection (a rush, flash, or thrill) may or may not be present, and the constipation associated with this class of drugs increases. Because morphine loses its potency when given orally (an oral dose is one-fiftieth as potent as an intravenous administration), it is primarily given by injection.

Intravenous administration of narcotics purchased on the street has given rise to many complications. These complications primarily result from the ingredients used to dilute the narcotics. The injected particulate matter (quinine, lactose, powdered milk, fruit sugars) may go directly to the lungs and cause an acute embolic phenomenon or a chronic granuloma formation (Becker, 1979). While narcotics exhibit little effect on the heart, an injection by unsterile methods may give rise to infectious complications such as abscesses and cellulitis at the injection site, septic thrombophlebitis, serum hepatitis, septic arthritis, and less commonly, tetanus, bacterial endocarditis, meningitis, and brain or spinal epidural abscesses.

The diagnosis of an addict is usually made when the patient says that he or she is using and needs drugs. Urinary tests are now available to determine if a dose of a narcotic has been taken in the last twenty-four hours. Naloxone, a narcotic antagonist, can be employed in a medical setting. The individual must be made aware of the proceedings, and a medical professional must be present. One dose of 0.4 mg. is given intravenously, very slowly. The procedure is stopped when pupillary dilatation, increased respiratory rate, lacrimation, rhinorrhea, sweating, and excessive yawning are manifested. If none of these symptoms appear after five to ten minutes, a second dose is given. If there are still no signs, the individual is not dependent upon narcotics. If the symptoms do appear, this confirms addiction. They become evident within five minutes, and last no more than three hours. In the case of a meperidine addict, the naloxone won't precipitate abstinence symptoms unless the daily dosage has been above 1,600 mg. The abstinence syndrome is characterized by increased respiratory rate, sweating, lacrimation, yawning, rhinorrhea, piloerection, tremor, anorexia, irritability, anxiety, and dilated pupils. These are seen approximately eight to twelve hours after the last dose of the drug. Later signs—which occur twenty-four to forty-eight hours after the last dose—include insomnia, nausea, vomiting, diarrhea, weakness, abdominal cramps, tachycardia, hypertension, involuntary muscle spasms, and chills alternating with sweating and flushing. This abstinence syndrome gradually subsides over a period of seven to ten days, and it is immediately reversible upon the administration of an opiate. Methadone withdrawal symptoms are the same, but the time period is altered: symptoms appear in twenty-four to forty-eight hours, and the total syndrome lasts up to three weeks. Methadone is the best drug to use for clinical detoxification. Also, it is the only legal one to use at this time (Khantzian and McKenna, 1979).

The program for detoxification must be performed in a federally approved treatment facility. This process must be accomplished gradually to delay appearance of the abstinence syndrome. After the abstinence syndrome appears, an initial oral dose of methadone is given (Green, Meyer, and Shader, 1978). If symptoms of intoxication appear, too much has been given. Small doses of 5–15 mg. every twenty-four hours may be given if the initial dose is unable to abate the abstinence symptoms. In the case of a documented tolerance to more than 40 mg. of methadone, the doses may be increased to 20 mg. in every twelve-hour period. After a two- to three-day period, the dose is adjusted to stabilize the individual. Once the individual is stabilized, detoxification can proceed. Then the dose, usually 20 mg. per day in one or two administrations, and rarely more than 40 mg. per day, can be reduced by 5 mg. or a maximum of 15 to 20 percent daily. This allows detoxification to occur in seven to ten days. The Food and Drug Administration has set a limit of twenty-one days for detoxification. At this rate of detoxification, the individual may experience mild abstinence symptoms resembling a bout with the flu. In some cases, where the methadone dose is greater than 50 mg. per day, the reduction is 5 mg. per day until the level of 20 mg. per day is reached; then reduction occurs more gradually.

The long-term treatment must attend to any medical complications accrued during the dependency period, and must help the addict to overcome his or her drug-craving tendencies. Drug-free programs do not use pharmacotherapy to abate the drug craving. Rather, they use a live-in experience to stimulate a change in the individual resulting in a drug-free life. The most common method known is the methadone maintenance program. In this program, a daily dose of methadone is supplied to the addict. This is thought to blunt the craving for heroin, as well as reduce the effects of injected heroin. Once the addict becomes tolerant to the methadone, he or she can function in life without exhibiting signs of intoxication. This program is initiated prior to detoxification, and daily doses range from 40 to 120 mg.

There are several drug-drug interactions with methadone (Martin, 1978). These include other CNS depressants, the tricyclic antidepressants, and the monoamine oxidase inhibitors.

Naltrexone and cyclazocine, narcotic antagonists, have been used after detoxification. These agents render the individual refractory to the euphoria produced by narcotics. Research is currently being done on L-alpha acetylmethadol (LAAM), a long-acting methadone-like drug. The effects last for seventy-two hours, and dosing is necessary only three times a week. Also, buprenorphine is under investigation as a low-abuse analgesic, and as a maintenance drug for narcotic addiction. They are not yet available for general use at this time.

The pharmacological programs that have been presented here are but a fraction of what is needed for the total care of the addict, and psychotherapy is greatly needed to fulfill the total treatment plan.

Minor Tranquilizers

The minor tranquilizers (also termed "anxiolytics" or "antianxiety agents") are closer in action to the sedative-hypnotics than to the major tranquilizers, or neuroleptics. The minor tranquilizers may be considered as daytime sedatives, since they primarily suppress anxiety rather than produce sleep (Swonger and Constantine, 1976). There are two major classes: the propanediols and the benzodiazepines.

In the propanediol class, meprobamate (Equanil) is practically the only drug abused today. It is a CNS depressant having properties similar to the barbiturates, namely sedation and tranquilization. It is used to treat anxiety and tension, and to promote sleep. Physical and psychological dependence, as well as abuse, have been reported for this compound. Its effects include drowsiness, ataxia, slurred speech, weakness and/or fatigue, visual disturbances, syncope, and euphoria. Long-term effects are hematological disorders, REM suppression, and cardiac abnormalities. Normal doses range in the 0.8 to 2.0 g. per day range. Daily doses of 1.6 to 3.2 g. for about 270 days are required to produce a physical dependency. Once the drug is stopped, the onset of withdrawal symptoms takes approximately eight to twelve hours (Inaba and Katcher, 1978). Acute intoxication or overdose produce stupor, coma, convulsions, and both circulatory and respiratory collapse. Upon withdrawal from the drug, in a dependent individual, delirium and convulsions are frequently seen. Other symptoms may include tremors, ataxia, headache, and insomnia. This withdrawal syndrome resembles that for alcohol. The clinical use of this drug is declining, since the benzodiazepines have all but replaced it as an antianxiety agent.

"Each day about 40 billion doses of benzodiazepine drugs are consumed throughout the world" (Tyrer 1980). Diazepam is at the top of the list of most widely prescribed drugs (Zimberg, 1982). Benzodiazepines are prescribed for insomnia, acute reactive anxiety, and chronic anxiety; as a pre-anesthetic medication; for alcoholic withdrawal syndrome, seizures, and neuromuscular disorders such as backache; for cerebral palsy, tetanus, and various other problems. Also, they are widely used as recreational drugs. These drugs, if taken alone, are relatively safe, even in large quantities (Moire and Sellers, 1979).

The benzodiazepines include diazepam (Valium), chlordiazepoxide (Librium), clorazepate (Tranxene), flurazepam (Dalmane), lorazepam (Ativan), and oxazepam (Serax). All exhibit similar properties, with the major differences being in potency and in duration of action. The primary location of CNS action is in the reticular activating system. All benzodiazepines increase the seizure threshold. Therefore, they can be used as anticonvulsants. Effects seen on the cardiovascular and respiratory systems are minimal. Action on the CNS manifests as drowsiness, ataxia, fatigue, slurred speech, and other indicators of CNS depression. Diazepam's normal dose range is 5–40 mg. With doses of 80–120 mg. for forty-two days, a physical dependence can occur. Chlordiazepoxide's doses range between 10 and 100 mg. Doses of 300–600 mg. for sixty to eighty days are required for the production of a physical dependence. Normal clorazepate doses range between 7.5 and 60 mg. To produce physical dependence, doses of 150–180 mg. for thirty days are needed. Since these drugs are eliminated slowly, physical dependence is difficult to unmask. Diazepam and chlordiazepoxide require twelve to twenty-four hours after cessation before withdrawal symptoms occur, and five to eight days before peak withdrawal symptoms are manifested (Inaba and Katcher, 1978). This may be due to their long half-lives and their conversion into active compounds. Also, this grace period may allow dependent individuals time to acquire more benzodiazepines if they run out, thus preventing or reversing withdrawal symptoms. For the other benzodiazepines, there is little proof of abuse.

Treatment of overdose is primarily support of cardiovascular function and respiration. Treatment of dependence is similar to that for barbiturates. More important is the prevention of dependency. The indications for use of these agents rarely exceed four weeks, and as long as doses are not excessive, physical dependency should not occur. Another aid in avoidance of dependency is to interrupt courses of therapy. This minimizes the development of tolerance, which in turn lowers the possibility for dependency.

Marijuana

Marijuana is obtained from the *Cannabis sativa* plant, which is a herbaceous annual. Both the male and female plants contain active ingredients; however, the highest concentration is found in the flowering tops.

The principal psychoactive ingredient in marijuana is delta-9-tetrahydrocannabinal, or THC. One average marijuana cigarette contains 2.5 to 5 mg. of THC (Jaffe, 1975). In examining marijuana smoke, approximately 150 compounds have been identified. Benzopyrene, a carcinogen that has been shown to be tumor-producing when applied to the skin of laboratory animals, is 70 percent more abundant in marijuana smoke than tobacco smoke. Also, more "tar" is contained in marijuana smoke than in the high-tar tobacco cigarettes. The body's breakdown of THC is very complex, and the THC has been found to be metabolized to over thirty-five products.

Acute effects of THC seen when a person is "high" include impairment of intellectual and psychomotor tasks involving digit symbol substitution, choice-reaction time, repeatability of order of digits, reading comprehension, concept formation, and speech. Marijuana most commonly interferes with the transfer of material to long-term memory storage—an effect that is detrimental to classroom functioning and the acquisition of knowledge. The drug also impairs driving ability and alters driver perception, as evidenced in increased risk-taking when "high." The most common psychological effect of THC seems to be a loss of perspective: anxiety and paranoia are brought on by a drug-induced distortion of reality.

Marijuana smoking causes local irritation of the bronchial mucous membranes, which leads to increased secretions and a chronic bronchitis. The cilia (fine, hairlike projections) which help in the removal of foreign material from the lungs are adversely affected by the smoke. This all leads to extensive lung inflammation and possible degeneration. While there haven't been any published reports of abnormal infants whose parents took marijuana, THC does decrease the sperm count and its motility. THC also has been shown to cause a shortening of the luteal phase of the menstrual cycle (and hence a shortened time span of potential fertility) and lower levels of prolactin (a hormone responsible for producing adequate levels of mother's milk); also, it has been shown to pass into the milk of nursing mothers (Levin, 1979).

THC has been shown to increase heart rate, but the effects are considered benign so far. THC has not been clearly implicated in chromosomal aberrations, alteration of cell metabolism, or brain damage (cerebral atrophy).

It has been well established that tolerance to THC develops with chronic use, but this may be a negative or positive tolerance. In other words, it may take more or, oddly enough, less to get the same result as was previously achieved. A mild abstinence syndrome has been observed upon discontinuation of THC after continuous intoxication. Symptoms may include anorexia, tremor, perspiration, irritability, cramps, diarrhea, nausea, and disturbances in sleep (Denber, 1979).

Since treatment of THC abuse primarily entails abstinence and psychotherapy, there is no need to discuss it further in this chapter. But something should be said about the newer therapeutic implications of this substance. THC has been used to combat nausea and vomiting associated with cancer chemotherapy. The results thus far have been promising, as evidenced by improved appetite and lessened weight loss. The drug is in a soft gelatin capsule form, and doses of 2.5–5 mg. have been given throughout the day. The best results have been seen in younger patients. Sedation and euphoria are the main side-effects (Denber, 1979). Marijuana has been shown to decrease intraocular pressure associated with open-angle glaucoma. It has worked better when used concomitantly with other pressure-reducing medications than when used alone.

Much work, however, is needed to establish marijuana as a safe therapeutic agent and to evaluate the possible long-term results of administration.

References

Becker, C. E. Medical complications of drug abuse. In G. H. Stollerman (ed.), *Advances in Internal Medicine*, vol. 24. Chicago: Year Book Medical Publishers, 1979.

———. Pharmacotherapy in the treatment of alcoholism. In J. H. Mendelson and N. K. Mello (eds.), *The Diagnosis and Treatment of Alcoholism*. New York: McGraw-Hill Book Co., 1979.

Boyer, J. L. Hepatic disorders. In K. L. Melmon and H. F. Morrelli (eds.), *Clinical Pharmacology*, 2nd ed. New York: Macmillan Publishing Co., 1979.

Coleman, J. H. Affective disorders. In M. A. Koda-Kimble, B. S. Katcher, and L. Y. Young (eds.), *Applied Therapeutics for Clinical Pharmacists*, 2nd ed. San Francisco: Applied Therapeutics, 1978.

Daniels, T. C., and Jorgensen, E. C. Metabolic changes of drugs and related organic compounds. In C. O. Wilson, O. Gisvold, and R. F. Doerge (eds.), *Textbook of Organic Medicinal and Pharmaceutical Chemistry*, 7th ed. Philadelphia: J. B. Lippincott Co., 1977.

Denber, H. C. *Clinical Psychopharmacology.* New York, Stratton Intercontinental Medical Book Corp., 1979.

The Extra Pharmacopoeia, 27th ed. London: The Pharmaceutical Press, 1978.

Forrest, G. G. *Intensive Psychotherapy of Alcoholism.* Springfield, Ill.: Charles C. Thomas, 1984.

Gold, M. S., and A. C. Pottash. Neurobiological aspects of opiate addiction and withdrawal. In E. Gottheil, K. A. Druley, T. E. Skoloda, and H. M. Waxman (eds.), *Etiologic Aspects of Alcohol and Drug Abuse.* Springfield, Ill.: Charles C. Thomas, 1983.

Green, A. I., Meyer, R. E., and Shader, R. I. Heroin and methadone abuse: acute and chronic management. In R. I. Shader (ed.), *Manual of Psychiatric Therapeutics.* Boston: Little, Brown & Co., 1978.

Greenblatt, D. J., and Shader, R. I. Treatment of the alcohol withdrawal syndrome. In R. I. Shader (ed.), *Manual of Psychiatric Therapeutics.* Boston: Little, Brown & Co., 1978.

Harvey, S. C. Hypnotics and sedatives. L. S. Goodman and A. Gilman (eds.), *The Pharmacological Basis of Therapeutics,* 5th ed. New York: Macmillan Publishing Co., 1975.

Hollister, L. E. *Clinical Pharmacology of Psychotherapeutic Drugs.* New York: Churchill Livingstone, 1978.

Hurt, R. D., Higgins, J. A., Nelson, R. A., Morse, R. M., and Dickerson, E. R. Nutritional status of a group of alcoholics before and after admission to an alcoholism treatment unit. *American Journal of Clinical Nutrition,* 1981, *34* (*3*), 386–392.

Inaba, D. S., and Katcher, B. S. Drug abuse. In M. A. Koda-Kimble, B. S. Katcher, and L. Y. Young (eds.), *Applied Therapeutics for Clinical Pharmacists,* 2nd ed. San Francisco: Applied Therapeutics, 1978.

Jaffe, J. H. Drug addiction and drug abuse. In L. S. Goodman and A. Gilman (eds.), *The Pharmacological Basis of Therapeutics,* 5th ed. New York: Macmillan Publishing Co., 1975.

———, and Martin, W. R. Narcotic analgesics and antagonists. In L. S. Goodman and A. Gilman (eds.), *The Pharmacological Basis of Therapeutics,* 5th ed. New York: Macmillan Publishing Co., 1975.

James, J. D., Braunstein, M. L., Karig, A. W., and Hartshorn, E. A. *A Guide to Drug Interactions.* New York: McGraw-Hill Book Co., 1978.

Khantzian, E. J., and McKenna, G. J. Acute toxic and withdrawal reactions associated with drug use and abuse. *Annals of Internal Medicine,* 1979, *90,* 361–372.

Levin, R. H. Teratogenicity and drug excretion in breast milk (maternogenicity). In E. T. Herfindal and J. L. Hirschman (eds.), *Clinical Pharmacy and Therapeutics,* 2nd ed. Baltimore: Williams & Wilkins Co., 1979.

Martin, E. W. *Hazards of Medication.* Philadelphia: J. B. Lippincott Co., 1978.

Modern Drug Encyclopedia and Therapeutic Index, ed. A. J. Lewis. New York: Dun-Donnelley Publishing Corp., 1977.

Moire, S. J., and Sellers, E. M. Use of drugs with dependence liability. *Canadian Medical Association Journal,* 1979, *121* (*1*), 717–724.

Neuhaus, O. W., and Orten, J. M. *Human Biochemistry,* 9th ed. Saint Louis: C. V. Mosby Co., 1975.

Petersen, R. C. *Marijuana and Health: Eighth Annual Report to the U.S. Congress from the Secretary of Health and Human Services.* Rockville, Md.: National Institute on Drug Abuse, 1980.

Quail, I., and Karelse, R. H. Disulfiram psychosis; a case report. *South African Medical Journal,* 1980, *57,* 551–552.

Ritchie, J. M. The aliphatic alcohols. In L. S. Goodman and A. Gilman (eds.), *The Pharmacological Basis of Therapeutics,* 5th ed. New York: Macmillan Publishing Co., 1975.

Robinson, G. M., Sellers, E. M., and Janecek, E. Barbiturate and hypnosedative withdrawal by a multiple oral phenobarbital loading dose technique. *Clinical Pharmacology and Therapeutics,* 1981, *30* (*1*), 71–76.

Sellers, E. Barbiturate withdrawal. *Journal of American Medical Association,* 1979, *241* (*14*), 1444–1448.

Stedman's Medical Dictionary. Baltimore: Williams and Wilkins Co., 1977.

Swonger, A. K., and Constantine, L. L. *Drugs and Therapy.* Boston: Little, Brown and Co., 1976.

Tong, T. G., and Bernstein, L. R. Alcoholism. In E. T. Herfindal and J. L. Hirschman (eds.), *Clinical Pharmacy and Therapeutics,* 2nd ed. Baltimore: Williams and Wilkins Co., 1979.

Tyrer, P. Dependence on benzodiazepines. *British Journal of Psychiatry,* 1980, *137,* 576–577.

Victor, M., and Adams, R. D. Alcohol. In K. J. Isselbacher, R. D. Adams, E. Braunwald, R. G. Petersdorf, and J. D. Wilson (eds.), *Harrison's Principles of Internal Medicine,* 9th ed. New York: McGraw-Hill Book Co., 1980.

———. Opiates and synthetic analgesics. In K. J. Isselbacher, R. D. Adams, E. Braunwald, R. G. Petersdorf, and J. D. Wilson (eds.), *Harrison's Principles of Internal Medicine,* 9th ed. New York: McGraw-Hill Book Co., 1980.

Wilson, A. Patient management in disulfiram implant therapy. *Canadian Journal of Psychiatry,* 1979, *24* (*6*), 537–541.

Wooddell, W. J. Liver disease in alcohol-addicted patients. In S. V. Davidson (ed.), *Alcoholism and Health.* Germantown, Md.: Aspen Publications, 1980.

Young, L. Y., and Barriere, S. L. Tuberculosis. In M. A. Koda-Kimble, B. S. Katcher, and L. Y. Young (eds.), *Applied Therapeutics for Clinical Pharmacists,* 2nd ed. San Francisco: Applied Therapeutics, 1978.

Zimberg, S. *The Clinical Management of Alcoholism.* New York: Brunner/Mazel, 1982.

3

Stress and Alcoholism

J. Kelley Yost / Robert A. Mines

Selye (1956) defined stress as the nonspecific response of the body to any demand made on it. Included in these demands were the normal physiological responses one would expect from walking into the cold from a warm house or engaging in an exhilarating activity. Over the years people came to use the word "stress" in a negative fashion, encompassing all the aversive events that may affect an organism. In response to this, Selye coined the term "eustress" to encompass the "positive" stresses.

Selye's original experiments were done on rats. When he injected the rats with cattle-ovary extract, they showed the following symptoms: (1) enlargement of the adrenal glands, (2) decrease in the size of the thymus and other bodily defense systems, and (3) deep bleeding ulcers of the stomach and duodenal linings.

Selye found that upon exposure to stimuli, animals underwent three distinct stages. The *alarm reaction,* a generalized "call to arms" of the defensive forces of the organism, was the first. If the animal did not die from initial exposure, it necessarily moved to the second stage, the *stage of resistance.* Physiological reactions during the resistance stage were almost the opposite of the alarm reaction. Whereas during the alarm reaction there was considerable discharge of glandular secretions, the stage of resistance showed a buildup of glandular secretions. If exposure to the noxious stimuli continued, the *stage of exhaustion,* which was quite similar to the alarm reaction, was reached. The end result was death, but a death due to premature aging from wear and tear. Selye called this three-stage response sequence the General Adaptation Syndrome (GAS).

In describing the three-stage model, Selye called it adaptive because defenses were stimulated in order to maintain the homeostatic balance within the body. Homeostasis refers to bodily systemic balance or consistency. It is this second stage of the GAS that we will largely be concerned with how people resist noxious stimuli in order to maintain homeostasis.

The Effects of Stress on Human Beings

We differentiate between two types of stress: acute and chronic. Acute stress occurs when danger arises. The stress is immediate and must be responded to instantaneously. Frequently people report being very clear in their thoughts during this phase. The body is in danger and must respond correctly and quickly. Chronic stress is prolonged and unabated (Pelletier, 1977), and can result in severe hypertension due to kidney damage.

No organ is immune to the stress response. Either through genetics or selective conditioning, it may affect one specific area in a particular individual—say, the kidney—but it is only a matter of time before the whole body is involved. Since stress causes a weakening of the immunological response, stress-ridden people are more sickly than those who are relatively free of stress, and the ultimate effect is death.

Adaptive work is whatever process of change the body goes through in order to adjust to the stress stimulus in stage 2 of the GAS. Selye devised the construct "adaptation energy" for the process experienced in adaptive work. He considered the amount available to any one being to be finite. When this is used up, death soon results, as the body is no longer able to maintain homeostasis in the presence of noxious stimuli. In Selye's opinion, no one dies from old age. If old age was indeed a cause of death, one would expect all the body's organs to wear out at the same time. This does not happen. Without adaptive energy, individual organs (the heart, lungs, and so on) cannot survive the environment's demands.

Individual Differences in Reactions to Stress

Stress does not produce negative physiological responses until the stimulus affects the psychological state of the beholder and is perceived as stressful (Pelletier, 1977). People react differentially to certain specific stimuli, phobias being an obvious example. Some people are petrified of snakes, yet others keep them as house pets. What factors cause people to experience stressful stimuli differently?

Perceived Control. The objective magnitude of a crisis of work or living situation is not as significant as the extent to which the individual perceives the situation to be threatening and therefore stressful. The amount of control the individual has over a stressful situation has a significant impact on his or her response. Overcrowding does not seem to be a factor in stress until people feel a loss of control (Tanner, 1976). Studies done on reduction in electrothermal response when the subject is able to control the aversive stimuli show significant reductions in measured levels of stress as compared to situations without control (Haggard, 1946; Champion, 1950; Corah and Boffa, 1970). However, it is not only actual control that reduces stress; perceived control will also result in lower levels of stress (Stotland and Blumenthal, 1964; Corah and Boffa, 1970; Glass and Singer, 1972). For Glass and Singer, this was true also on their measures of social and physical stressors: discrimination and bureaucracy. As long as the perception of control exists, whether justified or not, stress is reduced.

One way the perception of control can be maintained is through adaptation, either by changing the organism or by having the organism change the environment. Of the population in general, those who have difficulty in adapting to challenging situations, however mundane, are those who exhibit a major proportion of the illnesses (Pelletier, 1977). Put another way, that organism which is most adaptable is that organism which will survive (Bandler and Grinder, 1979).

Occupational Effects. A frequent topic of newspaper articles, television specials, and research studies is the relatively high rate of alcoholism among certain occupational groups. Three groups come to mind as examples: air traffic controllers, physicians, and police officers. Air traffic controllers, when compared to commercial cargo pilots, were found to have significantly greater incidences of high blood pressure, diabetes, and peptic ulcers (Tanner, 1976). Pearson (1975) reported that there is increasing evidence of emotional disturbance among physicians, and one effect associated with the stress physicians experience has been an increase in alcoholism. Nordlicht (1979) notes that stress factors among police officers are primarily due to the demands of the department, the community, and family life. The stresses that police officers experience include rejection due to their occupation, limited exposure to a wider world, disruptive work schedules, inability to give attention and love to their children, and a shortage of communication with their spouses. Nordlicht concluded that the most serious result of these stresses is alcoholism.

Another factor currently receiving publicity is the effect of post-Vietnam trauma. Lacoursier, Godfrey, and Ruby (1980) discuss how the stress trauma of Vietnam combat, among other things, has caused some veterans to "self-medicate" themselves with alcohol to the point of abuse.

There does seem to be a correlation between high-stress jobs and alcoholism, but one important point remains. Despite increased rates of alcoholism among certain occupational groups, the majority of people in these groups do not become alcoholics. If each subgroup was exposed to approximately the same levels of stress, why did some people turn to alcohol when others did not? How do the alcoholic subjects differ from the nonalcoholic subjects?

Alcoholics' and Nonalcoholics' Reactions to Stress. There is evidence of stress-related differences between alcoholics and nonalcoholics. Litz (1979) reported that among a group of alcoholic and nonalcoholic women, the alcoholic group subjectively "felt" the impact of stress more than the nonalcoholic group. In another study of women, Eddy (1978) had similar findings: Alcoholic women had greater levels of trait anxiety than nonalcoholic women on the State-Trait Anxiety Inventory. Horn (1978) matched groups of twenty male alcoholics and twenty male nonalcoholics and measured them on self-report and behavioral tests of assertive behavior. Although there were no differences in assertive behavior, alcoholics reported more assertive discomfort on both tests.

Thus it appears that given approximately equal amounts of stress, the alcoholic reports more perceived stress. Each situation is more stressful for the alcoholic subject than the nonalcoholic subject.

Interpersonal Failure as a Stressor. A second difference perhaps explains and expands upon the first. Forrest (1978) suggests that interpersonal failure is the basic rationale for alcoholic and problem drinking. Failure, he writes, "may be the single most important behavioral issue in the developmental pathology of alcohol addiction." Forrest characterizes interpersonal failure as a life-style where there is a very significant lack of interpersonal skills. His assumption is that a large part of the alcoholic population was not wanted, was raised by grandparents, foster parents, or other surrogates. The result was a poor self-concept and a general feeling of not being wanted, inadequacy, and inferiority. Forrest (1983; 1984) also cites the same general process among children in affluent, intellectual, seemingly well-adjusted families. Interpersonal relations may, on the surface, appear good, but in reality these relations are a composite of double messages and distorted communications. This failure identity promotes continued life failures, although the opposite effect can certainly be seen. The "successful" hard-driving business person who takes on a counter-identity in a continual struggle to prove his or her ability and worth is a prime example. At the core of the struggle is the failure identity, and poor interpersonal and coping skills.

There are data to support this premise. Allman, Taylor, and Nathan (1972) studied a group of three chronic alcoholics and exposed them to stress and a social situation. They found that subjects drank most when stress and social interaction coincided. While the study suffered from small sample, it does link stress, social interaction, and drinking behavior. Parker, Gilbert, and Thoreson (1978) note that there appear to be social-skill deficits in alcoholics versus nonalcoholics.

Interpersonal failure, then, can be a potent stressor. Certainly everyday living requires socialization with spouse, children, and co-workers, yet each interaction involves some stress. For an individual with poor interpersonal and coping skills, every interaction becomes a stressor, the anticipation of an interaction is a stressor, and remembering the interaction is a stressor. If almost every interaction places a person under stress, it is easy to see that this person must adapt more often than someone who does not find social situations so difficult. Alcoholics seem to respond to many social situations by being stressed. They also drink in order to extinguish this socially defined stress.

Is there a common factor that holds together this differential perception of stress and interpersonal failure? As we have previously mentioned, stress does not have an effect unless there is perceived lack of control. When there is perceived control, stress is less arousing (Glass and Singer, 1972). Since alcoholics seem to perceive more stress, it follows that they must also perceive less control or fewer alternatives for coping.

Are there group differences which would lead to this perception of less control? The difference seems to lie in the ability to use Selye's adaptive energy to develop alternative stress-reducing behaviors. Berman (1969) reported that drinking represents an exclusion of alternate, more adaptive behavior. Drinking does have adaptive consequences (Davis et al., 1974), but this behavior is only one response out of an infinite number of possibilities. This is in contrast to stress-resistant people, who tend to have common personality traits and coping styles. They are usually flexible in their attachments to other people, groups, and goals. They readily shift to other relationships when established ones are disrupted (Tanner, 1976). In other words, they are highly adaptive. Alcoholics rarely form other than superficial relationships and are stuck in their one overlearned behavior pattern, drinking.

Stress is differentially perceived. Each individual's reaction is related to a complex interaction of perceived control, actual control, learned coping skill, range of coping alternatives, and an attitudinal component of openness and flexibility.

Social Learning and Alcoholism

The premise of this chapter is that alcoholism is a multidimensional syndrome with its basis in social learning. Although a genetic predisposition may be able to account for differential physiological reactions to alcohol, we still have to account for how people learn to use alcohol and continue using alcohol.

The majority of people in this country have parents who modeled various types of drinking behavior as well as a myriad of coping skills or lack thereof. We learn our strategies for coping with stress and tension from our parents or other caretakers. We learn to take a drink after work, withdraw, ask for support, play, meditate, pray, respond socially, or respond irrationally from these models.

Social learning explains that individuals are exposed to differentially effective models. Parent A may model the use of alcohol as a way of "unwinding" after work by having a drink or two. This same person may also be modeling good interpersonal skills with his or her spouse, reliable work habits, flexibility in problem solving, the regular use of exercise, and so on. On the other end of the continuum, Parent B may model having a few drinks after work, abusive behavior toward the spouse, periodically missing work because of hangovers, poor relationships with friends and family, and other ineffective behavior patterns.

These two examples have different types of coping behaviors. Depending on the effectiveness of these behaviors, the individual will experience varying degrees of stress reduction or even an increase in stress. At this point operant conditioning helps to explain the maintenance of the drinking behavior. Parent A models a variety of responses which have the potential to reduce stress and be reinforcing in terms of secondary gains (i.e., money to live on, recognition at work and home, reduced perceived level of tension). These reinforcers are more potent than they would be if the person only had alcohol consumption as an effective tension-reducing technique.

If alcohol consumption is the most effective behavior in the person's response repertoire for reducing tension, it will have greater potency as a reinforcer (Lawson, Peterson, and Lawson, 1983). Thus there is an interactive effect of the number of effective coping alternatives modeled and the relative reinforcing potential of the alcohol consumption. Those individuals who use alcohol to reduce stress probably have had models with fewer coping alternatives.

Modeling is the predominant modality for learning most of our interpersonal and coping skills. Alcoholics have models on a variety of levels. The first aspect of modeling is the attitude of Western culture toward drinking: namely, that for one reason or another, almost every adult consumes varying quantities of alcohol. What party is without a certain amount of alcohol consumption? Edwards et al. (1972) surveyed 306 male adults who reported drinking at least once or twice a month. They reported that alcohol was used primarily for psychotropic effects, for its taste at meals, and in response to environmental pressures. Sadava, Thistle, and Forsythe (1978) studied 370 nonalcoholics, 51 percent of whom were women. They found, among other things, a positive attitude toward alcohol use. This positive attitude certainly implies some powerful modeling.

There are two frequently occurring models: peers and family. DeRicco (1978) found a direct effect of modeling on drinking rates. In this study, subjects drank with a pair of confederates. It was found that the subjects consistently matched the drinking rate of the confederates whether the confederates modeled a high or low consumption rate and regardless of the sex of either confederates or subjects. Familial modeling (Wegscheider, 1981) is perhaps even more powerful, if only because it is more longstanding. A review of studies conducted over four decades showed that on the average, one-third of any sample of alcoholics had at least one parent who was an alcoholic. In every study of families of alcoholics and nonalcoholics, the incidence of alcoholism was greater among families of alcoholics. One could argue for a genetic predisposition toward alcoholism, but this cannot account for all the data. Various cultures do show different drinking patterns. In different studies of rates of alcoholism among ethnic groups, the Irish-Americans show consistently greater rates than the population as a whole (Bales, 1946). Yet in terms of per capita consumption of alcohol, the Irish in Ireland rank rather low (Forrest, 1978).

In addition to specifically modeling drinking in families, alcoholic parents do not model many other coping responses. In a study of 186 adolescents, Rouse, Walker, and Ewing (1973) found significant differences on measures of psychological stress and activities used to relieve depression. Children of heavy drinkers indicated more stress but utilized fewer effective adaptive methods of dealing with anxiety and depression. In other words, these adolescents were already excluding appropriately adaptive responses to stress other than the drinking response, and they were limited in their repertoire of coping skills.

In addition to social learning and modeling effects, operant conditioning can also partially account for the use of alcohol as a coping response. Operant conditioning holds that an event or behavior which is reinforced will tend to reoccur with greater frequency than others which are not reinforced. When perceived tension is eliminated through drinking, the operant (drinking) behavior is reinforced negatively. Various studies on alcohol and operant conditioning (Mello and Mendelson, 1965; Mendelson and Mello, 1966; Narrol, 1967; Nathan et al., 1970; Cohen, Liebson, and Faillace, 1971) have focused on changing contingencies for drinking behavior, thus showing that at least some alcoholic drinking can be regarded as an operant response and manipulated accordingly.

Our view of alcoholism, while not applicable to every client, suggests that problem drinkers and alcoholics drink, at least initially, to remove aversive stimuli. A person suffering from job tension, family tension, or some other disagreeable condition takes a drink and feels better. Because the person finds that alcohol consumption reduces the effects of an aversive stimulus, drinking is reinforced, with the expected increase in frequency.

Critics of the tension-reduction hypothesis, or TRH (Mendelson, 1964; McNamee, Mello, and Mendelson, 1968; Nathan and O'Brian, 1971), have pointed out that among chronic alcoholics, tension actually increased upon consumption of alcohol. While we do not question the results of these studies, consider the following points: (1) The TRH may work best at a prealcoholic level (Edwards et al., 1972); (2) among problem drinkers, drinking behavior is overlearned (Forrest, 1978); and (3) in later stages, consumption of alcohol itself may be considered a stressor, as the individual has probably experienced repeated negative consequences from his or her drinking and reacts to the drinking, at least on the cognitive level, as a stressor.

Thus an explanation for resolving the apparent conflicts in the TRH might be that this model best fits those individuals in a pre-chronic alcoholic stage of drinking. They are the ones for whom a drink probably reduces tension. This behavior becomes overlearned, that is, learned to the point of excluding other more adaptive, more appropriate behaviors. Additionally, at the point that drinking behavior affects the life of the drinker, be it at work or in social and familial situations, the consumption of alcohol itself, paradoxical as it may seem, may cause an increase in the drinker's level of anxiety. Also, those who point to the measured maladaptiveness of drinking behavior may be overlooking an important factor: the strength of a response that it is intermittently reinforced. If the overlearned response is intermittently reinforced, then it will continue in spite of other, negative consequences.

If one is to accept the premise that alcoholism is a behavioral coping response to stress, the following areas must be addressed: Does alcohol reduce stress, and if so, how?

Does alcohol reduce the symptoms of stress? Animal studies which have attempted to determine if stress is a causal link in alcoholism have had mixed results. In a review of these studies, Cappell and Herman (1972) reported the data to be "equivocal, negative and even contradictory" and felt that the tension-reduction hypothesis had perhaps outlived its usefulness. On the other hand, a more recent review by Hodgson, Stockwell, and Rankin (1979) argues that a TRH is supported by animal research in most cases where an appropriate paradigm to explain the behavior has been used.

Selye (1956) found an increase in adrenocortical secretions during the alarm stage of the GAS. Does alcohol have a chemical effect on common physiological measures of stress? In a study of nonalcoholic humans, it was found that levels of corticosteroids were reduced by a low dose of ethanol (Pohorecky et al., 1980). In this study, foot shock was used as a stress-inducing aversive stimulus. Since alcohol ingestion reduced corticosteroid levels, the authors felt this was supporting evidence that alcohol reduced the biochemical consequences of stress. Other studies of nonalcoholic clients (Geber and Anderson, 1967; Stassen, Neff, and Meittinen, 1976) showed a normalization of the physiological responses to stress upon ingestion of alcohol. Greenberg and Carpenter (1957) and Lienent and Traxel (1959) studied the effects of alcohol on galvanic skin response (GSR). They found that among nonalcoholic clients, large amounts of alcohol reduced the GSR.

Among alcoholic clients, similar results have been shown (Gross et al., 1978; Begleiter and Platz, 1972; Naitoh, 1972). It seems fairly conclusive that ingestion of alcohol can reduce the physiological manifestations of stress.

Alcoholic behavior can be partially accounted for by social learning and operant conditioning as a response for reducing tension. There is support for this on the cognitive, behavioral, and physiological levels. If alcohol use, as a coping response to stress and tension, is learned, then, theoretically, alternative tension-reduction responses can also be learned. The remainder of the chapter will focus on those techniques.

Treatment Interventions

A number of interventions that have been used to reduce tension and/or anxiety in nonalcoholic clients may also have utility in helping alcoholics whose condition seems to be precipitated by stress, or as a learned coping response to stress. Techniques that have been reported to be useful in reducing tension are various types of biofeedback such as electromyogram feedback, finger-temperature feedback, alpha wave feedback, relaxation training, meditation, autogenic training, and aerobic exercise. These interventions have been shown to generally reduce oxygen consumption, respiration rate, heart rate, muscle tension, and in some cases blood pressure. In addition, an increase in alpha wave production and skin resistance have been demonstrated.

Biofeedback and Relaxation Training

Since biofeedback and relaxation training are often confounded in the research, the literature on these two areas is discussed together. The three types of biofeedback treatments reviewed in this chapter are electromyogram (EMG), electroencephalogram (EEG) for alpha wave training, and finger-temperature feedback.

Electromyogram. The use of EMG feedback assumes that tension in alcoholics is manifested in muscle tension. The studies reviewed all use the frontalis muscle as the dependent variable to indicate reduced tension.

Kurtz (1974) was one of the first investigators to look at the potential of EMG and EEG training as means of reducing tension in alcoholics. He assigned thirty-five inpatient alcoholics to a treatment group which received the regular therapy program and EMG and EEG biofeedback training ninety minutes a day, five days a week, instead of group therapy. An additional thirty-five alcoholic inpatients were used as controls, receiving their regular therapy program and going to group therapy during the biofeedback time. The subjects stayed in the program a minimum of twenty-eight days, with a maximum of six weeks and a mean stay of thirty days. Their blood pressure and pulse were taken before and after each training session. The in-session change in blood pressure decreased 7 mm. systolic, 5 mm. diastolic, with the pulse decreasing 4.3 beats per minute. Over the course of the treatment the experimental group's blood pressure decreased an average of 17.4 mm. systolic, 8.8 mm. diastolic, while the control group's blood pressure increased 7.7 mm. systolic and 2.57 mm. diastolic. No followup data or drinking behavior data was reported. Steffen (1975) trained four chronic alcoholics over a three-day period to reduce frontalis muscle tension. During the second phase of the study, liquor was available as long as the blood alcohol level did not exceed 250 mm. % on a given day over a twelve-day period. Phase 3 involved detoxification until the blood alcohol level was reduced to zero percent over a two-day period. Phase 4 consisted of fourteen sessions of general, forearm, and frontalis tension reduction training with and without EMG feedback. The cycle was repeated for forty-one days. The results indicated that the training led to decreased subjective mood disturbance, lowered EMG activity level, and lowered blood alcohol levels. There was no decrease in the number of drinks ordered.

Eno (1975) investigated the use of EMG-assisted relaxation training for reducing the tension level of fifty institutionalized male alcoholics. She had five groups: a no-treatment control group, a relaxation training group, a biofeedback-only group, a combined relaxation and biofeedback training group, and a control group enrolled in an established rehabilitation program. The results demonstrated that the combined biofeedback and relaxation group attained the lowest EMG level. There were significant changes in EMG level in the biofeedback only, relaxation training only, and the combined group, but not in the control groups. The relaxation training–only group had lower EMG levels than the biofeedback-only and the two control groups. The control groups did not change in EMG level. There was no significant difference between and within the groups on the self-reporting State-Trait Anxiety Inventory scores from pre- to post-test. Drinking behavior data was not reported.

Strickler et al. (1977) investigated the effect of one session of systematic relaxation training on the EMG tension level of abstinent alcoholics participating in an outpatient Antabuse maintenance treatment program. The subjects were given relaxation instructions or neutral material prior to listening to a tape recording of drinking-related stimuli. It was found that brief instruction in relaxation was adequate to significantly reduce the subjects' frontalis EMG levels; the exposure to the drinking-related stimuli significantly increased these EMG levels; and prior relaxation instructions protected the subjects from the EMG tension-inducing effects of the drinking-related tape.

Lenigen (1977) used a component control design to study the effect of EMG biofeedback and relaxation training on the performance of alcoholics under stress. He divided forty-one patients into a feedback-only group, a relaxation training–only group, an EMG plus relaxation training group, and a control group in which the subject merely rested for twenty-six minutes for five sessions. The dependent variable was frontalis muscle tension. In addition, cervical paraspinal muscles were monitored to measure generalization of training effects. The response latency measures on a post-test task were also used an indirect indices of autonomic nervous system balance. Lenigen found that the biofeedback treatments without supportive interventions did not reduce muscle tension during training or improve the performance on the post-test. The relaxation training reduced the frontalis muscle tension but did not generalize to the cervical paraspinal muscles. The relaxation training had no effect on the response latency post-test. In addition, the alcoholics were neither unusually anxious according to two psychological tests nor were they more muscularly tense than nonalcoholics. No drinking behavior data was reported. Lenigen suggested that the data does not support the theory that alcoholics, who are theoretically anxious and use ethanol to maintain autonomic nervous system balance, are good relaxation candidates.

In an attempt to be more prescriptive in the use of biofeedback, Page and Schaub (1978) studied EMG biofeedback applicability for differing alcoholic personality types. Thirty-two male inpatient alcoholics were divided into two groups on the basis of their Minnesota Multiphasic Personality Inventory (MMPI) profile. Group 1 consisted of tense and anxious subjects, while group 2 was a more heterogeneous collection of personality types. Eight subjects from each group received fourteen days of progressive relaxation training and EMG biofeedback, while control subjects were given sessions of taped music and EMG monitoring. The group 1 relaxation and EMG feedback component had lower EMG levels than group 2 or the control group. All of the groups reported an increase in improved mood states, but there was no difference in improved mood level between groups. Alcohol consumption data was not reported. The highly anxious subjects achieved lower EMG readings more rapidly than the heterogeneous group did with identical treatment. The researchers concluded that clients can be selected differentially for relaxation-biofeedback training through the use of the MMPI, and that clients who exhibit significant anxiety and tension can achieve lower levels of tension during training than clients with lower levels of pretreatment anxiety.

Hitchcox (1979) investigated the effectiveness of EMG-assisted biofeedback relaxation training in helping recovering women alcoholics to reduce their responsivity to stressful life events. She trained six recovering female alcoholics with five to nine sessions of frontalis EMG feedback and relaxation training, plus four to five sessions of exposure to stressful imagery in a single-subject replication multiple baseline design. The theme of the imagery was social stress. The dependent variables were frontalis and trapezius muscle tension level, hand temperature, self-awareness of relative tension levels, and subjective report of relaxation. The results indicated that frontalis feedback was effective in reducing high and moderate levels of tension to a normal range. The relaxation training was as effective as EMG feedback in facilitating relaxation. There was no relationship between the EMG level and hand temperature. Those subjects who had a low baseline temperature demonstrated a decrease in EMG level and an increase in hand temperature. There was some evidence of a reduction in responsivity to stress. The five subjects who completed training (one subject dropped out and had started drinking again) showed a significant reduction in current craving for alcohol, perceived helplessness, and intensity of psychophysiological complaints. They also demonstrated a substantial concordance between the subjective and the objective indices of relative relaxation and tension. Continued sobriety was associated with successful practice involving the stress-reduction techniques and the imagery.

McWilliams (1979) studied the effects of EMG-induced relaxation with relaxation training as an adjunct to a regular rehabilitation program for alcoholics. He hypothesized that the learning of self-regulation of psychophysiological events such as muscle relaxation would facilitate otherwise stressed alcoholics to cope with tension in a more effective manner. He assigned sixty male alcoholics to an EMG relaxation training group or an attention placebo group. The State-Trait Anxiety Inventory and the Physiological Manifestation of Anxiety Scale were used as dependent-variable measures. The results suggest strong evidence for the efficacy of EMG feedback–induced relaxation training with muscle relaxation training, but there was a limited correlation with the subjects' report of anxiety. The alcoholics receiving EMG training indicated more awareness of physiologically manifested anxiety symptoms. There was no followup on drinking behavior.

Rosenberg (1980) assumed that alcoholism is a multiple-syndrome group of disorders and hypothesized that relaxation therapy would be an effective treatment for alcoholic clients whose drinking is highly related to anxiety. He assigned fifty-nine male outpatient alcoholics to an EMG biofeedback-assisted relaxation group, with relaxation practice between sessions (six 30-minute sessions), or to a control group that received six 30-minute sessions of alcohol education. The State-Trait Anxiety Inventory and the Alcohol Use Inventory were used to measure aspects of the dependent variables. The results suggested that EMG-assisted relaxation was effective in reducing transitory states of subjective discomfort and physiological tension.

The relaxation subjects who scored high on anxiety related to drinking demonstrated a significantly greater improvement on all of the alcohol-use measures than did the control subjects who scored high on anxiety related to drinking. In contrast, no differences on any of the alcohol-use measures were reported between the experimental and control subjects who were not high on anxiety related to drinking. Additionally, the experimental subjects who frequently used the relaxation technique outside the treatment sessions demonstrated a significantly greater improvement on two or three of the alcohol-use measures than those subjects who infrequently used the relaxation technique. Rosenberg concluded that anxiety reduction may be expected to produce a decrease in alcohol use only for subjects whose drinking is highly related to anxiety.

EMG biofeedback has been effective in reducing the EMG level in institutionalized alcoholics, according to all the studies reported here (Eno, 1975; Steffen, 1975; Strickler et al., 1977; Page and Schaub, 1978; Hitchcox, 1979), with the exception of Lenigen (1977). Self-report data indicated reduced tension (Steffen, 1975; Page and Schaub, 1978; Hitchcox, 1979; McWilliams, 1979; Rosenberg, 1980), with the exception of Eno (1975). Finally, EMG is effective in reducing blood pressure and pulse rate (Kurtz, 1974). Minimal data indicate that EMG biofeedback is not successful in reducing drinking behavior, yet is related to reduced blood alcohol level in inpatient alcoholics (Steffen, 1975). It also has some initial promise in assisting recovering alcoholics to remain sober (Hitchcox, 1979). The majority of studies in this area have not reported drinking behavior data. In addition, many of the studies have confounded the treatment results by combining EMG biofeedback and relaxation training (e.g., Strickler et al., 1977; Page and Schaub, 1978; Hitchcox, 1979; Rosenberg, 1980). In those studies utilizing a component control design, a combination of EMG biofeedback and relaxation training or relaxation training alone was found to be superior to EMG biofeedback alone in reducing muscle tension. Since anxiety and tension can be manifested in various systems differentially (i.e., specific muscles and/or the cardiovascular system), reducing frontalis muscle tension will not necessarily reduce tension manifested in other parts of the body. Therefore a more general approach such as relaxation training has a higher probability of being successful. To date, the use of EMG warrants consideration as an intervention; however, further research is needed to demonstrate that specific types of anxious alcoholics exhibit their tension muscularly, and that the frontalis muscle is the appropriate feedback site. Furthermore, it still needs to be demonstrated that EMG feedback to develop tension-reduction skill is more effective than the other techniques. The research does not support the clinical use of EMG feedback for tension reduction in alcoholics.

Alpha Wave Biofeedback. An alternative to the EMG training has been to teach alcoholics to increase their alpha wave production. The rationale for this approach is that the "relaxation state" is associated with increased alpha wave production and thus such production may be an effective technique for reducing anxiety or tension. A secondary consideration is that increased alpha wave production has been associated with altered states of consciousness in meditation and thus may be an alternative vehicle for those alcoholics who use alcohol to "get altered." The research in this area is unimpressive to date. Wong

(1976) assigned twenty-four male inpatient alcoholics to either an experimental or control group. The experimental group was trained during fifteen hour-long sessions to increase the production of alpha waves, while the control group received an attention placebo treatment consisting of a placebo form of alpha wave biofeedback. No alpha wave production data was reported, nor was drinking behavior data reported. Wong found that the experimental group experienced more congruence between actual and ideal self-concept as well as greater improvement in scores on the repression-sensitization scale following treatment. Kurtz (1974) reports significant reductions in blood pressure as a result of EMG and EEG training but does not describe the relative contributions of these training procedures to the effect. Jones and Holmes (1976) tested the assumption that alcoholics produce fewer alpha waves than nonalcoholics. They trained twenty chronic alcoholic inpatients and twenty nonalcoholic, nonhospitalized subjects during three sessions of alpha wave feedback. There were no significant differences in ability to produce alpha. Jacobson, Wilson, and LaRocca (1977) trained thirty abstinent alcoholics and thirty nonalcoholic controls over five sessions in one of three experimental groups: accurate feedback, inaccurate feedback, and a no-treatment control group. They found no significant differences, as none of the groups demonstrated success in producing alpha. Passini et al. (1977) assigned twenty-five alcoholics to an experimental group which received two sessions of finger-temperature training and ten hour-long sessions of alpha wave training over three weeks. Twenty-five matched subjects were assigned to a no-treatment control group. The two groups were equal in regard to the amount of alpha produced with eyes open and closed in the pre-session assessment. The control group demonstrated no change after the experimental training period, while the experimental group was able to produce a significant increase in alpha waves. The alpha training appeared to significantly reduce self-reported anxiety, but no other measures demonstrated change. Drinking behavior data was not reported.

The utility of alpha wave training in reducing anxiety in alcoholics is uncertain. The studies reporting no effect may not have allowed an appropriate training period (three sessions, Jones and Holmes, 1976; five sessions, Jacobson, Wilson, and LaRocca, 1977). The studies reporting anxiety reduction (Kurtz, 1974; Passini et al., 1977) are confounded with EMG and finger-temperature training. To date, the relationship of alpha training to reduced or abstinent drinking behavior has not been demonstrated. The usefulness of alpha wave training with alcoholics remains to be seen, as well as its cost-effectiveness compared to other biofeedback or relaxation interventions.

Finger-Temperature Biofeedback. Temperature biofeedback is appropriate for tension that is manifested in the cardiovascular system. At this time, no data exists which demonstrates that anxious alcoholics do or do not manifest their tension in their cardiovascular system. The only studies employing temperature feedback either confounded it with other biofeedback information (i.e., alpha training—Passini et al., 1977) or consisted of anecdotal data (Green, Green, and Walters, 1974). According to the latter, preliminary investigations indicate that decreased alcohol consumption among a colleague's clients was associated with finger-temperature training. As this data is so minimal at this time, all that can be said is that the utility of finger-temperature biofeedback for tension reduction in alcoholics is unknown and awaits further research.

Relaxation Training. Relaxation training is the most promising tension-reducing technique for use with alcoholics. Litman (1974) used an intensive case study design to investigate the relationship between craving for alcohol and drinking to relieve unpleasant feelings in a 28-year-old male inpatient alcoholic and a 31-year-old female inpatient alcoholic. The subjects rated the strength of their negative feelings and cravings before and after each of eight to ten group therapy sessions (considered stressful situations) and seven to eight relaxation training sessions. Greater anxiety and craving were indicated in the woman but no changes were noted in the man after the group sessions. After relaxation training, less anxiety and craving were noted in both clients. Craving was related to anxiety in the woman and to somatic symptoms in the man. The preliminary data from this study supports the assumption that craving for alcohol may vary across subtypes of alcoholics, and relaxation training may minimize the craving and tension in some of the subtypes.

Meshboum (1977) studied the efficacy of experimental focusing and the use of visual imagery. She formed three groups of twenty inpatient alcoholics. The experimental group received three hour-long training sessions in progressive muscle relaxation and the technique of image focusing. The placebo control group received three lectures on alcoholism. The third group was a no-treatment control. The subjects were rated three times on the Gendlins Experiencing Scale and selected subscales of the Orlinsky-Howard Therapy Session Report (used as a measure of progress over four weeks), plus the Belts Test of Vividness of Imagery (before and after treatment). Meshboum concluded that training in imagery had a strong positive effect on patients' in-therapy behavior and that it was a successful method for improving prognosis for alcoholics in psychotherapy. Physiological data and outcome data were not reported. The relaxation training and training in imagery were confounded in the experimental group, thus limiting any conclusions that may be drawn from this study.

In a study designed to evaluate the effect of assertion training and relaxation training as adjunctive treatments in an ongoing inpatient rehabilitation program, Krummel (1977) argued that alcoholics experience stress and react with anxiety because they have below-average interpersonal and tension-reducing skills. He hypothesized that training in assertion and relaxation should assist in the alcoholics' recovery. Fifty-seven male inpatients were randomly assigned to one of three conditions: an assertion group that included behavioral rehearsal, vicarious observation, and homework assignments; a progressive relaxation group that practiced outside of the group twice a day; and an attention placebo control group that participated in unstructured activities such as making macrame and ceramics. The groups met two times a week for ninety minutes over a four-week period. The Assertiveness Questionnaire, the Locus of Drinking Control Scale, the Locus of Control Scale, the State-Trait Anxiety Inventory, and a semantic differential of self were used as pre- and post-test measures. A six-month follow-up showed no improvement of either abstinence or reduced drinking compared to the control group. In addition, no significant differences were noted on any of the self-report measures. This study confounds a number of treatment variables in the groups, reports no physiological data, and uses self-report as a dependent measure. The strength of this study is that it is one of the few that has a behavioral follow-up. One can tentatively infer that assertion and relaxation training adds little to the rehabilitation of chronic alcoholics.

In yet another type of treatment-comparison study, Henricksen (1979) compared a progressive relaxation group, a meditation group, and a placebo control group on mood stability, state-anxiety, and their effect on perceived locus of drinking control. The subjects were alcoholic inpatients, who received fourteen 35-minute daily sessions. The study found significant differences only for the confusion-bewilderment factor, reflecting a difference in an organized/disorganized aspect of emotion. There was no significant difference in mood stability or state-anxiety across the categories and treatment groups. Significant decreases in state-anxiety were reported for alcoholic subjects classified as having an external perceived locus of drinking control, as opposed to those subjects having an internal locus of control. The externals also reported higher pre- and post-test anxiety scores than internals. Hendricksen did not report physiological data nor any behavioral follow-up data.

Gilbert, Parker, and Claiborn (1978) compared the effects of progressive relaxation, meditation training, and quiet rest on the mood levels of thirty male alcoholics in an inpatient setting. The Profile of Mood States was used for pre- and post-test measures. The progressive relaxation and meditation conditions produced significant decreases in self-reported tension, while the quiet-rest group reported no change on any of the six subscales of the profile. The progressive relaxation group also reported decreased depression as well as a trend toward increased vigor. The meditation group seemed to exhibit a restful alertness, while the progressive relaxation group seemed to experience an energizing effect from the treatment.

Parker, Gilbert, and Thoreson (1978) compared the effects of progressive relaxation training and meditation training on autonomic arousal in alcoholics in an inpatient setting. The subjects were randomly assigned to one of three groups: a progressive relaxation training group, a meditation group, or a quiet-rest control group. The groups met for three weeks. During the training period blood pressure, heart rate, galvanic skin response, and state-anxiety (according to the State-Trait Anxiety Inventory) were measured. The researchers found that the progressive relaxation and meditation groups were successful in reducing blood pressure. In addition, the meditation training group had blood pressure decreases at an earlier point in the training period, and meditation had an effect on systolic blood pressure that progressive relaxation training did not. No drinking behavior data was reported. In a related study reporting the same subject information and using the same design and dependent measures, Parker and Gilbert (1978) also report that the two treatment groups did not show an increase in blood pressure but the control group did. These results support the hypotheses that tension may be manifested in different systems in the body and that various tension-reducing techniques may differentially affect them. These studies by Parker, Gilbert, and Thoreson (1978), Parker and Gilbert (1978), and Gilbert, Parker, and Claiborn (1978) indicate that relaxation training and meditation can be effective according to physiological measures and subjective self-reports. However, none of the above studies report any drinking behavior data or follow-up data on continued use of the techniques.

Alcoholics are thought to be deficient in social skills as well as coping responses to stress. Teare (1978) suggested that we need to assess individual differences in alcoholics' response to intrapersonal and interpersonal stress in order to determine the most suitable therapy for specific alcoholics. She assigned forty-four outpatient alcoholics to one of the following groups: hatha yoga, human relations training, and relaxation training. The subjects received sixty to ninety minutes of their treatment per day during an eleven-day period of a twenty-day "eclectic" six-hour-a-day therapy program. The Maximult, the Social Competence Scale, and "several measures of anxiety and depression" were given as pretests. Post-test measures were completed by three therapists and a friend or spouse. None of the three treatments produced significant improvement (significance level set at $p < .05$ according to post-test measures of anxiety, depression, hypochondriasis, and schizophrenia. This study's results are probably attributable to other treatment variables or expectancy effects due to the confounding of the treatments with the other treatment components of the outpatient setting. In addition, no physiological data, drinking behavior data, control data, or follow-up data were reported.

Frank (1979) investigated the use of guided versus nonguided imagery, combined with progressive muscle relaxation, for the treatment of chronic alcoholics in a Salvation Army rehabilitation program. Ninety chronic alcoholics were randomly assigned to two experimental treatment groups on two consecutive days for ninety minutes or to a control group, which had an informal conversation hour. The two experimental groups significantly reduced the alcoholics' level of state-anxiety when compared to the no-treatment control. There was no difference between the guided and nonguided imagery groups. This study confounded the imagery treatment with the use of progressive muscle relaxation. The results were most likely due to expectancy effects or to the relaxation training. Since the alcoholics were reported to have poor control over the capacity for visual imagery, a relaxation-only group and an imagery-only group would need to be added to the design to aid in our understanding of these interventions. Physiological data, drinking behavior data, and follow-up data would also be needed in order to better understand the impact of the above treatments.

In one of the better-designed analogue studies, Strickler et al. (1977) studied the effect of relaxation training in reducing the impact of antecedent stress on alcohol consumption. They assigned twenty-four male students, ages twenty-one to twenty-nine, designated as heavy social drinkers, and matched on duration of drinking behavior, to one of three experimental conditions: relaxation instructions; a sensitization, stress-enhancing condition; and a neutral control consisting of listening to a tape of a section of *National Geographic*. All of the subjects were told they would have to give a public speech and told to wait and listen to a tape. Drinking style and amount of alcohol consumed were measured in an ad lib drinking session in which the subjects were told to wait for their turn to get a drink and they could drink if they wanted to. Galvanic skin response was used as a measure of arousal. The post-test drinking rates significantly differed between the groups. The post-test drinking rates in the stress sensitization group were significantly higher, while the relaxation group had significantly lower drinking rates and there was no difference in the neutral group. Relaxation training reduced arousal and the sensitization conditions increased arousal. The relaxation group drank significantly less than the other two groups. In fact, the relaxation subjects slowed down their initial drinking rate in the presence of an anticipated stressful event. The stress-influenced changes in drinking style represented a shift toward more abusive drinking.

The results from Strickler et al. (1977) suggest that relaxation training may in some way insulate the individual's drinking style from environmental stress. The researchers noted that some responses to stress cues (e.g., rumination) were associated with significant increases in sip rate and therefore alcohol consumption. Relaxation during stress seems to minimize the impact of stress on drinking rate and amount. The Strickler study (Strickler et al., 1977) suggests that relaxation training in conjunction with a behavioral focus on drinking rate may increase the probability that a moderate drinking style will be practical in stress situations. Furthermore, additional research on the impact of antecedent stimuli on drinking patterns of young social drinkers may indicate that improving their repertoire of effective coping behaviors can reduce the likelihood of later progression to a more abusive drinking style (Strickler et al., 1977).

The Strickler study is one of the few to examine a stress-reduction technique as a preventive intervention and to use drinking behavior as a dependent variable. The study is an analogue study with heavy social drinkers, and thus further research with alcoholics is needed to demonstrate the utility of this technique as a preventive or remedial treatment.

The relaxation-training techniques have the most promise for use with alcoholics. Progressive muscle or autogenic relaxation has been shown to reduce self-reported anxiety or tension for inpatient alcoholics (Litman, 1974; Gilbert, Parker, and Claiborn, 1978; Teare, 1978; Frank, 1979) and for subpopulations of anxious alcoholics (Hendricksen, 1978). The techniques have also reduced alcoholic craving (Litman, 1974) and blood pressure (Parker, Gilbert, and Thoreson, 1978). Krummel (1977) did not find significant changes in self-reported anxiety or drinking behavior with a chronic inpatient population and his results were confounded with other treatments.

In the one experimental analogue study (Strickler et al., 1977), the results were impressive. With heavy social drinkers, relaxation training not only reduced the anxiety level but also aided in restraining drinking behavior. This study is encouraging insofar as we may be able to teach relaxation training in alcohol education programs as an alternative coping technique. This finding is consistent with the assumption that a subgroup of individuals who drink do so to reduce tension and anxiety. Thus training them in alternate coping techniques may have a great deal of promise in alcoholism prevention programs.

The relaxation training outcome literature indicates that inpatient and abstinent alcoholics can learn to reduce their anxiety level in regard to self-perceived and physiological tension. However, at this time we do not know if this type of training will have any impact on their drinking behavior. The drinking behavior is the most important outcome variable and we have to start including it in our outcome research. After all, what good will it do us as therapists to have more relaxed drunks on our hands?

Meditation

Techniques such as mantra meditation, zen meditation, or yoga meditation have been effective in reducing oxygen consumption, respiration rate, and heart rate; increasing alpha wave production and skin resistance (Benson, Beary, and Carol, 1974; Swinyard, Chaube, and Sutton, 1974); and decreasing blood pressure (Parker, Gilbert, and Thoreson, 1978). These meditation techniques hold promise for reducing tension in alcoholics (Swinyard, Chaube, and Sutton, 1974). The most commonly used meditation technique studied is the mantra meditation. In a mantra meditation the subject focuses his or her attention on a nonsense syllable or personally meaningless word, repeating it over and over for a period of fifteen to twenty minutes twice a day.

The early research in the use of meditation was descriptive. Benson (1974) did a retrospective study of alcohol intake associated with meditation. He analyzed questionnaire data from 1,081 males and 781 females who had practiced transcendental meditation, or TM (a mantra meditation), for at least three months as part of their training to become TM teachers. The results indicated a decrease in consumption of hard liquor after starting TM, and after twenty-seven to thirty-three months of practicing TM their consumption dropped to 0.4 percent of what it had been when they started the program. This data was retrospective and no information was available on the number of alcoholics in the sample. As these people were already interested in TM, applicability to treatment of alcoholism is at best speculative. In a similar study, Shafti, Lavely, and Jaffe (1975) investigated the frequency of alcohol use among transcendental mediators (N = 126) and a matched control group (N = 90). Forty percent of the meditators who had meditated for two years stopped drinking after six months.

After twenty-five to thirty-nine months 60 percent had stopped drinking. None of the control group had stopped drinking. Finally, 45 percent of the meditators versus one percent of the control group had stopped drinking hard liquor. This was a descriptive study subject to the same limitations as Benson's (1974) study.

The outcome research is minimal. Kline (1976) trained thirteen recovering alcoholics in transcendental meditation over three months. He pre- and post-tested the experimental and no-treatment control groups with the MMPI, Rotter's Internal-External Locus of Control, and the Tennessee Self-Concept Scale. No meaningful results were found. This was probably due to the small sample size, two inappropriate dependent variables, and/or a lack of physiological data. Nuerenberger (1977) investigated the effect of meditation on personality variables of inpatient alcoholics. He assigned 143 male inpatient alcoholics to one of the following: a four-week meditation training group, a pretest control group, or a post-test control group. The experimental group received meditation training twice a day and the pretest control group received two 30-minute didactic sessions on positive psychological health. There were no significant differences between the group on any of twenty-four personality scales, while the pretest control and experimental groups showed improvement on the Personal Orientation Inventory, a measure of self-actualization. This study offers little to the outcome literature, as it used dependent variables that are of little consequence to the clinician who needs to help the client reduce anxiety and reduce or stop drinking behavior. No physiological or drinking behavior data was reported. Gilbert, Parker, and Claiborn (1978), Parker, Gilbert, and Thoreson (1978), and Parker and Gilbert (1978), whose research was discussed in the relaxation training section, found that meditation and relaxation both resulted in self-reported decreases in tension and reduced blood pressure. In addition, meditation training induced decreases in blood pressure faster than relaxation training and affected decreases in systolic pressure that progressive relaxation training did not. Heart rate and galvanic skin response were not affected. Drinking behavior data was not reported.

These studies indicate that alcoholics using meditation can experience tension reduction as indicated by self-reports and physiological data. However, the data is preliminary in what we do not know what types of alcoholic, if any, differentially benefit from the meditation versus the relaxation technique, as the two techniques did result in somewhat different outcomes. Meditation training may be a useful adjunct as a tension-reduction tool, particularly as some clients may be more attracted to meditation than the various kinds of relaxation training.

Autogenic Training

Autogenic training has been widely used and researched in Europe. It involves a series of six standard exercises (e.g., "My arms and legs are heavy and warm, my heartbeat is calm and regular") and six advanced mental imagery exercises. Luthe and Schultz (1969) present a synthesis of this data and suggest that the exercises "have been found helpful in the treatment of habitual alcoholism." Autogenic training has comparable physiological effects to relaxation training and meditation, and thus has potential for treating stress in alcoholics. Luthe and Schultz report that "the exercises have been particularly praised by patients who once used to seek in alcohol a relief from intolerable tension and rising anxiety." They note that one group of thirty alcoholics treated in a state hospital had not had one relapse in a two-year follow-up. These authors report similar results in terms of tension reduction, improvement in sleep patterns, and increased motivation. Luthe and Schultz found that reduction in anxiety seems to be a reinforcing event, which, through stimulus generalization, is transferred to the entire treatment program and increases the probability of the client persisting in therapy. Since sleep disturbances are also associated with alcoholism, this effect is important. At this time the preliminary reports are encouraging. However, further outcome research in this country is needed to establish the utility of the exercises here.

Aerobic Exercise

Little or no research has been done to investigate aerobic exercise as a tension-reduction technique for alcoholics. Gary and Guthrie (1972) assigned ten male alcoholic inpatients to a jogging group that worked out five days per week for four weeks or until twenty miles had been reached. Ten control subjects completed their normal daily routine. The researchers found significant improvement in cardiovascular conditioning and self-esteem after only twenty days of training. Sleep disturbances were reduced. This was an important finding, as the difficulty many alcoholics have in getting a good night's rest contributes to their level of stress. No improvement in drinking was noted on the follow-up. Pelletier (1977) reports the psychological effects of running on a nonalcoholic population. Subjects were found to be more intelligent, stable, venturesome, tender-minded, imaginative, experimenting, self-sufficient, sober, expedient, and self-assured. It was noted that the subjects experienced increases in creativity and energy, became more self-disciplined, and had a higher level of motivation; sexual activity decreased but sexual satisfaction increased. Finally, the subjects slept less and had a lower level of anxiety. This study does not apply directly to treating alcoholics but demonstrates that the potential exists for using aerobic exercise with alcoholics. The experience of one of the authors adds anecdotal support to the use of aerobic exercise for reducing tension and moderating drinking behavior (six to twelve beers per week dropped to two or even fewer per week after three months of training).

Aerobic exercise has been shown to reduce heart rate, blood pressure, cholesterol level, and self-reported tension, as well as improve sleep and increase energy level. These are all areas of deficiency in the various types of alcoholics, and thus they may benefit from the inclusion of aerobic exercise in their treatment plan.

Conclusions

This chapter was based on the assumptions that (1) alcohol use, for a portion of the alcoholic population, is a socially learned coping response used to reduce tension, and (2) drinking behavior is enhanced or diminished as a function of social facilitation or modeling for subgroups of alcoholics. On the basis of these assumptions, teaching alcoholics tension-reducing coping skills is a logical component of the treatment process. The empirical findings on use of tension-reduction interventions with alcoholics are promising but inconsistent. The outcome studies generally indicate that subtypes of alcoholics report reduced tension and experience reduced muscle tension, reduced blood pressure, and improved sleep patterns. In addition, recovering alcoholics and heavy social drinkers demonstrate reduced craving and reduced alcohol consumption. Chronic alcoholics present a mixed picture. There seems to be a subgroup of alcoholics who are completely internally cued, drink under any conditions, and do not experience any benefits from these tension-reduction interventions. On the other side, chronic alcoholics who report higher levels of anxiety and/or are externally cued in their drinking behavior experience greater reductions in tension than the other chronic alcoholics.

The interventions are differentially effective. Progressive relaxation and autogenic training have the best support to date. Meditation (mantra) and EMG biofeedback have weaker support, particularly the EMG feedback. The EMG feedback was less effective than relaxation training and ineffective in some cases. This is most likely due to the specificity of the target area of EMG feedback versus the more general effect of the other three interventions. Alpha wave feedback is not supported, with the exception of Passini et al. (1977). Finger-temperature training remains to be investigated. Finally, aerobic exercise has promise but also has not been systematically studied.

Clinical Recommendations

Progressive relaxation, autogenic training, and the other techniques are appropriate for teaching alcoholics alternative ways to reduce self-perceived tension and physiologically manifested tension. The techniques are not sufficient treatments by themselves, but should be employed with other therapeutic components such as cognitive behavior therapy. The stress-reduction interventions can be used as a preventative technique with adolescents and heavy social drinkers. They also have promise for reducing blood pressure and improving sleep patterns in chronic alcoholics—common problems for this population. As a final note, the techniques can be used by abstinent alcoholics to reduce craving and to provide an "inoculation" effect for coping with stress in their lives. These stress-reduction treatments have two major benefits; (1) alcoholics can experience reduced tension on a variety of levels, which is an important treatment goal in and of itself; (2) those alcoholics who drink to reduce stress may be able to show a concomitant reduction in drinking behavior, although the data to support this is still preliminary.

Research Recommendations

As with most areas of mental health treatment, the clinical application of stress-reduction techniques with alcoholics is ahead of the research. To aid in our understanding of these techniques the following research is needed. In the areas of basic research, we need data on the various physiological systems in which alcoholics do or do not manifest tension, so that we can be more precise in our application of biofeedback techniques. Research needs to be continued on the learning history and characteristics of alcoholics who may differentially benefit from the use of these interventions. We need to use multiple dependent measures (Emrick, 1975; Emrick, 1983) with follow-up in the outcome studies such as self-report, physiological data on a variety of systems, and drinking behavior. As we become more refined in our use of these techniques, we will need cross–treatment effectiveness data. Finally, research is needed to examine the issue of differential effectiveness of the treatments across subtypes of alcoholics.

Alcoholism is a multidimensional syndrome and its complexity should be reflected in prescriptive treatment appraoches. The integration of stress-reduction techniques with skills training, cognitive-behavior therapy, family therapy, and group therapy is an important step toward this goal.

References

Allman, L. R., Taylor, H. A., and Nathan, P. E. Group drinking during stress: effects on drinking behavior, affect, and psychopathology. *American Journal of Psychiatry,* 1972, *129*(6), 669–678.

Bales, R. F. Cultural differences in rates of alcoholism. *Quarterly Journal of Studies on Alcohol,* 1946, *6,* 480–499.

Bandler, R., and Grinder, J. *Frogs into Princes; Neuro-Linguistic Programming.* Moab, Utah: Real People Press, 1979.

Begleiter, H., and Platz, A. The effects of alcohol on the central nervous system of humans. In B. Kissin, and H. Begleiter (eds.), *The Biology of Alcoholism,* vol. 2. New York: Plenum Press, 1972.

Benson, H. Decreased alcohol intake associated with the practice of meditation: a retrospective investigation. *Annals of the New York Academy of Sciences,* 1974, *233,* 174–177.

———, Beary, J. H., and Carol, M. P. The relaxation response. *Psychiatry,* 1974, *37,* 37–46.

Berman, M. I. Alcoholism-obesity "sans" teeth. *Maryland State Medical Journal,* 1969, *18*(3), 56–58.

Cappell, H., and Herman, C. P. Alcohol and tension reduction: a review. *Quarterly Journal of Studies on Alcohol,* 1972, *33,* 33–64.

Champion, R. A. Studies of experimentally induced disturbance. *Australian Journal of Psychology,* 1950, *2,* 90–99.

Cohen, M., Liebson, I., and Faillance, L. The modification of drinking of chronic alcoholics. In N. K. Mello and J. H. Mendelson (eds.), *Recent Advances in Studies of Alcoholism.* Washington, D.C.: U.S. Government Printing Office, 1971.

Corah, N. L., and Boffa, J. Perceived control, self-observation, and response to aversive stimulation. *Journal of Personality and Social Psychology,* 1970, *16,* 1–14.

Davis, D., Berenson, D., Steinglass, P., and Davis, S. The adaptive consequences of drinking. *Psychiatry,* 1974, *37,* 209–215.

DeRicco, D. A. Effects of peer majority on drinking rate. *Addictive Behavior,* 1978, *3,* 29–34.

Eddy, C. C. The effects of alcohol on anxiety in problem and non-problem drinking women. *Dissertation Abstracts International,* 1978, *39*(4–B), 1951–1952.

Edwards, G., Hensman, C., Chander, J., and Petro, J. Motivation for drinking among men: survey of a London suburb. *Psychological Medicine,* 1972, *2*(*3*), 260–271.

Emrick, C. D. A review of psychologically oriented treatment of alcoholism: II. The relative effectiveness of different treatment approaches and the relative effectiveness of treatment versus no treatment. *Journal of Studies on Alcoholism,* 1975 *36,* 88–108.

———, and Hansen, J. Assertions regarding the effectiveness of treatment for alcoholism: fact or fantasy? *American Psychologist,* 1983, *38,* 1078–1088.

Eno, E. H. A comparison study of the level of state-trait anxiety and muscle tension of alcoholics when treated by electromyograph biofeedback relaxation training and other clinical techniques. *Dissertation Abstracts International,* 1975, *36,* 1914.

Forrest, G. G. *The Diagnosis and Treatment of Alcoholism,* 2nd ed. Springfield, Ill.: Charles C. Thomas, 1978.

Forrest, G. G. *Alcoholism, Narcissism and Psychopathology.* Springfield, Ill.: Charles C. Thomas, 1983.

———. *Intensive Psychotherapy of Alcoholism.* Springfield, Ill.: Charles C. Thomas, 1984.

Frank, L. L. Anxiety reduction in alcoholics by means of selected imagery techniques. *Dissertation Abstracts International,* 1979, *39,* 4576.

Gary, V., and Gutherie, D. The effect of jogging on physical fitness and self-concept in hospitalized alcoholics. *Quarterly Journal of Studies on Alcohol,* 1972, *33,* 1073–1078.

Geber, Q., and Anderson, T. Ethanol inhibition of autogenic stress induced cardiac hypertrophy. *Experientia,* 1967, *23,* 734–736.

Gilbert, G. S., Parker, J. C., and Claiborn, C. D. Differential mood changes in alcoholics as a function of anxiety management strategies. *Journal of Clinical Psychology,* 1978, *34,* 229–232.

Glass, D., and Singer J. *Urban Stress: Experiments on Noise and Social Stress.* New York: Academic Press, 1972.

Green, E. E., Green, A. M., and Walters, E. D. Biofeedback training for anxiety and tension reduction. *Annals of New York Academy of Sciences,* 1974, *233,* 157–161.

Greenberg, L., and Carpenter, J. Effect of alcoholic beverages on skin conductance and emotional tension: wine, whiskey and alcohol. *Quarterly Journal of Studies on Alcohol,* 1957, *18,* 190–211.

Gross, M., Goodenough, D., Hasty, J., Rosenblatt, S., and Lewis, E. Sleep disturbances in alcoholic intoxication and withdrawal. In N. Mello, and J. Hendelson (eds.), *Recent Advances in Studies of Alcoholism.* Washington, D. C.: U. S. Government Printing Office, 1971.

Haggard, E. A. Some conditions determining adjustment during and readjustment following experimentally induced stress. In S. S. Tomkins (ed.), *Contemporary Psychopathology.* Cambridge, Mass.: Harvard University Press, 1946.

Hamilton, F., and Maisto, S. A. Assertive behavior and perceived discomfort of alcoholics in assertion-required situations. *Journal of Consulting and Clinical Psychology,* 1979, *47(1),* 196–197.

Hendricksen, N. E. The effects of progressive relaxation and meditation on mood stability and state anxiety in alcoholic inpatients. *Dissertation Abstracts International,* 1978, *39,* 981.

Hitchcox, C. F. EMG feedback training of women alcoholics: an alternative coping response to stress and helplessness. *Dissertation Abstracts International,* 1979, *39,* 3516–3517.

Hodgson, R. H., Stockwell, T. R., and Rankin, H. J. Can alcohol reduce tension? *Behavior Research and Therapy,* 1979, *17(5),* 459–466.

Horn, D. L. The use of alcohol by women as a stress reducer in interpersonal relations: the 86-proof solution. *Dissertation Abstracts International,* 1978, *3a(3–B),* 2987.

Jacobson, G. R., Wilson, A., and LaRocca, L. Perceptual field dependence and biofeedback training (EEG alpha) among male alcoholics. In R. A. Seixas (ed.), *Currents in Alcoholism,* vol. 2. New York: Grune & Stratton, 1977.

Jones, F. W., and Holmes, E. S. Alcoholism, alpha production, and biofeedback. *Journal of Consulting and Clinical Psychology,* 1976, *44,* 224–228.

Kline, K. S. Effects of transcendental meditation program on personality and arousal. *Dissertation Abstracts International,* 1976, *36,* 6386–6387.

Krummel, R. P. An investigation into selected effects of adding relaxation and assertion training to an existing treatment program for alcoholics. *Dissertation Abstracts International,* 1977, *38,* 4990–4991.

Kurtz, P. S. Treating chemical dependency through biofeedback. *Hospital Progress,* 1974, *55,* 68–70.

LaCoursiere, R. B., Godfrey, K. E., and Ruby, L. M. Traumatic neurosis in the etiology of alcoholism: Vietnam combat and other trauma. *American Journal of Psychiatry,* 1980, *137(8),* 966–968.

Lawson, G., Peterson, J. S., and Lawson, A. *Alcoholism and the Family,* Rockville, Md.: Aspen Publications, 1983.

Lenigen, R. W. The effect of electromyographic biofeedback and relaxation on the performance of alcoholics under stress. *Dissertation Abstracts International,* 1977, *38,* 1888–1889.

Lienent, G., and Traxel, W. The effects of meprobamate and alcohol on galvanic skin response. *Journal of Psychology,* 1959, *48,* 329–334.

Litman, G. K. Stress, affect, and craving in alcoholics: the single case as a research strategy. *Quarterly Journal of Studies on Alcohol,* 1974, *35,* 131–146.

Litz, J. E. Life stresses and alcoholism in women. *Dissertation Abstracts International,* 1979, *39(7–B),* 3525–3526L.

Luthe, W., and Schultz, J. H. *Autogenic Therapy. Vol. 3, Applications in Psychotherapy.* New York: Grune and Stratton, 1969.

McNamee, H. B., Mello, N. K., and Mendelson, J. H. Experimental analysis of drinking patterns of alcoholics: concurrent psychiatric observations. *American Journal of Psychiatry,* 1968, *124,* 1063–1064.

McWilliams, J. O. EMG feedback training and relaxation training in alcoholics. *Dissertation Abstracts International,* 1979, *39,* 3530.

Mello, N. K., and Mendelson, J. H. Operant analysis of drinking patterns of chronic alcoholics. *Nature,* 1965, *206,* 43–46.

Mendelson, J. H. Experimentally induced chronic intoxication and withdrawal in alcoholics. *Quarterly Journal of Studies on Alcohol.* Supplement no. 2, 1964.

———, and Mello, N. K. Experimental analysis of drinking behavior of chronic alcoholics. *Annals of New York Academy of Science,* 1966, *133,* Articles 2–3, 828–845.

Meshboum, R. K. Visual imagery and experiential focusing in psychotherapy with alcoholics. *Dissertation Abstracts International,* 1977, *38,* 4472.

Naitoh, P. The effect of alcohol on the autonomic nervous system of humans: a psychophysiological approach. In B. Kissin, and H. Begleiter (eds.), *The Biology of Alcoholism,* vol. 2. New York: Plenum Press, 1972.

Narrol, H. G. Experimental application of reinforcement principles to analysis and treatment of hospitalization. *Quarterly Journal of Studies on Alcohol,* 1967, *28,* 105–115.

Nathan, P. E., and O'Brien, J. S. An experimental analysis of the behavior of alcoholics and non-alcoholics during prolonged experimental drinking. *Behavior Therapy,* 1971, *2,* 455–476.

———, Titler, N. A., Lowenstein, L. M., Solomon, O., and Rossi, A. M. Behavioral analysis of chronic alcoholism. *Archives of General Psychiatry,* 1970, *22,* 419–430.

Nordlicht, S. Effects of stress on the police officer and family. *New York State Journal of Medicine,* 1979, *79(3),* 400–401.

Nuerenberger, E. P. The use of meditation in the treatment of alcoholism. *Dissertation Abstracts International,* 1977, *38,* 1413.

Page, R. D., and Schaub, L. H. EMG biofeedback applicability for differing personality types. *Journal of Clinical Psychology,* 1978, *34,* 1014–1020.

Parker, J. C., and Gilbert, G. S. Anxiety management in alcoholics: a study of generalized effects of relaxation techniques. *Addictive Behaviors,* 1978, *3,* 123–127.

Parker, J. C., Gilbert, G. S., and Thoreson, R. W. Reduction of autonomic arousal in alcoholics: a comparison of relaxation and meditation techniques. *Journal of Consulting and Clinical Psychology,* 1978, *46,* 879–886.

Passini, F. T., Watson, C. G., Dehnel, L., Herder, J., and Watkins, B. Alpha wave biofeedback training therapy in alcoholics. *Journal of Clinical Psychology.* 1977, *33,* 292–299.

Pearson, M. M. Drug and alcohol problems in physicians. *Psychiatric Opinion, 1975, 12(4),* 14–18.

Pelletier, K. *Mind as Healer, Mind as Slayer: A Holistic Approach to Preventing Stress Disorders.* New York: Dell Publishing, 1977.

Pohorecky, L., Rossi, E., Weiss, J., and Michulak, V. Biochemical evidence for an interaction of ethanol and stress: preliminary studies. *Alcoholism,* 1980, *4,* 423–426.

Roebuck, J. B., and Kessler, R. G. *The Etiology of Alcoholism.* Springfield, Ill.: Charles C. Thomas, 1972.

Rosenberg, S. D. Relaxation training and a differential assessment of alcoholism. *Dissertation Abstracts International,* 1980, *40,* 3963–3964.

Rouse, B. A., Walker, P. F., and Ewing, J. A. Adolescent stress levels, coping activities, and father's drinking behavior. *Proceedings of the 81st Annual Convention of the American Psychological Association,* 1973, *8,* 683–684.

Sadava, S. W., Thistle, R., and Forsythe, R. Stress, escapism, and patterns of alcohol and drug use. *Journal of Studies on Alcohol,* 1968, *39(5),* 725–736.

Selye, H. *The Stress of Life,* New York: McGraw-Hill Book Co., 1956.

Shafti, M., Lavely, R., and Jaffe, R. Meditation and the prevention of alcohol abuse. *American Journal of Psychiatry,* 1975, *132,* 942–945.

Stassen, W., Neff, R., and Meittinen, O. Alcohol consumption and non-fatal myocardial infarction. *American Journal of Epidemiology,* 1976, *104,* 306–308.

Steffen, J. J. Electromyographically induced relaxation in the treatment of chronic alcohol abuse. *Journal of Consulting and Clinical Psychology,* 1975, *43,* 275.

Stotland, E., and Blumenthal, A. The reduction of anxiety as a result of the expectation of making a choice. *Canadian Journal of Psychology,* 1964, *18,* 139–145.

Strickler, D., Bigelow, G., Wells, D., and Liebson, I. Effects of relaxation instructions on the electromyographic responses of abstinent alcoholics to drinking-related stimuli. *Behavior Research and Therapy,* 1977, *15,* 500–502.

Swinyard, C. A., Chaube, S., and Sutton, D. B. Neurological and behavioral aspects of transcendental meditation relevant to alcoholism: a review. *Annals of the New York Academy of Science,* 1974, *233,* 162–173.

Tanner, O. *Stress.* New York: Time-Life Books. 1976.

Teare, J. L. An evaluation of changes in alcoholic patients following three different treatments. *Dissertation Abstracts International,* 1978, *39,* 1971–1972.

Wegscheider, S. *Another Chance: Hope and Health for the Alcoholic Family.* Palo Alto, Calif.: Science and Behavior Books, 1981.

Wong, D. Biofeedback as an adjunct to the treatment of alcoholism. *Dissertation Abstracts International,* 1976, *36,* 5824.

Part Two

ASSESSMENT OF SUBSTANCE ABUSE AND ALCOHOLISM

IN THE FIRST CHAPTER in this part (Chapter 4), Janice F. Kauffman, Howard Shaffer, and Milton E. Burglass point out that professional groups (physicians, nurses, psychologists, and social workers) traditionally experience little, if any, formal training for their work with substance abusers. The chapter discusses the traditional medical use, appropriate dose levels, duration of effects, and physiological, psychological, and behavioral effects of narcotics and related analgesics, sedative-hypnotics, stimulants, hallucinogens, and phencyclidine, cannabis, and inhalants.

The second chapter in this part (Chapter 5) evaluates the medical aspects of alcohol use and assesses the risk of physical damage. Ruth Segal and Barry Sisson describe the acute and chronic effects of alcohol use. Alcohol-related medical complications are summarized by body systems. The concepts of intoxication, blood alcohol level (BAL), tolerance, dependence, withdrawal, and blackout are elucidated. The effects of alcohol upon the gastrointestinal system, pancreas, liver, brain and nervous system, heart and cardiovascular system, hematological system, endocrine system and malnutrition are also thoroughly explored.

The third chapter in this part (Chapter 6) evaluates the therapeutic effectiveness of Alcoholics Anonymous. The authors, Alan C. Ogborne and Frederick B. Glaser, suggest that a number of behavioral, personality, and social characteristics are associated with A.A. membership. The authors believe that evaluative studies of A.A. are possible and that such studies could lead to a better understanding of the specific indications for making referrals. It is suggested that the pervasive influence of A.A. inhibits innovations, alienates early problem drinkers, and limits treatment strategies.

The fourth chapter in this part (Chapter 7) considers the psychotherapeutic process with alcoholics and substance abusers, treatment outcome assessment, and clinical evaluations. Ernest Matuschka discusses types of therapy, personality theory, measurement of success and failure in therapy, and the neuropsychology of alcoholism. Passivity-confrontation techniques represent an effective system of psychotherapy with alcoholics and substance abusers.

The final chapter in Part Two (Chapter 8) discusses methadone maintenance and the "myth" of metabolic disorder theory. Thomas E. Bratter, Matthew C. Pennacchia, and DeAnne Gauya point out that the psychiatric and medical establishment has traditionally viewed heroin addiction as an incurable disease. The authors provide an extensive review of the pharmacological properties of methadone, morphine, naloxone, and cyclazocine. The authors also point out that the Food and Drug Administration, Federal Drug Administration, and Bureau of Narcotics and Dangerous Drugs permitted the number of methadone patients to escalate from 22 in 1963 to more than 125,000 in less than a decade.

4

The Biological Basics: Drugs and Their Effects

Janice F. Kauffman / Howard Shaffer / Milton E. Burglass

Responsibility for evaluating, treating, and referring individuals with drug problems is shared by a heterogeneous group of practitioners representing a diverse set of disciplines and ideologies. Professional groups such as physicians, nurses, social workers, and psychologists acquire varying degrees of knowledge and experience in working with psychosocial problems but traditionally have little, if any formal training for their work with a substance-abusing population. The majority of clinical drug treatment workers, particularly those who have direct (front-line) contact with the drug-involved client, have less academic training, and work, therefore, much as technicians (see Burglass and Shaffer, 1981, for a detailed analysis of this situation and its implications for the delivery of drug treatment services). "One characteristic of the work of a technician is that successful use of a technique does not require a command of the theory of that technique" (Burglass and Shaffer, 1981, p. 27).

Recent theorists (Burglass and Shaffer, 1981; Gambino and Shaffer, 1979; Shaffer, 1977; Shaffer and Gambino, 1979–1983) conclude that

Special thanks are extended to the staff and clients of the Drug Problems Resource Center for their helpful feedback during the preparation of this chapter. Preparation of this chpater was supported in part by the National Institute on Drug Abuse, #86140.

the addictions lack a paradigm capable of integrating the various scientific disciplines and philosophical perspectives for all workers in the field. Nonetheless, a pragmatic clinical approach to the assessment or treatment of drug-involved clients requires a working knowledge of the current commonly used drugs and their effects. The present chapter addresses the practitioner's need for this basic technical information; although detailed and specific, it is intended to be neither exhaustive nor definitive. The psycho- and neuropharmacology of virtually all the currently used recreational drugs have been extensively investigated and reported. New drugs and new patterns of use appear continuously; even old drugs, whose effects may be documented when prescribed in traditional therapeutic doses and conditions, may not be understood when used in new ways and combined with other psychoactive substances. Accordingly, the reader is advised to approach the acquisition of knowledge about drugs and drug effects not as a one-time study event, but rather as an *ongoing* learning process necessitating periodic review and reassessment.

Drug Categories

"A variety of old and new substances and drugs with powerful psychotropic effects have come into common use during the past decade" (Khantzian and McKenna, 1979). The consequences of involvement with these substances include: benign recreation, tragic, "experimental," social use, long-term habituation, toxic reactions, medical-psychologic complications, overdose, and death. Although clinicians tend to analyze and explain many patterns of drug use in terms of various psychodynamic, sociologic, and behavioral theories, all of these perspectives begin with the biological and pharmacological effects produced by the various drugs. During the assessment process the clinician can avoid much confusion by systematically generating hypotheses to clarify and distinguish these *direct* tropic effects from the *indirect* multiform behavioral effects of the drug in question.

Commonly used drugs conveniently can be grouped into six basic categories reflecting the primary action of each: (1) narcotics and related analgesics; (2) sedative-hypnotics (including barbiturates, nonbarbiturate sedatives, minor tranquilizers, and alcohol); (3) stimulants (including amphetamines, cocaine, and others); (4) hallucinogens; and substances like (5) phencyclidine and (6) cannabis and inhalants, which do not readily fit the other categories. In an attempt to economically organize and clarify the mass of specific information about each category of drug and its effects, six tables in this chapter present (a) the traditional medical use, (b) appropriate dose levels, (c) duration of effects, and (d) the physiological, psychological, and behavioral effects (including signs of intoxication, withdrawal, and overdose reactions). Each of these tables will be discussed separately in the sections that follow.

Considering these categories will help the clinician generate relevant hypotheses to determine the extent and pattern of a patient's abuse; the presence or absence of psychological or physiological dependence and/or addiction; and the nature and extent of any long-term consequences.

A grounding in the "biological basics" for each drug serves as excellent protection against thinking based upon the many stereotypes and generally unwarranted assumptions that abound in this field. For example, it is commonly assumed that drugs capable of producing physical dependence, with its characteristic withdrawal syndrome, are inherently more "dangerous" than those which do not. The biological basics, however, indicate otherwise. "The effects of abrupt cessation of long-term amphetamine and cocaine use, consisting of severe depression and lassitude, are often more disabling than the abrupt withdrawal of opiates, which produce a dramatic and very uncomfortable abstinence syndrome, but with less long-term disability" (Khantizian and McKenna, 1979, pp. 361–362). Without *specific* technical knowledge, the diagnostician/therapist is likely to become confused and lost in a bewildering maze of psychodynamic, behavioral, social, and cultural data.

Narcotics and Related Analgesics

To the uninformed clinician, the illicit use of narcotics often is thought to be the most dangerous pattern of drug use possible. Reference to the biological basics, however, reveals that the "dangerousness" of narcotic use arises not from the drug itself, but from nonpharmacologic factors associated with its use—i.e., the preference for injection as the major route of administering the drug, the use of impure drugs and contaminated apparatus, and the life-style typically associated with narcotic use (Brecher, 1972). Although many factors influence the way the general public (including politicians) perceives narcotics, it is incumbent upon the clinician to understand and separate fact from myth. Such distinctions are necessary to identify correctly drug effects and problems that require immediate rather than elective intervention.

Natural and synthetic narcotics are used in medicine primarily for the relief of pain, i.e., as analgesics. Although these drugs have a high potential for producing psychological and physical dependence, there is evidence that narcotics *can* be utilized safely and effectively if there is medical supervision (Powell, 1973; Zinberg, Harding, and Winkeller, 1977; Zinberg and Jacobson, 1976). However, on the "street," a nonmedical setting, the use of narcotics is often risky. Heroin, the most widely used narcotic, is available in the United States only through illicit channels. Thus, for a street addict it is difficult to determine whether the substance being sold as heroin is, in fact, heroin. Not surprisingly, therefore, heroin tends to be sold in adulterated form, "cut" with volume-expanding substances known to increase the risk of attendant medical complications (Baden, 1972; Perry, 1974). Table 4–1 presents in summary form the biological basics for narcotics. For further study see Jaffe (1980); Jaffe and Martin (1980); Khantzian and McKenna (1979).

The "Dangers" of Narcotics Use and Withdrawal

Professionals and nonprofessionals often consider the illicit use of narcotics life-threatening. Categorically speaking, narcotics use is neither dangerous nor life-threatening; however, certain associated factors may be. For example, the long-reported phenomenon of sudden death among users following intravenous administration of street heroin traditionally has been referred to as a narcotics "overdose." This reaction, however, cannot be attributed to the central depressant effects of an excessive amount of heroin; thus, technically, it is not an overdose. More recently, this reaction has come to be known diagnostically as "Syndrome X" (see Baden, 1972, and Brecher, 1972, for interesting discussions). A number of hypotheses have been offered to explain the syndrome, including (1) the toxic and allergenic effects of quinine, a frequently used street adulterant; (2) bacterial and other contaminants sometimes found in street heroin; and (3) the rapid injection of heroin into a body already burdened with detoxifying and metabolizing other central nervous system depressants (e.g., barbiturates and/or alcohol). The problem remains both compelling and intriguing (see Cherubin, 1967; Helpern and Rho, 1966; Hoffman, 1983).

It is also assumed that rapid withdrawal from narcotics referred to in many sources as the "abstinence syndrome") can be life-threatening. Although "dramatic and temporarily disabling, withdrawal represents the least life-threatening or permanently disabling danger when compared with effects of other classes of drugs, unless there is concurrent disabling illness or cardiac disease" (Khantzian and McKenna, 1979, p. 362). See Table 4–1 for additional details of opiate withdrawal.

Some Important Exceptions. Although many natural and synthetic narcotics share common effects, there are three specific exceptions of clinical significance.

First, when meperdine (Demerol) is used, even in high doses, "the tolerant addict may show *dilated* pupils, increased muscular activity, twitching, tremors, mental confusion and, occasionally, grand mal seizures" (Jaffe, 1980).

Second, propoxyphene (Darvon), a synthetic narcotic analgesic, also has been reported to produce delusions, hallucinations, confusion, and seizures both *with use in high doses and in withdrawal* (Jaffe and Martin, 1980). These life-threatening properties are important to note because they occur with none of the other narcotic analgesics, resembling instead the withdrawal syndrome associated with sedative-hypnotics. See Table 4–2 for details of sedative-hypnotic withdrawal.

Third, pentazocine (Talwin), another synthetic narcotic analgesic, can concurrently act as a weak *antagonist* of other narcotics. Its use by a person physically dependent on narcotics could precipitate a withdrawal reaction.

To reiterate, with the exception of meperdine and propoxyphene, withdrawal from narcotics and related analgesics is an uncomfortable but *not* life-threatening process.

Sedative-Hypnotics and Other Central Nervous System Depressants

The sedative-hypnotics frequently are misunderstood because the effects of these drugs vary enormously as a function of dose. In low-to-moderate doses these agents decrease inhibitions, relieve anxiety, inhibit higher cortical regulatory centers, and produce a short-term sense of euphoria and elation (Harvey, 1980; Smith and Wesson, 1974). "In higher doses, the main danger and fatal consequences of these drugs reside in their depressant action on vital central nervous system sites, particularly brainstem arousal and respiratory centers" (Khantzian and McKenna, 1979, p. 363). The synergistic depressant effect produced by combining two sedative-hypnotic drugs (for example, alcohol and a barbiturate) is the primary factor in the severe morbidity and mortality associated with use of drugs in this class. See Harvey (1980) and Khantzian and McKenna (1979) for a thorough description of these drugs and their effects.

Special Reactions. All of the drugs in this category demonstrate partial or complete cross-tolerance; that is, one drug can be substituted

TABLE 4–1. Narcotic Analgesics

Drug	*Common Street Names*	*Therapeutic Dose*	*Medical Use*	*Duration of Effects*	*Toler*
HEROIN (Diacetylmorphine)	H. Dougee, Junk, Smack, Dope, Scag, Horse, Narco, Stuff	Street availability only—see opium	None (in the U.S.A.)	3–6 hours	YE
MORPHINE (Morphine hydro-cloride)	Drugstore dope	8–15 mg. q3h prn oral or parenteral	Analgesic	3–6 hours	YE
DILAUDID (Hydromorphone hydrochloride)	DL's, "4's"	2.0 mg. prn oral or prenteral	Analgesic Antidiarrheal Antitussive	3–6 hours	YE
NUMORPHONE (Oxymorphone)	New Blues	1–1.5 mg. q4–6 IM or S/C 2–5 mg. q4–6h Rectal 10 mg. q4–6h oral	Analgesic Antidiarrheal Antitussive	3–6 hours	YE
OPIUM (Thebaine, narcotine, papaverine, Dover's powder, paregoric)		4 ml prn po. cough 60 mg. prn (powder) rectal or oral 300 mg. oral (Dover's powder) 0.6 ml prn oral (tincture)	Analgesic Antidiarrheal	3–6 hours	YE
CODEINE (Codeine sulfate)		15–30–60 mg. q3–4h oral or parenteral	Analgesic Antitussive	3–6 hours	YE
PERCODAN Oxycodone and aspirin)	Perks	1–2 tablets every 3–4 hours oral	Analgesic Antidiarrheal Antitussive	3–6 hours	YE
VICODIN (Hydrocodone and tylenol)		1–2 tablets q3–4h oral	Analgesic Antidiarrheal Antitussive	3–6	YE
DEMEROL (Meperidine hydrochloride; pethidine), Pethadol		25–100 mg. q3–4h oral or parenteral	Analgesic	3–6 hours	YE
METHADONE (Methadone hydro-chloride), Dolo-phine, Methadose	Dollies, Done	5–10 mg. q3–4h oral or parenteral NOTE: Parenteral dose = ½ oral dose	Antitussive Analgesic for terminal illness Treatment of narcotic abstinence syndromes	24–36 hours in addicts 8–18 hours as an analgesic	YE

ological endence	*Physiological Dependence*	*Overdose*	*Intoxication*	*Withdrawal*
I	HIGH	* Slow and shallow breathing * Clammy skin * Miotic pupils * Depressed levels of consciousness * Hypotension with tachycardia sometimes present * Wheezes, rales on occasion * Convulsions * Coma * Death * Syndrome "X" * Anaphlactoid reaction to drug or cutting agent	* Drowsiness * Euphoria * Apathy * Difficulty in concentration * Nausea and vomiting * Respiratory depression * Slowed speech * Miotic pupils * Decreased physical activity * Track marks * Drooling * Nodding * Analgesia * No motor ataxia * Peripheral vasodilation * Warm flushing of skin sensations in lower abdomen ("rush") * Orgasm * Spontaneous orgasm * Itching	Develop within 2–48 hours Peak at 72 hours Duration 7–10 days *Initial* * Pleas * Demands * Manipulations Although the above are more often associated with narcotics, not exclusive to narcotics. *8–12 hours* * Diaphoresis * Nausea * Anxiety * Lacrimation * Rhinorrhea * Yawning * Irritability *12–48 hours* * Vomiting * Anorexia * Gooseflesh * Mydriatic Pupils * Sneezing * Abdominal spasms * Diarrhea * Chills * Flushing * Coryza * Yawning—more intense * Elevated temperature, pulse, respirations, and blood pressure * Lower back pain, pain neck and extremities * Weight loss * Dehydration * Ketosis * Acid/base imbalance * Depression
I	HIGH			
I	HIGH			
I	HIGH			
	HIGH			
ERATE	MODERATE	SAME AS ABOVE	SAME AS ABOVE	
	HIGH	SAME AS ABOVE	SAME AS ABOVE	
	HIGH	SAME AS ABOVE	SAME AS ABOVE	
	HIGH	SAME AS ABOVE	SAME AS ABOVE	Begins within 3 hours peaks 8–12; few symptoms remain after 4–5 days Muscle twitching worse
	HIGH	SAME AS ABOVE	Same as short acting— onset longer and less dramatic	More slowly developed Prolonged, less intense No symptoms until 24–48 hours after last dose

Table 4–1 continued on next page

TABLE 4–1. Narcotic Analgesics (*Continued*)

	Common Street Names	*Therapeutic Dose*	*Medical Use*	*Duration of Effects*	*Tolera*
Other Analgesics					
DARVON (Propoxyphene)		30–60 mg. q4–6h Oral	Analgesic Mild-moderate pain	3–6 hours	YE
DARVON-N (Propoxyphene napsylate)	N's	1–2 (50–100 mg.) tablets q4h oral	Analgesic Mild-moderate pain	3–6 hours	YE
DARVON-N w/ASA	Darvon compound "Comps"	1 tablet q4h Oral	Analgesic Mild-moderate pain	3–6 hours	YE
DARVOCET-N (Propoxyphene napsylate with acetaminophen)		100 mg. (1 tablet) q4h p.o.	Analgesic Mild-moderate pain	3–6 hours	YE
TALWIN (Pentazocine hydrochloride)	"T's" (as in T's and Blues) Sets	1–2 tablets (50–100 mg.) q3-4h oral 50–100 mg. IM every 3–4 hours	Analgesic	3–4 hours	Ye

for any other in the category, thereby maintaining the physically dependent state and suppressing the manifestations of withdrawal. Consequently, the signs and symptoms of intoxication, overdose, or withdrawal from *any* of the sedative-hypnotics are virtually the same.

Like narcotics, sedative-hypnotics have a high potential for psychological and physiological dependence (Hoffmann, 1983). Unlike narcotics, however, sedative-hypnotics have a withdrawal syndrome that *is* life-threatening, specifically as a result of seizure and delirium tremens (the "DTs"). This most important point of distinction may not be appreciated by the naive clinician because sedative-hypnotics typically are ingested orally and are assumed not to be as "dangerous" as drugs that are injected. The biological basics, however, reveal that persons dependent on sedative-hypnotics *never* must be withdrawn

ychological ependence	Physiological Dependence	Overdose	Intoxication	Withdrawal
DERATE	HIGH	* Delusions, * Hallucinations and confusion * Pulmonary edema	Similar to morphine * Convulsions * Toxic psychosis—delusions, hallucinations, confusion	* Mild abstinence * Pneumonia
DERATE	HIGH	SAME AS ABOVE	SAME AS ABOVE	SAME AS ABOVE
DERATE	HIGH	SAME AS ABOVE	SAME AS ABOVE	SAME AS ABOVE
DERATE	HIGH	SAME AS ABOVE	SAME AS ABOVE	SAME AS ABOVE
DERATE	HIGH	* Marked respiratory depression * Increased blood pressure * Tachycardia	Similar to narcotics * Side effects differ somewhat—sweating, sedation, dizziness, lightheaded nausea, vomiting less common	Similar to narcotics but milder * Abdominal cramps, anxiety, chills, increased temperature, vomiting, sweating, lacrimation * Drug seeking behavior * NOTE: Antagonistic actions as well as sedation

RCES: All the tables in Chapter 4 were prepared from materials gathered from the following resources: holism and Drug Addiction Research Foundation, 1980 (a) and (b); Byck, 1970; Cherubin, 1957; Falconer ., 1968; Grinspoon and Bakalar, 1979; Harvey, 1980; Hoffer and Osmond, 1967; Jaffe, 1980; Jaffe and tin, 1980; Khantzian and McKenna, 1979; Mulé, 1976; McCarron et al., 1981 (a) and (b); Pevnick, Jasinski, Haentzen, 1978; Ritchie, 1970; Sharp and Brehm, 1977; Smith and Wesson, 1974; Surgeon General, 1981; ner, 1980.

abruptly. To do so entails a substantial risk of sensory confusion, seizures, functional brain damage, and even death. The patient's level of dependence must be carefully assessed and strict detoxification protocols must be followed (Khantzian and McKenna, 1979; Smith and Wesson, 1974). Given careful medical treatment, the vast majority of sedative-hypnotic-dependent patients can be safely withdrawn (detoxified) without disenabling complications. *Sedative-hypnotic detoxification requires careful and frequent technical monitoring of the patient* and always should be done on an inpatient basis.

All the sedative-hypnotics (barbiturates, nonbarbiturate sedatives, minor tranquilizers, and alcohol) demonstrate the same potential side effects and progressive complications. There are, however, certain special properties of two specific agents that should be noted.

TABLE 4–2. Sedative-Hypnotics

Drug	*Common Street Names*	*Therapeutic Dose*	*Medical Use*	*Duration of Effects*	*Toleran*
BARBITURATES:					
Nembutal (pentobarbital sodium)	Yellow Jackets	100–200 mg. h.s. Oral or Rectal Parenteral	Sleep Sedation	4–8 hours	YES
Seconal (secobarbital sodium)	Reds	100–200 mg. Oral or Rectal	Same as above but shorter duration of action	2–6 hours	YES
Tuinal (secobarbital sodium and amobarital sodium)	Tuey's	50–200 mg. h.s. Oral	Same as above	4–8 hours	YES
Amytal (amobarbital)		20–40 mg. Oral	Same as above	4–8 hours	YES
Fiorinal		1–2 tablets or capsules every 4 hours not to exceed 6 per day	Tension headache Psychic tension Muscle contraction in head, neck and shoulders	4–6 hours	YES
phenobarbital (Luminal)		15–60 mg. Oral, up to qid (anti-convulsant)	(Anti-convulsant Sedation	1–16 hours	YES
OTHER DEPRESSANTS:					
Quaaludes (Methaqualone) Sopor, Parest, Optimil	Ludes, 714's	75 mg. p.c. and h.s. 150–300 mg. h.s. Oral	Sedation Sleep	4–8 hours	YES
Doriden (glutethimide)		250 mg. tid p.c. Oral 500 mg.-lgm. h.s. Oral	Sedation Sleep	4–8 hours	YES
Placidyl (ethchlorvynol)		50–100 tid or qid Oral 200–400 mg. h.s. Oral	Sleep, sedation, Anti-anxiety	4–8 hours	YES
Noludar (methyprylon)		50–500 mg. h.s. Oral (hypnotic) 200–500 mg. bld or tid Oral (Sedative)	Sleep, sedation Anti-anxiety	4–8 hours	YES
Chloral Hydrate (Lorinal, Noctec, Somnos)		250–600 mg. h.s. Oral liquid or capsules	Sleep Sedation	5–8 hours	PROBA
Dalmane (flurazepam hydrochloride)		15–30 mg. h.s. Oral	Sleep, Hypnosis	4–16 hours	YES

Psychological Dependence	*Physiological Dependence*	*Overdose*	*Intoxication*	*Withdrawal*
HIGH	HIGH	* Somnolence * Confusion * Shallow respiration * Cold, clammy skin * Loss of deep tendon reflexes * Apnea * Decreased/absent response to painful stimuli * Difficulty in arousal * Shock * Dilated pupils * Hypotension * Coma * Death	ACUTE: * Slowed mental functioning * Slowed physical activity * Relation * Drowsiness * Slurred speech * Ataxia * Impaired thinking * Poor concentration * Memory disturbances * Decreased reaction time * Poor judgement * Limited attention span * Disinhibition of impulses * Labile mood swings * Exaggerated personality traits * Irritability * Combativeness * Release of sexual and aggressive impulses (high doses) * Bizarre and paranoid thoughts * Erratic and suicidal behavior CHRONIC All of the above plus— * Nystagmus * Diplopia * Strabismus * Pseudoptosis * Vertigo * Positive Romberg sign * Hypotonia * Dysmertria (motor) * Decreased superficial and deep tendon reflexes * Pupil response and sensations unaltered * Decreased REM sleep * Thick slurred speech * Signs of overdose	*12–24 hours* * Tremors (coarse and rhythmic) * Weakness * Insomnia * Diaphoresis * Restlessness * Postural hypotension * Nausea and vomiting * Anorexia * Dry mouth * Headache * Malaise * Frequent dreaming * Nightmares * Restless sleep * Deep tendon hyperreflexia * Apprehension * Acute anxiety * Irritability * Remorsefulness * Depression *24–72 hours* * Myoclonic muscular contractions * Spasmodic jerking of extremities * Bizarre movement patterns * Grand mal seizures * Status epilepticus 3–8 DAYS * Hallucinosis ("The Horrors") -visual, haptic (tactile), auditory, often persecutory in nature * Delirium tremens
HIGH	HIGH			
HIGH	HIGH			
HIGH	HIGH			
MODERATE	MODERATE			
HIGH	HIGH			
HIGH	HIGH	SAME AS BARBITURATES		
HIGH	HIGH	NOTE: * Doriden and Placidyl remains in stomach longer-reabsorption can lead to coma * Entero-hepatic circulation stores in fat		
POSSIBLE	POSSIBLE			
POSSIBLE	POSSIBLE			
POSSIBLE (rare)	POSSIBLE (rare)			
MODERATE	MODERATE			

Table 4–2 continued on next page

TABLE 4–2. Sedative-Hypnotics (*Continued*)

Drug	*Common Street Names*	*Therapeutic Dose*	*Medical Use*	*Duration of Effects*	*Tolera*
TRANQUILIZERS:					
Valium (diazepam)	V's,	2–5–10 mg. tid or qid Oral 2–10 mg. IM/IV q3-4h	Anti-anxiety, Sedation, sleep Anti-convulsant	4–12 hours	YES
Librium (chlordiazepoxide hydrochloride)		5–10–25 mg. tid or qid Oral 100 mg. q4–6h 1M. Dosage individually adjusted	Anti-anxiety, Sedation, sleep	4–12 hours	YES
Serax (oxazepam)		10–30 mg. tid or qid Oral	Sedation, muscle relaxant, tranquilizer	4–8 hours	YES
Vistaril (Hydrochloride Ataraz, Hydroxyzine)		10–100 mg. Oral 500 mg. IM/IV 10 mg/5ml syrup	Sedation, Muscle relaxant, Tranquilizer	4–8 hours	YES
meprobamate (Equanil, Miltown)		400 mg. tid or qid Oral	Anti-anxiety Sedation Muscle relaxant	4–8 hours	YES
ALCOHOL:	Juice, Booze, Sauce	1–2 oz. (20–80 proof) p.c. or h.s.	Spinal-headache, Sedation, Digestive aid, Decrease uterine contractions	2–8 hours Highly variable	YES

Glutethimide (Doriden), a nonbarbiturate sedative-hypnotic, poses a special hazard since the range between the drug's lethal and therapeutic doses is quite narrow. The ratio of the lethal to the therapeutic dose of a drug is known as the "therapeutic index" and is one measure of that drug's safety. More worrisome, however, is the fact that glutethimide "remains in the stomach longer than barbiturates, because reabsorption will occur and can produce coma *after* a patient appears to be recovering from overdose" (Khantzian and McKenna, 1979). Special care must be taken when assessing patients who currently are or recently have been using glutethimide.

Diazepam (Valium), one of the several benzodiazepine anti-anxiety agents currently in wide clinical use, is the most frequently prescribed drug in this country) Brecher, 1972). When alcohol (in any form) is combined with diazepam, a particularly potent synergistic effect obtains which, even with low doses of each drug, can result in massive, often fatal central nervous system depression. Although diazepam may have a lesser potential for physical dependence than do other sedatives, regular use in moderate to high doses quickly can result in dependence.

ychological ependence	Physiological Dependence	Overdose	Intoxication	Withdrawal
SSIBLE	POSSIBLE	SAME AS BARBITURATES		NOTE—Valium * Onset of withdrawal delayed * Symptoms minimal for first 5 days; peak between 5th-9th day.
SSIBLE	POSSIBLE			
SSIBLE	POSSIBLE			
SSIBLE	POSSIBLE			
DERATE	MODERATE			
GH	HIGH	SAME AS BARBITURATES		

Since individual tolerances and rates of metabolism for sedatives vary widely, no precise level of dose or duration of use can be indicated as consistently problematic.

The signs and symptoms of diazepam withdrawal are the same as those seen with the other sedative-hypnotics (including alcohol), with one very significant difference: the time of onset of Valium withdrawal symptoms is *frequently delayed* in comparison to that of the other agents in this class. Whereas the signs and symptoms of sedative withdrawal typically appear within the first seventy-two hours after the last dose, in the case of Valium these signs and symptoms may be minimal for up to five days or more, attaining peak levels between the fifth and ninth days (Khantzian and McKenna, 1979; Pevnick, Jasinski, and Haentzen, 1978). The relative absence of withdrawal signs and symptoms during the first five days or so must not be assumed to mean that the diazepam-dependent patient already has emerged from or will not enter a withdrawal phase. Careful clinical monitoring needs to be continued for at least seven days after a patient's last dose of diazepam.

Central Nervous System Stimulants

Included in this category are amphetamines, nonamphetamine stimulants, cocaine, nicotine, and caffeine. These drugs share a number of common properties, but vary in (1) duration and intensity of action, (2) usual route of administration, and (3) street availability. Comprehensive consideration of the many agents in this category is beyond the scope of this chapter; consequently, the following discussion will focus on two of the more commonly used central nervous system stimulants: amphetamines and cocaine. Exclusion of nicotine and caffeine from this discussion in no way means that these two extensively and intensively used drugs are without their own special untoward effects and substantial risks. See Table 4–3 and Alcoholism and Drug Addiction Research Foundation (1980a) for a more detailed account of nicotine and a caffeine.

"Ingestion of high doses of central nervous system stimulants by a nontolerant person can produce effects ranging from enjoyable subjective states of euphoria to acute psychotic states and dramatic physiologic reactions such as extreme tachycardia, arrhythmia, hypertensive crises, cardiovascular collapse, and death" (Khantzian and McKenna, 1979, p. 368). Initially, the effects of amphetamines and cocaine can be characterized as increased mental and physical well-being. With increased doses and/or chronic use, the risk of toxicity increases and the user may experience tremulousness, muscle tension, jitters, irritation, outbursts of anger, violent assaultive behavior, paranoia, delusional thinking, visual and auditory hallucinations, or any combination of these symptoms. Memory and orientation, however, generally are not affected except when extremely high doses are taken (Jaffe, 1980; Khantzian and McKenna, 1979; Weiner, 1980). The patterns of toxic-stimulant effects are quite heterogeneous: amphetamine toxicity can closely resemble schizophrenic, hypomanic, emotionally labile, and obsessive-compulsive states. These latter states can be differentiated from those induced by stimulants only by the demonstration of stimulants or their metabolites in the body or by a diagnostically discriminating premorbid history (Khantzian and McKenna, 1979; Hofmann, 1983).

Khantzian (1975) has suggested that individuals who become heavily involved with stimulant drugs do so in an attempt to better cope with mild but chronic feelings of depression. Wurmser (1978) also views the compulsive use of stimulants as a form of self-medication, arguing that these agents "provide a sense of aggressive mastery, control, invincibility and grandeur."

Despite the fact that earlier reports on stimulant use and abuse made few distinctions between cocaine and the amphetamine-like drugs, there are important differences. Although both types of drug stimulate both the cardiovascular and central nervous systems, cocaine exerts its energizing effects predominantly via direct action on the cerebral cortex, while the effects of the amphetamine group are mediated mainly through cardiac acceleration. The 1979 national survey on drug abuse (Fishburne, Abelson, and Crisin, 1980) reveals that the patterns of cocaine and amphetamine use are quite different, and that the dramatically increased incidence and prevalence of cocaine use in recent years has not been paralleled for the amphetamines. In an earlier study, Brecher (1972) postulated that the relative preference of stimulant users for either cocaine or amphetamines is largely a function of the price and availability of each. In a recent study of the development of *psychological* dependence on cocaine, Burglass and Milligan (1979) note that chronic users of low-dose intranasal cocaine reported neither antecedent histories of depression (mild or severe) nor any significant previous or concurrent use of amphetamines. These researchers, however, do find evidence of a number of specific cognitive, psychodynamic, and affective changes that developed in users while they were involved with drugs.

Unlike narcotics and sedative-hypnotics, the stimulants do not produce a clear-cut abstinence (withdrawal) syndrome. Convincing evidence does exist that a "transitory subjective/psychological reaction results after abrupt cessation of the drugs" (Khantzian and McKenna, 1979). On the street this experience is referred to as "crashing." Importantly, the absence of a physiologic abstinence syndrome does not reduce the hazards associated with chronic stimulant use. As a result of the subjective depression following cessation of use, suicidal thoughts and attempts are not uncommon clinical events. In fact, marked depression can persist for months. The extent of this depressive reaction is influenced by dose level, duration of use, and a number of individual metabolic, endocrine, and nutritional factors. Depressive reactions can occur following cessation of use of both the amphetamines and cocaine, but are more commonly observed in amphetamine users.

Warning: Stimulant-Sedative Combination Drugs. Several of the amphetamines are commercially marketed in combination with barbiturate sedatives, in preparations used for weight control. The somewhat dubious rationale for this merchandising practice is that a low dose of a sedative will counter the unpleasant effects of any excess physical stimulation produced by the amphetamine.

The combination of dextroamphetamine and amobarbital, mar-

TABLE 4–3. Stimulants

Drug	*Common Street Names*	*Therapeutic Dose*	*Medical Use*	*Duration of Effect*	*Toler[e]*
AMPHETAMINE:					
BENZEDRINE (Amphetamine Sulfate)	Speed	10–20 mg daily (divided doses) Oral	Hyperkinesis/MBD[a] Narcolepsy Mild depression	2–4 hours	YE[S]
DIDREX (Benzphetamine hydrochloride)	Speed	25–150 mg daily (divided doses) Oral	Mild depression	2–4 hours	YE[S]
DEXEDRINE (Dextoampheta-mine Sulfate)	Speed	5–10 mg. bid-qid or divided doses 10 mg. spansules bid	Hyperkinesis/MBD Narcolepsy Mild depression	2–4 hours Spansules—up to 12 hours	YE[S]
DESOXYN (Methamphetamine hydrochloride)	Speed, Methedrine, Crystal	2/5–7.5 mg. bid or qid oral 15–30 mg. IM/IV	Hyperkinesis/MBD Narcolepsy Mild depression	2–4 hours	YE[S]
BIPHETAMINE (l-Amphetamine and d-Amphetamine)	Black Beauties Speed	7.5 mg, 12.5 and 20 mg Oral lowest effective dose	MBD Narcolepsy Mild depression	2–4 hours	YE[S]
DEXAMYL (Dextroampheta-mine sulfate and amobarbital)	Speed	5 mg dextroamphet-amine and 32 mg, (½ gr.) amobarbital per tablet lowest effective dose	Mild depression	2–4 hours Spansules—up to 12 hours	YE[S]
NON AMPHETAMINE STIMULANTS:					
PRELUDIN (pheumetrazine hydrochloride)		50–75 mg. 25 mg. bid/tid ½h a.c. oral 75 mg sustained released o.m. 15–30 mg o.m. oral	Weight control	2–4 hours	YE[S]
RITALIN HYDRO-CHLORIDE (Methyl-phenidate hydrochloride)		5–20 mg. bid or tid oral 10–50 mg parenteral prn	Hyperkinesis/MBD Narcolepsy Mild depression	2–4 hours	YE[S]
CROSSROADS	Crossroads		None	2–4 hours	YE[S]
CYLERT (Pemoline)		37.5 mg → 150 mg qd oral	MBD	8–24 hours 1/day dose children	YE[S]

iological endence	Physiological Dependence	Overdose	Intoxication	Withdrawal
I	POSSIBLE	*Excessive Stimulation:* * Restlessness, dizziness, increased reflexes, tremor, insomnia, irritability, confusion, assaultiveness hallucinations, panic states. Chills, pallor or flushing, sweating, palpitation. Hypertension or hypotension, arrhythmias, anginal pain, circulatory collapse, nausea, vomiting, diarrhea abdominal cramps. Convulsion, coma. *Excessive Stimulation:* (see above) *Excessive Sedation:* (from amobarbital) * Respiratory depression Decreased superficial and deep reflexes Decreased urine formation	*Effects:* * Mood elevation * Sense of energy and alertness * Decreased appetite * Mild ketosis * Sense of improved task performance * Anxiety, irritability * Insomnia * Transient drowsiness *IV Use:* * Enhanced physical strength and mental capacity * Delayed orgasm * "Subjective rush" *Toxicity:* * Bruxism * Touching and picking face and extremities * Suspiciousness—paranoia * Stereotyped repetitious behavior * Preoccupations * Toxic psychosis Compulsive behavior Vivid auditory, visual sometimes tactile hallucinations * Delusions of parasitosis (formication) * Looseness of associations * Slight elevation of blood pressure * Hypertensive crisis may occur	* Drug craving * General fatigue * Prolonged sleep (12–24 hours) * Depression * Lassitude * Hyperphagia * Suicidal Ideation High doses—crashes
SIBLE	POSSIBLE			
H	POSSIBLE			
H	POSSIBLE			
H	POSSIBLE			
H	POSSIBLE			
H	POSSIBLE			
H	POSSIBLE	See Excessive Stimulation		
H	POSSIBLE			
LIKELY	UNLIKELY			

Table 4–3 continued on next page

TABLE 4–3. Stimulants (*Continued*)

Drug	*Common Street Names*	*Therapeutic Dose*	*Medical Use*	*Duration of Effect*	*Toler*
COCAINE HYDROCHLORIDE	Coke, Blow, Toot Snow, Lady	1–10% solution Topical	Local anesthetic Vasoconstrictor ENT surgery Intubation	1–2 hours	YE
CAFFEINE	Coffee/tea/colas Java, mud, brew Cocoa	100–300 mg daily	Adjuctive medication in migraine preparations and other analgesics to slow absorption	5 min.-4 hours peak 30 minutes	YE
NICOTINE	Weeds, fags, butts tobacco products	None	None		YES

ychological)ependence	Physiological Dependence	Overdose	Intoxication	Withdrawal
GH	QUESTIONABLE	* Seizures; respiratory collapse; cardiac failure arrhythmias Florid hallucinations (all modes)	* CNS effects-Cardiac Effects * Increased sense or mastery, capacity * Increased blood pressure * Increased pulse	Not well documented May involve cravings, depression, or increased psychomotor agitation after prolonged IV use
GH	HIGH Not reported	*Large Doses in Non-Users:* * Headache * Jitters * Nervousness * Delirium *Long-Term Toxic Effects* (Above 8 cups/day): * Chronic insomnia * Persistent anxiety * Depression * Stomach upset	PHYSIOLOGICAL EFFECTS: * General metabolism and body temperature may increase * Tachycardia * Increase in peripheral blood flow (except in brain) * Elevated blood pressure especially during stress * Increase urination * Stimulate secretion of gastric acid * Inhibits glucose metabolism—increased blood sugar levels * Motor tremulousness BEHAVIORAL EFFECTS: * Variable * Interference with sleep (delays onset, shortens time, reduces depth, increases REM sleep early in night but reduces it Overall) * Postpones fatigue * Enhance endurance * Brighter affect * Mild increase energy * Decreased boredom	* Fatigue * Tremulousness * Severe headache * Irritation
GH	HIGH		PHYSIOLOGICAL EFFECTS: * Increased heart rate and blood pressure * Drop in skin temperature * Increased respiration * Diarrhea and vomiting * CNS stimulation but paradoxically relaxation can occur in habitual users * Inhibition of stomach contractions * Long term effects on bronchopulmonary and cardiovascular systems	* Craving * Labile emotions * Nervousness and agitation * Restlessness * Dullness * Drowsiness * Sleep disturbances * G-I disturbances * Headache * Impairment of concentration, judgement, and psychomotor performance

IBD = Minimal Brain Dysfunction

TABLE 4–4. Hallucinogens

Drug	*Dosage*	*Duration of Effect*	*Sensitization*	*Common Objective Effects*	*Common Subjective Effects*
1. LSD or ACID (D-lysergic diethylamide)	Street use highly variable Average 50–200 mcgm	45 min.—8–12 hours *peak* 2–3 hours *half-life*—2 hours	YES develops quickly	* Nausea, chills (early) * Pupil dilation * Increase deep tendon reflexes * Increase pulse, temperature, and blood pressure * Mild dizziness * Tingling, trembling * Slow deep breathing * Loss of appetite * Insomnia	PERCEPTUAL CHANGES: * Fascination or enchantment with ordinary objects * Heightened esthetic responses to color, texture, spatial arrangements, contours, music * Heightened body awareness, vision, depth, distortion, afterimages * Physiognomies * Synesthesia * Slowing of time EMOTIONAL CHANGES: * Heightened sensitivity to faces, gestures * Feelings magnified—love, lust, hate, joy, anger, pain, terror, despair, etc. * Experience two incompatible emotions simultanteously * Fear of losing control, paranoia, panic * Euphoria, bliss * Impairment short term memory * Introspective reflection * Profound changes in sense of sel[illegible] THOUGHT: * Regression * Projection of self into dreamlike images * Experiences of birth, death, and incarnation * Encounters with gods and demons * Identification with animals

2. MESCALINE (3, 4, 5-trimethylyloxyphenyl-ethylamide)	200 mg. or 3–5 peyote buttons	45 min.—8–10 hours *peak*—2–3 hours *half-life* 2 hours	YES	* Resembles LSD * Bitter and nauseating * Vomiting (peyote buttons) * More intense autonomic symptoms than LSD	* Similar to LSD * More sensual and perceptual * Less change in thought, mood, and sense of self
3. PSILOCYBIN AND PSILOCIN	4–6 mg. usual dose 10–20 mg. dried—5–10 gm. 30 times stronger than mescaline	4–6 hours	YES	Like LSD but gentler	* Similar to LSD * More strongly visual * Less intense * More euphoric * Fewer panic reactions * Less change in thought mood, and sense of self
4. MORNING GLORY SEEDS (lysergic acid amide) HEAVENLY BLUE, PEARLY GATES, FLYING SAUCERS	100 ololiuqui seeds or 4–8 Hawaiian baby woodrose seeds = 100 mcgm LSD DRINK		Contro-versial	* Similar to LSD * Nausea * Diarrhea	* Similar to LSD
5. MDA (methyl dioxymphetamine)	50 mg. usual dose 100–150 mg.	45 min.—8–12 hours peak 1–2 hours	Contro-versial	* Feeling of relaxation and physical well-being * Sweating * Tension in jaw and facial muscles * Skin reaction * Alleged aphrodisiac	* Feelings of esthetic delight, empathy, serenity, joy, insight * Self awareness without perceptual change, loss of control, or depersonalization * Eliminates anxiety and defensiveness * Invites self-exploration/ LSD demands * Age-regression * Relives childhood experiences * Affectionate * Melting boundaries with others * Distorts perceptions less * Causes fewer unpleasant emotions

Table 4–4 continued on next page

TABLE 4–4. Hallucinogens (*Continued*)

Drug	*Dosage*	*Duration of Effect*	*Sensitization*	*Common Objective Experience*	*Common Subjective Experience*
6. DMT (dimethyltrypt-amine)	50 mg. smoked or injected	seconds—30 min. *peak* 5–20 min.	YES only after frequent use	* Resembles LSD * Dilated pupils * Heightened blood pressure *Above symptoms more intense than with LSD*	* Resembles LSD but more intense * Thoughts and visions crowd in at a great speed * Sense of transcending time * Objects lose form and dissolve into a play of vibrations
7. DOM or STP (2, 5 dimethoxy-4-methylamphet-amine)	under 5 mg.—resembles DOET 5 mg. and above—resembles LSD	high doses—16–24 hours low doses—6–8 hours	YES	* Resembles amphetamine or LSD	* Experience feels like amphetamine combined with LSD * Long ebbing and returning effects—feels like it never ends * Prolonged psychosis * Flashbacks
8. DOET (2, 5-dimethoxy-4-ethylamphetamine)	1.5 mg. = 2–3 mg. DOM	5–6 hours	YES	* Dilates pupils * Little effect on pulse, blood pressure, and respiration	* Resembles MDA * Mild euphoria * Enhanced self awareness, insight * Body image awareness * Close eye imagery * Talkativeness * No perceptual or cognitive impairment

keted under the trade name Dexamyl, is widely prescribed and also heavily used on the "street." Patients who are heavily involved with this or similar combination drugs may present at evaluation with the signs and symptoms of either stimulation or sedation. Particular caution needs to be exercised during the withdrawal phase, since abrupt cessation of the drug might result in *both* a "crash" from the amphetamine and the acute life-threatening sedative-hypnotic withdrawal state.

Hallucinogens

The subjective experience of using a hallucinogen is unlike any of the drug effects described thus far. The hallucinogens bear little resemblance to narcotics, sedative-hypnotics, or stimulants except that mild tolerance to these drugs may develop. There is, however, no hallucinogen withdrawal reaction or syndrome, even after prolonged high-dose use. In addition, although individual reactions to these drugs vary enormously, the primary effects tend to involve changes in thought content, perception, and subjective emotional experience. Hallucinogens primarily differ in the intensity and duration of the drug experience produced. For a more detailed examination of these drugs, see Grinspoon and Bakalar (1979) and Hoffer and Osmond (1967).

Although the hallucinogen experience is typically one that is desired by the user, on rare occasions (most commonly with a first-time user) a panic reaction can occur. Known as a "bad trip," this type of intensely dysphoric experience can occur at any time, even when many previous LSD and PCP experiences have been pleasant and nontraumatic. During a bad trip, the individual often feels that the reaction to the drug will never end; a panic reaction ensues, and the user is unable to distinguish the drug induced subjective experience from socially validated reality. Further, Becker (1967) has argued that bad trips may result from a novice user's unfamiliarity with the drug's effects rather than from any direct chemical effects. Persons who have experienced bad trips are more likely to report having "flashbacks" (the spontaneous recurrence of the drug experience without the drug being used) than are users who have not experienced bad trips. Flashbacks appear to occur predominantly during periods of stress and anxiety. Prolonged psychotic states following use of a hallucinogen are thought by some to be indicative of an acute schizophrenic reaction rather than a direct drug effect; however, this issue remains controversial and actively disputed (Khantzian and McKenna, 1979).

Phencyclidine (PCP)

Phencyclidine, most commonly known as "PCP" or "angel dust," has been used recreationally with increasing frequency since the late 1950s. Phencyclidine commonly has been classified as a hallucinogen because in toxic doses it typically produces severe agitation, excitement, and quasi-psychotic reactions including paranoid delusions and auditory hallucinations. In low to moderate doses there may be little or no hallucinosis, and reactions may include drowsiness, ataxia, excitability, and nystagmus. Note that all these latter signs and symptoms are similar to those produced by low-dose sedative-hypnotics. Because

TABLE 4–5. Phencyclidine (Sernyl, Sernylan)

Common Street Names	*Dosage*	*Medical*	*Duration of Effect*	*Tolerance*	*Psychological Dependence*
Crystal, PCP, Angel dust, Hog, Rocket fuel, Super weed, Peace pill, Elephant tranquilizer, Dust, *THC*— Although PCP is not THC, many report THC use when actually ingesting PCP	*Low* Under 5 mg *Moderate* 5 to 10 mg High 100 mg or more Oral, IV, or smoked on mint, parsley or marijuana High variability on street	Veterinary anesthetic tranquilizer and sedation in large animals	Variable Approx 4–6 hours Residual effects up to 24 hours Half life—1–3 days Remains in fat, blood and urine as long as a week	YES	Yes, but degree unknown

of the multiform reactions to this drug and the difficulty in correlating dose levels with effects, phencyclidine will be considered separately.

PCP is a frequent adulterant of other street hallucinogens. In fact, it is not uncommon for PCP to be sold as THC (tetrahydrocannabinol), the active ingredient of marijuana, or as LSD or mescaline. PCP can be distributed in a variety of forms ranging from a powder (often sprinkled on parsley leaves, marijuana, or other herbs) to variously colored tablets, pastes, capsules, and a liquid. Conversely, biological toxins such as rat poison and hairspray on occasion have been sprayed on herb leaves and marijuana and sold on the street as phencyclidine! What PCP users think is PCP may or may not be correct. Therefore

Physiological Dependence	*Possible Effects*	*Intoxication*		*Withdrawal*
egree unknown	* Highly variable Dose and time–related. *Physiological:* * Nystagmus * Increased blood pressure * Sweating * Nausea * Numbness * Floating sensation * Relaxation * Warmth and tingling * Increase heart rate * Lethargy * Slowed reflexes *Cognitive:* * Altered body image * Altered perception of time and space * Impaired immediate and recent memory * Decreased concentration * Dyscalculia * Paranoid thoughts * Delusions * Disordered and confused thoughts *Behavior:* * Blank staring * Catatonic immobility * Uncharacteristic violence	Minor Patterns: Highly Variable 1. Lethargy/Stupor * Rare autonomic signs * 67% clear in 6 hours Blank staring common 2. Bizarre Behavior 98% alert without delusions/hallucinations * Symptoms last from 30 min.-6 hours in 80% cases 3. Violent Behavior * Lasts only a few hours in most cases * Restraints and neuroleptic drugs often necessary 4. Agitation * Usually less than 6 hours * Marked increased motor activity 5. Euphoria * Sense of well-being without above patterns * May be described as tingling * No specific complaints * Nystagmus present in about 68% of cases	Major Patterns: Possibly Dose-Related 1. Coma * Mild, moderate or severe 2. Catatonic Syndrome * Posturing, catalepsy, rigidity * Mutism, staring, negativism * Excitement, possible violence * Stupor 3. Toxic Psychosis * Hallucinations/delusions (visual/auditory, often bright colored lights) * Bizarre behavior * Ingestion of PCP commonly up to 7 days before onset of symptoms * Duration 1–30 days; average 3–4 days 4. Acute Brain Syndrome * Disorientation * Confusion, loss of recent memory * Inappropriate behavior (labile) * Violence	Syndrome not reported—degree unknown

TABLE 4–6. Cannabis (Marijuana)

Drug	Common Street Names	Dosage	Medical Use	Duration of Effect
9-Tetra-hydrocannab-inol (THC) Marijuana Hashish Hash oil	Bhang, Kif, Gangja, Dope, Grass, Pot, Smoke, Hemp, Joint, Weed, Bone, Mary-Jane, Herb	* One cigarette (joint) might contain 1% THC delivers 2.5 mg. to lungs smoked, oral	* Relief of nausea and side effects of chemo-therapeutic agents in cancer patients * Glaucoma	3–5 Hours *Smoked* Onset—within minutes Peak—10–30 min. Duration—2–3 hours *Oral* Onset—30 min. to 1 hour Peak—2–3 hours Effect—3–5 hours

Inhalants (Toxic Vapors)

Drug	Common Street Names	Dosage	Medical Use	Duration of Effect
Glue sniffing Gasoline Paint Thinner Naphtha Solvents—Toluene	Fumes Chemicals	Difficult to determine	None	Undetermined Quick onset

the evaluating clinician may find it difficult to identify a pattern of effects consistent with PCP as the putative agent, and users may be unable to accurately judge their own response, thereby increasing the probability of a panic reaction (Becker, 1967) and further complicating the already difficult task of assessment. For a detailed discussion see McCarron et al. (1981a, 1981b).

Marijuana

"Marijuana is probably the most widely used drug in our society other than tobacco, alcohol, and caffeine" (Khantzian and McKenna, 1979). Despite much current debate, there is no conclusive evidence that marijuana is physically or psychologically damaging to the user. Marijuana does not seem to produce tolerance or physiological dependence (Babor et al., 1975). Although panic reactions associated with mari-

Tolerance	*Psychological Dependence*	*Physiological Dependence*	*Possible Effects*	*Withdrawal*
No—Sensitization	Moderate	Not reported	* Euphoria * Relaxed inhibitions * Increased appetite * Disoriented behavior * Mild stimulant * Tranquilizer *Toxic Reactions:* (rare) * Panic reactions * Paranoid ideation * Fatigue * Possible psychosis	*Not Reported* Possible Effects *Upon Cessation* * Hyperactivity * Insomnia * Decreased appetite * Anxiety
Unknown	Mild to Moderate	Degree unknown	*Varied* * Mild intoxication * Disorientation * Acute and severe pulmonary crisis * Toxicity to various organ systems * Possible damage to bone marrow, kidney, liver, and brain * Psychosis * Peripheral neuropathy	Unknown

juana use have been reported, these are "most often seen in first-time users who are unaware of the drug's effects and who may have taken the drug in an unfamiliar setting" (Khantzian and McKenna, 1979). Finally, there is no evidence of physical withdrawal syndrome associated with marijuana, although mild hyperactivity, insomnia, decreased appetite, and anxiety have been reported in some cases.

Inhalants (Toxic Vapors)

The intentional use of inhalants (for example, "glue sniffing") appears to be a phenomenon of the past and rarely is seen now (almost never in adults). Earlier reported reactions to glue sniffing ranged from mild intoxication and/or disorientation to coma. Conflicting reports can be found regarding damage to bone marrow, the kidneys, the liver, and central and peripheral neural tissue, but little consistent data on the actual effects of recreational inhalant use has been reported. See Sharp and Brehm (1977) for a thorough review of the psychological and physiological aspects of inhalant use.

A Closing Caveat

Pharmacological effects can mislead and/or complicate the process of clinical assessment. Substances often appear in more than one category because many share a common chemical structure or because their effects on the central nervous system (brain and spinal cord) may be similar. The generation of biological hypotheses during assessment is necessarily complicated, since the intoxication effects of one drug may be quite similar to the withdrawal effects of another. For example, the disorientation and hallucinosis associated with sedative-hypnotic withdrawal may be superficially indistinguishable from hallucinogen intoxication. While in some contexts final responsibility for diagnostic determination and therapeutic planning will be the responsibility of the physician, the nonmedical front-line worker is obliged to have a detailed and current working knowledge of the specific effects of specific drugs. Without this level of expertise, drug evaluation and treatment can be at best irrelevant and at worst lethal.

References

Alcoholism and Drug Addiction Research Foundation. *Facts About Caffeine.* Toronto, Canada, Jan. 1930(a).

———. *Facts About Tobacco.* Toronto, Canada, Jan. 1980(b).

Angrist, B. M., and Gershon, S. Amphetamine abuse in New York City—1966–1968. *Seminars in Psychiatry,* 1969, *1,* 195–207.

Babor, T. F., Mendelson, J. H., Greenberg, I., and Kuehnle, J. C. Marijuana consumption and tolerance to physiological and subjective effects. *Archives of General Psychiatry,* 1975, *32,* 1548–1552.

Baden, M. M. Narcotic abuse: a medical examiner's view. *New York State Journal of Medicine,* 1972, *72,* 834–840.

Becker, H. S. History, culture, and subjective experience: an exploration of the social biases. *Journal of Health and Social Behavior,* 1967, *8,* 163–176.

Brecher, E. M., and Editors of *Consumer Reports. Licit and Illicit Drugs,* Boston: Little, Brown Co., 1972.

Burglass, M. E., and Milligan, J. E. Cocaine: cognitive and dynamic aspects in the development of psychological dependence. Paper presented at the National Drug Abuse Conference, New Orleans, Aug. 1979.

Burglass, M. E., and Shaffer, H. The natural history of ideas in the treatment of addiction. In H. Shaffer and M. E. Burglass (eds.), *Classic Contributions in the Addictions.* New York: Brunner/Mazel, 1981.

Burton, J. D., Zawadski, E. S., Weatherbell, H. R., and Moy, T. W. Mainliners and blue velvet. *Journal of Forensic Sciences,* 1965, *10,* 466–472.

Byck, R. Drugs and the treatment of psychiatric disorder. In L. S. Goodman and A. Gilman (eds.), *The Pharmacological Basis of Therapeutics.* New York: Macmillan Publishing Co., 1970.

Cherubin, C. E. The medical sequelae of narcotic addiction. *Annals of Internal Medicine,* 1967, *67,* 23–33.

Falconer, M. W., Norman, M. R., Patterson, H. R., and Gustafson, E. A. *The Drug, the Nurse, the Patient.* Philadelphia: W. B. Saunders Co., 1968.

Fishburne, P. M., Abelson, H. I., and Crisin, I. *National Survey on Drug Abuse: Main Findings 1979.* Rockville, Md.: National Institute on Drug Abuse, 1980.

Gambino, B., and Shaffer, H. The concept of paradigm and the treatment of addiction. *Professional Psychology,* 1979, *10,* 207–223.

Grinspoon, L., and Bakalar. J. B. *Psychedelic Drugs Reconsidered.* New York: Basic Books, 1979.

Harvey, S. C. Hypnotics and sedatives. In A. G. Gilman, L. S. Goodman, and A. Gilman (eds.), *The Pharmacological Basis of Therapeutics,* 6th ed. New York: Macmillan Publishing Co., 1980.

Helpern, M., and Rho, Y. M. Deaths from narcotism in New York City. *New York State Journal of Medicine,* 1966, *66,* 2391–2408.

Hoffer, A., and Osmond, H. *The Hallucinogens.* New York: Academic Press, 1967.

Hoffmann, F. G. *A Handbook on Drug and Alcohol Abuse: The Biomedical Aspects.* New York: Oxford University Press, 1983.

Jaffe, J. H. Drug addiction and drug abuse. In A. G. Gilman, L. S. Goodman, and A. Gilman (eds.), *The Pharmacological Basis of Therapeutics,* 6th ed. New York: Macmillan Publishing Co., 1980.

———, and Martin, W. R. Opioid analgesics and antagonists. In A. G. Gilman, L. S. Goodman, and A. Gilman (eds.), *The Pharmacological Basis of Therapeutics,* 6th ed. New York: Macmillan, 1980.

Khantzian, E. J. Self-selection and progression in drug dependence. *Psychiatry Digest,* 1975, *36,* 19–22.

———, and McKenna, G. J. Acute toxic and withdrawal reactions associated with drug use and abuse. *Annals of Internal Medicine,* 1979, *90(3),* 361–372.

Lazare, A. Hypothesis testing in the clinical interview. In A. Lazare (ed.), *Outpatient Psychiatry: Diagnosis and Treatment.* Baltimore: Williams and Wilkins, 1979.

Mulé S. J. (ed.). *Cocaine: Chemical, Biological, Clinical, and Social Treatment Aspects.* Cleveland: CRC Press, 1976.

McCarron, M. M., Schulze, B. W., Thompson, G. A., Conder, M. C., and Goetz, W. A. Acute phencyclidine intoxication: incidence of clinical findings in 1,000 cases. *Annals of Emergency Medicine,* 1981(a), *10,* 237–242.

———. Acute phencyclidine intoxication: clinical patterns, complications, and treatment. *Annals of Emergency Medicine,* 1981(b), *10,* 290–297.

Perry, D. C. Heroin and cocaine adulteration. *Pharmchem Newsletter,* 1974, *3*(2), 1–4.

Pevnick, J. S., Jasinski, D. R., and Haentzen, C. A. Abrupt withdrawal from therapeutically administered diazepam: report of a case. *Archives of General Psychiatry,* 1978, *35,* 995–998.

Powell, D. H. A pilot study of occasional heroin users. *Archives of General Psychiatry,* 1973, *28,* 586–594.

Ritchie, J. M. The aliphatic alcohols. In L. S. Goodman and A. Gilman (eds.), *The Pharmacological Basis of Therapeutics.* New York: Macmillan Publishing Co., 1970.

———, and Greene, N. M. Local anesthetics. In A. G. Gilman, L. S. Goodman, and A. Gilman (eds.), *The Pharmacological Basis of Therapeutics,* 6th ed. New York: Macmillan, 1980.

Shaffer, H. Theories of addiction: in search of a paradigm. In H. Shaffer (ed.), *Myths and Realities: A Book About Drug Users.* Boston: Zucker, 1977.

———, and Gambino, B. Addiction paradigms. Part 2: Theory, research, and practice. *Journal of Psychedelic Drugs,* 1979, *11,* 299–304.

Sharp, C. W., and Brehm, M. L. (eds.). *Review of Inhalants: Euphoria to Dysfunction.* National Institute on Drug Abuse Research Monograph No. 15. Rockville, Md.: National Institute on Drug Abuse, 1977.

Siegel, H., Helpern, M., and Ehrenreich, T. The diagnosis of death from intravenous narcotism. *Journal of Forensic Science,* 1966, *11,* 1–16.

Smith, D. E., and Wesson, D. R. *Diagnosis and Treatment of Adverse Reactions to Sedative-Hypnotics.* Rockville, Md.: National Institute on Drug Abuse, 1974.

Surgeon General. *The Health Consequences of Smoking—the Changing Cigarette,* pp. 16–26. Rockville, Md.: U.S. Department of Health and Human Services, 1981.

Weiner, N. Norepinephrine, epinephrine, and the sympathomimetic amines. In A. G. Gilman, L. S. Goodman, and A. Gilman (eds.), *The Pharmacological Basis of Therapeutics,* 6th ed. New York: Macmillan Publishing Co., 1980.

Wurmser, L. *The Hidden Dimension.* New York: Jason Aronson, 1978.

Zinberg, N. E., Harding, W. M., and Winkeller, M. A study of social regulatory mechanisms in controlled illicit drug users. *Journal of Drug Issues,* 1977, *7*(2), 117–133.

Zinberg, N. E., and Jacobson, R. C. The natural history of chipping. *American Journal of Psychiatry,* 1976, *133,* 37–40.

5

Medical Complications Associated with Alcohol Use and the Assessment of Risk of Physical Damage

RUTH SEGAL / BARRY V. SISSON

THE PSYCHIC OR BEHAVIORAL manifestations of acute alcohol intoxication reflect the increasing depression of the central nervous system (CNS) as the blood alcohol level (BAL) rises. The initial euphoria and disinhibition of emotion and conversation is followed by a progressive dulling of perception and impairment of judgement. In intoxication in which drinking continues there is a gradual reduction of the level of consciousness. The chronic drinker who has developed tolerance may be able to conceal these changes much longer than the occasional drinker given the same amounts of alcohol. The chronic drinker often tolerates an alarmingly high BAL without appearing intoxicated or developing symptoms of withdrawal (Hore and Rossall, 1979). Eventually muscular incoordination, depression of reflexes, and sensory disturbances such as double vision, ringing in the ears, and numbness may occur. Generally the face is flushed, the pulse becomes rapid, and the blood pressure is lowered. Loss of consciousness is usually gradual, but coma may also occur at this time. The intoxicated patient needs to be evaluated medically to rule out potential causes of coma such as subdural hematoma from head injury, alcohol-induced hypoglycemia, and epilepsy leading to coma.

Blood Alcohol Level (BAL)

A drinker's blood alcohol level depends on the amount consumed, the rate of drinking, the food in the stomach, and the drinker's size and build. A 154-lb. (70 kg.) man's BAL will reach 0.05 percent by taking two ordinary-sized drinks over a short period. In a 120-lb. (54 kg.) woman, one and a half drinks will do the same. A BAL of 0.05 percent produces impairment in most people. The lethal BAL of human beings is about 0.5 percent. Blood alcohol levels are expressed as the concentration of *absolute* alcohol in the bloodstream. In order to estimate the BAL, the following formula may be used.

$$\text{BAL} = \frac{80 \times \text{g.}}{\text{f} \times \text{w}} = \text{mg./100 ml.}$$

The number 80 is used because blood absorbs 80 percent of the alcohol in body tissue water.

g. = no. grams absolute alcohol consumed by subject	This number can be derived by multiplying the number of standard drinks × 13.6 gs. of alcohol/standard drink.
f = subject's body water expressed as a decimal fraction of body weight/type	Since alcohol is water-soluble but not fat-soluble and since individuals vary in their fat, one must account for this factor by using one of the following decimal fractions in the formula: Lean/Muscular .7 Average .6 Fat .5
w = subject's weight in kilograms	$\frac{\text{Wt. in lbs.}}{2.2} = \text{kg.}$

Let us assume that an *average* individual weighing 150 lb. has consumed four bottles of 5 percent beer in one hour. The entire calculation in this example would be as follows:

g. = no. grams alcohol consumed
$4 \times 13.6 = 54.4$ g.
(average build) = .6

$$\frac{\text{w.} = 150 \text{ lb.}}{2.2 \text{ kg./lb.}} = 68 \text{ kg.}$$

$$\text{BAL} = \frac{80 \times 54.4}{.8 \times 68} = \frac{4352}{41} = \begin{matrix}106 \text{ mg./100 ml.} \\ (106 \text{ mg. \%})\end{matrix}$$

The calculated BAL must then be corrected for the amount of time elapsed since the beginning of the drinking episode. Each hour, the liver reduces the BAL by a factor of 0.015 g./100 ml. (or 15 mg./100 ml.). This is the average rate of metabolism for human beings in a *healthy* state (the rate is slower with liver disease).

Thus, after one hour the BAL would be estimated to be

$$.106 - .015 = .091 \text{ g./100 ml. or } 91 \text{ mg./100 ml.}$$

Characteristics of Chronic Alcohol Use

The acute effects of alcohol are distinct from the chronic or long-term changes it produces in animals and human beings. Whereas the former are immediately and readily apparent, the results of repeated alcohol use over long periods of time are subtle, less readily recognized, and more difficult to define. They are termed "tolerance," "dependence," and "withdrawal" (abstinence syndrome).

Tolerance

Pharmacologically, tolerance is said to develop when the response to the same dose of a drug (in this discussion, alcohol) is decreased with repeated use. Cicero (1980) asserts that tolerance must be demonstrated in two ways: first, there will be reduced effect at the same dose level, and second, a greater dose will be necessary to produce the same effect in the tolerant animal as in one which is alcohol-naive. Cicero (1980) refers to animal and human research to elucidate the concept of "tolerance."

The term "alcohol-naive" is used here in only a relative manner because a person is exposed from early life onward to small amounts of alcohol produced more or less regularly in his own intestine (Blomstrand, 1971; Cicero, 1980). Turner (1980) reported that results of research have shown that an adult, whether an alcohol user or not, produces on average about 18 g. (¾ oz.) of ethanol daily.

Cicero (1980) describes three aspects of tolerance. The first is "acute" tolerance, which develops after a single dose of alcohol and which may be a precursor of "protracted" tolerance. Protracted tolerance develops after a period of chronic alcohol ingestion. The third type of tolerance is "innate" tolerance or "initial sensitivity." There are strong individual, racial, ethnic, and animal-strain differences in sensitivity to the effects of alcohol that may have little to do with tolerance; therefore the term "initial sensitivity" may be more precise. People working with drug- and alcohol-dependent persons are usually referring to protracted tolerance when they describe someone as tolerant to alcohol or a drug (Zinberg, 1981).

An important semantic point should be noted here. Simply because the individual develops tolerance to alcohol or a drug one cannot infer that the body tolerates the substance used in a less harmful fashion. Indeed, the opposite is likely the case. Because tolerance develops, many people drink throughout the day but seldom seem to be intoxicated. These people may work reasonably well and their condition may go unacknowledged until social or physical complications result or they experience withdrawal symptoms. Even though they seldom appear inebriated, the damage is dose-related and cumulative, and is probably related to their total lifetime alcohol consumption.

Dependence

The term "dependence" is used to signify both psychological dependence and physical dependence. Psychological dependence refers to repetitive and excessive self-administration of alcohol due to its reinforcing properties (Cicero, 1980). Furthermore, Cicero believes that the terms "need" or "craving" are as imprecise and inaccurate as the term "psychological dependence," and that it is more precise to speak of "repetitive self-administration behavior." This state is present when alcohol becomes so central to a person's thought, emotions, and activities that it is virtually impossible to stop using it. Edwards (1967) states simply that psychological dependence is present when drinking goes beyond a "take it or leave it affair."

The Physician's Manual of the Addiction Research Foundation (1981) describes psychological dependence as "a psychic drive for a feeling of satisfaction that requires periodic or continuous administration of the drug to produce a desired effect or to avoid discomfort. Psychological dependence is clearly the most important contributing cause of persistent drug use by patients. From the operational point of view, a dependent patient (physically or psychologically) is one who continues to take a drug at any particular time when the specific medical need is no longer present" (or when its use is deleterious). The *Manual* further states: "Physical dependence is a physiological state of adaptation to a drug, normally following the development of tolerance, which results in a characteristic set of withdrawal symptoms (often called the 'abstinence syndrome') when administration of the drug is stopped" (p. 32). It is not usually a factor in the persistence of drug-taking behavior of most patients.

Stated another way by Cicero (1980), dependence refers to a series of behavioral, physiological, and psychological disturbances which occur on abrupt withdrawal after alcohol has been administered for a prolonged period of time. The term "physical dependence" suggests (perhaps incorrectly) that certain biological processes have adapted to the point where alcohol is now a required biochemical factor. There is some evidence but no proof of this. It is therefore better simply to describe and quantify the signs and reactions during withdrawal.

The consistent drinker becomes tolerant to, then dependent on, alcohol over a period of time. Dependence on alcohol, as on other drugs, is not an absolute or fixed phenomenon, but more akin to a dynamic continuum: the user moves in and out of phases depending on the pattern of use and many other factors. Since dpendence is accepted as a normal component of our lives, it is inappropriate to categorically reject persistent drug use by patients as bad. The question to be evaluated, therefore, is not whether dependence can occur but whether dependence in a given case results in physical, psychological, or social harm.

Dr. Harold Kalant (1982, p. 12), in an address to the Canadian Psychological Association in Montreal, concurred that physical dependence generally accompanies tolerance. He said: "I believe they are two manifestations of the same phenomenon, a biologically adaptive phenomenon which occurs in all living organisms and with many types of stimuli. He would prefer to avoid the use of the word "dependence" (other than in a limited sense). The acute effects of ingestion of alcohol or any other psychoactive drug can be classified as aversive and positively reinforcing. This dichotomy of effects depends not only on the substance used but on the user's psyche and the immediate socioenvironmental circumstances. The balance between aversive and reinforcing effects will determine the probability of repeated exposures, and hence the probability of developing tolerance and dependence.

Gilbert (1982), sums up the situation thus: "Each new subtlety that is discovered about the involvement of the environment during drug administration helps to strengthen arguments that drug dependence is not a simple matter of pharmacology and physiology but (also) a complex interaction between the abuser's body and the world around it" (p. 5).

Withdrawal

Isbell et al. (1955) demonstrated that physical dependence developed in human volunteers who consumed alcohol daily for 48 days. This was evidenced by severe withdrawal syndromes, including epileptic seizures and some characteristics of delirium tremens, occurring in the subjects on abrupt cessation of drinking. This finding was confirmed by Mendelson (1964), whose ten subjects, after drinking whisky for twenty-four days, experienced withdrawal tremors and hallucinations on stopping.

The withdrawal symptoms for any drug are generally opposite to the effects induced by the drug itself. However, no one who is physically dependent on alcohol and stops drinking necessarily has the same set of withdrawal symptoms as everyone else. Different phases in withdrawal have been described in association with alcohol. Although they can be separated for purposes of discussion, clinically the distinctions are not so clear. Taken together they constitute a continuum.

The earliest and most common syndrome of withdrawal is tremulousness, which begins within four to six hours after consuming the last drink. It may be accompanied by irritability, retching, nausea, vomiting, and sweating. It is this tremulousness which often prompts the alcoholic to have a morning drink. When the physically dependent person abstains completely, there is a marked increase of tremulousness. The appearance is one of stimulation. The alcoholic startles easily and feels irritable. A fast pulse, sweating, dilated pupils, and a flushed face may appear. Sleeping is difficult. As a rule any significant drinking will produce withdrawal symptoms within six to eight hours after termination of alcohol intake. More serious withdrawal results from heavier drinking. The peak effects of minor withdrawal occur within twelve to forty-eight hours from the last drink.

A second and later syndrome of alcoholic withdrawal, alcoholic hallucinosis, may occur in up to 25 percent of persons withdrawing from alcohol. This syndrome does not imply true hallucinations. Rather, it represents a confusional state in which the person misinterprets existing stimuli. Visual or tactile misperceptions, together with disorientation, give rise to restlessness and sometimes fearfulness, with feelings of paranoia.

Auditory hallucinations accompanying withdrawal are a separate syndrome. Usually these hallucinations are of voices familiar to the patient, probably family and friends. Often they are threatening, demeaning, and invoke guilt. Since they are true hallucinations, the individual thinks they are real and acts as if they are. This can lead to the subject doing harm to himself and others. Auditory hallucinations are more commonly associated with drug use and withdrawal than with alcohol withdrawal.

Another phenomenon of alcohol withdrawal is convulsive seizures. These seizures are major motor seizures; the eyes roll back into the head, the body muscles contract and extend rhythmically, and there is loss of consciousness and breath-holding leading to cyanosis. Seizures are not intrinsically dangerous, and treatment is limited to preventing injury. They usually occur within forty-eight hours of the last drink.

Delirium tremens (DTs) is the most serious form of alcohol withdrawal syndrome. "Delirium" refers to hallucinations, confusion, and disorientation. "Tremens" refers to the heightened autonomic nervous activity producing tremulousness, agitation, fast pulse, and fever. The terrifying nature of the hallucinations and delusions is captured by a slang phrase for the DTs, "the horrors." They may occur as early as one or two days after the last drink and as late as fourteen days. The acute phase can last from two days to a week. Although predictions cannot be made about who will have DTs, the most likely candidate is a daily drinker who has consumed over a fifth of a gallon a day for a week and who has been a heavy drinker for ten years—especially if, during previous periods of abstinence, the person has already had DTs, or convulsions, extreme agitation, marked confusion, and disorientation.

Management of Alcohol Withdrawal. The proper management of withdrawal reactions depends largely on full assessment and early treatment. Full assessment is intended to detect factors that increase the morbidity of withdrawal, and early treatment is intended to prevent signs and symptoms from progressing to a major reaction. The severity of the alcohol withdrawal reaction depends on both the intensity and duration of alcohol consumption. Generally this withdrawal is mild and requires little medical treatment. However, even mild withdrawal may progress to the major withdrawal syndrome of delirium tremens, the mortality of which may be as high as 15 percent. In the large doses taken by alcoholics, alcohol has a depressant action on the central nervous system. When alcohol ingestion is abruptly decreased or discontinued, the compensatory increase in neuronal excitability produces most of the signs and symptoms characteristic of the alcohol withdrawal reaction.

Jacob and Sellers (1977) provide a practical overview of the management of patients in alcohol withdrawal. Mild to moderate reactions can be treated initially in the emergency room and then safely managed at home. Patients with severe uncontrolled withdrawal reactions or complicating problems require hospitalization. General emergency management includes reassurance in surroundings that are well-lighted and quiet, monitoring of vital signs as frequently as clinically indicated, hydration, correction of electrolyte abnormalities, and administration of thiamine, 100 mg. parenterally.

Drug therapy for alcohol withdrawal reactions is intended to relieve symptoms, prevent or treat more serious complications, and prepare the patient for long-term rehabilitation without introducing new drug-dependence problems or therapy-related toxicity. Various drugs are more effective than placebos for accomplishing these objectives. However, the benzodiazepines have replaced most of the older drugs because of their wide margin of safety. They prevent reactions from becoming more severe by decreasing anxiety, restlessness, tremor, and frequency of seizures.

Although phenytoin is usually used, there is uncertainty about its therapeutic and prophylactic value in alcohol withdrawal seizures. Phenytoin need not be continued past the withdrawal period (five days) except in patients with a preexisting seizure disorder. The butyrophenones cause less sedation or hypotension than chlorpromazine and are frequently tried for control of hallucinations, particularly after the risk of seizures has passed. Concurrent use of a benzodiazepine will decrease the risk of haloperidol-induced seizures.

Jacob and Sellers (1977) suggested guidelines for the hospitalization of patients in withdrawal:

1. Presence of a medical or surgical condition requiring treatment.
2. Hallucinations, tachycardia > 100 beats per minute, severe tremor, extreme agitation, or a history of severe withdrawal symptoms.
3. Fever ≥ 38.50° C.
4. Wernicke's encephalopathy, which includes confusion, nystagmus, and opthalmoplegia.
5. Confusion or delirium.
6. Seizures: generalized seizure occurring for the first time in the withdrawal state; focal seizures; status epilepticus; seizures in patients withdrawing from a combination of alcohol and other drugs.
7. Recent history of head injury with loss of consciousness.
8. Social isolation.
9. Patients withdrawing from a combination of alcohol and other drugs, particularly barbiturates and nonbarbiturate hypnotics.

Blackouts

One of the most frequent symptoms accompanying heavy drinking (Forrest, 1983) is disturbances in memory, particularly memory related to the drinking period. The amnesic periods (usually called "blackouts") may extend for as long as several days. More typically, however, the memory disturbance is that of morning amnesia: the drinker is unable to recall the events surrounding the previous night's drinking. During these amnesic periods the person may appear to be fully orientated and in contact with his or her surroundings, and may carry out tasks in an efficient manner.

Medical Complications Associated with Alcohol Abuse

Alcohol abuse is a debilitating chronic condition. It is also one of the Western world's oldest and most prevalent disorders, recognized as such since earliest times. Ethanol exerts its toxic effects on virtually all organ systems. Carried by the bloodstream, it passes the blood-brain and placental barriers and is dispersed into all tissues in relatively uniform concentrations, with the significant exception of fat or adipose tissue. Those organs with the highest rate of circulation receive a greater uptake of alcohol and therefore tend to sustain greater impact or damage. Furthermore, the more highly specialized tissues are more susceptible to toxic effects and are affected earlier and more profoundly than less highly developed cells, where the functional threshold is less critical. It is not surprising, then, that organs such as the brain, liver, peripheral nerves, pancreas, and endocrine glands show early and serious impairment. They sustain this damage in proportion to the BAL and the frequency and duration of their exposure to alcohol.

The exact dosage level which can be said to constitute abuse is not certain, but it is clear that as the knowledge and understanding of the effects of alcohol on the body become more precise, the estimation of dangerous consumption levels becomes progressively lower. Some authorities would maintain that there is no absolutely safe drinking level. Eventually one must determine in practical terms what constitutes hazard. Perhaps the most one can do empirically is distinguish reversible from irreversible damage. This too, however, cannot be differentiated except in a somewhat imprecise fashion, since a minute amount of damage from even a single drinking episode may be permanent. With each successive episode the damage may be cumulative. It is generally agreed that the extent of damage from alcohol consumption is directly related to the total lifetime consumption.

There are many confounding factors, however, which upset this deceptively simple formula. Some heavy drinkers of many years' duration appear to go relatively unscathed, while others develop complications early (e.g., after five years) in their drinking careers. Some develop brain damage; others, liver disease; still others, both. The reasons for this are simply not known, but numerous hypotheses have been advanced by different investigators. Among the most likely variables postulated are nutritional factors; immunological (protective) mechanisms, which vary between blood groups and races; and genetic differences. Verifying these physiological claims is likely to take considerable time.

Certainly the toxic effects of alcohol in chronic alcoholics who already have significant changes in cellular functioning are bound to be more serious than the acute effects of drinking in "normal" individuals. For clinical purposes the effects of alcohol and their severity are dose-dependent, even though what constitutes an excess dose will vary considerably between individuals. Since excess alcohol use leads to a variety of specific pathological and functional consequences, this section outlines, in a system-oriented fashion, the major alcohol-related problems.

The Gastrointestinal System

Beverage alcohol enters the body and is absorbed into the bloodstream largely through the upper intestine. While small amounts of alcohol may be absorbed through the buccal mucosa and more from the stomach, it is mainly absorbed through the small intestine—duodenum, jejunum, and ileum (Holt, 1980). Its effects on the mouth and esophagus are transient and negligible. However, the incidence of cancer of the esophagus is increased when more than 40 grams of alcohol are consumed per day (Péquignot and Tuyns, 1975), but this is difficult to separate from the effects of tobacco use and the urban environment (Schoenberg, Bailar, and Fraumeni, 1971).

In the stomach and small intestines alcohol acts in a variety of ways. Even moderate amounts can disturb and alter the normal functioning of this system. Alcohol inhibits peristalsis, the muscular contractions that pass food through the intestinal tract (possibly by exerting a relaxant effect on the smooth muscle). Alcohol tends to stimulate the secretion of hydrochloric acid and the release of pepsin, a digestive enzyme. This combination, in the absence of food, appears to irritate the gastric mucosa (stomach lining). The mucosa becomes hyperemic and swollen, and small erosions appear in the distended cells, with consequent bleeding. Symptoms—if there are any—vary from severe heartburn and gnawing pain to nausea or vomiting, possibly with some blood-streaked mucus. Despite the production of gastritis with erosions and bleeding in the stomach, there is little evidence to suggest that alcohol causes or predisposes an individual to peptic ulcers, though drinking may aggravate an existing ulcer.

Gastroesophageal reflux, the regurgitation of stomach contents backward past the cardia (the muscle at the junction of the stomach and esophagus), may give rise to similar symptoms. When this becomes chronic, ulcerations of the lower esophagus may result. If neglected, scarring and stricture of the area may follow. Nausea with retching and vomiting may be so severe as to cause mechanical tears in the esophageal lining and bring on massive bleeding (the Mallory-Weiss syndrome). If, in addition, the alcoholic has esophageal varices as a result of cirrhosis and portal hypertension, rupture of the veins causes a hemorrhage, which may be fatal.

Although there are no specific diseases of the small and large intestines directly attributable to alcohol abuse, diarrhea frequently occurs and hemorrhoids are common. The diarrhea is thought to result in part from the impairment of water and electrolyte absorption from the jejunum. Coupled with the malabsorption of water and electrolytes there may be malabsorption of vitamin B_{12} (cyanocobalamin), especially in alcoholics with severe pancreatic disease. In alcoholics with inadequate dietary intake there is a more profound disturbance in absorption. Whether poor nutrition predisposes to malabsorption or vice versa is a complex and not yet fully understood issue. Undoubtedly both malabsorption and insufficient dietary intake contribute to the multiple vitamin deficiencies found in alcoholics. Other factors such as inability to utilize nutrients at the cellular level and inability to store these substances as a result of hepatocellular damage possibly play a major role in the production of malnutrition. The evidence for this is that simply supplying the lacking nutrients does not necessarily restore nutritional balance.

The Pancreas

The pancreas is both an exocrine and endocrine gland. Its exocrine secretions (proteolytic enzymes), which empty into the duodenum, are responsible in part for the breakdown of proteins into amino acids: the basic body tissue–building elements. Its major endocrine function is the production of insulin from special cells in the Islets of Langerhans. Insulin is secreted into the bloodstream in response to a rise in the blood sugar level after food is eaten.

Pancreatitis (inflammation of the pancreas) occurs frequently in those alcoholics who usually present with recurrent attacks of upper abdominal pain, often with nausea and severe vomiting. (A significant proportion may present without any history of preceding pain.) It is not likely that a single drinking binge in nonalcoholics will produce an attack of pancreatitis. Usually damage from chronic drinking precedes an episode.

Pancreatitis is classified as "acute" or "acute relapsing" if the gland returns clinically and functionally to normal when the cause of trouble is eliminated; and as "chronic" or "chronic relapsing"—the usual pancreatic disease of alcoholism—whom anatomical and functional damage persists. The mechanism(s) whereby alcohol produces pancreatic injury are not fully understood. One explanation (Sarles et al., 1979) suggests that obstruction of the pancreatic exocrine ducts by proteinacious plugs produces retention of pancreatic secretions and autodigestion of the blocked glandular segments. The ensuing changes in the gland include local inflammation with swelling, necrosis (tissue death), fibrotic scarring, and occasional hemorrhage. When 90 percent of the gland is destroyed, pancreatic insufficiency, with steatorrhea, weight loss, and diabetes, usually follows. About 75 percent of patients with chronic pancreatitis in the U.S.A. are alcoholics (Fairclough and Clark, 1980).

The diagnosis is suggested by a history of upper abdominal pain, often with nausea and vomiting, and the presence of an elevated serum amylase. Tests may show elevated liver function, and there may be mild jaundice. Radiologically, the presence of calcifications in the pancreas strongly suggests chronic pancreatitis. A CAT scan (using computerized axial tomography) or ultrasonic scan, gastric barium meal X-ray, and gall bladder studies are occasionally necessary to rule out other conditions with similar presentation.

Alcoholic Liver Disease and Its Complications

Alcoholic liver disease is a major physical illness. The liver is an extremely versatile and complex organ performing many functions. It is responsible for the breakdown of wastes or end-products of metabolism, and neutralization of toxic substances. It manufactures essential proteins, including clotting factors. It also produces bile, a digestive juice. It stores certain vitamins such as B_{12} (essential for red blood cell metabolism) and glycogen (sugar) to help regulate the blood sugar level. It stores and burns fats, its main fuel. Impairment of its function, therefore, can cause a wide range of adverse and far-reaching effects.

Liver disease occurs because the presence of alcohol disturbs the metabolic machinery of the liver. Metabolizing alcohol is always a priority liver function. Hence, when alcohol is present, the liver is "distracted" from other normal and necessary functions. It is a liver enzyme, alcohol dehydrogenase, which begins the detoxification of alcohol to acetaldehyde; then to acetic acid, and then to carbon dioxide and water. Apart from the toxicity of alcohol alone, another mechanism in the production of liver damage—hypoxia—has been postulated (Israel et al., 1977). Chronic alcohol consumption leads to a hyperthyroid-like increased rate of alcohol metabolism (in humans and other animals) without a corresponding increase in T_3 or T_4. This appears to be due to an increased rate of general metabolism of the liver and an increased liver mass. These factors, and many other conditions which occur in alcoholics more often than in the general population, increase the liver's demand for oxygen, making it more vulnerable to a variety of conditions that reduce oxygen availability. It is suggested that hypoxia or ischaemia resulting from these conditions may play a role in the production of liver lesions in the alcoholic. However, the use of anti-metabolic drugs (anti-thyroid medications) such as propylthiouracil may reduce the risk of liver damage.

Alcoholic liver disease is classified into three types, which are distinct from each other but tend to overlap: (1) fatty liver, (2) alcoholic hepatitis, and (3) cirrhosis. Liver biopsies may show evidence of one type only or may have characteristics of any combination of them. A probable explanation for this is that the dynamic processes of liver cell destruction, healing, and fat storage occur simultaneously.

Fatty Liver. In this condition (the commonest response to alcohol) the liver becomes infiltrated with fat, which is stored while the liver "burns off" alcohol. The source of the fat is either dietary or fatty (adipose) tissue mobilized from other sites in the body. It occurs whenever 30 percent or more of the dietary calories are in the form of alcohol. Fatty liver is the most prevalent form of alcoholic disorder and may occur in minor form even in nonalcoholics after an atypical binge. The most severe forms, naturally, occur in alcoholics who drink heavily and steadily (daily) without giving the liver any respite.

Recognition of fatty liver may be difficult, especially in mild forms and when there are no symptoms. Generally there may be diffuse smooth enlargement of the liver with variable overlying tenderness. Jaundice may be present in a small proportion of cases. Liver function tests vary from normal to abnormal depending on the extent of the fatty infiltration. Most cases resolve spontaneously with abstinence. Very rarely they may terminate fatally, especially if drinking is continued.

Alcoholic Hepatitis. Alcoholic hepatitis is a more sinister form of liver disease, which often follows a severe prolonged bout of drinking. Usually it is superimposed on an already damaged alcoholic liver. There may be no intervening stage of fatty liver. Microscopically the liver shows all the changes of inflammation, with swelling and necrosis (death) of some liver cells and the presence of white blood cells around them. A very characteristic finding is the presence of Mallory bodies—a hyaline substance deposited in the cells.

Patients with alcoholic hepatitis present a wide array of symptoms depending on the severity of the inflammation. Symptoms may be minimal and the disorder unrecognized by the patient except as a mild flulike indisposition which clears almost entirely with abstinence. With clinically significant hepatitis, however, the symptoms begin just after or during a heavy drinking episode. The liver is enlarged, and there is abdominal pain, vomiting, weakness, low-grade fever, fatigability, and loss of appetite. An elevated white blood cell count is common and jaundice is very frequent. More severe cases may present the additional signs of ascites (fluid in the abdominal cavity) and weight loss. There may be enlargement of the spleen and gastrointestinal hemorrhaging. Other causes of jaundice must be excluded, including viral hepatitis and cancer of the pancreas, and a history of heavy drinking is necessary for the diagnosis. Elevation of the liver enzymes and serum bilirubin and prolongation of the prothrombin time are usually present, but are nonspecific in differentiating hepatitis from the other forms of alcoholic liver disease. They are probably most useful in monitoring the course of the disease. With strict abstinence from any alcohol, the provision of proper nutrition, enforced rest, and treatment/prevention of complications, the majority of cases of alcoholic hepatitis will recover completely. There is a fatal outcome in a sizeable proportion of the most severe cases. Some will progress to cirrhosis.

Alcoholic Cirrhosis. The tertiary, or end, stage of alcoholic liver disease, often preceded by fatty liver and alcoholic hepatitis, is cirrhosis. With it there is widespread destruction of liver cells, which are replaced by fibrous (scar) tissue. As a consequence of this destruction—which is believed to be caused by the direct toxic effect of alcohol on the liver—a vast reduction in the overall functional capacity of the liver occurs. Cirrhosis is not an all-or-nothing phenomenon, and persisting islands of viable liver cells exist in inverse proportion to the extent of scarring (Wooddell, 1984). As previously stated, adjacent areas of the liver may show changes of fatty infiltration and hepatitis. The fibrosis and scarring is likely to be irreversible. As fibrosis proceeds, contraction of the fibrous tissue produces a smaller, harder, nontender liver with small or large nodules on its surface representing surviving cells proliferating to compensate for loss of liver function. While many alcoholics will die from liver failure or hemorrhage from esophageal varices before this stage is reached (particularly if they continue drinking even modest amounts of alcohol), complete abstinence from all forms of alcohol markedly improves the outlook for survival.

Clinically cirrhotics present to physicians with enlarged liver, variable tenderness over the liver, loss of appetite, weight loss, nausea, and fatigue. In some cases symptoms may be absent. In more advanced stages the liver has shrunk to the point where it cannot be felt. There may be evidence of liver failure manifested by jaundice and/or ascites or by the appearance of a confusional or comatose state (hepatic encephalopathy), a complication of cirrhosis. Liver function tests may all be normal or abnormal depending on whether the cirrhosis is "active" or "inactive." Occasionally the diagnosis is first made when a hemorrhage from weakened esophageal varices sends the victim to the hospital.

Though the foregoing makes one suspicious of cirrhosis, the exact diagnosis may only be made by liver biopsy or at necropsy. The overall five-year survival rate of patients with diagnosed alcoholic cirrhosis is 50 percent. Those without the complications of jaundice, ascites, or significant gastrointestinal hemorrhage, who also cease drinking entirely, have a much greater five-year survival expectation. The treatment of cirrhosis requires abstention from alcohol, correction of malnutrition, watchful, supportive care to forestall or correct the many intercurrent incidental diseases (particularly infection) to which alcoholics are prone, and prompt, adroit management of the specific complications of cirrhosis.

Complications of Cirrhosis. With the onset and progress of cirrhotic scarring in the liver, there often develops resistance or impedance to its venous circulation. Whereas vessels from the intestines normally carry nutrients, toxins, and other substances to the liver for disposal, there is now back pressure from compressed vessels in the liver as well as resistance to venous outflow from the liver to the inferior vena cava and hence to the heart. In short, the hemodynamics of the liver are disturbed, resulting in increased portal pressure, or "portal hypertension" (not to be confused with systemic hypertension). It is as a direct result of this portal hypertension that the main complicating conditions of cirrhosis occur. These include: (1) ascites, (2) esoaphageal varices, and (3) hepatic or portal encephalopathy. While these conditions are very serious, they are not necessarily of themselves fatal or irreversible.

Ascites, the presence of excessive abnormal free fluid in the abdominal cavity, occurs in up to three-quarters of patients with cirrhosis (Ratnoff and Patek, 1942; Powell and Klatsin, 1968), but other causes of ascites must be excluded. The abdomen becomes progressively distended and taut as the fluid accumulates. The process is complex and requires the existence of portal hypertension, hypoproteinema (low serum protein) and water and sodium retention (related to increased aldosterone production) to develop. It involves a buildup of extracellular fluid in the liver and increased hepatic lymph flow. The end result is the seepage of fluid under pressure from the surface of the liver into the abdominal cavity.

This ascitic fluid provides an ideal nutrient for any bacteria which may travel there. When bacteria invade the ascitic fluid, a "bacterial peritonitis" develops. When this occurs without any apparent source of infection, it is referred to as spontaneous bacterial peritonitis. The ascitic patient usually has abdominal pain, tenderness, and fever, although signs may be minimal. About 50 percent of cases of bacterial peritonitis terminate fatally (Gerding, Hall, and Schierl, 1977). The treatment of ascites includes sodium and fluid restriction, and diuretics combined with watchful support and careful monitoring of weight (fluid) loss. For peritonitis, appropriate antibiotics are given.

Esophageal varices, or varicose veins in the lower esophagus (as well as those in the stomach and rectum), develop with cirrhosis as a result of a rerouting of blood from the liver due to the back pressure there. The veins become dilated, weak, and thin-walled from increased venous pressure and are prone to rupture, especially if they become eroded and/or if the patient retches violently causing a sudden surge in pressure. The varices may be found by esophagoscopy when suspected, but sometimes they are discovered only when they rupture and the patient vomits fresh blood. The bleeding may vary from a small transient leak to a massive and sometimes fatal hemorrhage. The impairment of the blood clotting process due to lack of essential factors which the diseased liver cannot produce can make the hemorrhage more profuse and difficult to control.

The management of this emergency requires involvement of the surgical service from the start. The initial treatment is medical and includes: the immediate establishment of an intravenous line; cross-matching and securing blood for possible transfusion; constant monitoring of vital signs; passing a D-tube; ice-water lavage; measures (vasopressin) to reduce portal hypertension. According to Mullin (1980), the mortality rate in patients with such bleeds remains near 50 percent. An acute hemorrhage may precipitate hepatic encephalopathy in patients with chronic liver disease, and this may result in death, even if the hemorrhage is controlled.

Hepatic encephalopathy (also called *precoma* and *coma*) is a diseased state of the brain which complicates liver disease. It is not restricted to alcoholic liver disease. The signs and symptoms are often subtle and vary widely in degree. Mental functioning is progressively impaired and is characterized by emotional and behavioral changes covering a wide spectrum from slowing of mental processes, apathy, variable euphoria or depression, sleep disturbance, increasing confusion, and deepening level of unconsciousness to coma. The syndrome may be accompanied by electroencephalographic (EEG) changes, fetor hepaticus (liver breath or smell), and asterixis, a flapping tremor of the hyperextended wrists when the arms are outstretched. It may be precipitated by hemorrhage, excess protein intake, infection, porto-caval shunt surgery, electrolyte disturbances, or excess diuresis. Management requires the removal/treatment of any precipitating or perpetuating cause; discontinuation of any narcotic, sedative, or tranquilizer drugs; elimination of protein ingestion (initially); reduction of intestinal ammonia using neomycin or lactulose; and complete abstention from alcohol.

The biochemical mechanisms giving rise to hepatic encephalopathy are complex and not entirely clear. Ammonia produced in the intestine by bacterial action on protein may accumulate in the blood when impaired liver function fails to reduce it to urea for excretion. This rise in serum ammonia, however, does not occur in all cases of hepatic encephalopathy and may be simply one biochemical trigger for a complicated chain of chemical events in the brain.

The Brain and Nervous System

The effects of chronic ingestion of alcohol on the brain are apparent both immediately and over the long term. Some effects are transient and others are irreversible (Zimberg, 1982). It has been suggested that even one or two drinks may cause the death of some brain cells. There is no documented proof of this, but the thought of the possibility is sobering enough. How fast irreversible damage occurs is strictly a guess (except in fatal alcohol poisoning!).

Nerve cells, being among the most highly developed in the body, are also somewhat more susceptible to alcohol toxicity than cells of more primitive origin. Chronic excessive alcohol use may lead to varying degrees of dementia and organic brain dysfunction. The mechanisms by which the brain is injured through alcohol abuse are diverse. These may be direct toxic effects; metabolic, biochemical, traumatic, or nutritional effects; or combinations of any of the foregoing.

Acute intoxication has already been discussed. The common misconception that alcohol is a stimulant arises from the lay observations that increased talkativeness and motor activity, as well as euphoria, accompany mild intoxication. In fact these behaviors result from alcohol depressing the higher cortical and (critical) functions of the forebrain, thereby releasing from their inhibitory influence the more primitive areas of the brain stem and midbrain.

The effects of a drinking binge of a day or two may not be completely resolved even as long as several weeks after abstinence. Particularly affected are short-term memory, visuomotor and visuospatial coordination, and abstract reasoning. The longer the excessive drinking continues, the more refractory these changes become. Late in the alcoholic's drinking career may come Wernicke's syndrome or Korsakoff's psychosis or the Wernicke-Korsakoff syndrome.

The Wernicke-Korsakoff Syndrome. Clinically, a person with Wernicke's syndrome (encephalopathy) usually appears confused, apprehensive, and semidelirious. A characteristic dysfunction of the eye muscles called "nystagmus," which causes jerky, unsteady eye movements, is present. There may be paralysis of some eye muscles resulting in a cross-eyed or wall-eyed (divergent foci) appearance. Ataxia (uncoordinated, unsteady walking) due to peripheral nerve or cerebellar damage is present. This syndrome is thought to be caused primarily by thiamine (vitamin B_1) deficiency. Certainly its manifestations often respond dramatically to the parenteral administration of thiamine within hours. Thiamine deficiency occurs in alcoholics for several reasons: (1) inadequate dietary intake; (2) poor intestinal absorption; (3) inability of the body to utilize it; (4) in advanced cirrhosis, interference with the metabolism of thiamine. Failure to obtain treatment for Wernicke's encephalopathy may result in death; if not, the more permanent, indeed irreversible changes of Korsakoff's psychosis may ensue.

Korsakoff's psychosis presents a somewhat different picture. It is marked by severe memory loss with confabulation. Because of severe brain dysfunction, the patient cannot process and store information. To fill in memory gaps the person fabricates stories (confabulation) which vary with each repetition. In addition, there is general disorientation and confusion, with overall intellectual deterioration probably due to widespread rather than focal brain damage. Inability to learn and retain new material is characteristic. There may be evidence of peripheral neuropathy with the Wernicke-Korsakoff syndrome. Recovery or improvement in Korsakoff's psychosis, even with the best treatment, is the exception. Patients who suffer from it will probably require permanent nursing home care.

Chronic Brain Syndrome (nonspecific brain damage). A variety of less distinct clinical changes may occur independently of the foregoing syndromes. Though these changes may focus more in one or another area of the brain, they are widespread, and they may be accompanied by few, if any, obvious signs of intellectual deterioration. They are real nevertheless. When damage focuses mainly in the cerebellum (a late complication), the patient develops a slow, broad-based lurching gait, as if he or she is about to fall over; however, there may be no obvious cognitive or mental dysfunction. The development of more sophisticated neuropsychological tests tend to substantiate the view that there is evidence of widespread damage of a subtle and not readily apparent nature. Standard tests of brain dysfunction often do not reveal this. Overall intellectual deterioration is not seen until very late in the course of alcoholism. The IQ of most alcoholics remains relatively constant. There occur, however, other specific defects, including decreased ability to solve problems, a lessened ability to perform complex psychomotor tasks, and a decreased ability to use/grasp abstract concepts. Most of the impaired function is not obvious.

The advent of the computerized axial tomography (CAT) scan has greatly augmented former methods in revealing the anatomical concomitants of this type of damage. The EEG is often normal and air encephalography may show little change. According to Mullin (1980), CAT scans have confirmed that there is an actual reduction of brain volume in up to 50 percent of long-term alcoholics. The exact nature of this change is not certain; that is, whether the "shrinkage" of the brain is due to atrophy and necrosis (death of brain cells) or to a reduction in connective tissue substance is not clear. With prolonged abstinence, however, improvement often occurs and the brain volume may return to near normal. Improvement in brain function may also occur.

Subdural Hematoma. While not a direct consequence of alcoholism, subdural hematoma is a very common complication of drinking, resulting from a fall or a blow to the head (often trivial) while the individual is intoxicated or undergoing withdrawal. Alcohol-induced brain atrophy is believed to predispose to it. If recognized in time, it is usually completely curable; without surgical intervention it may be fatal or produce varying degrees of permanent brain damage and disability.

Anatomically it is a hemorrhage beneath the outer fibrous brain covering (the "dura mater"), followed by clot formation which produces pressure on and displacement of the adjacent brain area, with subsequent damage or death of brain tissue. It results from rupture of the veins passing from the inner coverings and brain to the dura mater. The hemorrhage may be worse in alcoholics because of their load's reduced clotting ability.

The head injury may not be apparent and the incident that caused it may not be recalled by the patient; symptoms which may be similar to those of other brain syndromes may be obscured by intoxication and may not appear for widely varying intervals following the incident. Persistent or increasing headache is the hallmark symptom; this, coupled with signs of increased intracranial pressure, confusion, dizziness, and a unilateral dilated pupil, should alert one to the possibility of this problem. The occurrence of unusual behavioral and personality changes may partially obscure the situation, but subdural hematoma should always be suspected in one who presents as described. A deepening level of consciousness is a sinister sign requiring prompt action, while oscillations in the above-mentioned symptoms should increase one's suspicion. A CAT brain scan usually confirms the diagnosis. Surgical evacuation of the clot is effective in most cases.

Peripheral Neuropathy. Nerve tissue other than that in the brain is susceptible to damage from chronic alcohol use and is frequently seen in cases of Wernicke/Korsakoff syndrome. Clinically this is most commonly found in the feet and legs. Less frequently the hands and forearms may be affected. The patient notes numbness and tingling, burning, or a pins-and-needles sensation in these areas. Less often a painful toothache-type pain occurs. These symptoms may be accompanied by hyper- or hypo-aesthesia on testing the skin. Loss or reduction of vibration sense, tested by using a tuning fork, is usual. The local deep tendon reflexes may be reduced or absent in the affected limbs. Varying degrees of weakness in the muscles may be present (see "Alcoholic Myopathy," pp. 160–161), as well as evidence of muscle wasting.

While the cause of the neuropathy is largely nutritional (lack of thiamine) due to inadequate intake, absorption, or utilization, a direct toxic action of alcohol on the nerve cells may also play a part. In any event, most mild to moderate cases respond well to abstinence and the administration of thiamine. In advanced cases residual weakness and diminished sensation with or without muscle wasting may persist.

The Heart and Cardiovascular System

The means by which alcohol affects the heart and its functioning are not yet fully elaborated. It is possible that several mechanisms are involved, including (1) a direct toxic effect on the muscle fibers; (2) a direct effect of alcohol on nerve impulse conduction in the heart; and (3) a deficiency of thiamine, which may also affect the innervation of the heart (see the preceding discussion of neuropathy). The biochemical and histopathological mechanisms by which these actions may occur are exceedingly complicated and beyond the scope of this text.

Alcoholic Cardiomyopathy. This term implies disease of the heart muscle. Excessive alcohol is responsible for this uncommon form of heart disease (Regan et al., 1969; Forrest, 1978). It is a serious condition in which the heart muscle is weakened, and it is characterized by some degree of congestive heart failure in alcoholics, usually fifty years of age or under, who have no other cause of heart disease and in whom the condition reverses with permanent abstinence and prolonged rest. The ECG shows nonspecific changes. The symptoms include shortness of breath, fatigue, and occasionally cyanosis and peripheral edema. There may be palpitations (irregular heart rhythms) and enlargement (dilation) of the weakened heart muscle. In addition there may be pulmonary edema (fluid in the lungs) and an enlarged (congested) liver. The outcome is usually fatal if drinking continues, but fair to good with abstinence from alcohol. The true incident of the disease is unknown, and it may exist in subclinical (symptomless) form in many alcoholics.

Beriberi Heart Disease. This is a more specific form of heart problem which produces congestive heart failure. It is related to thiamine deficiency and usually responds dramatically to large doses of the vitamin if there are no significant complicating factors. Virtually not seen in alcoholics in Western culture, the disease is mainly found in persons undergoing gradual starvation on diets which are bereft of thiamine.

Hypertension. This condition, persistent elevation of blood pressure, is more prevalent in alcoholics than in the general population (Dyer et al., 1977; Klatsky et al., 1974; Ashley and Rankin, 1979). Mullin (1980), reports a correlation of hypertension with moderate to high alcohol intake which is apparently independent of sex, age, race, smoking, obesity, or previous heavy drinking. It would seem probable that this form of hypertension is reversible on cessation of drinking. In view of the high morbidity and mortality from hypertension, further research and public education in this area are needed.

Coronary Artery Disease. In this condition there is atheromatous narrowing of the arteries supplying the heart muscle. Extra stress (exercise, fright, etc.) placed on the heart in this state gives rise to coronary insufficiency, or "angina pectoris," characterized by chest pain. Further narrowing of an artery occludes the blood supply to that part of the heart, which consequently dies. This is in essence a coronary occlusion, or "heart attack." If the patient survives, the dead muscle cells are in time replaced with fibrous scar tissue constituting a myocardial infarction.

Recent studies have produced somewhat conflicting evidence on the question of whether alcohol in moderate to light use may play a protective role against the development of coronary artery disease (Klatsky et al., 1974; Dyer et al., 1977; Hennekens, 1979; Yano, Rhoads, and Kagan, 1977); the matter is still contentious. However, there is no doubt that heavier drinkers are at greater risk for circulatory disorders and higher mortality from all causes, including coronary artery disease, than are light drinkers or abstainers.

Cardiac Dysrhythmias. Popularly referred to as "palpitations," these are either intermittent or sustained episodes of abnormal heart rhythms. They may take the form of arrhythmias (irregularities of rhythm) or a slowing (bradycardia) or speeding (tachycardia) of the heart. Dysrhythmias may be induced by amounts of alcohol as low as two or three standard drinks, but this occurs infrequently in a healthy heart. The extent of the roles of nicotine and caffeine (heart muscle irritants) in the production of dysrhythmias is difficult to separate from that of alcohol. The mechanism by which alcohol evokes a change in the heart rhythm is unclear. It is known that alcohol disrupts the electrodynamics of the nerves in the heart which govern rate and rhythm by affecting conduction time and action potential duration (Gould et al., 1978). There may be other mechanisms involved. The drinker may experience "palpitations" (a fluttery sensation in the mid-chest) of varying duration when the heart skips beats or beats rapidly. Minor manifestations may go unnoticed and only appear incidentally on an ECG. Most dysrhythmias are transient, harmless, and disappear shortly with abstention. Occasionally, in the presence of an underlying heart disorder, a serious or fatal dysrhythmia (ventricular tachycardia) may be provoked. Such events may be a cause of sudden unexplained deaths among alcoholics.

The Hematological System (*and Infection*)

Blood and the vascular tree constitute the body's main transportation network. The blood carries oxygen to the tissues and removes waste products of combustion to the kidneys and lungs for disposal. It also carries nutrients and hormones to the cells and protects the body from infection with the white blood cells it contains. The platelets and other components protect against hemorrhage.

In chronic alcoholics white blood cell production in the bone marrow is often suppressed and the function of the white blood cells in phagocytizing (surrounding) invading organisms is impaired, as is chemotaxis (the movement of white cells at the site of infection). Hence alcoholics are especially vulnerable to contracting infectious diseases and have increased difficulty combating them. Platelet production in the bone marrow is depressed from acute exposure to alcohol; this quickly reverts with abstinence.

Other hematological problems in the alcoholic population include the occurrence of several types of anemia. Iron deficiency anemia secondary to acute or chronic blood loss and aggravated by prolongation of bleeding time is not uncommon. The changes which may occur in the blood with cirrhosis include decreased coagulation factors, thrombocyctopenia (low platelet levels), and depression of thrombopoiesis (platelet formation). Macrocytosis occurs in many forms of liver disease, including alcoholic liver disorders. In alcoholics with a folate (folic acid) deficiency from faulty nutrition a megaloblastic anemia may occur. Beer drinkers are less likely to develop this type of anemia, since beer contains adequate amounts of folate whereas wine and spirits contain only traces. A hemolytic anemia may occur in association with cirrhosis due to a shorter red-cell life span, which may be only half that in people with normal livers.

The Endocrine System

The endocrine, or ductless, glands manufacture hormones, chemicals essential for many different body functions, e.g., growth, metabolism, and sexual reproduction and function. These chemicals are excreted directly into the bloodstream in response to demand and exert their effects on various target tissues throughout the body.

Alcohol alters the normal systemic hormonal balance. The main functions affected are the sexual ones (including sexual performance and secondary sexual attributes—especially in men) and carbohydrate metabolism. The biochemical mechanisms responsible for these changes are multiple, very complex, and not yet fully elucidated. However, with regard to sexual function, their net result in men is reduced libido (sexual arousability), testicular atrophy, reduction or loss of production of spermatozoa, reduced growth of secondary sexual hair, and gynecomastia. The probable cause is that alcohol suppresses production of testosterone (the male sex hormone) in the testes; in cirrhotics there is not only a decrease in testosterone but an increase in estrogen production.

In addition to the foregoing, an alcohol-related pseudo–Cushing's syndrome—with typical moon face, proximal muscle wasting, truncal obesity, bruising, hypertension, buffalo hump, and abdominal striations—may occur. This can only be differentiated from true Cushing's syndrome when with abstinence the symptoms and signs revert to normal. The condition results from a disturbance of the hormonal balance in the hypothalamic-pituitary-adrenocortical axis and is characterized, as is true Cushing's syndrome, by impairment of glucose metabolism, elevated plasma cortisol levels, and other biochemical changes. The pseudo–Cushing's syndrome may reappear with resumption of drinking.

Malnutrition

Nutritional deficiencies are common in alcoholic patients, and the consequences affect all systems of the body (Forrest, 1978). However, the mechanisms of tissue injury caused by alcohol have not been completely elaborated. Chronic alcoholism–related damage is a major cause of long-term hospitalization and disability, while lesser degrees of injury frequently are undocumented and often disregarded. The existence and importance of such changes may become more apparent with the greater availability of more sophisticated methods of measuring changes, such as computerized axial tomography. Although the exact mechanism by which alcohol causes tissue injury remains uncertain, it is clear that nutrition does play a key role in limiting and repairing the induced damage. A comprehensive, detailed discussion of this topic is provided by Thompson, Ral, and Majumdar (1980).

Alcoholic Myopathy

Geller (1981) describes three types of muscle disease in the alcoholic: acute, subclinical, and chronic alcoholic myopathy. The onset of the acute form, as first described by Hed (1955), is usually abrupt and dramatic, evidenced by muscular pain, aching, or cramps; marked tenderness on palpation; and muscle swelling. Muscle weakness may be limited to only one limb or group of muscles, or it may involve multiple muscle groups, and it may even be diffuse. There may be acute muscle necrosis, with resultant myoglobinuria and renal failure.

The syndrome of subclinical alcoholic myopathy also exists. According to Ekbom et al. (1964), it can be identified by elevation of specific serum enzymes, abnormal electromyographic patterns, and minor but significant histopathologic alterations. The incidence of subclinical alcoholic myopathy is unknown, because cases are only recognized when individuals are subjected to study. However, it has been estimated that 38 percent of chronic alcoholics have this disease (Oh, 1972).

In chronic alcoholic myopathy, subjects present with progressive muscle weakness which has been gradual and insidious in its development and is painless. Muscle involvement is generally symmetrical, and the proximal muscles, particularly those of the lower extremities, are the most conspicuously involved. Many alcoholics have no symptoms, but do have evidence of myopathy demonstrable as muscle tenderness or by electromyography or biochemical derangements. Muscle atrophy may be prominent and is usually more severe proximally, but may be diffuse.

The relation between the acute and chronic forms is not clear. Astrom (1970) commented on the evidence in this regard by emphasizing that the acute and chronic forms of alcoholic myopathy are clinically and pathogenetically discrete entities, although they may occasionally coexist. Complete removal of alcohol from the diet is the most effective therapeutic approach. Recovery is usually prompt and eventually complete. In chronic alcoholics, the duration of weakness after cessation of alcoholic intake may be proportional to the length of time of alcoholism (Tarter and Jones, 1971).

Hereditary and Genetic Factors

Hore (1981) summarizes the work of a number of investigators. In discussing genetic factors and alcoholism one could çonsider the inheritance of a specific metabolic syndrome or the inheritance of basic personality types. Evidence relating to genetic influences has come from attempts to link genetic theories with genetic markers, family studies, twin studies, and studies in relation to adoptees.

It is generally agreed that families of alcoholics have an increased incidence of alcoholism compared with families of nonalcoholics, but whether this trend is genetically determined or acquired cannot be stated. The genetic studies carried out in adoptees which Hore (1981) discusses suggest that some genetic factor is important in the etiology of alcoholism, although the genetic mechanism is obscure, and whether it is specific or related to nonspecific variables remains unclear. In the studies of adoptees (Goodwin et al., 1973; Schukit, Goodwin, and Winokur, 1972) the children from alcoholic biological parents who were subsequently adopted were found to become alcoholic significantly more often than a controlled group of adopted children. It was also found that the children of alcoholic parents developed alcoholism at an almost identical rate, whether they had been reared by an alcoholic or nonalcoholic biological parent.

The response to alcohol varies widely between individuals and between all species. It is also clear that there are differences between races. Cutaneous facial flushing, nausea, headache, and tachycardia sometimes occur in about 75 percent of Orientals who ingest even small amounts of alcohol (Goodwin, 1979). This reaction indicates a physiological intolerance to alcohol and may in part account for the low rate of alcoholism among Orientals.

Assessment of Risk of Physical Damage

The Toxicity of Ethanol

While it is important to understand the medical complications and the various phenomena associated with alcohol use, it is also necessary to understand the relationship between these and levels of consumption, and to translate the information into practical guidelines for use by persons in the areas of assessment and counseling. The estimation of physical risk is based on information collected about pattern of use, frequency, style of drinking, level of consumption, other drug use, gender, body type, weight, and general health.

As with any drug, the acute effects of alcohol depend on the amount taken at one time, the previous experience of the user (tolerance), and the circumstances. The acute behavioral effects of consuming different amounts are well known to experienced drinkers. Also, the serious effects of heavy, regular consumption on physical health have been outlined in the earlier part of the chapter. On the other hand, the *precise* level of chronic intake at which the risk of developing an alcohol-related disease or shortening the life-span becomes significantly increased is to some degree a matter of conjecture (Popham and Schmidt, 1978). There is some evidence (Péquignot et al., 1974; Tuyns, Jensen, and Péquignot, 1977) that a level as low as three to four standard drinks (40 to 60 grams) of absolute alcohol daily for a 150-pound healthy person who smokes carries significant risks of liver cirrhosis and cancer of the esophagus. Péquignot (1963) has noted that a level of six or more standard drinks (80 grams) daily incurs a definite risk for the development of cirrhosis. Obviously, periodic episodes of acute intoxication interspersed with periods of abstinence are also fraught with this and other risks.

Alcohol-Drug Interactions

A good overview of this topic is presented by Holloway and Marshman (1977). Alcohol alters the effects of many drugs either directly or indirectly. The most widely recognized type of interaction is enhancement by alcohol of the depressant properties on the central nervous system (CNS) of anxiolytic agents, sedative-hypnotics, narcotics, and various other drugs including antihistamine and propoxyphene. Because of the high risks associated with driving or operating machinery after ingestion of such drug combinations, and because of their potentially fatal consequences in high doses as a result of respiratory depression, it is important that individuals be warned not to mix alcohol and drugs of this type. Although alcohol abusers have considerable tolerance to the (CNS) depressant effects of these drugs, they remain at risk because of excessive quantities they may consume.

A number of other alcohol-drug interactions which are less widely recognized and less common merit attention. Some evidence exists to indicate that drug absorption may be altered after alcohol consumption. It has been shown by Barboriak and Meade (1970) that alcohol prior to a meal decreases the rate of gastric emptying; therefore, it is reasonable to expect that the time course of any medication taken with or immediately after a meal may be altered if alcohol is consumed as an aperitif. More generally, individuals taking large amounts of ASA or those with gastrointestinal damage should avoid alcohol because of the possibility of anemia resulting from chronic occult blood loss due to the gastric mucosal damage.

Patients taking anticoagulants must be monitored carefully, because acute doses of alcohol enhance the anticoagulant effect. The anticoagulant effect of warfarin, given to patients with chronic consumption, is impaired because its metabolism is enhanced. A drastic change in alcohol consumption levels may adversely affect the steady state. Careful monitoring of anticoagulant blood levels is advisable, and patients should be aware of signs of toxicity or lack of anticoagulant effect.

Patients who take oral hypoglycemic medications or insulin should avoid alcohol because of the unpredictable fluctuations in serum glucose. Otherwise hyperglycemia or hypoglycemia may result.

It is generally wise to avoid alcohol when using antidepressants, especially if driving or operating hazardous equipment. There may be enhancement, reduction, or no alteration of CNS-depressant activity. With phenytoin, an anticonvulsant medication, small to moderate alcohol intake is not likely to be dangerous, but phenytoin levels should be closely monitored by a physician if sudden drastic changes in drinking habits occur. With chronic alcohol use (as a result of enhanced metabolism) there may be decreased anticonvulsant blood levels, which could lead to convulsive seizures.

When various drug-alcohol interactions are superimposed on inherent interpatient variability and complicated further by diverse disease states, it becomes apparent that making good predictions of alcohol impact on drug therapy is not only extremely difficult but also a critical matter for consideration which has often been overlooked.

Sex Differences

Some investigators found suggestive evidence indicating that women are more susceptible to alcoholic liver disease than men. Spain (1945) noted that the mean age of death in alcoholic women was eight years younger than in alcoholic men. Schmidt and De Lint (1969) found that in male alcoholics the mortality from cirrhosis was eleven times that of the general population, but in female alcoholics it was twenty-five times greater. Other studies (Viel, Donoso, and Salcedo, 1968; Wilkinson, Santamaria, and Rankin, 1968) have shown the prevalence of cirrhosis in female alcoholics to be twice that found in male alcoholics. Though various hypotheses have been advanced to account for these apparent sex differences—e.g., endocrine mechanisms, genetic differences, and different styles of drinking—the explanation is still uncertain.

Risks at Various Ethanol Consumption Levels

The Concept of a Standard Drink. In discussing alcohol intake it is necessary to establish a common method of quantification that refers to approximately the same amount of alcohol regardless of the type of beverage concerned. North American drinkers generally express quantity of alcohol in terms of the number of "drinks" or ounces they consume. Although consumers are aware that distilled spirits contain more alcohol than beer or wine, they often have little knowledge of the actual alcohol content of various beverages. In North America beer usually contains between 2.5 and 6.5 percent alcohol by volume; table wine, 7 to 14 percent; fortified wine, up to 20 percent; and distilled spirits or liquor, approximately 40 percent. The concept of a standard drink makes it possible to arrive at a useful expression of a client's total alcohol intake. The term "standard alcoholic drink" refers to the quantity of alcohol typically offered to a consumer in a single drink. Thus:

$$\text{1 standard drink} = \begin{cases} \text{1½ oz. spirits} \\ \text{3 oz. port or sherry} \\ \text{5 oz. table wine or champagne} \\ \text{12 oz. beer (5 percent).} \end{cases}$$

It is also important to appreciate that a "drink" is meaningful chiefly to the nonaddicted drinking public. Those with an estimated dependence on alcohol are concerned with large volumes and think in terms of bottles of wine or spirits and cases of beer. An expanded presentation of alcohol equivalents for common alcoholic beverages appears in Table 5–1.

The Risk-o-Graph. For healthy males, as noted earlier, the best evidence indicates that consumption of more than three to four standard

TABLE 5–1. Alcohol Equivalents for Common Alcoholic Beverages

Beverage	*Usual Serving*	*Standard Drinks* [a] *per Serving*	*Usual Size Bottle*	*Standard Drinks* [a] *per Bottle*
Beer 6.5%	12 oz. bottle	1.3	12 oz.	1.3
6 %	12 oz. bottle	1.2	12 oz.	1.2
5 %	12 oz. bottle	1.0	12 oz.	1.0
4 %	12 oz. bottle	0.8	12 oz.	0.8
3 %	12 oz. bottle	0.6	12 oz.	0.6
2.5 %	12 oz. bottle	0.5	12 oz.	0.5
Table wine	5 oz.	1.0	26 oz.	5.2
			35 oz.	7.0
Fortified wine	3½ oz.	1.0	26 oz.	7.4
Spirits	1½ oz.	1.0	12 oz.	8.0
			26 oz.	17.3
			40 oz.	26.7

[a] One standard drink is equal to 13.6 gms. of alcohol. The "average, healthy" individual will metabolize approximately 7–10 gms. of alcohol each hour.

drinks daily by an individual of 70 kg. (155 lbs.) carries an increasing risk to health. Consumption of six or more standard drinks daily by an individual of similar size is commonly accepted as the level at which definite physical damage begins to accrue. The graph in Figure 5–1 assumes a steady rate of daily ingestion; however, one may have a low average daily intake yet still drink hazardously on sporadic occasions. This carries great risk of acute physical damage, accidents, and death, even though average daily consumption is in the minimal-risk range.

The effects of alcohol depend on the amount taken (dose), and the consumer's frequency of consumption, rate of absorption, metabolic rate, body weight, proportion of body water, and general state of health. These factors all vary somewhat not only *between* individuals but *within* a given individual at different times. However, with few exceptions body weight, dose, and frequency are the major relevant variables which predict the risk of damage from drinking in healthy individuals. The longer a given level of drinking is maintained (weeks, months, years), the greater the probability of permanent damage.

Figure 5–1 provides a graphic representation of the risks of *physical* damage associated with various levels of alcohol consumption, for individuals of various weights. However, it must be recognized that with certain types of diseases the risk increases faster than the graph indicates. It should be emphasized that the boundaries between risk levels

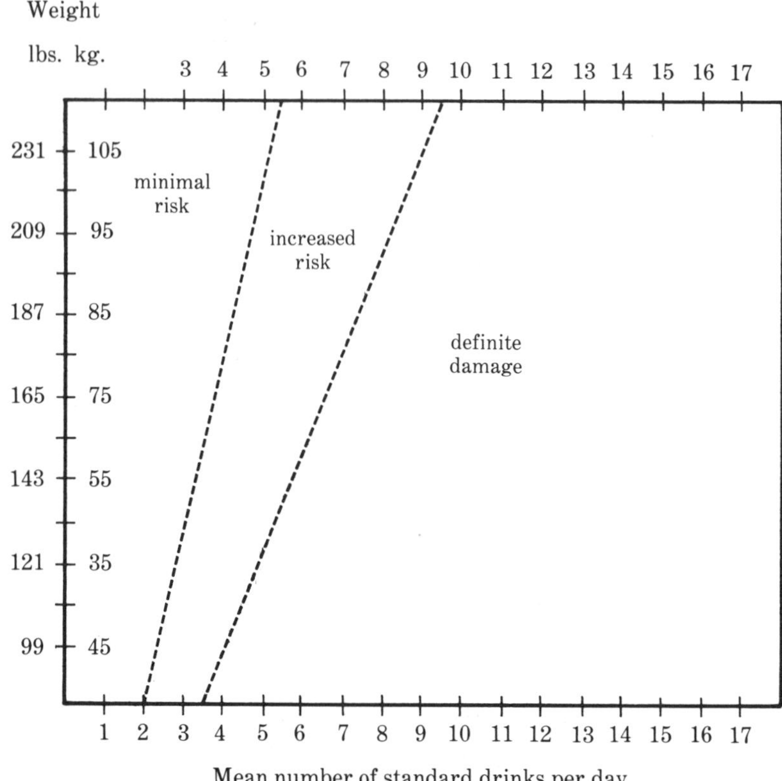

Figure 5-1. Risk-o-Graph. A graphic representation of the risk of physical damage from alcohol consumption as a function of average daily alcohol intake and body weight for a person of medium fat content. For fatter persons (less body water by proportion) the risk is greater. For leaner individuals the risk is a bit less.

Reprinted from *An Initial Interview for Clients with Alcohol Problems* (*ICAP*) with permission of the Addiction Research Foundation, Toronto, Canada (1981).

are arbitrary and the increasing risk is part of a continuum. When in doubt one should err on the side of caution in assessing the hazards of physical damage.

Determination of Alcohol Consumption Level. Increasing the scientific literature presents data on alcohol consumption levels in terms of grams of (absolute) alcohol per kilogram of body weight per day; therefore it may be desirable to describe a person's drinking level in these units to facilitate comparisons. Data obtained relating to level of alcohol consumption described in terms of number of standard drinks can be readily converted to grams (absolute) alcohol/kg. body weight/ day by use of the Table 5–2.

Using this unit of measurement from Table 5–2, "minimal risk" levels of alcohol consumption are considered to be those less than 0.69 grams alcohol/kg./day. Levels between 0.69 grams alcohol/kg./ day and 1.1 grams alcohol/kg./day are associated with increased risk, and levels at or above 1.2 grams alcohol/kg./day are associated with definite damage.

While the numbers appear to lend an aura of precision to the determination of the risk of physical damage, it should be emphasized that these numbers refer to the so-called "average" person. In fact, a great deal of other information is required to assess the risk of damage. As noted earlier, it is important to learn as much as possible about the length of the drinking history, the style, the frequency, the usual dose, the use of other drugs, and the presence of certain types of disease. As also noted earlier, these factors all vary somewhat not only *between* individuals but *within* a given individual at different times. Because of the variability of these factors, it must be recognized that for many individuals the risk increases *faster* than the graph in Figure 5–1 indicates. It cannot be emphasized enough that the risk levels are arbitrary and the increasing risk is part of a continuum.

In the process of assessing or counseling a patient, it is important to include clinical judgment in weighing the impact of all possible factors on the risk level, so that the individual can be told whether his or her risk is likely to increase faster than the graph indicates.

Method for Estimation of Average Daily Alcohol Consumption. This section provides a working guideline for estimation of average daily alcohol consumption. Two columns have been provided in the event that the individual has two drinking styles—usual and secondary. The number of days of each kind in a typical month must be determined and a mean number of standard drinks per day calculated according to the following method:

Usual Type of Drinking Pattern (e.g., weekdays)	*Secondary Type of Drinking Pattern* (e.g., weekends, binges, holidays)
(a) ___ Average no. standard drinks of beer/ day	(a) ___
(b) ___ Average no. standard drinks of table wine/day	(b) ___
(c) ___ Average no. standard drinks of fortified wine/day	(c) ___

TABLE 5–2. Conversion Table for Determination of Rate of Alcohol Consumption as Grams Alcohol/Kg. Body Weight/Day According to Number of Standard Drinks Consumed Daily

Body Weight (Kg.)

No. Standard Drinks Consumed/Day	40	45	50	55	60	65	70	75	80	85	90	95	100	105	110	115	120
	=88 lb.	=99 lb.	=110 lb.	=121 lb.	=132 lb.	=143 lb.	=154 lb.	=165 lb.	=176 lb.	=187 lb.	=198 lb.	=209 lb.	=220 lb.	=231 lb.	=242 lb.	=253 lb.	=264 lb.
1	0.34	0.30	0.27	0.25	0.23	0.21	0.19	0.18	0.17	0.16	0.15	0.14	0.14	0.13	0.12	0.12	0.11
2	0.68	0.60	0.54	0.50	0.45	0.42	0.39	0.36	0.34	0.32	0.30	0.29	0.27	0.26	0.25	0.24	0.23
3	1.0	0.91	0.82	0.74	0.68	0.63	0.58	0.54	0.51	0.48	0.45	0.43	0.41	0.39	0.37	0.36	0.34
4	1.4	1.2	1.1	0.99	0.91	0.84	0.78	0.73	0.68	0.64	0.60	0.57	0.54	0.52	0.50	0.47	0.45
5	1.7	1.5	1.4	1.2	1.1	1.1	0.97	0.91	0.85	0.80	0.76	0.72	0.68	0.65	0.62	0.59	0.57
6	2.0	1.8	1.6	1.5	1.4	1.3	1.2	1.1	1.0	0.96	0.91	0.86	0.82	0.78	0.74	0.71	0.68
7	2.4	2.1	1.9	1.7	1.6	1.5	1.4	1.3	1.2	1.1	1.1	1.0	0.95	0.91	0.87	0.83	0.79
8	2.7	2.4	2.2	2.0	1.8	1.7	1.6	1.5	1.4	1.3	1.2	1.2	1.1	1.0	0.99	0.95	0.91
9	3.1	2.7	2.4	2.2	2.0	1.9	1.7	1.6	1.5	1.4	1.4	1.3	1.2	1.2	1.1	1.1	1.0
10	3.4	3.0	2.7	2.5	2.3	2.1	1.9	1.8	1.7	1.6	1.5	1.4	1.4	1.3	1.2	1.2	1.1
11	3.7	3.3	3.0	2.7	2.5	2.3	2.1	2.0	1.9	1.8	1.7	1.6	1.5	1.4	1.4	1.3	1.3
12	4.1	3.6	3.3	3.0	2.7	2.5	2.3	2.2	2.0	1.9	1.8	1.7	1.6	1.6	1.5	1.4	1.4
13	4.4	3.9	3.5	3.2	3.0	2.7	2.5	2.4	2.2	2.1	2.0	1.9	1.8	1.7	1.6	1.5	1.5
14	4.8	4.2	3.8	3.5	3.2	2.9	2.7	2.5	2.4	2.2	2.1	2.0	1.9	1.8	1.7	1.7	1.6

15	5.1	4.5	4.1	3.7	3.4	3.1	2.9	2.7	2.6	2.4	2.3	2.2	2.0	1.9	1.9	1.8	1.7
16	5.4	4.8	4.4	4.0	3.6	3.4	3.1	2.9	2.7	2.6	2.4	2.3	2.2	2.1	2.0	1.9	1.8
17	5.8	5.1	4.6	4.2	3.9	3.6	3.3	3.1	2.9	2.7	2.6	2.4	2.3	2.2	2.1	2.0	1.9
18	6.1	5.4	4.9	4.5	4.1	3.8	3.5	3.3	3.1	2.9	2.7	2.6	2.5	2.3	2.2	2.1	2.0
19	6.5	5.7	5.2	4.7	4.3	4.0	3.7	3.5	3.2	3.0	2.9	2.7	2.6	2.5	2.4	2.2	2.2
20	6.8	6.0	5.4	5.0	4.5	4.2	3.9	3.6	3.4	3.2	3.0	2.9	2.7	2.6	2.5	2.4	2.3
21	7.1	6.4	5.7	5.2	4.8	4.4	4.1	3.8	3.6	3.4	3.2	3.0	2.9	2.7	2.6	2.5	2.4
22	7.5	6.7	6.0	5.4	5.0	4.6	4.3	4.0	3.7	3.5	3.3	3.2	3.0	2.9	2.7	2.6	2.5
23	7.8	7.0	6.3	5.7	5.2	4.8	4.5	4.2	3.9	3.7	3.5	3.3	3.1	3.0	2.8	2.7	2.6
24	8.2	7.3	6.5	5.9	5.4	5.0	4.7	4.4	4.1	3.8	3.6	3.4	3.3	3.1	3.0	2.8	2.7
25	8.5	7.6	6.8	6.2	5.7	5.2	4.9	4.5	4.3	4.0	3.8	3.6	3.4	3.2	3.1	3.0	2.8
26	8.8	7.9	7.1	6.4	5.9	5.4	5.1	4.7	4.4	4.2	3.9	3.7	3.5	3.4	3.2	3.1	3.0
27	9.2	8.2	7.3	6.7	6.1	5.7	5.3	4.9	4.6	4.3	4.1	3.9	3.7	3.5	3.3	3.2	3.1
28	9.5	8.5	7.6	6.9	6.4	5.9	5.4	5.1	4.8	4.5	4.2	4.0	3.8	3.6	3.5	3.1	3.1
29	9.9	8.8	7.9	7.2	6.6	6.1	5.6	5.3	4.9	4.6	4.4	4.2	3.9	3.8	3.6	3.4	3.3
30	10.0	9.1	8.2	7.4	6.8	6.3	5.8	5.4	5.1	4.8	4.5	4.3	4.1	3.9	3.7	3.6	3.4

Grams of Alcohol/Kg. Body Weight

Reprinted from *An Initial Interview for Clients with Alcohol Problems* (*ICAP*) with permission of the Addiction Research Foundation, Toronto, Canada (1981).

Usual Type of Drinking Pattern (e.g., weekdays)	*Secondary Type of Drinking Pattern* (e.g., weekends, binges, holidays)
(d) ___ Average no. standard drinks of spirits/day	(d) ___
(e) ___ Total no. standard drinks/day (i.e., total of a–d above)	(e) ___
(f) ___ Number of drinking days/month	(f) ___

For the client with two types of drinking patterns, the mean number of standard drinks/day is calculated as follows:

$$\frac{\text{e(usual)} \_\_\_ \times \text{f(usual)} \_\_\_ + \text{e(secondary)} \_\_\_ \times \text{f(secondary)} \_\_\_}{\text{30 days}} = \text{average no. standard drinks per day}$$

According to the Risk-o-Graph, what risk level characterizes the client's/patient's mean alcohol consumption?

___ minimal risk ___ increased risk ___ definite damage

According to the conversion table (Table 5–2), what is the client's/patient's mean alcohol consumption in grams of alcohol/kg. body weight/day? ___

In order to understand and fully appreciate the calculations for estimation of average daily alcohol consumption, the following two practice exercises will illustrate a few important points.

1. Mr. Smith claims to have no problem with his drinking. Although he drinks frequently, he feels he can stop at any time. He reports the following pattern of consumption: four beers after work during the week and two shots of Scotch; on weekends he rarely drinks beer but usually has three drinks before dinner and approximately half a bottle of wine with his evening meal. Mr. Smith weights 132 lbs.

   Calculate his mean alcohol consumption in grams of alcohol/kg./day ___

   What risk category is he in? ___

Estimation of Average Daily Alcohol Consumption

	Usual Type of Drinking Day	*Secondary Type of Drinking Day*
(a)	4 Average no. standard drinks of beer/day	___
(b)	___ Average no. standard drinks of table wine/day	3
(c)	___ Average no. standard drinks of fortified wine/day	___
(d)	2 Average no. standard drinks of spirits/day	3
(e)	6 Total no. standard drinks/day (i.e., total of a–d above)	6
(f)	22 Number of drinks days/month	8

For the client with two types of drinking patterns, the mean number of standard drinks/day is calculated in the following manner:

$$\frac{[\text{e(usual)}\ \underline{6} \times \text{f(usual}\ \underline{22}] + [\text{e(secondary)}\ \underline{6} \times \text{f(secondary)}\ \underline{8}]}{30\ \text{days}} = \underline{6}\ \text{avg. no. std. drinks per day}$$

$$\frac{6 \times 22 + 6 \times 8}{30} = \frac{132 + 48}{30} = \frac{180}{30} = 6$$

According to the Risk-o-Graph, what risk level characterizes the client's/patient's mean alcohol consumption?

___ minimal risk ___ increased risk _*_ definite risk

According to the conversion table (Table 5–2), what is the client's/patient's mean alcohol consumption in grams of alcohol/kg. body weight/day?

1.4 gms./kg./day

Mrs. Jones is a 99-lb. lady who has been "sipping" a total of four standard drinks of sherry per day for ten years. Mr. Smith is a 231-lb. construction worker who has been consuming a mickey of Scotch/day for ten years. Calculate their mean alcohol consumption in grams of alcohol/kg./day. Which person incurs greater risk of physical damage?

Usual Type of Drinking Day			*Secondary Type of Drinking Day*	
Mr. Smith	*Mrs. Jones*		*Mr. Smith*	*Mrs. Jones*
(a) ___	(a) ___	Average no. standard drinks of beer/day	(a) ___	(a) ___
(b) ___	(b) ___	Average no. standard drinks of table wine/day	(b) ___	(b) ___
(c) ___	(c) 4	Average no. standard drinks of fortified wine-day	(c) ___	(c) ___
(d) ___	(d) ___	Average no. standard drinks of spirits/day	(d) ___	(d) ___
(e) 8	(e) 4	Total no. standard drinks/day (i.e., total of a–d above)	(e) ___	(e) ___
(f) 30	(f) 30	Number of drinking days/months	(f) ___	(f) ___

For the client with irregular consumption levels, the mean number of standard drinks/day is calculated as follows:

Mrs. Jones

$$\frac{\text{e(usual)}\ \underline{4} \times \text{f(usual)}\ \underline{30} + \text{e(secondary)}\ \underline{0} \times \text{f(secondary)}\ \underline{0}}{30\ \text{days}} = \underline{4}\ \text{avg. no. std. drinks per day}$$

Mr. Smith

$$\frac{\text{e(usual) } \underline{8} \times \text{f(usual) } \underline{30} + \text{e(secondary) } \underline{0} \times \text{f(secondary) } \underline{0}}{\text{30 days}} = \underline{8} \text{ avg. no. std. drinks per day}$$

(g) According to the Risk-o-Graph, what risk level characterizes the client's/patient's means alcohol consumption?

Mrs. Jones:

__ minimal risk   __ increased risk   __ definite damage

Mr. Smith:

__ minimal risk   __ increased risk   __ definite damage

(h) According to the conversion table (Table 5–2), what is the client's/patient's mean alcohol consumption in gram of alcohol/kg. body weight/day? __

Mrs. Jones: 1.2 gms. alcohol/kg.

Mr. Smith: 1.0 gms. alcohol/kg.

Summary

In this chapter we have attempted to provide a brief overview of the most common medical complications associated with alcohol use. It has been our impression that a gap has existed between the many technical discussions about these medical complications and the translation of these into operational guidelines for use by persons in the areas of assessment and counseling.

We have attempted to provide information about the complications of alcohol use and to relate their development to various levels of alcohol consumption and the consequent risk of the individual developing physical damage. Hopefully, this information and data will enable alcoholism counselors and treatment personnel to provide the alcoholic patient with more effective and holistic treatments.

References

Addiction Research Foundation of Ontario. *The Physician's Manual,* 1981.

Ashley, M. J., and Rankin, J. G. Alcohol consumption and hypertension—The evidence from hazardous drinking and alcoholic populations. *Australia and New Zealand Journal of Medicine,* 1979, *9,* 201–206.

Astrom, K. E. Metabolic myopathies. *Acta Neurologica Scandinavica,* 1970, *46,* 177–193.

Barboriak, J. J., and Meade, R. C. Effect of ethanol on gastric emptying in man. *American Journal of Clinical Nutrition,* 1970, *23,* 1151.

Blomstrand, R. Observations on the formation of ethanol in the intestinal tract in man. *Life Sciences,* 1971, *10,* 575–582.

Cicero, T. J. Alcohol self-administration, tolerance, and withdrawal in humans and animals: Theoretical and methodological issues. In H. Rigter and J. C. Crabbe (eds.), *Alcohol Tolerance and Dependence.* New York: Elsevier/North Holland Biomedical Press, 1980.

Dyer, A. R., Stamler, J., Paul, O., Berkson, D. M., Lepper, M. H., McKean, H., Shekelle, R. B., Lindberg, H. A., Garside, D. Alcohol consumption cardiovascular risk factors, and mortality in two Chicago epidemiologic studies. *Circulation,* 1977, *56,* 1067–1074.

Edwards, G. The meaning and treatment of alcohol dependence. *British Journal of Hospital Medicine,* 1967, *2,* 272–281.

Ekbom, K., Hed, R., Kirstein, L., and Astrom, K. E. Muscular affections in chronic alcoholism. *Archives of Neurology,* 1964, *10,* 449–458.

Fairclough, P. D., and Clark, M. L. Alcohol related diseases of the gastrointestinal tract. In P. Clark and L. J. Kricka (eds.), *Medical Consequences of Alcohol Abuse.* Toronto, Canada: John Wiley and Sons, 1980.

Geller, S. A. Muscle disease in the alcoholic. In P. Clark and L. J. Kricka (eds.), *Medical Consequences of Alcohol Abuse.* Toronto, Canada: John Wiley and Sons, 1980.

Gerding, D. N., Hall, W. H., and Schierl, E. A. Antibiotic concentrations in ascitic fluid of patients with ascites and bacterial peritonitis. *Annals of Internal Medicine,* 1977, *86,* 708–713.

Gilbert, R. Conditioned responses and drug abuse. *The Journal,* Alcoholism and Drug Addiction Research Foundation, September 1982, p. 5, cols. 1–4.

Goodwin, D. W., Schulsinger, F., Hermonson, L., Guze, S. B., and Winokur, G. Alcohol problems in adoptees reared apart from alcoholic biological parents. *Archives of General Psychiatry,* 1973, *28,* 238–242.

———. Alcoholism and heredity. *Archives of General Psychiatry,* 1979, *36,* 57–61.

Gould, L., Reddy, R., Becker, W., Oh, K.-C., and Kim, S. G. Electrophysiologic properties of alcohol in man. *Journal of Electrocardiology,* 1978, *11,* 216–226.

Hed, R. Three cases of non-familial myoglobinuria. *Acta Medica Scandinavica,* 1955, *152,* 459–463.

———, Lundmark, C., Fahlgren, H., and Orell, S. Acute muscular syndrome in chronic alcoholism. *Acta Medica Scandinavica,* 1962, *171,* 584–599.

Hennekens, C. H. Effects of beer, wine and liquor in coronary deaths. *Journal of American Medical Association,* 1979, *242,* 1973–1974.

Holt, S. Observations on the dependence of alcohol absorption on the rate of gastric emptying. *ARF Substudy,* Alcoholism and Drug Addiction Research Foundation, 1980, *1086.*

Hore, B. D. The aetiology of drinking problems. In P. Clark and L. J. Kricka (eds.), *Medical Consequences of Alcohol Abuse.* Toronto, Canada: John Wiley and Sons, 1981.

———, and Rossall, C. Intoxication and withdrawal assessment scales. *British Journal of Alcohol and Alcoholism,* 1979, *14,* 2–6.

Isbell, M., Fraser, H. F., Wikler, A., Belleville, K. D., and Eisenmen, A. J. An experimental study of the aetiology of delirium tremens. *Quarterly Journal of Studies on Alcohol,* 1955, *16,* 1–33.

Israel, Y., Orrego, H., Khanna, J. M., Stewart, D. J., Phillips, M. J., and Kalant, H. Alcohol induced susceptibility to hypoxic liver damage: Possible role in the pathogenesis of alcoholic liver disease? In M. M. Fisher and J. G. Rankin (eds.), *Alcohol and the Liver.* New York: Plenum Press, 1977.

Jacob, M. S., and Sellers, E. M. Emergency management of alcohol withdrawal drug therapy. *Hospital,* April 1977, *2(4),* 28–34.

Kalant, H. Drug research is muddied by sundry dependence concepts. *The Journal,* Alcoholism and Drug Addiction Research Foundation, September 1982, p. 12, cols. 1–5.

Klatsky, A. L., Friedman, G. D., and Siegelaub, A. B. Alcohol consumption before myocardial infarction. Results from the Kaiser–Permanente epidemiologic study of myocardial infarction. *Annals of Internal Medicine,* 1974, *81,* 294–301.

Leevy, C. M. Clinical diagnosis, evaluation and treatment of liver disease in alcoholics. *Federation Proceedings,* 1967, *26,* 1474–1481.

Lieber, C. S., Jones, D. P., and De Carli, L. M. Effects of prolonged ethanol intake: Production of fatty liver despite adequate diets. *Journal of Clinical Investigations,* 1965, *44,* 1009–1021.

Mendelson, J. H. (ed.), *Quarterly Journal of Studies on Alcohol,* May 1964, Supplement no. *2.*

Mullin, C. S. *The Medical Consequences of Chronic Alcohol Abuse.* Boston: Massachusetts Department of Public Health, 1980.

Oh, S. J. Alcoholic myopathy: A critical review. *Alabama Journal of Medical Science,* 1972, *9,* 79–95.

Péquignot, G. Les Enquêtes par interrogatoire permettent—Elles de déterminer la frequence de l'étiologie alcooleque des cirrhoses du foie? *Bulletin National du Médicin,* 1963, *147,* 90–97.

———, Chabert, C., Eydoux, H., and Courcoul, M. A. Augmentation du risque de cirrhose en fonction de la ration d'alcool. *Revue Alcoholisme, 1974, 20,* 191–202.

Péquignot, G., and Tuyns, A. Symposium Franco–Britannique sur l'alcoholisme. *Inserm,* 1975, *54,* 33–43.

Popham, R. E., and Schmidt, W. The biomedical definition of safe alcohol consumption: A crucial issue for the researcher and the drinker. *British Journal of the Addictions,* 1978, *73,* 233–235.

Powell, W. J., and Klatskin, G. Duration of survival in patients with Laennec's cirrhosis. *American Journal of Medicine,* 1968, *44,* 406–420.

Ratnoff, O. D., and Patek, A. J. The natural history of Laennec's cirrhosis of the liver. *Medicine* (Baltimore) 1942, *21,* 207–268.

Regan, T. J., Levinson, G. E., Oldewurtel, H. A., Frank, M. J., Weisse, A. B., and Moschos, C. B. Ventricular function in noncardiacs with alcoholic fatty liver: Role of ethanol in the production of cardiomyopathy. *Journal of Clinical Investigations,* 1969, *48,* 397–407.

Rydberg, U., and Skerfving, S. The toxicity of ethanol: A tentative risk evaluation. In M. Gross (ed.), *Alcohol Intoxication and Withdrawal.* New York: Plenum Press, 1977.

Sarles, H., Sahel, J., Staub, J. L., Bourry, J., and Laugier, R. Chronic pancreatitis. In H. T. Howat and H. Sarles (eds.), *The Exocrine Pancreas.* London: W. B. Saunders, 1979.

Schmidt, W., and De Lint, J. Mortality experience of male and female alcoholic patients. *Quarterly Journal of Studies on Alcohol,* 1969, *30,* 112–118.

Schoenberg, B. S., Bailar, J. C., and Fraumeni, J. F., Jr. Certain mortality patterns of oesophageal cancer in the United States. *Journal of the National Cancer Institute,* 1971, *46,* 63–73.

Schukit, M. A., Goodwin, D. A., and Winokur, G. A study of alcoholism in half siblings. *American Journal of Psychiatry,* 1972, *128,* 1132–1136.

Spain, D. Portal cirrhosis of the liver: A review of 250 necropsies with reference to sex differences. *American Journal of Clinical Pathology,* 1945, *15,* 215–218.

Tarter, R. E., and Jones, B. M. Motor impairment in chronic alcoholics. *Diseases of the Nervous System,* 1971, *32,* 632–636.

Thompson, A. D., Ral, S. A., and Majumdar, S. K. Malnutrition in the alcoholic. In P. Clark and L. J. Kricka (eds.), *Medical Consequences of Alcohol Abuse.* Toronto, Canada: John Wiley and Sons, 1980.

Turner, T. B. Clinical aspects of ethanol tolerance and dependence. In H. Rigter and J. C. Crabbe, Jr. (eds.), *Alcohol Tolerance and Dependence.* New York: Elsevier/North Holland Biomedical Press, 1980.

Tuyns, A. J., Jensen, O. M., and Péquinot, G. Le cancer de l'oesophage en Ille-et-Vilaine en fonction des niveaux de consommation d'alcool et de tabac; des risques qui multiplient. *Bulletin du Cancer,* 1977, *64,* 45–60.

Viel, B., Donoso, S., and Salcedo, D. Alcoholic drinking habit and hepatic damage. *Journal of Chronic Disease,* 1968, *21,* 157–166.

Wilkinson, P., Santamaria, J. N., and Rankin, J. G. Epidemiology of alcohol cirrhosis. *Australasian Annals of Medicine, 1968, 18,* 222–226.

Yano, K., Rhoads, G. G., and Kagan, A. Coffee, alcohol and the risk of coronary heart disease among Japanese men living in Hawaii. *New England Journal of Medicine,* 1977, *297,* 405–409.

Zinberg, N. E. Alcohol addiction: Toward a more comprehensive definition. In M. H. Bean and N. E. Zinberg (eds.), *Dynamic Approaches to the Understanding and Treatment of Alcoholism.* New York: Free Press, 1981.

6

Evaluating Alcoholics Anonymous

Alan C. Ogborne / Frederick B. Glaser

Alcoholics Anonymous is regarded by many professional and lay alcoholism workers as the most significant treatment resource available to people with drinking problems. Referral to A.A. is routine in some programs and regular attendance at A.A. meetings is required in others. A number of important treatment programs are based entirely upon the A.A. philosophy and many others have incorporated much of this philosophy into their operations (Glaser, Greenberg, and Barrett, 1978).

The hegemony of A.A. is not, however, without its critics. Tournier (1979), for example, argues that the pervasive influence of A.A. inhibits innovations, alienates early problem drinkers, and limits treatment strategies. Others (e.g., Goodwin, 1979) have speculated that A.A.'s insistence that any drinking by a recovered alcoholic inevitably leads to loss of control can become the basis for a self-fulfilling prophecy. Thus, the erstwhile abstainer who, for whatever reason, takes a drink may in effect be induced to go on a spree by the belief that this is inevitable. Spree drinking could also be induced by the fact that status in A.A. is correlated with length of sobriety. Years of sobriety with their attendant symbols and status can be obliterated by one slip, so the social cost of a single drink is as great as the cost of an all-out binge.

Despite these criticisms there is no doubt that A.A. helps many thousands of people who do not find relief elsewhere. Questions about the overall value of A.A. should thus be rephrased to address the specific utility of the A.A. approach to problem drinkers with specific characteristics. Both critics and advocates of A.A. seem to accept that A.A. helps some, but not all, problem drinkers. Therefore it would be a most useful line of inquiry to determine the characteristics of problem drinkers for whom A.A. is the treatment of choice. How might one select clients whose needs and affinities would match more closely what A.A. has to offer?

In this chapter we present the main outcomes and conclusions of an extensive literature review which was undertaken to seek evidence and ideas about the kinds of people for whom A.A. might be most appropriate. We also argue that contrary to widely held beliefs about the impossibility of scientific studies of A.A.'s efficacy, such studies have been done and should continue to be done. Hopefully, the following material will stimulate relevant studies.

Characteristics Associated with A.A. Affiliation

Personality

Canter (1966) examined the personality characteristics of fifty hospitalized male alcoholics who were free to attend A.A. meetings or group therapy, to take disulfiram, or to obtain conditioned-reflex treatment. He found that those who went to A.A. meetings scored higher on the California F-Scale, a measure of authoritarianism, than those who sought other forms of therapy. No other investigators have considered authoritarianism experimentally in relationship to A.A. membership, though it is often listed in the catalogue of attributes of the likely A.A. candidate (Baekeland, 1977).

Trice and Roman (1970) followed up 378 white male problem drinkers from an A.A.-based hospital program in Maryland. All subjects had been given a variety of tests on admission to the program. Stepwise regression analysis was used to determine which tests best predicted affiliation with A.A. subsequent to discharge. Patients were considered to have "successfully" affiliated with A.A. if they had attended meetings at least twice a week for a year since discharge. Trice and Roman do not state the proportion of their sample who became successful A.A. affiliates.

Twenty-four variables were found to discriminate A.A. affiliates from nonaffiliates, and these were used in the regression analysis. Fourteen of these were scores on personality tests [16 personality factors (PF), Minnesota Multiphasic Personality Inventory] or ratings of mood (Clyde Mood Scale). These fourteen variables together accounted for 25 percent of the variance in the dependent variable, successful A.A. affiliation. The remaining ten variables* accounted for an additional 11 percent.

Trice and Roman interpret their results as indicating the importance of personality factors in determining A.A. affiliation and suggest that such affiliation is associated with high affiliative and group dependency needs, a proneness to guilt, and all individual's "considerable experience of social processes which have labeled him as deviant." Deviance can be measured by the number of (hospitalizations, scale Am on the MMPI, and years of alcoholism). Trice and Roman did not find that ego strength predicted affiliation with A.A. In contrast, Seiden (1960), using the Bender-Gestalt error score as a measure of ego strength, did find that A.A. members were superior to nonmembers. A number of other studies (e.g., Mindlin, 1964; Hantmann, 1951; Trice, 1959) also suggest a relationship between affiliative needs and membership in A.A.

Machover and Puzzo (1959) administered three projective tests (the Thematic Apperception Test, the Blacky Test, and the Rorschach) to forty-six male problem drinkers and attempted to discriminate those who subsequently became A.A. affiliates from the others. The results suggested that A.A. affiliates tend to identify with their mothers, to be prone to rationalizations, to lack social inhibition, and to use the defenses of reaction formation, obsession-compulsion, or overcontrol. These results are not, however, very convincing, since the measures used are of uncertain reliability and validity.

Only one published study failed to detect any significant differences between problem drinkers who had or had not affiliated with A.A. This study, by Haertzen et al. (1968), involved administering a wide range of scales from the Addiction Research Center Inventory to problem drinkers in various hospital settings. Those who were A.A. members did not differ from nonmembers. Typically, however, the A.A. members tested had all "failed" in A.A., since they required hospitalization for their drinking problem.

In general, then, these studies do suggest that people with certain types of personalities are more likely to affiliate with A.A. than others, a conclusion consistent with clinical observations (e.g., Cohen, 1962; Ginther and Brillant, 1967; Pattison, Coe, and Dorr, 1973). More research, however, is needed. In particular it would be useful to have

* These were history of sibling alcoholism; number of prior hospitalizations for alcoholism; age; years of alcoholism; American nativity of parents; father's occupation; alcoholism in family; health status; time of follow-up; EEG pathology rating.

more longitudinal studies which use well-standardized psychological tests.

Perceptual Style and Related Matters

The perceptual styles of normal individuals, and of those belonging to various deviant and nondeviant subgroups, have been extensively studied for many years. An important group of such studies has addressed the dimension of field dependence/field independence. The perceptual style of a field-independent person is to see each element in a perceptual field as a discrete entity; it is an analytic style which focuses upon the separation of the figure from the ground. At the opposite pole of this perceptual continuum is the field-dependent person, whose style of perception is dominated by the overall organization of the surrounding field; it is a synthetic style which tends to view figures as inseparable from the context of the ground. Classical methods of measuring individual differences along this continuum have included the Rod-and-Frame Test and the Embedded Figures Test.

Persons with drinking problems have been among the groups most extensively studied with such measures of perceptual style. Over time, there has been an evolution of the conclusions drawn from these studies. Early investigations (Bailey, Hustmyer, and Kristofferson, 1961; Karp, Poster, and Goodman, 1963; Rhodes and Yorioka, 1968; Witkin, Karp, and Goodenough, 1959; Goldstein and Chotlos, 1965) were interpreted as showing that problem drinkers were strongly (and very likely irrevocably) field-dependent. However, in due course it has become clear that problem drinkers in fact vary considerably along the dimension of field dependence/independence, as field-independent samples of problem drinkers have been identified (Burdick, 1969; Hayes et al., 1978). Evidence has also developed that field dependence is not necessarily a fixed attribute, but that it varies over time and may be decreased by abstinence, by therapy, and by other means (Goldstein and Chotlos, 1966; McWilliams, Brown, and Minard, 1975; Jacobson, 1968).

Many correlates of field dependence and field independence have also been explored, among them their possible interactions with various forms of intervention. A summary statement from a comprehensive review article is instructive in this regard:

> The evidence suggests that therapists more often assign their field-dependent patients to supportive therapy, in which a well-defined structure is provided for them; in contrast, field-independent patients are more often assigned to modifying therapy, in which the patient's role is less highly structured. . . . field-dependent persons show a strong interest in people,

> prefer to be physically close to others, are emotionally open, and favour real-life situations that will bring them into contact with people; in contrast, field-independent persons are less interested in people, show both physical and psychological distancing from others, and favour impersonal situations. . . . field-independent people are relatively immune to the effects of a group context. (Witkin and Goodenough, 1977, pp. 667, 672, 675)

Obviously, one would predict on the basis of these conclusions that field-dependent individuals would be much more likely to affiliate with Alcoholics Anonymous. Evidence of just such a close, specific relationship is indeed found in the literature. In a direct study of this relationship (Reilly and Sugarman, 1967; Brook, 1962), which also examined the related dimension of cognitive simplicity/cognitive complexity, two groups of problem drinkers, one which had affiliated successfully with A.A. and one which had not, were examined. Twenty-nine of the thirty successful affiliates, or 96.7 percent, were field-dependent. On the other hand, fourteen of the fifteen field-independent subjects in this study, or 96 percent, were A.A. nonaffiliates.

In contradistinction to these striking results, an earlier study concluded that A.A. members were *less* field-dependent than other alcoholics (Karp, Witkin, and Goodenough, 1965). While this initially seems contentious, a close reading of the study and the addition of a temporal perspective suggests that the results of the two studies may actually be congruent. Clearly a good deal remains to be learned about the relationship of perceptual style to suitability for different modes of therapy. But there is presumptive evidence of a compatibility between field-dependent problem drinkers and Alcoholics Anonymous. Moreover, there are intriguing leads which link research on perceptual style with several other areas of research.

For example, the Brook study (1962) linked cognitive simplicity with field dependence. Given the proposed need of field-dependent persons for structure, one may ask whether field dependence and cognitive simplicity are not also linked with a need for authoritarianism. If so, then Brook's results would support those of Canter (1966). McLachlan (1972, 1974), in similar fashion, has provided evidence of a match between clients with what he terms "low conceptual level" and highly structured therapy. This has a familiar ring, especially when one recognizes that both dimensions of "low/high conceptual level" and "cognitive simplicity/complexity" are measured by means of similar sentence-completion tests. The suggestion of Fontana, Dowds, and Bethel (1976) that alcoholics with a preference for "formistic thinking" would be more accepting of A.A. is in the same vein. Formistic thinking is an unusual concept which seems to relate both to field dependence and authoritarianism. Finally, autokinesis, a perceptual phenomenon in which a stationary pinpoint of light in an otherwise darkened room appears to move about, is closely related to field dependence, and is also thought to predict successful affiliation with A.A. (Vota, 1968). Thus there may be a close relationship between this group of perceptual and cognitive variables, on the one hand, and affiliation with Alcoholics Anonymous on the other.

Social Characteristics and Social Functioning

Traditionally, A.A. members have tended to be middle-aged and male. Changes in the age and sex composition of A.A. groups have been noted (Leach and Norris, 1977), and recently groups for young people and for women have been started. The appropriateness of A.A. for women has, however, been questioned (e.g., Curlee, 1971; Davidson, 1976).

Several studies suggest that A.A. appeals more to the socially stable problem drinker than to the skid row inebriate. Also, there are suggestions that A.A. is more attractive to middle- and upper-class problem drinkers than it is to lower-class problem drinkers (Canter, 1966; Leach and Norris, 1977; Bailey and Leach, 1965). Pattison, Coe, and Doerr (1973) see the A.A. member as one whose life is not too bad if he does not drink and as a person whose drinking has, in a very real sense, significantly threatened or disrupted a valued life-style. Such a person can be contrasted with an individual whose drinking is but one of a host of mutually compounding problems, which are not readily resolved by becoming abstinent.

The "social" nature of A.A. suggests that it would appeal to people who could function in groups, and a study by Mindlin (1964) confirms that this is so. Mindlin administered an attitude questionnaire to inpatient alcoholics who had at various times been A.A. members or in psychotherapy or who had never had any contacts with A.A. or psychotherapy. Mindlin found that patients who had been in A.A. were less likely to describe themselves as isolated, lonely, or socially ill at ease.

Drinking History and Drinking Problems

The model of alcoholism emphasized by A.A. lays great stress upon "hitting bottom," physical dependence, and loss of control. "Hitting bottom" (Mumey, 1984) refers to a belief current among A.A. members that it is the person who comes to A.A. after a prolonged adverse interaction with alcohol, rather than the younger initiate, who is most likely to affiliate and benefit. There is a considerable amount of research support for such a belief (e.g., Popham and Schmidt, 1976; Miller and Joyce, 1979), which relates it particularly to A.A.'s universal goal of total lifetime abstinence. Despite evidence that a small proportion of persons with long histories of heavy drinking may achieve successful rehabilitation without attaining such a goal (Davis, 1962), it has not yet proven possible to distinguish the few who will from the many who will not. Thus, abstinence for those with lengthy histories continues to make sound common sense, and a careful drinking history may assist in selecting suitable candidates for Alcoholics Anonymous.

Physical dependence and loss of control were two of the principal elements (along with the related phenomena of tolerance and adaptive cell metabolism) used by Jellinek (1960) to characterize what he termed "gamma alcoholism." Gamma alcoholism, said Jellinek, "is what members of Alcoholics Anonymous recognize as alcoholism to the exclusion of all species." This being so, A.A. would be more likely to attract gamma alcoholics than those whose drinking problems take other forms. Jellinek's own research bore this out. He found, for example, that the majority of A.A. members reported loss of control. Those who did not Jellinek considered as belonging to another category completely, "alpha alcoholics," who, he said, "conform their language to A.A. standards." Instruments are now available for the psychometric measurement of both physical dependence (Hodgson et al., 1978) and loss of control (Wanberg, Horn, and Foster, 1977), and these could be used to test Jellinek's notions in a prospective manner.

Recent data from the Addiction Research Foundations's assessment unit is relevant to this point. In a sample of 192 consecutive admissions to the unit, 88, or 46 percent, claimed that at one time they had attended A.A. meetings regularly. These A.A. attenders scored significantly higher ($p = .052$) than nonattenders on the loss of control scale of the Alcohol Use Inventory (Wanberg, Horn, and Foster, 1977), when age, sex, social class, and quantity of alcohol consumed were controlled. A number of other writers have made passing reference to the possibility that A.A. could be seen as specializing in helping alcoholics who experience loss of control, but there is no other empirical data directly relevant to this suggestion. The high incidence of negative social reactions by A.A. members to the continued drinking of their fellow members has been documented (Trice and Roman, 1970; Edwards et al., 1967). Thus drinkers with a relatively lengthy history of heavy drinking, with a pattern of binge drinking, and those who exhibit physical dependence and loss of control can be identified and should be particularly suitable candidates for Alcoholics Anonymous.

Values, Attitudes, and Beliefs

Alcoholics Anonymous is based upon a particular model of alcoholism and offers its members a course of action for the management of their drinking problem (Kurtz, 1982). In addition, A.A. members (Mumey, 1984) seem to endorse a range of values, attitudes, and beliefs about "how to live" which extend beyond the question of living without drinking. These values, attitudes, and beliefs are both implicit and explicit in A.A.'s "twelve steps" and "twelve traditions" and in the writings and statements of A.A. members.

A.A.'s beliefs about alcoholism are that it is a progressive disease for which there is no cure. Those who suffer from the disease must accept that they are powerless over alcohol and assume responsibility (with the help of God) for adjusting their lives accordingly. Since there is no cure, the only alternative to problem drinking is abstinence. While A.A. is not a religious organization, many of its basic tenets have a strong religious flavor (Jones, 1970). Thus, central to A.A.'s prescriptions for dealing with alcoholism is the assumption that the sufferer must come to accept that only a power greater than himself can help restore his "sanity." An early step in recovery, therefore, is to make a decision to "turn our will and our lives over to the care of God as we understand him."* Five of A.A.'s twelve steps make a specific reference to God. No particular god is mentioned, and the phrase "as we understand him" occurs twice. In addition, one step mentions a "power greater than ourselves" and the final step talks of a "spiritual awakening." Whether or not A.A. appeals primarily to people who have a basic sympathy to religion or a belief in some form of god is unknown. Of interest, however, is the fact that the movement was in the early days, at least, greatly influenced by the Oxford Group movement—an evangelical Christian movement which emphasized self-survey, public confession, restitution, and service to others.

Among the values most commonly stressed by speakers at A.A. meetings are friendship, honesty, humility, faith, courage, helping others, spirituality, personal responsibility, and "getting on" in the world (Murphy, 1953; Bratter, 1980). Other researchers (e.g., Pattison, Coe, and Doerr, 1973; Jones, 1970) have noted A.A.'s concern with "respectability." If not frankly religious (see above), such a complex of values can be viewed as reflecting existential concerns (Frankl, 1969). Examined from this perspective, A.A. appears attuned to, and highly effec-

* The past tense is used in the twelve steps since they are presented as a record of the experience of people who have already accepted the A.A. philosophy.

tive in dealing with, the existential concerns of its members (Holmes, 1970).

A number of potentially relevant and operationally feasible conclusions may be drawn from this material regarding suitable candidates for Alcoholics Anonymous. The simplest is that individuals with viable ties to organized religious bodies might be most likely to affiliate. At a more abstract level, since the first of A.A.'s twelve steps requires an admission of powerlessness, some measure of the subjective sense of powerlessness or, as it has been phrased in the psychological literature, of a perceived external locus of control of reinforcement (Rotter, 1966, 1975) might predict successful affiliation (Hinrichsen, 1976). It has been demonstrated (Abramowitz et al., 1974) that persons with a perceived external locus of control respond more favorably to directive forms of psychotherapy, a result which would accord well with the postulates and the strong directiveness provided by A.A. Finally, the presence of existential concerns can also be readily measured (Crumbaugh and Meholick, 1964; Crumbaugh, 1968). A significant proportion of persons with alcohol problems score in the high range on this measure (Strom and Tranel, 1967; Crumbaugh, 1972; Jacobson, Ritter, and Mueller, 1977; Crumbaugh and Carr, 1979). Such persons tend to show greater improvement than others upon receiving forms of treatment which are responsive to existential concerns (Crumbaugh, 1972; Crumbaugh and Carr, 1979); and, as noted, A.A. is quite responsive to such concerns (Holmes, 1970). Thus it is reasonable to suppose that clients with alcohol problems who have particularly severe existential concerns represent superior candidates for Alcoholic Anonymous (Giannetti, 1981).

Group Processes and Affiliation

The general psychological and social-psychological literature on group processes and affiliation furnishes a number of concepts that would be useful to consider in further studies of A.A. The "conformity" literature, for example, suggests that extreme conformists have (in contrast to those who conform less) less ego strength, lower impulse control, less tolerance for ambiguity, less ability to accept responsibility, less self-insight, less spontaneity and originality, more authoritarian and prejudicial attitudes, and more parental idealization; they also place a greater emphasis on external socially approved values (Crutchfield, 1955). This rather unflattering portrait is somewhat reminiscent of the personality traits found or thought to be associated with A.A. membership. Moreover, some of the criticisms that have been made of A.A. concern the "difficult" personalities of some of its members

(Leach and Norris, 1977). If the most ardent A.A. members are indeed characterized by the traits listed by Crutchfield, then some difficulties in working with A.A. would be expected.

The social-psychological literature on the functions of groups also suggests useful ways of analyzing the A.A. movement. The tendencies for "birds of a feather to flock together" and for "misery to love company" seem basic to the development of any social movement among people with a common problem which is stigmatized by the broader society. Also A.A., like other social groups, can serve a number of other functions for its members. For example, the "deindividuation" which Festinger, Pepitone, and Newcomb (1952), Zimbardo (1970), and others find generally relevant to understanding why people join groups may be especially relevant to A.A., which stresses "anonymity" and "powerlessness." While A.A. members are encouraged to accept responsibility for their actions, they can, at the same time, lose a sense of uniqueness and individuality by identifying with the movement as a whole and adopting its codes of behavior. Deindividuation can also cause or increase normally unacceptable behaviors, including the admission of deviance. Such behavior is encouraged by A.A. and may well be facilitated by anonymity and other aspects of A.A. philosophy.

The potential for affiliation with others, in a similar plight, to reduce individual anxieties has been commented on and researched by a number of social psychologists. Early studies by Schachter (1959) showed how the manipulation of anxiety levels affected people's desire to be with others in a similar condition. Schacter also found individual differences in the propensity to affiliate under conditions of anxiety; a remarkably high correlate of this propensity was ordinal position of birth. Firstborn and only children are more likely than others to want to be with others in anxiety-producing situations.

Other social psychologists who have studied groups have noted that groups offer their members a frame of reference for self-definition as well as friendships, social approval, support, and prestige. Such functions are clearly relevant to understanding the value of A.A. to some of its members. These needs in prospective A.A. members reinforce group affiliation.

Summary of the Literature

In general the empirical evidence supports clinical impressions and deductions from psychological theory and suggests that problem drinkers who affiliate with A.A. are in various ways different from those who do not. Table 6–1 summarizes suggestions and evidence as to what these differences might be. This table should not be taken too

TABLE 6–1. A Summary of Individual Attributes Which May Be Associated with Differential Affiliation with Alcoholics Anonymous

Attributes of Successful Affiliators	*Attributes of Unsuccessful Affiliators*
Male	Female
Over forty years of age	Under forty years of age
White	Non-white
Middle or upper class	Working class
Socially stable	Not socially stable
Firstborn or only child	Other birth order
Heavy drinking	Other drinking histories
Binge drinking	Other drinking patterns
Physical dependence on alcohol	Not physically dependent on alcohol
Loss-of-control drinking	Controlled drinking
Authoritarian personality	Other personality configurations
High affiliative needs	Normal affiliative needs
High group dependency needs	Normal group dependency needs
Prone to guilt	Not prone to guilt
External locus of control	Internal locus of control
Field-dependent	Field-independent
Cognitive simplicity	Cognitive complexity
Low conceptual level	High conceptual level
Formistic thinking	Other cognitive patterns
High autokinesis scores	Low autokinesis scores
Religious orientation	Nonreligious orientation
Existentially anxious	Not existentially anxious
Conformity orientation	Nonconformist orientation
Deindividuation potential	Lack of deindividuation potential

seriously. Evidence that some of the listed attributes are associated with A.A. affiliation is weak, and specific attributes are unlikely to prove independent of all others. The table is primarily presented in the hope that it will provoke suggestions for further exploration. It is also hoped that the table will be helpful to referral agencies who must decide whether or not particular clients would be good candidates for A.A.

Are Controlled, Evaluative Studies of A.A. Possible?

Most attempts at the evaluation of A.A. have been based upon multivariate studies involving A.A. attendance as one factor (Rohan, 1970; Tomsovic, 1970; Rossi, 1970; Kish and Herman, 1971; Oakley and Holden, 1972; McCance and McCance, 1969; Robson, Paulus, and Clarke, 1965); upon uncontrolled studies of A.A.-based programs (Smith, 1941; McMahon, 1942); or upon longitudinal or cross-sectional studies of

A.A. members (e.g., Bailey and Leach, 1965; Jones, 1970; Bill, 1965). Such studies have done little more than reinforce clinical impressions that A.A. is helpful to some problem drinkers. Due mainly to problems of research design, they have not added significantly to knowledge of the general efficacy of A.A. as a treatment resource (Bebbington, 1976; Bratter, 1980).

Thus it remains unclear (1) what proportion of any population of problem drinkers would either accept or benefit from a referral to A.A.; (2) whether or not benefits to be derived from involvement with A.A. are greater than those to be gained from other programs; and (3) whether or not involvement with A.A. has any detrimental effects on those concerned. These critically important questions can, of course, only be convincingly answered with well-controlled studies in which various groups of problem drinkers are randomly assigned to A.A. or to some other form of intervention. Clearly the informal and voluntary nature of A.A. rules out some such studies (Goodwin, 1979). However, any agency which provides assessment, referral, and follow-up services could, in principle, conduct controlled studies in which referral to A.A. was but one of a series of options to which selected clients could be assigned at random. Those assigned to A.A. could be linked with a potential sponsor who would be asked to facilitate affiliation with the movement in the normal manner by taking assigned clients to A.A. meetings and introducing them to other members. The issues of client acceptance of the A.A. "treatment," attrition, and other dimensions of noncompliance would be similar to those posed in all other controlled studies of psychosocial interventions.

Lest any readers be skeptical that such studies could be carried out, we call to witness the fact that studies have already been reported (Ditman et al., 1967; Brandsma, Maultsby, and Welsh, 1980). Such studies involve the random assignment of problem drinkers to Alcoholics Anonymous or to other interventions. These, as well as other studies already cited, demonstrate beyond any doubt that A.A. is not mysteriously impenetrable to analytic scrutiny. Indeed, it is our impression that there is an unusually rich literature which suggests promising ways in which A.A. might be studied. The leads which it provides can be examined through the medium of carefully controlled experimental designs involving A.A. as well as other available alternatives (Glaser and Ogborne, 1982).

Future studies, however, might benefit greatly from a more judicious application of the matching perspective. Neither of the above mentioned experimental studies produced results favorable to A.A.; the opposite was in fact the case. Some might thereby conclude that controlled studies have proven A.A. to be therapeutically inefficacious. We feel that this is an overinterpretation of the data. While the two studies strongly indicate that A.A. is not effective for *all* kinds of persons with alcohol problems, this is not, as noted above, an unexpected result. Both studies had a high proportion of court referrals and of lower socioeconomic status clients, whom one would not expect to find A.A. congenial. Our survey suggests that randomized controlled trials of Alcoholics Anonymous (as well as other interventions) are most appropriately directed toward those clients whom previous work suggests are likely to find the intervention appropriate along as many dimensions (affective, attitudinal, cognitive, and so forth) as possible. We predict that a series of such trials would provide evidence for the efficacy of Alcoholics Anonymous for a particular, identifiable subgroup of persons with alcohol problems.

References

Abramowitz, C. V., Abramowitz, S. I., Roback, H., and Jackson, C. Differential effectiveness of directive and nondirective group therapies as a function of client internal-external control. *Journal of Consulting and Clinical Psychology,* 1974, *42,* 849–53.

Baekeland, F. Evaluation of treatment methods in chronic alcoholism. In B. Kissin and H. Begleiter (eds.), *Treatment and Rehabilitation of the Chronic Alcoholic.* Vol. 5, *The Biology of Alcoholism.* New York: Plenum Press, 1977.

Bailey, M. B., and Leach, B. *Alcoholics Anonymous, Pathways to Recovery.* New York: National Council on Alcoholism, 1965.

———, W., Hustmyer, F., and Kristofferson, A. Alcoholism, brain damage, and perceptual dependence. *Quarterly Journal of Studies on Alcohol,* 1961, *22,* 387–393.

Bebbington, P. E. The efficacy of Alcoholics Anonymous: the elusiveness of hard data. *British Journal of Psychiatry,* 1976, *128,* 572–580.

Bill, C. The growth and efficacy of Alcoholics Anonymous: the elusiveness of hard data. *British Journal of Psychiatry,* 1976, *128,* 572–580.

Bill, C. The growth and effectiveness of Alcoholics Anonymous in a southwestern city 1945–1962. *Quarterly Journal of Studies on Alcohol,* 1965, *26,* 279–284.

Brandsma, J. M., Maultsby, M. C., and Welsh, R. J. *Outpatient Treatment of Alcoholism: A Review and Comparative Study.* Baltimore: University Park Press, 1980.

Brook, R. R. Personality correlates associated with differential success of affiliation with Alcoholics Anonymous (Doctoral dissertation, University of Colorado, Boulder, 1962.)

Burdick, A. J. A field-independent alcoholic population. *Journal of Psychology,* 1969, *73,* 163–166.

Canter, F. M. Personality factors related to participation in treatment of hospitalized male alcoholics. *Journal of Clinical Psychology,* 1966, *22,* 114–116.

Cohen, F. Personality changes among members of Alcoholics Anonymous. *Mental Hygiene,* 1962, *46,* 427–437.

Crumbaugh, J. C. Cross-validation of purpose-in-life test based on Frankl's concepts. *Journal of Individual Psychology,* 1968, *24,* 74–81.

———. Changes in Frankl's existential vacuum as a measure of therapeutic outcome. *Newsletter for Research in Psychology* (VA Center, Bay Pines, Fla.), May 1972, *14,* 35–37.

———, and Carr, G. L. Treatment of alcoholics with logotherapy. *International Journal of the Addictions,* 1979, *14,* 847–853.

Crumbaugh, J. C., and Meholick, L. T. An experimental study in existentialism: the psychometric approach to Frankl's concept of nosogenic neurosis. *Journal of Clinical Psychology,* 1964, *20,* 200–207.

Crutchfield, R. S. Conformity and character. *American Psychologist,* 1955, *10,* 191–198.

Curlee, J. Sex differences in patient attitudes toward alcoholism treatment. *Quarterly Journal of Studies on Alcohol,* 1971, *32,* 643–650.

Davidson, A. F. An evaluation of the treatment and after-care of a hundred alcoholics. *British Journal of Addiction,* 1976, *71,* 217–224.

Davis, D. L. Normal drinking in recovered alcohol addicts. *Quarterly Journal of Studies on Alcohol,* 1962, *23,* 94–101.

Ditman, K. S., Crawford, G. G., Forgy, E. W., Moskowitz, H., and MacAndrew, C. A controlled experiment on the use of court probation for drunk arrests. *American Journal of Psychiatry,* 1967, *124*(2), 160–163.

Edwards, G., Henseman, C., Hawker, A., and Williamson, V. Alcoholics Anonymous: the anatomy of self-help. *Social Psychiatry,* 1967, *1,* 195–204.

Festinger, L., Pepitone, A., and Newcomb, T. Some consequences of deindividuation in a group. *Journal of Abnormal and Social Psychology,* 1952, *47,* 382–389.

Fontana, A. F., Dowds, B. N., and Bethel, M. H. A.A. and group therapy for alcoholics: an application of the World Hypotheses scale. *Journal of Studies on Alcohol,* 1976, *37,* 675–682.

Frankl, V. E. *The Will to Meaning: Foundations and Applications of Logotherapy.* New York: World Publishing Co., 1969.

Giannetti, V. J. Alcoholics Anonymous and the recovering alcoholic: an exploratory study. *American Journal of Drug and Alcohol Abuse,* 1981, *8,* 363–370.

Glaser, F. B. The origins of the drug-free therapeutic community. *British Journal of Addiction,* 1981, *76,* 13–25.

———, Greenberg, S. W., and Barrett, M. *A Systems Approach to Alcohol Treatment.* Toronto: Addiction Research Foundation Books, 1978.

Glaser, Frederick B., and Ogborne, A. C. Does AA really work? *British Journal of Addiction,* 1982, *77,* 123–29.

Goldstein, G., and Chotlos, J. W. Stability of field dependence in chronic alcoholic patients. *Journal of Abnormal Psychology,* 1966, *71,* 420.

Goldstein, G. and Chotlos, J. Dependency and brain damage in alcoholics. *Perceptual and Motor Skills,* 1965, *21,* 135–150.

Goodwin, D. W. Comments on the article by R. E. Tournier. *Journal of Studies on Alcohol,* 1979, *40,* 318–319.

Gynther, M. D., and Brillant, P. J. Marital status, readmission to hospital, and intrapersonal and interpersonal perceptions of alcoholics. *Quarterly Journal of Studies on Alcohol,* 1967, *28,* 52–58.

Hanfmann, E. The life story of an ex-alcoholic. *Quarterly Journal of Studies on Alcohol,* 1951, *12,* 405–443.

Hayes, W. R., Schwarzbach, H., Schmierer, G., and Stacher, G. Hospitalized chronic alcoholic patients without field-dependent performance in the rod-and-frame test. *Journal of Psychology,* 1978, *99,* 49–52.

Hinrichsen, J. J. Locus of control among alcoholics: some empirical and conceptual issues. *Journal of Studies on Alcohol,* 1976, *37,* 908–16.

Hodgson, R., Stockwell, T., Rankin, H., and Edwards, G. Alcohol dependence: the concept, its utility and measurement. *British Journal of Addiction,* 1978, *73,* 339–342.

Holmes, R. M. Alcoholics Anonymous as group logotherapy. *Pastoral Psychology,* 1970, *21 (202),* 30–36.

Jacobson, G. R. Reduction of field dependence in chronic alcoholic patients. *Journal of Abnormal Psychology,* 1968, *73,* 547–549.

———, Ritter, D. B., and Mueller, L. Purpose in life and personal values among adult alcoholics. *Journal of Clinical Psychology,* 1977, *33,* 314–316.

Jellinek, E. M. *The Disease Concept of Alcoholism.* New Haven, Conn.: College and University Press, 1960.

Jones, R. K. Sectarian characteristics of Alcoholics Anonymous. *Sociology,* 1970, *4,* 181–195.

Karp, S. A., Poster, D. C., and Goodman, A. Differentiation in alcoholic women. *Journal of Personality,* 1963, *31,* 386–393.

Karp, S. A., Witkin, H. A., and Goodenough, D. R. Alcoholism and psychological differentiation: effect of achievement of sobriety on field dependence. *Quarterly Journal of Studies on Alcohol,* 1965, *26,* 580–585.

Kish, G. B., and Herman, H. T. The Fort Meade alcoholism treatment programme: a follow-up study. *Quarterly Journal of Studies on Alcohol,* 1971, *32,* 628–635.

Kurtz, E. The intellectual significance of Alcoholics Anonymous. *Journal of Studies on Alcohol,* 1982, *43,* 38–80.

Leach, B., and Norris, J. L. Factors in the development of Alcoholics Anonymous (A.A.). In B. Kissin and H. Begleiter (eds.), *Treatment and Rehabilitation of the Chronic Alcoholic.* Vol. 5, (*The Biology of Alcoholism.*) New York: Plenum Press, 1977.

Machover, S., and Puzzo, F. S. Clinical and objective studies of personality variables in alcoholism. Part 2: Clinical study of personality correlates of remission from active alcoholism. *Quarterly Journal of Studies on Alcohol,* 1959, *20,* 520–542.

McCance, C., and McCance, P. F. Alcoholism in north-east Scotland: its treatment and outcome. *British Journal of Psychiatry,* 1969, *115,* 189–198.

McLachlan, J. F. C. Benefit from group therapy as a function of patient-therapist match on conceptual level. *Psychotherapy: Theory, Research, and Practice,* 1972, *9,* 317–323.

———. Therapy strategies, personality orientation, and recovery from alcoholism. *Canadian Psychiatric Association,* 1974, *19,* 25–30.

McMahon, H. G. The psychotherapeutic approach to chronic alcoholism in conjunction with the Alcoholics Anonymous program, *Illinois Psychiatric Journal,* 1942, *2,* 15–20.

McWilliams, J., Brown, C. C., and Minard, J. G. Field dependence and self-actualization in alcoholics. *Journal of Studies on Alcohol,* 1975, *36,* 387–394.

Miller, W. R., and Joyce, M. A. Prediction of abstinence, controlled drinking, and heavy drinking outcomes following behavioral self-control training. *Journal of Consulting and Clinical Psychology,* 1979, *47,* 773–775.

Mindlin, D. F. Attitudes toward alcoholism and toward self: differences between three alcoholic groups. *Quarterly Journal of Studies on Alcohol,* 1964, *25,* 136–141.

Mumey, J. *The Joy of Being Sober.* Chicago: Contemporary Books, Inc., 1984.

Murphy, M. M. Values stressed by two social class levels at meetings of Alcoholics Anonymous. *Quarterly Journal of Studies on Alcohol,* 1953, *14,* 576–585.

Oakley, S., and Holden, P. H. Alcoholic Rehabilitation Centre follow-up survey 1969. *Quarterly Journal of Studies on Alcohol* (abstract), 1972, *33,* 873.

Pattison, E. M., Coe, R., and Doerr, H. O. Population variation among alcoholism treatment facilities. *International Journal of the Addictions,* 1973, *8,* 199–229.

Popham, R. E., and Schmidt, W. Some factors affecting the likelihood of moderate drinking by treated alcoholics. *Journal of Studies on Alcohol,* 1976, *37,* 868–882.

Reilly, D. H., and Sugerman, A. A. Conceptual complexity and psychological differentiation in alcoholics. *Journal of Nervous and Mental Disease,* 1967, *144,* 14–17.

Rhodes, R. J., and Yorioka, G. N. Dependency among alcoholic and non-alcoholic institutionalized patients. *Psychological Reports,* 1968, *22,* 1343–1344.

Robson, R. A. H., Paulus, I., and Clarke, G. C. An evaluation of the effect of a clinic treatment program on the rehabilitation of alcoholic patients. *Quarterly Journal of Studies on Alcohol,* 1965, *26,* 264–278.

Rohan, W. P. A follow-up study of hospitalized problem drinkers. *Diseases of the Nervous System,* 1970, *31,* 259–265.

Rossi, J. J. A holistic treatment program for alcoholism rehabilitation. *Medical Ecology and Clinical Research,* 1970, *3,* 6–16.

Rotter, J. B. Generalized expectancies for internal versus external control of reinforcement. *Psychological Monographs,* 1966, *80* (1, whole No. 609).

———. Some problems and misconceptions related to the construct of internal versus external control of reinforcement. *Journal of Consulting and Clinical Psychology,* 1975, *43,* 56–67.

Schachter, S. *The Psychology of Affiliation.* Stanford, Calif.: Stanford University Press, 1959.

Seiden, R. The use of Alcoholics Anonymous members in research on alcoholism. *Quarterly Journal of Studies on Alcohol,* 1960, *21,* 506–509.

Smith, P. L. Alcoholics Anonymous. *Psychiatric Quarterly,* 1941, *15,* 554–562.

Strom, K. R., and Tranel, N. N. An experimental study of alcoholism. *Journal of Religion and Health,* 1967, *6,* 242–249.

Tomsovic, M. A follow-up study of discharged alcoholics. *Hospital and Community Psychiatry,* 1970, *21,* 94–97.

Tournier, R. E. Alcoholics Anonymous as treatment and as ideology. *Journal of Studies on Alcohol,* 1979, *40,* 230–239.

Trice, H. M., and Roman, P. M. Sociopsychological predictors of affiliation with Alcoholics Anonymous: a longitudinal study of "treatment success." *Social Psychiatry,* 1970, *5,* 51–59.

Vota, A. C. Autokinesis and alcoholism. *Quarterly Journal of Studies on Alcohol,* 1968, *26,* 412–422.

Wanberg, K. W., Horn, J. L., and Foster, F. M. A differential assessment model for alcoholism: the scales of the Alcohol Use Inventory. *Journal of Studies on Alcohol,* 1977, *38,* 512–543.

Witkin, H. A., and Goodenough, D. R. Field dependence and interpersonal behavior. *Psychological Bulletin,* 1977, *84,* 661–689.

Witkin, H. A., Karp, S. A., and Goodenough, D. R. Dependence in alcoholics. *Quarterly Journal of Studies on Alcohol,* 1959, *20,* 493–504.

Zimbardo, P. The Human Choice. *Nebraska Symposium on Motivation 1969.* Lincoln, Nebraska: University of Nebraska Press, 1970.

7

Treatment, Outcomes, and Clinical Evaluation

Ernest Matuschka

How does one determine success or failure of psychotherapy with alcoholics? While abstinence is the most common criterion of treatment success, many investigators have incorporated controlled drinking and general improvement as criteria in evaluating treatment outcome. Reviewing 271 studies that evaluated outcome following some psychologically oriented treatment of alcoholism, Emrick (1974) classified change, during the entire follow-up period, into nine categories: (1) abstinence; (2) drinking but never to excess (controlled); (3) abstinent or controlled; (4) improved but having one or two periods of drinking to excess (much improved); (5) improved but having more than one or two periods of drinking to excess (somewhat improved); (6) sometimes much improved and sometimes totally abstinent; (7) totally improved; (8) unchanged; (9) worse (drinking more). These results show that many evaluators used more than total abstinence in measuring treatment outcome. However, Hoffman and Noem (1976) investigated the criteria for the differentiation of successful and failed treatment outcomes of alcoholics. On the basis of their results, the term "improvement" might be defined by the following areas: financial and employment status, social involvement, self-reliance supplemented with help and support from others, positive attitude toward treatment, few occasions on which they drive while intoxicated, and a bright future outlook, in addition to the traditional concept of abstinence.

Criteria used to determine recovery or successful treatment depend on the goals set forth in the treatment program (Lowe and Thomas, 1976). If the goal of the program emphasizes occupational adjustment, criteria for success are determined by job attendance and performance. If the desired goal is abstinence or controlled drinking, then a reduction in drinking would constitute success.

Forrest (1973; Forrest, 1984) utilizes continued intoxication versus termination of drinking behavior as units of measurement for successful treatment. In his research he reported that 45 percent of the research sample remained abstinent nine months after treatment and a total of 75 percent of the same nine-month sample group remained abstinent or achieved a reduction in alcohol consumption (Forrest, 1975).

Much controversy exists among professionals in trying to determine whether psychotherapy with the alcoholic is effective or not. Eysenck (1952) seems to be a benchmark for suggesting that no psychotherapy with neurotics was as valuable as psychotherapy with neurotics. Needless to say, this created a heated argument, with Eysenck defending his position a number of times. Bergin (1971) reviewed forty-eight research studies and reported that experienced psychotherapists were more successful than inexperienced psychotherapists. Meltzoff and Kornreich (1970) also report successful treatment via psychotherapy, as does Malan (1963). The general conclusion of all researchers with the possible exception of Eysenck is that psychotherapy is helpful and is of value to the client. If the client will stop destructive behavior and begin positive goal-directed behavior, this change constitutes successful psychotherapy for both the client and the therapist.

In the field of alcohol and drug abuse, responsible drug and alcohol use would indicate successful treatment. For many alcohol and drug abusers, *responsible* alcohol and *responsible* drug use may mean *total abstinence* from alcohol and drugs.

Does the successful treatment of alcohol and substance abuse and other forms of self-destructive behavior depend upon the skill of the therapist? Is therapeutic skill a legitimate way to manipulate a client into non-self-destructive behavior? Apparently the answer is "yes" to both questions. When a client enters a therapeutic relationship with a therapist, a contract is established. That implied contract reads in part that the therapist will use his or her skill in helping the client stop destructive behaviors and begin productive behaviors. In the context of this chapter, termination of alcohol and substance abuse is the therapeutic goal for an abusing client and it should become the basis of the contract between the client and the therapist.

Some systems of psychotherapy deal largely with the affective domain. Feeling needs to be translated into thoughts and then into behavioral change. The usefulness of exploring feelings may be in understanding how the client got that way and in the client's understanding that giving up negative feelings will facilitate growth.

Cognitive therapies deal with thought processes before feelings. "Guts don't make you well, cortexes do" may have come from Eric Berne; a psychotherapist can challenge or confront dysfunctional thinking. If there is inappropriate affect, confronting inappropriate feelings is appropriate as well, but if the thinking becomes clearer—that is, more responsible—better feelings about oneself usually follow.

Confrontation and confrontation therapy techniques are part of every psychotherapeutic relationship, whether it be in an individual or a group setting. "Confrontation" can be defined as going against the flow of the client or as becoming a counterforce or barrier to the individual's destructive behavior. The word "confrontation" may seem harsh, but confrontation is and can be gentle. In many ways a passive suggestion is confrontational and can be very powerful. The range of behavior for a confrontational therapist can be as varied as all human behavior. A therapist who does not accept a client's craziness is confrontational as well as therapeutic.

Denton (1981) discusses the interrelationship of feelings, thoughts, and behavior with an aim at development of appropriate "life skills" to facilitate maturational growth. His contention is that often the personality of the alcoholic is an incomplete, immature one lacking information, behaviors, and skills for coping with life's stresses and crises. Denton further states: "This basic incomplete personality represents a condition that long preceded any addictive behavior and . . . whenever the stresses and/or crises occur the structure of the personality is highly vulnerable to inappropriate actions" (pp. 18–19). Life skills, according to Denton, "are needed by the alcoholic to function effectively and with health in his perceptual world. These skills require a reordering of thinking and the learning of healthy habits of need fulfillment. Feelings change as thinking and habitual behavior is modified" (pp. 18–19). Denton has proposed a "thinking structure" to be utilized by therapists as well as a "feeling structure" to provide a cognitive map for therapy of alcoholics. The thinking structure encompasses the identification of the alcoholic's "belief system"; his "expectations" relating to his own and other persons' behavior; and, as therapy continues, his perception of how one makes personal "decisions" by operating from these "basic beliefs" and "expectations." The feeling structure consists of examining one's "basic needs"; the "emotional-behavioral bonding" that relates to how one satisfies these needs and thus receives emotional satisfaction; and, lastly, the "habitual-behavioral response," or repeated habitual pattern, and the strength of such a habit utilized in fulfilling a basic need. Change occurs as old "basic beliefs" that are unhealthy are replaced with more functional, healthy, accepting ones, and as new behaviors are developed to satisfy basic needs.

Many clinicians agree with Blane (1968; Black, 1981) that there are certain observable behavioral characteristics in the alcoholic personality. Of those found in the literature, dependency, denial, depression, emotional instability, impulsivity, self-destructive themes, and paranoia are common. Elements of passive-aggressive and passive-dependent behaviors are found as well. Most therapists recognize that "passives" are difficult individuals to work with. Of the systems of psychotherapy available, *passivity confrontation techniques,* based upon the work of Schiff and Schiff (1971), are productive and worthy of review.

Passivity Confrontation Therapy

A person being treated according to this system is known as a "passive," and substance abusers, like other passives, do not want to assume more than minimum, if any, responsibility for their behavior.

"Passivity," defined as behavior which is non-problem-solving and dependency-provoking, usually arises out of an unresolved oral symbiotic relationship between the mother and the child. The passive seems determined to get other people to do things for him and to have others become more responsible for problem solving than he is. It is important to note that during therapy a client of this type is motivated to make the therapist more uncomfortable with passive behavior than he himself is. The passive says "I can't think" and behaves as though he cannot. If the therapist submits to the nonthinking of the passive, the therapist is, in fact, hooked into the passive's game and becomes part of the problem. Therefore, much of the therapist's energy is spent in keeping himself out of the passive relationship. The opposite of passive-dependent behavior or passive-aggressive behavior is defined as assertive, effective, responsible behavior that acknowledges ownership of problems and responsibility for their solutions.

In all probability, the etiology of passivity begins when the mother does not give enough nurturance to the child. The mother does not give enough physical stroking nor psychological breast feeding. The child suffers from stimulus hunger, tries to maintain a symbiotic relationship with the mother, and continues to play weak and helpless to reinforce the symbiotic relationship. It is generally felt that two or more personalities must be involved to foster passivity in an individual. "Caretaker" parents foster passivity in a child when they accept more responsibility for what the child is doing than the child does himself. For example, when it is more important for the caretaker parents than it is for the child to get good grades in school, mow the lawn, wash the dishes, clean up the bedroom, the parents encourage a passive relationship. Caretaker parents assume the responsibility for the child because the child appears too dumb or too irresponsible to complete the tasks required. The child willingly accepts the position of being dumb and irresponsible, which then creates and maintains the symbiotic relationship.

Grandiosity is verbal or nonverbal communication used by both caretakers and passives to develop and maintain the passivity. Grandiosity is an excuse or rationalization projected onto other people. It provides the passive with the power to control and manipulate. "I can't stand it" or "I lose control" or "I did it because I was so angry" or "I was petrified with fear" or "I can't think" or "I don't know" are examples of grandiosities, which seem to cancel out any rational thought or problem-solving ability. If someone says "I don't know," the general assumption is that the person does not possess certain facts, and there is some legitimacy to an "I don't know" response when information truly beyond the comprehension or grasp of the individual is in question. However, a passive who says "I don't know" if asked when he is going to clean his room is essentially saying, "I don't know, you know for me, or you be responsible for me."

Schiff and Schiff (1971) discuss four behaviors used by passives: (1) doing nothing; (2) overadaptation; (3) agitation; (4) incapacitation or violence. All these passive behaviors are not relevant to problem solving and are intended to maintain a symbiotic relationship with the caretaker parents.

1. *Doing nothing:* In order to maintain symbiosis and not solve a problem, the passive does nothing. Grandiosities are "I can't think," "I can't do it," or "I was too scared (stoned) (drunk) to think." Attempts to elicit problem-solving behavior on the part of the client can be frustrating for the therapist, who, if he provides answers for the client can find himself caught in a symbiotic relationship.

2. *Overadaptation:* Overadaptation occurs when the passive moves from the do-nothing position. The passive does not identify goals or problem-solving abilities for himself, but tries to imagine what someone else would want him to achieve. He then decides that achieving someone else's expectations is too difficult or impossible, and therefore he returns to the do-nothing position. The grandiosity in this position is "I can't do as much as you expect or demand of me, and therefore I will do nothing."

3. *Agitation:* When overadaptation is escalated, the passive may

become agitated. Agitated behavior can also be non–problem solving. The passive has the knowledge that he could solve the problem by doing something, but this, of course, would destroy the symbiosis. At this juncture the passive is in conflict. The suggestion "sit down and think about your problem" will return the passive to overadaptation or the do-nothing position. "Don't just sit there, do something" will lead the passive into believing that any activity is problem solving—pacing the floor, worrying, smoking, drinking, eating, or rearranging the files. Both of the above examples are grandiosities. Agitated behavior can continue until the energy is dissipated and the passive can return to a do-nothing position and feel that the problem cannot be solved.

4. *Incapacitation or violence:* This behavior is the most pathological of all passive behavior because no thinking can be identified in this stage. The grandiosity of this stage is "I can't stand it!" which gives the passive permission to be incapacitated and retreat into isolation, alcohol, substance abuse, migraine headaches, unconsciousness, or catatonic behavior. Violent behavior is also built on the same grandiosity, and "I can't stand it!" gives the passive license to be violent, destructive, homicidal, or suicidal. The violent behavior indeed proves to the caretaker parents that the passive cannot think or function and he needs to be taken care of.

The passive's goals are to avoid solving his problems; to force someone else to solve them and take control of him; and to maintain the symbiosis.

The first three passive behaviors can be confronted in an office setting; however, it is inappropriate to confront a violent passive in an office. Passive patients may escalate into violence to prove that they are out of control and need to be taken care of. It is possible to do effective confrontation therapy without escalating a passive into violence in an office setting.

Discounting is a behavior initiated by caretaker parents who want to do their part in maintaining the symbiotic relationship with the child. Parental discounts can then become integrated beliefs and behaviors of the passive. There are four ways of discounting: (1) discount the problem; (2) discount the significance of the problem; (3) discount the solvability of the problem; (4) discount the person. The following examples represent the integrated belief of the passive.

1. *Discount the problem:* A substance abuser says, "What problem?" or "There is no problem, that's just the way I am," or "I don't drink that much," or "I only had two drinks." Discounting the problem is a denial that the problem exists or that drinking behavior is causing a problem. "Sure I drink, but I'm not an alcoholic."

2. *Discount the significance of the problem:* This tactic devalues

the problem—it isn't important enough to solve. The client says, "I only drink after work or on weekends," or "I only had two beers," or "It's not important anyway."

3. *Discount the solvability of the problem:* In this case the passive feels that nothing can be done to change his situation. He says, "I know I drink but I can't help it," or "I've tried but I can't control it," or "If I would stop drinking I would probably do something worse," or "I tried but they won't let me."

4. *Discount the self:* This is the most pathological of the discounting behaviors. The client says, "I am so nervous," or "I don't know how," or "I don't care anymore." When the person discounts his own ability to solve a problem or even refuses to recognize that he has problem-solving ability, the therapist should recognize that here is a passive in trouble.

Effective confrontation therapy with passives means that the therapist can recognize and confront a grandiosity, a discounting behavior, and a passive behavior. This system of therapy is most effective when the therapist restrains from interpreting or analyzing the client and only confronts the three abovementioned passive behaviors.

Psychotherapy should follow a logical order of events. In the following section, step 1 needs to be solved before the therapist can move to step 2.

1. Most passives begin in a doing-nothing position. They have a good reason for staying in that position (to maintain a symbiotic relationship) and need a reason to change. The therapist can discuss a richer life-style, in terms of productivity and satisfaction, with the client. If this sounds like a sell job, it is. But remember that clients may have to be sold good mental health and a positive life-style before they will consider giving up past self-defeating and damaging behaviors.

2. If a caretaker parent is in the environment, he or she must be willing to stop discounting and rescuing behavior. Many young alcoholics and substance abusers live with a caretaker parent. Getting the caretaker parent to stop discounting behavior is an extremely difficult task, and in some cases the passive may have to leave the environment. However, the age of the passive and lack of a more desirable environment may make relocation difficult.

3. Teach the passive and caretaker parent the terminology of this system. Inform them that you will point out (confront) when they are engaging in passive behavior, discounting, or grandiosities.

4. If the passive has accepted the above premises and stated a willingness to change (to give up passive behavior and to develop problem-solving behavior), the therapist is in a good position to be helpful. Confrontation takes place when the client displays long-standing pas-

sive behavior and is not owning his problems or being responsible for their solution.

The passive may be in the overadapted position to begin with, but that is the healthiest of the four positions. At this point he may be adapting to the therapist's resistive suggestion to "think and develop some positive alternatives to your behavior." If the client is engaging in overadaptation, or any of the other passive behaviors, the therapist may be in a symbiotic relationship. Most therapists do not want to be part of the problem, and therefore, should this occur, the alert therapist will confront this passive behavior as well.

As mentioned earlier, escalation of a passive into violent behavior is not desirable in an office setting. It may be more appropriate in a group setting, where a number of persons can help the passive "blow through" his violence. However, escalating a passive from doing nothing to overadapting, or de-escalating the passive from agitation to overadapting, is appropriate for office psychotherapy. If a passive in overadaptation asks, "What do you want me to do?" the therapist can help explore any number of healthy alternatives to the current destructive behavior. Exploring alternatives is thinking, which is seen as productive behavior.

Confrontation therapy is not discounting a client when the therapist attends to the client's "here and now" existence. Straightforward information about starting and stopping behavior is also appropriate. After saying to a client who is picking at a sore or pulling his hair or digging his fingernails into his body, "You are not supposed to hurt yourself, so stop that," the therapist may add, "You may want to think about what hurting yourself means to you." The purpose of that confrontation is to make the passive uncomfortable with old behavior so as to produce change into new behavior.

Psychotherapy with passives, drinking or nondrinking, is a difficult task. A course in courage could be added to a curriculum in psychotherapy. Forrest (1982, p. 29) points this out:

> Psychotherapists, as a group, tend to be rather passive individuals, and as such tend to rather passively absorb the aggressive confrontations of their alcoholic patients. Many competent therapists avoid or eventually leave the therapeutic arena with alcoholic patients as a result of the confrontations of their patients. Characterologically, the alcoholic patient is angry, aggressive, a manipulator, and psychodynamically of extreme importance, the alcoholic experiences marked interpersonal difficulties with authority figures (Bratter, 1979). All of these matters can prove difficult for the psychotherapist. If the therapist is to establish a productive therapeutic alliance with the alcoholic patient, he must be able to tolerate these abrasive and often threatening behaviors of the patient. In order to do this, the therapist must actively deal with the patient's manipulative,

angry and exploitive behaviors. Confrontation is but one significant tool in the therapist's interpersonal repertoire for helping accomplish this task.

Passivity confrontation is an effective system of psychotherapy whether it is used in individual, group, or family therapy. When passivity confrontation techniques are used in group therapy, group members often pick up on the techniques and confront each other. Confrontation can lead individuals and groups into some good cause-and-effect thinking, and such thinking can help individuals understand that consequences follow behavior.

Group Therapy

Individual therapy can be done in a one-to-one setting, or group therapy can be conducted with other individuals present. The classification "group therapy" implies that more than one therapist and more than one client are present in the setting.

An excellent definition of group therapy is offered by Forrest (1975, p. 93):

> Group psychotherapy is essentially an interpersonal transaction involving a group leader who, by virtue of a particular type of educational training and life experience, can potentially help facilitate behavioral growth and change on the part of other group members, who, in this particular context, share the same problem of alcohol addiction.

Group psychotherapy, whether it is inpatient or outpatient, offers a dimension not found in individual psychotherapy. In group therapy not only is the wisdom of the therapist available to the group, but the collective wisdom of the group is also present. A definition of group wisdom includes collective experiences (both successful and unsuccessful) and the ability of the group to utilize another person's experiences. The group offers a certain amount of psychological protection for all members including the therapist. Some former group participants may disagree with the above statement if they have experienced "hot seat" or "Synanon" tactics, but nevertheless, the group and therapist, unless totally pathological, will afford each participant protection.

Most importantly, a group can establish goals for growth and move individual members of the group toward those goals.

Research shows that group therapy is an effective form of treatment. Cartwright and Zander (1968) show that the group puts considerable pressure on its members to conform to group norms. An extensive review of literature regarding outcomes of different forms of group intervention can be found in Rose (1977), where he discusses six different group designs and documents the results. As in individual psychotherapy, the literature is rich in research and results.

In general, group therapy is as successful as any other form of psychotherapy providing the goals are established by the group members and the group leadership is solid. There is a cohesive element to a group which may make group therapy less abrasive than individual therapy, but that depends upon the group and the style of leadership.

Group leaders are in a powerful position and should be considered as such. Psathas and Hardert (1966) showed that the group leader's remarks usually determined the group norms, while Shapiro and Birk (1967) showed that when a group leader would make a remark to one member, the other members would indicate acceptance of those remarks in subsequent meetings. Not only does the group leader suggest and set norms, but he becomes a role model for personal behavior in and out of the group. Group members are sensitive to the leader's conduct and will imitate his method of handling both content and process in the group.

Unfortunately, subcertification for group leaders per se is not possible yet. Group leaders and leadership styles are as widely diversified as the groups they lead. Training and certification are left more to the imagination of trainers and future leaders than to a rigorous training program. The alarm bells should go off when someone who has participated in a weekend encounter group decides that by virtue of that experience he can conduct his own group utilizing the same techniques. Group members are trusting, naive, and gullible, and assume that if a person says he is a group leader, he is qualified to be one. Unfortunately it doesn't work that way, and for all practical purposes it cannot, because, as Yalom (1970) points out, "there are a bewildering array of approaches" and no practical way of monitoring all of the groups. A minimum requirement for a group leader should be membership in the American Group Psychotherapy Association.

Group leaders or members may select their own goals and directions for growth or change. Open participation in the group to determine individual and group goals would encourage a willingness for group members to support or confront each other. Matuschka (1971) utilized an Intra-Group Rating Scale (IGRS) as a method of helping groups determine group values and as a way of measuring group progress at various intervals along the way. The IGRS was modeled after the Multiple Peer Rating System used by the United States Air Force (1952).

The Intra-Group Rating Scale is designed to measure personal characteristics of the members of a group. The rating of group members can be accomplished by the peer group members, by the group leader, or by observers of the group. The IGRS is designed so that the group members are confronted with a one-to-one dyadic interface on a single personal characteristic. The dyadic interface allows the user to concentrate upon one other person in relationship to another without having to be concerned with a total group relationship. The group members are asked to evaluate one person against another person as well as themselves.

Admittedly, the IGRS results deal with a subjective impression, but many concepts and goals in psychotherapy are subjective. The exception might be the stopping and starting behaviors suggested by behavioral therapists. Stop-start behaviors can be objectively reported in a group, but behaviors such as more or less feeling, warmth, or empathy are subjective evaluations.

The group members and the group leader can select characteristics for group growth. The characteristics must be defined, understood, and accepted by the group as goals that the group will try to achieve. Several characteristics may be used simultaneously with a group if the group has felt comfortable with the process. However, in utilizing the IGRS only one variable at a time should be rated. If several characteristics are to be measured, it is better to use different IGRS forms.

For example, suppose the group chooses empathy or empathic understanding as a desirable characteristic and hence a group goal. The leader can provide the group with the definition of empathy and a model of empathic behavior. While the group is in progress, members will become sensitive to their own empathy and to the empathic behavior of others. Some will learn faster and better than others, while some members may fake empathy. However, to be entirely successful at faking, a group member must be skilled enough to "fool all the people all the time." If that happens, the group members may need to sharpen their observation skills.

The directions for administering the IGRS are given on the example in Figure 7–1.

Scoring of the IGRS consists of counting the T's in each column and the S's in each row. The T's are added to the S's, and that aggregate number is recorded in the column so indicated on the right side of the IGRS matrix. A rank order can be determined, showing the person highest in the characteristic measured, the next-highest person, and so on, down to the lowest person. The rater can see how he rated himself in relationship to how he rated other group members.

A group analysis can be made by tabulating all of the scores on the IGRS Group Analysis Worksheet (Figure 7–2, p. 205).

By following the same procedure—summing T's, summing S's, and adding T's to S's—a rank order of the entire group can be made. An individual's rank order can be compared with the way the individual

Your Name ______________________________

On this scale you are asked to make an evaluation of each individual in your group, including yourself. The scale is designed so that you will rate each individual against each other individual.

First, read the personal characteristic below and use only this personal characteristic in your evaluation of each individual.

Now, ook at the first name which appears at the top of the matrix. It is coded "A." Go down the column to the first row on the left side of the page where there is a name. For example, let's say row "K" contains the first name. The intersection of "A" and "K" will be where you make your first evaluation.

Ask yourself the question "Does 'A' or 'K' show the greatest amount of the characteristic to be rated?" If you feel that the person whose name is at the top (in this case "A") possesses a greater amount of the characteristic than the person on the side (in this case "K"), place a "T" (for *top*) in the cell at the intersection of "A" and "K." If, on the other hand, you feel that the person on the side possesses a greater amount of the characteristic, place an "S" (for *side*) at the intersection "A-K." Continue this rating until you have rated each individual in the group, including yourself.

Personal characteristic ______________________________

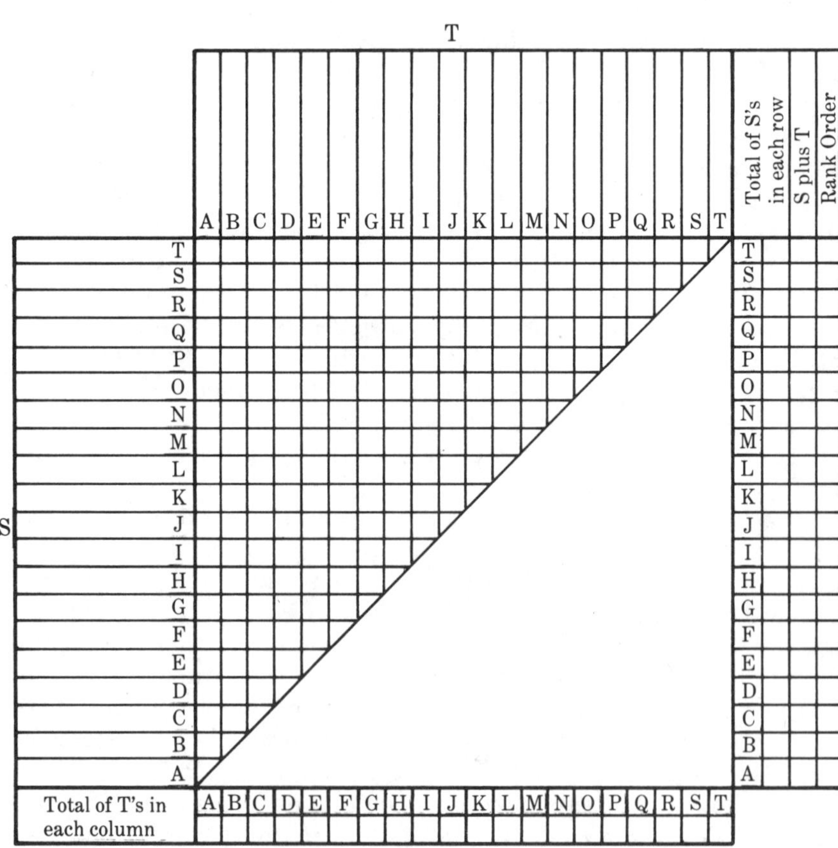

Figure 7–1. Intra-group rating scale

	A	B	C	D	E	F	G	H	I	J	K	L	M	N	O	P	Q	R	S	T		1	2	3
T																					T			
S																					S			
R																					R			
Q																					Q			
P																					P			
O																					O			
N																					N			
M																					M			
L																					L			
K																					K			
J																					J			
I																					I			
H																					H			
G																					G			
F																					F			
E																					E			
D																					D			
C																					C			
B																					B			
A																					A			
	A	B	C	D	E	F	G	H	I	J	K	L	M	N	O	P	Q	R	S	T				

(1) After computing rank order for each member of the group, those rank orders can be placed in the corresponding columns of this worksheet.
(2) Summate the rows and record in column 1.
(3) Rankorder the summations in column 2. This produces a group rank order.
(4) An independent rank order made by the group leader may be put into column 3. Any individual rank order may be compared with the group rank order or group leader rank order.
(5) The steady state cells, A to A, B to B, etc., show a single individual's self-ranking.

Figure 7–2. **Group analysis worksheet, intra-group rating scale**

ranks himself. The individual's rank of himself is found in the steady state cells, A to A, B to B, etc.

The usefulness of the IGRS depends upon feedback to group members. Without elaborating, one can easily see that the rankings can elicit discussion, particularly with members ranking lower on the scale. Few instruments facilitate honesty and openness as quickly and effectively as the IGRS.

The IGRS can also be used in researching growth, content, and progress in groups. For example, those counseling characteristics suggested by Truax and Carkhuff (1967) can be compared with the same variables, assessed in a client-submitted Barrett-Lennard Relationship Inventory (BLRI) (1962). The relationship between a self-perceived characteristic and the way the group sees an individual member is an area for research. Any subscale of any standardized personality or personal growth scale can be compared with the same subjective description measured on the IGRS.

Utilizing the peer group as raters of group growth is a very successful technique and allows the group to assume responsibility for their own growth. Group members will assume responsibility for other group members and will encourage the members to strive for a common group goal (group personality). The role of the group leader is to ensure that group goals are healthy for all individuals, and that in the process of growth a certain amount of safety and protection is afforded all members.

Family Therapy

Family therapy, a variation of group therapy, has become a popular method of treating drug and alcohol abusers. The family therapist suggests that substance abuse is a family illness (Stanton, 1978; Wegscheider, 1981). In examining families, the family therapist looks for dysfunctional relationships in the marriage and determines how that pathology extends into the family proper. The interrelatedness of families makes each family member part of, and a sustainer of, the problem. The alcoholic or substance abuser within the family structure is often prevented from changing because of the unwillingness of family members to consider a different (nonalcoholic) life-style. To complicate matters, many families have poly-drug abuse problems and each individual family member gets reinforcement for his or her pathological behavior from other abusing family members. Consider, if you will, a hypothetical family of four: the father, an alcoholic; the mother, a foodaholic; and two teenage children, poly-drug abusers. Families like this say they want to change; however, any disruption in the pathology of such a family will be met with passive, aggressive, sabotaging behavior.

The role of the family therapist (Stanton, 1978) is to reconstruct the family. It takes courage just to consider this kind of therapy.

Family members try to create a homeostatic climate to survive as individuals and as a unit. Changes that occur within the family such as illness, trauma, drunkenness, or sobriety create an imbalance, and family members as a team try to return the family to the status quo, including returning to a pathological position. This explains in part why family members try to keep the alcoholic drunk even though they insist they do not want to.

Steinhauer (1970) discusses four basic principles of family equilibrium: (1) All members are assigned and assume roles that relate to each other in characteristic ways. (2) Each family has a set of rules that govern the members and the way they relate to each other. (3) Any attempt to shift the family equilibrium from within or without will result in resistance and an effort to return to the status quo. (4) No matter how pathological a family appears to an outside observer, the established equilibrium is the family's way of minimizing threats of disruption and pain.

In most cases the request for intervention comes from the nonalcoholic spouse. As Forrest (1980) points out: "Spouses of problem drinkers head the list of those most affected by the pathological drinking patterns of others!" The nonalcoholic spouse risks physical abuse, family breakup, and excessive emotional pressure when outside intervention is sought. In most cases the risk is worth taking. First, no one known by this therapist ever started drinking with "becoming an alcoholic" as a long-term goal. Secondly, no person or family who has completed psychotherapy sober and intact would ever return to the alcoholic days.

The effort that families put into adjusting to and maintaining a pathological unit is phenomenal. Jackson (1954) mentions the stages of family adjustment to alcoholism: (1) an attempt to deny the problem; (2) an attempt to eliminate the problem; (3) disorganization of the family; (4) an attempt to reorganize in spite of the problem; (5) efforts to escape the problem; (6) reorganizing of part of the family; (7) recovery and reorganization of the whole family. She further points out that the family develops a trial-and-error system to find adjustments to maintain stability.

The effectiveness of family therapy lies in the fact that all members contributed to the family pathology and therefore it is imperative that all members contribute to reconstructing the family along healthy, productive lines. Helping the substance abusers in a family to refrain from abusing is only the beginning. Nonalcoholic spouses may indicate that alcohol or drugs were the only problem—all the while remaining blind to their own contribution to the pathological relationship. Getting an alcoholic or substance abuser to quit may be the beginning of treatment, but sobriety does not guarantee that wellness will follow. In many cases, sobriety brings out a number of changes in family structure and leads to more problems than anyone had imagined. Berenson (1976) indicates that therapy has two phases. The first is to get the alcoholic to stop drinking; the second is to deal with family dynamics after the achievement of sobriety. Neither of these are easy for the family therapist to accomplish with the alcoholic/abusing family. The achievement of sobriety is the primary goal, but it is necessary to work with family problems, adjustments, and changes concurrently.

In conducting therapy with families of alcoholics, a wise therapist will utilize many sources of help. The first source is Alcoholics Anonymous—both the organization and the individual helping members within that organization. The alcoholic must transfer his or her dependence to something other than alcohol. Alcoholics Anonymous offers alcoholics consistency in their lives. Spouses and children need support and reeducation, which can be found in Al-Anon, Alateen, and Alatot. The clergy (if the person has a church of choice), social workers, probation counselors, alcoholism counselors, welfare workers, mental health workers, physicians, lawyers, and friends can also be helpful, if their involvement is healthy and appropriate.

Wegscheider (1981) states that counseling with families is always challenging, but counseling a family whose thinking is clouded by alcohol or substance abuse is additionally complicated by the defenses of denial and delusion. As each family member strives to get his or her needs met, it becomes the therapist's task to facilitate that growth in a positive way. Helping the family build a positive support group is essential to their long-term rehabilitation. Therefore, as stated above, therapists need to draw upon a number of other groups, because family therapy is difficult and therapists need all the help they can get.

Coercive Approaches

Suppose you were told by your boss, "Stop drinking or submit your resignation." Or told by the county judge, "You may choose thirty days in jail or thirty days in an alcoholism treatment center." Or told by your spouse, "Move out until you have maintained a period of sobriety."

Motivation for behavioral change comes in many forms, but none so shocking or dramatic as those which leave an individual with limited choices. The approach is coercive; the results are quite positive. The most dramatic cases are those individuals who have been arrested for drinking while intoxicated (DWI) for the third through tenth time and are eyeball to eyeball with a disgusted judge. Given the choice of jail or treatment, in most cases the offender chooses a stay in a treatment center. The progression from drunk to detox to treatment may be rapid.

Most individuals entering treatment do so because they are feeling at least a subtle coercion. Alcoholics rarely seek treatment voluntarily, since at the core of the problem rests denial! Therefore, as Selzer and Hollway (1952) suggest, the coercive approach is a viable alternative.

Treatment which carried a coercive element has been shown to have a higher cure ratio than treatment without a coercive element. Mindlih (1960) reported that 32 percent of a coerced group benefited from treatment, while only 12 percent of a non-coerced group benefited. Dana (1964) reported that 50 to 75 percent of a group of coerced alcoholics returned to society and were productive at work and at home. Many coerced alcoholics may choose to use Antabuse as an extra guarantee that they will not drink.

Coercion, subtle or obvious, is still coercion. Therapy should be seen as a necessary and positive function in a substance abuser's life, which offers an alternative to continued drinking, abusing, and other destructive behaviors. The coercive approach is a way of saying to the abuser "You don't have to bottom out, you can (and will) get help now."

Whether the coercive therapy is performed in individual, group, or family settings, one of the major ingredients of effective psychotherapy is the therapist.

Matching Clients to Psychotherapists

The granting of a degree or the issuance of a license or certificate has meaning. It should mean that the individual has received an appropriate academic background, passed supervised internship requirements, and received the blessing of a graduate committee concerned with scholarly research. Licensing or the granting of a certificate to practice psychotherapy is based in part upon academic background, internship requirements, and the passing of a standardized examination.

Membership in the American Psychiatric Association, American Psychological Association, American Group Psychotherapy Association, American Association of Marriage and Family Therapists, or any other organization means that the individual adheres to the ethical standards of that organization. Any reasonable consumer of psychological services in the general public would therefore believe that a degree, a license, and membership in a professional organization means that the therapist is competent. Therein lies the problem. Degrees, licenses, or certificates do not guarantee effective psychotherapy. Licenses, degrees, academic standards, membership in organizations, and ethical standards do afford the general public some indications of quality. The personality of the therapist interacts with the client's personality. This interaction is the basis for effective or ineffective psychotherapy.

Bioenergetics, a therapy created by Lowen (1958, 1965, 1967, 1970, 1971, 1972, 1975), refers to character structure as an individual's defensive positions. Lowen (1958) draws upon Fenichel (1945) and Reich (1949) for his early concepts of character formation and character structure. He discusses the following character or personality types: (1) oral; (2) masochistic I; (3) masochistic II; (4) hysterical I; (5) hysterical II; (6) phallic-narcissistic; (7) passive feminine; (8) schizophrenic, and (9) schizoid.

Compare Lowen's list with the list of personality disorders in the *Diagnostic and Statistical Manual* (1980): (1) paranoid; (2) schizoid; (3) schizotypal; (4) histrionic; (5) narcissistic; (6) antisocial; (7) borderline; (8) avoidant; (9) dependent; (10) compulsive; (11) passive-aggressive; (12) atypical; (13) mixed; and (14) other.

Later Lowen (1975) condensed his original group of nine into five basic types. It is with this list of five personality types as reference that therapists' personality types can be explored. The five types are: (1) schizoid; (2) oral; (3) psychopathic; (4) masochistic; and (5) rigid. In general it is accepted that clients have personality types. It is proposed in this section that therapists also have personality types. The purpose of this section is to extract and summarize the material in bioenergetics that pertains to psychotherapists as people. For a beginning understanding of the bioenergetic therapy the reader may wish to read Lowen (1971 and 1975). For those who do not have a complete understanding of bioenergetics, suffice it to repeat that for this discussion, personality types and therapist personality types are drawn from the same material.

Schizoid therapist personality types are individuals who think but are split from their feelings and who may have little awareness of their own behavior. These individuals seem to have a weakened ego structure with a poor concept of self. They seem fearful of rejection, and therefore avoid intimate, feeling relationships. Physically, they represent themselves as tense in the upper part of the body, with a masklike face and eyes that do not make contact. There is an "as if" quality to their behavior. That is, they act "as if" they feel but they do not express feelings. It is as if the schizoid type is most fearful of rejection. The fear of rejection leads to covert hostility on the part of the therapist—perhaps toward a client.

The second type is the oral therapist personality disorder. Orality has its roots in infancy and is represented by traits of weakness, dependence, clinging behavior, decreased aggressiveness, and a need to be held, supported, and taken care of. Therapists of this type may need to keep clients in therapy longer than necessary. While a client is in therapy, such therapists may try to get their own oral needs met. Many oral character types show signs of exaggerated independence, which collapses into dependence under stress. The oral type is most fearful of deprivation, and exhibits mood swings and a longing for people.

The third personality type is the psychopathic therapist, whose basic modality is denial of feelings, particularly sexual feelings. The psychopathic personality may choose one of two modalities, bullying or seducing, to gain the necessary powers. The bullying type has a strong need to overpower, dominate, and control the therapy and the clients. This need may be expressed orally, since psychopathic individuals have been described as having an oral fixation. The need to control and overpower is closely allied to the fear of being controlled and overpowered. The seductive type uses seductive, sly behavior to gain power and control. The seductive psychopath may have his (or her) etiology in unresolved Oedipal feelings. This seductive relationship may lead to a sexual liaison with a client; however, the sexual pleasure is secondary to power, control, and conquest.

Fourth, we find the character structure of the masochistic therapist, who may be outwardly submissive and cooperative but have underlying feelings of hostility, negativity, superiority, and spitefulness. Submissiveness is the most common masochistic tendency; the person whimpers, whines, and complains a great deal. There is a stagnation of feelings, which need to be released before this therapist can function freely and effectively with clients.

Lastly, the rigid therapist personality type is one who holds back and is afraid to give in. There is a certain guardedness as this therapist holds back impulses to be open and transparent, and to reach out to other people. While therapists of this type have much better contact with reality than the four other types described, they will meet their needs through workaholic striving rather than pleasure. They may be too involved in work and production to allow clients to work or stumble through their own problems and find their own solutions. Male rigid therapists may be phallic-narcissistic character types, while the female rigid therapist may be tempted to use her sex as a defense against her own sexuality (hysterical).

The above discussion of therapist personality types illustrates how a therapist can express the need for love, intimacy, closeness, and pleasure. The schizoid personality represents an extreme withdrawal from intimacy. The oral personality needs warmth and support in an infantile way. The psychopathic personality needs those who need to be controlled by him, while the masochistic personality establishes closeness based upon his submissive attitude. The halfway-symbiotic relationship of the masochist with his clients is more intimate than that of the first three types, but like the first two, he needs to grow and develop. The rigid personality type can develop better interpersonal relationships but hinders himself because he remains guarded.

As in the quest for the Holy Grail, there must be a perfect therapist model. Staying within the description of bioenergetic therapy, the following ideas are paraphrased. Personality growth and good mental health are the process and end-result of a person becoming aware of his or her human rights. Schizoids have a right to exist and to be. Orals have a right to be secure in their own needing. Psychopathic types have the right to be autonomous and independent, while masochists have the right to be assertive. Rigid character types have the right to satisfy their wants openly and directly. An effective therapist has developmentally progressed through the five basic positions and has evolved into a responsible human being who can facilitate growth in clients and be an effective role model for others.

If assumptions based upon Lowen's theories (1975) are true, then psychotherapy offered by a therapist with a personality disorder would be detrimental to a client. Recently the question was asked, "Can a person who is even slightly screwed up be an effective psychotherapist?" The answer: "No, psychotherapy is too sensitive and too important to be left to individuals who are slightly screwed up!" The answer might have been harsh, but a psychotherapist should not be allowed to practice until he or she has had extensive psychotherapy from another competent therapist. Ideally, training institutions need to be populated with staff members who also have received extensive psychotherapy. The notion that psychotherapists or teachers of psychotherapists should be allowed to function in a state of arrested development or with a fixated personality disorder should not be condoned. Growth in personality types can take place in individual or group psychotherapy.

As mentioned earlier, degrees, licenses, and memberships are important first steps. However, the therapist's personality is important too. A healthy therapist can be very facilitative for a client's growth, whereas unhealthy matches in personality types between therapist and client can be very detrimental to both.

Neurological Deficits in Alcoholics

In evaluating the progress of neurological deficits or organic brain damage and its relationship to alcoholism, two questions need to be considered. The first is whether the excessive use of alcohol causes brain damage. The second question deals with a more elusive concept: whether the brain and neurological system shows partial or complete reversibility of cognitive function.

The relationship of alcohol to brain pathology has been a frequent topic in alcoholism literature for a number of years. The controversy has ranged from no relationship between alcohol and brain damage to the concept that consuming over one ounce of alcohol per hour causes immediate and irreversible brain damage. Wilkinson and Carlen (1980) state that neurological deterioration in alcoholics was suggested by Stewart and Wernicke in 1881 and by Korsakoff in 1889, marking the beginning of the study of brain behavior and alcoholism. Talland (1969) considers Korsakoff's syndrome and Wernicke's disease as the same disease and suggests six components of Korsakoff-Wernicke disease. They are: (1) anterograde amnesia, inability to form new memories; (2) retrograde amnesia, loss of old memories; (3) confabulation, making up stories rather than admitting to a memory loss; (4) meager content in conversation, a lack of spontaneity and creativity; (5) lack of insight, unawareness of one's memory defects; (6) apathy, loss of interest in ongoing activities.

The cause of Korsakoff-Wernicke disease is attributed to a deficiency of thiamine (vitamin B_1). It is generally believed that there is damage in the medial thalamus as well as the mammillary bodies of the hypothalamus. The vitamin B_1 deficiency causing Korsakoff's syndrome is linked to lesions caused by the combination of the consumption of alcohol and a poor diet.

After the pioneering work of Stewart, Wernicke, and Korsakoff, research progressed to the point where it was generally accepted that a relationship between alcohol consumption and brain damage did exist. Therefore, the next logical step was to find a suitable measure to prove or disprove this assumption. Reitan (1955), proponent and developer of the Halstead-Reitan Neuropsychological Test Battery, utilized that battery plus the Wechsler-Bellevue Battery to generate an enormous amount of research differentiating brain-damaged from normal populations. Rather than reference all of Reitan, it is suggested that a reader may want to start with *Clinical Neuropsychology: Current Status and Applications* by Reitan and Davidson (1974).

Reitan's work with the Halstead Battery, and his improvement upon procedures to test for brain damage, led to a number of research projects relating neurological deterioration to alcoholism. O'Leary et al. (1979) examined seventy-six alcoholic and nonalcoholic males with the Wechsler-Bellevue Intelligence Test (W-B) and the Halstead-Reitan Test Battery. They found a significant difference between alcoholics and nonalcoholics and further indicated that nine of the subtests were useful in differentiating between the two groups. Those subtests of the W-B found to be sensitive to differentiating between alcoholics and nonalcoholics were: Block Design, Digit Symbol, Picture Completion, Arithmetic, Picture Arrangement, and Object Assembly. From the Halstead-Reitan Battery, the Category Test, Tactile Performance Test (TPT) (both hands), and Part B of the Trail Making Test were also discriminating tests. Prior research by Fitzhugh, Fitzhugh, and Reitan (1960, 1965), and Smith, Burt, and Chapman (1973), also showed that the W-B and Halstead-Reitan Battery are sensitive in discriminating between alcoholics and nonalcoholics.

Løberg (1977) studied 111 male alcoholics with the Halstead-Reitan Battery as well as sensorimotor testing and the W-B. Sensitive and nonsensitive tests were essentially the same as in many other studies. Løberg also studied the hypothesis of asymmetrical involvement that suggested alcohol affected the right hemisphere more than the left. The results of the sensorimotor tests did not support this concept of lateralization. It is gratifying to note that Løberg's research may be developed to a point where localization and lateralization of brain function may be studied with the intent of further differentiating alcoholic brain dysfunction.

Cognitive deficits in alcoholics as discussed by Parsons (1980) show impairment in perceptual-motor and problem-solving abilities as well as general cognitive abilities. Parsons also discusses cognitive dysfunction in social drinkers without being definitive about which components of the cognitive domain are dysfunctional. Wilkinson and Carlen (1980) report that computerized tomography (CT) scores showed cerebral atrophy in both neurologically normal alcoholics and neurologically impaired alcoholics. However, the neurologically impaired alcoholics did more poorly on the Halstead-Reitan Impairment Index. Atrophy was defined as the sum of the widths of the eight largest visible sulci. The researchers report two other findings showing that some subjects function quite well despite cerebral atrophy and that atrophy may be more closely related to aging than to excessive drinking. This leads to the question of brain morphology and its usefulness. Perhaps brain function is a more valuable measure than brain morphology as studied by CT scan results.

The concept of brain aging suggested by Reitan (1973) and followed by Schau, O'Leary, and Chaney (1980) suggests that there is a decrease in intellectual functioning with advancing age. Reitan suggests that the following tests are brain-sensitive: Halstead's Category Test, Tactile Performance Test, Time and Localization Components, and Trail Making Test, Part B; and the Block Design and Digit Symbol subtests of the Wechsler-Bellevue Intelligence Test. Reitan adds Information, Comprehension, Similarities, and Vocabulary from the W-B as tests which are educationally sensitive. He developed a conversion table based upon brain-related variables and called the results the "brain-age quotient."

Schau, O'Leary, and Chaney (1980) utilized the brain-age quotient in studying the amount of cognitive recovery from deterioration of functional problem-solving ability due to excessive consumption of alcohol. By using the brain-sensitive tests and measuring brain-age quotient, a researcher may determine whether the brain age is at an expected or average level for persons of a given chronological age.

The concept of premature aging of the brain due to alcoholism has been discussed by Blusewicz (1975), Fitzhugh, Fitzhugh, and Reitan (1965), Goldstein and Shelly (1971), Kleinknecht and Goldstein (1972), Schau and O'Leary (1977), Williams, Ray, and Overhill (1973), and Schnechenberg, Dustman, and Bech (1972), with most of the research agreeing that the ingesting of large amounts of alcohol causes some cerebral dysfunction. Even though this dysfunction is short of organic brain damage, the amount of impairment present in alcoholics is worthy of the classification "premature aging."

Alcohol, even though there may be an equal distribution in the bloodstream (blood alcohol level), affects various parts of the brain and neurological system differently. Whether researching the lateralization and localization effect of alcohol on the brain is valuable or an academic exercise is yet to be determined. Well-documented orderly research which can be replicated will add to the general understanding of the problem. Research, of course, must be translated into practical suggestions for psychotherapy if it is to have any ultimate value.

Research by Golden (1981) suggests that neurological impairment in chronic alcoholics tends to fall into three major categories: (1) frontal lobe skill; (2) limbic lobe disorders of emotion and memory; and (3) right brain disorders, including the loss of spatial skills. There are also evidences of drawing disorders (construction dyspraxia) involving loss of the total gestalt when dealing with data. In regard to frontal lobe skill, Golden points out that the frontal lobes of the brain are responsible for planning, performing, and evaluation of all voluntary behaviors. The frontal area excludes the motor strip and sensorimotor area and its contralateral control. The secondary frontal area is responsible for reacting to past movements and meeting environmental demands. The tertiary area is responsible for planning, structuring and evaluating voluntary behavior.

The left frontal lobe is responsible for external and internal speech. A disruption of this area would lead to thought disorders as well as garbled, slow speech or no speech at all. Impairment of the right frontal lobe does not result in a loss of speech but may result in loss of ability to sing (try to tell a drunk that). Most importantly, the right frontal tertiary area may show impairment of spatial ability and visual spatial integration, causing problems with maze learning and nonverbal visual memory.

Those neurological tests that measure frontal lobe function are the Category Test and Trail Making Test, Part B. Left frontal function is also measured with the Category Test and Trail Making, Part B, as well as the Digit Span subtest of the Wechsler tests. The Aphasia Test is sensitive to central dysarthria (slurring and mispronunciation of complex words) and to dysgraphia (loss of writing skills).

Neurological deficits in the right frontal area are the most difficult to measure or recognize. They seem to be largely asymptomatic. The Picture Arrangement and Digit Span subtests of the Wechsler, and the Memory for Design Test (Graham and Kendall, 1960), are sensitive indicators. Spatial construction tasks are measured by the Bender-Gestalt Test (Bender, 1938) or the Benton Visual Retention Test (Benton, 1945, 1963, 1974). The Purdue Pegboard, Tactile Performance Test, and slowness in finger tapping of the nondominant hand would indicate spatial impairment in the posterior right frontal lobe.

Tests sensitive to temporal lobe involvement measure hearing acuity and sensorimotor involvement. Lesions in the temporal lobes are difficult to diagnose because of the close association to the limbic system. Nothing the differences between the left and right temporal lobes yields better diagnostic information. The left temporal lobe is sensitive to the Seashore Rhythm Test and speech-sound perception tests. These tests are valuable in diagnosing lesions in these areas. The Aphasia Screening Test, Digit Span subtest, and Sentence Learning Test are also sensitive indicators.

Picture Arrangement, Object Assembly, Memory for Designs, pitch perception, and the Seashore Rhythm Test are most sensitive to right temporal lobe dysfunction.

The right parietal lobe is sensitive to sensory defects on the left side of the body. Right parietal lesions are seen in low scores in Block Design, Picture Arrangement, Drawing the Greek Cross of the Aphasia Test, the Trail Making Test, and other drawing tests like the Bender-Gestalt.

The left parietal lobe is sensitive to the sensory input of the right side of the body. Any number of expressive problems can be present when this left lobe is dysfunctional: for example, dyslexia (inability to read), dysnomia (inability to name objects), and dysgraphia (inability to write).

Lesions of the occipital lobe cause partial or complete loss of vision. Lesions along the visual pathways may result in visual field defects, and therefore an inability to relay visual information to the visual cortex. A standard visual field examination will screen out any evidence of visual deficits.

Visual recognition, analysis, and synthesis of information is necessary for successful performance on the Block Design and Object Assembly subtests of the Wechsler. Visual agnosia is the inability to recognize objects through the visual senses or because of mental deterioration in the visual cortex. A number of separate forms of agnosia are now recognized: (1) visual object agnosia; (2) simultaneous agnosia; (3) visuospatial agnosia; (4) agnosia for faces; (5) color agnosia; and (6) agnostic alexia (Walsh, 1978). The research question that remains in examining the concept of visual agnosia is whether it implies lesions in the occipital lobes and whether alcohol and/or alcoholism can produce these lesions.

Possibly the understanding of brain/behavior relationships is more advanced than the psychometric devices available to elicit that information. Research should travel in the direction of finer measurements with more specific and detailed answers to the question, rather than in the direction of shortcuts and abbreviated forms of neuropsychological testing. The clinical neuropsychologist may only want to know whether brain damage is present and does not have the time or energy for a full examination. In this case the decision to use an abbreviated examination may be warranted. However, researchers should be encouraged to refine psychometric procedures and develop new ways to ferret out the intricacies of brain/behavior relationships.

In summary, psychoneurological examinations suggest that the performance subtests of the Wechsler differentiate between brains impaired by the use of alcohol and those that are not (controls). Arithmetic is the only verbal subtest which suggests that relationship. Those tests of the Halstead-Reitan Battery sensitive to impairment in alcoholics are the Category Test, Tactile Performance Test, Time and Localization Test, and the Trail Making Test, Part B (Parsons, 1980).

Other tests have been mentioned in the preceeding discussion which did not make Parsons's final list in his review of fifteen studies relating intelligence, as measured by the Wechsler tests, and neuropsychological functioning, as measured by the Halstead-Reitan Battery. (Parsons, Table 6, p. 335, in Filskov and Boll, 1981). The assumption made above still seems valid; that is, new, refined systems of examining alcoholic brain/behavior relationships need to be developed. Reitan's (1973) concepts of "brain-age quotient" and "problem-solving ability" should lead research in the direction of better neuropsychological examinations and their contributions to understanding the function or dysfunction of the alcoholic brain.

The question of recoverability of the dysfunctional brain needs to be addressed. For those individuals involved in psychotherapeutic treatment of alcoholics, the alcoholic's inability to "problem solve" is detrimental to recovery. To this add rigidity in thought and rigidity in personality, plus confabulation and memory defects—all of which complicate the life and recovery of the alcoholic. A small number of researchers have studied this problem (Goodwin and Hill, 1975; Carlen et al., 1978; Hansen, 1977; Cermak, 1977). In general, alcoholics who abstain do show some recoverability of brain function, while those who continue to consume alcohol do not. Those alcoholics who abstain and go through cognitive-intellectual training programs do better in listening skills, of memory for direction finding, spatial analysis, and abstract reasoning.

Neuropsychologists would do well to study the results of gerontologists and their concepts regarding reversible versus irreversible organic brain syndrome. Two classifications of brain disease are considered irreversible. The first, senile dementia, involves a gradual and progressive decline in intellectual and cognitive abilities. The second is arteriosclerotic brain disease where there is localized death of brain tissue due to occlusive arterial disease (Pfeiffer, 1975).

Those organic brain syndromes which are considered reversible due to temporary malfunction of a significant area of cortical cells are generally grouped into the categories of metabolic malfunction or drug intoxication (Engle and Roman, 1959). Such diseases would include diabetic acidosis, liver failure, dehydration, uremia, emphysema, hypothyroidism, electrolyte imbalance, cardiac arrhythmia, and ineffective cardiac output (Butler and Lewis, 1977). Drug intoxication can be caused by the sensitivity to drugs of elderly persons. Drug-to-drug interaction as well as drug intoxication can be "iatrogenic," that is, a result of the medical treatment itself. In many cases, a reevaluation of treatment and reduction or elimination of the offending drug will produce reversibility of organic brain syndrome.

This research would suggest that the use of alcohol could cause reversible or irreversible organic brain syndrome depending upon the amount of alcohol ingested as well as the length of time the alcoholic has been drinking.

Adams, Grant, and Reed (1980), in reexamining some subjects of their earlier study (Grant, Adams, and Reed, 1979), found that the men who had been abstinent for eighteen months showed more similarities to a nonalcoholic group than to a recently detoxified group on the neuropsychological examinations. Alcohol does damage the neurological system. How much damage it does, and the severity and duration of the damage, is a necessary bit of research that remains to be done.

Summary

There are parameters to psychotherapy, which were presented from the vantage point of a clinical psychologist and generalized into the areas of alcohol and substance abuse. Even though there is disagreement concerning who can treat whom and where, there is a general consensus that effective individual, group, and family psychotherapy does produce desired and beneficial results for the client. Passivity confrontation techniques represent an effective system of providing psychotherapy for alcohol and substance abusers.

The Intra-Group Rating Scale was adopted for use with groups and is an effective feedback device.

Fully qualified and licensed therapists may still need to examine their own personality (Lawson, Ellis, and Rivers, 1984). To need to do this and yet not do so is a question of ethics, or is it? It could be a sign of the personality dysfunction itself.

In the last section, neuropsychological diagnosis, brain/behavior relationships, and the influence of alcohol were examined. This topic is another area which is fertile for research, particularly in answering the question of rehabilitating the brain and nervous system of the alcoholic.

References

Adams, K. M., Grant, I., and Reed, R. Neuropsychology in alcoholic men in their late thirties: one-year followup. *American Journal of Psychiatry,* 1980, *137.*

American Psychological Association. A model for state legislation regulating the practice of psychology. Washington, D.C.: American Psychological Association, 1977.

Barrett-Lennard, G. T. Dimensions of therapist response in causal factors in therapeutic change. *Psychological Monographs,* 1962, *76* (*43*), 1024–1030.

Bender, L. A visual motor gestalt test and its clinical use. *Journal of American Orthopsychiatry,* 1938.

Benton, A. L. A visual retention test for clinical use. *Archives of Neurological Psychiatry,* 1945, *54,* 16–21.

———. *The Revised Visual Retention Test.* New York: The Psychological Corp., 1963.

———. *The Revised Visual Retention Test.* New York: The Psychological Corp., 1974.

Berenson, D. A family approach to alcoholism. *Psychiatric Opinion,* 1976, *13,* 3–5.

Berger, M. M. *Beyond the Double Blind.* New York: Brunner/Mazel Publishers, 1978.

Bergin, A. E. The evaluation of therapeutic outcomes. In A. E. Bergin and S. L. Garfield (eds.), *Handbook of Psychotherapy and Behavior Change.* New York: John Wiley & Sons, 1971.

Black, C., *It Will Never Happen to Me.* Denver: M.A.C., 1981.

Black, H. C. *Black's Law Dictionary.* St. Paul, Minn.: West Publishing Co., 1968.

Blane, H. T. *The Personality of the Alcoholic.* New York: Harper & Row, 1968.

Blusewicz, M. J. Neuropsychological correlates of chronic alcoholism and aging. Ph.D. dissertation, Pennsylvania State University, University Park, Pa., 1975.

Bratter, T. E. The psychotherapist as a twelfth-step worker in the treatment of alcoholism. *Family and Community Health,* 1979, *2*(*2*), 31–58.

Butler, R. N., and Lewis, M. I. *Aging and Mental Health: Positive Psychosocial Approaches.* St. Louis: C. V. Mosby Co., 1977.

Carlen, P. L., Wortzman, G., Holgate, R. C., Wilkinson, D. A., and Rankin, J. G. Reversible cerebral atrophy in recently abstinent chronic alcoholics measured by computerized tomography scans. *Science 200,* 1978.

Cartwright, D., and Zander, A. (eds.). *Group Dynamics: Research and Theory.* New York: Harper & Row, 1968.

Cermak, L. S. Improving retention in alcoholic Korsakoff patients. In O. A. Parsons (chm.), *Behavioral Assessment of Cognitive Functioning in Alcoholics: Treatment Implications.* Symposium presented at the NATO International Conference on Experimental and Behavioral Approaches to Alcoholism, Bergen, Norway, 1977.

Dana, A. *The Constructive Element of Coercion.* Paper delivered before Alcoholism Workshop of the 17th Annual Meeting of the Florida Psychological Association, April 1964. Report #10 of the North American Association of Alcoholism Programs, Miami, Fla.

Denton, J. L. Maturation: the development of life skills. Unpublished manuscript, 26 pp., Kearney State College, Kearney, Neb., 1981.

Diagnostic and Statistical Manual of Mental Disorders, 3rd ed. Washington, D. C.: American Psychiatric Association, 1980.

Emrick, C. D. A review of psychologically oriented treatment of alcoholism. Part 1: The use and interrelationships of outcome criteria and drinking behavior following treatment. *Quarterly Journal of Studies on Alcohol,* 1974, *35,* 523–549.

Engle, G. L., and Roman, J. Delirium, a syndrome of cerebral insufficiency. *Journal of Chronic Diseases,* 1959, *9.*

Engler, B. *Personality Theories: An Introduction.* Boston: Houghton Mifflin Co., 1979.

Eysenck, H. J. The effects of psychotherapy: an evaluation. *Journal of Consulting Psychology,* 1952, *16,* 116–132.

Fenichel, O. *The Psychoanalytic Theory of Neurosis.* New York: W. W. Norton, 1945.

Filskov, S. B., and Boll, T. J. (eds.), *Handbook of Clinical Neuropsychology.* New York: John Wiley & Sons, 1981.

Fitzhugh, L. C., Fitzhugh, K. B., and Reitan, R. M. Adaptive abilities and intellectual functioning in hospitalized alcoholics. *Quarterly Journal of Studies on Alcohol,* 1960, *21,* 112–116.

———. Adaptive abilities and intellectual functioning in hospitalized alcoholics: further considerations. *Quarterly Journal of Studies on Alcohol,* 1965, *26,* 920–937.

Forrest, G. G. *The Effect of Group Psychotherapy upon Levels of Anxiety, Depression, and Hostility Within an Alcoholic Population.* Fort Gordon, Ga.: Alcohol and Drug Rehabilitation Center, 1973.

———. *The Diagnosis and Treatment of Alcoholism.* Springfield, Ill.: Charles C. Thomas, 1975.

———. *How to Live with a Problem Drinker and Survive.* New York: Atheneum, 1980.

———. *Confrontation in Psychotherapy with the Alcoholic.* Holmes Beach, Fla.: Learning Publications, 1982.

———. *Alcoholism, Narcissism and Psychopathology.* Springfield, Ill.: Charles C. Thomas, 1984.

Golden, C. J. *Diagnosis and Rehabilitation in Clinical Neuropsychology.* Springfield, Ill. Charles C. Thomas, 1981.

Goldstein, G., and Shelly, C. H. Field dependence and cognitive, perceptual, and motor skills in alcoholics: a factor-analytic study. *Quarterly Journal of Studies on Alcohol,* 1971, *32.*

Goodwin, D. W., and Hill, S. Y. Chronic effects of alcohol and other psychoactive drugs on intellect, learning, and memory. In J. G. Rankin (ed.), *Alcohol, Drugs, and Brain Damage.* Toronto: Addiction Research Foundation, 1975.

Graham, F. R., and Kendall, B. S. Memory for designs test: revised general manual. *Perceptual and Motor Skills,* 1960, *11,* 62–66.

Grant, I., Adams, K., and Reed, R. Normal neuropsychological abilities of alcoholic men in their late thirties. *American Journal of Psychiatry,* 1979, *136.*

Hansen, L. Treatment of reduced intellectual functioning in alcoholic patients. In O. A. Parsons (chm.), *Behavioral Assessment of Cognitive Functioning in Alcoholics: Treatment Implications.* Symposium presented at the NATO International Conference on Experimental and Behavioral Approaches to Alcoholism, Bergen, Norway, 1977.

Hoffman, H., and Noem, A. A. Criteria for the differentiation of success and failure in alcoholism treatment outcome. *Psychological Reports,* 1976, *39,* 101–113.

Jackson, J. K. The adjustment of the family to the crises of alcoholism. *Quarterly Journal of Studies on Alcohol,* 1954, *15.*

Kleinknecht, R. A., and Goldstein, S. G. Neuropsychological deficits associated with alcoholism: a review and discussion. *Quarterly Journal of Studies on Alcohol,* 1972, *33,* 1011–1019.

Lawson, G. W., Ellis, P. C., and Rivers, P. C. *Essentials of Chemical Dependency Counseling.* Rockville, Md.: Aspen Publications, 1984.

Løberg, T. Dimensions of alcohol abuse in relation to neuropsychological deficits. In O. A. Parsons (chm.), *Behavioral Assessment of Cognitive Functioning in Alcoholics: Treatment Implications.* Symposium presented at the NATO International Conference on Experimental and Behavioral Approaches to Alcoholism, Bergen, Norway, 1977.

Lowe, W. C., and Thomas, S. D. Assessing alcoholism treatment effectiveness: a comparison of three evaluative measures. *Journal of Studies on Alcohol,* 1976, *37,* 772–784.

Lowen, A. *Physical Dynamics of Character Structure.* New York: Grune & Stratton, 1958.

———. *Love and Orgasm.* New York: Signet Books, 1965.

———. *The Betrayal of the Body.* New York: Collier Books, 1967.

———. *Pleasure: A Creative Approach to Life.* New York: Penguin Books, 1970.

———. *The Language of the Body.* Toronto: Collier-Macmillan, 1971.

———. *Depression and the Body.* Baltimore: Penguin Books, 1972.

———. *Bioenergetics.* New York: Penguin Books, 1975.

Malan, D. *A Study of Brief Psychotherapy.* London: Tavistock, 1963.

Matuschka, E. P. The Intra-Group Rating Scale. Unpublished manuscript, 9 pp., Kearney State College, Kearney, Neb., 1971.

Meltzoff, J., and Kornreich, M. *Research in Psychotherapy.* Chicago: Atherton, 1970.

Mindlin, D. F. Evaluation of therapy for alcoholics in a workhouse setting. *Quarterly Journal of Studies on Alcohol,* 1960, *21.*

O'Leary, M. R., Donovan, D. M., Chaney, E. F., Walker, R. D., and Schau, E. J. Application of discriminate analysis to level of performance of alcoholics and nonalcoholics on the Wechsler Bellevue and Halstead-Reitan subtests. *Journal of Clinical Psychology,* 1979, *35,* 205–214.

Parsons, O. A. Cognitive dysfunction. *Journal of Studies on Alcohol,* 1980, *41,* 1304–1318.

———, and Farr, S. P. The neuropsychology of alcohol and drug use. In S. B. Filskov and T. J. Boll (eds.), *Handbook of Clinical Neuropsychology.* New York: John Wiley & Sons, 1981.

Pfeiffer, E. Successful aging. In L. E. Brown and E. O. Ellis (eds.), *Quality of Life: The Later Years.* Boston: Publishing Science Group, 1975.

Psathas, G., and Hardert, R. Trainee interventions on normative patterns in the T-group. *Journal of Applied Behavioral Science,* 1966, *2.*

Reich, W. *Character Analysis.* New York: Orgone Institute Press, 1949.

Reitan, R. M. The relation of the Trail Making Test to organic brain damage. *Journal of Counseling Psychology,* 1955, *19.*

———. *Behavioral manifestations of impaired brain function in aging.* Paper presented at the Annual Meeting of the American Psychological Association, Montreal, 1973.

———, and Davidson, L. A. (eds.). *Clinical Neuropsychology: Current Status and Applications.* New York: Halstead, 1974.

Rogers, C. R. The necessary and sufficient conditions of therapeutic personality change. *Journal of Consulting Psychology,* 1957, *21.*

Rose, S. D. *Group Therapy: A Behavioral Approach.* Englewood Cliffs, N.J.: Prentice-Hall, 1977.

Schau, E. J., and O'Leary, M. R. Adaptive abilities of hospitalized alcoholics and matched controls: the brain-age quotient. *Journal of Studies on Alcohol,* 1977, *38,* 741–760.

———, and Chaney, E. F. Reversibility of cognitive deficits in alcoholics. *Journal of Studies on Alcohol,* 1980, *41,* 922–930.

Schiff, A. W., and Schiff, J. E. Passivity. *Transactional Analysis Journal,* 1971, *1(1).*

Schnechenberg, T., Dustman, R. E., and Bech, E. C. Cortical evoked responses of hospitalized geriatrics in three diagnostic categories. Paper read at the 80th Annual Convention of the American Psychological Association, Montreal, Canada, 1972.

Selzer, M. L., and Hollway, W. H. A followup of alcoholics committed to a state hospital. *Quarterly Journal of Studies on Alcohol,* 1952, *18.*

Shapiro, D. and Birk, L. Group therapy in Experimental Perspective. *International Journal of Group Psychotherapy,* 1967, *17.*

Smith, J. W., Burt, D. W., Chapman, R. F. Intelligence and brain damage in alcoholics: A study in patients of middle and upper social class. *Quarterly Journal of Studies on Alcohol,* 1973, *34,* 177–191.

Stanton, M. D. Some outcome results and aspects of family therapy with drug addicts. In D. Smith, S. Anderson, M. Buxton, T. Chung, N. Gottlieb, and W. Harvey (eds.), *A Multicultural View of Drug Abuse: Selected Proceedings of the National Drug Abuse Conference, 1977.* Cambridge, Mass.: Schenkman Publishing Co., 1978.

Steinhauer, P. D. Introductory lecture on family therapy. *Quarterly Journal of Studies on Alcohol,* 1970, *31,* 277–284.

Talland, G. A. *The Pathology of Memory.* New York: Academic Press, 1969.

Truax, C. B., and Carkhuff, R. R. *Toward Effective Counseling and Psychotherapy: Training and Practice.* Chicago: Aldine, 1967.

United States Air Force. *Officer Candidate School Peer Rating Scale.* Lackland AFB, Texas, 1952.

Walsh, K. W. *Neuropsychology: A Clinical Approach.* Edinburgh, Scotland: Churchill Livingstone Publishing, 1978.

Wegscheider, S. *Another Chance: Hope and Health for the Alcoholic Family.* Palo Alto, Calif.: Science and Behavior Books, 1981.

Williams, J. D., Ray, C. G., and Overhill, J. E. Mental aging and organicity in an alcoholic population. *Journal of Consulting and Clinical Psychology,* 1973, *41,* 62–77.

Wilkinson, D. A., and Carlen, P. L. Neuropsychological and neurological assessment of alcoholism: discrimination between groups of alcoholics. *Journal of Studies on Alcohol,* 1980, *41(1),* 1641–1655.

Yalom, I. D. *The Theory and Practice of Group Psychotherapy.* New York: Basic Books, 1970.

8

The Clinical Assessment and Diagnosis of Addiction

Hypothesis Testing

HOWARD SHAFFER / JANICE KAUFFMAN

THIS CHAPTER EXAMINES the merits of a hypotheses-testing model and its role in the clinical assessment and diagnosis of drug dependence, abuse, and addiction. Discussion will focus primarily on the clinical interview as the setting within which the hypotheses-testing model can be utilized. Consequently, this chapter also will consider some useful interview strategies designed to facilitate the hypotheses-testing approach and will examine some potential procedural problems that can occur during the assessment process.

Historically, clinical assessment has played a central role in the intervention process. Only recently, however, has the assessment process in particular received formal and detailed attention; a variety of excellent resources have organized and explicated this process (e.g., Barlow, 1981; Butcher, 1972; Weiner, 1975, 1976; Megargee, 1966; Korchin, 1976; Hersen and Bellack, 1976; Cimenaro, Calhoun, and Adams, 1977; Lazare, 1979a; Renner, 1979; Jackson and Messick, 1967; Kendall and Hollon, 1981; Sullivan, 1970; Paolino, 1981; Merluzzi, Glass, and

The authors express their thanks to Dr. Milton E. Burglass, Dr. Blase Gambino, Dr. John A. Renner, Jr., Dr. Edward J. Khantzian, Mary Gardiner, Charles Neuhaus, and Carolyn Dyer for their helpful comments on earlier drafts of this chapter.

The preparation of this chapter was supported, in part, by funds provided by The National Institute on Drug Abuse, #86140.

Genest, 1981; Mendelson and Mello, 1979; Miller, 1980; Mischel, 1968; Nicholi, 1978; Wilson, 1980; Woody, 1980; Zimberg, 1982).

It is important to note that the procedures of clinical assessment are dictated by the various assumptions upon which unique theoretical systems rest. Therefore, the utility of any assessment procedure is a function of its theoretical foundations. Thus, assessment from a psychodynamic framework proceeds differently and has different functions than assessment from a behavioral or neurological framework. In general, there are four functions of clinical assessment: (1) problem description, (2) category diagnosis, (3) selection of treatment procedure(s), and (4) evaluation of treatment outcome and process. As already noted, the prominence of these functions during the assessment process is determined by the clinician's theoretical orientation.

The process of clinical assessment typically utilizes information obtained from a variety of sources. These may include (1) direct interviews with the identified patient, (2) observation of the patient in varied settings, (3) interviews with significant others who have information about the patient, (4) psychometric instruments, (5) self-report and significant-other reporting forms, (6) case histories (social, medical, drug, etc.), and (7) physiological measurement. The hypothesis-testing approach described here may utilize each of these sources as the basis for the generation of clinically relevant hypotheses, and, through the process of confirmation and disconfirmation, direct future choices of source material. This chapter, therefore, will emphasize the testing of hypotheses rather than the use of the traditional sources of assessment information listed above. This approach will be illustrated within the *clinical interview* setting. This focus is due primarily to the limitations of space and time; nevertheless, a hypotheses-testing approach is readily generalized to other types of assessment activities in a variety of settings.

The present chapter has an additional limiting organizational strategy: a focus on *drug*-related addiction. This attention is neither the result of chauvinism with respect to other habitual behaviors (e.g., gambling) nor an attempt to restrict the techniques offered here to the assessment of drug addiction only; rather, the assessment of drug addiction is intended to illustrate the use of these techniques for application to the other areas of "addictive" behavior. In order to assist the clinician, researcher, or student interested in pursuing issues in greater detail than space permits here, we will include key references that provide points of entry into the relevant literature. Finally, for the reader unfamiliar with the semantics of addiction, Appendix 1 contains a glossary of essential definitions relevant to the assessment of diagnosis of addictive behaviors.

Clinical Assessment: General Considerations

Diagnosis

> . . . [I]n order to solve a problem it is necessary (if not sufficient) to "diagnose" it correctly. Whether we are considering a malfunctioning TV, a person in distress, or nations in conflict, the route to solution starts with knowledge of the problem's nature and causes. In this broad and commonsensical meaning, diagnosis is as necessary to mental health intervention as to action in any other realm. It is an inevitable part of the clinical process, whether or not special procedures are involved. (Korchin, 1976, p. 123)

In general usage, and in the DSM II (*Diagnostic and Statistical Manual of Mental Disorders,* 3rd edition), diagnosis "refers to the process of identifying specific mental or physical disorders. Some, however, use the term more broadly to refer to a comprehensive evaluation that is not limited to the identification of specific disorders" (American Psychiatric Association, 1980, p. 358). Diagnosis, in the nosological sense, has not proved particularly useful in facilitating the decision concerning what therapies should be applied to which specific problems (for pertinent discussions about this phenomenon, see Bentler, 1979; Goldstein and Stein, 1976). Because of the current limited prescriptive and evaluative usefulness of establishing diagnostic categories, we will consider the concept of diagnosis under the more generic term "clinical assessment." This avoids the common misconception implied by "diagnosis" that all individuals described as having the same mental disorder are alike in all important ways. Although individuals described as having the same disorder show at least the defining features of the disorder, they may well differ in other important ways, which can affect clinical management and outcome (American Psychiatric Association, 1980).

Finally, Menninger (1963, p. 333) further clarified the relationship between treatment and diagnosis: "Treatment depends upon diagnosis, and even the matter of timing is often misunderstood. One does not complete a diagnosis and then begin treatment; the diagnostic process is also the start of treatment. Diagnostic assessment is treatment; it also enables further and more specific treatment."

Assessment

"Clinical assessment is the process by which clinicians gain understanding of the patient necessary for making informed decisions" (Korchin, 1976, p. 124). Clinicians may proceed to form impressions and identify attributes of their patients via *formal* and *informal* processes. Formal assessment, which is a specialized segment of the clinical process, includes the systematic study of the patient based upon special procedures (e.g., psychological testing, structured interviews, formal behavioral measurements). Alternatively, informal assessment refers to less intentional ways that the clinician observes and forms impressions about the nature and vicissitude of a patient's difficulties. Clinical assessment may include the evaluation of simple or complex variables; the process might utilize a single, specialized psychometric instrument or a complex battery of devices. Korchin (1976, p. 124) suggests that clinical assessment taps

> multiple levels of functioning, in historical as well as contemporaneous perspective . . . this orientation puts the clinician rather than the test at the center of the assessment process. The clinician conceptualizes the questions to be answered, the techniques to use, and finally has to integrate the many findings into a coherent whole. At all stages, clinical judgement and inference are required and the effectiveness of the assessment depends on the skill and wisdom of the clinician.

Perhaps Megargee (1966, p. xiii) summarized it best: "Clinical assessment is a complex, frustrating, and fascinating activity. From small samples of behavior the clinician attempts to come to some understanding of each unique personality with which he deals." Both Korchin and Megargee emphasized the inferential and organizational activity that the clinician engages in while attempting to (1) understand the nature of a patient's presenting problem as well as (2) come to an understanding of the patient as a unique and distinct human being. The issues associated with understanding both the patient's *presenting problem* and the *patient* reflect the juxtaposition of diagnosis and clinical assessment.

Diagnosis Versus Assessment: Understanding the Problem and the Patient

It is essential for a clinician to gain a *comprehensive understanding* of each patient in order to perform effectively as a therapeutic agent. Such an understanding may be based as much on "art" as "science" (e.g., Deese, 1972; Sederer, 1977; Korchin, 1976). Uncodified, intuitive experience (i.e., "art" according to Deese, 1972) constitutes much of the assessment process. Such "artistic" skill is often the result of months and years of experience gained by interviewing, evaluating, and observing large numbers of patients over extended periods of time.

Weiner (1975) emphasized the important differences between a therapist (1) understanding the patient's problem and (2) understanding the patient, by comparing *clinicial* and *dynamic* formulations. Each of these concepts involves much more than a categorical diagnosis.

> A working clinical formulation consists of more or less traditional diagnostic judgments about the nature and severity of a patient's psychological condition . . . an initial evaluation is not complete until the therapist has reached three general diagnostic conclusions: (a) whether his patient is suffering primarily a psychotic, characterological, or psychoneurotic disorder; (b) whether the presenting symptoms are primarily psychogenic in origin or instead related to organic brain dysfunction or some toxic condition that requires medical evaluation; and (c) whether the patient's psychological difficulties are so slight as not to require ongoing psychotherapy or so severe as to call for immediate supportive intervention. (Weiner, 1975, pp. 57–58)

Thus, a clinical formulation suggests a diagnostic category but also provides some guidance to the development of a treatment plan; just enough information is required to decide if treatment is necessary and which type of treatment is appropriate.

A dynamic formulation involves a more complete understanding of the person than a clinical formulation.

> A working dynamic formulation consists of a general impression of what the patient is like as a person and how he got to be that way. Included in this formulation are some fairly clear ideas of the nature of the conflicts the patient is experiencing; the defenses he uses against the anxiety these conflicts produce; his style of coping with social, sexual, and achievement-related situations; his attitudes toward significant people in his life and what he perceives their attitudes to be toward him; and how his past and present life experiences have contributed to his becoming distressed and seeking help. (Weiner, 1975, p. 58)

From this perspective it seems apparent that dynamic formulations are rarely, if ever, complete. These formulations may/should be reorganized and revised throughout the course of treatment. Taken together, they offer a clinical heuristic for the vicissitudes of both diagnosis and treatment—without emphasizing the traditional diagnostic categories, which can be stigmatizing and dehumanizing (Laing, 1967).

Assessment and Addiction

Shaffer and Gambino (1979) have noted that there is little agreement among theorists as to the causes of addiction and even less agreement among practitioners as to the course of proper treatment. The field of addictions is in a pre-paradigm stage of development (Gambino and Shaffer, 1979; Shaffer and Gambino, 1979; Khantzian and Shaffer, 1981; Shaffer and Burglass, 1981; Shaffer and Gambino, 1984). As a result, clinicians typically have been left to their own devices to develop and adopt a "working" model of addiction. In spite of the variety of pre-paradigmatic perspectives offered to explain addictive behavior (e.g., moral turpitude, intrapsychic conflict, social deprivation, metabolic deficiency, developmental regression, pharmacological "defense" mechanisms), practitioners continue to apply *their own* ideas about addiction, addicts, treatment strategies, and the goals of treatment (e.g., abstinence versus "controlled" substance use). This confusing state of affairs is complicated further by the plethora of drugs (and associated effects) that are available for use/abuse, and therefore may become objects of assessment. To illustrate, users of psychoactive drugs may be involved with substances from four major categories: (1) narcotics; (2) sedative-hypnotics; (3) central nervous system stimulants; and/or (4) hallucinogens. Accurate assessment of abuse, addiction, and/or the need for medical treatment for such use requires a range of information and observational/interactive skills. Thus, for example, the ability to distinguish a generalized anxiety response from narcotic withdrawal requires a working knowledge of the multiform manifestations of anxiety and of narcotics and their effects, as well as the observational skills necessary to assess signs of intoxication or withdrawal (e.g., pupil size, vital signs). Since heavy drug use may precipitate shifts in personality (Zinberg, 1975) and complicate the assessment process, it may be necessary to gather additional information about the patient's prior behavior patterns from parents or friends, in conjunction with patient interviews.

How did addictive behavior become the object of clinical assessment? To this point, we have assumed that "addictive" behavior properly and deservedly should be considered as an object of clinical assessment; the observation that prior to the present century drugs were not considered objects of addiction (Szasz, 1974) casts this assumption in considerable doubt. As Szasz (1974, p. 7) has noted, "the diagnosis of 'drug addiction' became officially recognized only in 1934, when it was included for the first time among the 'mental illnesses' listed in the American Psychiatric Association's Standard Classified Nomenclature of Diseases." Presumably, however, "some persons have always 'abused' certain drugs—alcohol for millennia, opiates for centuries" (Szasz, 1974, p. 6). Thus we can assume that addictive behavior became the object of assessment not for clinical but for *social* reasons.

> [P]eople who *poison other people* are criminals. What we do with them is not a problem for science or pharmacology to solve, but a decision for

> legislators and the courts to make. But is it any less absurd to include, in the compass of medicine or pharmacology, the problem of what to do with those persons who *poison themselves,* or who do not even harm themselves but merely violate certain social norms or legal rules? (Szasz, 1974, p. 10)

Illicit drug users/abusers violate social codes and norms. Do they engage in such behavior as an act against authority or as an assertion of self-control? Has society determined the legal status of drugs based on its need to develop leverage and control over counterculture groups or from a need to self-regulate the system and insure its survival? Although rhetorical, these questions illustrate that the *phenomenon* of drug addiction has a long history; the *field* which has developed around it is of more recent origin.

Throughout history society has demonstrated an interest in regulating the substances ingested by its members. This interest can be traced historically by the succession of religious and secular rules, laws, sanctions, and policies that have served to define certain substances, such as "food" or "drugs," as acceptable or unacceptable. In addition, these legal limits, mores, and folkways have determined that certain forms and patterns of ingestion are defined as proper use or in some cases abuse.

> Contemporary society, scientifically informed and religiously pluralistic, continues this tradition of regulating ingestible substances, though now less explicitly in the name of religion as in earlier times and more so in the cause of public health and safety. The ill-specified nature of these latter-day causes and the zeal and fervor with which regulatory activities are pursued has led some observers to characterize our present food and drug laws, their medical and scientific "justifications" notwithstanding, as religious in intent, purpose and effect, as being in fact the dietary and liturgical laws of the modern secular religion of science. (Burglass and Shaffer, 1981, p. xix)

During the early part of this century, the church yielded primary responsibility for the promulgation of values and the regulation of individual conduct to the state. Consequently, the phenomenon of the addictions came to be seen as a social problem, and, as such, the object of formal inquiry and intervention vis-à-vis the social sciences. Such inquiry and intervention primarily was directed at identifying causal factors that could prevent or stop individuals from using certain substances in certain ways. This concern has stimulated a plethora of theoretical explanations designed to explicate the etiology and treatment of addiction.

The earliest explanations of addiction emphasized personal responsibility; "the moral turpitude of the individual was cited as the cause;

and addiction, like poverty and ignorance, was understood as the consequence of spiritual weakness" (Burglass and Shaffer, 1981, p. x). As society became more urban and a greater variety of people were represented among addicts, explanations of drug addiction were less personally condemning; moral turpitude gradually yielded to psychological defect as the preferred explanation for addiction (e.g., Abraham, 1908; Rado, 1933). It was during this historical transition that addicts became *patients* to be cured by *treatment* rather than sinners to be saved by piety. Thus, in an effort to understand a complex pattern of behavior and comprehend the causal structure of their environment (Kelley, 1967, 1972), theorists offered psychological explanations of addiction and the need for assessment emerged. Less dramatic, but equally responsible for confirming the need for assessment were the explanatory perspectives that followed: psychoanalytic, sociologic, psychosocial, metabolic, learning/conditioning, political-legal. Each of these perspectives generated a need for a particular type of assessment. Currently, there are numerous popular assessment models that apply to the area of addiction and drug abuse: *behavioral* (Barlow, 1981; Cone and Hawkins, 1977; Cimenaro, Calhoun, and Adams, 1977; Sobell and Sobell, 1976; Krasnegor, 1980; Mash and Terdal, 1976; Callner, 1975; Gilbert, 1976; Goldfried, 1976; Wikler, 1965, 1973), *cognitive-behavioral* (Kendall and Hollon, 1981; Kendall and Korgeski, 1979; Burglass, 1974; Meichenbaum, 1977; Rathjen, Rathjen, and Hiniker, 1978), *multidimensional* (American Psychiatric Association, 1980; Lazare, 1979a; Renner, 1979; Mischel, 1968, 1977), *multimodal* (Lazarus, 1976; Nay, 1979), *attributional* (Jones and Berglas, 1978; Metalisky and Abramson, 1981), *motivational* (Carr, 1977), *psychodynamic* (Vaillant, 1975; Khantzian, 1974, 1975; Paolino, 1981), *psychoanalytic* (Rado, 1933; Zinberg, 1975; Khantzian, Mack, and Schatzberg, 1974; Glover, 1956; Wurmser, 1974), *biologic* (Khantzian and McKenna, 1979; Dole and Nyswander, 1965, 1968; Keller and Manschreek, 1979), *sociologic* (Lindesmith, 1938, 1947, 1968; Becker, 1967; Chein et al., 1964), *psychosocial* (Ausubel, 1961; McLemore and Benjamin, 1979; Zinberg, Harding, and Winkeller, 1977; Weissman, 1975), and *biosocial* (Millon, 1969). For the clinician, such a plethora of approaches may be overwhelming and confusing. Assessment protocols within each of these areas also vary, adding to the confusion. Nevertheless, these theoretical orientations and popular paradigms are generally responsible for determining (1) the focus of the assessing clinician, (2) the data that will be considered important and relevant, (3) the data that will be ignored, and as a consequence, (4) the system of organization that will be implemented to organize the data obtained during the assessment process.

The clinician, who attempts to understand and develop a treatment plan for an addicted client, needs to consider a vast array of intrapersonal (e.g., psychodynamic, biologic) and interpersonal (e.g., environmental, familial, social) factors during the course of assessment. Failing to attend to the *multiplicity* of *interacting* variables only can reduce the efficacy of treatment. Encouraging multidimensional assessment, Mischel (1977, p. 246) warned that

> complex human behavior tends to be influenced by many determinants and reflects that almost inseparable and continuous interaction of a host of variables both in the person and in the situation . . . if human behavior is determined by many interacting variables—both in the person and in the environment—then a focus on any one of them is likely to lead to limited predictions and generalizations.

Zinberg (1974) introduced a conceptual schema to facilitate and organize our understanding of the variety of interacting factors that influence drug use and the effects that are produced by such use. Zinberg considered that the many factors associated with drug use could best be understood by examining the interactive role of (1) *set* (psychological/psychodynamic processes); (2) *setting* (sociocultural influences); and (3) *substance* (psychoactive drug). Although relatively simple, this model has served as an important clinical and empirical heuristic for the field of drug use and abuse since it was originally published.

More recently, Lazare (1976, 1979a) and Renner (1979) have clarified the process of assessment further by offering a multidimensional model based on hypotheses generation and testing. This model proposes that assessment efforts be directed toward the testing of clinical hypotheses generated by *biologic, sociologic, psychodynamic,* and *behavioral* perspectives. Lazare (1973) has noted that during the clinical assessment process a variety of perspectives are implicitly utilized but rarely articulated (see Shaffer and Gambino, 1979, for a discussion of this issue in the area of addiction treatment). Lazare noted that the biologic, sociologic, psychodynamic, and behavioral models are the most commonly used, unarticulated, clinical perspectives. In the next section of this chapter, each of these viewpoints will be introduced, and typical hypotheses will be offered to illustrate the corresponding clinical model.

Testing hypotheses along these four dimensions fosters an approach that successfully: (1) reduces the assessment process to manageable proportions; (2) provides a "cognitively economical" (Mischel, 1979) paradigm for clinical assessment; (3) establishes a model that permits either a narrow or eclectic (Dimond and Havens, 1975; Dimon, Havens, and Jones, 1978) approach to clinical assessment; and (4) facilitates the organization of clinical material fundamental to the assessment of drug abuse and addiction. Consequently, the following discussion of the clinical assessment process and associated various techniques will be conducted from the perspective of Lazare's hypotheses generation and testing model.

Assessing the User, Abuser, or Addict: Hypotheses to Be Tested

Lazare's (1979a; 1979b) concept of "hypotheses" is essentially analogous to a *partial psychodynamic formulation.* These hypotheses are considered partial formulations "because any one alone is insufficient to provide adequate understanding of any given patient. In the process of bringing these partial formulations to the interview for consideration, they become hypotheses to be tested" (Lazare, 1979b, p. 132). By identifying a variety of hypotheses from each of the four areas presented above, this approach "(1) helps the clinician make efficient use of limited time in attempting to be comprehensive, (2) guards the clinician from coming to premature closure in the collection of data, and (3) provides a stimulus for the exploration of relevant but neglected clinical questions" (Lazare, 1979a, p. 132). In addition, this schema permits the following discussion to focus specifically on hypotheses relevant to drug abuse and addiction; the reader interested in references explicating a more general hypotheses-testing approach to assessment is referred to Lazare (1973, 1976, 1979a, 1979b).

A caveat is in order: Although the following hypotheses are specifically relevant to addiction, we are not suggesting that they be tested instead of other more general hypotheses appropriate to comprehensive assessment. Hypotheses associated with addiction should be included for testing within the typical assessment regimen: Substance abuse and addiction disorders transverse all other diagnostic categories and should not be casually disregarded as a possibility during an assessment. The following discussion is a brief review of hypotheses that we have found useful in our assessments of drug-involved patients.

Biologic Hypotheses

Biologic hypotheses consider psychiatric disorders as the manifestation of disease process. "For each disease, it is supposed that there eventually will be found a specific cause related to the functional anatomy of the brain" (Lazare, 1979c, p. 4). Identifying and understanding the particular disease process involved determines the clinician's choice of treatment.

Can the patient's problem be understood as a result of drug intoxication or withdrawal? Is the patient evidencing any signs of intoxication, overdose, or withdrawal? Signs of intoxication or withdrawal require an immediate decision: Does the patient require hospitalization? As we noted earlier, "Drug use does not exempt individuals from other psychiatric conditions. . . . For that reason, patients need to be evaluated carefully for evidence of schizophrenia, major affective disorders, or other psychiatric conditions of an organic nature that may require specific medication and treatment" (Renner, 1979, p. 465).

Has drug use altered the patient's neurologic/psychologic functioning? Is there any evidence (e.g., impaired memory, impaired sensorium, abstraction) that permits the patient's problem to be understood as a function of organic impairment? Such impairment may be due to the acute effects of (1) intoxication or withdrawal, (2) residual organic deficiencies resulting, perhaps, from long-term use, or (3) complications associated with an attempted suicide. These possible relationships need to be tested and clarified by the assessor.

Psychodynamic Hypotheses

Psychodynamic hypotheses focus on the mind, and the associated mental, cognitive, and affective processes that influence human behavior. According to this model, "the developmental impasse, the early deprivation (Forrest, 1983), the distortions in early relations, and the confused communication between parent and child lead to the adult neuroses and vulnerabilities to certain stresses" (Lazare, 1979c, p. 4). Psychodynamically oriented therapy is directed toward resolving intrapsychic conflict; strengthening the ego; permitting the experience of overwhelming dysphoric affect; and learning to understand the meaning of thoughts, feelings, and behaviors.

Can the patient's drug use be understood as an attempt to reduce dysphoria? Wurmser (1974) and Khantzian (1974, 1975) have suggested that the specific pharmacologic effects of opiates may serve a progressive effect, whereby regressive, dysphoric states may actually be reversed. Wurmser considered that narcotics may be used adaptively by addicts in order to compensate for defects in affect defense, particularly against feelings of rage, hurt, shame, and loneliness. Khantzian stressed the use of narcotics as a drive defense; he considers that narcotics may act to reverse regressive states by the direct anti-aggression action of opiates. Opiates are considered to counteract the disorganizing influences of rage and aggression on the ego. Both Khantzian and Wurmser suggest that the psychopharmacological effects of drugs can substitute for defective or nonexistent ego mechanisms of defense;

in addition, both theorists consider developmental impairments, severe predisposing psychopathology, and problems in adaptation as central issues in understanding the etiology of addiction. Thus it is essential for the clinician to ask and understand what drug use accomplishes, intrapsychically, for the patient and how the drug attains this end. Khantzian (1975) has considered that drugs may be selected by users specifically for the differential psychopharmacological effects produced (e.g., containment, energy, release of inhibition). Only a thorough drug use history (including psychological effects produced) will provide a clue as to the possible role of these psychodynamic issues in drug use, abuse, and addiction. It is vital to understand that the drug a patient is actually using (chosen from those drugs that are practically available) and the drug he or she would prefer to use if it were available may be different (Hartford, 1978).

Generally, a drug history will reveal a pattern of episodic use—often involving "trial and error" with a variety of drugs—in a specific social context; gradually such use may escalate to a point perceived by the patient to be out of control, and typically it is associated with psychological and/or physical dependence. Renner (1979) has underscored that addicts may have great difficulty acknowledging their underlying psychological difficulties. It may be easier for addicts to present their problems as being medical (e.g., adverse drug reactions) rather than psychological in nature (e.g., depression, rage, low self-esteem). The assessor might consider accepting "the existence of some 'real' medical problem while explaining that such problems may also be caused or aggravated by psychological stress." After a firm therapeutic alliance has been established and the patient feels reassured that the therapist does not believe that he is worthless and hopeless, it will be possible for him to admit more easily to his psychological difficulties (Renner, 1979, p. 466).

Can the patient's drug use be understood as compulsive or controlled: is the patient's problem due to addiction, "chipping," or some intermediate level of controlled use? Zinberg, Harding, and Winkeller (1977) and Zinberg and Jacobson (1976) have demonstrated, contrary to popular belief, that not all drug use is compulsive. It is possible—perhaps even common—for drug use to be "controlled" in some fashion (e.g., cultural, contextual, religious); patients may be aware of these controls, or they may not. In order to properly address the issue of controlled use, abuse, and addiction, the assessor needs to probe for evidence that clarifies the extent of compulsive or controlled drug use and the conditions under which these occur—perhaps differentially.

Can the patient's difficulties be understood as antecedent or consequent to drug use? Zinberg's (1975) now classic paper on addiction and ego function noted that "psychopathology" or ego deficiencies actually may be a *consequence* of drug use rather than a predisposing factor. During assessment, the clinician must clarify and discriminate pre–drug involved behavior patterns from post-involvement patterns. Psychological regression and dysphoria may be the result of "hustling" for drugs and being involved in an illicit activity instead of some predisposing "psychopathy."

Sociologic Hypotheses

Sociologic hypotheses "focus on the way in which individuals function in their social system. Symptoms are traced not to conflicts within the mind and not to manifestations of psychiatric disease, but to the relationship of the individuals to their manner of functioning in social situations, i.e., in the type and quality of their 'connectedness' to the groups which make up their life space. Symptoms may therefore be regarded as an index of social disorder" (Lazare, 1979c, p. 5). Treatment from the sociologic perspective (Heath, 1983) consists of interventions designed to change the relationship(s) that exist between patients and their social milieu.

Does the patient's drug use occur in limited or varied environmental contexts? Typically, substances are used within a variety of contextual conditions and not within others. An assessment of these conditions will permit the clinician to understand which social situations encourage, precipitate, or inhibit drug taking. What do these environments have in common? What are the differences? For example, specific situations have similar characteristics that have been considered to elicit cognitions and/or expectations that may or may not initiate a sequence of drug-taking behavior (e.g., Wikler, 1965, 1973). In addition, there are many cultural rituals and attitudes that tend to naturally control drug use (e.g., the cocktail party, the "happy hour," negative attitudes toward drinking before lunch). These ceremonies and attitudes tend to restrict potentially disruptive and/or abusive behavior patterns to specified places and times. Is the patient's problem behavior restricted to sanctioned events, or does it tend to generalize (perhaps, compulsively) to a wide variety of contexts? If so, perhaps the patient is attempting to alter consciousness and/or mood rather than participate in a ceremony or ritual.

Can the patient's behavior be viewed as an attempt to focus attention on a familial problem or difficulty? "Often, a patient's drug use can be seen as a cry for help or an effort at social communication" (Renner, 1979, p. 467). Adolescents may be using drugs to express individuality, rebellion, or hostility toward their parents when channels of communication are limited. Drug use can also be a desperate attempt to communicate to placating parents (or others) that one is "out of control," experiencing serious psychological distress, and in need of "special" attention (e.g., treatment).

Can the patient's drug use behavior be understood as a response to peer group pressure? Initial drug use (Forrest, 1983) often occurs in the company of one's "best" friend. Using drugs in the context of a social group that has established "reasonable" limits for such use should not be considered as "psychopathology" unless there are other specific problems that can be identified during assessment. Are the drugs used within the limits established by the reference group or beyond? Are the drugs used and the pattern of such use indicative of self-destructive tendencies that are reflected in other patterns of behavior? If so, then perhaps other psychiatric problems are evident; however, "while clinicians cannot condone an individual's participation in illegal activities, it is not appropriate to suggest that such people are in need of psychiatric treatment purely because they choose to use illegal drugs" (Renner, 1979, p. 466).

Behavior Hypotheses

The emphasis implicit in the following behavioral hypotheses is that addictive behavior can be viewed as a set of learned behaviors rather than a result of deep-seated psychological or social trauma or physical illness. The behavioral treatment that emerges from this view involves applying procedures and techniques, derived from known principles of learning, to modify, reduce, or eliminate maladaptive behavior and to foster the acquisition of more adaptive behavior patterns (see Krasnegor, 1980; Callner, 1975; Sobell and Sobell, 1976, for important reviews of the behavioral literature).

Can the patient's problems be understood as contingent upon the "reinforcing" properties of the drugs they have used or are using? Does the use of drugs provide (1) primary positive or negative reinforcement (e.g., euphoria versus relief-from-withdrawal syndrome); or (2) secondary positive or negative reinforcement (as a result of classicial conditioning)?

Can the patient's problems be understood by understanding the mediation between his or her cognitive and behavioral activities? Wikler (1965, 1973) considered the mediating role of cognitions to be an essential assessment area for understanding addictive behavior. Every drug user, abuser, and/or addict has thought, feelings, motives, ideas, and attributions that occur during the acquisition, maintenance, and extinction of addictive behavior.

The Interview

In order to generate and test hypotheses in practice, the assessor must understand some basic interview strategies, the structure of the interview, and the client's and therapist's role, expectations, treatment goals, and communication problems. Although these areas are important to all types of clinical interviews (Sullivan, 1970) this section will focus specifically on the major issues that are relevant to hypotheses testing within the assessment interview with drug abusing and addicted clients.

Basic Strategies and Techniques

Once the clinician generates several hypotheses to be tested, strategies must be selected that provide an adequate opportunity to test these considerations. A specific strategy should be selected on the basis of its capacity for generating observable evidence that will either confirm or refute the hypotheses being considered. As Lazare (1979b, p. 138) has noted, this data can be collected using a wide variety of methods, for example, "direct questioning, sitting in silence, employing the associative anamnestic technique, encouraging free association, speaking to the family, testing the patient's memory, paying attention to his [therapist's] own subjective responses, stressing the patient." In addition, Snyder and his colleagues have demonstrated that although individuals are capable of eliciting evidence that would disconfirm a particular hypothesis (Snyder and White, 1981), there is an overwhelming preference to collect only data that will confirm hypotheses (Snyder and Campbell, 1980). Such a strategy may restrict the utility of clinical evidence; awareness of this tendency should facilitate the use of disconfirming strategies for data collection. A strategy or data collection method can be judged effectively only by determining whether or not the information generated by the chosen strategy adequately supports or refutes the hypothesis being tested. Such adequacy depends, in part, on the interviewing skills of the clinician and the responsiveness of the patient. Lazare warned that particular methods may have to be withheld if these are antitherapeutic. "For example, the stress of extended silence may yield useful data, but may impair the treatment relationship" (1979b, p. 138). As a result, clinicians must consider carefully the possible adverse consequences of the strategies they select, the skills they have available for successfully implementing a strategy, the patient's capacity to tolerate a particular method, the "strength" of the therapeutic alliance, and the purpose of the assessment interview.

Establishing a Purpose. Assessment interviews may be conducted for many reasons, e.g., hiring personnel in a job setting; collecting data for a research project; getting to know a potential roommate; or gathering data for clinical assessment, diagnosis, and treatment planning. From the onset, it is important for the clinician and client to understand the reasons for the interview. In addition, discussing the purpose of the interview can provide the opportunity to generate initial hypotheses and set the tone for the remainder of the sessions. The purpose of the interview also determines, in part, the process, detail, type of inquiry, and clinical goals of the interaction.

The Interview Process

Once the purpose of the interview has been clarified between the client and the therapist and beginning steps are made to set the tone of the interview, the next step involves a preview of the process. As in all psychiatric interviews, it is helpful to outline for the client the areas that will be covered during the interview. These areas generally include a childhood and family history, a social relationships history, and a medical history. Since these are common areas of exploration for all psychiatric assessments, the reader is referred to Edinburg, Zinberg, and Kelman (1975), Sullivan (1970), Weins (1976), Nicholi (1978), and Korchin (1976) for several important points of entry into the assessment interview literature. During an assessment interview with a drug-involved client, a detailed drug history and investigation of the current pattern of substance use needs to be included.

Providing an outline of the interview process with clients prepares them for the experience ahead and provides them the opportunity to ask questions or share concerns—further offering the clinician an opportunity for hypotheses generation and testing. From this discussion of the early stages of the assessment interview it should be apparent that many hypotheses can be generated and tested without the clinician interfering with the "flow" of the interview. In addition, "it is neither necessary nor desirable to systematically ask questions about each successive hypothesis. Such a procedure would reduce the interview to a disjointed interrogation. The clinician, in gathering the relevant information, is as active and directive as necessary for diagnostic completeness. At the same time, he remains as non-directive as possible to preserve the free flow of the patient's thoughts" (Lazare, 1979b, p. 138). For example, during the interview it is possible to discard the hypothesis that a patient may be suffering from drug withdrawal or intoxication if the patient is fully oriented, does not manifest physical signs, appears in good physical health, and appears physically comfortable with concurrent normally paced speech and nonverbal cues (e.g., has normal speed of movement, doesn't have slurred or slowed speech or gait, isn't ataxic, has normal pupils). When direct questioning is necessary to test specific hypotheses, these questions (or, perhaps, other strategies) can and should be utilized within the natural flow of the interview (Lazare, 1979b). Lazare (1979b) has suggested that all of the available hypotheses be reviewed at two specific times during the clinical examination: first, when the hypotheses that are generated during the initial ten to fifteen minutes of an assessment fail to adequately make clinical sense of the evidence; and second, five to ten minutes prior to the completion of the interview. The first review provides clinicians with an organized opportunity to (1) generate new ideas, (2) redirect their approach or assessment strategy, and (3) provide a useful dynamic formulation for information that was not relevant to the discarded hypotheses. The second review provides an opportunity to be certain that the clinical formulation is complete; if the clinician determines that it is not, there is still ample opportunity to elicit the information that is necessary to complete such a formulation.

Taking a Drug History and Understanding Current Patterns of Use

Gathering a detailed drug use history can be accomplished in four basic ways: (1) it can be gathered separately from other areas of history-taking; (2) it can be integrated as part of a developmental and social history—exploring drug use along with preadolescent, adolescent, and early adult experiences; (3) it can be derived secondarily from the medical/physical phenomena relating to illness; or (4) it can be studied as a function of a precipitating life crisis. No matter which approach the clinician selects, it is essential that very detailed, precise information be gathered. These details should support or refute the clinician's hypotheses regarding what signs are observed during the interview, what symptoms are reported by the client, the social setting and context of drug use, and the distinction between (1) use, (2) abuse, (3) physical and psychological dependence, and (4) addiction. *Unless the data are detailed enough to distinguish these states, and therefore test relevant hypotheses, a precise assessment and diagnosis of drug dependence will be unmanageable and unavailable.*

In our experience, a drug history and the current pattern of drug use is easier and most simply recorded and reported chronologically: that is, beginning with the first drugs used (often coffee, tea, cigarettes, or alcohol) and proceding in an orderly fashion to the current pattern of use, or, conversely, beginning with the current pattern of drug use and then transitioning back to the initial drugs used. The clinician needs to include six crucial areas in the drug history: (1) the *four major drug categories*—narcotic analgesics, sedative-hypnotics, stimulants, and hallucinogens—as well as cannabis, inhalants, and phencyclidine, and the way in which each drug used affects the patient's thinking, mood, affect, and behavior; (2) the *amount* used and *route* of administration (e.g., oral, intranasal, or intravenous injection), the *frequency* of use (e.g., daily, twice daily), and the *duration* of use (i.e., over what period of time—two weeks, four months, three years, etc.); (3) the *setting* in which the drug is used (e.g., alone, with friends, at home, at parties); (4) how the client *acquires* the drug (e.g., stealing, cashing prescriptions, "dealing" drugs, robbing drugstores); (5) significant *life issues* related to drug use (e.g., a precipitating crisis, hospitalization); and (6) any reports of *drug overdose.* Chronologically organized, a comprehensive drug use history will generally provide all the information necessary to test specific biologic (e.g., dependence), sociologic (e.g., reference group influence), psychodynamic (e.g., self-medication), and/or behavioral hypotheses (e.g., classically conditioned discriminative stimuli leading to use). Such a history does not, however, preclude the necessity for gathering additional information in order to test specific additional psychodynamic, sociologic, biologic, and behavioral hypotheses.

The following is a sample drug history gathered during a clinical assessment:

1962 (12 y.o.): First use of *cigarettes*—smoked on weekends ½–1 pack. Usually with friends. Increase use at 14 y.o. to ½–1 pack daily.

1964 (14 y.o.): First use of *alcohol*—drank only on weekends with friends (mostly beer). Use didn't increase until 17 y.o.—drank vodka twice weekly and on weekends continually.

1964 (14 y.o.): Used *marijuana* on occasion—smoked with friends—weekends. Increased use between 17 and 20 y.o. and dropped off again on weekends.

1968 (18 y.o.): Tried *LSD* with friends—had pleasant experience. At 19 y.o. used every weekend for 3 months. Stopped use—reports having difficulty concentrating.

1968–1970 (18–20 y.o.): Used various *amphetamines* (benzedrine, crossroads, methedrine, black beauties); used orally except two experiences snorting methedrine. Used mostly to study in college, but on occasion to get high on weekend. Reports no intravenous (IV) use, gets drugs from kids on campus.

1968–70 (18–20 y.o.): Experimented with *sedative-hypnotics,* mainly Valium, Quaalude, and Tuinal. Reports using on occasion by mouth. Increased Quaalude use at age 20; began to use daily, up to 8–12 per day orally. Reports "shooting" once. Used with alcohol. Reports getting drugs on campus and from a nearby physician. Reports one overdose—brought by friends to the hospital. Hospitalized, referred for detox. Reports father contracting cancer 6 months prior to overdose. Continued use of sedatives, mostly Quaalude, on and off until recently.

1970–1971 (20–21 y.o.): Reports use of *heroin* a few times. Snorted it twice, IV use once. Reports being sick on heroin and discontinued use. Denies use of any other narcotics. Dropped out of college at the end of his junior year.

1971–present: Continued use of *Quaalude*—reports oral use only—reports using 8–10 daily prescribed by a physician for anxiety. Reports 2 seizures in the last year. Currently unemployed; living in Boston with girlfriend. Reports occasional use of alcohol, usually with Quaalude and some marijuana. Denies use of any other substances except sometimes substitutes Valium, Nembutal, and other sedatives for the Quaalude. Later the client reported some current dealing to support drug use. The patient does not report any use of phencyclidine or inhalants. Drinks coffee and tea on occasion.

This history provides a cornucopia of information. It illustrates the *sequence* and *progression* of the patient's patterns of drug use: mostly experimental use as a young adolescent, then habitual use of sedatives during college. In addition, the data describes the amount, frequency, route of administration, duration, and contextual settings of drug use: mostly social at the beginning of use, but later, a more regular, and habitual pattern of use. The patient also revealed a preference for sedative-hypnotics and a dislike for narcotics. The history also reflects that the client obtained drugs on the "secret" (from friends, illicitly) but later got drugs from a physician (legal prescriptions). In addition, it is important to note that related psychosocial factors in this individual's history might have contributed to the observed patterns of use. For example, the patient reported that when he was 20 years old, his father was diagnosed as having cancer; about that time, drug use increased, an overdose was reported, and the patient dropped out of college.

In sum, this history provides data that permits hypotheses to be tested along the four dimensions of assessment discussed above: biological (i.e., actual use, overdose), psychodynamic (i.e., life crisis and ability to cope), sociological (i.e., use of drugs with friends, then later regular use and dealing), and behavioral (i.e., habitual use of sedatives).

Person Perception: Shortcomings of Clinical Inference—Some Caveats

The process of forming "accurate" impressions about another individual's emotional and cognitive dispositions often becomes imprecise because of the subjective nature of the observations. Just when a clinician begins to formulate tentative hypotheses about a patient's character, situations may develop that cast these conclusions in doubt. More often, however, new information that competes or is inconsistent with early impressions is discounted (Shaffer and Gambino, 1978).

In addition, some theorists describe a "fundamental attribution error"; that is, observers have a "tendency to overestimate the importance of personal or dispositional factors relative to environmental influences" (Ross, 1977). The reasons for these and other distortion phenomena in the person perception process are many, but there are emerging themes (see Nisbett and Ross, 1980; and Ross, 1977, as important points of entry into this literature).

In order to survive in an often unpredictable world, individuals may hold beliefs for reasons other than rationality (Abelson, 1974; Nisbett and Ross, 1980). Heider (1944) noted that "man grasps reality, and can predict and control it, by referring transient and variable behavior and events to relatively unchanging underlying conditions." These underlying conditions were considered by Heider to be the dispositional properties of an individual or the environment. Attribution theory is concerned with the process of perceiving and/or inferring these dispositional properties. Only recently, however, has attribution theory and research had substantial impact on clinical practice (e.g., Kendall and Hollon, 1981; Carroll, 1978; Bandura, 1977; Kopel and Arkowitz, 1975; Jones and Berglas, 1978; Miller and Norman, 1979; Brehm, 1976; Valins and Nisbett, 1972).

During the assessment process, particularly the interpersonal interview, the clinician is flooded with information that must be processed, simplified, and reduced in order to avoid what might be considered a "cognitive overload." Mischel (1979) has considered "cognitive economics" as responsible for such data reduction. Since clinicians and laypersons both appear to be susceptible to errors of interference (Ross, 1977; Ross, Lapper, and Hubbard, 1975; Chapman and Chapman, 1967, 1969), cognitive economics can be expected to influence the assessment process. Consequently, it is essential that the clinician maintain a "wait-and-see" attitude toward prospective patients—particularly during the assessment or data collection phase of treatment. This deferral of forming impressions is vital because "once an action, outcome, or personal disposition is viewed as the consequence of known or even postulated antecedents, those antecedents will continue to imply the relevant consequence even when all other evidence is removed" (Ross, 1977, p. 207). Simply stated, all drug users are not abusers or addicts! Once initial impressions are formed, these cognitive structures serve to "distort" subsequently considered evidence (Ross, Lapper, and Hubbard, 1975). For example, information that is consistent with previously formed dispositional impressions (e.g., dope "fiends," junkies, or the "addicted personality") is viewed as *support* for these impressions, while contradictory evidence may be attributed to chance or situational pressure; thus, information obtained after a clinical impression has been formed serves as independent support for such a judgment (Snyder & Uranowitz, 1978).

"[I]t is hardly possible to take up one's residence in the kingdom of the ill unprejudiced by the lurid metaphors with which it has been landscaped" (Sontag, 1979, p. 3). Addiction has become a metaphor for a fiendishly evil, impulse-ridden, psychopathic personality. Drug dependence also has been considered "suicide on the installment plan." These perspectives, biased by the metaphorical meanings of addiction and dependence, can insidiously influence even the most skilled clinicians—perhaps even if they are astutely aware of the genesis and existence of these restricting views. For example, Chapman (1967) first identified illusory correlation: one mechanism that biases the diagnostic process. Chapman defined illusory correlation as "the report of observers of the correlation between two classes of events which, in reality, (a) are not correlated, or, (b) are correlated to a lesser extent than reported, or (c) are correlated in the opposite direction from that which is reported" (1967, p. 151).

In their classic study on the genesis of popular but erroneous psychodiagnostic observations (i.e., illusory correlations), Chapman and Chapman (1967) reported the findings of six studies that bear directly on the assessment process. "Beginning clinicians" observed diagnostic test protocols of patients and were informed of a "variety of their reported symptoms." These observers significantly identified correlates in the psychodiagnostic tests (i.e., Draw-a-Person and Rorschach) with those observed in the symptom statements. The correlates that were "erroneously reported corresponded to associative connections between symptoms and drawing characteristics, and also correspond to what clinicians expect to see before they actually observe" (Chapman and Chapman, 1967).

Recently there have been two attempts to reduce the illusory correlation phenomenon by training subjects to beware of such judgmental errors (Golding and Rorer, 1971; Kurtz and Garfield, 1978). Both these studies replicated the basic findings of Chapman and Chapman, and, more importantly, *failed* to reduce the illusion effect by training subjects. Fischhoff (1976) has warned that "the very feeling that we have explained, or made sense out of, an event may be the best guarantee that we are not learning anything from it that will improve our predictive efficacy" (see Fischhoff, 1974, 1975, and Fischhoff and Beyth, 1975, for excellent examinations of hindsight and its effect on judgment).

Finally, Kandler et al. (1975) asked *senior* members of the department of psychiatry at Albert Einstein College of Medicine to predict the performance of psychiatric residents during their three years of residency. Prospective residents were assessed by structured interviews and a Resident Applicant Scale (RAS), i.e., formal assessment. The RAS was comprised of items that the faculty had come to believe were related to training experience and clinical performance. When residents' performances were evaluated against these measures at the end of each year, no correlations were found!

"When we manage to explain the past, we feel that we have increased our ability to predict the future" (Fischhoff, 1976). If we accept the assumption that explanation and prediction are formally identical (Hempel, 1965), then clinical ability to assess cause and prescribe treatment under conditions of uncertainty must be questioned. Thus, the relationship between dynamic formulations and treatment plans based on these formulations must be constantly evaluated and reviewed; such scrutiny must be based empirically on observable evidence.

Further Biases. Three major factors consistently complicate, confuse, and confound the assessment process and implicitly bias the person perception process still further; these are (1) situation, (2) time, and (3) socioeconomic status. First, the *situation* or *context* within which patients are evaluated can greatly affect the assessment process. For example, one is more likely to perceive the patient who is restrained (either chemically or physically—either self-medicated or other) as "aggressive and acting-out" then the nonrestrained patient. It has also been shown that clinicians who assess patients within inpatient settings are more likely to make the diagnosis of psychosis than those working in outpatient settings (see Rosenhan, 1973, for a particularly interesting and important examination of these issues).

Second, the *time* that a patient is examined will greatly affect the outcome of assessment, since a patient's behavior will naturally vary from one day to the next (as does the behavior of all individuals). For example, after reviewing the literature, Zubin (1969) concluded that the consistency over time of nonorganic disorders is quite low. Edelman (1969) provided additional support for this conclusion by reporting results that indicate 25 percent of diagnostic impressions change by the fourth interview or therapy session.

> The typical procedure for establishing a diagnosis is a single unstandardized interview, the results of which may be augmented by psychological testing. An implicit assumption of this procedure is that interviewee behavior has been adequately sampled in the alloted time span and that the interviewee is sufficiently motivated to reveal all pertinent information. Yet, there are numerous studies which indicate that interviewee behavior is mediated by complex process variables suggesting that such assumptions may not always be justified. (Edelman, 1969, p. 395)

Third, and finally, there is a great deal of evidence suggesting that *socioeconomic* and *cultural background* of both client and interviewer influence psychiatric judgements (Hollingshead and Redlich, 1958). "The influence of the client's socioeconomic class in facilitating the attribution of some, and impeding the application of other, nosological designations is particularly well documented. . . . [T]he findings converge in suggesting social distance as the mediating variable. Across socioeconomic or other subcultural lines, the middle-class diagnostician is prone to assign categories of severe psychopathology" (Phillips and Draguns, 1971, pp. 447, 467). Lee and Temerlin (1970) have demonstrated that diagnoses generated by psychiatric residents were highly influenced by their imagined socioeconomic history of the patient and by the perceived diagnosis of prestigious psychiatrists; these diagnostic impressions were independent of the clinical picture that the patient presented. In sum, a lower socioeconomic history tends to bias the diagnostic process toward psychiatric judgments of greater illness and poorer prognosis.

Conclusions

Is the assessment of addiction, with its state of pre-paradigm chaos and the attributional biases inherent in person perception, still possible? Yes—but it becomes a viable endeavor only when clinicians minimize the uncertainty often associated with the clinical assessment task by (1) attending to and gathering explicit, observable, valid, and reliable information about drug use and its effects (i.e., physiological, psychological, behavioral, and sociological) and (2) testing relevant hypotheses within the clinical setting to ensure and confirm/disconfirm their observations, inferences, and assumptions.

The hypotheses-testing approach promotes a comprehensive and avoids a narrow unidimensional approach to assessment. This approach does not *guarantee* increased assessment accuracy, since support for such accuracy is an empirical question—one we think is worthy of investigation. Be that as it may, the hypotheses-testing approach originally proposed by Lazare and applied here to the problems associated with the assessment of addiction does: (1) ensure comprehensivity of approach; (2) permit "eclecticism"; (3) reduce the assessment process to manageable proportions; (4) improve the clinician's capacity to elicit, understand, and organize patient information; (5) permit students to learn a teachable assessment system; and finally, (6) provide a check-and-balance system simplifying the clinician's task of self-review and self-observation.

Appendix: The Semantics of Addiction

In order to understand the clinical assessment of drug addiction, it is essential to explicate the "targets" of assessment (e.g., drug use, abuse, dependence, addiction). The language of addiction theory and treatment tends to be rich with connotative, confusing, and associative meaning (Apsler, 1978; Shaffer and Burglass, 1981): Is "intoxicated" the opposite of "nontoxic" (poisoned versus pure), or is being "high" the opposite of being "low" (euphoric versus dysphoric), or is "stoned" the opposite of "straight" (different versus normal)?

Semantic precision is essential to a solid integration of theory, research, and practice (Gambino and Shaffer, 1979; Shaffer and Gambino, 1979; Pattison, 1984). Such precision (1) facilitates the development of explicit practice principles (Shaffer and Gambino, 1979), (2) reduces the "crisis" of competing categories that exists presently in addiction theory (Burglass and Shaffer, 1981), and (3) contributes to the development of the addictions as a more "mature" discipline (see Burglass and Shaffer, 1981, for an examination of scientific immaturity in the addictions). "Not all facts are, or become genuine scientific knowledge; they must survive lengthy and rigorous processes of testing and transformation. These take place in the course of the evolution of the different components of a solved problem" (Ravetz, 1971, p. 192). Although Ravetz was not discussing the addictions, his comments are relevant; in order to scientifically understand addictive behavior, we must apply rigorous experimental principles. This can only be

We are indebted to Dr. Milton E. Burglass, Maxine James, Robert Potter, Bruce Jason, Sheila Zangwill, Susan Grosdov, and Carolyn Dyer for their assistance in the development of the definitions in this appendix.

accomplished after careful theoretical construction, including the clarification of theoretical constructs and operational definitions as well as the syntax that guides these relationships.

Definitions

Too often "drugs" are considered to be only illicit substances; licit substances tend to be viewed as "medicine" or "food" and are even occasionally ignored during the assessment process. In order to conceptualize the term "drug" in an effective, useful, and parsimonious manner, we have adopted the following definition:

Drug: Any chemical agent (natural or synthetic) that affects living processes.

"Drug abuse" varies as a function of the context (e.g., cultural, medical, social, or individual) within which drugs are used. Consequently, *drug abuse* may be defined as the use (usually by self-administration) of any drug in a manner that deviates from the approved religious, medical, or social patterns within a given culture. This term conveys the notion of *social disapproval;* it is not necessarily descriptive of any particular pattern of drug use or its potential adverse consequences.

The use of drugs may lead to psychological or physical dependence.

Psychological dependence: When the effects produced by a drug or the conditions associated with its use are perceived by the user to be *necessary* to maintain an optimal state of well-being, interpersonal relations, or skill performance, the individual is considered psychologically dependent on this drug. The dependence may vary in intensity from a "mild" desire to a "craving" or "compulsion" to use the drug(s). In most contexts, such a compulsion is socioculturally dystonic; thus, when a drug is used to the point that psychological dependence develops, such use is generally considered "drug abuse."

Physical dependence: An altered *physiological* state produced by the repeated administration of a drug which necessitates its continued administration to *prevent* the appearance of a stereotypical syndrome of unpleasant effects characteristic of the particular drug, that is, the *withdrawal* or *abstinence* syndrome.

The development of physical dependence is facilitated by the phenomenon of *tolerance.* A tolerant state has developed when, after repeated administration, a given dose of a particular drug produces a decreased effect. Conversely, tolerance exists when increasingly larger or more frequent doses of a drug must be administered in order to obtain the effects observed with the original dose. The use of nearly all psychoactive or somatic drugs yields a tolerance effect; the rate at which tolerance develops varies widely across drugs and the context within which drug use occurs.

The concept of addiction is often used and more often abused! In fact, some semantic critics have suggested that the concept has lost its utility. Be that as it may, "addiction" is such a popular term in everyday usage that it may be more useful to clarify it than discard it.

Addiction: A *behavioral* pattern of compulsive drug use characterized by *overwhelming involvement* (e.g., disruption of typical day-to-day patterns of living) with the use of a drug and the securing of its supply, as well as a strong tendency to relapse after completion of withdrawal. Considered from this perspective, "addiction" is an extreme of a continuum of involvement with drug use and refers quantitatively rather than qualitatively to the extent that drug use pervades the total life activity of the user. Consequently, anyone currently addicted would be considered drug-dependent; but those who are psychologically or physiologically dependent may not necessarily be addicted.

An illustration should further clarify the meaning and application of these terms. For example, consider the most commonly used licit substance: alcohol. When alcohol is used for a dinner beverage, a toast, a religious ceremony, or a remedy for insomnia, its use is considered *drug use,* since it is being used for recreation, celebration, and medication, respectively. Drug use in these contexts is not only condoned but often encouraged.

The use of alcohol is not considered abuse unless it is used in a socially unacceptable manner. For example, drinking a quantity of alcohol with dinner and becoming loud, threatening, and abusive can no longer be considered simple drug use; it is now likely to be defined as drug abuse. Substance or drug abuse is not necessarily determined by the amount of the substance used, but rather by its effect on individuals within their social context. In addition, what might be drug use for one may be drug abuse for another. That is, people react to alcohol, for example, in a variety of ways (e.g., becoming playful, destructive, sleepy). Playfulness at a party may be a desirable effect of alcohol (use) but at an important business luncheon an inappropriate consequence (abuse).

If a person *feels* it *necessary* to drink in order to tolerate a social affair, *feel* confident at a luncheon meeting, or relax at night, then such use of alcohol might be considered indicative of psychological dependence. Conversely, when one must have a drink before a family function, or a business meeting, in order to prevent shakiness, anxiety, nausea, sweating, weakness, etc., then the person is manifesting *signs* of physical dependence. Both of these dependent states are considered drug abuse. Finally, when one becomes so *overwhelmingly* involved with alcohol that its use is compulsively carved into one's daily routine (e.g., hiding a flask at work, or slipping alcohol into one's morning orange juice), then the pattern of substance use becomes addiction.

It is important to note the significance of *tolerance* in the examples above. People who use drugs but do not abuse them may still develop a tolerance. For example, if the first time a person drinks one glass of wine, s/he feels relaxed, drowsy, and/or silly, that person is demonstrating a low tolerance to the wine. If the same person, several months later, drinks the same amount of wine and exhibits no effects, but feels sleepy and silly only after larger quantities of wine, then the person has demonstrated an increased tolerance to the wine. Tolerance, therefore, can develop without the presence of (1) abuse, (2) psychological dependence, or (3) physical dependence.

Tolerance can also vary from person to person, depending on variables such as metabolism and body weight. Two people who drink at the same frequency—only with dinner on weekends, for example—can have very different tolerances. One person may feel the effects of the wine after one glass; the other feels no effect until three glasses. The fact that tolerance may be different in these people does not indicate the presence or absence of psychological and/or physical dependence. It is important to note that identifying tolerance contributes little to the clinician's ability to distinguish drug use from drug abuse, dependence, or addiction.

In sum, understanding the drug use lexicon is essential during assessment. What might be drug use for one may be abuse for another. An accurate assessment requires an understanding of the drug, its context of use, whether the drug is necessary for the maintenance of psychological well-being and/or physical equilibrium, and finally, the patterns of substance involvement.

References

Abelson, R. Social psychology's rational man. In G. W. Mortmev and S. I. Benn (eds.), *The Concept of Rationality in the Social Sciences.* London: Routledge & Kagen Paul, 1974.

Abraham, K. The psychological relation between sexuality and alcoholism. In *Selected Papers of Karl Abraham.* New York: Basic Books, 1960. (Originally published, 1908.)

Ajzen, I. Intuitive theories of events and the effects of base rate information on prediction. *Journal of Personality and Social Psychology,* 1977, *35,* 303–314.

American Psychiatric Association. *Diagnostic and Statistical Manual of Mental Disorders,* 3rd ed., 1980.

Apsler, R. Untangling the conceptual jungle of drug abuse. *Contemporary Drug Problems,* 1978, *7,* 55–80.

Ausubel, D. P. Causes and types of narcotic addiction: a psychosocial view. *Psychiatric Quarterly,* 1961, *35,* 523–531.

Bandura, A. Self-efficacy: toward a unifying theory of behavioral change. *Psychological Review,* 1977, *84,* 191–215.

Barlow, D. H. (ed.). *Behavioral Assessment of Adult Disorders.* New York: Guilford Publications, 1981.

Becker, H. S. History, culture, and subjective experience: an exploration of the social bases. *Journal of Health and Social Behavior,* 1967, *8,* 163–176.

Bentler, L. E. Toward specific psychological therapies for specific conditions. *Journal of Consulting and Clinical Psychology,* 1979, *47,* 882–897.

Brehm, S. *The Application of Social Psychology to Clinical Practice.* Washington, D.C.: Hemisphere Publishing, 1976.

Burglass, M. E. *The Thresholds Method of Program: Teacher's Guide and Manual.* Cambridge: Correctional Solutions Foundation Press, 1974.

———, and Shaffer, H. The natural history of ideas in the addictions. In H. Shaffer and M. E. Burglass (eds.), *Classic Contributions in the Addictions.* New York: Brunner/Mazel, 1981.

Butcher, J. N. *Objective Personality Assessment: Changing Perspectives.* New York: Academic Press, 1972.

Callner, D. A. Behavioral treatment approaches to drug abuse: a critical review of the research. *Psychological Bulletin,* 1975, *82(2),* 143–164.

Carr, E. G. The motivation of self-injurious behavior: a review of some hypotheses. *Psychological Bulletin,* 1977, *84(4),* 800–816.

Carroll, J. S. Causal attributions in expert parole decisions. *Journal of Personality and Social Psychology,* 1978, *36(12),* 1501–1511.

Chapman, L. J. Illusory correlation in observational reports. *Journal of Verbal Learning and Verbal Behavior,* 1967, *6,* 151–155.

———, and Chapman, J. P. Genesis of popular but erroneous psychodiagnostic categories. *Journal of Abnormal Psychology,* 1967, *72,* 193–204.

———. Illusory correlation as an obstacle to the use of valid psychodiagnostic signs. *Journal of Abnormal Psychology,* 1969, *74,* 271–280.

Chein, I., Gerard, D. L., Lee, R. S., and Rosenfeld, E. Personality and addiction: a dynamic perspective. In *The Road to H: Narcotics, Delinquency, and Social Policy.* New York: Basic Books, 1964.

Cimenaro, A. R., Calhoun, K. S., and Adams, H. E. *Handbook of Behavioral Assessment.* New York: John Wiley & Sons, 1977.

Cone, J. D., and Hawkins, R. P. (eds.). *Behavioral Assessment: New Directions in Clinical Psychology.* New York: Brunner/Mazel, 1977.

Deese, J. *Psychology as Science and Art.* New York: Harcourt Brace Jovanovich, 1972.

Dimond, R. E., and Havens, R. A. Restructuring psychotherapy: toward a prescriptive eclecticism. *Professional Psychology,* 1975, *6,* 193–200.

———, and Jones, A. C. A conceptual framework for the practice of prescriptive eclecticism in psychotherapy. *American Psychologist,* 1978, *33,* 239–248.

Dole, V. P., and Nyswander, M. A. A medical treatment for diacetylmorphine (heroin) addiction. *Journal of the American Medical Association,* 1965, *193(8),* 80–84.

———, and Warner, A. Successful treatment of 750 criminal addicts. *Journal of the American Medical Association,* 1968, *206(12),* 2708–2711.

Edelman, R. I. Intra-therapist diagnostic reliability. *Journal of Clinical Psychology,* 1969, *25,* 394.

Edinburg, G. M., Zinberg, N. E., and Kelman, W. *Clinical Interviewing and Counseling: Principles and Techniques.* New York: Appleton-Century-Crofts, 1975.

Fischhoff, B. Hindsight: thinking backward? *Oregon Research Institute Research Monograph,* 1974, *14(1).*

———. Hindsight ≠ foresight: the effect of outcome knowledge on judgment under uncertainty. *Journal of Experimental Psychology: Human Perception and Performance,* 1975, *1(3),* 288–299.

———. Attribution theory and judgment under uncertainty. In J. Harvey, W. Ickes, and R. Kidd (eds.), *New Directions in Attribution Research,* vol. 1. Hillsdale, N.J.: Lawrence Erlbaum Associates, 1976.

———, and Beyth, R. "I knew it would happen"—remembered probabilities of once-future things. *Organizational Behavior and Human Performance,* 1975, *13,* 1–16.

Gambino, B., and Shaffer, H. The concept of paradigm and the treatment of addiction. *Professional Psychology,* 1979, *10,* 207–223.

Gilbert, R. M. Drug abuse as excessive behavior. *Canadian Psychological Review,* 1976, *17,* 231–240.

Glover, E. On the etiology of drug addiction. In E. Glover (ed.), *On the Early Development of Mind.* New York: International Universities Press, 1956.

Goldfried, M. R. Behavioral assessment. In B. Weiner (ed.), *Clinical Methods in Psychology.* New York: John Wiley & Sons, 1976.

Golding, S. L., and Rorer, L. G. "Illusory correlation" and the learning of clinical judgment. *Oregon Research Institute Bulletin,* 1971, *11(10).*

Goldstein, A. P., and Stein, N. *Prescriptive Psychotherapy.* New York: Pergamon Press, 1976.

Hartford, R. J. Drug preferences of multiple drug abusers. *Journal of Consulting and Clinical Psychology,* 1978, *46,* 908–912.

Heider, F. Social perception and phenomenal causality. *Psychological Review,* 1944, *51,* 358–373.

Hempel, C. G. *Aspects of Scientific Explanation.* New York: Free Press, 1965.

Hersen, M., and Bellack, A. S. (eds.). *Behavioral Assessment: A Practical Handbook.* New York: Pergamon Press, 1976.

Hollingshead, A. B., and Redlich, F. C. *Social Class and Mental Illness.* New York: John Wiley & Sons, 1958.

Jackson, D. N., and Messick, S. (eds.). *Problems in Human Assessment.* New York: McGraw-Hill Book Co., 1967.

Jones, E. E., and Berglas, S. Control of attributions about the self through self-handicapping strategies: the appeal of alcohol and the role of underachievement. *Personality and Social Psychology Bulletin,* 1978, *4*(*2*), 200–206.

Kandler, H., Plutchik, R., Cone, H., and Siegal, B. Prediction of performance of psychiatric residents: a three-year follow-up study. *American Journal of Psychiatry,* 1975, *132,* 1286–1290.

Keller, M. B., and Manschreek, T. C. The biologic approach. In A. Lazare (ed.), *Outpatient Psychiatry: Diagnosis and Treatment.* Baltimore: Williams & Wilkins, 1979.

Kelley, H. H. Attribution theory in social psychology. *Nebraska Symposium on Motivation,* 1967, *15,* 192–238.

———. Attribution in social interaction. In E. E. Jones, D. Kanouse, H. H. Kelley, R. E. Nisbett, S. Valins, and B. Weiner (eds.), *Attribution: Perceiving the Causes of Behavior.* Newark, N.J.: General Learning Press, 1972.

Kendall, P. C., and Hollon, S. D. (eds.). *Assessment Strategies for Cognitive-Behavioral Interventions.* New York: Academic Press, 1981.

Kendall, P. C., and Korgeski, G. P. Assessment and cognitive-behavioral intervention. *Cognitive Therapy and Research,* 1979, *3*(*1*), 1–21.

Khantzian, E. J. Opiate addiction: a critique of theory and some implications for treatment. *American Journal of Psychotherapy,* 1974, *27,* 59–70.

———. Self-selection and progression in drug dependence. *Psychiatry Digest,* 1975, *36,* 19–22.

———, and McKenna, G. J. Acute toxic and withdrawal reactions associated with drug use and abuse. *Annals of Internal Medicine,* 1979, *90*(*3*), 361–372.

Khantzian, E. J., Mack, J. E., and Schatzberg, A. F. Heroin use as an attempt to cope: clinical observations. *American Journal of Psychiatry,* 1974, *131,* 160–164.

Khantzian, E. J., and Shaffer, H. A contemporary psychoanalytic view of addiction theory and treatment. In J. H. Lowinson and P. Ruiz (eds.), *Substance Abuse: Clinical Problems and Perspectives.* Baltimore: Williams & Wilkins, 1981.

Kopel, S., and Arkowitz, H. The role of attribution and self-perception in behavior change: implications for behavior therapy. *Genetic Psychology Monographs,* 1975, *92,* 175–212.

Korchin, S. J. *Modern Clinical Psychology.* New York: Basic Books, 1976.

Krasnegor, N. A. Analysis and modification of substance abuse: a behavioral overview. *Behavior Modification,* 1980, *4*(*1*), 35–56.

Kurtz, R. M., and Garfield, S. L. Illusory correlation: a further exploration of Chapman's paradigm. *Journal of Consulting and Clinical Psychology,* 1978, *46,* 1009–1015.

Laing, R. D. *The Politics of Experience.* New York: Ballatine Books, 1967.

Lazare, A. Hidden conceptual models in clinical psychiatry. *New England Journal of Medicine,* 1973, *288,* 345–351.

———. The psychiatric examination in the walk-in clinic. *Archives of General Psychiatry,* 1976, *33,* 96–102.

———. Hypothesis testing in the clinical interview. In A. Lazare (ed.), *Outpatient Psychiatry: Diagnosis and Treatment.* Baltimore: Williams & Wilkins, 1979(a).

——— (ed.). *Outpatient psychiatry: Diagnosis and Treatment.* Baltimore: Williams & Wilkins, 1979(b).

———. A multidimensional approach to psychopathology. In A. Lazare (ed.), *Outpatient Psychiatry: Diagnosis and Treatment.* Baltimore: Williams & Wilkins, 1979(c).

Lazarus, A. A. (ed.). *Multi-model Behavior Therapy.* New York: Springer Publishing Co., 1976.

Lee, S. D., and Temerlin, M. K. Social class, diagnosis, and prognosis for psychotherapy. *Psychotherapy: Theory, Research, and Practice,* 1970; *7,* 181.

Lindesmith, A. R. A social theory of drug addiction. *American Journal of Sociology,* 1938, *43,* 593–613.

———. *Opiate Addiction.* Bloomington, Ind.: Principia Press, 1947.

———. *Addiction and Opiates.* Chicago: Aldine Publishing Co., 1968.

Mash, E. J., and Terdal, L. G. (eds.). *Behavior Therapy Assessment: Diagnosis, Design, and Evaluation.* New York: Springer Publishing Co., 1976.

McLemore, C. W., and Benjamin, L. S. Whatever happened to interpersonal diagnosis? *American Psychologist,* 1979, *34,* 17–34.

Megargee, E. I. (ed.). *Research in Clinical Assessment.* New York: Harper & Row, 1966.

Meichenbaum, D. *Cognitive-Behavior Modification.* New York: Plenum Press, 1977.

Mendelson, J. H., and Mello, N. K. (eds.). *The Diagnosis and Treatment of Alcoholism.* New York: McGraw-Hill Book Co., 1979.

Menninger, K. *The Vital Balance: The Life Process in Mental Health and Illness.* New York: Viking Press, 1963.

Merluzzi, T. V., Glass, C. R., and Genest, M. (eds.). *Cognitive Assessment.* New York: Guilford Publications, 1981.

Metalisky, G. I., and Abramson, L. Y. Attributional styles: toward a framework for conceptualization and assessment. In P. C. Kendall and S. D. Hollon (eds.), *Assessment Strategies for Cognitive-Behavioral Interventions.* New York: Academic Press, 1981.

Miller, W. (ed.). *The Addictive Behaviors.* New York: Pergamon Press, 1980.

Miller, I. W., III, and Norman, W. H. Learned helplessness in humans: a review and attributional-theory model. *Psychological Bulletin,* 1979, *86(1),* 93–118.

Millon, T. *Modern Psychopathology: A Biosocial Approach to Maladaptive Learning and Functioning.* Philadelphia: W. B. Saunders, 1969.

Mischel, W. *Personality and Assessment.* New York: John Wiley & Sons, 1968.

———. On the future of personality assessment. *American Psychologist,* 1977, *32,* 246–254.

———. On the interface of cognition and personality: beyond the person-situation debate. *American Psychologist,* 1979, *34,* 740–754.

Nay, W. R. *Multimethod Clinical Assessment.* New York: Gardner, 1979.

Nicholi, A. M., Jr. History and mental status. In Armand M. Nicholi, Jr. (ed.), *The Harvard Guide to Modern Psychiatry.* Cambridge: Harvard University Press, 1978.

Nisbett, R. E., and Ross, L. D. *Human Inference: Strategies and Shortcomings of Informal Judgment.* Englewood Cliffs, N.J.: Prentice-Hall, 1980.

Paolino, T. J., Jr. *Psychoanalytic Psychotherapy.* New York: Brunner/Mazel, 1981.

Phillips, L., and Draguns, J. G. Classification of the behavior disorders. In *Annual Review of Psychology,* vol. 22. Palo Alto, Calif.: Annual Reviews Press, 1971.

Rado, S. The psychoanalysis of pharmacothymia (drug addiction). *The Psychoanalytic Quarterly,* 1933, *2,* 1–23.

Rathjen, D. P., Rathjen, E. D., and Hiniker, A. A cognitive analysis of social performance: implications for assessment and treatment. In J. P. Foreyt and D. P. Rathjen (eds.), *Cognitive Behavior Therapy.* New York: Plenum Press, 1978.

Ravetz, J. R. *Scientific Knowledge and Its Social Problems.* New York: Oxford University Press, 1971.

Renner, J. A. Drug abuse. In A. Lazare (ed.), *Outpatient Psychiatry: Diagnosis and Treatment.* Baltimore: Williams & Wilkins, 1979.

Rosenhan, D. L. On being sane in insane places. *Science,* 1973, *179,* 250–258.

Ross, L. The intuitive psychologist and his shortcomings: distortions in the attribution process. In L. Berkowitz (ed.), *Advances in Experimental Social Psychology,* vol. 10. New York: Academic Press, 1977.

———, Lepper, M. R., and Hubbard, M. Perseverance in self-perception and social perception: biased attributional processes in the debriefing paradigm. *Journal of Personality and Social Psychology,* 1975, *32,* 880–892.

Sederer, L. I. The importance of seeing psychiatry as more than a science. *Psychiatric Opinion,* 1977, *14,* 27–29.

Shaffer, H., and Burglass, M. E. (eds.). *Classic Contributions in the Addictions.* New York: Brunner/Mazel, 1981.

Shaffer, H., and Gambino, B. Order effects and context: discounting resurrected. *Psychology—a Journal of Human Behavior,* 1979, *15(4),* 1–13.

———. Addiction paradigms. Part 2: Theory, research, and practice. *Journal of Psychedelic Drugs,* 1979, *11,* 299–303.

———. Addiction paradigms III: From theory-research to practice and back. *Advances in Alcohol and Substance Abuse,* 1983, *3,* 135–152.

Shaffer, H., and Milkman, H. Crisis and conflict in the addictions. In H. Milkman and H. Shaffer (eds.), *The Addictions: Multidisciplinary concepts and treatments.* Lexington, Mass.: Lexington Books, 1984.

Snyder, M., and Campbell, B. Testing hypotheses about other people: the role of the hypothesis. *Personality and Social Psychology Bulletin,* 1980, *6,* 421–426.

Snyder, M., and Uranowitz, S. W. Reconstructing the past: some cognitive consequences of person perception. *Journal of Personality and Social Psychology,* 1978, *36,* 941–950.

Snyder, M., and White, P. Testing hypotheses about other people: strategies of verification and falsification. *Personality and Social Psychology Bulletin,* 1981, *7,* 39–43.

Sobell, M. B., and Sobell, L. C. Assessment of addictive behavior. In M. Hersen and A. S. Bellack (eds.), *Behavioral Assessment: A Practical Handbook.* New York: Pergamon Press, 1976.

Sontag, S. *Illness as Metaphor.* New York: Vintage Books, 1979.

Sullivan, H. S. *The Psychiatric Interview,* pp. 3–182. New York: W. W. Norton & Co., 1970.

Szasz, T. *Ceremonial Chemistry: The Ritual Persecution of Drugs, Addicts and Pushers.* Garden City, New York: Doubleday, 1974.

Vaillant, G. E. Sociopathy as a human process: a viewpoint. *Archives of General Psychiatry,* 1975, *32,* 178–183.

Valins, S., and Nisbett, R. E. Attribution processes in the development and treatment of emotional disorders. In E. E. Jones, D. Kanouse, H. H. Kelley, R.E. Nisbett, S. Valins, and B. Weiner (eds.), *Attribution: Perceiving the Causes of Behavior.* Newark, N.J.: General Learning Press, 1972.

Weiner, I. B. *Principles of Psychotherapy.* New York: John Wiley & Sons, 1975.

——— (ed.). *Clinical Methods in Psychology.* New York: John Wiley & Sons, 1976.

Weins, A. N. The assessment interview. In B. Weiner (ed.), *Clinical Methods in Psychology.* New York: John Wiley & Sons, 1976.

Weissman, M. M. The assessment of social adjustment. *Archives of General Psychiatry,* 1975, *32,* 357–365.

Wikler, A. Conditioning factors in opiate addiction and relapse. In D. I. Wilner and G. G. Kassebaum (eds.), *Narcotics.* New York: McGraw-Hill Book Co., 1965.

———. Dynamics of drug dependence: implications of a conditioning theory for research and treatment. *Archives of General Psychiatry,* 1973, *28,* 611–616.

Wilson, N. (ed.). *Colorado Client Assessment Record (CCAR)*, pp. 1–37. Denver, Colo.: Department of Institutions, Division of Mental Health, 1980.

Woody, R. H. (ed.). *Encyclopedia of Clinical Assessment.* San Francisco: Jossey-Bass, 1980.

Wurmser, L. Psychoanalytic considerations of the etiology of compulsive drug use. *The Journal of the American Psychoanalytic Association,* 1974, *22,* 820–843.

Zinberg, N. E. *High States, a Beginning Study,* pp. 1–50. *National Drug Abuse Council,* 1974.

———. Addiction and ego function. *The Psychoanalytic Study of the Child,* 1975, *30,* 567–588.

———, Harding, W. M., and Winkeller, M. A study of social regulatory mechanisms in controlled illicit drug users. *Journal of Drug Issues,* 1977, *7*(*2*), 117–133.

Zinberg, N. E., and Jacobson, R. C. The natural history of "chipping." *American Journal of Psychiatry,* 1976, *133*(*1*), 37–40.

———, and Harding, W. M. Social sanctions and rituals as a basis for drug abuse prevention. *American Journal of Drug and Alcohol Abuse,* 1975, *2*(*2*), 165–182.

Zubin, J. Classification of behavior disorders. *The Annual Review of Psychology,* Vol. 18. Palo Alto, Calif.: Annual Reviews Press, 1969.

9

From Methadone Maintenance to Abstinence

The Myth of the Metabolic Disorder Theory

THOMAS EDWARD BRATTER / MATTHEW C. PENNACCHIA / DEANNE C. GAUYA

HEROIN ADDICTION has been long and heavily debated. More than a century ago, for example, Day (1868) recognized that the medical profession could not agree about the most effective method to treat opium habituation. More recently the debate concerning the treatment of heroin addiction has been exacerbated because various disciplines have claimed competence and have assumed antagonistic positions. Anslinger and Tompkins (1953) and Rossdies (1971) argue that addiction is a crime. In 1914 the Harrison Narcotic Act, according to Eldridge (1962), "set out to control the non-medical use of narcotics and evolved into the prohibition of non-medical uses and the control of medical uses." Physicians did not protest when politicians demanded that law enforcement personnel control the medical uses of narcotics.

The psychiatric and medical establishment traditionally has viewed heroin addiction to be an incurable disease. In the 1940s and the 1950s, Prescor (1943) and O'Donnell (1964) report, many hospitals discontinued addiction treatment programs as economically unwarranted because longitudinal studies documented recidivism rates to exceed 90 percent. Simmel (1929), Rado (1935), and Krystal and Raskin (1970) believe that the addictive process can be resolved through psychoanalysis. Freud (1953, pp. 295–296) concluded that "life as we find it is too hard for us; it entails too much pain, too many disappointments, impossible tasks. We cannot do without palliative remedies. . . . There are perhaps three of these means: powerful diversions of interest, which lead us to care little about our misery; substitutive gratifications, which lessen it; and intoxicating substances, which make us insensitive to it."

Sugarman (1974), and Bratter (1981) describe a self-help approach which utilizes recovered addicts as the primary catalytic agents for change. The treatment of addiction by means of pharmacological agents gained acceptance because it enabled physicians to regain control of addiction—an approach which, in comparison to other approaches, appeared cheaper, shorter, and more effective. Nyswander (1956), Dole, Nyswander, and Kreek (1966), Martin and Gorodetsky (1965), Martin et al. (1965), and Martin, Gorodetsky, and McClane (1966) view addiction as essentially a medical problem which can be treated pharmacologiclly. There are, of course, many tautological theories regarding heroin addiction, but they fall outside the purview of this chapter. The metabolic disease theory, which postulates that addicts require opiates for relief of a biochemical deficit, has been described by Dole and Nyswander (1966a) as a psychotherapeutic orientation, and will be examined later in this chapter.

Shaffer (1977) laments that the field of heroin addiction lacks a paradigm which explains addictive behavior, and this lack creates treatment and research problems. Despite the Dole and Nyswander effort to substantiate a metabolic disorder, Cochin (1974) concedes that "although we have learned a great deal about tolerance and dependence, the mechanisms responsible for their initiation, maintenance, and loss still remains obscure." Shaffer (1977) contends that addiction research and theory must be based on a new paradigm that takes into account the interactive, contextual, and temporary features of the phenomena as these occur in real life and the consequences of those phenomena as observed in practice. Shaffer and Burglass (1981a, p. 485) list five principles which must be considered before any paradigm for addictive behavior can be devised:

> First, it is important to come to terms with the individual differences among drug users if explanations of addiction are to be relevant and practical. Second, drug users are self-determining agents; an adequate model of addiction should include an examination of drug-use motivation. Third, an analysis of the settings and contexts within which drugs are used is fundamental to a complete understanding of addiction. Particular interest should be paid to the dynamics of social and cultural rituals and ceremonies that implicitly and explicitly control drug use. Fourth, an adequate explanation of addiction must allow for unconsciously motivated behavior. Fifth, . . . drugs alter the perceived experience of the user; thus, after drug use, a user's experience is altered. This change in experience (both the

expected and the unexpected) notes the importance of the cybernetic aspects of drug use.

Until the Dole and Nyswander version of addiction is expanded to consider the holistic elements, the metabolic theory will have limited appeal because there is no continuum which spans etiology, treatment, and detoxification (i.e., abstinence). Individuality and personal idiosyncrasies are ignored. The concept of personal choice and responsibility is deemed irrelevant. Nowhere is there a scientific discussion concerning the relative merits of high dosages of methadone versus low dosages of methadone and their respective relationship to the metabolic dysfunction. When no paradigm exists, there can be no consensus, no scientific validation, and no consistent treatment regimen. Paradigms are accepted examples of actual scientific practice that provide models from which spring peculiar coherent traditions of scientific research. Dole and Nyswander (1967b) contend that "heroin is a medical problem—one that can be solved by medical research or not at all." Peele (1981) refutes the Dole and Nyswander contention when he writes:

> Despite the considerable resources invested in it, pharmacological research devoid of an awareness of the psychological needs of the addict and his or her social setting has succeeded in creating new drugs to which people may become addicted. What brought about this substantial miscalculation was the failure to understand that those who become addicted welcome the elimination of troubling sensation and the dulling of awareness that all of these drugs produce. This means that any drug which is effective for analgesic or related purposes will be addictive by definition, since it is this very experience the person seeks in an addiction.

Pharmacological Properties of Methadone and Morphine: Is the "Cure" More Toxic Than the Solution?

Methadone was synthesized as a byproduct of meperidine research by the Germans during World War II, when their supply of morphine was depleted. Despite the shortage of painkillers in Germany, methadone was not utilized because large doses resulted in a substantial incidence of side effects. German scientists recognized that methadone, an analgestic, could produce an insensitivity to pain by sedation—depression of both the respiratory and central nervous systems—with a concurrent relaxation of smooth muscle.

Methadone hydrochloride (4,4 diphenyl-6-demethylamino-hepanone-3 hydrochloride) is a synthetic opiate-type narcotic that has analgesic effects which are similar to those of morphine. Newmeyer et al. (1972) have described methadone as a "second-rate, semi-synthetic narcotic analgestic." Unlike other synthetic narcotic analgesics, methadone has effects that last between twelve and forty-eight hours. Dole, Nyswander, and Warner (1968) claim that a single dose of methadone is sufficient to prevent the patient who uses heroin from experiencing abstinence symptoms or the usual euphoria. Nyswander (1969) propose that the effectiveness of methadone in neutralizing heroin addiction is its ability to block not only euphoric effects but also a craving for the opiate, without any deleterious physical and psychological reactions. Brill and Jaffe (1968), Wieland (1969), and Wieland and Chambers (1970) believe that methadone produces a cross-tolerance to the opiates and their analogs which not only stabilizes patients but also reduces their drug craving.

When asked to prepare a critical commentary on the Second National Methadone Treatment Conference, Martin (1970, p. 550) warned:

> Methadone is a dangerous drug and the doses used for maintenance are highly toxic to the nontolerant individual. Methadone is a narcotic and produces in nontolerant patients a type of euphoria . . . that is similar to heroin. Further, it produces a type of tolerance and physical dependence that is indistinguishable from that of heroin and morphine. It has a high abuse potentiality. Finally, in all probability, it produces, like morphine, long-lasting physiological and psychological abnormalities. Therefore, it seems obvious that because of the toxicity of methadone, it should be used cautiously and as a last resort when the therapist is quite certain that the consequences of methadone maintenance will be less detrimental to the individual than the consequences of continued illicit drug taking, and after less dangerous treatment modalities have failed or have been rejected.

Both the Food and Drug Administration and the Bureau of Narcotics and Dangerous Drugs have been mandated to maintain rigorous pharmacological criteria before any chemical will be approved and subsequently released for public consumption under medical supervision. While criticism by Hughes and Brewin (1979) is perhaps only tangentially relevant to methadone, they cast some doubt on the scientific integrity of the Food and Drug Administration not only in recognizing but also warning the public about the potential dangers and toxicity of drugs.

Randal (1982, p. 114) describes the process to which the F.D.A. insists that the pharmaceutical industry conform before a new drug can be marketed:

> The animal testing, which can require several years, the literature search comes first. When these results are passed on to the F.D.A., approval is almost always granted for Investigational New Drug status, which means human testing can begin. The first phase of testing is simply for toxicity

> and metabolic effects. The trial group is ordinarily limited to up to 80 healthy young men (drug company testing, even for drugs aimed at a female clientele, is conducted almost solely with male volunteers). If nobody gets sick, the next F.D.A. phase allows the drug to be tested for effectiveness on about 200 patients who suffer from the disease it is intended to treat. If the drug passes muster on safety and efficacy at this stage—and less than half do—it goes on to clinical tests with about 1,000 patients. If these final tests for infrequent side effects are successful, the drug is granted approval by the F.D.A. and can be readied for market. Depending on the drug, the pharmaceutical companies often bear the costs of all trials.

Although this testing process sounds rigorous, it is not rigorous enough. For example, despite the compelling evidence linking Miltown, Valium, and Librium with birth defects, it was only after a decade and a half of abuse that the F.D.A. finally decided to challenge the drugs' manufacturer, Hoffmann–La Roche. Hughes and Brewin (1979, pp. 82–83) write:

> While tranquilizers, such as Miltown, Librium, or Valium, have been routinely prescribed for many years during pregnancy and have been considered relatively benign substances by both mother and physician, a growing body of scientific evidence now implies a causal relationship between these drugs and birth defects. Reports of birth abnormalities associated with Miltown, Librium, and Valium have been routinely forwarded by doctors to both the drug manufacturers and the F.D.A., but it was not until 1976 that the F.D.A. finally took heed of this growing evidence and put a warning label on all the minor tranquilizers, cautioning against their use by pregnant women. Hoffmann–La Roche steadfastly maintains that one of its products, Valium, has not been implicated in birth defects, despite the F.D.A.'s warning notice.

Will there be another insidious repetition of the Food and Drug Administration's dismal performance with methadone? Time will be the judge.

Methadone initially was classified as an "experimental" and "investigational" substance. The Federal Registrar (1970, p. 9014) warns: "Though methadone is a marketed drug approved through the new-drug procedure for specific indications, its use in maintenance treatment of narcotic addicts is an investigational use for which substantial evidence of safety and effectiveness is not available." Dole (1970, pp. 360–361), in contrast, claims that "in no case has it been found that methadone has had any dangerous toxic effects. No patient has shown signs of somatic damage that could be related to the medication. . . . These findings have been confirmed by clinicians using methadone maintenance in other treatment programs. So far as I can tell . . . almost everyone agrees that methadone treatment is safe." Bloom and Sudderth (1970), twenty-five years after Isbell and Vogel (1949), question the government's findings and refute Dole's contentions. They discovered some clinical side effects such as "constipation and insomnia . . . pitting, pedal edema . . . myoclonic jerks . . . drowsiness . . . sexual impotence."

Dole consistently has denied that methadone has any toxic effects. Dole et al. (1971, p. 541) have written: "When taken by the maintenance patients, whose special tolerance for narcotics decreases the pharmacologic effects of this medication, this dose produces no sedation, no impairment of respiration, or other adverse effects. However, the same dose will cause severe respiratory depression if taken by nontolerant subjects who are not on the methadone program, and is likely to be fatal in children." Fraser (1971), however, has challenged this assumption because he believes "with increasing use of any drug, new manifestations of its toxicity are recognized. It is hoped that this report may both alert physicians and stimulate further investigation into the mechanism and spectrum of its [methadone] toxicity." Baden (1972) concurs with Fraser and suggests that "the persistence of the pharmacologic effects, particularly the respiratory depression, was not appreciated by attending physicians in a few instances of fatal methadone poisoning." Gardner (1970) has discussed methadone misuse and deaths. Ratcliffe (1963) was perhaps the first to discuss methadone poisoning in children. Aronow, Paul, and Wooley (1972) lament that children find it easier than adults to acquire methadone, which has proved to be fatal in nontolerant people. Bruchner et al. (1972), who validate the concept of methadone poisoning, suggest that naloxone can be the antidote of choice for methadone overdoses. Datta and Antopol (1973) and Grove and Amith (1973) have conducted experimental studies with mice which document the toxicity of methadone. Thornton and Thornton (1974) mention that incidents of adverse reactions to methadone maintenance, though limited, appear to be increasing. Kjeldgaard, Halm, and Heckenlively (1971) describe a former heroin addict who, after ingesting 80 milligrams of methadone, developed pulmonary edema. Kreek (1973) discovered liver function abnormalities in 57 percent of those who were enrolled in a methadone maintenance treatment program. Unquestionably, with the rise of deaths which have been attributed directly to the use and abuse of methadone, there is urgent reason to resolve the issue of the cure which can be a killer. Pierson, Howard, and Kleber (1972) suggest some of the questions which must be asked and answered. "Did the methadone taken during pregnancy cause subtle and detrimental physiological or immunological changes in the infant? Did any of the other drugs addicts use to get a 'high' cause such changes?"

In 1972, after extensive chemcial tests were conducted by the National Institute of Mental Health and the Bureau of Narcotics and Dangerous Drugs, the Food and Drug Administration changed the status of methadone to an approved drug. The Federal Registrar (1972), however, still warned:

> The use methadone presents difficult and unique questions of medical judgment, law enforcement, and public policy that have not previously been encountered with other new drugs. Methadone presently represents the only drug for which there is substantial evidence of effectiveness in the treatment of heroin. Although the short-term use of the drug has been shown to be relatively safe from a toxicity standpoint, more information is necessary on the toxicity of long-term use.

Despite the Federal Registrar's warning, the numbers of patients who were being treated with methadone began to escalate dramatically. Dobbs (1971, pp. 1536–1541), who, in the main, is cautious but optimistic about methadone, has compiled a list of thirteen side effects of methadone on the basis of a random sample of one hundred patients, which constituted 20 percent of an outpatient clinic: (1) "high" effects, drowsiness, and "nodding"; (2) constipation; (3) excessive sweating; (4) interference with sexual functioning; (5) menstrual irregularities; (6) difficulties in urinating; (7) gastrointestinal tract complaints such as pain or nausea and vomiting; (8) bradycardia or lowered blood pressure; (9) symptoms of impaired lung functioning or chronic bronchitis; (10) transitory allergic skin rashes; (11) a definite pitting edema of extremities; (12) nightmare-type drams; (13) death or near-fatal coma from accidental overdose. Senay (1971, p. 183) engages in some interesting, but contradictory, rhetoric when he reports that

> patients taking methadone for two or three years have reported a belief that methadone is a "worse" habit to get rid of than heroin. . . . Many patients also voice the conviction that methadone "gets in your bones" or similar ideas which give expression to the feeling that methadone becomes a part of the person in a way which is not true of heroin. Scientifically, there appears to be no basis for such convictions; rather, they appear to be related to the fear generated by the uncertainty and novelty of methadone.

After indicating a skepticism about subjective patient complaints, Senay continues:

> Patients who have been taking methadone for a decade, however, have not suffered from serious side effects; it may be that such long-term use with its attendant psychologic dependence will turn out to have been necessary. However, until sufficient resources are available to find out what is possible, indefinite maintenance appears to be safe and to be far preferable to "ripping and running," hustling, shooting up, etc.

Senay and Renault (1971) conclude that the "long-term outcome of methadone maintenance is not yet known; while there is no reason for anxiety, critics have seized on the uncertainty." Kafer (1973), Marks and Goldring (1973), Soin, Thomashow, and Wagner (1973), Veebely and Kutt (1973), and Wiley, Hunt, and Peters (1973) describe the short- and long-term adverse side effects of methadone maintenance.

Why the Federal Registrar neglects to include the clinical observations of Bloom and Sudderth (1970) and Dobbs (1971), as well as the more recent investigations, is a matter of conjecture. Why the government has not reissued a statement in view of these studies raises questions similar to those Hughes and Brewin (1979) asked about Valium, Librium, and Miltown. Bratter (1980) wonders whether or not methadone maintenance treatment programs have been misguided management of heroin addicts. Langrod, Lowinson, and Ruiz (1981, p. 951), apparently oblivious of the studies which have discussed the potential toxicity and complications of methadone, conclude that "maintenance is a validated treatment. The medical safety of the medication and the procedure have been documented. . . . There are no medical contradictions which could prevent the utilization of methadone maintenance for a large heterogeneous addict population. However, further research in the psychophysiologic sphere is certainly warranted to increase our knowledge in this field."

The Physicians' Desk Reference (1982, p. 1122) contends, however, that methadone hydrochloride is a

> synthetic narcotic analgesic with multiple actions quantitatively similar to those of morphine . . . which can produce drug dependence of the morphine type and, therefore, has the potential for being abused. Psychic dependence, physical dependence, and tolerance may develop upon repeated administration of methadone, and it should be prescribed and administered with the same degree of caution appropriate to the use of morphine.

But what is morphine? Tatum, Steevers, and Collins (1929) proposed a dual-action hypothesis, which described the development of physical dependence on morphine: (1) morphine causes a concurrent depression and stimulation in the integrated nervous system; (2) during the initial drug reaction, depression will neutralize the stimulant effects; (3) inasmuch as stimulation exceeds depression, the final phase of the reaction will be hyperexcitability; (4) with increasingly larger dosages, stimulation is commensurately intensified and can produce tetany and convulsions; (5) since tolerance is prolonged until the depressant effects of morphine terminate, any increase in dosage will result in intensified excitatory effects. It has also been suggested that direct morphine stimulation may temporarily summate with, and thus enhance the intensity of abstinence especially during nalorphine-induced withdrawal.

Kolb and Himmelsbach (1938) and Himmelsbach (1942b) recognized that in addition to drugs of the phenanthrene series, i.e., morphine and its derivatives, Demerol was also addictive. Himmelsbach was perhaps the first to recommend that methadone (also known as 10820, amidone, and dolophine) be classified as a potent analgesic which had a similar pharmacologic action to morphine and consequently required scientific investigation regarding its addictive liability. Isbell and various associates (1947a, 1947b, 1948a, 1948b) studied the addiction liability of methadone. Isbell and Vogel (1949, p. 914) concluded that "the results leave absolutely no doubt that methadone is a dangerous addicting drug. . . . The drug in sufficient dosage produces a type of euphoria which is even more pleasant to some morphine addicts than is the euphoria produced by morphine." Because of Isbell's warning regarding abuse potential, methadone was included in the Harrison Narcotic Act. What appears significant and startling to any serious researcher is the omission of these significant works from any of the early Dole and Nyswander studies. It appears, in retrospect, almost as if the entire methadone maintenance bureaucracy neglected to acknowledge any historical precedent. A reasonable explanation is that increasingly more sophisticated scientific technology and methodology made these studies simply look too crude, and they could not be replicated. Unfortunately, nowhere have the Himmelsbach and Isbell studies been repudiated.

The Metabolic Disorder Theory of Addiction: A Pharmacodynamic Solution with No Psychotherapy

During the late 1950s, Dole, a biochemist, a Nyswander, a psychiatrist, attempted to discover a pharmacological cure for heroin addiction. The husband-and-wife team have postulated that the primary reason for heroin addiction is an altered response to narcotics which suggests a metabolic change within the central nervous system. The rationale for a narcotic substitution therapy rests on the assumption that a metabolic change in the structure of the cells creates a systemic dysfunction and narcotic hunger. Dole and Nyswander (1966a) explicitly have stated that heroin addicts suffer from a metabolic disease or biochemical deficit which requires opiates for relief. This is the basis for the pharmacodynamic approach which includes a narcotic substitution therapy. It is interesting, though not particularly significant, that almost half a century before Dole and Nyswander's work, Ferenczi

(1912), a disciple of Freud, proposed that alcoholics and drug addicts might be deficient in endogenous psychotoxins. Ferenczi believed that addiction was caused by the efforts of the individual to compensate for pain by self-medication, and he deduced that there was a metabolic or endocrine imbalance. Perkins (1972, p. 461) has written:

> The mechanism by which methadone acts is not understood; nor is the metabolic theory of addiction—the underlying rationale of methadone maintenance—yet established. These observations alone are not disquieting. After all, a tradition of empiricism permits a therapeutic agent to be used, and results to be studied, before precise knowledge of the mechanism of action is in hand. Furthermore, a theory of pathogenesis need not to be demonstrably correct in order to provide a scaffolding for work to be advanced.

The 'metabolic deficiency' hypothesis has . . . never been adequately explained or in any way substantiated. However, it has played a crucial role in shaping methadone programming. Until very recently, the role of ancillary services was underplayed and the involvement of professional personnel, apart from nurses and medical doctors, minimized. Bowden and Maddux (1972, p. 436), after concluding there is no evidence to support the contention that addiction to narcotics creates a metabolic disorder, offer two observations which reject the metabolic imbalance theory:

> First, if it were correct, abstinent ex-addicts should not be able to function well without narcotics. . . . Many recovered addicts do function well without the use of narcotics and other drugs. Second, an adequate dose of methadone or other narcotic should abolish narcotic craving, but we know that many patients receiving methadone continue to use heroin, even when they are receiving doses that produce complete cross-tolerance to the morphine-like effects of narcotics.

Dole and Nyswander suggest that a "narcotic blockage" can be created when sufficient methadone has been prescribed. This treatment regimen substitutes controlled amounts of equally addicting methadone, which, in maintenance dosages, blocks the addict's craving for heroin. "By establishing tolerance to methadone and subsequently maintaining the tolerant state with a constant daily oral dose, we found it possible to block the action of heroin and eliminate the hunger for narcotic drugs" (Dole and Nyswander, 1966b, p. 640). Patients who have been blockaded experience no narcotic effects but concurrently lose their compulsive desire for heroin. In their first publication, Dole and Nyswander (1965), who stabilized twenty-two former heroin addicts with oral methadone hydrochloride, contend that methadone "appears to have two useful effects: (1) relief of narcotic hunger, and (2) induction of sufficient tolerance to block the euphoric effect of an average illegal dose of diacetylmorphine." Nyswander (1971, p. 24) has written:

> we have found that, taken orally, methadone could assuage narcotic hunger without giving the disabling euphoria of heroin. Also, while dosage had to be increased regularly for a while to achieve this effect, it eventually could be leveled off to a stable requirement. And through a mechanism of cross-tolerance for other opiates, methadone blocked the effect of a heroin shot. Despite large challenge doses of morphine, heroin, dilaudid, or methadone, patients and physicians both reported that the euphoric effects of those narcotics were absent.

In a well-documented overview, Goldstein (1972, p. 297) offers a rational proposition:

> If heroin addiction is truly a "metabolic disease" without a cure, then patients, even in the best-run methadone programs, will never be able to achieve or maintain the abstinent state; they will have to take methadone indefinitely. It is important, however, to find this out by an adequate trial. At least until solid evidence is forthcoming to support the position that methadone maintenance should be of unlimited duration, it is better to act upon the more cautious view that major factors in perpetuating heroin addiction are psychologic, and that they can be modified by reeducation, retraining, and reconditioning.

There still remain many unanswered questions regarding the validity of the metabolic lesion "theory." Jaffe (1970) asks: "What is the essential feature of the methadone approach: the alleviation of 'narcotics hunger' or the 'blockade' of heroin-induced euphoria?" Casriel and Bratter (1974, p. 362) inquire:

> Does a metabolic dysfunction exist at birth or is it created by a physiologic reaction to heroin abuse? If the metabiologic disorder is a biochemical reaction to heroin, how many applications of the opiate are needed to produce a genetic change? Is a metabiologic change permanent or ephemeral? How specifically does the application of methadone restore/neutralize the metabiologic disorder? What is the optimal dosage of methadone needed to be a blockade? If methadone is the chemotherapeutic cure, why does a significant patient population continue to purchase additional illicit methadone to augment their dose?

Why do many methadone patients continue to abuse other drugs, such as alcohol, barbiturates, or amphetamines? While admittedly an early reaction, the Committee on Alcoholism and Drug Dependence of the American Medical Association stated in 1967 its belief that the efficacy of methadone maintenance programs remained unproved and required additional evaluation. Fifteen years later, these concerns persist.

In retrospect, utilizing metabolic disorder to explain the cause of heroin addiction appears reductionary because no data has been produced which either can validate or disprove the Dole and Nyswander contentions. Freedman (1968a) first observed that the controversy over whether there is an "addictive personality" or an innate metabolic disorder has not been resolved. Is the individual born with a metabolic disorder which creates a craving for heroin, or is such a disorder caused by abusing heroin? Dole and Nyswander have not explained the abrupt detoxification from heroin undergone by those who become incarcerated or enter drug-free programs. The metabolic disorder explanation is questioned indirectly by two studies about Vietnam servicemen. Zinberg (1974) discovered that a significant number of servicemen who used relatively pure heroin in high dosages in Vietnam never became addicted and experienced little difficulty becoming abstinent when they completed their tour of duty. Robins, Davis, and Goodwin (1974), who confirmed Zinberg's findings, concluded that since less than 10 percent of the returning servicemen continued their drug-related activities, "contrary to conventional belief, the occasional use of narcotics without becoming addicted appears to be possible even for men who had previously been dependent on narcotics."

The pharmacological explanation for addiction ignores the psychological and environmental factors which, at least partially, produce addiction. Perhaps more insidious and countertherapeutic is that the physiological view eliminates from consideration the concepts of personal responsibility, choice, and individual accountability. Horney (1945, p. 241) has defined the goal of psychotherapy to help the individual:

> To assume responsibility for himself, in the sense of feeling himself the active, responsible force in his life, capable of making decisions and of taking the consequences. With this goes an acceptance of responsibility toward others, a readiness to recognize obligations in those values he holds whether they relate to his children, parents, friends, employees, colleagues, community, or country.

Nyswander (1956) has written about the heroin addict as a patient, but does not mention psychotherapeutic strategies and elects to discuss the pharmacological, physiological, psychological (distinguished from psychotherapeutic), and demographic aspects of addiction. This tendency to emphasize the pharmacological causes of addiction needs to be viewed carefully, since it influences both the conceptualization and implementation of methadone maintenance. The Dole and Nyswander (1966) work was presented in 1966 at the Association for Research in Nervous and Mental Diseases, a group concerned with the biochemcial-pharmacological-physiological rather than the psychological causes of addiction. Freedman (1968a), who cautioned against a simplistic single-dimensional approach regarding etiology, proposed that addiction was a multifactor phenomenon and that societal, psychic, and metabolic factors needed to be studied before any definitive conclusion could be achieved. Dole and Nyswander throughout their research never have provided tautological specific reasons why they have not referred or responded to the works of Kolb (1925), Levy (1925), Glover (1932), Rado (1926, 1933, and 1957), Lindesmith (1938), Crowlay (1939), Gerard (1955), Ausubel (1958), Hill, Haertzen, and Glaser (1960), Chein et al. (1964), and other sociological and psychological works pertinent to heroin addiction. The omission of antecedent and contemporary sociological and psychological literature becomes critical when attempting to comprehend how Dole and Nyswander (1966b) and Kreek (1973) derive the theory of a metabolic deficiency, because this omission has affected the conceptualization and implementation of methadone maintenance programs worldwide.

Dole and Nyswander have rejected the psychogenic theory of the cause of addiction, and consequently have rejected the two arguments which, they believe, would corroborate such a theory. The first of these arguments is the character-disordered hypothesis, which they dismiss because, they contend, there is no evidence that sociopathetic traits precede addiction. Dole and Nyswander (1968, p. 362) write:

> The decisive proof of a psychogenic theory would be a demonstration that potential addicts could be identified by psychiatric examination before drug usage had distorted behavior and metabolic functions. However, a careful review of the literature has failed to disclose any study in which a characteristic psychopathology or "addictive personality" has been recognized in a number of individuals prior to addiction. Retrospective studies, in which a record of delinquency before addiction is taken as evidence of sociopathic tendencies, fail to provide the comparative data needed for diagnosis of deviant personality. . . . There is no known way to identify the future addicts among delinquents. No study has shown a consistent difference in behavior or pattern of delinquency of adolescents who later become addicts and those who do not.

Dole and Nyswander (1968, p. 362) reject the notion of any preaddictive personality because

> crime statistics show both the force of drug hunger and its specificity; almost all of the crimes committed by addicts relate to the procurement of drugs. The rapid disappearance of theft and antisocial behavior in patients on the methadone maintenance program strongly supports the hypothesis that the crimes that they had previously committed as addicts were a consequence of the drug hunger, not the expression of some more basic psychopathology. The so-called sociopathic personality is no longer evident in our patients.

Dole and Nyswander dismiss the contention that addicts are unable to control their drug hunger, because this evaluation, they claim, is subjective and dependent upon the respective personal experiences of both the interviewer and the addict. Dole and Nyswander (1968, p. 362) pejoratively label those who researched the preaddictive characteristics as being both "critics" and "moralists," who, "having won their own struggles for self-control, measure the character of others by what they presume they would do if addicted." The authors go on to say (p. 363):

> Moralists generally assume that opiates are dangerously pleasant drugs that can be resisted only by the strength of character. The pharmacology is somewhat more complicated than this. For most normal persons, morphine and heroin are not enjoyable drugs—at least not in the initial exposures. Given to a postoperative patient, these analgesics provide a welcome relief of pain. . . . When given to an average pain-free subject, morphine produces nausea and sedation, but rarely euphoria. What, then, is the temptation to become an addict? So far as can be judged from the histories of addicts, many of them found the first trials of narcotics in some sense pleasurable or tranquilizing, even though the drug caused nausea and vomiting. Perhaps their reaction to the drug was abnormal, even on the first exposure.

Dole and Nyswander (1968, p. 363) rhetorically ask the fundamental question on which they base the methadone maintenance rationale: "Does the abnormal reaction which can be observed after the narcotic drug has become euphorigenic stem 'from a basic weakness of character or is [it] a consequence of drug use'?" They answer their question by stating: "When drug hunger is blocked without production of narcotic effects, the drug-seeking behavior ends."

On the basis of their experience with 304 addicts over a fourteen-month period, the research team concludes that the etiology of addiction is metabolic more than characterological. Dole and Nyswander (1968, pp. 363–364) extrapolate the final conclusion:

> We are not aware of any comparable success in treatment of addicts by psychotherapy. This casts some doubt on the psychogenic theory of addiction, but of course does not disprove it. Conceivably, a basic character defect might lead to drug use, and in turn, to an irreversible addition in which the subsequent behavior of the subject is determined by conditioned reflexes or by metabolic changes in neurones following repeated exposure to narcotic drugs. This argument, however, represents a considerable departure from a purely psychological theory of addiction and relapse.

While Dole and Nyswander (1967a) recognize the need for counseling and additional supportive services, nowhere do they describe specific psychotherapeutic and ancillary approaches. They have written (1967a, p. 365):

> Any program that ignores the social deficits of the street addict will fall short of making him a productive citizen in a free society. Acquisition of the drug habit is only the first step in the social deterioration of the street addict and likewise, stopping the use of heroin is only the beginning of rehabilitation. When an adolescent becomes addicted to heroin, his maturation ceases. The normal experiences of school, family life, vocational training, and assumption of responsibility are blocked and his energies become diverted to the means of getting money for heroin. If he was not delinquent before becoming addicted, he becomes so; his alienation from society widens with exposure to the addict world and jail. This is the path that must be retraced in therapy.

Dole and Nyswander (1967a) suggest that formal psychotherapy may be unnecessary in a carefully supervised methadone maintenance program. When treatment failures occur in methadone maintenance programs, Dole (1970, pp. 361–362) attributes them to the inability of therapists to rehabilitate patients who have stopped heroin use: "Individuals who have stopped heroin use with methadone treatment but continue to steal, drink excessively, or abuse non-narcotic drugs, or are otherwise antisocial, are failures of the rehabilitation program but not of the medication." The Dole and Nyswander logic appears to be contradictory. On the one hand, the physicians suggest that psychotherapy is not required; but on the other, they explain treatment failures as a result of the psychotherapeutic rehabilitation program. Dole and Nyswander (1967a) in their original design did offer counseling but reported that "no specific psychiatric treatment was provided. . . . There has, however, been very little need for psychotherapy, and no indication that structured group therapy would contribute to rehabilitation." They continued to stress the metabolic basis for heroin addiction, which, it can be assumed, was their rationale for minimizing the need for any kind of psychotherapy.

Dole and Nyswander (1967b) admit that "problem patients, the disturbed individuals with psychopathology independent of addiction, respond less well" to methadone maintenance. This finding, which negates their claim of only a metabolic dysfunction, has been confirmed by Ramer, Zaslove, and Langan (1971), who discovered that the continued abuse of heroin by methadone patients concealed the existence of significant psychopathology. Both these studies appear to question the original Dole and Nyswander hypothesis that heroin addiction is caused by a metabolic disorder. Dole and Nyswander do not resolve their ambivalence regarding the efficacy of psychotherapy. This confusion and controversy characterized the methadone maintenance programs of the late 1960s and early 1970s. Karkus (1973) reflects this confusion and believes that "formal psychotherapy has little place in a methadone program even with serious problem patients, provided that patients receive help in solving day-to-day problems and are allowed to develop self-confidence and respect." Unfortunately, Karkus does not describe the process by which patients can develop self-confidence and respect.

In their review of the literature, Dole and Nyswander only surveyed studies of psychoanalytic approaches, which have proved to be less than effective with an addicted subpopulation. Dole and Nyswander neglected to consider some of the more innovative, learning-based, reality-oriented, confrontative psychotherapeutic programs. Their apparent assumption that psychoanalysis and psychotherapy are synonymous could explain their ambivalence—an ambivalence which permits Dole (1972) to state: "It has been my privilege during the past seven years to witness the emergence of a new branch of medicine: the medical treatment of narcotics addiction." Apparently, Dole assumes he is an originator of the pharmacological treatment of heroin addiction; he neglects to recognize that the works of Eddy, Isbell, Martin, and Wikler precede his.

Dole and Nyswander view the indefinite administration of methadone as the only legitimate treatment goal. Nowhere have they discussed the procedure for any detoxification from methadone. During the discussion of his presentation at the Second National Methadone Treatment Conference, Dole (1970) was asked by Eddy (1947a, 1947b, and 1955), a pioneer in analgesic research, to clarify a most significant issue: Dole's contention that "people cannot be taken off methadone without a reversion to heroin." Dole (1970, p. 372) responded:

> I did not say that a person taken off methadone is sure to revert to heroin. What he does with this compulsion is, of course, another matter. There are a number of people who are able to live with drug hunger and remain abstinent. Withdrawal of methadone, therefore, is not the same thing as dooming them to relapse to heroin. But in our experience the return of heroin is a consistent phenomenon of the withdrawal of methadone. What they return to pharmacologically after withdrawal of methadone is the status they had prior to treatment with methadone.

The Classical Conditioning Model of Heroin Addiction: Neurochemical Determinants of Behavior

While, perhaps, only tangentially relevant both to the metabolic disorder theory of addiction and methadone as subsequent treatment, other pharmacotherapeutic techniques appear to contradict much of the Dole and Nyswander thinking. Gold and various associates (1978, 1979, 1980a, 1980b, and 1981) and Washton, Resnick, and Rawson (1980) conclude that clonidine can be utilized for effective detoxification from opiates before patients receive naltrexone, which is a narcotic antagonist. Using double-blind experimental procedures when comparing clonidine to methadone for detoxification, Washton and Resnick (1981) found that of the eighteen subjects who elected to discontinue their detoxification, eight "returned to the opiates in response to some form of psychological stress (i.e., relationship problems, job pressures, dysphoric state)." Six attributed their relapse to an uncontrollable craving for opiates, and the remaining four said they were unable to endure the physical withdrawal discomfort. Any study which utilizes such a small sample (N = 18) must be placed into perspective. The findings, nevertheless, appear to reject the metabolic disorder theory. More likely, the eight who suffered a relapse due to an "uncontrollable craving for opiates" can be explained more by the conditioning theory proposed by Wikler (1952, 1953, 1965, and 1970). Wikler amalgamated pharmacological, physiological, psychoanalytical, and learning theory to explain addiction as a conditioned, or learned, phenomenon. Wikler (1973, pp. 611–612) writes:

> Drug dependence is defined as . . . habitual, non-medically-indicated drug-seeking and drug-using behavior which is contingent for its maintenance upon pharmacological and usually, but not necessarily, upon social reinforcement. . . . Pharmacological reinforcement is viewed as the result of interactions between certain pharmacological effects of the drug and sources of reinforcement, i.e., organismic variables upon which the reinforcing properties of the drug are contingent. Pharmacological reinforcement is said to be direct if such sources of reinforcement had not been engendered by the drug itself, or indirect if the contrary is true. Furthermore, sources of direct pharmacological reinforcement may be intrinsic (built into the central nervous system) or developmental (acquired in the course of personality development or otherwise. . . . Also, direct or indirect pharmacological reinforcement may be primary (unconditioned) or secondary (conditioned).

Ironically, while Wikler based the classical conditioning model of addiction on his work with animals in a laboratory environment, he portrayed heroin addicts in a humanistic perspective. Rather than being considered the victims of conditioning, and, therefore, not amenable to psychotherapy (the metabolic dysfunction theory exculpates any personal responsibility for becoming addicted due to the existence of a predetermined physiological condition), addicts are, Wikler suggests, products of the interplay between cognitive, emotional, and behavioral phenomena. Wikler believes that stimuli which are connected to previous withdrawal attempts elicit the conditioned responses. Rejecting the power of euphoric drug effects to create addiction or to cause relapse, Wikler (1973) suggests that a conditioned withdrawal sickness can cause a relapse. Dews (1958, p. 1025), who analyzed the effects of psychopharmacological agents in animals, describes four variables which are critical for research with animals:

1. What the animal is; the species chosen and the particular class chosen.
2. What the animal is doing: (a) the nature of the response chosen for study, and (b) the frequency with which it is occurring under control conditions.
3. What the environment is doing to the animal; the eliciting, reinforcing, and discriminative stimuli playing on the animal. . . .
4. What has happened to the animal in the past; the nature of training to which the animal has been exposed, and also previous administrations of drugs leading to the possibilities of adaptation, tolerance or cumulation.

Expanding on Dews's work, Laties and Weiss (1969, p. 123) discussed the impact of environmental stimuli on the drug-behavior of the animal: "When a response is reinforced in the presence of a particular stimulus, that stimulus acquires a measure of control over the response in the sense that presenting it increases the probability of responding." Laties and Weiss describe the variables which influence behavior: experimental history, the schedule of reinforcement, the pattern and rate of responding, and the character of the discriminative stimuli available to the organism. Wikler's (1965) theory of relapses of heroin addicts, which utilizes an operant conditioning perspective, considers environment and drug effect but rejects the notion of personality factors which may predispose an individual to initial drug behavior. Teasdale (1973, p. 278) writes: "Conditioned withdrawal symptoms were only one of a number of possible factors leading to the resumption of drug use and even if treatment had successfully eliminated abstinence symptoms conditioned to a whole range of environmental stimuli, these other factors might still be operative and lead to the resumption of drug use." McAuliffe validates Wikler's theory of relapse because he believes that narcotics can ameliorate withdrawal sickness while concurrently not only producing euphoria but also resolving psychological problems. McAuliffe (1982, pp. 30–31) suggests there are four variables which contribute to relapse after a successful withdrawal:

1. Addicts who experience conditioned withdrawal sickness would be conscious of the experience at least a good part of the time.
2. Conditioned withdrawal symptoms would consist of relatively specific,

recognizable abstinence signs (e.g., yawning, tearing eyes, runny nose) rather that merely craving. . . .

3. Respondents would usually be able to remember having experienced conditioned withdrawal sickness. . . .
4. Addicts would understand why they relapsed.

Teasdale (1973) and O'Brien et al. (1977), who studied heroin addicts, have produced results similar to the Wikler hypothesis which do not eliminate other causes of recidivism.

Undeniably, a significant number of individuals become addicted because, as Vaillant (1977) suggests, they wish either to self-medicate themselves against frustration, fear, and failure in growing up or to prolong their adolescence. Khantzian, Mack, and Schatzberg (1974) view heroin addiction as an attempt to cope with emotional pain, stress, and dysphoria. These authors suggest that addicts have not successfully established familiar defensive, neurotic characterological, or other common adaptive mechanisms as a way of dealing with their distress. . . . Their attempt to cope with stress and anxiety by reverting repeatedly to the use of opiates as an all-powerful device, thereby precluding other solutions that normally develop and that might better sustain them. After examining Federal Bureau of Narcotics records from 1955 until 1960, Winick (1962) concluded that a majority of addicts simply "matured out" of their addiction. Hunt and Odoroff (1962) validated the Winick hypothesis that aging can be an important determinant in the voluntary cessation of addiction. Duvall, Locke, and Brill (1963) discovered that abstinence increased in relationship to age. Ball and Snarr (1969) replicated the earlier studies with men who returned to Puerto Rico after having been at Lexington Hospital. Vaillant (1966a, 1966b, 1973) confirmed the maturing-out hypothesis but concluded that a significant additional variable was the imposition of probation and parole. Snow (1973), who followed New York City addicts, as did Vaillant, from 1964 until 1968, found that 23 percent matured out of their addiction. Snow achieved results similar to the original Winick survey.

Like the Dole and Nyswander generalizations, Wikler's hypotheses need to be validated by empirical inquiry. Shaffer and Burglass (1981b, p. 338) suggest that

> by considering addiction as a "learned phenomenon," Wikler's formulations permit the development and implementation of precise treatment techniques, e.g., extinguishing specific conditioned responses which maintain addictive behavior patterns. . . . Wikler's consideration and theoretical inclusion of the perceptual, cognitive, and internal events which mediate behavior placed his "conditioning approach" twenty years ahead of his contemporaries in cognitive-behavioral psychological theory.

Other Pharmacological Approaches: Naloxone and Cyclazocine

During the late 1950s, and the 1960s, as Jaffe (1968) reports, the government encouraged much exploration to discover (1) pharmacological agents which could be utilized in the treatment of heroin addiction and opiate withdrawal symptoms, (2) analgesics with low abuse potential, and (3) narcotic antagonists. Antagonists have similar structures to opiates and their derivatives and utilize the same sites within the nervous system; in so doing, they prevent or reverse the pharmacological action of narcotics. Narcotic antagonists appear to neutralize the effects of opiates.

The interest in psychopharmacology and neurophysiology paralleled the discovery that both the central nervous system and the brain produced significant chemical activity. Fisher (1969, p. 61) cogently describes the chemical stimulation of the brain:

1. Neurotransmitter actions. Selective release of, and response to, these "chemical messengers" has been found essential for most synaptic conduction.
2. Decreases in threshold. Many hormones, as well as some drugs, probably act as threshold modulators rather than as neural triggers. In these instances, release of a neurotransmitter substance by afferents to the cell is nonetheless required to initiate function.
3. Selective effects on neurotransmitter function. Increased or decreased firing of selective chemical action which circumvents, mimics, enhances, or blocks neurotransmitter action. Most psychoactive drugs work in such ways.

Marshall (1894) and Strong (1895) were the first to recognize a dichotomy between original pain and the psychological reaction to the initial sensation. Beecher et al. (1951), one of the first to study the effects of methadone, discovered that experimental pain which was induced under laboratory conditions did not respond to the administration of morphine. However, Beecher (1955, 1959, and 1960) and Beecher et al. (1953) conclude that morphine could ameliorate pathological pain and disease. Martin was the first to propose the use of narcotic antagonists in the treatment of heroin addiction. Martin et al. (1963) studied the tolerance of morphine in rats. Abstinence can also be conditioned in rats. Martin and Gorodetzky (1965) discovered that the administration of nalorphine could demonstrate high levels of tolerance and that dysphoric and sedative reactions could result. [Martin, Gorodetzky, and McClane (1966) found that patients who were given large doses of cyclazocine became refractory to the euphoric and dependence-producing qualities of morphine.] Martin (1967) prepared an extensive technical overview of the antagonist literature which discussed clinical applications. Eddy (1966) detailed the antagonistic effects of nalorphine against morphine and its analogs. Jasinski, Martin, and Haertzen (1967) have indicated that naloxone, a new antagonist, possesses relatively few antagonistic actions. Naltrexone, a cyclopropylmethyl of naloxone, has been found by Blumberg, Dayton, and Wolf (1967) to possess (in animals) both a longer duration and antagonistic potency than naloxone. Schecter and Grossman (1975) contend that naltrexone has a longer duration and appears more effective than previously tested narcotic antagonists. Scientists attempted to discover an antagonist which would be analgesic to individuals but sufficiently potent to discourage the use and abuse of the opiates and their derivatives. Freedman (1968b) discusses the application of cyclazocine, a benzomorphan with potent antagonist qualities, to precipitate a withdrawal–abstinence reaction to morphine.

Perhaps the most conservative assessment is that there earlier existed controversy, confusion, and uncertainty concerning the basic biological mechanisms of heroin addiction. After assessing the few existing developmental psychopharmacological studies, Young (1967) concludes: "Generally speaking, there is an abhorrent lack of knowledge concerning the effects of biochemical intervention on developing behavioral systems." More study is required to understand the pharmacologic actions of morphine and its analogs and the neurotropic interactions. Most of the studies performed have utilized animal subjects. For example, De Salva and Oester (1960) used cats as subjects in their research and concluded that opiates and their analogs inhibit synaptic conduction in the spinothalamic tracts, which depresses the action of reticular formation.

Some neurochemical investigations purport to demonstrate the transfer between learned behavior and biochemical substances which are produced in the process and subsequent crossover. Conditioned behavior seems to have a chemical compound whereby a pseudoenzyme can be formed. Ungar and associates (1965a and 1969), studying morphine, claimed that tolerance could be transferred from one animal to another. Ungar and Oceguera-Navarro (1965b, p. 46) contended: "The information of previous exposure to the drug recorded in the nervous system could modify the pharmacologic responses. If the information is recorded in a chemical code, tolerance could be transferred to other animals by the administration of the substance containing the code." Unger and associates (1965b and 1968), after conditioning rats to fear darkness, extracted their brain tissue and transferred it by intraperitoneal injection to unexposed subjects; they found there was a crossover of that fear. Whether this is applicable to human beings has not been substantiated thus far. In Dole and Nyswander's only attempt to examine the experimental animal research, they attempt to generalize the findings to human subjects (Dole, 1972). He discusses the neurochemical determinants of behavior. Way and Adler (1960 and 1962) reviewed the biological disposition of morphine and its analogs between 1940 and 1960. Way (1968) concludes that "the pharmacological effects of morphine appear to correlate well with concentrations of the drug in the brain."

Numerous studies—of which the overwhelming majority use rats as subjects—have assessed the reaction of morphine and its derivatives on the oxidative metabolism of various body tissues. Takemori (1968) attempts to discuss the relationship between cellular adaptation and the cerebral cortex. Mule (1968) suggests that morphine and nalorphine affect phospholipid metabolism in brain tissue. Interestingly, nowhere do Dole and Nyswander refer to this research, and, therefore, there has been no conclusive evidence linking the salutary effects of methadone with the metabolic disorder findings.

Jaffe (1969, p. 358), whose research includes work with both cyclazocine and methadone, concludes:

> The antagonists appear to have values for treatment that are independent of the conditioning hypothesis. Since they can prevent a patient who uses narcotics intermittently from becoming physically dependent, the antagonists may make it possible for the patient to continue work or to participate in a rehabilitative program, even if he fails to achieve total abstinence from narcotics. . . . Obviously, a drug that prevents the action of narcotics in and of itself cannot change an individual's well-established life patterns, nor can it give him vocational skills. . . . The advantage of the antagonists in comparison with menthadone is that they are not narcotics. They have virtually no abuse potential and may, therefore, be given to patients for self-administration without fear of illicit redistribution. Additionally, although discontinuation of antagonists may give rise to some symptoms, these are far less distressing than the opiate withdrawal syndrome. When a patient has been doing well for some time, cyclazocine may be discontinued in order to determine if the improvement will be maintined.

The Role of the Self-Fulfilling Prophesy

Fisk, Hunt, and Luborsky (1970) contend that in any psychotherapeutic relationship between psychologist and client or between physician and patient, "expectancies are always present in both therapist and patient." The logic of their contentions seems irrefutable. Forrest (1984) recognizes that the treatment relationship has major impact for influencing the patient's feelings, beliefs, and behavior.

The literature is replete with studies which extol the therapeutic virtues of methadone maintenance. Chambers, Babst, and Warner

(1971), in fact, have provided a clinical rationale for the use of methadone by stating that "the retention power of the methadone maintenance modality is without equal in the addiction field." Another justification for methadone maintenance has been offered by Ling et al. (1976), who contend that "addicts can be rehabilitated while remaining addicted to a medically administered opiate." Cattes (1973), Chappel, Skolnick, and Senay (1972), Novick (1973), Riordan and Rapkin (1972) also enthusiastically endorse methadone maintenance as a viable therapeutic response to addiction. In methadone maintenance treatment programs, furthermore, after a prolonged period of participation many patients desire to become drug-abstinent (i.e., to become detoxified). Unfortunately, the clinical staff will frequently discourage this desire by stating they believe the patient has not demonstrated sufficient responsible and productive behavior to warrant detoxification. The staff thus communicates a negative, self-fulfilling prophesy which condemns patients to perpetuated dependencies on methadone. Such reasoning can be a direct result of an acceptance of the Dole, Nyswander and Warner hypothesis (1968, p. 2711) that addicts who stop taking methadone will relapse: "We have not, however, considered it desirable to withdraw medication from patients who are to remain in the program, since those who have been discharged have experienced a return of narcotic drug hunger after a removal of the blockade, and most of them have promptly reverted to the use of heroin. It is possible that a very gradual removal of methadone from patients with several years of stable living . . . might succeed, but this procedure has not yet been adequately tested." Newman (1975), in contrast, complains that "no one has the temerity to question the medical or empirical basis for concluding that detoxification must be for the universal good." There is insufficient data to correlate successful detoxification from methadone with the treatment goals of a maintenance program and the attitudes of that program's staff. Indeed, Dole and Nyswander wrote in 1965 that they viewed the indefinite administration of methadone as the only legitimate treatment goal. Nor did their later works (1967a) contain provisions for any detoxification from methadone.

The negative self-fulfilling prophesy can be exemplified most dramatically by examining the critical question of whether detoxification or methadone maintenance are realistic treatment goals. When drug programs adopt the concept of a metabolic lesion, methadone maintenance becomes the legitimate treatment goal. Bourne (1975) reports that "the goals of these programs are to rehabilitate socially the addict by a continued dependence on methadone. Responding to a patient's emotional distress by increasing his dosage of methadone furthers his drug dependence." Gould (1971, p. 22) discusses a countertherapeutic reaction by patients when he poses the question, "Do not some of the patients on methadone interpret this treatment as a final judgment—society's way of telling them, in effect, 'You are a hopeless addict who is so weak (psychologically) and so destroyed (physically) that you must remain an addict all your life'?" Any program which adopts the Dole and Nyswander methodology would be most reluctant to detoxify any patient. The explicit message which the staff implicitly communicated to patients was that they not only were "sick" but also required more methadone to feel "normal." Bowen and Maddux (1972, p. 436) contend:

> Responding to missed doses by reducing the dosage gives the message that the main aim of the program is continued dependence on methadone. Responding to a patient's emotional distress by increasing his dosage of methadone furthers his drug dependence. Instead, such circumstances should be used as opportunities to help the person understand and perhaps modify his own reaction patterns and coping skills.

Scher (1973, p. 962) warns against the potential problems of premature detoxification from methadone, and, curiously, minimizes the ethical right of patients to determine when they wish to discontinue medication. Scher contends that physicians, by virtue of their training, can make the decision:

> Abstinence may provide the greatest jeopardy to a patient. It may expose him . . . to the vagaries and vicissitudes of his own emotional fluctuations, social contacts, psychochemical responses, and unreliability of will. The memory of the "high" alone may be enough to set him off, without any other outside stimulation, emotional stress, etc. It is for these reasons that we have begun to feel that in some cases at least, despite the urge on the part of the patient to detoxify, he must be discouraged strongly from doing so. . . . Furthermore, the implications of detoxification must be properly understood. . . . A thorough assessment of personality factors, social stability, family structure, and other personal sustainers must be undertaken before staff agreement to allow a patient to detoxify. Otherwise, we surely run the risk of exposing many of these hasty patients to the possibility of . . . an overdose, which may in all too many cases prove fatal.

Scher agrees with Dole (1972) when he proposes that "psychological factors are only triggers for relapse, the underlying cause of which is a persistent neurochemical disturbance."

Unfortunately, the majority of physicians who prescribe the methadone regimen remain pessimistic about the possibility of a successful detoxification. Dumont (1972, p. 43) suggests that the medical-psychiatric establishment believes "addicts are not in control of their own behavior and are not curable by any known treatment. Until one is found, the best we can hope for is to block the addict's craving, monitor his social behavior and reduce the profit of an illegal market in heroin." Patients, tragically, internalize this negative predisposition toward detoxification. Despite the fact that questions remain about the ethical employment of methadone as a synthetic opiate, the long-term effects have not been assessed and the government still classifies methadone as an experimental drug. Brecher (1972, p. 161) has concluded:

> It is unfortunate, of course, that patients must continue to take methadone year after year, just as it is unfortunate that diabetics must continue to take insulin or some other diabetes drug year after year. But the heroin addict's need for continuing medication is not the result of methadone; it arises out of his initial addiction to heroin. Methadone relieves the patient of life-shattering effects of that need.

Despite almost total support by the medical-psychiatric establishment in 1972, the Department of Health, Education, and Welfare made it mandatory for all programs to adopt detoxification as their primary treatment goal. We do not claim that detoxification from methadone can be accomplished easily. When programs, however, establish effective treatment alliances with patients—for example, as described by Raubolt and Bratter (1974a) and Lowinson, Langrod and Berle (1975)—there the achievement of a drug-free state becomes a realistic treatment goal. The senior author (Bratter, 1975b) formerly directed a small methadone clinic which stressed detoxification as a viable and realistic treatment goal. One of the authors, a former member of that program, has more than a decade of abstinence and is living proof that detoxification can be achieved.

Detoxification from Methadone: A Realistic and Attainable Treatment Goal

Unquestionably, in comparison to morphine and heroin addiction, addiction to methadone hydrochloride is preferred, because methadone is longer-acting and can be administered orally. This in no way negates the findings of Martin and associates (1973), who have proved that methadone dosages of 100 milligrams can produce sedation, apathy, reduction in sexual drive, hemodilution, and edema. The concerns expressed by Walsh more than ten years ago (1970) that methadone does not cure heroin addiction but substitutes a dependence on a relatively inexpensive substance remain valid. When methadone is used as a transitory remedy, it provides patients with an opportunity to stabilize themselves so that they are more amenable to psychotherapy.

The treatment problem is self-evident. In general, addicts have chosen to medicate themselves so they could escape from a reality which they feel is too painful and devoid of promise to endure. Viewed from this perspective, the addictive process is more psychological than physiological. Sensitive, weak individuals become involved with and then imprisoned by heroin because they have made a conscious choice (i.e., to abuse drugs). Any treatment regimen which will be effective needs to help individuals extricate themselves from the constaining shell of addiction. By stressing the psychological explanations of the cause of addiction, the metabolic lesion theory commensurately is deemphasized. Trussell (1970) notes that treatment failures can occur when there is inadequate staff support: "It is not just the methadone that results in our data of success, it is the various supporting services that go along with achieving freedom from drug hunger." Cheek et al. (1973) recognize that while methadone can ameliorate heroin addiction, it cannot replace the self-destructive life-style typically associated with drug-related behavior. These authors suggest the introduction of behavior modification techniques which can facilitate social rehabilitation—a prerequisite for structuring a more positive life-style. Addiction to heroin is viewed more as a manifestation of irresponsible, infantile, impulsive, and self-destructive behavior than as a problem with a pharmacological solution such as the permanent dispensing of methadone. Renner and Rubin (1973, p. 980), who favor detoxification, write: "Amid all the controversy about the treatment of addiction, detoxification has been overlooked as a significant treatment approach . . . it is vitally important that approaches to detoxification be reevaluated to learn how this procedure can be used more effectively to engage addicts in treatment." Even though methadone hydrochloride is addictive and produces feelings of euphoria, it is unlike heroin in that it does not permit patients to withdraw totally into a narcissistic tranquility, so consumed with themselves that they are not interested in anything else. Methadone partially satisfies patients' needs to reduce their psychological pain, but, more important, as Levine et al. (1972) have written, it permits them, while they are participating in the treatment process, to consider constructive alternatives to their addictive life-styles. When individuals elect to modify their behavior and attitudes, then it becomes possible to discuss the concepts of habituation and rehabilitation. Most methadone programs, however, stress the metabolic disease construct and do not consider attitudinal alterations. They stress the acceptance of the existence of a metabolic disorder over which individuals have no personal control.

Nevertheless, there is, as Brown, Jansen, and Benn (1975, p. 218) explain, a recently emerging tendency to use methadone as an interim treatment modality rather than perpetuate the maintenance model:

Dependence on methadone, even to permit normal responsibility taking, simply does not fit well with views of proper adult, i.e., independent functioning. For many, such dependence betokens not simply individual weakness, but is viewed as being morally wrong. Even the efforts to characterize heroin as the master of the addict-slave would seem to make more difficult the public's and the client's ability to accept a related drug, methadone, as his or her aid. For the addict, the use of any such drug must smack of an attack on his or her personhood.

Ironically, one of the first to discuss psychotherapy as a major contributor to the eventual withdrawal from heroin was Nyswander (1968, p. 366), who writes:

> The withdrawal treatment of the drug addict is, in itself, a fairly simple process. . . . Group psychotherapy as well or in conjunction with individual psychotherapy is helpful to some adolescent addicts and should be suggested or tried with all. The major problem in psychotherapy with the adolescent is: (1) to really involve him; (2) to keep therapeutic contact with him even though he may relapse to the use of drugs; and (3) to insure his return to psychotherapy after subsequent hospitalization.

The New Haven methadone maintenance program directed by Kleber was one of the first not only to emphasize comprehensive psychiatric-social-educational-vocational treatment but also to encourage patient participation in planning overal operations. Kleber (1969), who recognizes that addicted individuals have significant psychopathology, decided to implement intensive psychiatric services. Wishing to utilize corrective group pressure to curtail drug-related problem behavior, Kleber (1970, p. 451) initiated a group orientation which enabled some patients to discontinue their reliance on methadone: "The emphasis in the groups is on confrontation, on facing up to the reality aspects of their lives and behavior. We tend not to do much probing into earlier genetic factors but tend to be concerned very much with the here and now." This program helped patients secure upwardly mobile jobs so they could begin to acquire some positive experience while simultaneously regaining their self-respect.

DeAngelis and Lehmann (1973) have demonstrated that "adolescents can be successfully initiated, maintained, and detoxified from methadone when they are provided with a high-intensity, supportive program." Kuncel (1981, p. 421) more recently confirms that augmentation of rehabilitative services would contribute positively:

> (1) . . . the regularity of counseling is central to successful rehabilitation of the client, and (2) . . . the client who is employed is in the most critical need for supportive counseling. It was all too common an observation at the MMTP studied for the newly employed client to interrupt counseling

> and return to heroin use. The necessity for the client to participate in counseling should not only be emphasized at the point of client entry into the MMTP but also be strongly supported at the point the client begins employment.

From an empirical point of view, there can be no doubt that psychotherapy increases commensurately the chances not only for detoxification from methadone but also for eventual recovery. Brill (1977) contends that "it becomes clear during the 1950s and 1960s that the traditional techniques of psychoanalysis were minimally effective" in the treatment of opiate addiction. There virtually was no debate that psychoanalysis was ineffectual for addicts who were treated on an outpatient basis. Yet there was question whether psychoanalytic thought provided the concerned clinician with any treatment options. The analytic approach cannot be considered apart from issues of premorbid psychodynamic influences but becomes relevant only after reviewing the myriad factors likely to have been involved in addicts' life experiences. The psychoanalytic orientation, which remains imprecise and generated after the fact, has been predicated upon unconscious needs and obsessions. Psychoanalysis remains reductionistic by proposing that patients' etiology originates from past unresolved, unconscious sexual and aggressive instincts. Psychoanalytic research has failed to produce anything relevant beyond the discovery that opiate addiction has been caused by a psychopathogenic fixation at the oral phase of development and/or by disturbances of early object relationships. In truth, these psychoanalytic insights may be valid, but they miss the point. Tragically, self-medication may be the only activity whereby addicted individuals can derive a sense of relief from their desperate attempts to escape from pressures, responsibilities, and feelings of loneliness, inadequacy, and failure which are too debilitating to endure.

The sine qua non of a psychotherapeutic orientation with impulsive, self-destructive individuals is constant confrontation with an attempted therapeutic control of their behavior. Therapeutic control appears necessary because it prevents continued self-deception and self-destructive behavior. Confrontation also becomes a challenge for addicted individuals to improve their performances. It shatters the barriers of resistance which they have erected to insulate themselves from being hurt or helped. Raubolt and Bratter (1974) write that while confrontation can be "painful, it is also a nurturing, supportive, and caring act." Confrontation (Forrest, 1982) can stimulate an intense and intimate relationship which becomes the central tenet of a treatment alliance with addicted persons. Unless addicted individuals accept the responsibility for their addiction, rather than rationalizing the cause to be a metabolic lesion, they will not feel they have the power to change (i.e., to adopt more reasonable, realistic, and responsible behavior). Addicted individuals must learn that they can control their behavior because they retain the element of choice.

Bratter (1976, p. 247) has described the seven basic sequential principles of this humanistic, learning-based, educational, and psychotherapeutic confrontation orientation:

1. Confrontation attacks the malignant and dysfunctional aspects of behavior.
2. Confrontation penetrates the facade of justification of behavior.
3. Confrontation forces the individual to accept total responsibility for his behavior.
4. Confrontation helps the person evaluate his behavior.
5. Confrontation assists the individual to be aware and to anticipate the consequences and payoffs of his behavior.
6. Confrontation challenges the person to mobilize his resources.
7. Confrontation defines a directionality so that the person can continue his growth and development.

Kooyman and Bratter (1980) and Bratter and Kooyman (1981) report that rehabilitation successes are facilitated when a confrontational, reality-oriented psychotherapeutic model is adopted. In addition to the confrontation model which has been explicitly described by Bratter (1976), any effective program must be sensitive to a concern voiced by Perkins (1972) and Perkins and Wolkstein (1976, p. 11):

> Methadone maintenance patients manifest a wide range of social, educational, and vocational levels. Few patients come to the program with occupational skills. The vast majority present sporadic work histories and negative vocational experiences. Given such varied and unique levels of work among patients, the vocational rehabilitation counselor generally finds himself faced with four categories of patient problems: the first, a patient who requests job upgrading; the second, a patient who has a spotty, irregular work history; the third, a patient with an ambiguous attitude toward work; and lastly, a patient who is functioning poorly in all aspects of vocational adjustment and essentially appears to be a non-worker.

If methadone programs want to encourage patients to improve themselves, clearly there must be emphasis on vocational and educational opportunities. When the components of psychotherapy and vocational-educational training become the focus rather than the dispensing of methadone, the chances for recovery from a chemical-dependent and abusive life-style are maximized. Methadone becomes an adjunct to treatment rather than being the treatment. Detoxification and abstinence become realistic and attainable goals after individuals receive psychotherapy and are exposed to positive and productive eductional-vocational opportunities.

Conclusion: "Let the Buyer (Methadone Maintenance Patient) Beware"

Despite the unsubstantiated claims relative to the validity of the metabolic lesions "theory" and the comparative "harmlessness" of methadone maintenance, there remains much confusion, controversy, and camouflage. How the Food and Drug Administration, the Federal Drug Administration, and the Bureau of Narcotics and Dangerous Drugs permitted the number of methadone patients to escalate from 22 in 1963 to more than 125,000 in less than a decade certainly behooves an explanation. The distressing observations of Pekkanen (1973) and Hughes and Brewin (1979) regarding the lack of integrity of governmental agencies and the pharmaceutical industry cannot be dismissed, because there appears to be a parallel between the uncritical acceptance of the methadone maintenance "theory" and the history of the acceptance and subsequent use of tranquilizers. Pekkanen (1973, p. 337) warns:

> As the drug industry continues to both forestall and weaken the effectiveness of the laws, and at the same time fails to adequately regulate itself, it maintains for itself uninterrupted profit. But this attitude could allow another major and sudden drug catastrophe like thalidomide, a catastrophe which some government officials now privately predict is inevitable. This attitude is leading our country more deeply into a drug-reliant and drug-accustomed society. But as we move close to a system of socialized medicine and the government assumes a larger role in health care, it may be forced to assume direct control of the drug industry.

Will methadone become another thalidomide? Only time will be the judge. Critical to any unbiased inquiry would be the vested interests of some of the researchers. It would be significant, indeed, to ascertain what specific payments and stock options were granted to the methadone and narcotics researchers and scientists who not only designed the experiments but also gathered the data and wrote the conclusions. How much, if any, of the research scientists' annual salaries were paid directly by pharmaceutical companies? Such an inquiry falls outside the purview of this chapter but certainly must be considered most relevant, because vast sums of money could be involved. Has methadone maintenance produced an iatrogenic circumstance which has placed addicted patients in a "no win," "no exit" labyrinth? Has Bratter's (1974) conclusion been disproved or has it remained relevant almost a decade later?

Scientifically, until many of the medical issues regarding the short- and long-term physiologic effects are resolved, methadone maintenance remains an unproved enigma. Medically, to subject approximately 100,000 human beings to a potent chemical without adequate controls is malpractice of the most insidious sort. Legally, to imprison marijuana smokers and heroin addicts as criminally dangerous while concurrently maintaining that methadone addicts are law-abiding is a travesty of justice. Philosophically, to confuse deliberately the concept of "treatment" with the concept of "social control" is fraudulent. Psychologically, to convince addicts that they have a mystical metabolic disorder and must remain dependent on a potential poison rather than strive for their autonomy is a conspiracy. Ethically, any conspiracy which places people in "no win" situations and mitigates against their growth and development must be considered a criminal act.

References

Anslinger, H. J., and Tompkins, W. F. *The Traffic in Narcotics.* New York: Funk & Wagnalls Co., 1953.

Aronow, R., Paul, S. D., and Wooley, P. V. Childhood poisoning: an unfortunate consequence of methadone availability. *Journal of the American Medical Association,* 1972, *219,* 321–324.

Ausubel, D. P. *Drug Addiction: Physiological, Psychological, and Sociological Aspects.* New York: Random House, 1958.

Baden, M. Narcotic abuse: a medical examiner's view. *New York State Journal of Medicine,* April 1, 1972, p. 840.

Ball, J. D., and Snarr, R. N. A test of the maturation hypothesis with respect to opiate addiction. *United Nations Bulletin on Narcotics,* 1969, *21,* 1–7.

Beecher, H. K., Deffer, P. A., Fink, F. E., and Sullivan, D. B. Field use of methadone and levo-isomethadone in a combat zone. *U. S. Armed Forces Medical Journal,* 1951, *2,* 1269–1276.

Beecher, H. K., Keats, A. S., Mosteller, F., and Lasanga, L. The effectiveness of oral analgesics (morphine, codeine, acetylsalicylic acid) and the problem placebo: "reactors" and "nonreactors." *Journal of Pharmacology and Experimental Therapeutics,* 1953, *109,* 393–400.

Beecher, H. K. The powerful placebo. *Journal of the American Medical Association,* 1955, *159,* 1602–1606.

———. *Measurement of Subjective Responses: Quantitative Effects of Drugs.* New York: Oxford University Press, 1959.

———. Increased stress and effectiveness of placebos and "active" drugs. *Science,* 1960, *132,* 91–92.

Bloom, W. A., and Sudderth, E. W. Methadone in New Orleans: patients, problems, and police. *International Journal of Addictions,* 1970, *5,* 468–469.

Blumberg, H., Dayton, H. B., and Wolf, P. S. Analgesic and narcotic antagonist properties of noroxymorphone derivatives. *Toxicology and Applied Pharmacology,* 1967, *10,* 401–406.

Blumberg, H., Pachter, I. J., and Matossian, Z. US Patent 3,322,950. July 1967.

Bourne, P. *Methadone Benefits and Shortcomings.* Washington, D. C.: Drug Abuse Council, 1975.

Bowen, C. L., and Maddux, J. F. Methadone maintenance: myth and reality. *American Journal of of Psychiatry,* 1972, *129,* 436.

Bratter, T. E. The crime of methadone maintenance treatment programs: a conspiracy against the heroin addict. In L. Miller (ed.), *Abstracts of the Third International Symposium on Drug Abuse.* Jerusalem: Graphpress, 1974.

———. From methadone treatment programs to involuntary electronic behavior control: legacy of heroin addiction in 1984? *Corrective and Social Psychiatry,* 1975(a), *21*(2), 1–7.

———. Methadone, try it. You'll hate it! *Addiction Therapist,* 1975b, *1,* 48–59.

———, T. E. Confrontation group: the therapeutic community's gift to psychotherapy. In P. Vamos and J. J. Devlin (eds.), *Proceedings of the First World Conference on Therapeutic Communities.* Montreal: The Portage Press, 1976.

———. Confrontation groups: the therapeutic community's gift to psychotherapy. In P. Vamos and J. J. Devlin (eds.), *The First World Conference on Therapeutic Communities.* Montreal: Portage Press, 1977.

———. Methadone maintenance: misguided mismanagement of heroin addicts in the United States. In G. Schakel and M. Sikkens (eds.), *Readings of the Fifth World Conference of Therapeutic Communities.* The Hague: Samson Sijthoff, Publishers, 1980.

———. Some pre-treatment group psychotherapy considerations with alcoholic and drug-addicted individuals. *Psychotherapy: Theory, Research and Practice,* 1981, *18,* 508–515.

———, and Pennacchia, M. C. Methadone maintenance: a negative self-fulfilling prophecy. In J. H. Lowinson, B. J. Primm, and S. D. Coletti (eds.), *Critical Concerns in the Field of Drug Abuse.* New York: Marcel Deeker, 1978.

Bratter, T. E., and Kooyman, M. A structured environment for heroin addicts: the experiences of a community-based American methadone clinic and a residential Dutch therapeutic community. *International Journal of Social Psychiatry,* 1981, *27,* 189–203.

Brecher, E. M., and Editors of Consumer Reports. *Licit and Illicit Drugs: The Consumers Union Report of Narcotics, Stimulants, Depressants, Inhalants, Hallucinogens, and Marijuana—Including Caffeine, Nicotine, and Alcohol.* Mount Vernon, N. Y.: Consumers Union, 1972, p. 161.

Brill, L. The treatment of drug abuse: evolution of a perspective. *American Journal of Psychiatry,* 1977, *134*(2), 157.

———, and Jaffe, J. The relevancy of some never American treatment approaches for England. *British Journal of the Addictions,* 1968, *62,* 375–386.

Brown, B. S., Jansen, D. R., and Benn, G. J. Changes in attitude toward methadone. *Archives of General Psychiatry,* 1975, *32,* 218.

Bruchner, L. H., Cimino, J. A., Raybin, H. W., and Stewart, B. Naloxone reversal of methadone poisoning. *New York State Journal of Medicine,* Sept. 15, 1972, pp. 2305–2309.

Casriel, D. H., and Bratter, T. E. Methadone maintenance treatment: a questionable procedure. *Journal of Drug Issues,* 1974, *4(4),* 359–375.

Cattes, D. What is a successful patient and must detoxification be a factor? In *Proceedings of the Fifth National Conference on Methadone Treatment.* R. L. DuPont and R. S. Freeman (eds.). New York: NAPAN, 1973.

Chambers, C. D., Babst, D. V., and Warner, A. Characteristics predicting long-term retention in a methadone maintenance program. In *Proceedings: Third National Conference on Methadone Treatment.* New York: NAPAN, 1971.

Chappel, J., Skolnick, V. B., and Senay, E. C. Techniques of withdrawal from methadone and their outcome over six months to two years. In *Proceedings of the Fifth National Conference on Methadone Treatment.* R. L. DuPont and R. S. Freeman (eds.). New York: NAPAN, 1972.

Cheek, F. E., Tomarchio, T., Standen, J., and Albahary, R. S. Methadone plus—a behavior modification training program in self-control for addicts on methadone maintenance. *International Journal of the Addictions,* 1973, *6,* 969.

Chein, I., Gerard, D. L., Lee, R. S., and Rosenfeld, E. *The Road of Narcotics, Delinquency, and Social Policy.* New York: Basic Books, 1964.

Cochin, J. Factors influencing tolerance to and dependence on narcotic analgesics. In S. Fisher and A. M. Freedman (eds.), *Opitate Addiction: Origins and Treatment.* Washington, D. C.: Winston Press, 1974.

Committee on Alcoholism and Drug Dependence of the American Medical Association. Management of narcotic-drug dependence by high dosage methadone HCL techniques: Dole-Nyswander program. *Journal of the American Medical Association,* 1967, *124,* 956–957.

Crowlay, R. M. Psychoanalytic literature of drug addiction and alcoholism. *Psychoanalytic Review,* 1939, *26,* 39–54.

Datta, R. K., and Antopol, W. Effects of combined treatment with sulfapyridine and metahdone on behavior of mortality of mice. *Pharmacology,* 1973, *10,* 104–110.

Day, H. G. *The Opium Habit with Suggestions as to Remedy.* New York: Harper & Brothers, 1868.

DeAngelis, G. G., and Lehmann, W. Adolescents and short-term, low-dose methadone maintenance. *International Journal of Addictions,* 1973, *8(5),* 861.

DeSalva, S. J., and Oester, Y. T. The effect of central nervous system depressants on certain spinal reflexes in the acute high cervical cat." *Archives of Internal Pharmacodynamie,* 1960, *124,* 255–262.

Dews, P. B. Analysis of effects of psychopharmacological agents in behavioral terms. *Federation Proceedings,* 1958, *17,* 1025.

Dobbs, W. H. Methadone treatment of heroin addicts. *Journal of the American Medical Association,* 1971, *218,* 1536–1541.

Dole, V. P., and Nyswander, M. A medical treatment for diacetylmorphine (heroin) addiction: a clinical trial with methadone hydrochloride. *Journal of the American Medical Association,* 1965, *193,* 646.

———. Narcotic blockage. *Archives of Internal Medicine,* 1966(a), *118,* 304–309.

———. Rehabilitation of heroin addicts after blockade with methadone. *New York State Journal of Medicine,* 1966(b), *66,* 2011.

———. Addiction—a metabolic disease. *Archieves of Internal Medicine,* 1967(a), *120,* 19–24.

———. Rehabilitation of the street addict. *Archives of Environmental Health,* 1967(b), *14,* 477–480.

———, and Kreek, M. J. Narcotic blockage: a medical technique for stopping heroin use by addicts. *Archives of Internal Medicine,* 1966(a) *118,* 304.

Dole, V. P., Nyswander, M., and Warner, A. Successful treatment of 750 criminal addicts. *Journal of the American Medical Association,* 1968, *206,* 2711.

Dole, V. P., and Nyswander, M. E. Methadone maintenance and its implications for theories of narcotic addiction. In A. Winkler (ed.), *The Addictive States.* Baltimore: Williams & Wilkins Co., 1968, pp. 359–366.

Dole, V. P., Foldes, E. F., Trigg, H., Robinson, J. W., and Blatman, S. Methadone poisoning diagnosis and treatment. *New York State Journal of Medicine,* 1971 (71), 541.

Dole, V. P. Research on methadone maintenance treatment. *International Journal of Addictions,* 1970, *5,* 361–362.

———. Methadone maintenance treatment for 25,000 heroin addicts. *Journal of the American Medical Association,* 1971, *215,* 1131.

———. Pharmacological treatment of drug addiction. *Modern Medicine,* May, 1972, *62,* 19.

———. Narcotic addiction, physical dependence, and relapse. *New England Journal of Medicine,* 1972, *286,* 988–992.

Dumont, M. D. Methadone maintenance? It's more than a clinical question. *Medical Insight,* 1972, *4,* 43.

Duvall, H., Locke, B., and Brill, L. Follow-up of narcotic drug addicts five years after hospitalization. *Public Health Reports,* 1963, *78,* 185–193.

Eddy, N. B. A new morphine-like analgesic. *Journal of the American Pharmacological Association,* 1947(a), *8(11),* 536–540.

———. Synthetic substances with morphine-like effect: Methadone. *Journal of the American Pharmacological Association,* 1947(b), *8,* 84–91.

———. The phenomenon of tolerance. In M. G. Sevag, R. D. Reid, and O. E. Reynolds (eds.), *Origins of Resistance to Toxic Agents.* New York: Academic Press, 1955.

———. The chemotherapy of drug dependence. *British Journal of Addiction,* 1966, *61,* 155–167.

Eldridge, W. B. *Narcotics and the Law: A Critique of the American Experiment in Narcotic Drug Control.* Chicago: University of Chicago Press, 1962, p. 9.

Eli Lilly & Co. *Product Information Leaflet.* Indianapolis: 1971, p. 1.

Faigel, H. C. Methadone maintenance for treatment of addiction. *Journal of the American Medical Association,* 1971, *215,* 299.

Federal Registrar. "Conditions for Investigational Use of Methadone for Maintenance Programs for Narcotic Addicts." 21 CFR Part 130.44 (June 11, 1970).

Ferenczi, S. Alkohol und Neurosen. (Antwort auf die Kritik Bleulers.) *Psychoanalytic Psychopathology,* 1912, *3,* 56–121.

Fink, M., Zaks, A., Sharoff, R., Mora, A., Brunner, A., and Freedman, A. Naloxone in heroin dependence. *Clinical Pharmacology Therapeutics,* 1968, *9,* 568–577.

Fisher, A. E. Chemical stimulation of the brain. In P. Black (ed.), *Drugs and the Brain: Papers on the Action, Use, and Abuse of Psychotropic Agents.* Baltimore: The Johns Hopkins Press, 1969.

Fisk, D., Hunt, H., and Luborsky, L. Planning of research on effectiveness of psychotherapy. *Archives of General Psychiatry,* 1970, *22,* 27.

Forrest, G. G. *Confrontation in Psychotherapy with Alcoholics.* Holmes Beach, Fla.: Learning Publications, 1982.

Forrest, G. G. *Intensive Psychotherapy of Alcoholism.* Springfield, Ill.: Charles C. Thomas, 1984.

Fraser, D. W. Methadone overdose: illicit use of pharmaceutically prepared parenteral narcotics. *Journal of the American Medical Association,* 1971, *217,* 1388–1389.

Freedman, A. M. Drug addiction: an eclectic view. *Journal of the American Medical Association,* 1966, *197,* 878–882.

———. Toward a rational approach to the treatment of narcotic addiction: basic notions. *Research Publication of the Association of Research in Nervous and Mental Disorders,* 1968(a), *46,* 378–386.

———. Clinical studies of cyclazocine in the treatment of narcotic addiction. *American Journal of Psychiatry,* 1968(b), *124,* 57–61.

Freud, S. *The Future Progress of Psychoanalytic Theory.* Vol. 2 of *Collected Papers.* London: Hogarth, 1953, pp. 285–296.

Gambino, B., and Shaffer, H. The concept of paradigm and the treatment of addiction. *Professional Psychology,* 1979, *10*(2), 219.

Gardner, R. Methadone misuse and death by overdose. *Briish Journal of the Addictions,* 1970, *65,* 113–118.

Gerard, L., and Kornetsky, C. Adolescent opiate addiction: a study of control and addict subjects. *Psychiatric Quarterly,* 1955, *29,* 457–486.

Glover, E. On the aetiology of drug addiction. *The International Journal of Psychoanalysis,* 1932, *12(3),* 298–328.

Gold, M. S., Redmond, Jr., D. E., and Kleber, H. D. Clonidine blocks acute opiate withdrawal symptoms. *Lancet,* 1978, *2,* 599–602.

Gold, M. S., Pottash, A. L. C., Sweeney, D. R., and Kleber, H. D. Opiate withdrawal using clonidine. *Journal of the American Medical Association,* 1980(a), *243,* 343–346.

Gold, M. S., Pottash, A. L. C., Extein, I., and Kleber, H. D. Clonidine in acute opiate withdrawal. *American Journal of Psychiatry,* 1980(b), *302,* 1421–1422.

Gold, M. S., Byck, R., Sweeney, D. R., and Kleber, H. D. Endorphin-locus coeruleus connection mediates opiate action and withdrawal. *Biomedicine,* 1979, *30,* 1–4.

Gold, M. S., Pottash, A. L. C., Extein, I., and Stoll, A. Clinical utility of clonidine in opiate withdrawal. In L. S. Harris (ed.), *Problems of Drug Dependence,* 1981. Washington, D. C.: National Institute on Drug Abuse, 1981.

Goldstein, A. Heroin addiction and the role of methadone in its treatment. *Archives of General Psychiatry,* 1972, *26,* 297.

Gould, R. E. Methadone reconsidered. *Drug Therapy,* 1970, *1,* 22.

Grove, R. N., and Amith, J. M. Methadone pretreatment and ethanol toxicity in mice. *Pharmacologist,* 1973, *15,* 243.

Hill, H. E., Haertzen, D. A., and Glaser, R. Personality characteristics of narcotic addicts as indicated by the MMPI. *The Journal of General Psychology,* 1960, *62,* 127–139.

Himmelsbach, C. K. Studies on the addiction of Demerol (D-140). *Journal of Pharmacology and Experimental Therapeutics,* 1942(a), *75,* 57–71.

———. Clinical studies of drug addiction: physical dependence, withdrawal, and recovery. *Archives of Internal Medicine,* 1942(b), *69,* 766–771.

Horney, K. *Our Inner Conflicts: A Constructive Theory of Neurosis.* New York: W. W. Norton & Co., 1945, p. 241.

Hughes, R., and Brewin, R. *The Tranquilizing of America: Pill Popping and the American Way of Life.* New York: Harcourt Brace Jovanovich, 1979, pp. 82–83.

Hunt, G. H., and Odoroff, M. E. Follow-up study of narcotic drug addiction after hospitalization. *Public Health Reports,* 1962, *77,* 41–54.

Isbell, H., and Vogel, V. H. The addiction liability of methadone (amidone, dolophine, 10820) and its use in the treatment of morphone substance abstinence syndrome. *American Journal of Psychiatry,* 1949, *105,* 914.

Isbell, H., Wikler, A., Eisemman, A. J., Daingerfield, M., and Frank, K. Liability of addiction to 6-dimethylamino-4, 4-diphenyl-3-heptanone (methadone, amidone or 10820) in man. *Archives of Internal Medicine,* 1948(a), *82,* 362–393.

Isbell, H., et al. The effects of single doses of 6-dimethylamino-4, 4-diphenylheptanone-3 (amidone, methadone, or 10820) on human subjects. *Journal of Pharmacology and Experimental Therapeutics,* 1948(b) *92,* 80–88.

———. Tolerance and addiction liability of 6-dimethylamino-4-4-diphenyl-heptanone-3 (methadone). *Journal of American Medical Association,* 1947(a), *135,* 39–47.

———. Treatment of the morphine abstinence syndrome with 10820 (4-4-diphenyl-6-dimethylamine-heptanone-3). *Federation Proceedings,* 1947(b), *6,* 338–349.

Jaffe, J. H. Psychopharmacology and opiate dependence. In D. Efron (ed.), *Psychopharmacology: A Review of Progress, 1957–1967.* Washington, D. C.: U. S. Government Printing Office, 1968.

———. Pharmacological approaches to the treatment of compulsive opiate use: their rationale and current status. In P. Black (ed.), *Drugs and the Brain: Papers on the Action, Use, and Abuse of Psychotropic Agents.* Baltimore: Johns Hopkins Press, 1969.

———. Further experiences with methadone in the treatment of narcotics users. *International Journal of Addictions,* 1970, *5(3),* 376.

Jasinski, D. R., Martin, W. R., and Haertzen, C. A. The Human pharmacology and abuse potential of N-allyinoroxymorphone (naloxone). *Journal of Pharmacology and Therapeutics,* 1967, *157,* 420–426.

Kafer, E. R. Primary hypoventilation. *British Journal of Anaesthesia,* 1973, *45,* 622.

Karkus, H. Methadone vs. psychotherapy in the treatment of heroin addiction. *International Journal of Addictions,* 1973, *8,* 433.

Khantzian, E. J., Mack, J. F., and Schatzberg, A. F. Heroin use as an attempt to cope. *American Journal of Psychiatry,* 1974, *131,* 162–164.

Kjeldgaard, J. M., Halm, G. W., and Heckenlively, J. R. Methadone-induced pulmonary edema. *Journal of the American Medical Association,* 1971, *218,* 882–883.

Kleber, H. D. Narcotic addiction—the current problem and treatment approaches. *Connecticut Medicine,* 1969, *33,* 113–116.

———. The New Haven methadone maintenance program. *International Journal of the Addictions,* 1970, *5,* 451.

Kolb, L. Pleasure and deterioration from narcotic addiction. *Mental Hygiene Reports,* 1925, *9,* 699–724.

———, and Himmelsbach, C. K. Clinical studies of drug addiction. Part 3: A critical review of the withdrawal treatments with method of evaluating abstinence syndromes. *American Journal of Psychiatry,* 1938, *94,* 759–799.

Kooyman, M., and Bratter, T. E. De Noodzaak van Confrontatie en Structuur bij de Behandeling van Drugverslaafden. *Tijdschrift Voor Alcohol, Drugs En Andere Psychotrope Stoffen,* 1980, *6,* 27–34.

Kreek, M. J. Medical safety and side effects of methadone in tolerant individuals. *Journal of the American Medical Association,* 1973, *223,* 665–668.

Krystal, H., and Raskin, H. A. *Drug Dependence: Aspects of Ego Function.* Detroit: Wayne State University Press, 1970.

Kuncel, E. E. Effects of intensive counseling on client outcome in a methadone maintenance program. *International Journal of the Addictions,* 1981, *16,* 421.

Langrod, J., Lowinson, J., and Ruiz, P. Methadone treatment and physical complaints: a clinical analysis. *International Journal of the Addictions,* 1981, *16,* 951.

Laties, V. G., and Weiss, B. Behavioral mechanism of drug action. In P. Black (ed.), *Drugs and the Brain: Papers on the Action, Use, and Abuse of Psychotropic Agents.* Baltimore: Johns Hopkins Press, 1969.

Levine, D. G., Levin, D. B., Sloan, I. H., and Chappel, J. N. Personality correlates of success in a methadone maintenance program. *American Journal of Psychiatry,* 1972, *129,* 456.

Levy, L. The psychology of the effect produced by morphia. *International Journal of Psycho-Analysis,* 1925, *6,* 313–316.

Lindesmith, A. R. A sociological theory of drug addiction. *American Journal of Sociology,* 1938, *43,* 593–613.

Ling, W., Charuvastra, V. C., Kaim, S. C., and Klett, J. L. Methadyl acetate and methadone as maintenance treatments for heroin addicts. *Archives of General Psychiatry,* 1976, *33,* 709.

Lowinson, J., Langrod, J., and Berle, B. Detoxification of long-term methadone patients. In *Developments in the Field of Drug Abuse,* E. Senay, V. Shorty, and H. Alksne (eds.). Cambridge: Schenkman Publishing Co., 1975.

McAuliffe, W. E. A test of Wikler's theory of relapse: the frequency of relapse due to conditioned withdrawal sickness. *International Journal of the Addictions,* 1982, *17,* 30–31.

Maddux, J. F., and Bowden, C. L. Critique of success with methadone maintenance. *American Journal of Psychiatry,* 1972, *129,* 446.

Marks, C. E., and Goldring, R. M. Chronic hypercapinia during methadone maintnence. *American Review of Respiratory Disease,* 1973, *108,* 1088–1093.

Marshall, H. P. *Pain, Pleasure, and Anesthetics.* London: Macmillan, 1894.

Martin, W. R., and Fraser, H. F. A comparative study of psychological and subjective effects of heroin and morphine administered intravenously in postaddicts. *Journal of Pharmacology and Experimental Therapeutics,* 1961, *133,* 388–399.

Martin, W. R., Wikler, A., Erdes, C. G., and Prescor, F. T. Tolerance to and physical dependence on morphine in rats. *Psychopharmacologia,* 1963, *4,* 247–260.

Martin, W. R., and Gorodetzky, C. W. Demonstration of tolerance to and physical dependence on N-allylnormophone (nalorphine). *Journal of Pharmacology and Experimental Therapeutics,* 1965, *150,* 437–442.

Martin, W. R., Fraser, H. F., Gorodetzky, C. W., and Rosenberg, D. E. Studies of the dependence-producing potential of the narcotic antagonist 2-cyclopropylmethyl-2-hydroxy-5, 9-dimethyl-6, 7-benzomorphan (cyclazocine, Win 20,740, ARC II-C-3. *Journal of Pharmacological and Experimental Therapeutics,* 1965, *150,* 426–436.

Martin, W. R., Gorodetzky, C. W., and McClane, T. K. An experimental study in the treatment of narcotics addicts with cyclazocine. *Clinical Pharmacological Therapeutics,* 1966, *7,* 455–465.

Martin, W. R. Commentary on the Second National Conference on Methadone Treatment. *International Journal of the Addictions,* 1970, *5,* 550.

———. Opioid antagonists. *Pharmacological Reviews,* 1967, *19,* 463–521.

Martin, W. R., Jasinski, D. R., and Mansky, P. A. Naltrexone, an antagonist for the treatment of heroin dependence. *Archives of General Psychiatry,* 1973, *28,* 784–791.

Martin, W. R., Jasinski, D. R., Haertzen, C. A., Kay, D. C., Jones, B. E., Mansky, P. A., and Carpenter, R. W. Methadone—a reevaluation. *Archives of General Psychiatry,* 1973, *28,* 286–295.

Mezritz, M. F., Slobetz, H., Kleber, H., and Riordan, C. A follow-up study of successfully detoxified methadone maintenance patients. In *Developments in the Field of Drug Abuse,* E. Senay, V. Shorty, and H. Alksne (eds.). Cambridge: Schenkman Publishing Co., 1975.

Mule, S. J. Effect of morphine and nalorphine on brain phospholipid metabolism. In A. Wikler (ed.), *The Addictive States.* Baltimore: The Williams & Wilkins Co., 1968.

Myerson, D. J. Methadone treatment of addicts. *New England Journal of Medicine,* 1969, *281,* 390–391.

Newman, R. G. Methadone maintenance: it ain't what it used to be. In *Developments in the Field of Drug Abuse,* E. Senay, V. Shorty, and H. Alksne (eds.). Cambridge: Schenkman Publishing Co., 1975.

Newmeyer, J. A., Gay, G. R., Corn, R., and Smith, D. E. Methadone for kicking and for kicks. *Drug Forum,* 1972, *1,* 390.

Novick, M. The role of detoxification in the long-term treatment of the drug abuser. In *Proceedings of the Fifth National Conference on Methadone Treatment,* R. L. DuPont and R. S. Freeman (eds.). Washington, D. C.: NAPAN, 1973.

Nyswander, M. *The Drug Addict as a Patient.* New York: Grune & Stratton, 1956.

———. The withdrawal treatment of adolescent drug addicts. In E. Harms (ed.), *Drug Addiction in Youth.* Oxford: Pergamon Press, 1968.

———. Methadone therapy for heroin addiction: Where are we? Where are we going? *Drug Therapy,* 1971, *17,* 24.

O'Brien, C., and Greenstein, R. Naltrexone in a behavior treatment program. In D. Julius and P. Renault (eds.), *Narcotic Antagonists: Naltrexone Progress Report.* Springfield, Va.: National Technical Information Service, 1976.

O'Brien, C. P., Testa, T., O'Brien, T. J., Brady, J. P., and Wells, B. Conditioned narcotic withdrawal in humans. *Science,* 1977, *195,* 1000–1002.

O'Donnell, J. A. A follow-up of narcotic addicts: mortality, relapse, and abstinence. *Journal of Orthopsychiatry,* 1964, *34,* 948–954.

Peele, S. Reductionism in the psychology of the eighties: Can biochemistry eliminate addiction, mental illness, and pain? *American Psychologist,* 1981, *36*(*8*), 816–817.

Pekkanen, J. *The American Connection: Profiteering and Politicking in the "Ethical" Drug Industry.* Chicago: Follett Publishing Co., 1973, p. 337.

Perkins, M. E. Methadone maintenance: expanding the concept of service. *American Journal of Psychiatry,* 1972, *129,* 461.

———, and Wolkstein, E. Vocational rehabilitation of patients in a methadone maintenance treatment program: society's responsibility. *American Journal of Orthopsychiatry,* 1976 (42), pp. 321–322.

Pierson, P. S., Howard, P., and Kleber, H. D. Sudden deaths in infants born to methadone-maintained addicts. *Journal of the American Medical Association,* 1972, *220,* 1733–1734.

Prescor, M. J. Follow-up study of treated narcotic addicts. *Public Health Reports Supplement,* 1943, *170,* 1–18.

Rado, S. The psychic effects of intoxicants: an attempt to evolve a psychoanalytical theory of morbid cravings. *International Journal of PsychoAnalysis,* 1926, *7,* 396–413.

———. The psychoanalysis of pharmacothymia (drug addiction). *Psychoanalytic Quarterly,* 1933, *2,* 1–23.

———. The psychoanalysis of pharmacothymia. *Psychiatric Quarterly,* 1935, *2,* 2–23.

———. Narcotic bondage: a general theory of dependence on narcotic drugs. *American Journal of Psychiatry,* 1957, *114,* 165–170.

Ramer, R. S., Zaslove, M. D., and Langan, J. Is methadone enough? The use of ancillary treatment during methadone maintenance. *American Journal of Psychiatry,* 1971, *127,* 80–84.

Randal, J. The orphan drug game. *Science: The American Association for the Advancement of Science,* 1982, *3,* p. 39.

Ratcliffe, S. G. Methadone poisoning in a child. *British Medical Journal,* 1963, *1,* 1069–1070.

Raubolt, R. R., and Bratter, T. E. Treating the methadone addict: a confrontation and reality therapy model. *Journal of Drug Education,* 1974(a), *4,* 51–60.

———. Games addicts play: implications for group treatment. *Corrective and Social Psychiatry,* 1974(b), *20,* 7.

Rawson, R. A., Washton, A. M., Rasnick, R. B., and Tennant, Jr., R. S. Clonidine hydrochloride detoxification from methadone treatments: the value of naltrexone aftercare. In L. S. Harris (ed.), *Problems of Drug Dependence, 1980.* Washington, D. C.: National Institute on Drug Abuse, 1981.

Raynes, A. E., and Patch, V. D. Improved detoxification techniques for heroin addicts. *Archives of General Psychiatry,* 1973, *29,* 417–419.

Renner, J. A., and Rubin, M. L. Engaging heroin addicts in treatment. *American Journal of Psychiatry,* 1973, *130,* 980.

Resnick, R. B., Fink, M., and Freedman, A. M. Cyclazocine treatment of opiate dependence: a progress report. *Comprehensive Psychiatry,* 1971, *12,* 491–587.

Resnick, R. B., Washton, A. M., and Stone-Washton, N. Psychotherapy and naltrexone in opioid dependence. In L. S. Harris (ed.), *Problems of Drug Dependence, 1980.* Washington, D. C.: National Institute on Drug Abuse, 1981.

Riordan, C., and Rapkin, R. Detoxification as a final step in treating the successful long-term methadone patient. In *Proceedings of the Fourth National Conference on Methadone Treatment.* A. Goldstein (ed.). Washington, D. C.: NAPAN, 1972.

Robbins, L. N., Davis, D. H., and Goodwin, D. W. Drug use by U. S. Army enlisted men in Vietnam: a follow-up on their return home. *American Journal of Epidemiology,* 1974, *99,* 48.

Rossdies, E. T. Drug scourage—a top priority. *New York Law Journal,* Dec. 6, 1951, pp. 3–32.

Sapira, J. D., Ball, J. C., and Cottress, E. S. Addiction to methadone among patients at Lexington and Fort Worth. *Public Health Reports,* 1968, *83,* 691.

Schecter, A., and Grossman, D. Experiences with naltrexone: a suggested role in drug abuse treatment programs. In E. Senay, V. Shorty, and H. Alksne (eds.), *Developments in the Field of Drug Abuse.* Cambridge, Mass.: Schenkman Publishing Co., 1975.

Scher, J. M. A chemical alternative to the narcotic antagonist thesis. *International Journal of Addictions,* 1973, *8,* 962.

Senay, E. C., and Renault, P. F. Treatment methods for heroin addicts: a review. *Journal of Psychedelic Drugs,* 1971, *3,* 54.

Senay, E. C. Methadone: some myths and hypotheses. *Journal of Psychedelic Drugs,* 1971, *4,* 183.

Shaffer, M. Theories of addiction: in search of a paradigm. In H. Shaffer (ed.), *Myths and Realities: A Book About Drug Issues.* Boston: Zucker Publishing Co., 1977.

Shaffer, H., and Burglass, M. E. Epilogue: reflections and perspectives on the history and future of the addictions. In H. Shaffer and M. E. Burglass (eds.), *Classic Contributions in the Addictions.* New York: Brunner/Mazel, 1981(a).

———. Behavioral approaches to addiction. In H. Shaffer and M. E. Burglass, *Classic Contributions in the Addictions.* New York: Brunner/Mazel, 1981(b).

Simmel, E. Psycho-analytic treatment in a sanatorium. *International Journal of Psychoanalysis,* 1929, *10,* 70–89.

Singhai, R. L., Kacew, S., and Lafreniere, R. Brain adenylate cyclase in methadone treatment of morphine dependency. *Journal of Pharmacy and Pharmacology,* 1973, *25,* 1022–1024.

Snow, M. Maturing out of narcotic addiction in New York City. *International Journal of the Addictions,* 1973, *8,* 937.

Soin, J. S., Thomashow, D. F., and Wagner, H. N. Increased sensitivity of regional measurements in detection of pulmonary abnormalities in narcotic addicts. *Chest,* 1973, *64,* 408–409.

Strong, C. A. The psychology of pain. *Psychological Review,* 1895, *2,* 329–347.

Sugarman, B. *Daytop Village: A Therapeutic Community.* New York: Holt, Rinehart & Winston, 1974.

Takemori, A. E. The effects of morphine, other opioids, and their derivatives on the metabolism of the cerebral cortex. In A. Wikler (ed.), *The Addictive States.* Baltimore: The Williams & Wilkins Co., 1968.

Tatum, A. L., Steevers, M. H., and Collins, K. H. Morphine addiction and its physiological Interpretation based on experimental evidence. *Journal of Pharmacology and Experimental Therapeutics,* 1929, *36,* 447–475.

Teasdale, J. D. Conditioned abstinence in narcotic addicts. *International Journal of the Addictions,* 1973, *8,* 278.

Thornton, W. E., and Thornton, B. P. Narcotic poisoning: a review of the literature. *American Journal of Psychiatry,* 1974, *131,* 869.

Trussell, R. E. Treatment of narcotics addicts in New York City. *International Journal of the Addictions,* 1970, *4,* 353.

Ungar, G., and Oceguera-Navarro, C. Transfer of habituation by material extracted from brain. *Nature,* 1965b, *207,* 296–307.

———. Transfer of morphine tolerance by material extracted from brain. *Federation Proceedings,* 1965a, *24,* 541–549.

———. Chemical transfer of learning: its stimulus specificity. *Federation Proceedings,* 1966, *25,* 201–209.

———, and Cohen, M. Induction of morphine tolerance by material extracted from brain of tolerant animals. *International Journal of Neuropharmacology,* 1967, *5,* 181–189.

Ungar, G., Galvan, L., and Clark, R. H. Chemical transfer of learned fear. *Nature,* 1968, *217,* 1257–1262.

Ungar, G. Chemcial transfer of passive avoidance. *Federation Proceedings,* 1969, *28,* 642–649.

Vaillant, G. E. A twelve-year follow-up of New York City addicts. *American Journal of Psychiatry,* 1966(a), *122,* 727–737.

———. A twelve-year follow-up of New York narcotic addicts. Part 3: Some social and psychiatric characteristics. *Archives of General Psychiatry,* 1966(b), *15,* 599–609.

———. A twenty-year follow-up of New York narcotic addicts. *Archives of General Psychiatry,* 1973, *29,* 237–241.

———. *Adaptation to Life.* Boston: Little, Brown & Co., 1977.

Veebely, K., and Kutt, H. The effect of a single dose on the steady state methadone plasma level. *Pharmacologist,* 1973, *15,* 167.

Walsh, J. Methadone and heroin addiction: rehabilitation without a cure. *Science,* 1970, *168,* 684–686.

Washton, A. M., Resnick, R. B., and Rawson, R. A. Clonidine for outpatient opiate detoxification. *Lancet,* 1980, *1,* 1078–1079.

Washton, A. M., and Resnick, R. B. Clonidine vs. methadone for opiate detoxification: double-blind outpatient trials. In L. S. Harris (ed.), *Problems of Drug Dependence, 1980.* Washington, D. C.: National Institute on Drug Abuse, 1981.

Way, E. L., and Adler, T. K. The pharmacologic implications of the fate of morphine and its surrogates. *Pharmacological Review,* 1960, *12,* 121–129.

———. *The Biologic Disposition of Morphine and Its Surrogates.* Geneva: World Health Organization, 1962.

Way, E. L. Distribution and metabolism of morphine and its surrogates. In A. Wikler (ed.), *The Addictive States.* Baltimore: The Williams & Wilkins Co., 1968.

Wieland, W. F. Methadone treatment of chronic narcotic addiction. *New Physician,* 1969, *18,* 210–211.

———, and Chambers, C. D. Methadone maintenance: two stabilization techniques. *International Journal of the Addictions,* 1970, *5,* 645–659.

Wikler, A. A psychodynamic study of a patient during self-regulated readdiction to morphine. *Psychiatric Quarterly,* 1952, *26,* 264–274.

———. *Opiate Addiction: Psychological and Neurophysiological Aspects in Relation to Clinical Problems.* Springfield, Ill.: Charles C. Thomas, 1953.

———. Conditioning factors in opiate addiction and relapse. In D. M. Wilner and G. G. Kassebaum (eds.), *Narcotics.* New York: McGraw-Hill Book Co., 1965.

———. Interaction of physical dependence and classical operant conditioning in the genesis of relapse. *American Journal of Nervous and Mental Disorders Proceedings,* 1968, *46,* 280–287.

———. Some implications of conditioning theory for problems of drug abuse. In P. H. Blanchy (ed.), *Drug Abuse: Data and Debate.* Springfield, Ill.: Charles. C. Thomas, 1970.

———. Dynamics of drug dependence: implications of a conditioning theory for research and treatment. *Archives of General Psychiatry,* 1973, *28,* 611–612.

Winick, C. Maturing out of narcotic addiction. *United Nations Bulletin on Narcotics,* 1962, *14,* 1–7.

Wiley, T. J., Hunt, G. M., and Peters, M. A. Computer analysis of methadone effects on the electroencephalogram. *Electroencephalography and clinical neurophysiology,* 1973, *34,* 715.

Young, R. D. Developmental psychopharmacology: a beginning. *Psychological Bulletin,* 1967, *67,* 73.

Zinberg, N. The search for rational approaches tq heroin use. In P. G. Bourne (ed.), *Addiction.* New York: Academic Press, 1974.

Part Three

TREATMENT MODALITIES

THE FIRST CHAPTER in Part Three (Chapter 10) delineates the psychodynamically oriented treatment of alcoholism and substance abuse. Gary G. Forrest considers the history of psychodynamic theory and dynamically oriented treatment strategies. He elucidates a comprehensive psychodynamic theory of addiction and substance abuse, and develops a psychodynamically oriented approach to the psychotherapy of addiction and substance abuse. Efficacious psychodynamic psychotherapy with addictive patients involves (1) the establishment of a working and productive therapeutic alliance; (2) "genetic reconstruction" work; (3) enhanced patient insight and self-awareness; (4) an ever-present focus on addiction; and (5) an ongoing commitment to the psychotherapy process and self-help treatment.

The second chapter in this part (Chapter 11) discusses the individual treatment of substance abusers within an independent practice setting. The author, Herbert J. Freudenberger, points out that most therapists have viewed the "hardcore" chemical abuser as not amenable to independent practice treatment. Specific treatment procedures and assessment strategies, as well as the personality, behavioral characteristics, and ego structure of substance abusers are discussed in this chapter. The role of the therapist in the treatment process is also considered. The therapist needs to understand and control his or her countertransference feelings and also realize that addicted patients' regressions do precipitate therapist countertransference feelings of anger, hopelessness, and guilt. Therapists who treat addicts in independent practice settings are prone to the process of "burning out."

The third chapter in this part (Chapter 12) discusses group psychotherapy interventions with adolescent substance abusers. The authors, Arnold W. Rachman and Richard R. Raubolt, indicate that since the early 1970s there has been a decline in professional interest in the problems associated with adolescent drug abuse. In this chapter, the intrapsychic adjustment of the adolescent drug abuser, social issues associated with adolescent drug abuse, and the rationale for utilizing group psychotherapy to treat adolescent substance abusers are presented. Several confrontation techniques that are useful in such group psychotherapy are also delineated.

The fourth chapter in this part (Chapter 13) elucidates the dynamics of the alcoholic family system and provides strategies of family therapy for the treatment of alcoholism. Edward Kaufman points out that mental health professionals in the family therapy field still manifest negative attitudes toward alcoholics and tend to focus solely on family dynamics and ignore the alcoholism. The author describes four family systems in which alcoholism is present; children in alcoholic family systems; family patterns after alcoholics return to sobriety; and principles of family intervention with alcoholics. Modifications of family therapy for alcoholism includes the therapeutic contract, use of therapeutic paradoxes, interpretation, reenactment techniques, marking boundaries, education and teaching, and use of the total family network.

The fifth chapter in this part (Chapter 14) addresses the family and drug abuse. The author, M. Duncan Stanton, indicates that the family system is very important in symptom maintenance. This chapter includes a discussion of family boundaries; intergenerational coalitions; triads; family homeostasis; the scapegoat for a family's problems, who is identified by the other family members as the "patient"; and family roles, symptoms, and change. The patterns and structures of drug abuser families are delineated. The prototypical drug abuser family is one in which one parent is intensely involved with the abuser, while the other is more punitive, distant, or absent. Family treatment techniques are also presented.

The sixth chapter in this part (Chapter 15) explores the differential therapy of alcoholism. This treatment approach is systems-oriented. The authors—Frederick B. Glaser, Helen M. Annis, Shelby Pearlman, Ruth L. Segal, and Harvey A. Skinner—point out that alcoholism has traditionally been viewed as a unitary problem which might succumb to a single effective treatment approach. In this chapter, the structural and functional properties of differential alcoholism treatments and treatment research systems are described, together with their implications for and impact upon clinical services.

The seventh chapter in this part (Chapter 16) considers Antabuse treatment. Gary G. Forrest indicates that Antabuse maintenance can be an effective alcohol-antagonizing treatment for alcoholism. Antabuse causes the accumulation of a toxin in the body which makes an individual extremely sick following the ingestion of alcohol. This chapter includes a discussion of the pharmacology of Antabuse, Antabuse "myths," and Antabuse treatment guidelines. Antabuse treatment is most efficacious in combination with other treatment modalities. However, the global efficacy of Antabuse treatment remains questionable. Emergency measures to help counteract an Antabuse-alcohol reaction are outlined.

The eighth chapter in this part (Chapter 17) discusses the American self-help residential therapeutic community as a treatment approach for addicts. The authors—Thomas E. Bratter, Ernest A. Collabolletta, Allen J. Fossbender, Matthew C. Pennacchia and John R. Rubel—discuss the evolution of therapeutic communities, Alcoholics Anonymous, the psychology of addiction, the role of "choice" in recovery, confrontation in treatment, and the self-help concept. The authors believe that there is a need for integrating the therapeutic community with more traditional mental health services. The challenge is for recovered persons to work with credentialed mental health practitioners to keep the self-help residential therapeutic community a viable treatment modality for addicts.

The ninth chapter (Chapter 18) explores the role of behavioral contracting in psychotherapy with alcoholics. The author, Gary G. Forrest, defines and discusses the various parameters of the term "behavioral contract," which clinicians tend to use in reference to various and often divergent treatment techniques. The behavioral contract can be a viable treatment outcome assessment tool, a method for evaluating patient commitment to the treatment process, and even a measure of patient readiness for therapy. The legal ramifications of behavioral contracting in psychotherapy are touched upon.

The final chapter in this part (Chapter 19) discusses special therapeutic concerns for alcoholic and drug-addicted individuals. The author, Thomas E. Bratter, reports that traditional psychoanalytic and psychotherapeutic approaches are relatively ineffective in the treatment of addiction. This chapter includes sections that consider therapeutic limit setting, political antecedents that are associated with the treatment process, the threat of suicide, forced treatment, confidentiality, family involvement in matters of confidentiality, therapeutic trust, and self-disclosure. Dr. Bratter advocates that professional organizations and societies begin to consider and debate the special clinical concerns of addicts which require special therapeutic action.

10

Psychodynamically Oriented Treatment of Alcoholism and Substance Abuse

Gary G. Forrest

Orthodox psychoanalysis is rarely used in the treatment of alcoholism and other addictions (Forrest, 1978; Bratter; 1980). Freud (1953) wrote extensively about the psychoanalytic treatment of hysteria, depression, anxiety, and a diversity of other neurotic conditions, and, like the other early psychoanalysts, he wrote a great deal about the development of personality, character structure, and psychopathology. These same clinicians (Horney, 1936; Adler, 1963; Reich, 1942; Stekel, 1949; Freud, 1953; Sullivan, 1953) have contributed very little to the understanding of addiction and substance abuse. Clearly, there is a historic dearth of psychoanalytic literature dealing with the psychopathology and treatment of these tragic problems.

Freud (1953) did indicate that the alcoholic is orally fixated. However, none of Freud's extensive clinical case studies involved alcoholics. Therefore, he did not provide basic treatment guidelines for this population of patients. This is very much in contrast to Freud's exhaustive development of relatively specific psychoanalytic treatment techniques for hysterical patients, anxiety neurotics, and depressives.

Most of the orthodox Freudians (Fenichel, 1945; Reik, 1948), the neo-Freudians (Sullivan, 1953; Fromm, 1955), and the psychoanalytically oriented psychotherapists (Alexander, 1956) share Freud's basic lack of clinical experience in the realm of addiction treatment. Fenichel (1945) and Stekel (1952) were among the most knowledgeable and clinically experienced of the early psychoanalysts in addiction psychopathology and treatment. Many of Stekel's case studies and therapy vignettes include alcoholics, "drunkards," and patients who would be evaluated as "problem drinkers" by contemporary clinicians (Forrest, 1978; 1983a). Fenichel (1945) briefly delineated the psychopathology and psychoanalytic therapy of drug addiction. According to Fenichel (p. 772), "addicts represent the most clear-cut type of impulsives." Furthermore, "addicts are persons who have a disposition to react to the effects of alcohol, morphine, or other drugs in a specific way, namely, in such a way that they try to use these effects to satisfy the archaic oral longing which is sexual longing, a need for security, and a need for the maintenance of self-esteem simultaneously." The addict's pre-morbid personality is the decisive factor in the development of addiction. Fenichel pointed out that the addicted person experiences the drug of choice as food and warmth. Addicts are intolerant of tension and they cannot endure pain and frustration. Such persons manifest reality-oriented conflicts and they progressively withdraw from reality. The addict is fixated at various infantile levels of sexuality.

Fenichel (1945) did address a number of clinical issues which he explicitly associated with the psychopathology of alcohol addiction. Escape from misery, escape into pleasurable fantasies, and the blocking of inhibitions are significant dynamic factors which contribute to the development of alcohol addiction. The unconscious impulses (Fenichel, 1945) in alcoholics are very often homosexual as well as oral in nature. Periodic drinking disorders are similar to manic-depressive states. Fenichel also noted that psychotic episodes in addicts are frequently precipitated during periods of abstience. Knight (1937) indicated that symptomatic family constellations involving oral frustrations during childhood play an important role in the etiology of chronic alcoholism.

Knight (1936, 1937) and Fenichel (1945, 1953) have written about the psychoanalytic treatment of alcoholics and other addicts. Fenichel (1945) indicates that addicted patients are amenable to psychoanalytic treatment. According to Fenichel, in the absence of psychoanalysis or other psychotherapeutic treatment following a "withdrawal cure," the patient can be expected to return to the use of the drug. Knight (1937) suggests that the appropriate time to begin psychoanalytic treatment with the addicted patient is during or immediately after withdrawal. These authors also point out that it is unrealistic to expect the addicted patient to remain totally abstinent or drug-free throughout the course of psychoanalytic treatment. Periodic regressions involving substance abuse can be expected during analysis. Fenichel

(1945) was of the opinion that addicts "are to be analyzed in institutions rather than as ambulatory patients." He did not provide therapists with guidelines pertaining to the control of the patients' addiction or substance abuse. Fenichel (1945) very astutely conceptualized addiction as a "chronic disintegrating process." It was also his belief that "the most important consideration from a therapeutic point of view is at what stages of disintegration the analysis is begun." The "drug addict" is viewed as an individual with a very different relationship to reality and with very different capacities for establishing tranference.

The alcoholic was frequently referred to as a "drunkard" in the early psychoanalytic literature and the neo-Freudian literature. Fenichel (1945) stated that "an addiction begins as a search for a protective guard against painful stimulation" and theorized that in the case of drunkards, drinking is "essentially a retreat from unbearable external conditions." These general viewpoints are consistent with current psychodynamic theory (Forrest, 1983a) pertaining to the etiology of alcoholism and the addictions. However, the analytic viewpoint that therapy for addicts "will be of no avail" as long as the external contributing conditions persist and "would become unnecessary if they were changed" (Fenichel, 1945) is unacceptable to modern-day clinicians involved in the treatment of alcoholics and other substance abusers (Forrest, 1978, 1980b; Bratter, 1980; Knauert, 1980).

Object relations theory represents a recent development within the realms of psychoanalysis and psychoanalytic theory (Kernberg, 1975; Hartocollis, 1977; Kernberg, 1976, 1980). The object relations theorists, according to Kernberg (1975), have not developed their psychoanalytic theories and treatment techniques via extensive clinical experience with addicts and substance abusers. In contrast to many other contemporary insight and analytically oriented therapists the object relations theorists (Gunderson, 1977; Kernberg, 1976) do focus upon the various patterns of substance abuse and addictive behavior which their borderline patients frequently manifest.

Forrest (1983a) suggests that many alcoholics manifest a character structure which is very much akin to the borderline. Although the borderline personality is generally felt to be a specific nosologic or diagnostic category (Apfelbaum, 1979), these individuals often abuse chemicals and are prone to addiction. The overt behavior, interpersonal style, and internal world of the alcoholic and borderline are similar (Forrest, 1980b, 1983a). Kernberg (1975) refers to the following "presumptive" diagnostic elements of borderline personality organization: (1) chronic, diffuse, free-floating anxiety; (2) multiple phobias (phobias relating to body and physical appearance in contrast to phobias involving external objects, phobias involving severe social inhibitions, and paranoid trends and obsessive-compulsive symptoms); (3) polymorphously perverse sexual trends; (4) prepsychotic personality structure (paranoid, schizoid, hypomanic, or "cyclothymic" personality organization); (5) impulse neurosis and addiction (including alcoholism, drug addiction, kleptomania, and certain forms of psychogenic obesity); and (6) "lower level" character disorder.

More specifically, Kernberg (1975, pp. 64–65) states that the "main problem" with patients manifesting a narcissistic personality structure

> appears to be the disturbance of their self-regard in connection with specific disturbances in their object relationships. On the surface, these patients do not appear to be severely regressed; some of them may function socially, very well. These patients present an unusual degree of self-reference in their interactions with other people, a great need to be loved and admired by others. Their emotional life is shallow. They experience little empathy for the feelings of others, they obtain very little enjoyment from life other than from the tributes they receive from others or from their own grandiose fantasies, and they feel restless and bored when external glitter wears off and no new sources feed their self-regard. They envy others, tend to idealize some people from whom they expect narcissistic supplies, and to depreciate and treat with contempt those from whom they do not expect anything (often their former idols). In general, their relationships with other people are clearly exploitative and sometimes parasitic. It is as if they feel they have the right to control and possess others and to exploit them without guilt feelings, and behind a surface which very often is charming and engaging, one senses coldness and ruthlessness. Very often such patients are considered to be "dependent" because they need so much tribute and adoration from others, but on a deeper level they are completely unable really to depend on anybody because of their deep distrust and depreciation of others.
>
> Their haughty, grandiose, and controlling behavior is a defense against paranoid traits related to the projection of oral rage, which is central in their psychopathology.

The psychoanalysis and psychoanalytically oriented treatment of the borderline patient has been explored at length (Kernberg, 1975, 1976; Hartocollis, 1977; Apfelbaum, 1979; Bauer, 1979; Kernberg, 1980; Lowen, 1983). Kernberg (1975) has written extensively about the psychoanalytic treatment of the borderline patient. The technical requirements for the psychoanalytic psychotherapy of borderline patients include (Kernberg, 1975, p. 74):

> (1) systematic elaboration of the negative transference in the "here-and-now" only, (2) interpretation of the defensive constellation of these patients as they enter the negative transference; (3) limit-setting in order to block

acting-out of the transference, with as much structuring of the patient's life outside the [treatment] hours as necessary to protect the neutrality of the analyst; (4) non-interpretation of the less primitively determined, modulated aspects of the positive transference to foster the gradual development of the therapeutic alliance.

It is generally thought (e.g., Apfelbaum, 1979; Kernberg, 1980) that interpretive, confrontive therapeutic interventions with borderline patients are more productive and efficacious than supportive therapeutic techniques. Transference psychosis is a frequent complication in the treatment of individuals with borderline personality organization.

It is apparent to clinicians who are experienced in the treatment of addicts and substance abusers that the personality, character structure, and psychotherapeutic treatment of these persons are generally congruous with those of the borderline patient.

In general, psychoanalysts and insight therapists appear to be reluctant to treat addicts and substance abusers. The addicted patient is particularly difficult to treat within the confines of psychoanalysis and psychoanalytically oriented psychotherapy (Knight, 1937; Menninger, 1938; Fenichel, 1945, 1953; Stekel, 1952; Freud, 1953; Reich, 1942; Sullivan, 1953). A recent research investigation (Bratter, 1979) indicated that over one-third of practicing psychiatrists refuse to treat substance abusers. Many psychologists and other psychotherapists choose not to work with addicts and substance abusers. A widely accepted misconception among the behavioral science professions is that alcoholics and addicts cannot be rehabilitated or successfully treated by any psychotherapeutic method. The unfounded and irrational belief "once an alcoholic, always an alcoholic" is perhaps as prevalent among clinicians and behavioral scientists as it is among the general population!

Analytically oriented therapists from diverse schools of counseling and psychotherapy tend to think that addicted individuals have a poor treatment prognosis. Dynamically oriented psychotherapists and clinicians have contributed very little data to the research literature dealing with treatment outcomes of alcoholics and substance abusers (Forrest, 1983a). Recent treatment outcome research data pertaining to alcoholics and substance abusers (Emrick, 1975; Forrest, 1978; Armor, Polich, and Stambul, 1978; Emrick, 1980; Bratter, 1980) suggests that 50 to 80 percent of these individuals are significantly benefited by a diversity of treatment interventions. Indeed, the overall treatment prognosis for most populations of alcoholics, problem drinkers, and substance abusers is very similar to that for various other psychiatric/psychological populations entering psychotherapy.

Psychodynamic Theory of Addiction and Substance Abuse

A diversity of etiological theories of addiction and substance abuse have evolved during the past four decades (Forrest, 1978; Catanzaro, 1978; Pattison, 1980). Current theories of addiction emphasize the roles of genes and heredity, conditioning and learning, affective disturbance, psychiatric disorder, and interpersonal milieu. As indicated earlier, psychodynamically oriented explanations of addictive behavior tend to be rather truncated and fragmented. In this section of the chapter, I will construct a comprehensive psychodynamically oriented model of alcoholism and substance abuse.

Narcissistic need and entitlement deprivation are key ingredients in the etiology of addiction (Forrest, 1978, 1983a, 1984). Alcoholics and other addicts have experienced pervasive narcissistic injury during the early periods of life, as well as during the various stages of adolescence and adulthood. Elsewhere (Forrest, 1983a, pp. 35–36). I have indicated that

> narcissistic injury is used, as a concept, interchangeably with the concept of narcissistic need and entitlement deprivation. Most fundamentally, narcissistic needs refer to the life-sustaining needs of the human organism. Oxygen, food, appropriate temperature control, physical contact and the maintenance of excretory functions are narcissistic needs. These needs of the infant and young child must be managed by significant others (mother, father and family system). Such needs are self-oriented, thus narcissistic and life-sustaining. Should significant others fail to meet the narcissistic needs of the infant death may occur.
>
> Narcissistic entitlement deprivation refers essentially to those psychological and interpersonal processes which convey a basic sense of dignity, love, respect, worth, esteem, concern and trust to the infant and child. As human beings we are entitled to feel loved, worthwhile, adequate and respected within the context of our relationships with significant others. Such needs are lifelong.
>
> Narcissistic needs pertain to essentially physiological processes, while entitlement needs refer more to interpersonal and psychological processes. However, narcissistic needs and entitlement needs clearly include physiological and psychological components.
>
> Narcissistic injury occurs when the narcissistic needs and entitlements of the evolving person are inadequately managed by significant others. Narcissistic need and entitlement deprivation most catastrophically affects the growth and development of the person under pervasive and chronic circumstances. Narcissistic need and entitlement deprivation is an interpersonal process. Throughout life all people must consistently be able to manage their narcissistic needs and entitlements through relationships involving self and significant others.

Quite simply, the addict has consistently been hurt by significant others throughout much of his or her life. Many addicted individuals can vividly recall having been physically abused and neglected very early in life. Psychological abuse by parents, surrogate parents, and significant others is central to the interpersonal historicity of virtually all addicts and most substance abusers. As a part of the narcissistic injury rubric, approximately one-half of addicted patients have been parented by an addictive parent or surrogate parent. These individuals are "programmed" to become addicted (Forrest, 1978).

It is important to emphasize that the addict has experienced consistent narcissistic injury within the context of his or her significant interpersonal relationships throughout the various developmental stages of life. The lifelong interpersonal modus vivendi of alcoholics and other addicts is destructive and pathologic. Poor social skills are one long-term consequence of inadequate parenting and narcissistic injury in early life. Feelings of inadequacy, low self-esteem, a sense of worthlessness, an inability to love and work effectively, and chronic depression are but a few of the internal conflicts of the addict which help create chronic intrapersonal pathology. The intrapersonal and interpersonal pathology of the addicted person is actively reinforced via academic failures, peer adjustment problems, dating and sexual difficulties, marital discord, vocational problems, and parenting inadequacies. In sum, the basic characterological pathology of the addict which is associated with early-life narcissistic injury is consistently reinforced and exacerbated through a multiplicity of subsequent developmental inadequacies and failures. These developmental inadequacies and failures pertain to virtually every aspect of daily living.

The psychopathology of addiction is focally associated with early-life pervasive and chronic narcissistic need and entitlement deprivation. Orally addictive persons (alcoholics, compulsive overeaters, prescription and other "pill" addicts, and heavy marijuana smokers) have experienced intense anxiety within the context of their mothering relationships during the initial weeks and months of life. As such, the anxiety-oriented conflicts of the addict are initially interpersonally determined. Juxtaposed to this the addicted person inconsistently experiences a significant degree of orally oriented anxiety reduction during the early weeks and months of life. Feeding and eating experiences result in a significant degree of intermittent anxiety reduction. These factors contribute to the overdetermined orality of addicts. The early-life anxiety which the addict prototaxically experiences within the context of the mothering relationship involves matters pertaining to rejection, abandonment, and annihilation. In essence, the addict is a person who has experienced intense and chronic early-life anxiety as a result of prototaxically fearing destruction and annihilation by significant others.

The pervasively anxious relationship which the addict experiences with his or her mother and significant others during the early developmental epochs of life results in a less than adequately consolidated nuclear sense of self (Forrest, 1983a). Thus, the self-system of the addict is fragmented. Addicted persons are chronically vulnerable to the experience of intense anxiety; they are prone to regression; and they experience consistent problems pertaining to a blurring of the ego boundaries. In short, the addict struggles with chronic identity conflicts. These factors are also associated with ego-splitting (Kernberg, 1975) and the utilization of overdetermined oral methods of binding anxiety and stress.

Addicts are forever in search of an answer to the question "Who am I?" Most basically, this is a struggle associated with nuclear identity. Matters of masculinity and femininity are also central to an addict's search for identity. It is within the context of warm, loving, and essentially anxiety-free early life mothering relationships that the evolving person is able to primitively experience a consistent sense of consensual validation which fosters the development of an adequately consolidated nuclear sense of self. The addict has not experienced this form of healthy mothering relationship.

The addicted person develops an avoidance defense system (Forrest, 1983a,b) in order to cope with the catastrophic anxiety associated with early-life narcissistic need and entitlement deprivation. The avoidance defense system is developed during the first three years of life and is basic to the lifelong characterological makeup of the addict. In essence, this system consists of a tripartite set of primitive defense mechanisms. Denial, distortion, and projection are the core defense mechanisms of the avoidance defense system. The purpose of the system is to "protect" the addict from basic human relatedness, contact, and intimacy. The contact-oriented, intimate experiences of the addict during infancy and childhood have been consistently anxiety-ridden. Furthermore, addicts learn from these pathological early-life experiences that intimate human relationships and encounters are very often dangerous and potentially life-threatening. Therefore, the addict compulsively attempts to avoid intimate human encounters and relationships during subsequent developmental epochs.

The function of the avoidance defense system also includes an avoidance of the self. Many addicts and substance abusers are painfully aware of themselves. Therefore, the avoidance defense system constitutes an interpersonal and intrapersonal characterological style. Addicts not only fear and thus avoid the intimacy and contact associated with interpersonal relationships, they also fear and therefore avoid the intimacy and contact associated with self-awareness, personal feelings, and self-oriented cognitions, fantasies, and behaviors (Lowen, 1983). For these reasons, the alcoholic denies that he or she is an "alcoholic." In reality, "one or two drinks" usually means many drinks in the real world of alcoholism. This is distortion. The drinking behavior or substance abuse is caused by spouses, children, or "the boss." This is projection.

Clinicians and psychotherapists very often fail to realize that addiction per se is a life-style of avoidance. Addicts maintain a constant avoidance of self, significant others, and the phenomenal world via the ingestion of chemicals and addictive substances. Indeed, the addicted person experiences self, others, and the world through the medium of what might be called a "semipermeable membrane" (Forrest, 1978, 1983a). This semipermeable membrane can be alcohol, heroin, marijuana, Valium, or any other addictive substance. It should also be noted that addicts employ virtually all of the defense mechanisms in the service and maintenance of their addiction.

Addicts experience chronic depressive symptomatology. Indeed, the addict often manifests depression of an endogenous nature (Forrest, 1983a). The depressive struggles of addicts and substance abusers are chronic and evolve as a result of pervasive infantile and childhood narcissistic injury. The alcoholic is hurt, sad, and depressed as a result of having been rejected, chronically criticized, and simply hurt by significant others. Many alcoholics and other addicts verbalize that they have "never been depressed." Such individuals may not appear to be clinically depressed during the initial hours of psychotherapeutic treatment. However, these patients tend to begin to evidence clear-cut clinical depression following the establishment of total sobriety or drug-free living. A few addicts experience a short-term depressive psychosis early in the treatment process. Successful psychotherapy and rehabilitation with addicted persons is often contingent upon the therapist's ability to help the patient resolve and overcome his or her acute depression associated with the establishment of drug abstinence. Addiction can thus be viewed as a neurotic defense against depression.

The addict is pathologically dependent. Dependency-oriented pathology is closely associated with overdetermined orality and depression. The etiology of the addicted person's pathological dependency is pervasive infantile and childhood narcissistic need and entitlement deprivation. Frequently, addicts attach themselves to people who are "mother substitutes." The addicted person chronically searches for a "mother" or significant other who can provide the love, warmth, nurturing, and healthy parenting which was absent during the early months and years of life. This process can be viewed as the addict's lifelong attempt to undo his or her interpersonal historicity. Obviously, addicts are addicted to mood-altering chemicals. They are dependent upon substances. Addicts maintain a long-term "love affair" with alcohol and other addictive substances (Forrest, 1978; Knauert, 1979; Forrest, 1983a, 1984). The addict experiences a sense of importance, adequacy, warmth, and power while under the influence of alcohol and other drugs.

Some addicts and substance abusers, most notably alcoholics and problem drinkers, have been labeled "counterdependent personalities." Behaviorally this label can appear to be clinically appropriate. Internally, affectively, and even behaviorally this label is ultimately inappropriate. Aggressive, overly assertive, and seemingly gregarious alcoholics and problem drinkers are dependent, contrary to appearances. The apparently counterdependent addict attempts to neurotically deny his or her pathologic dependency via the development of an overly assertive, aggressive, independent adjustment style. Addiction per se is the example par excellence of dependency!

Addiction is an obsessive-compulsive disorder. The obsessive-compulsive dynamism is both a defense against anxiety and a neurotic means of "binding" anxiety. Thus, early infantile and childhood narcissistic injury contributes to the development of an obsessive-compulsive character structure. During the initial years of life, the addict has experienced intense and chronic interpersonal anxiety associated with narcissistic injury. In order to control and bind chronically ego-threatening levels of anxiety the addicted person develops an obsessive-compulsive character structure. The addict tends to be rigid, perfectionistic, orderly, preoccupied with matters of time, and highly structured. Many addicts are floridly anal in character structure. This particular character structure and personality makeup is a central ingredient in being "programmed" for addiction. An obsessive-compulsive cognitive and behavioral style dictates that alcoholics and other addicts obsessively ruminate about alcohol and other addictive substances. Furthermore, the addict uses and abuses addictive substances in a compulsive manner. Alcoholics are not people who can consistently drink "one or two" alcoholic beverages. The alcoholic drinks compulsively. This usually means taking one drink after another until reaching the point of gross intoxication. People who are addicted to prescription drugs may ingest these substances compulsively for years.

Addicted individuals spend an inordinate amount of time thinking and ruminating about the substance or substances upon which they are dependent. The addict learns to use mood-altering substances in order to feel in control of himself or herself. Addicts are literally obsessed with the issue of control. They attempt to control themselves, significant others, and their phenomenal world via their addiction and use of addictive substances. Paradoxically, the addict is always a person who is out of control! The obsessive-compulsive addict eventually thinks of alcohol and other mood-altering substances as "magic" solutions to anxiety and control problems.

Addicts and substance abusers are also prone to acting-out. Indeed, addiction is an impulse disorder. The addict is unable to internalize conflict and thus maladaptively resolves intrapersonal and interpersonal problems via a plethora of impulsive, poorly controlled acting-out behaviors. Virtually all addicted persons manifest low frustration tolerance. The specific acting-out behaviors of addicts and substance abusers include anxiety, anger and rage, sexuality, manipulation and exploitation, low frustration tolerance, and generalized irresponsibility (Forrest, 1980a, 1984). In the case of alcoholics and other substance abusers, acting-out serves the purpose of binding intense intrapersonal and interpersonal anxiety associated with early-life narcissistic injury. Many addicts consciously fear becoming "insane" or "going crazy." Addicts are also catastrophically afraid of dying. Acting-out solutions to internal threat and dissonance also represent neurotic attempts to feel important, worthwhile, adequate, and powerful. The acting-out behaviors of the addict represent a defense against feelings of inadequacy, inferiority, and personal impotence. A physiological result of ingesting many addictive substances is also behavioral acting-out.

The acting-out dimensions of the addictive character structure and personality makeup are etiologically associated with early-life narcissistic need and entitlement deprivation (Kernberg, 1975; Forrest, 1978, 1983a). Addiction and substance abuse per se represent acting-out solutions to the many difficult and painful realities of life. However, many addicts and substance abusers do not manifest a psychopathic or sociopathic character structure. Fewer than 10 percent of chronic alcoholics manifest a psychopathic character structure (Forrest, 1983a). These are often perplexing clinical matters for the therapist and research psychotherapist. For these reasons, an accurate differential diagnosis (Knauert, 1980) is essential to the process of successful psychotherapy with alcoholics, other addicts, and substance abusers. The alcoholic is impulsive, manipulative, and prone to generalized acting-out (Forrest, 1978; Knauert, 1980; Forrest, 1980a, 1983a). However, the vast majority of alcoholics are intensely anxious, guilty, remorseful, depressed, and affectively disturbed. This symptom structure precludes the diagnosis of psychopathic or sociopathic personality. Thus, only a very small percentage of alcohol-addicted persons can accurately be diagnosed as manifesting a psychopathic adjustment style.

Addiction is also a disorder of sadism and masochism, thus sadomasochism. Addicts very often physically—and psychologically—destroy themselves and significant others via their addiction and addictive behaviors. Pain is the central ingredient in the addict's sadomasochistic adjustment style.

Early-life narcissistic injury determines the addict's sadomasochistic character pathology. The addict is consistently hurt by significant others during the initial months and years of life. Some addicts have been physically abused by their parents and significant others. Virtually all addicts have been psychologically abused and hurt by those closest to them during infancy and childhood. In effect, the addict has been taught by significant others, "You deserve to be punished." As a result of prolonged learning experiences of this variety, the addict begins to behave, think, and feel according to the dictate "I deserve to be punished." Most addicts do not consciously understand the self-defeating, sadomasochistic dimensions of their addictive behavior.

Pervasive early-life narcissistic injury predisposes the addict to a life-style of angry, resentful, and sadistic attacks against significant others. The addict unconsciously attempts to "get even" with his or her parents and significant others via criticism, sarcasm, and sometimes outright physical assult. However, in the end the addicted person is always the victim of his or her self-destructive and masochistic character structure. The alcoholic who sadistically destroys another human being in an automobile accident is eventually "punished" by the legal system and at the same time becomes the victim of his or her own superego. Thus, addicts ultimately become the victims of their masochism. Sadistic attempts at retaliation result in masochistic self-punishment and often self-destruction.

Addicts and substance abusers manifest a paranoid characterological makeup (Kernberg, 1975; Forrest, 1978, 1983a,b). Indeed, in some individuals (Meissner, 1978) addiction can precipitate a florid paranoid decompensation. Paranoid symptomatology is associated with ego-deficit and self-system fragmentation (Freud, 1953; Meissner, 1978; Forrest, 1983a). Intense and chronic early-life narcissistic injury results in ego-deficit, ego-splitting (Kernberg, 1975, 1976, 1980; Forrest, 1983a) and self-system fragmentation. Many addicts go through life paranoically wondering what is wrong with them and why they are so unlovable. Thus, paranoid symptomatology is basic to the addictive character structure.

The paranoid character structure of the addict is closely associated with sexual role and identity confusion. Addicts tend to be confused about their sexuality. Many addicted persons fear the possibility of being homosexual. A small percent of addicts are primarily homosexual with regard to sexual object choice. These individuals struggle with paranoid pathology associated with both their addiction and sexual adjustment style. An inadequately consolidated nuclear sense of self (Forrest, 1983b) is perhaps the initial characterological prerequisite to the addict's paranoid symptomatology.

Many addicts and substance abusers are chronically guilt-ridden. Guilt is a major psychodynamic component in alcoholism and alcohol abuse (Forrest, 1978, 1979a, 1980a). However, some addicts pathologically lack the capacity to experience guilt (Cameron, 1963; Sutker, 1971; Forrest, 1978). Heroin addicts and many so-called "hard-drug" addicts and abusers seem to lack the superego development essential to experiencing intense and chronic guilt.

The chronically guilt-ridden addict or substance abuser tends to have struggled with a plethora of guilt-oriented conflicts since childhood. These individuals are neurotically guilty about their unresolved childhood feelings of inadequacy, worthlessness, and "unlovability." Pervasive narcissistic injury (Forrest, 1983a) creates neurotic guilt. In effect, many addicts and substance abusers are neurotically guilty as a result of their interpersonal experiences with significant others, which have taught them very early in life to feel inadequate, worthless, and unlovable. Alcoholics experience chronic and intense feelings of guilt which are associated with an early-life sense of "non-well-being."

Addictive persons make themselves feel guilty (Ellis, 1979); they engage in a plethora of socially unacceptable behaviors. Frequently, addicts inflict psychological and even physical pain upon other people. Intoxicated drivers kill thousands of innocent people each year. It is both rational and appropriate for the addict to experience guilt in these situations. The addict consistently exacerbates his or her more neurotically oriented guilt conflicts via a multiplicity of chemically determined, irresponsible behaviors. The addict's guilt operates in the service of his or her addiction.

The various psychodynamic factors discussed thus far constitute the psychopathology of addiction and substance abuse (Forrest, 1983a). A basic understanding of these pathological dynamisms and their various interrelationships is essential to the successful psychotherapeutic treatment of addicts and substance abusers. It is imperative that clinicians and psychotherapists adequately understand the character structure, personality makeup, and adjustment style of their addictive patients prior to initiating intensive psychotherapy and other rehabilitation strategies.

Psychodynamically Oriented Psychotherapy

This section of the chapter includes a discussion of the basic ingredients in psychodynamically oriented psychotherapy with addicts and substance abusers. Efficacious therapy of this type involves (1) the establishment of a working and productive therapeutic alliance; (2) a reconstruction of the patient's interpersonal and intrapersonal historicity; (3) the development of the patient's capacity for insight and self-awareness; (4) an ever-present focus upon the patient's addiction, addictive behaviors, and the various dynamics associated with the addiction process; and (5) fostering the patient's commitment to ongoing therapy and active involvement in adjunct strategies of rehabilitation and change.

The Therapeutic Alliance

Chemically dependent patients are believed to be poor candidates for intensive dynamically oriented psychotherapy (Forrest, 1978; Bratter, 1979; Forrest, 1984). Many clinicians claim that psychotherapeutic treatment is contraindicated for addicts and substance abusers. Myths and grossly erroneous clinical dogmas of this variety steer many psychotherapists away from treatment relationships with addicted persons. It must be stressed that many chemically dependent persons respond very favorably to psychotherapeutic treatment. Psychotherapy and rehabilitation outcome studies (Emrick, 1975; Forrest, 1978; Armor, Polich, and Stambul, 1978; Emrick, 1980) consistently indicate that 50 to 75 percent of alcoholic and substance-abusing patients are successfully treated. Such studies tend to employ a diversity of outcome assessment criteria: total abstinence, reduced drug usage, social skills, job performance, and marital and family relationship stability, to name only a few.

The productive therapeutic alliance encompasses the therapist's basic belief and awareness that addicted patients can benefit from psychotherapy. Furthermore, the psychotherapist expects his or her addictive patients to (1) terminate the use of all addicting substances; (2) modify or extinguish the behavioral repertoire which maintains and supports the addiction process; and (3) grow and change in myraid ways which are often tangential to the addiction process.

It is essential to the process of successful psychotherapy with addicted persons that the therapist simply be comfortable with addicts. Many clinicians and psychotherapists report that they are uncomfortable with addicted and substance-abusing patients (Forrest, 1978). Some therapists openly dislike addicts and refuse to work with them in therapy (Bratter, 1980). Therapists who are able to like their addicted patients tend to be successful in their treatment relationships with these individuals.

Productive and working therapeutic alliances evolve as a process;

they are not established within a matter of two or three therapy hours. While the initial therapy hours represent a critically important barometer of therapist-patient potential for establishing a working and productive therapeutic alliance, it takes several sessions to develop the therapy relationship into a meaningful vehicle of change. The therapeutic alliance is constructed via the development of mutual trust, respect, and concern. As discussed in the previous section of this chapter, addicts experience intense anxiety when involved in close human relationships. The therapist must understand this, and must sensitively and supportively communicate to the patient that the treatment relationship will not result in the patient's destruction or annihilation. To the contrary, the initial anxiety inherent within the therapist-patient relationship is grist for exploration, interpretation, and resolution. Addictive patients experience a sense of comfortableness and trust once the interpersonal anxiety of the early therapy sessions has been openly discussed and worked through. This process is basic to the patient's ability to develop an ongoing commitment to therapy. Obviously, the cement of the productive and working therapeutic alliance involves the patient's ability to remain committed to the psychotherapeutic process.

The central ingredients in the development and maintenance of a productive therapeutic alliance with addicted patients are the therapist's nonpossessive warmth, empathy, and genuineness (Truax and Carkhuff, 1967; Forrest, 1978, 1984). Briefly, these ingredients pertain to the therapist's ability to (1) accept the patient unconditionally; (2) be affectively and cognitively attuned to what the patient is currently feeling and experiencing, and be able to communicate this understanding to the patient; and (3) be open to his own experience within the therapeutic encounter, so as to be honestly capable of expressing these feelings to the patient—i.e., the therapist is a "real person" in the therapeutic encounter. There are numerous other essential ingredients in the process of dynamically oriented psychotherapy with addicts and substance abusers. However, these "core" conditions are essential to successful therapy. Effective psychotherapists are able to consistently provide high levels of nonpossessive warmth, empathy, and genuineness throughout their treatment relationships with addictive patients.

The therapeutic alliance is nurtured and strengthened by the therapist's consistent communication of respect for the addicted patient during treatment sessions. Addicted patients respond favorably to therapists who are able to communicate to them a sense of dignity, respect, and worth. Psychotherapists who work with addicts and substance abusers must also be consistently and rationally confrontive (Forrest, 1982) in their treatment relationships! In essence, the therapist displays respect and concern for the patient by caring enough to be confrontively involved in the patient's various problems and life struggles. Effective confrontation strategies in psychotherapy with addictive persons (Forrest, 1982) evolve as an essential ingredient in the therapeutic alliance. The therapist's nonpossessive warmth, empathy, genuineness, and respect are basic ingredients in the use of confrontation strategies.

Therapists who simply provide their addictive patients with the "core conditions" of therapy may actually fail in their treatment relationships. The essential therapist ingredients, or core conditions, in effective psychotherapy are necessary but not sufficient to create personality and behavioral change and growth in most addicted persons. Dynamically oriented psychotherapy with addicts and substance abusers requires a good deal of therapist activity. Passive, reflective, supportive, or simply analytic psychotherapists consistently fail in their treatment efforts with addicts. Interpretation, confrontation, self-disclosure (Jourard, 1964; Forrest, 1970; Hountras and Forrest, 1970), social skills training, homework assignments, and an active reinforcement of patient involvement in self-help modalities are but a few of the treatment strategies which the addiction psychotherapist must utilize. These strategies of intervention are ingredients in the ongoing process of dynamic psychotherapy. They become a part of the transference–countertransference mosaic of psychotherapy with addicted and substance-abusing persons.

The more traditional analytically oriented models of psychodynamic psychotherapy do not "work" with addicts and substance abusers. I have found (Forrest, 1978, 1980a, 1984) that most addicted patients will not remain committed to the process of analytically oriented psychotherapy. A therapist's silence, lack of involvement and activity, ambiguity, and premature focusing upon feelings and intrapersonal pathology routinely drives addicted patients away. Addicted patients require (Bratter, 1980) therapist support, structure, and concreteness in order to establish a productive and working therapeutic alliance.

Recall

"Genetic reconstruction" in psychodynamically oriented psychotherapy refers to the therapist's structuring of the treatment relationship in a manner which focuses upon the patient's early life experiences, behaviors, feelings, and cognitions. The experiential past of the addicted patient is "grist for the Mill" in the psychotherapeutic process. This therapeutic stance is somewhat of a paradox. Addicts and substance abusers are pathologically fixated in the past and future, and their temporal style (Forrest, 1978, 1983a) is oriented to the past and/or future. The patient's addiction represents a neurotic solution to painful and traumatic narcissistic injuries which have in reality occurred in the past. Addicts attempt to avoid and deny their experiential histories by using a wide variety of mood-altering substances. The paradoxical task of the psychotherapist is that of helping the addicted patient explore fully and in-depth his or her past in the absence of chemical intoxication.

The process of genetic reconstruction in psychotherapy with addicts and substance abusers is basic to the development and maintenance of a working therapeutic alliance. During initial therapy sessions, addictive patients tend to be quite ambivalent about dealing with their early life experiences. The therapist must understand this ambivalence and the resistance associated with it. Furthermore, during the early treatment sessions it is the task of the psychotherapist to supportively help the addicted patient begin to explore and understand the many painful realities of his or her past. This therapeutic technique eventually enables the patient to rationally come to grips with the "pain of the past." As this process begins to unfold, the patient begins to discover that he or she no longer feels the compulsion to escape the past through chemical intoxication. The patient learns to overcome severe and chronic *feelings* (Lowen, 1983) of anxiety, depression, anger, and guilt associated with the past. Patients no longer ruminate endlessly about their earlier experiences in life. In sum, genetic reconstruction in psychotherapy with addicts and substance abusers is a treatment strategy which helps the patient adaptively resolve the bondage of the past.

It is most efficacious for the therapist to focus the initial six to ten sessions almost exclusively in the realm of the patient's childhood and early adolescent history. Anxiety and a plethora of uncomfortable affects usually accompany this procedure—which is initiated following the patient's commitment to total drug abstinence. Obviously, the patient fears this process of uncovering. Yet, for many addicted individuals, this therapeutic procedure results in a tremendous sense of release and catharsis. Many addicts and substance abusers have never before discussed their personal historicity in an open, honest, and drug-free manner with another human being. The therapeutic alliance is greatly strengthened by the use of this technique. In addition, the therapeutic relationship becomes more intense and depth-oriented, and the patient learns to trust another human being.

Genetic reconstruction work is an integral part of the ongoing process of successful psychodynamic psychotherapy with addicts and substance abusers. The therapeutic focus upon the patient's early life experiences is much more intensive during the initial treatment hours. After the initial six to ten sessions, the therapy continues to include a focus upon the patient's past. However, as the therapy relationship evolves into the middle and later stages of treatment (Forrest, 1978), the focus on genetic reconstruction is much less intense, and the psychotherapist shifts the temporal focus into the here-and-now. As a part of the evolving here-and-now focus, the therapist continues to make associations and dynamic interpretations which link the patient's past and present feelings, experiences, behaviors, and cognitions.

By focusing upon past history, the psychotherapist soon discovers the genetic basis for the patient's feelings of inadequacy, inferiority, and worthlessness. In essence, the patient's extended history of narcissistic injury becomes grist for the psychotherapeutic process. The patient's pathological personality makeup and characterological structure have been determined during infancy and childhood. As discussed earlier in the chapter, pervasive and chronic narcissistic need and entitlement deprivation is genetic to the personality makeup and character structure of addicts and most substance abusers. Conflicts of this variety can only be resolved through genetic reconstruction work.

The patient's current anxieties, depression, anger and rage, identity conflicts, sexual problems, interpersonal difficulties, and generally self-defeating behaviors are better understood by the psychotherapist vis-à-vis genetic reconstruction work. The patient's defensive style and avoidance defense system are also elucidated by the utilization of this treatment strategy. Addicted individuals tend to deny their drug dependence. They also deny depression, anxiety, and other psychological problems. Addicts avoid their painful pasts in a multiplicity of ways. Genetic reconstruction work in intensive psychotherapy helps the addict modify his or her overdetermined use of primitive defense mechanisms. The addict must learn how to stop neurotically avoiding and denying the past in order to establish a chemically free life-style. Indeed, the defensive armoring of the addict is exceedingly rigid. The process of genetic reconstruction work in therapy enables the addicted person to (1) accept the reality of being addicted and (2) modify the pattern of characterological rigidity which is fundamental to all addictions. This pattern of characterological rigidity is none other than the avoidance defense system (Forrest, 1978, 1983a), and the basic mechanisms of this system are denial, distortion, and projection. Recovery from addiction is contingent upon the ability of the therapist-patient dyad to significantly modify the patient's avoidance defense system. The addicted person must develop the capacity for an interpersonal recovery. This process is actively fostered by the psychotherapy relationship.

Alcoholics and many other chemically dependent patients (Forrest, 1978) continuously struggle with hypernarcissism and low self-esteem. Such patients vascillate between feelings and perceptions of personal omnipotence, grandiosity, and megalomania, on the one hand, and severe depression and a sense of inadequacy and total worthlessness, on the other. Process genetic reconstruction work with these individuals is essential to a resolution of the power fantasy ideation (Forrest, 1978, 1984), which determines radical shifts in self-esteem. The majority of addicted and substance-abusing patients are clearly depressive and experiencing some form of life crisis when initially seen in outpatient psychotherapy (Forrest, 1979b). These patients tend not to be overtly grandiose and omnipotent at the point of treatment engagement. It is after a patient has resolved the life crisis which fostered the decision to enter psychotherapy, and after the establishment of a working therapeutic alliance, that narcissistic, egocentric, and perhaps floridly omnipotent cognitions and fantasies, behaviors and self-perceptions, begin to emerge in the treatment sessions. Indeed, the therapeutic resolution of the addicted patient's power fantasy ideation may constitute the major work of genetic reconstruction during the middle and later stages of the psychotherapeutic process.

The Development of Insight and Self-Awareness

A major goal in psychodynamicallyoriented psychotherapy with addicts and substance abusers is that of fostering patient insight and self-awareness. This is another paradoxical aspect of the process of psychotherapy with addictive persons. Addicts tend to be unconsciously and preconsciously aware of many of their historic as well as present neurotic conflicts. Prior to being involved in intensive psychodynamicallyoriented psychotherapy, addicts neurotically attempt to deny, avoid, and repress insight and self-awareness. Indeed, many addicts try to block out and suppress their sensitivity and self-awareness through intoxication. This process may be based upon a conscious element of insight and self-awareness. Some addicts consciously choose to avoid their painful feelings and perceptions through the medium of a mood-altering chemical. More typically, addicts and substance abusers are preconsciously or unconsciously aware of their various neurotic patterns of behavior. Addicted people are afraid of themselves. Therefore, they fear self-awareness.

The development of a patient's insight and self-awareness (Forrest,

1982) is accompanied by fear and intense anxiety. Personality growth and behavior change are potential results of insight and enhanced self-awareness. A psychotherapist understands this aspect of the treatment process. As such, he or she actively structures the treatment relationship in a manner which is conducive to the patient's development of a greater capacity for personal insight and self-awareness. This means that the patient must be helped in the endeavor of struggling with the pain, fear, and anxiety associated with greater personal awareness. This process is facilitated by two factors. First of all, the therapeutic alliance provides a relationship context which actively facilitates a patient's self-exploration and openness. The therapist's qualities of nonpossessive warmth, empathy, genuineness, self-disclosure, support, and concreteness (Truax and Carkhuff, 1967) play a very important role in the patient's evolving and growing capacity for insight and heightened self-awareness. Secondly, the psychotherapist's consistent use of the technique of interpretation within the context of the therapeutic relationship (Forrest, 1984) eventually elevates the patient's unconscious and preconscious self-oriented perceptions and processes to the conscious level of experience. Appropriately timed therapist's interpretations also help to modify the addicted patient's overdetermined use of repression and the avoidance defense system. It should be noted that these therapeutic strategies prove most efficacious after the addicted patient is committed to complete drug abstinence. Indeed, the paradox of successful psychotherapy with addicted persons is that the therapist requires the patient to be committed to total drug abstinence prior to the initiation of psychotherapeutic treatment!

Interpretation is the most fundamental technique in the psychotherapist's armamentarium for potentiating patient insight and self-awareness (Kernberg, 1975, 1980), but these are also facilitated by a number of other therapeutic strategies: reflection, clarification, exploration of feelings, confrontation, and suggestion. Psychodynamically oriented psychotherapy represents an approach to the treatment of addiction and substance abuse which utilizes all of these treatment techniques in order to facilitate patient self-awareness and insight. A basic tenet of such therapy is that increased or heightened patient insight and self-awareness are the essential ingredients in personality change and growth and behavioral change.

An initial treatment task is that of fostering patient insight in the explicit realm of drug use, abuse, and addiction. Addictive persons scotomize their relationships with mood-altering substances. The "drug–person" relationship is grist for the therapeutic process. Drug-dependent persons tend to manifest numerous neurotic insights and perceptions relating to themselves. Their perceptions of significant others and the external world also tend to be parataxic and generally distorted. The clinician must initiate the process of reality-oriented and rational perceptions, beliefs, and insights upon the part of the addicted patient.

Addicted persons deny that they are physicologically and psychologically dependent upon a mood-altering substance. The patient's insight is severely impaired in this realm. Most addicts and substance abusers are anxious and uncomfortable about the therapeutic process of exploring early parenting and familial experiences. Patient beliefs, recall, and feelings in respect to mothers and surrogate mothers are grossly distorted and lacking in insight (Forrest, 1978). The sexual and acting-out conflicts of addicts reflect a limited capacity for self-awareness and an insight deficit. Addicts manifest impaired and ditorted self-awareness in virtually all areas of human living.

One salient reason for genetic reconstruction work in psychotherapy with addictive persons is simply that of resolving neurotic perceptions, insights, affects, and cognitions of the past. It is even more important for the psychotherapy process to foster here-and-now insight and self-perceptions which are not parataxic and neurotically distorted. Recovery is contingent upon the patient's ability to learn new and more accurate insights pertaining to self, significant others, and the phenomenal world. Indeed, accurate self-awareness is basic to the recovery process.

Much of the work of psychodynamically oriented psychotherapy with addicts and substance abusers involves helping the patient better understand and deal with affects and feelings. The feelings and internal affects of the patient tend to be in the service of the addiction. Addicts and substance abusers cannot openly and productively explore their internal struggles and feelings early in the psychotherapy process. Therefore, an intensive focus upon feelings and affect is strategically appropriate during the middle and later stages of the therapy relationship. A premature and intense focus upon affect tends to make addicts run away from therapy (Forrest, 1984).

A major process goal is that of facilitating patient insight into narcissistically determined pathology. Indeed, it is imperative that the patient come to grips with his or her history of narcissistic injury (Lowen, 1983). The vicissitudes of narcissistic disturbance—which is global in terms of character structure, cognitive style, interpersonal relations, affect, and behavior—encompass the addicted patient's struggle with depression, denial, avoidance, anxiety, low-self esteem, guilt, megalomania, manipulation, and self-destruction. Resolution of the narcissistic pathology only occurs within the context of long-term psychodynamically oriented psychotherapy. Most addictive individuals are not emotionally capable of understanding their narcissistic disturbance early in treatment, but successful psychotherapy is contingent upon an eventual resolution of this pathology (Forrest 1983a). In-depth exploration and interpretative work and an intensive therapeutic focus on the patient's narcissism is basic to the middle and later stages of successful psychotherapy.

It is important to indicate that insight and self-awareness are not the only requirements for effective psychotherapy of addicts and substance abusers. However, a patient's capacity for personality growth, behavioral change, and recovery is quite limited in the absence of a psychotherapeutic relationship which fosters the development of accurate insight and self-awareness.

Maintaining an Addiction Focus

The traditional psychiatric viewpoint maintains that addiction and substance abuse are symptoms of underlying and more serious psychopathology (Forrest, 1978; Wegscheider, 1981). Hence many psychiatrists and psychotherapists are primarily concerned with treating an addict's underlying problems with depression, anxiety, and impulse control. These clinicians are far less concerned with the actual psychotherapeutic treatment of the patient's addiction or substance abuse. Accordingly, they do not usually maintain a primary addiction focus during the process of therapy.

A crucial modification in the psychodynamic psychotherapy of addiction is the maintenance of an ever-present addiction focus throughout the course of treatment. The therapist must continually explore the patient's historic and present use and abuse of mood-altering substances. An active and ongoing therapeutic exploration of the patient's feelings about using alcohol and other drugs is essential. It is helpful for addicted individuals to gain insight into the various mechanisms and conflicts that facilitate their addictive behavior.

One of the technical requirements of successful psychodynamic psychotherapy with addicts is the patient's commitment to total drug abstinence during the process of treatment. Therefore, it is also important for the therapist to explore the patient's thoughts and feelings about future drug-taking behaviors during the process of therapy. The psychotherapist actively reinforces the patient's commitment to a drug-free life style throughout the treatment process.

Addicts and substance abusers abuse chemicals in order to avoid and neurotically extinguish myraid unpleasant feelings and conflicts. The clinician uncovers, explores, and interprets the various genetic and present factors which contribute to the patient's pattern of drug abuse or addiction. This process fosters patient self-awareness and insight as well as trepidation, anxiety, and even fear. Anxiety is essential to personality change and growth (May, 1977), because it is closely associated with self-discovery. Psychotherapeutic modification of the addicted patient's character structure and overdetermined utilization of denial, distortion, repression, projection, and other primitive defenses often results in feelings of acute anxiety associated with unconscious and/or preconscious fears of decompensation. Drug abstinence can create a conscious fear of insanity or loss of control. More prototaxically, addicts tend to experience acute death anxiety subsequent to becoming drug-abstinent.

The process of psychodynamic psychotherapy with addicts and substance abusers fosters personality growth and change through the resolution of fear, anxiety, and pain. An ongoing and consistent therapeutic focus upon the addiction process is germane to long-term recovery. The addicted patient experiences a sense of "freedom from bondage" as he or she begins to grow and change through the mediums of fear, anxiety, and pain while totally drug-abstinent and committed to the psychotherapeutic process. Addictive persons eventually learn that they will not lose control and become insane following a prolonged commitment to a chemically free life-style. Indeed, the growth and personal discovery involved in this aspect of the psychotherapeutic process is essential to ongoing creative recovery.

Many psychotherapists fail to maintain a consistent addictive focus throughout the course of their treatment relationships. These same therapists consistently fail in their treatment efforts with addicts and substance abusers. The addict interprets the psychotherapist's avoidance of addiction focus in therapy as "permission" to indulge (Forrest, 1979b). Addicts and substance abusers will literally use any of the therapist's verbal messages, behaviors, and other communications in the direct service of their addiction. Therefore, the clinician must maintain a keen awareness of the messages which he or she communicates to the addictive patient relative to past, present, and future drug-taking behaviors. This matter also pertains to the drug-taking behaviors of the psychotherapist. Psychotherapists with drinking and other drug problems very quickly become the hopeless victims of their own countertransference pathology. Their treatment efforts are destined to failure, and they very readily become the instruments of iatrogenic psychotherapy.

Addicts and substance abusers do experience "slips" or drug-facilitated "massive regressions" while involved in psychodynamic psychotherapy (Forrest, 1984). In fact, it is highly unrealistic to expect most or all addictive patients to remain totally drug-abstinent throughout and following psychotherapeutic treatment. Drug-taking behavior by a patient during therapy can be an index of the appropriateness of the therapist's addiction focus. Frequently, the experienced and skilled therapist senses that a patient is setting himself or herself up for a regressive return to drinking or other drug usage. At these junctures the therapist actively explores and interprets the patient's regressive and self-defeating behaviors, cognitions, and affects. When "slips" do occur in psychotherapy, it is imperative that the therapist-patient dyad explore the various dynamics associated with the regressive episode. In these situations the psychotherapist must continue the addiction-focused aspects of the treatment relationship while at the same time perhaps strengthening or in other ways modifying the strategy of addiction focus. Addiction is a lifelong disorder. In accord with this reality, an ever-present addiction focus is essential to successful psychodynamic psychotherapy with addicts and substance abusers.

Patient Commitment to Long-term Treatment and Adjunctive Strategies of Change

Brief psychotherapy is of little benefit to chronic alcoholics, other addicts, and most substance abusers (Forrest, 1978; Silverstein, 1982). The psychotherapist openly shares this reality with the addicted patient at the time of treatment engagement. It is simply not realistic to expect a person who has been chronically intoxicated for thirty years to radically modify his or her pattern of drinking behavior following five to ten hours of psychotherapeutic treatment. It is even more unrealistic for the psychotherapist to believe that such a person will evidence significant personality growth and life-style change after a few hours of therapy.

Most addicts require an active involvement in psychotherapy for several months in order to terminate their addiction and evidence significant gain in other areas of daily living. Drug abstinence is a primary goal in the psychodynamically oriented psychotherapy of addiction and substance abuse. However, abstinence is but one of the goals of such treatment. The therapist explains to the addicted patient that a drug-free life-style, personality change, and life-style change are usually associated with an on-going commitment to the psychotherapeutic process. During the initial one to three therapy sessions it is appropriate for the therapist to openly discuss with the patient the matter of commitment to treatment. By the same token, the clinician informs the addicted patient early in the treatment process that it is highly unrealistic to expect to achieve drug abstinence, personality change, interpersonal conflict resolution, and life-style alterations following a few hours of psychotherapy. Some patients are overtly very resistant to making a commitment to weekly therapy for a period of several months. In such cases it is usually inappropriate for the psychodynamically oriented psychotherapist to attempt to initiate the treatment process. After an exploration of these issues within the context of the initial few sessions, the therapist may decide to refer the patient to another therapist, an agency, or a self-help group.

It is also unrealistic to expect all addicts and substance abusers entering psychotherapy to remain committed to treatment and persist to the stage of mutual termination. Even seemingly highly motivated addicted patients terminate treatment prematurely. Many of these premature treatment terminations occur after the patient experiences a "massive regression" (Forrest, 1978).

I have found (Forrest, 1975) that approximately 50 percent of chronic alcoholic patients remaining actively committed to outpatient psychotherapy for a period of six to eight months remain totally abstinent from alcohol for at least five years following treatment termination. Roughly 25 percent of this sample of chronic alcoholics have now been totally abstinent from alcohol for at least seven years. Emrick (1974, 1975, 1980) reports similar treatment outcome and follow-up data for alcoholics receiving a diversity of "treatments." As Pattison (1980) points out, treatment outcomes for alcoholics and other addicts are a function of the "matching" of patient with therapist, treatment modality, and treatment facility. Moreover, the successful psychodynamic psychotherapy of addicts and substance abusers entails a diversity of parameters beyond simple drug abstinence.

It is of paramount importance for the psychotherapist to share these basic realities of therapy process and outcome with the addicted patient. This procedure can contribute to the development of a working and productive therapeutic alliance by facilitating realistic expectations about the course of therapy on the part of both clinician and patient. The therapist can assess the addicted patient's readiness to make a commitment to therapy by exploring these matters during the initial sessions. Psychotherapeutic outcome is directly associated with the patient's ability to remain committed to the treatment process for a period of several months. Therefore, the therapist must reinforce the patient's commitment to treatment throughout the course of therapy. Commitment to therapy and change are ongoing dynamic issues in the treatment of addicted persons.

Psychodynamically oriented psychotherapy is not a "cure-all" for all addicts and substance abusers. All models and strategies of psychotherapy are limited. The model of psychodynamically oriented psychotherapy presented in this chapter is modified. Another salient aspect of this model of modified psychodynamically oriented therapy with addicts and substance abusers includes the patient's active involvement in adjunctive self-help modalities as an integral part of the psychotherapeutic process. Very early in this process the therapist actively supports and reinforces the addicted patient's involvement in self-help modalities such as Alcoholics Anonymous, Pills Anonymous, Narcotics Anonymous, a routine exercise program, weight control, diet and nutrition, meditation and relaxation, and perhaps organized religion.

The therapist and patient must explore these self-help alternatives on an individual basis. Some patients need the continuous support and confrontation provided by an involvement in a self-help group such as Pills Anonymous or Alcoholics Anonymous. Most addicts are in poor physical condition and thus need to be involved in a regular program of physical exercise. Some addicts and substance abusers are grossly overweight. The therapist and patient need to explore these various adjunct treatment modalities and develop an individually designed program of recovery for the patient. A few addicted patients resist involvement in adjunct self-help treatments, and such resistance is grist for the psychotherapeutic process.

It is important to point out that the psychodynamically oriented psychotherapists have not historically utilized adjunctive self-help treatment alternatives, but, as stated earlier, self-help modalities are essential to the successful psychotherapy of addiction and substance abuse. It is appropriate for the clinician to consistently and actively reinforce the addicted patient's involvement in self-help treatment, and, subsequent to the patient's termination of intensive psychodynamically oriented therapy, an ongoing and long-term involvement in Pills Anonymous, Alcoholics Anonymous, or other self-help strategies is recommended.

Summary

This chapter includes a discussion of (1) the basic historical perspectives associated with the psychodynamic theory and psychotherapy of addiction and substance abuse; (2) a current psychodynamically oriented theory of addiction and substance abuse; and (3) a psychodynamically oriented model of psychotherapy for addiction and substance abuse.

Psychoanalytic and psychodynamically oriented clinicians have contributed very little to the behavioral science literature dealing with addiction and substance abuse. Psychotherapists from these "schools" view the addict as an inappropriate candidate for therapeutic treatment. Many analysts and analytically oriented psychotherapists refuse to treat addicts and substance abusers. Therapists from a diversity of theoretical orientations tend not to treat addicts and substance abusers. Indeed, the vast majority of gestalt, rational emotive, client-centered, interpersonal, cognitive-behavioral, reality, and Adlerian therapists do very little clinical work with addictive patients. The clinicians who have developed these various schools of psychotherapy have not constructed their theoretical assumptions about the process and techniques of therapy via extensive clinical practice with addicts and substance abusers.

Psychodynamically oriented theories of addiction and substance abuse have been truncated and fragmented. A comprehensive psychodynamic theory of addiction is delineated in this chapter. Addicts have experienced pervasive narcissistic need and entitlement deprivation. The addict experiences profound early-life narcissistic injury. The interpersonally determined process of narcissistic injury continues throughout the addict's childhood, adolescence, and adult years. Narcissistic need and entitlement deprivation is etiologically associated with the addict's intense interpersonal anxiety, identity defusion, depression, dependence, orality, rage, obsessive-compulsive character style, sadomasochism, acting-out, paranoia, sexual problems, and guilt. The psychopathology of addiction and substance abuse involves the interacting mosaic of all of these characterological dynamisms.

Psychodynamically oriented psychotherapy with addicts and substance abusers entails (1) the establishment of a working and productive therapeutic alliance; (2) genetic reconstruction work; (3) fostering patient insight and self-awareness; (4) maintaining an ever-present addiction focus; and (5) facilitating patient commitment to long-term treatment and adjunct strategies of change. Modified psychodynamically oriented psychotherapy is very effective in the treatment of addiction and substance abuse. The relationship dimensions of such therapy provide the curative basis for patient growth and personality change. The techniques of exploring the patient's past in depth, fostering insight and self-awareness through active interpretation, consistently focusing upon the patient's addiction and addictive behaviors, and actively reinforcing the patient's commitment to therapy and adjunct strategies of change are the essential ingredients of effective psychotherapy with these individuals.

Modified psychodynamically oriented psychotherapy of addiction and substance abuse employs a diversity of behavioral therapy techniques. Additionally, the patient is encouraged to attend such self-help groups as Alcoholics Anonymous and Pills Anonymous. Patients may be encouraged to develop an exercise program, change eating and nutritional habits, and modify their life-style patterns.

Very few clinicians are trained and experienced in the realm of addiction treatment. Indeed, every addicted patient presents the psychotherapist with a multiplicity of challenges, caveats, and paradoxes.

Millions of people throughout the world are addicted to various life-threatening and socially destructive substances. In view of this reality, psychotherapists and behavioral scientists must begin to more actively attempt to understand and treat addicts and substance abusers.

References

Adler, A. *The Problem Child.* New York: Capricorn Publishing Co., 1963.

Alexander, F. M. *Psychoanalysis and Psychotherapy.* New York: W. W. Norton & Co., 1956.

Apfelbaum, S. A. To define and decipher the borderline syndrome. *Psychotherapy: Theory, Research and Practice,* 1979, *16*(*4*), 365–370.

Armor, D. J., Polich, J. M., and Stambul, H. B. *Alcoholism and Treatment.* New York: John Wiley & Sons, 1978.

Bauer, R. The use of trance in working with the borderline personality. *Psychotherapy: Theory, Research and Practice,* 1979, *16*(*4*), 371–375.

Bratter, T. E. Reality therapy training. Lecture presented at Psychotherapy Associates Fifth Annual "Treatment and Rehabilitation of the Alcoholic" Winter Workshop, Colorado Springs, CO, Jan. 30, 1979.

———. Advanced reality therapy techniques in the treatment of alcoholism and substance Abuse. Lecture presented at Psychotherapy Associates' Sixth Annual "Treatment and Rehabilitation of the Alcoholic" Winter Workshop, Colorado Springs, CO, Feb. 5, 1980.

Cameron, N. *Personality Development and Psychopathology: A Dynamic Approach.* Boston: Houghton Mifflin Co., 1963.

Catanzaro, R. J. *Alcoholism: The Total Treatment Approach,* 2nd ed. Springfield, IL: Charles C. Thomas, 1978.

Ellis, A. Rational emotive therapy training. Lecture presented at Psychotherapy Associates' Fifth Annual "Treatment and Rehabilitation of the Alcoholic" Winter Workshop, Colorado Springs, CO, Jan. 31, 1979.

Emrick, C. D. A review of psychologically oriented treatment of alcoholism. Part 1: The use and interrelationships of outcome criteria and drinking behaviors following treatment. *Quarterly Journal of Studies on Alcoholism,* 1974, *35,* 523–549.

———. A review of psychologically oriented treatment of alcoholism. Part 2: The relative effectiveness of different treatment approaches and the effectiveness of treatment versus no treatment. *Quarterly Journal of Studies on Alcoholism,* 1975, *36,* 88–108.

———. Perspectives in clinical research: relative effectiveness of alcohol abuse treatment. In S. V. Davidson (ed.), *Alcoholism and Health.* Germantown, MD: Aspen Systems Corp., 1980.

Fenichel, O. *The Psychoanalytic Theory of Neurosis.* New York: W. W. Norton & Co., 1945.

———. *The Collected Papers of Otto Fenichel,* 1st series. New York: W. W. Norton & Co., 1953.

Forrest, G. G. Transparency as a prognostic variable in psychotherapy. Unpublished doctoral dissertation, Univ. of North Dakota, Grand Forks, ND, 1970.

———. *The Diagnosis and Treatment of Alcoholism,* rev. 2nd ed. Springfield, IL: Charles C. Thomas, 1978.

———. Alcoholism, object relations and narcissistic theory. Lecture presented at Psychotherapy Associates' Fifth Annual "Treatment and Rehabilitation of the Alcoholic" Workshop, Colorado Springs, Colo., Jan. 29, 1979(a).

———. Negative and positive addictions. *Family and Community Health,* 1979(b), *2(1),* 103–112.

———. *How to Live with a Problem Drinker and Survive.* New York: Atheneum, 1980(a).

———. Alcoholism, identity and sexuality. Lecture presented at Psychotherapy Associates' Sixth Annual "Treatment and Rehabilitation of the Alcoholic" Workshop, Colorado Springs, Colo., Feb. 3, 1980(b).

———. Alcoholism, schizophrenia and defense. Lecture presented at Psychotherapy Associates' Eighth Annual "Treatment and Rehabilitation of the Alcoholic" Workshop, Colorado Springs, Colo., Feb. 1, 1982(a).

———. *Confrontation in Psychotherapy with Alcoholics.* Holmes Beach, Learning Publications, 1982(b).

———. *Alcoholism, Narcissism, and Psychopathology.* Springfield, Ill.: Charles C. Thomas, 1983(a).

———. *Alcoholism and Human Sexuality.* Springfield, Ill.: Charles C. Thomas, 1983(b).

———. *Intensive Psychotherapy of Alcoholism.* Springfield, Ill.: Charles C. Thomas, 1984.

Freud, S. The future prospects of psychoanalytic therapy. In *Collected Papers,* vol. 2. London: Hogarth, 1953.

Fromm, E. *The Sane Society.* New York: Holt, Reinhart & Winston, 1955.

Gunderson, J. G. Characteristics of borderlines. In *Borderline Personality Disorders,* ed. P. Hartocollis. New York: International Universities Press, 1977.

Hartocollis, P. (ed.). *Borderline Personality Disorders.* New York: International Universities Press, 1977.

Horney, K. *The Neurotic Personality of Our Time.* New York: W. W. Norton & Co., 1936.

Hountras, P. T., and Forrest, G. G. Personality characteristics and self-disclosure in a psychiatric outpatient population. *College of Education Record,* Univ. of North Dakota, 1970, *55,* 206–216.

Jourard, S. M. *The Transparent Self.* Princeton, N. J.: Van Nostrand, 1964.

Kernberg, O. F. *Borderline Conditions and Pathological Narcissism.* New York: Jason Aronson, 1975.

———. *Object Relations Theory and Clinical Psychoanalysis.* New York: Jason Aronson, 1976.

———. *Internal World and External Reality.* New York: Jason Aronson, 1980.

Knauert, A. P. The treatment of alcoholism in a community setting. *Family and Community Health,* 1979, *2*(*1*), 91–102.

———. Perspective from a private practice: the differential diagnosis of alcoholism. In S. V. Davidson (ed.), *Alcoholism and Health.* Germantown, Md.: Aspen Systems Corp., 1980.

Knight, R. The psychodynamics of chronic alcoholism. *Journal of Nervous and Mental Disorders,* 1936, *86,* 36–41.

———. Application of Psychoanalytic Concepts in Psychotherapy, MENN. Ball. I., 1937.

Lowen, A. *Narcissism-Denial of the True Self.* New York: Macmillan, 1983.

May, R. *The Meaning of Anxiety,* rev. ed. New York: W. W. Norton & Co., 1977.

Meissner, W. W. *The Paranoid Process.* New York: Jason Aronson, 1978.

Menninger, K. *Man Against Himself.* New York: Harcourt, Brace & World, 1938.

Pattison, E. M. Differential treatment of alcoholics. In Fann et al., *Phenomenology and Treatment of Alcoholics.* New York: SP Medical and Scientific Books, 1980.

Reik, T. *Listening with the Third Ear.* New York: Pyramid Books, 1948.

Reich, W. *The Discovery of the Orgone: The Function of the Orgasm.* New York: The Noonday Press, 1942.

Silverstein, L. Systematic suicide. Lecture presented at Psychotherapy Associates' Eighth Annual "Treatment and Rehabilitation of the Alcoholic" Workshop, Colorado Springs, Colo., Feb. 1, 1982.

Stekel, W. *Sadism and Masochism,* vol. 1. London: Liveright Publishing Co., 1949.

———. *Patterns of Psychosexual Infantilism.* New York: Washington Square Press, 1952.

Sullivan, H. S. *The Interpersonal Theory of Psychiatry.* New York: W. W. Norton & Co., 1953.

Sutker, P. B. Personality differences and sociopathy in heroin addicts and nonaddict prisoners. *Journal of Abnormal Psychology,* 1971, *78,* 247–251.

Truax, C. B., and Carkhuff, R. R. *Toward Effective Counseling and Psychotherapy: Training and Practice.* Chicago: Aldine Publishing Co., 1967.

Wegscheider, S. *Another Chance: Hope and Health for the Alcoholic Family.* Palo Alto, CA: Science and Behavior Books, 1981.

11

Individual Treatment of Substance Abusers in Independent Practice

HERBERT J. FREUDENBERGER

UNTIL RECENTLY, most therapists viewed the hardcore chemical abuser as not amendable to treatment in independent practice, and patients were limited largely to self-help groups or therapeutic communities (Freudenberger, 1975, 1976). The last fifteen years have seen some exciting breakthroughs: the work of Chein et al. (1964), Krystal and Raskin (1970), Zinberg and Robertson (1972), Khantzian (1974), Vaillant (1966) and Stanton and Todd (1982) has given impetus to the concept of treatment in private practice.

At the outset of this discussion, it is necessary to distinguish between working with patients from lower socioeconomic groups and working with members of the middle and upper classes. By and large, the clientele of an independent practice is drawn from middle and upper socioeconomic groups, and patients from these groups have usually sought treatment voluntarily or have entered treatment because they are under pressure from employers or members of the family. Their situation is often one of "If you do not seek help, you will lose your job," or "If you do not seek help, I will leave you." Young adults are usually threatened with placement in a residential facility and therefore come to treatment with a great deal of negativity and resistance and a "show-me" attitude. People from lower SES who manifest addiction problems rarely enter treatment with private practitioners. However, a few therapists in independent practice do treat such patients on a sliding-fee scale arrangement.

Factors in the slums (Freudenberger, 1981a)—such as degradation, emotional and economic impoverishment, the utilization of drugs as a substitute for an inadequate family, and the constant impacting of violence, prostitution, and criminality—initially make these clients poor candidates for exclusive treatment in private practice. It is realistic, however, once these individuals have terminated their compulsive drug-abusing cycle by participation in a therapeutic community, a methadone program, or an in-hospital treatment program, to consider them for follow-up treatment within the confines of private practice.

Freudenberger (1984) indicates there are significant factors that promote the middle- and upper-class person into treatment are the demands that are made upon them by family members, or they are requested by an employer to seek assistance once they are perceived as chemcial or alcohol abusers. The stress and burnout that has impacted upon them due to their desire for high achievement, performance, and sometimes setting impossible goals often set the stage for chemical abuse. The abuser is loathe to admit that he or she is involved to the degree that they are, but the pressure and threat of loss of employment serves as a valuable "motivator" for treatment. They enter treatment under duress, much like the adolescent.

In terms of working with adolescents in independent practice, Bratter (1980) writes that, "for the psychotherapist in indpendent practice, who work with unmotivated and self-destructive adolescent substance abusers, negotiating the therapeutic alliance and determining treatment goals can decide whether or not there will be any further relationship." Most adolescents who are seen in private practice, according to Norem-Heibesen and Hedin (1981), "manifest other forms of dysfunctional behavior." Activities such as dropping out of school, truancy, running away from home, theft, teenage pregnancy, and emotional problems—all contribute to their abuse of chemicals. The abuse, in turn, is often accompanied by impulsive behavior, irresponsibility, and other intellectual, cognitive, and behavioral malfunctioning. Each of these behaviors further are accompanied by attitudinal changes that range from negativism, low self-esteem to poor concentration. When an adolescent reaches private practice treatment it is often because of pressures from parents, school authorities, or the law. Once the authorities pressure the adolescent to seek treatment, the initial demeanor is not one conducive to promoting a positive attitude for the adolescent's remaining in treatment. It is therefore incumbent upon the therapist early in treatment to seek to promote a positive transference, and appropriate therapeutic alliance—an alliance within which the adolescent can function and continue treatment without feeling threatened, rejected, or dominated. Any deterrent factors or perceived threats may be used by a troubled young person to discontinue.

In many ways the adult middle-class person is significantly different from the adolescent. In addition to a chemical abuse, the personality dynamics that the middle-class person presents are usually accompanied by feelings of alone and loneliness, feelings of omnipotence, a sense of emptiness, not having an ability to be intimate and feeling depressed. These persons often refer to an overall sense of meaninglessness to their lives. Many are prone to impulsive behavior and are self-centered, narcissistic, self-destructive, dependent, helpless, and irresponsible. Also, many have affect deficiencies, use poor judgement, and do not feel authentic to, or with, anyone.

A major factor that needs to be overcome during treatment is to work on the individual's inability to be intimate. This is initially more profound for women than for men. Women, because of the sex-role stereotypes that have been attributed to them, often find that intimacy is a feeling that eludes them. Some of the drug dependent women are products of abuse, sexual exploitation, incest, and emotional neglect. Their drug abuse only serves to heighten their feelings of dependency, their inability to be assertive, and a sense that drugs are one way that they can rely on to avoid issues of life that often appear overwhelming.

Addicts of all socioeconomic classes believe that they have discovered a potent pharmacological solution for their agony, their fears, their frustrations, and their failures. They often feel lonely, empty, depressed, and are unable to form intimate relationships. Often they have feelings of omnipotence. Many are prone to impulsive behavior, are self-centered, narcissistic, self-destructive, dependent, helpless, irresponsible. They have affect deficiencies, use poor judgment, and do not feel authentic to, or with, anyone. They do not trust.

Khantzian (1981) offers some reflections on the ego functioning of alcoholics which is quite applicable to work with addicts. He states that "the alcoholic has been most vulnerable and impaired in two areas of functioning. One area involves functions of self-care, and the second area has been the alcoholic's inability to regulate his/her feelings." The issue of self-care becomes a profound one in working with addicts because the clinician must evaluate the client's capacity for reality testing, judgment, and rational decision making evaluation. When self-care, as Khantzian suggests, "is impaired, certain ego mechanisms of defense are prominent or exaggerated."

Treatment Procedures

Initially the private practitioner needs to evaluate the source of, and the purpose of, the referral. If the referral is a court- or attorney-recommended one, then the chances for initial success are low. This is because clients view the visits to a therapist as a major condition for their remaining out of jail. It takes much to motivate these individuals to commit themselves to treatment. In all cases their degree of involvement—how serious they think their problem is, e.g., threat of wife, husband, or job loss—will determine their treatment staying power and motivation.

Another component that I have found helpful in determining initial motivation is to ascertain who made the initial call—the client, or someone else. I have found it essential that the initial appointment be made by the addict, although it may be under duress. If the addict does not make the initial call, his or her staying power tends to be poor. Making the initial call gives some indication of the desire to seek out treatment, as well as giving a sense of how critically impaired this person perceives himself to be.

Once the patient has arrived, discussion centers around his or her degree of drug involvement. It is important to ascertain what kinds of drugs are being abused, the length of the abuse, and to what degree the drug is making inroads, of non-functioning, into their life. Some are able to maintain some job functioning, although they may be abusing cocaine, heroin, Quaaludes, amphetamines or barbiturates on a routine basis. It is not unusual for this type of client to walk in "high" in their initial visit. Of course when confronted they will usually deny that this is the case. Early in treatment, however, I point out to patients that if they arrive intoxicated they will be asked to leave a particular session. Talking to someone who is inebriated is often a waste of time because the individual may not remember what was said during the session.

The fee structure, the number of visits per week, and the length of the visits need to be clarified. A further initial request that I have found essential is that the client undergo a medical and dental evaluation, relatively early in treatment. This is generally not needed as much with the middle-class abuser as it is needed with individuals from lower socioeconomic groups who have less contact with medical personnel. This approach is critical, especially for long-term addiction-related problems, such as vitamin deficiencies, hormonal imbalances, venereal disease, hepatitis, dermatological problems, and/or dental decay. It is sensible for the therapist to establish a close relationship with a physician once withdrawal takes place, because of the medical complications that might occur during the course of treatment.

Dynamically, Freudenberger and North (1982) have recognized that most addicts are impaired in their capacity to regulate either their affect or ego functioning. They respond to many stimuli in impulsive, infantile ways, use poor judgment in their decision making, and tend to get involved in situations that are not thought out. One man, a thirty-year-old cocaine abuser of sixteen years' duration, tended to invite strangers to his home and then find to his "surprise" that many of his personal articles were missing after their departure. He is the son of a wealthy family and could not understand why anyone would steal from him after he had been kind enough to offer the hospitality of his home. He was extremely immature, and desperate in his desire to be liked and "cared about" by almost anyone he happened to meet in his wanderings about the city. He had extremely poor judgment, and the psychological testing that was done during the course of treatment indicated "severe affect deprivation." Addicts' impairment may include an inability to identify, relate to their feelings, tolerate frustrations, take initiative, be able to inhibit acting-out behavior, or cope with the anxious moments of daily living.

It is essential for the therapist to set the conditions of treatment in order to reflect a structured and consistent approach. Consistency is crucial to treatment, since the addicts' lives are replete with inconsistencies. They have often lived a life of minimum structure. Most of their homes reflect this. There is usually little or no food in the refrigerator, the home has not been cleaned in months, there is no laundry, or often no showers have been taken in weeks.

Most practitioners work with set appointments, within a prescribed time schedule. Initially I ask addict clients to arrive half an hour earlier than I would be able to see them. If this is not done, most tend to miss their appointments because they arrive too late, have overslept, have forgotten, or have a variety of other excuses why they could not make their appointment time. The resistances to treatment need to be presented and discussed with the client very early in the process. Once patients have become more consistent in their arrival, then the proper appointment time may be given.

As Bratter (1981, p. 509) reported:

> The avoidance-denial syndrome is prevalent. The more extreme pathological dependency on, and addiction to, chemicals can be seen as a desperate attempt to survive the painful and turbulent existences these individuals feel they have. This type of isolation creates a form of paranoia which needs to be resolved before any therapeutic trust can be established.

The resistances to treatment are ever-present during treatment and need to be continuously attended to. Clients will use all sorts of subterfuges to explain why they could not attend a session. Excuses such as "I forgot my money," "My cousin could not lend me his car," I thought you would not be here because it's a holiday," "I forgot the time," "I had a fight with my girlfriend and I was just too angry to come," or "My dog got sick" are just some of the stories that one hears during the course of working with substance abusers. Many times the reasons are a cover for avoiding what was talked of in a previous session, which could not be faced by the client. Not coming to a session may be a client's best technique of coping with anxiety, stress, or anger.

Because of addictive patients' ego deficiencies and their inability to concentrate for a reasonable period of time, scheduling for abbreviated twenty- to thirty-minute sessions seems warranted. This tends to diminish the frustration felt both by addicts—who may be nonverbal, negativistic, paranoid, untrusting, and noncommunicative—and the therapist, who desires to help. *Frequency of contact is essential;* five to six visits per week is a necessity in the beginning. This is necessary because the therapist is attempting to substitute himself/herself for the drug that is being abused, and is seeking to begin to establish a relationship with the patient. In time, the therapist will become the transitional object substitute for the gradually given up drug.

As to fee, it is mutually arrived at. I have found it appropriate to involve the client as early as possible in the mechanics of the treatment process. The fee discussion helps to ascertain another component of the client's motivation. In the beginning, daily payment is most appropriate. On a realistic level, it diminishes the possibility of the therapist's being cheated, and it helps the client to gain a sense of real "investment" in the treatment. If the client is unable to pay the complete fee, then a partial payment by him or her is appropriate, with the remainder paid by the family, an insurance company, or sometimes even the patient's employer.

A further initial request that this psychoanalyst has found essential is that the client undergo a medical and dental evaluation, relatively early in treatment. This is critical, especially for a long term abuser who has most likely been suffering from many secondary drug related problems, e.g., nutritional deficiencies, hormonal imbalances, venereal disease, hepatitis, dermatological problems, or dental decay. It is also imperative for the therapist to establish a close relationship with a physician, once withdrawal takes place, because of possible medical complications that might occur.

Initial treatment needs to be on an individual basis. This is in order to establish some degree of trust with the therapist and the therapeutic environment. It is important to indicate, however, that addicts, because of their infantile needs, readily find themselves in a dependent relationship with the therapist. Since most are ego-deficient, it may be appropriate to introduce a group therapy approach or include members of the family in treatment as early as possible. This allows, as Freudenberger (1982) has noted, for the individual to receive the additional support of members of the family, as well as members of a peer group. It also provides the therapist with indispensible information as to whether the patient is being honest and responsible, i.e., staying drug-free. Sometimes the client is informed that spot-check urine samples will be taken before a session. I believe that if the individual is living alone or is prone to consistent lying, the spot request for urine samples helps to keep him or her honest. Working out the arrangements for a 24-hour pickup by a local laboratory is the responsibility of the therapist.

The importance of peer groups cannot be overestimated. They may be utilized to monitor addicts outside of therapy, especially if members of the therapy group are committed to help each other. Reinforcement outside of therapy is further heighened if the patient is encouraged to join Alcoholics Anonymous, Gamblers Anonymous, or whatever self-help groups are available. This is in order for the self-help groups to serve as an additional support system for the individual.

Addicts who belong to self-help groups will also feel less threatened if they regress. The support of a peer or self-help group will better enable them to cope with the shame of failure, fear of rejection by the therapist, or a sense that all is hopeless. If the peer group support process is not used, there is a possibility that the addict might not return to treatment. This is due to the feeling of addicts that they will not "make it," as well as their tendency to believe that they have disappointed the therapist. As Wurmser (1981) suggested, "The increase in self-esteem is essential in the early treatment process" and its continued growth essential for the continuation of treatment. Another valuable source for ongoing support are the A.A., N.A., and G.A. groups. If the family is uninvolved, if a group process is either premature or unavailable in the therapists' practice, then the importance of the self-help groups cannot be overestimated enough. The self-help group serves to reinforce all that which is taking place in therapy. It assists the therapist to relieve some of the pressure on him/her especially if more than one addict is in need of so much energy and time at a particular treatment period. The members of self-help groups further serve as models for the individual, of what could be, if one works at it diligently. This therapist has found self-help groups to be invaluable in his work with the habituated.

As the patient begins to use less and less of the abused chemical or chemicals, a very crucial time in treatment occurs. As suggested, gradual withdrawal may need to be accomplished with the close cooperation of a physican. As addicts give up the drug, they tend to feel naked, exposed, shy, and hypersensitive. Some will become quite paranoid, or feel the loss of their sense of infantile omnipotence. This is a very important phase of treatment; it is here that many will seek to leave treatment, and it is at this point that many will seek to leave because of their anxiety, panic, confusion, and fear. As a teacher–colleague, Theodor Reik, once said to this therapist, "Never remove a crutch, before the patient has fashioned one of his own." It is at this point in treatment that the support of all involved becomes essential.

Additionally, this therapist has found that the patient and therapist will need, early in the treatment, to come to a resolution as to what are their goals for treatment—goals that both can agree upon. Is it a modification of drug abuse, or will it be total abstinence? Most habituated verbalize the desire to be abstinent as their best mode of self-control, but most will feel threatened if it is introduced too early in treatment as an ultimate goal. The alliance with and support of the therapist becomes a crucial element in the working through of the factors of the addiction. The need for support became most evident in this therapists' work with Vietnam veterans who were drug addicts, as Freudenberger (1974, 1975), has noted, where the continued support of the various members of the veterans' peer group were critical in allowing the working through of the problems predisposing to drug abuse.

The Role of the Therapist

The therapist needs to be an active participant in treatment. The therapist needs to be aware that many of the stories addicts relate about their life, and the rationalizations for their behaviors, may be symptomatic of both their personality and their choice of drug. Different dynamics exist for the heroin addict as opposed to the cocaine, amphetamine, LSD, or barbiturate abuser. Each has selected "his or her drug" based upon conscious, unconscious, and homeostatic needs. Amphetamines, for example, are usually abused by depressed individuals who are seeking to overcome their depression through the use of "uppers." Because they often have minimal insights into why compulsive drug behavior has become part of their life, ascertaining the nature of the drug and the rituals that accompany its use may often serve as crucial clinical insights into the dynamics of the addicted individual. Heroin addicts are often the products of an arrested psychic development. They have often not evolved or developed from the stage of infantile omnipotence to that to being able to delegate a sense of trust to another human being.

The analyst must act and serve as a transitional trust object for the patient. The active part of the therapist may be expressed in terms of verbalizing and setting limited goals on a daily, and eventually weekly, basis. Goals such as taking showers, eating regularly, and setting up a structure (e.g., attending self-help group meetings, or calling on the telephone if there is an urge to "shoot up") become all-important. This active therapeutic role is entered into because the addict has not developed a consistently reliable set of behaviors. Therefore the therapist must act as the first consistent and responsible person in the addict's life. If the therapist can not help the addict to break his or her life-style, then the addict will continue to cling to infantile omnipotence as the only source of felt safety and will make minimal, if any, progress in treatment.

Therapists, in understanding the personality of the abuser, need to have a good sense, and control, of their countertransference feelings, as well as an awareness of their potential for hopelessness, guilt, and anger—all of which might be generated by addicts' frequent regressions. Freudenberger (1979, 1981b) has discussed burnout, and the dangers of overidentification when working with addicts. The therapist who is treating addicts in an independent practice setting is prone to the process of burning out. The therapist's help, efforts, expectations, and identification with patients makes him or her vulnerable. Addicts are demanding because they require sustained ego investment, which concurrently can infuriate and deplete the therapist. Most therapists view themselves as dedicated individuals and high achievers. Part of the dynamic of a high achiever is to be a perfectionist, who needs to work hard, is compulsive, competitive, committed, initially needs to prove himself or herself, and may have unresolved feelings of guilt. Therapists may also be possessive and have a difficult time letting go of a patient as the patient makes progress. All of these are fertile ground for burnout of the therapist in work with addicts and for potential therapeutic failure.

The compulsive behavior of abusers often promotes within them an identity of being a victim. It becomes important for therapists not to fall into the trap of being or feeling victimized themselves. Addicts are often skilled liars, con artists who have survived by lying. If the therapist is seduced to respond to a crisis, rather than to the dynamics expressed in the behavior, the therapist may end up feeling angry, burned out, and emotionally "ripped off."

The overly dedicated and unaware therapist is especially prone to respond to this form of manipulation. The therapist will work harder and harder to reach this con artist, who may have no intention to make significant changes. The result: a frustrated, cynical therapist.

It is, parenthetically, important not to be seduced by patients' statements of progress, because they could be false, a flight into health, or a need to please the therapist. Initially, such comments often are *not* expressions of real change. The addict can feel threatened by progress and the possibility of returning to school, getting a job, or moving out of noxious relationships, and the resultant fear and panic can trigger an acting-out through taking more drugs. This may result when addicts' feelings of omnipotence are challenged, or they feel that they cannot meet the expectations that they believe the therapist or members of their families have of them.

Since the addict usually enters treatment with a minimum of coping mechanisms, a too-rapid intrusion into his psyche, by "brilliant" and insightful interpretations, may be so threatening that treatment is terminated before it ever started. Overly early intervention may promote panic and a flight from therapy. As Khantzian (1974) indicated, "a too early intervention that tends to ignore or deny the patient's real self, only serves to reproduce the patient's childhood experiences of not being acknowledged, or understood."

The patient's frequent display of helplessness, hopelessness, and fears of failure and defeat may subtly call to the fore the therapist's needs for omnipotence and desire to help. This can be counterproductive, and can hinder patients' ability to find themselves in their own space and period of time. Impatience for change, the need to see too early a glimmer of hope and change, is often a reflection of the needs of the therapist, members of the family, the court, or the referring corporation, *but not necessarily the patient.*

In sum, addicts may be treated in a private practice setting, but therapists need to recognize the tremendous wants, the deep sense of object loss, and the staggering ego deficiencies that beset the addict, as well as the many frustrations and countertransference issues that they themselves will have to confront. The reward, as always, is knowing that both the therapist and patient have made reasonable progress to accomplish what they set out to do together.

References

Bratter, T. E. Negotiating the therapeutic alliance with unmotivated, self-destructive adolescent substance abusers in independent practice: Some pre-treatment issues. In R. Faukinberry (ed.), *Drugs: Problems of the 70's, Solutions for the 80's.* Lafayette, Louisiana: Endac Enterprises Print Media, 1980.

———. Some pre-treatment group psychotherapy considerations with alcoholic and drug-addicted individuals. *Psychotherapy: Theory, Research and Practice,* 1981, *18,* 508–515.

Chein, I. G., Lee, D. L., Hill, R. S., and Rosenfeld, E. *The Road to H.* New York: Basic Books, 1964.

Freudenberger, Herbert J. The therapeutic community in private practice. *The Psychoanalytic Review,* 1972, *2,* 375–388.

———. A therapeutic marathon with Vietnam veteran addicts. *Voices,* 1973–74, 34–41.

———. How we can right what's wrong with our therapeutic communities. *Journal of Drug Issues,* 1974, *4,* 381–392.

———. The psychology of the Vietnam veteran and drug addiction. *Psychiatric Opinion,* 1975, *12,* 34–38.

———. The therapeutic community revisited. *American Journal of Drug and Alcohol Abuse,* 1976, *3*(*1*), 33–43.

———. The hazards of being a psychoanalyst. *Psychoanalytic Review,* 1979, *66,* 22.

———. The dynamics and treatment of the young drug abuser in an hispanic therapeutic community. In Richard H. Dana (ed.), *Human Services for Cultural Minorities.* Baltimore: University Park Press, 1981(a).

———. *Burnout: How to Beat the High Cost of Success.* New York: Bantam Books, 1981(b).

———, and North, Gail. *Situational Anxiety—Coping with Everyday Anxious Moments.* New York: Doubleday, 1982.

———. Counseling and dynamics: treating the end-stage person. In S. P. Whiton (ed.), *Job Stress and Burnout: Research, Theory and Intervention Perspectives.* Beverly Hills, California: Sage Publications, 1982.

———. Burnout and job dissatisfaction: impact on the family. In J. C. Hansen (ed.), *Perspectives on Work and the Family.* Rockville, Maryland: Aspen Publications, 1984.

Khantzian, E. J., Mack, J. F., and Schatzberg, A. F. Heroin use as an attempt to cope: clinical observations. *American Journal of Psychiatry,* 1974, *131,* 160–164.

———. Some treatment implications of the ego and self disturbances in alcoholism. In M. H. Bean and N. E. Zinberg (eds.), *Dynamic Approaches to the Understanding and Treatment of Alcoholism.* New York: Free Press, 1981, 163–188.

Krystal, H., and Raskin, H. *Drug Dependence: Aspects of Ego Functions.* Detroit: Wayne State University Press, 1970.

Norem-Hebeisen, A., and Hedin, D. Influences on adolescent problem behavior: Causes, connections, and contexts. In S. E. Gardner (ed.), *Adolescent Peer Pressure Theory, Correlates, and Program Implications for Drug Abuse Prevention.* Rockville, Maryland: National Institute on Drug Abuse, 1981, 21–46.

Stanton, M. D., and Todd, T. C. Principles and techniques for getting "resistant" families into treatment. In M. D. Stanton, T. C. Todd, and Associates (ed.), *The Family Therapy of Drug Abuse and Addiction.* New York: Guilford Press, 1982, 71–102.

Vaillant, G. E. A twelve year follow-up of New York narcotic addicts. Part 4: Some social and psychiatric characteristics of abstinence. *Archives of General Psychiatry,* 1966, *15,* 599.

Wurmser, L. Psychoanalytical considerations of the etiology of compulsive drug use. In H. Shaffer and M. E. Burglass (eds.), *Classic Contributions in the Addictions.* New York: Brunner/Mazel, 1981, 133–154.

Zinberg, N. E., and Robertson, J. A. *Drugs and the Public.* New York: Simon & Schuster, 1972.

12

The Clinical Practice of Group Psychotherapy with Adolescent Substance Abusers

Arnold W. Rachman / Richard R. Raubolt

Adolescent drug abuse is a significant social and psychological problem. To those working with adolescents today this may be an obvious statement. The state of affairs is not, however, currently reflected in the professional psychotherapy literature. Since the early 1970s, there has been a decline in professional interest in the problems associated with adolescent drug abuse. This is unfortunate, as the major burden of treatment in this area has fallen to paraprofessionals. While paraprofessionals are often effective, their insufficient professional training frequently leaves them without a broadly based understanding of human development and well-developed psychotherapy skills. Professionals often have much to offer in supplementing these skills. This chapter will seek to address these issues. We will describe adolescent drug abuse from both an intrapsychic and interpersonal context. We will also present our view that group therapy is the treatment of choice for adolescent drug abusers. Finally, we will discuss the practical considerations for successful group psychotherapy with this population, as well as the limitations and pitfalls of this treatment modality.

Adolescent Drug Abuse: Intrapsychic Considerations

The adolescent drug abuser, according to Bratter (1974), "attempts to reconcile his basic instinctual urges with the demands of reality through the use of chemicals." Since this drug-taking behavior is directed toward the pursuit of pleasure and reduction of pain, it is not surprising that, as Laskowitz (1968, p. 68) suggests, "the teenager usually presents a clinical picture of pervasive underdevelopment . . . emotionally, academically, vocationally . . . rather than a transient interruption of psychological growth occasioned by experimentation with drugs."

The distinction between chronic abuse and experimentation is a crucial one, as it points up, perhaps most clearly, the underlying developmental issues involved. Wieder and Kaplan (1969, p. 351) give a good description of the appeal of drugs to many adolescents: "In the matrix of anxiety, depression and physical discomfort engendered by the adolescent process, the regressive reappearance of magical thinking reinvests the concept of drugs with the seductive promise of relief without the need for active mastery and adaptation."

For most healthy adolescents this is a temporary experience, since they find that passive enslavement to drugs interferes with desire for active mastery, gratifying social relationships, and crystallization of their identity search. To the chronic drug user, however, there is a greater regressive disorganization during the process. Drug use is often begun in early adolescence and becomes the preferred method of conflict resolution. Weider and Kaplan describe this course of action, suggesting (1969, p. 351) that "intoxication at first offers a temporary resolution, palliating through alteration of psychic energy equilibrium. With chronic use, the ego becomes more compliant to id demands, more passive when confronted with anxiety, and increasingly relies on the drug effect as participant in its functioning."

Drugs for the chronic adolescent drug abuser often represent an attempt at self-medication. The user seeks to establish, via the repeated ingestion of chemicals, a psychological/physiological equilibrium. Such a state offers satisfaction and gratification, even if momentary, while also staving off, in the same temporary fashion, psychic distress.

Casriel (1973, pp. 204, 205) has referred to this form of adaptation as encapsulation:

> By successfully removing themselves from the pain of reacting to stress, [drug abusers and addicts] have detached themselves and spend their energy reinforcing, by encapsulating, their isolation to a nonpainful state of functioning. . . . Once this intrapsychic world with relatively little tension is evolved, the individual overtly or covertly fights anyone who attempts to remove him from his prison-fortress . . . from his encapsulative

shell of detachment. . . . The individual patient, though he hears cannot be reached . . . though he knows, he will not change.

The end result of this drug-induced encapsulation is an adolescent who is intolerant of frustration and unable to make satisfying personal relationships with either adults or peers. In the web of a "chemical cocoon" the adolescent developmental tasks of ego-identity formation, sexual role crystallization, and appropriate separation and individuation from the family have been suspended. In this vein, the chronic adolescent drug abuser may be described by the characteristics Brown (1978) developed in defining acting-out in adolescents:

1. Heightened narcissism, increased orality, and limited impulse control—the adolescent drug abuser is often demanding and egocentric. Little appears to exist for him or her beyond the gratification of physical and emotional needs, real or imagined.
2. Distortion in relation of action to speech in verbalized thought—communication for the drug-involved adolescent becomes pseudocommunication, "using speech to charm, attract and confuse, and much less often to reveal, explain and inform" (Brown, p. 463).
3. Acting-out (drug abuse) often in tandem with heightened visual eroticization. With the misuse of language, there is a reliance on the part of these adolescents on nonverbal communication. Particularly given the illicit nature of their activity, appearance becomes crucial, and a hypervigilant view of the world is often developed. This reliance on visual communication also reflects the underlying passivity of drug abusers; "on the outside watching the world go by," they have no direct emotional involvement.
4. Unconscious belief in magical action to gratify needs. While feeling unable to meet the developmental requirements of their age, many of these adolescents seek magical resolutions to conflicts through drugs. Often this belief is but a further manifestation of ego regression to an earlier stage of development, where "the supplier is often mother and [the] supplies are often mood food" (Wieder and Kaplan, p. 350). Drugs are attractive for their magical, relief-giving attributes.

Instead of making attempts at ego mastery, the chronic drug-abusing adolescent gives up. Sweeney, Tingling and Schmale (1970, p. 378) describe this giving-up reaction as including both helplessness and hopelessness.

Helplessness is defined as a feeling of being left out or abandoned where loss of gratification is perceived as caused by external events or objects. Deciding that gratification cannot be regained by active self-intervention the individual is forced to wait for some promising change in his environment. With hopelessness, on the other hand, the individual feels that he alone is responsible for the loss and that there is nothing he or anyone else can do about it.

The adolescent drug abuser has adopted a negative peer group affiliation (Rachman, 1975). Unable to achieve a personal sense of uniqueness, continuity, and affiliation by his/her own psychic efforts, the drug-abusing adolescent flees to a drug subculture. While making few emotional demands, this world offers a ceremonial group association complete with an esoteric language of drugs not often comprehended by outsiders. Perhaps most significantly, however, this affiliation, while tenuous, offers a sense of belonging, a second chance with a family. Unlike many healthy families, this family accepts aberrant behavior, requires little motivation and success, and values emotional distancing. It offers instead a place to belong where the sense of pain, despair, and hopelessness is masked and denied by the sheer force of shared group drug involvement. Drugs become the group's bond and claim to uniqueness and achievement. Unfortunately, our society today offers support for these false claims.

Adolescent Drug Abuse: Societal Considerations

Societal issues have been a prominent force in the continuing problem of adolescent drug abuse. In the 1960s, when drug abuse first recieved national attention, the civil rights movement was prominent, as was the divisive issue of the Vietnam war and concommitant issues of the draft and American foreign policy in general. Traditional cornerstones of the American culture, the family and church, were being attacked from many sides. The call was for "relevancy," and, with increased leisure time and affluence, there was a basic emptiness. Gratification of hedonistic desires was expected and society became focused on narcissistic satisfaction. There was, however, a basic optimism in the 1960s and the 1970s as far as adolescents and young adults were concerned. There was a belief that society could change. There was a belief that America should and could become more responsive to human needs. Racism, militarism, and poverty, it was thought, were problems only because of a callous lack of interest. In reality there were no problems, only solutions to be found.

Drugs represented this optimism initially, since the goal was to expand one's thinking and chart new courses with a sense of hope for the future. The expectations related to drugs have altered dramatically. We, today, have a generation of adolescents who have been brought up to think that nothing is more important than their hedonistic desires. Since there is little chance that these unreal expectations can be met, these youngsters often display bitterness, despair, and rage.

In essence, many adolescent drug abusers feel betrayed. They have seen and grown up with the Vietnam war on TV, with the numbing disgraces this country has been involved in, including Watergate. They have heard and seen the call for civil rights and societal change weaken and in some cases fall away, to be replaced with increased conservatism and self-centeredness. Quite often adolescent drug abusers, in addition to intrapersonal worries, do not possess any positive sense of this country or of the future.

The void being created by these trends, and by the demise of the nuclear family, is being filled by some of the muscial groups with a negative, hopeless view of the world. They are providing a voice for the despair and discouragement many adolescents experience. As a result, many of these adolescents band together and live out this message in feral packs. Many popular adolescent songs, fashions, and actions suggest angry, disenfranchised people. The anger is what becomes so self-destructive—it turns back on them. Many of these youngsters stick safety pins in their ears, wear torn clothing, and destroy their hair in self-directed anger. Banding together, furious at their parents and society, they don't know what to do with that anger. Turning it into a creative act by making music out of it is trying to communicate a message to adults: "Look, this is pain and this is anguish that we have, because of the way in which we see and feel our world."

The feral conditions, however, continue. Children are growing up disconnected from their parents, from positive peer group affiliation, and from society. They are searching for both affiliation and meaning. This, of course, encourages drug abuse, because adolescents need to work on and resolve their sense of ego identity. With no positive options in sight, they turn to negative, often chemical solutions. It is important to have positive alternatives for this resolution. When negative alternatives, or what appear to be no alternatives, occur, it increases the anxiety, confusion, and disorganization of the adolescent. In order to resolve this crisis, one can turn to substance abuse to relieve the pain and the suffering and to feel better. The simple fact of the matter is that drugs work—and to the extent that we make our adolescents vulnerable to pain and suffering, with no positive alternatives, we encourage drug abuse.

Adults often unwittingly glorify drug abuse for adolescents. We have to realize that when a place like Studio 54 in New York City receives publicity as a playground of glamorous Americans, where drugs are taken, this sends a profound message to our young people. This publicity creates a role model of adults abusing drugs as a desirable mode of living. It is also of interest to note that the same selection process that operated at Studio 54 has had to be implemented at many of the adolescent "punk rock" clubs throughout the country. These clubs have had to become selective because adults have been going there, apparently hungry for many of the same things as are our adolescents. They unfortunately are missing the message that many young people today are trying to give them. This demonstrates in dramatic form how confused our society has become about who we are and where we're going. In this time of profound societal change, we find ourselves in the unenviable position of having adults imitate adolescents even though the adolescents are saying, "Look, we're all screwed up." We need to develop favorable forums for ego-identity resolution where adult role models provide faith, hope, and direction. Therapy services offer one such place. In a safe, reliable, and accepting environment, many adolescents are able to face some of their painful feelings. Therapy can serve as a "life-saving device" (Rachman, 1975) through which a sense of personal meaning and authenticity may be developed. Group therapy, in particular, can provide the emotional context where both adult and adolescent can meet in a true empathic dialogue.

The Rationale for Group Psychotherapy with Adolescents

It is our view that group psychotherapy offers significant potential in addressing both intrapsychic and societal reasons for adolescent drug abuse. To fully appreciate the effectiveness of this approach to treatment, however, it is first necessary to understand the basic theoretical premises for the use of this modality with adolescents in general.

Adolescents often reveal very great fluctuations in behavior and attitudes, heightened by anxieties in developing a separate, stable ego identity and in mastering changes in drives. This turmoil and instinctual indulgence has made the adolescent very difficult to treat in both traditional psychoanalysis (Gittelson, 1948; Eissler, 1958) and individual psychotherapy (Noshpitz, 1963; Holms, 1964).

Group psychotherapy, however, offers special advantages in treating the disturbed adolescent by speaking directly to the above-noted resistances, and by recognizing the developmental tasks at hand (Ackerman, 1944; Brandes, 1964; Singer, 1974; Berkovitz and Sugar, 1975).

The adolescent, frequently weakened by inner turmoil resulting from very profound physical, emotional, and intellectual changes, often sees a therapy group as a reservoir of strength. Such a grouping offers support for independent strivings, as well as assistance in appropriate disengagement from parental figures. Additionally, many adolescents have had such difficult and punitive relationships with adults that they automatically take a counter-position to psychotherapeutic assistance offered by a adult. In a group, however, this defiance and rebelliousness is often counteracted by the feeling of group identification and the individual's realization that he or she is not exposed alone to the adult therapist.

Schulman (1952, p. 337) offers seven very explicit reasons for group psychotherapy with adolescents:

1. It is more convenient and inexpensive than individual psychotherapy for adolescents.
2. It is more easily accepted and less threatening to anxious and disturbed youngsters.
3. Group psychotherapy offers better opportuntities to work out social relationships in a live setting while serving to decrease individual resistance.
4. Group treatment permits reality testing in social relationships and provides the occasion to be accepted by peers and by an adult.
5. In groups, ego defenses are more easily broken in the protection of the group, which also permits the acceptance of the therapist.
6. A group approach offers opportunities to compare oneself with others and to understand and accept oneself.
7. Group psychotherapy with adolescents fosters the development of social interests and a willingness to accept group ideals or parental and gang ideals.

As we can see, one of the essential characteristics of group therapy with adolescents in the recognition of the central role of the peer group in adolescent development. The peer group often serves as the cornerstone during adolescence, as it offers a support system in a forum where adolescents can work for more highly developed and complete self-definition. It also serves as the crossroads for ego-identity formation, where one can clarify and begin to answer such questions as: What do I believe in or hold dear and cherish? What am I not sure of? Where do I belong? How do I fit in? How much am I willing to be known? What must I hold onto? Who makes my decisions? Who am I now and how do I accept myself?

This peer group influence in adolescence is capitalized on where other adolescents in a therapy group can coax, limit, and support, as well as share with and challenge, each other. The group is also able to provide sympathy and empathy, as well as assistance in controlling more effectively the acting-out behavior that is so prevalent during this phase of life. This effectiveness in controlling acting-out results from the limit setting that is an inherent part of the peer group, rather than being seen as arbitrary restrictions imposed by adults.

Similar thoughts are expressed by various writers on adolescent group psychotherapy (Kraft, 1961; Singer, 1974), but the potential impact and clinical implications of this position have perhaps been most explicitly stated by Berkowitz and Sugar (1975, p. 22) when they recommend group thearpy as means

> to support assistance in confrontation with peers; to provide a miniature real-life situation for studying change of behavior; to stimulate new ways of dealing with situations and developing new skills of human relations; to feel less isolated; to provide a feeling of protection from the adult while undergoing changes; as a bind to therapy to help maintain continued self-examination; to allow the swings of rebellion and submission which will encourage independence and identification; to uncover relationship problems not evident in individual therapy.

The most comprehensive rationale for adolescent group therpy comes from Erikson's monograph on ego identity (1959), where a developmental theory for the use of groups in the treatment of troubled adolescents may be found. As we have seen, a peer group affiliation is the crucial element in building a sense of ego identity. On the other hand, many adolescents are also threatened by a negative stage, identity confusion. Group membership becomes a "life-saving device." Adolescents will only develop their self-esteem by their own actions in a group of their peers that is meaningful, positive, and continuous.

In group therapy, adolescents can see and share in each other's ego-identity struggles. Such identification and mutual support leads to cohesiveness and trust, so that typical adolescent defensiveness is converted into psychological awareness and insight.

Group therapy also provides special experiences that foster and enhance adolescent development. Of speical importance in this regard is the belief that group therapy offers a unique arena to support the psychosocial moratorium (Erikson, 1959) so necessary to this developmental period. This adolescent moratorium is a period in which a lasting sense of "inner identity" is completed. This inner identity develops from an assured sense of inner continuity and a sense of social sameness. It becomes a bridge from childhood to adulthood, from what one was to what one is about to become. It also offers the individual a chance to accept his conception of the way he is recognized by the community.

Group psychotherapy with adolescents provides an opportunity for clarification and discussion of ego-identity issues on all three levels: interpersonal, intrapersonal, and philosophical. This may be accomplished by providing a moratorium that offers both peer and adult recognition in a relatively safe, supportive, and flexible environment.

Through such a process, group therapy can offer one avenue for a psychosocial moratorium by supporting a delay of premature adoption of adult roles and commitments and by encouraging free role experimentation and provocative playfulness.

Free role experimentation is particularly crucial in dealing with adolescent drug abusers. Such adolescents are in desperate need of developing new modes of positive problem-solving behavior and alternate forms of conflict resolution. Group psychotherapy, in particular, offers a secure arena to enter into healthy relationships with peers, as well as offering creative, growth-enhancing opportunities for psychosocial play. In essence, an ethos of action is created, where anger, frustration, and despair may be channeled in active, productive modes of behavior. Perhaps most succinctly stated, this action takes the group members' sense of hopelessness and challenges it, but it also gives them the same sense of excitement that they are seeking now in negative ways and turns that into positive excitement. The goal is the expressing of one's ideas in a powerful rather than a powerless way. Group therapy can offer the adolescent a sense of mastery over his or her confusion and disorganized behavior.

Surprisingly, given the scope of the problem with adolescent drug abusers, as well as the advantages of group psychotherapy with this age group, there have been few treatment procedures described in the literature.

Bartlett (1975) reports favorable results with multiple family therapy groups of adolescent drug addicts. While cautioning that this approach is not a panacea, she states (p. 280): "The M.F.T. group describes and illuminates the fact that this modality is helpful in reversing a trend where the patient and family are both in crisis and at the point of decision."

Zucker and Waksman (1972) report on the results of their inpatient therapy groups with young addicts. They report positive results, yet caution that the group psychotherapy program must be integrated into a total rehabilitation process. They also underscore the belief that group psychotherapy offers an active intervention that is necessary in helping patients bridge the gap from hospitalization to community placement.

Rachman (1975) suggests that group psychotherapy can provide an alternative to drug abuse by creating a positive context in which adolescents can find direction and meaning in a positive group affiliation. He goes on to suggest a variety of ways in which therapy groups can aid in this process:

1. Encouraging adolescents to bring their fantasies about drug experimentation before the actual experience.

2. Open, direct and honest confrontation of self-destructive drug abuse by both the therapist and the group.
3. Therapeutic exploration of actual drug experiences to find out the personal meaning to the individual involved.
4. Therapist sharing drug-related beliefs and serving as an ego-identity role model for alternatives to substance abuse.
5. Offering specific recommendations for curbing drug abuse, including total abstinence, reduction in drug abuse, or changes in drugs used, i.e., "hard" to "soft" drugs.
6. Encouraging extra group activities to supplement the treatment regimen, i.e., joining a drug rehabilitation program; encourageing family therapy sessions; supplemental individual psychotherapy sessions.
7. Developing and maintaining a positive emotional climate in groups where non–drug taking is considered virtuous. In essence, drug abstinence is reinforced as a positive, sought after life-style.

Bratter, perhaps the most prolific writer on group therapy with adolescent drug and alcohol abusers (1971, 1972, 1973, 1974a, 1974b), has combined reality therapy with confrontation in an approach that is reported to be highly effective. In describing his approach, Bratter (1972, p. 309) states: "Utilizing a confrontation/teaching/interpretive reasoning approach, the group demonstrates to the drug abuser the irresponsible and self-defeating aspects of his behavior. The individual becomes aware of the impact of his behavior, begins to understand the consequences of his actions, and attempts to become responsible to himself, others and society."

Raubolt and Bratter (1974), in describing the goal of this confrontation/reality therapy group model, suggest five sequential steps:

1. Eliminate overt self-destructive behavior (drugs, violence, manipulation).
2. Encourage (provoke) expression of current feelings (pain, fear, anger).
3. Operationalize current feelings in responsible, productive behavior.
4. Foster the development of confrontation, "responsible concern," and encouragement from group members (caring community).
5. Support independent, creative, self-enhancing thinking and action (art, music, political activism).

This emphasis on confrontation is drawn from the work of drug-free therapeutic communities directed in large part by ex-addicts. Bassin (1968), in describing this approach, suggests that what is perceived as a group "attack" is actually an act of love which is entwined with the assumption that if "we did not care about you or have concern for you, we would not bother to point out something for you that might save your life."

Rachman and Heller (1974), however, offer some caution and point out the antitherapeutic factors in this approach, particularly as it relates to adolescent drug abusers. They caution (p. 402) that

> there is a serious shortcoming within the theory and the practice of the T.C. (therapeutic community) in the understanding and treatment of adolescents. The experiences with the original population of adult addicts still pervade the thinking and functioning of most T.C.'s. Many programs report a high dropout rate with younger adolescents, which is directly related to this factor. . . . In addition, group practice becomes an antitherapeutic factor within the T.C. when the uniqueness of adolescent psychosocial development is not understood and incorporated into clinical practice.

A summary of the writings cited suggests that active, firm, consistent limit setting on behavior is important to the treatment of adolescent drug abusers. It is also important to note that adolescent drug addicts are often seen in a homogeneous group. Such an approach allows for direct confrontation of self-destructive drug abuse which may not be necessary or appropriate for other treatment populations, i.e., borderline schizophrenic patients, schizoid personalities, and acutely anxious, neurotic adolescents.

It would seem that an active/confrontation approach has merit with adolescents extensively involved in drug abuse, since it challenges their escapist methods of problem solving while also providing, in a therapeutic sense, involvement and excitement, which they appear to thrive on. For such an approach to be successful, however, there must be an understanding of adolescent development tasks (particularly a still-forming ego identity), and most importantly, a recognition of the individual ego strengths and limitations of each patient.

The Advantages and Limitations of Group Psychotherapy for Adolescent Substance Abusers

Substance abuse in adolescence is best treated by group psychotherapy, with certain qualifications. The qualifications concern the type of substance abuse; the intensity of the abuse; the ego strength and overall personal functioning of the individual; and the psychosocial environment in which the individual must function.

Type of Substance Abuse

The substances which are considered soft-core drugs are best treated by group psychotherapy intervention. These substances are the natural hallucinogens: e.g., marijuana, hashish, peyote, mescaline, all amphetamines, alcohol. The use of the so-called hard-core drugs—e.g., heroin, cocaine, LSD—presents a greater problem, but the experimental or curiosity-seeking use of hard-core drugs can also be successfully treated in adolescent groups. The labeling of substances as "hard-core" can be useful if it serves to caution the group leader to respect the powerful effects these drugs can have on the psychological and physiological functioning of the individual.

Although the old notion was that the use of marijuana is just a stepping-stone to heroin addiction, this is not widely accepted as either a scientifically verifiable behavior pattern or a psychologically effective device for scaring contemporary adolescents.

Adolescents today are very sophisticated. In some instances, they are more sophisticated about the drug literature and experience than the clinicians. If a clinician wants to discourage substance abuse, he or she must appeal to youth on the basis of informed, intelligent information without a panic reaction that insults the intelligence of the individual or causes a breach in the emotional relationship with the leader. This would mean reading up on the latest research on substance abuse as it affects individual functioning, and being knowledgeable about periodicals, music, and events which relate to the adolescent experience and drug use. We do need, however, to develop an ongoing "hovering attention" to the possibility that the use of hard-core drugs can have a negative powerful effect on the functioning of an adolescent with a still-developing ego and social patterns. What is more, in an adolescent with weak ego development, inadequate coping skills, poor family ties, and a negative environment, experimental use of heroin, cocaine, LSD, or any other powerful drug can become a habitual way to relieve pain, boredom, and inadequacy.

Intensity of Substance Abuse

The intensity of substance abuse is another significant factor in the potency of group therapy for adolescent substance abuse. The Drug Abuse Inquiry and Evaluation (Rachman, 1975) can assist the group leader in assessing the nature and intensity of substance use. The basic distinctions to be made concern "curiosity-seeking" use versus habitual use. Is the substance being used under nonpathologic conditions, experimentally or occasionally? There should be few indications of use in a regular pattern to relieve anxiety, avoid social problems, cover up personal inadequacies, or avoid coping with life's stresses?

Group psychotherapy can be very helpful in the nonpathologic stage of drug use, since it can act as a preventative measure (Rachman, 1975). Adolescents can ventilate their anxieties, adventures, and concerns with peers without receiving the overconcerned, sometimes hysterical, repressive reactions that well-meaning adult authorities, including psychotherapists, can easily be provoked into giving.

In our desire to help an adolescent avoid the pitfalls of drug abuse, and armed with special sensitivity, knowledge, and clinical experience, we are also susceptible to antitherapeutic responses. Sometimes being an expert in an area of human functioning contributes to an overly suspicious attitude and a zealous determination to "save" a youngster from a life of drug abuse. An adolescent group can provide a welcome antidote to our missionary zeal.

At the same time, on the basis of their own negative experiences, adolescents can appropriately caution a group member to crub experimental use of drugs. For example, an adolescent warning that experimentation with heroin can be a symptom of serious personal discontent is less likely to be rejected as an adult's hysterical reaction to a taboo drug. After all, the group member can speak from personal experience of the dependency, depression, and self-depreciation which can lead to heroin addiction.

Substance abuse which has become prehabitual or preaddictive can also be ameliorated by group psychotherapy. In these instances, the adolescent is regularly using some substances for the purpose of reducing anxiety, pain, inadequacy, or malfunctioning. While the youngster may not make the insightful connection between the increased use of a drug and a desired change in functioning, it is a compelling interpretation to the professional expert or an experienced drug abuser. Usually, youngsters at this point in their drug abuse behavior, when confronted with their prehabitual drug use, will respond by saying, "I know I shouldn't be taking that stuff every day. I've stopped using it for months and never missed it. I can stop using it anytime I want." These youngsters need to maintain their ego integrity by denying they are hooked on drugs, while asserting they are still in control and are not dependent children caught in a personal crisis from which they cannot extricate themselves.

Group psychotherapy alone is not effective with all levels of drug usage. It is not likely to produce significant change when the individual is habituated or addicted to a substance. Any serious substance abuse is a way of life, in which the individual is a prisoner of the habit.

Intervention must be dramatic and wholistically oriented. Only a drug rehabilitation program can provide the necessary direct, persistent confrontation (Forrest, 1982) necessary to break through the wall of denial which envelops the habitual substance abuser. It is also essential that the confrontation come from a group of peers who have been through the same life experiences, so that this confrontation is perceived as genuine.

Ego Strengths

The personality development and ego strength of the individual is another crucial variable for the use of group psychotherapy in the treatment of substance abuse. Adolescents who present serious personality problems (Forrest, 1983) in addition to their substance abuse need a psychotherapy experience. Drug rehabilitation programs rarely have the staff, experience, or desire to treat personality disorders on an individual basis or apply nonconfrontational methods. Severe neurotic, borderline, and psychotic conditions which are either the underlying cause of substance abuse or are its result demand ongoing psychotherapy. When severe substance abuse and severe personality disturbance are both present, it is necessary to work out a conjoint treatment program between the psychotherapist and a drug rehabilitation program. Actually, such a cooperative effort is not only in the interest of the individual substance abuser, but assures the success of both the drug rehabilitation program and the psychotherapy experience.

Degree of ego strength is a significant determinant both for inclusion in a group psychotherapy program and for application of confrontation. Being able to successfully function in interaction with others signifies a certain strength in ego functioning. When there are significant problems, concerning passivity, dependency, depression, mastery, self-esteem, and interpersonal withdrawals, it is difficult to come outside of oneself to either develop an emotional attachment or give to a group. When one of these factors is present in a significant degree or they are all present within an individual substance abuser, a period of individual psychotherapy may need to precede group participation. Depending on the extent of difficulty and response to therapy, conjoint individual and group psychotherapy may be indicated.

When ego strength is severely impaired, even the mildest and most gradual form of confrontation would be difficult. If an appraisal is made that confrontation is necessary and it could lead to personality disintegration, group therapy in a residential treatment center is advisable.

Psychosocial Environment

The psychosocial enviroment in which the substance abuser lives his or her life is a crucial variable in the overall treatment process. There are two primary group affiliations in the adolescent's world which affect the individual's rehabilitation—family and peer group. The family of a substance abuser often provides the antecedent conditons for alcohol and drug-dependent behavior. If the family, at the time of referral, is a primary source of substance abuse by example or by support, with no treatment affiliation (psychotherapy, self-help program, chemotherapy, etc.), it is unlikely that the adolescent will benefit from group psychotherapy. Therapy, however, can be helpful if the adolescent wishes to break away from the pathologic influence of his or her family and can use the group psychotherapy experience as a corrective family experience.

Affiliation with a negative, deviant, or pathologic peer group is, of course, one of the most serious deterrents to change in adolescence (Erikson, 1959). If a substance abuser's major peer affiliation is with a group of adolescents who are also substance abusers, group psychotherapy is not likely to be influential. Such an adolescent will perceive the group as having contradictory interests to his. If, however, the adolescent is or can be motivated to move away from the negative peer group, then group psychotherapy can be helpful. In the event that the adolescent substance abuser comes from a family where substance abuse has been ongoing, with no treatment affiliation, and his or her peer group affiliation is based upon the experience of shared substance abuse, referral to a drug rehabilitation program seems to be the treatment of choice. The drug rehabilitation program mandates removal from the negative peer group and parallel treatment involvement of the parents.

When group psychotherapy is employed, it is essential to encourage the adolescent to identify with the drug-free group philosophy and to question the motivation of peers who are encouraging self-destructive behavior. In addition, the family of the adolescent abuser must be involved in the therapy process in some constructive, cooperative manner.

The Group Therapist's Philosophy Regarding Substance Abuse

Although we are suggesting that the traditional therapeutic community rigidly adheres to a concept or philosophy of human behavior concerning the meaning of substance abuse and personality and behavior change, we are not suggesting that a philosophy about substance abuse and its amelioration is not needed. It is an essential part of group psychotherapy to have a philosophy about substance abuse, and to impart that notion in a direct, empathetic manner to adolescents. The leader's views, as has been mentioned, should be based on up-to-date information and thoughtful synthesis of the "advantages" and disadvantages of drug-taking behavior. By "advantages," we mean it has to be admitted that:

1. Drugs do have "positive" effects on the feelings, thoughts, and behavior of individuals. By "positive," we acknowledge that the ingestion of chemical and natural substances often produces an immediate alteration in consciousness associated with a feeling of well-being, an absence of anxiety, a diminution of conflict, a sense of euphoria, a feeling of power, a lifting of depression (depending upon the substance used).
2. The reason substances are used and abused is *their potency* to alter the mood, feeling, and behavior of individuals.
3. We are all desirous of and susceptible to wanting some substance to immediately and potently alter our modds, conflicts, anxieties, etc. There is nothing inherently "wrong," "bad," or "evil" in having such a desire. Rather, it is basic to human nature. When an individual is anxious, depressed, conflicted, unhappy, etc., it is natural to want to alleviate these negative states and feel happy, euphoric, peaceful.
4. It is *easier* to alter one's feelings, moods, and behavior by swallowing a pill, smoking a pipe or cigarette, sniffing some powder, or injecting a substance into the vein than it is to acknowledge, explore, confront, and work through the personal problem by the natural means of direct verbal dialogue with one or more caring individuals.
5. If substance use continues, the individual will be able to "forget" about his or her problems because an artificial consciousness is produced in which problems don't seem to exist, pain is erased, anxiety is diminished, and feelings are suppressed. After a while one enters a kind of twilight zone where the artificially produced state of consciousness becomes more real, more desirable, more interesting, more acceptable, and more peaceful than daily life.
6. Everyday living can be a "drag"—boring, difficult, conflictual, dull. There are days that are a washout. There are very few natural means of coping with such days that can match a drug's

capacity to quickly and easily alter the negative experience. There are some (like sex, affection, food, diaglogue, recreation), but they all take more effort and are not guaranteed to alter mood.

7. Substance ingestion can invariably guarantee the production of the desired effect. Chemical substances are manufactured for the express purpose of altering mood and behavior in a particular way. People and the environment are more complex than substances, and don't go directly to the brain or bloodstream. Sometimes they do the opposite of what you want them to do. Therefore, turning to people increases the possibility of dealing with disappointment and frustration.
8. It is "easier" to deal with life during these difficult times of family, economic, political, and social conflict by turning to drugs. There are so many problems to cope with in everyday life, with so few easy solutions, that drugs are a very tempting nonconflictual solution.

Admitting to the temptation and behavior-altering capacities of drugs does not mean that the group psychotherapist endorses substance use or abuse. It simply means that we are willing to confront reality square in the face; to face our adversary directly and honestly. Youth can only be influenced by honest, direct, vulnerable dialogue. They will not listen to, or be influenced by, defensive, hypercritical, uneducated, or dishonest interaction. Engaging them in direct and honest dialogues will also provide a role model for compassionate confrontation on difficult issues between caring significant others. It is also necessary to provide adolescents with some statement of a philosophy which challenges substance abuse. The following is a composite "drug rap" the group therapist can offer in total or in part when it is necessary to expound a stand on substance abuse. It should be clear that all adolescents want, need, and expect significant others, psychotherapists in particular, to make clear their philosophy regarding substance abuse. It is through the adult's clear, nonjudgmental, nonpunitive statement of a drug philosophy that an adolescent group can begin to rethink their involvement in substance abuse.

"I guess it is time for my lecture on drugs. Here's where I stand on drugs. I am basically a puritan when it comes to drug use. I firmly believe that any introduction of any chemical substance into my body is undesirable, and I try to avoid it whenever I can. I see all chemical substances introduced into my body as potential poisons. Any chemical or drug can become a body poison, if it is abused. By chemicals or drugs, I mean all drugs, everything—aspirin,

Alka-Seltzer, sleeping pills, tranquilizers, penicillin, Allerest, nicotine, alcohol, grass, acid, speed, goof balls, dope. Of course, there are some drugs that I take at some time or other: for example, aspirin, Excedrin, Allerest, alcohol, nicotine. So, I am also a drug user. But I try not to cop out. I try to be honest with myself. When I have a headache, nine times out of ten it's because of tension, anxiety. I'm probably pissed off about something I don't want to admit to. I should really sit down and have a talk with myself, and find out what (and who) I am angry at. Sometimes talking with myself works; sometimes it doesn't. I have to live with it not working all the time.

It's important to admit to yourself that taking drugs is a kind of copout—a magical, chemical, fairy-tale way of not dealing with the real thing that is bothering you. Take a look at TV any night and see how much of America and the adult population cops out and is into drugs. Commercials for aspirin, antacids, sleeping pills, and tension-relieving pills are all examples of how uptight many adults are, how much anxiety they have, and how much they turn to pills and drugs to get relief.

"I am not for smoking grass, on a regular basis, any more than I am for taking alcohol on a regular basis. Smoking grass or taking a drink on a recreational basis, on the weekends, occasionally at a party, to get high and feel good, and be part of the good time everyone is having, is no big deal. I've done that in the past and will probably do so in the future. But there is a big difference between being able to get high when you're under control and getting high because without drugs you can't enjoy a party or you don't feel comfortable relating to people. Any adult who needs a drink or two to feel comfortable or enjoy a party is in the same negative place as a teenager who smokes a joint before going to a high school dance. If you need to smoke a joint each time you go to a party and you are not free to deal with this situation without it, you have a problem you are not facing.

"I view all chemicals which are manufactured, synthesized, or created in home laboratories to be poisons, which should not be taken into the body. Any substance which can significantly alter body chemistry is potentially dangerous. *These drugs do cause dependence and habituation.* This list would include uppers, downers, tranquilizers, LSD, THC, STP, DMT, and whatever is the latest craze in drug abuse. Cocaine, although not physically addictive, *does cause serious dependence and habituation.* I abhor the glamorous image that cocaine has gained through its association with the "jet set," athletes, and the rich and famous. It is one of the most serious negative role models in our culture. Influential adults enjoying the recreational use of cocaine and promulgating it as an important aspect of their life-style provide adolescents with a desire to emulate serious drug abuse as a part of the *rites de passage* to adulthood and success.

Heroin is *physiologically addictive and psychologically demoralizing.* Any experimentation with this substance can lead to dependence, so that you lose control over the situation, and the drug controls you. If you feel the need to take this substance, you are in trouble. I urge you to talk to me and the group about it immediately. There are other ways to deal with your problems that can make you feel better and will not cost you your life."

Confrontation and Drug Rehabilitation

Confrontation as a therapeutic tool was pioneered in the drug rehabilitation movement for use with addicted individuals from disadvantaged backgrounds. Bratter (1972) has outlined his application of confrontation in working with difficult and unmotivated adolescent and young adult substance abusers from privileged families. Both the traditional approach to confrontation practiced in drug rehabilitation and Bratter's variation need to be still further adapted in order to be used in group psychotherapy with middle- or upper-class youngsters who have mild or moderate substance abuse problems.

All drug rehabilitation programs and most clinicians who work exclusively with substance abusers feel that confrontation is the most effective—indeed the only—clinical tool for changing serious substance abuse. While this position has both clinical and theoretical merit, we believe it has been overstated. The sole reliance on confrontation has actually produced a negative and antitherapeutic condition called "attack therapy" (Rachman and Heller, 1974).

Attack therapy develops from the sole reliance on confrontation as therapeutic intervention because:

1. In a confrontational atmosphere, individuals are often psychologically assaulted. Individuals who are rehabilitated from substance abuse can pay the price of losing their dignity, their freedom to disagree, or their sense of independence and opportunity to think, feel, or behave in a unique manner.
2. The mandate is to conform to a strict, unflexible code of behavior and philosophy known as "The Concept."
3. Confrontation is often used before a working alliance is developed.
4. There is a lack of therapeutic flexibility, so that a variety of helpful interventions are not integrated along with confrontation.
5. A ritualistic interaction develops in which individuals confront each other over and over again without genuine internal change occurring.

Members learn the "cop-to game" in response to attack. They learn to admit to transgressions in behavior in order to get the group leader, the members, the staff, and the administration "off their back." Confrontation when used exclusively encourages an increase in tension, anger, hostility, *and* resentment, to the exclusion of positive feelings, empathy, concern, or caring. The leader in such groups is "backed into a corner" where he or she escalates the use of confrontation, when at times support, dialogue, and exploration of family interpersonal or personal issues would be more helpful. The confrontation group experience resembles a harassment procedure or, at worst, brainwashing.

As a result of the exclusive use of confrontation, group participants feel attacked rather than helped to understand their substance abuse problems. They learn to admit to their problems as a way of placating the leader and their peers, as well as means of appearing to be benefiting from the group experience. They leave the group harboring great resentment toward the leader and the experience, vowing never again to be part of a therapeutic group experience. This negative side effect to the use of confrontation is likely to continue because of two basic issues. First, drug rehabilitation programs rely on group leaders who are graduates of their program but who do not receive any academic coursework or formal training in counseling or therapy. In addition, the drug rehabilitation community is often either disinterested in or hostile to a cross-fertilization of ideas and techniques with the psychotherapy community.

The Caring Confrontation

The basic technique and clinical practice for maximally effective group psychotherapy centers around creating a therapeutic climate which fosters direct confrontation of the substance abuser in an empathetic atmosphere of genuine concern, compassion, and caring. The uniqueness of group psychotherapy is centered in the leader's capacity to be "tough and tender." This is a special synthesis of the values and lessons learned from the drug rehabilitation movement and the contributions of traditional psychotherapy (despite the latter's failure to effect a significant change in serious substance abuse). The contribution of the drug rehabilitation movement is: (1) the use of confrontation to peel away the layers of defense against the awareness of the destructive effect of substance abuse; (2) the use of peers as the agents of change rather than traditional authority figures; (3) a here-and-now experimental approach to the individual's present functioning; (4) the realization that serious substance abuse involves a life-style and an identity which consumes the individual; (5) insistence that before personality change can occur, abstinence and a concentrated focus on the drug-taking behavior must be forthcoming; (6) insistence that the individual develop a sense of responsibility for his or her self-destructiveness and drug-oriented behavior; (7) the use of a total group approach as the treatment of choice for substance abuse; (8) the use of everyday nontechnical language in discussing psychological issues in personality functioning; (9) the development of the intense confrontation group to break open the wall of denial and defensiveness in habituated and addicted individuals.

Contributions from psychotherapy include both theoretical and clinical concerns about adolescent development. The use of confrontation as a major tool in helping adolescents deal with drug abuse is related to the development of active psychotherapy techniques for adolescents (Rachman, 1982). Greater activity and action in the process of psychotherapy has been recently accelerated by the human potential movement, drug rehabilitation programs, and clinical work with difficult patient populations. Interestingly enough, adolescent group psychotherapy originated from the application of traditional psychoanalytic precepts in an active manner to help disadvantaged and delinquent youngsters (Raubolt, 1979). The field lost sight of its active therapeutic roots as it strived to imitate adult therapy models which had established traditional psychoanalysis as the ideal guideline for therapeutic behavior.

Confrontation (Forrest, 1984) is a modern technique geared to helping adolescents own and explore self-destructive impulses which are denied to their awareness. It is particularly suited for helping adolescents face their self-destructive drug-abusing behavior. In fact, as drug rehabilitation has demonstrated, confrontation is the most significant tool for helping serious drug abuse. By expressing approval of confrontation, we are making a specific statement about the therapeutic value of an active, involved, and concerned psychotherapist. We also believe that to remain "neutral," "passive," or "solely interpretive" in response to drug abuse is antitherapeutic. The analogy that best suits this situation is the role and responsibility of "good" parents. A good parent may need to intervene, sometimes dramatically, in a child's life.

With these considerations in mind, we need to distinguish the conditions under which confrontation is best practiced to meet the needs of adolescents:

1. Confrontation is seen as one important parameter within the array of active or action techniques a psychotherapist can employ to help adolescents face their self-destructive behavior.
2. The use of confrontation is a judgment made by the leader based upon the personality structure of the individual and the group. For example, if an adolescent has a tendency to develop a paranoid attitude to a group confrontation, it behooves the leader to find a more suitable intervention to deal with the problem. The individual's need has priority over the technique.
3. Flexibility of leader and group functioning is encouraged. Other

interventions may be necessary to prepare for a confrontation, to deal with the resistance to confrontation, and to deal with the aftermath of the confrontation.

4. Confrontation often becomes necessary under special circumstances, when other responses (empathy, interpretation, information giving, etc.) do not deal effectively with the problem.
5. Confrontation is necessary when the individual's functioning is being seriously undermined by substance abuse.
6. Confrontation, although a deviation from standard psychotherapeutic technique, has a developing tradition in contemporary psychotherapy with the "difficult patient" (Adler and Meyerson, 1973; Buie and Adler, 1972; Corwin, 1972).
7. Several types of confrontation are helpful with adolescents:
   a. *gradual confrontation:* ongoing challenge of an individual by the group or leader, geared to the individual's capacity to integrate interventions. There is no emergency situation or immediate need to change.
   b. *intensive confrontation:* persistent "therapeutic pressure" is applied to an individual or group to face the substance abuse issue. The situation is considered very serious, approaching an emergency. Change is considered necessary.
   c. *the "showdown session":* the substance abuse issue is an emergency situation. Immediate, dramatic action is necessary. The entire session is devoted to intense confrontation, with the goal of a breakthrough in behavior. Usually, a time-extended session is necessary for this procedure.

The material to follow, an example of a composite session in adolescent group psychotherapy, illustrates the use of intense confrontation in a showdown session. Confrontation was used to attempt to persuade an adolescent substance abuser to admit to his drug habit and subsequently to accept a referral to a drug rehabilitation program.

A Composite Session

The therapist felt Josh's deep emotional distance. It was an extremely negative sign in a group that was as emotionally alive as this one. He wondered if it could indicate emotional disturbance. On the other hand, it could be an indication of continued drug use. Intuitively, he decided to go with the possibility that Josh was stoned.

"Josh, I'm going to lay something on you that'll probably piss you off, but I feel it's time to get into it," the therapist began.

"I'm getting sick of this," Josh backed off. "Just leave me alone."

"Sorry, Josh, I'm not going to leave you alone. I'm not trying to hurt you, but I feel there's something going on that you're not talking about, and it's getting in the way of your being part of the group right now. So I'd like to help bring it out in the open."

"Who am I to stop you when you go into your big authority number?" Josh was trying to bait the therapist.

"Here it goes," the therapist told Josh. "I think you've been on drugs during the entire marathon. You came up high and you've stayed high. My guess is that what Judy picked up this morning was that you were on downs. What's more, I think you've come stoned to the regular group sessions too."

The group felt stunned. They may have had their suspicions, but no one would have dared to blow his cover like this. It was almost an unspoken pact between them. There are certain things you don't talk about, but deep down they knew this had to come out, and it took the pressure off them to have a therapist who could handle it.

Josh's only response was an angry silence. The group leader knew he'd have to come down even harder, even if it meant alienating the rest of the group.

"Listen, I want an answer. What kind of shit are you on?"

"Hey, what are you? Some kind of Nazi? Fuck you."

"I said I want an answer."

"My answer is fuck off. Go pick on someone else for a change."

"No way, Josh. Right now it's you and me, and I don't want anyone else coming into this. I know the answer anyway; you're a junkie, man. You're probably strung out on smack today. That's why you're dragging your ass around. If that's the way you are every morning, then you've been hooked on heroin for years. What bullshit you handed me when I first saw you. You're a fucking liar. And I don't give a shit if you don't tell me. I don't trust you anyway."

Josh looked white and shaky now. "You're up your ass. I'm no junkie. And who cares what you think. You don't know shit about drugs anyway."

"I know a junkie when I see one. Every time I see you, you look strung-out. Your eyes are blurry. You walk like your feet are made of lead. You take twenty years to stay one sentence. Your energy is always shot to hell. And the only time I ever saw you get excited was the time you got drunk at our Christmas party. You're not only a junkie, Josh, you're an asshole. You've been sitting in this group over four months. You still don't give a shit about helping yourself."

Josh's defenses were beginning to crumble. The attack had finally reached his emotions. It looked like Josh was about to cry or scream.

"Hey, junkie, don't cry. If you're pissed, get angry. Let it out."

A strangled noise, half sob, half scream, pushed out of Josh's throat.

"Let it out, Josh. I can take it." He meant it. The attack was over, but he didn't want Josh's feelings to dissipate.

"Let me alone, let me alone," Josh moaned weakly.

"No, I won't let you alone. You won't get me off your back until you let it out. I'm not your parents. You can't fool me or turn me off. I'm not going to lay off till you tell me the truth."

"No," moaned Josh. "I can't take any more."

"You'll have to take it. I won't stop till you cop to your habit."

"You fucking bastard," Josh fought back. "Stop playing with my mind."

"Your're the one who's fucked up. You're the junkie who's playing the games. You're the one who's fucked me over. You've been lying to me all year."

"All right, I'll tell you the truth." Josh still sounded pleading. "I haven't stopped smoking pot. I can't get through a day without it. I'll cop to smoking a joint before sessions, but that's all, man. I'm not on smack. Nothing like it." Josh hoped that was all the punishment he'd have to take.

"What bullshit. Don't think you can tell me you're just a nice middle-class pot-head. I know a stoned junkie when I see one."

"I'm trying to come clean, and you just shoot me down again," Josh protested. "What do you want, my blood?"

"You can't throw me a bone with this marijuana crap. I want the truth. But obviously you're not going to be honest, so I'm going to have to take a more drastic step."

Josh was in a panic now. He had no idea of what the therapist was going to do, but he was frightened to death of it. The whole group, including the co-therapist, were alarmed.

The male therapist stood up. He looked intense. Wayne tensed to physically defend Josh. Judy felt panicky, Cathy had stomach cramps, and Maria was about to burst into tears.

"Okay, junkie. I know you've got the stuff. I'm going to search your luggage and find it."

As the therapist took the first steps, Josh struggled to his feet. "Touch my stuff and I'll kill you."

The therapist kept on walking toward the loft and Josh rushed after him shouting, "No, don't touch my stuff! I'll tell you everything you want to know."

At this point, the theapist took hold of Josh in the middle of the circle. "Let's have it out right now. What are you on?"

"I'm not on heroin," Josh tried to bargain.

"I said tell me what the fuck you're on."

Josh couldn't keep it together any longer. He began to choke and cried out, "Okay, you fucking bastard. I'm on pills; I take downs all the time. If you had my life, that's what you'd do. How else can I get through the week, including your fucking therapy sessions. And yes, bastard, I do take smack, but only when I can get it on the weekend."

"I've heard that weekend heroin bullshit before."

"I've told you the truth!" Josh screamed back. "It's the goddamned truth! That's it. There's nothing more."

Suddenly Josh's desperate rage turned to a desperate sadness and he began to weep uncontrollably, crying his guts out. "My whole life sucks, and I know it. Don't make me go through any more of this. There's nothing more. I've told you everything." He bent over, heaving with sobs.

The therapist said nothing. He knew he'd heard the truth. The confrontation was over. He stepped toward Josh and reached out to him. Josh looked up, hesitated for a moment, and then fell into his embrace, hanging onto him for dear life. He continued to sob for what seemed an hour.

The aftermath of the confrontation interaction is an integral part of the group therapeutic process. It is necessary for the therapist to practice flexible technique and now shift focus to become supportive, empathetic, and interpretative (Forrest, 1982). In so doing, the therapist helps the patient deal with present defensive behavior and characteristic behavior patterns, the origins of the substance abuse problem and its relationship to family psychodynamics, and the re-creation of the personal and interpersonal dynamics as they were re-created in the group therapy process.

The group therapist also explores the meaning and psychodynamics of the confrontation session with the group. The member who was confronted, and all the other group members, are encouraged to reveal and explore their own particular reactions to this kind of intense pressure to change on the part of an adult authority figure. The therapist, therefore, must be willing to deal therapeutically with direct expressions of anger, resentment, and hostility toward him. It is during this difficult period that the therapist must be willing to allow the full ventilation of these feelings, at the same time attempting to curb any expressions of defensive or countertransference reactions.

Finally, all members are encouraged to develop insight into their behavior with regard to the member who was confronted, as well as to their own particular issues regarding substance abuse.

References

Ackerman, N. W. Patterns in group psychotherapy. *Psychiatry,* 1944, *7,* 340–348.

Adler, G., and Meyerson, P. G. (eds.). *Confrontation in Psychotherapy.* New York: Jason Aronson, 1973.

Bartlett, D. The use of multiple family therapy with adolescent drug abuses. In M. Sugar (ed.), *The Adolescent in Group and Family Therapy.* New York: Brunner/Mazel, 1975.

Bassin, A. Daytop Village. *Psychology Today,* Feb. 1968, 48–52.

Berkovitz, I. H., and Sugar, M. Indications and contraindications for adolescent group psychotherapy. In M. Sugar (ed.), *The Adolescent in Group and Family Therapy.* New York: Brunner/Mazel, 1975.

Brandes, N. W. Challenges in the management of troubled adolescents. *Clinical Pediatrics,* 1964, *11,* 647–650.

Bratter, T. E. Treating adolescent drug abusers in a community-based interaction group program: some philosophical considerations. *Journal of Drug Issues,* 1971, *1,* 237–252.

———. Group therapy with affluent, alienated adolescent drug abusers: a reality therapy and confrontation approach. *Psychotherapy: Theory, Research and Practice,* 1972, *9,* 308–313.

———. Treating alienated, unmotivated, drug abusing adolescents. *American Journal of Psychotherapy,* 1973, *27,* 589–596.

———. Confrontation: a group psychotherapeutic treatment model for alienated, acting-out, unmotivated, adolescent drug abusers and addicts. Unpublished doctoral dissertation, Columbia University, 1974(a).

———. Reality therapy: a group psychotherapeutic approach with adolescent alcoholics. *Annals of the New York Academcy of Sciences,* 1974, *233,* 1974(b).

Brown, S. Acting out in adolescence: genesis and some treatment implications. In S. Feinstein and P. Grovacchini (eds.), *Adolescent Psychiatry: Developmental and Clinical Studies,* vol. 6. Chicago: University of Chicago Press, 1978.

Buie, D. H., and Adler, G. The uses of confrontation with borderline patients. *International Journal of Psychoanalysis and Psychotherapy,* 1972, *1*(3), 90–108.

Casriel, D. The acting-out neurosis of our times. *The Neurosis of Our Times: Acting Out,* eds. Donald S. Milman and George Goldman. Springfield, Ill.: Charles C. Thomas, 1973.

Corwin, H. A. The scope of therapeutic confrontation from routine to heroic. *International Journal of Psychoanalysis and Psychotherapy,* 1972, *1*(3), 68–89.

Eissler, K. R. Personal communication, July 1978.

Erikson, E. Identity and the life cycle. Monograph 1 of *Psychological Issues.* New York: International Universities Press, 1959.

Forrest, G. G. *Confrontation in Psychotherapy with Alocholics.* Holmes Beach, Fla.: Learning Publications, 1982.

Forrest, G. G. *How to Cope with a Teenage Drinker: New Alternatives and Hopes for Parents and Families.* New York: Atheneum, 1983.

Forrest, G. G. *Intensive Psychotherapy of Alcoholism.* Springfield, Ill.: Charles C. Thomas, 1984.

Gitelson, M. Character synthesis: the psychotherapeutic problem of adolescence. *American Journal of Orthopsychiatry,* 1948, *18,* 422–431.

Holmes, D. *The Adolescent in Psychotherapy.* Boston: Little, Brown & Co., 1964.

Kraft, I. A. Some special considerations in adolescent group psychotherapy. *International Journal of Group Psychotherapy,* 1961, *11,* 196–203.

Laskowitz, D. Psychological characteristics of the adolescent addict. In E. Harmes (ed.), *Drug Addiction in Youth.* Oxford, England: Pergamon Press, 1968.

Noshpitz, J. Opening phase in the psychotherapy of adolescents with character disorders. *Bulletin of the Menninger Clinic,* 1963, *21,* 153–164.

Rachman, A. W. *Identity Group Psychotherapy with Adolescents.* Springfield, Ill.: Charles C. Thomas, 1975.

———. Humanistic analysis in groups. *Psychotherapy: Theory, Research and Practice,* 1982, *18(4),* 422–430.

———, and Heller, M. Anti-therapeutic factors in therapeutic communities for drug rehabilitation. *Journal of Drug Issues,* 1974, *4,* 393–403.

Raubolt, R., and Bratter, T. E. Games addicts play: implications for group treatment. *Corrective and Social Psychiatry,* 1974, *20(4),* 3–10.

Raubolt, R. The history and development of adolescent group psychotherapy (monograph 19). American Group Psychotherapy Association Publications, 1979.

Schulman, I. The dynamics of certain reactions of delinquents to group psychotherapy. *International Journal of Group Psychotherapy,* 1952, *2,* 334–343.

Singer, M. Comments and caveats regarding adolescent groups in a combined approach. *International Journal of Group Psychotherapy,* 1974, *24(4),* 429–438.

Sweeney, D. R., Tingling, D., and Schmale, A. Differentiation of the "giving up" affects—helplessness and hopelessness. *Archives of General Psychiatry,* 1970, *23(10),* 328.

Wieder, W. L., and Kaplan, E. H. Drug use in adolescents: psychodynamic meaning and pharmacogenic effect. *Psychoanalytic Study of the Child,* 1969, *24,* 399–431.

Zucker, A., and Waksman, S. Results of group therapy with young drug addicts. *International Journal of Social Psychiatry,* 1972, *18,* 267–279.

13

Family Therapy in the Treatment of Alcoholism

EDWARD KAUFMAN

OVER THE PAST TWENTY YEARS there has been major progress in the development of differential treatment of alcoholism; that is, the matching of treatment methods to the unique needs of the alcoholic patient. Similar differential development of family therapy techniques to meet the problems of different types of families has occurred. However, as Orford (1975) has pointed out, each clinical field has developed as a specialty, with minimal interchange. As a result, the family therapy field has devoted little effort to the specification of family therapy techniques directed to the unique problems of families with alcohol problems. At the same time, in the field of alcoholism treatment, family treatment has been viewed as a generic treatment modality, with minimal reference to specific variations in family therapy.

There are several reasons for this situation. First, mental health professionals in the family therapy field still tend to hold stereotyped negative attitudes toward alcoholics (Pattison, 1977). Second, family therapists often may work with alcoholic families, but focus solely on family dynamics and ignore the alcoholism (Cohen and Krause,

The author wishes to acknowledge the assistance of E. M. Pattison, M.D., in the preparation of this chapter.

1971). Third, psychotherapists in alcoholism treatment programs have only recently adopted widespread use of family therapy, and are less likely to be informed about the many current family therapy techniques which may be modified for alcoholism treatment (Pattison, 1976).

This chapter stresses the *interaction* between family psychodynamics and the dynamics of alcoholic behavior. The chapter will identify *different* family patterns of alcoholism, which require different family therapy interventions. This is a clinical application of the concept of differential treatment, which Pattison has described elsewhere (Pattison, 1976, 1978; Pattison and Kaufman, 1979; Pattison, Sobell, and Sobell, 1977). Finally, techniques from several distinct schools of family therapy will be adapted and modified for the treatment of alcoholic families.

Alcoholism in Four Family Systems

Four different types of family systems in which alcoholism is a major problem will be described to indicate major family constellations. The differential treatment of each type and general treatment concepts will be described in detail in a later section, "Interventions with Different Family Systems."

The Functional Family System (*the family with an Alcoholic Member*)

These family systems are apparently stabilized and happy. The parents maintain a loving relationship with each other, with a relatively good sexual adjustment. They are successful as a parenting team; their children are well-adjusted, have good relationships with each other and with their peers. Drinking in the alcoholic partner(s) does not evolve as a result of family stresses, but primarily from response to social strains and/or personal neurotic conflict. Excessive drinking is often outside the home, in binges, at parties, or at bedtime. The existence of these functional family systems usually occurs in the early phases of the disease, since such systems may deteriorate as alcoholism progresses.

The Neurotic Enmeshed Family System (*the Alcoholic Family*)

In these families, drinking behavior interrupts normal family tasks, causes conflict, shifts roles, and demands adaptive responses from family members who do not know how to appropriately respond. Drinking also triggers anger in the drinker, despite his or her attempts to absorb the anger with alcohol. Alcoholism creates physical problems, including sexual dysfunction and debilitating cardiac, hepatic, and neurological disease, which in turn produce further marital conflicts and role realignments.

A converse dynamic also occurs, in that marital and family styles, rules, and conflict may evoke, support, and maintain alcoholism as a *symptom* of family system dysfunction or as a *coping mechanism* to deal with family dysfunction. In these families, excessive drinking occurs when family anxiety is high and stirs up higher anxiety in those dependent on the one who drinks. The anxiety causes everyone to do more of what they are already doing. Drinking to relieve anxiety, and family anxiety in response to drinking, can spiral into a crisis (Bowen, 1974).

Stresses in any single family member immediately affect the entire family. Communication is often not direct but through a third party. Likewise, conflicts are triangulated (projected) onto another family member (Bowen, 1974). Everyone in the family feels guilty and responsible for each other, but particularly for the alcoholic and his or her drinking.

These alcoholic marriages are often highly competitive. Each partner sees himself or herself as giving in to the other. The one who gives in most becomes "de-selfed" and is vulnerable to a drinking problem (Bowen, 1974). After the pattern of alcoholism is established, these couples continue in a highly competitive relationship. The alcoholic repeatedly tries to be controlling and avoid responsibility through passive-dependent techniques. The spouse tries to control by being forceful, active, blunt, and dominating, or by suffering. Neither ever clearly becomes dominant, but the fight continues indefinitely.

Fighting frequently occurs, as the spouses blame each other for the family's problems. This dual projection blinds the couple from seeing their respective roles in creating problems. They may fight endlessly about "who started it" and readily duplicate this position in therapy with the hope that the therapist will judge right and wrong.

The alcoholic may relinquish his or her role as a parent. Other roles involving household chores and maintenance are abandoned and given over to others. The role of the breadwinner is the last to go, and this stage may be necessary before treatment is sought. The nonalcoholic wife may encourage the older son to take over responsibilities abdicated by the father, placing the son in overt competition with the father.

As nonalcoholic members take over management of the family, the alcoholic is relegated to a child's status, which perpetuates drinking. Coalitions occur between the nonalcoholic spouse and children or in-laws which tend to further distance the alcoholic. Alcoholic fathers are prone to abuse their children through violence, sexual seduction, or assault. Alcoholic mothers are more prone to abuse their children through neglect. The nonalcoholic spouse may also neglect children in order to direct his or her attention to the alcoholic. Although not all alcoholics seriously abuse or neglect their children, many have difficulties in child rearing.

The Disintegrated Family System (*the Alcoholic Temporarily Separated from the Alcoholic Family*)

This is frequently a later state of the neurotic enmeshed system, although the functional system may also regress directly to a disintegrated system. There is a past history of reasonable life and family function, but at the point of entering treatment, the family system has collapsed. The family is separated and there may be no family contact. In this situation, alcoholics must first learn to take responsibility for themselves and stop blaming wife, family, friends, and employers. They often require three months or more of abstinence before vocational retraining and family reinvolvement can be *initiated.*

The Absent Family System (*the Alcoholic Permanently Separated from the Family*)

Although this may be an end-stage of deterioration, the more frequent pattern is total loss of family of origin early in the drinking career. Alcoholics in this situation have little or no family contact and few social or vocational relationships. Their significant others, such as providers of board and care or "bottle gang" buddies, provide minimal social support. Their contacts with the family of origin may be renewed after months of sobriety, but usually contact with their prior families of procreation is impossible. If individual therapy and social/vocational rehabilitation is successful, then they may form new nuclear families. This is unusual, but does occur in younger alcoholics of this type.

Alcoholism and the Family

There is a substantial literature on alcoholism and the family, which contains a variety of major issues. This will not be reviewed, but those themes and conclusions which are basic to the author's family therapy approach will be summarized. Several major reviews have recently been published which detail the literature (Ablon, 1976; Bailey, 1961; Hanson and Estes, 1977; Janzen, 1976; Krimmel, 1973; Paolino and McCrady, 1979; Scott, 1970; Steinglass, 1976).

Most early studies focused on the male alcoholic and his nonalcoholic wife. It was implied that the wife was neurotic and chose an alcoholic husband, or later that the wife became neurotic because of her husband's alcoholism (Ballard, 1959; Chassell, 1938; Karlen, 1965). Perhaps even more misogynist was the view that the wife "drove her husband to drink." In sum, the fable of the noxious wife is just that—a fable (Kogan and Jackson, 1965). There is no validity to several earlier typologies of "typical wives of alcoholics" (Edwards, Harvey, and Whitehead, 1973; Paolino et al., 1976; Tarter, 1976). The same problem obtains in the few studies of men who marry women alcoholics. They indicate often significant psychopathology among these men—but there is probably no specific type of male spouse of an alcoholic woman (Busch, Kormendy, and Feverlein, 1973; Rimmer, 1974).

A more fruitful approach has been the study of marital interactional dynamics, role perceptions, and marital patterns of expectations and sanctions concerning the use of alcohol. Couples with alcoholism demonstrate neurotic interactional behavior similar to other neurotic marriages: alcoholic and neurotic marriages are dissimilar from healthy marital interaction. Thus, alcoholic marriages are not unique; rather, they are neurotic marriages in which alcoholism is part of the neurotic interaction (Busch, Kormendy, and Feverlein, 1973; Rimmer, 1974; Becker and Miller, 1976; Billings et al., 1979; Bullock and Mudd, 1959; Drewery and Rae, 1969; Gorad, 1971; Haberman, 1969; Hanson, Sands, and Sheldon, 1968; Hersen, Miller, and Eisler, 1973; Mitchell, 1968; Rae and Drewery, 1972).

The Family and Alcoholism as a System Problem

Recent family research has moved away from a focus on the marital partners toward a consideration of the entire family system, including the families of origin, the life-style of children from alcoholic families, and the kin structures of the extended family system. This provides a much broader view of alcoholism as a family problem.

The first conclusion from experimental observations of family systems is that alcohol use in a family is *not* just an *individual* matter. The use of alcohol and the consequential behavior of drinking is dynamically related to events in the family system. Thus the use of alcohol is *purposeful, adaptive, homeostatic,* and *meaningful.* The problem of alcoholism is not just the consequences of drinking per se, but, more importantly, the *system functions* which drinking fills in the psychodynamics of the family system (Davis, et al., 1974; Davis, Stern, and Von Deusen, 1978; Steinglass, Weiner, and Mendelson, 1971). Thus we may properly consider alcoholism as a family system problem.

We can extend the systems approach to a larger consideration of the nuclear family embedded in generational and kinship systems. The problem of alcoholism is not just an individual problem, nor a problem of marital partners or even the nuclear family system, but can reflect *larger alcoholism-generating family systems.*

Alcoholism and Children in the Family System

Much of the literature on alcoholism in the family has focused primarily on the marital partners, while neglecting the roles and functions of children (Ackerman, 1983) in the family, and the consequences of alcoholism for the children. As Margaret Cork (1969) named the problem, they have been "the Forgotten Children." In the immediate situation of the alcoholic family, children are often the most severely victimized. They have growth and developmental problems, school and learning problems, and emotional problems, and frequently exhibit significant behavior dysfunctions (Chafetz, Blane, and Hill, 1971; El-Guebly and Offord, 1977; Fox, 1962; Mayer, Black, and MacDonald, 1978; Wilson and Offord, 1978). Further, these children are often subject to gross neglect and even abuse. Teenage children are not immune to these adverse consequences, even though they are often considered less vulnerable—perhaps a misperception (Smith, 1969; Paolino and McCrady, 1976; Steinglass, Davis, and Berenson, 1977; Steinglass, 1979; Ewing, Long, and Wenzel, 1961; Gliedman, 1957; MacDonald, 1958). Thus, family intervention must truly consider the needs of the juvenile and teenage members both in terms of short-range problems and longer-term preventive concerns.

Family Patterns After Sobriety

The spouse and family build up many defenses which create problems when and if the alcoholic gets sober. If alcoholics stop drinking, spouses may no longer fight with them about drinking, but about whether they will resume drinking, which paradoxically triggers resumption of drinking.

The alcoholic who is sober, and doesn't want to be, is still psychologically drunk and punishes everyone (Forrest, 1983) because he expects and doesn't receive exceptional rewards for giving up alcohol. The romance of sobriety wears off after a while, and the slightest stress may tip him off again. The grief work in giving up alcohol may last for months or years. This period of prolonged grief may produce the clinical phenomenon of the "dry drunk." If the family system is not worked with during this phase of the cycle, and if the family does not learn new patterns of relating to each other to replace those developed during alcoholism, then the old system will draw the alcoholic and the family back to symptomatic consumption of alcohol.

The Family as a Determinant of Rehabilitation

In keeping with the observation of alcoholism as a system problem, the attitudes, structure, and function of the family system has been shown to be a crucial variable in the successful outcome of alcoholism treatment. The alcoholic person enters treatment from a family system and returns to that family system. If the system is dysfunctional, it may vitiate any individual treatment gains. However, if the family changes or adapts more appropriate functions, it may sustain improvement and change in the alcoholic member (Bromet and Moos, 1977; Moos et al., 1979; Orford et al., 1976; Rae, 1972; Webb et al., 1978; Wright and Scott, 1978).

Development of Family Treatment for Alcoholism

The development of family treatment interventions for alcoholism has paralleled the development of the conceptual framework of alcoholism as a family systems problem. The first family treatment approaches were developed forty years ago in social work agencies, primarily as individual casework methods (Boggs, 1944). This was followed by marital therapy of alcoholic couples (Esser, 1968, 1971; Smith, 1969). A variant on this theme is the joint hospitalization of marital couples, although only one is alcoholic (Paolino and McCrady, 1976; Steinglass, Davis, and Berenson, 1977; Steinglass, 1979). Group therapy for the wives of alcoholics is another early treatment modality which has been used for about twenty years (Ewing, Long, and Wenzel, 1961; Gliedman, 1957; MacDonald, 1958). From there it was a short step to group therapy of alcoholic couples (Cadogan, 1973; Corder, Corder, and Laidlaw, 1972). More recent are clinical reports on specific family therapy of whole families with alcoholism as a problem focus (Ewing and Fox, 1968; Meeks and Kelly, 1970).

The importance of involving the total family system, including children, parents, and in-laws, in order to ameliorate or stop the drinking of the alcoholic is presently often neglected despite all the above evidence mandating such an approach. The ways that members of the entire three-generational system affect the alcoholic make it necessary to include all generations in family evaluation and treatment. For example: Young children may encourage parents to drink to quiet violence or to loosen controls to a point where affection is shown. Alcoholic parents may drink because of their inability to control their children's antisocial behavior, or teenagers may provoke a cycle of drinking and fighting in parents so that they are unable to set limits and enforce punishments. Parents of alcoholics may prevent them from relating to spouses by overprotecting and infantilizing them.

Clinical reports have also focused on more extended family systems. This includes Al-Anon as an adjunct social system for wives (Ablon, 1974; Bailey, 1965); support groups for children (Kern et al., 1978) and for adolescents (McElfresh, 1970); multiple family alcoholism groups who include at least one addicted member (McKany, 1976); the inclusion of relatives and friends in the "familization" of a hospital treatment program (Catanzaro, et al.); and the development of "social networks" of significant persons to form an effective social system in which to embed the alcoholic upon reentry into the community (Howard and Howard, 1978; Sands and Hanson, 1971; Ward and Faillace, 1970). This social network approach affords methods to deal with the generational family systems, kinship systems, and community systems which constitute the large social networks of individual and family structure, detailed by Pattison elsewhere (Pattison et al., 1975).

There is no one family therapy approach, but rather a variety of family intervention methods available, which can be utilized where appropriate to the needs of a specific alcohol problem and family constellation.

General Principles of Family Intervention with Alcoholics

In working with alcoholics and their families, the therapist is faced with a unique problem, that of "wet" and "dry" family systems. A wet system is one in which the alcoholic continues to drink problematically, while a dry system is one where active drinking is not a problem but the family's problems continue. Some therapists, particularly those who work in A.A.-oriented programs, will only work with dry systems. This should *not* be a precondition of treatment with family systems, in my opinion. A dry system is always preferable; however, it may be an unreasonable expectation for many families at the onset of treatment. It may be necessary to work with a wet system for some time to motivate nondrinking family members to continue in treatment if the alcoholic should drop out of treatment. In all families, the therapist should suggest measures to effect a dry state, at least temporarily, and in some instances the therapist should insist on these measures.

Achieving a Dry System

If the alcoholic is drinking so severely that he or she is unable to attend sessions without being under the influence, and/or if functioning is severely impaired, then the first priority is to interrupt the pattern of drinking. In these circumstances, the first goal is to persuade the family to pull together to initiate detoxification. This may be done on an outpatient basis, but if the drinking is severe, immediate short-term hospitalization may be required (Feldman et al., 1975). If the drinking is only moderately severe or intermittent, then the family should be offered alternatives to initiate a temporary alcohol-free state. These should include social detoxification centers, Alcoholics Anonymous, and Antabuse. In families of the neurotic enmeshed types, Antabuse should not be given to another family member for daily distribution to the alcoholic, as preoccupation with taking Antabuse tends to replace the family's overinvolvement with the alcoholic's drinking or not drinking. If the alcoholic refuses to initiate abstinence, then we are stuck with working with the wet system.

Working with Wet Systems

Since the wet system is a reality, the therapist should have techniques available to work with such families. When a member arrives at a session intoxicated, the therapist should not deal directly with this problem. Rather, he or she should ask the sober spouse and family members to deal with the intoxicated person. This offers an excellent opportunity to observe how the family interacts during intoxication, which is one of the most critical phases of family system function. In subsequent sessions this behavior can be reexamined, or videotapes of this behavior can be reviewed. In general, it is easier to ask the hyperfunctioning (sober) partner to change than the underfunctioning (alcoholic) one (Bowen, 1974).

In working with wet systems it is critical that the therapist not maintain the illusion that problems are being resolved because the family is "in therapy" when, in fact, the problems are still being reinforced. Provision of support systems for the other family members may help reduce the emotional intensity fixated on the alcoholic (or therapist). Al-Anon is a valuable support system, as are "significant others" and social network systems of relatives and friends. Other supports such as vocational training, jobs, social agencies, pastors, and attorneys may be essential. Groups for responsible drinkers may be helpful to alcoholics if they can keep their drinking from becoming destructive.

The therapist can offer the family three choices as their only alternatives (as outlined by Berenson, 1979):

1. Keep doing exactly what you are doing.
2. Detach, or emotionally distance, yourselves from the alcoholic.
3. Separate, or physically distance, yourselves.

When the family members choose to not change, it is overt; thus one can label what they are doing. When they do not choose alternative 2 or 3, the therapist can tell them that they are choosing 1. In choosing 2 they are not criticizing drinking, but are being asked to accept it, live with the alcoholic, and be responsible for their own reactivity regarding drinking (Berenson, 1979). Al-Anon reinforces alternative 2 by teaching sober spouses that they have no power over their partners' alcohol intake (the goal is to get the sober spouse to stop asking the alcoholic to control his or her drinking). If the family chooses 3, the alcoholic may frustrate attempts to get him or her out of the house, so the family may have to move out, which is initially considered impossible.

Thus, the family is presented with three choices, each of which may seem impossible. The problem is resolved by choosing one of three courses of action and following through or by experiencing the helplessness and powerlessness of these situations being repeated and clarified. The therapist should make it clear that these are the only options but should not expect one to be adopted right away. The family then shares despair and "hits bottom" sufficiently to become responsible for themselves rather than continue to try to change the alcoholic. When they do this, the alcoholic may get worse in order to get the family back into the entanglement. The therapist must prepare the family for this situation. If the family can say, in effect, "We prefer you not to kill yourself (or us) but we are powerless to help you," it is unlikely that the alcoholic will kill himself or someone else. These options, then, open the door to consideration of new family adaptations apart from whether the alcoholic is wet or dry (Berenson, 1979).

Interventions with Different Family Systems

Different schools of family therapy tend to utilize different languages, techniques, or strategies. There is little data to compare the efficacy of different family therapy methods, much less the application of such methods to alcoholism. I utilize an integration of structural, systems, psychodynamic, and behavioral methods. Each therapist must modify these techniques according to his or her own style, work setting, and types of family alcoholism problems encountered. Therefore, general principles for working with the four types of family systems previously described will be presented.

In the *functional family system,* families have learned to function with a minimum of overt conflict, so that they avoid psychologically oriented interventions. Here *family educative* approaches are often helpful. Explanation of the medical effects and the medical complications of alcoholism may be the most useful initial entry into family participation. Such families will often then participate in educative-cognitive exploration of family roles and explicit and observable behavioral interaction. Exploration of implicit family rules and behavioral expectations can be followed by the development of family contracts and behavioral role practicing. Intensive family exploration of personal and interpersonal dynamics may not be necessary or may be resisted because the family system protects the working homeostatic adjustment. Many will respond to the more cognitive and behavioral approaches outlined. In these families, Antabuse may be given to a family member for daily distribution, since it can be done with a minimum of conflict.

In the *neurotic enmeshed family system,* many of these same initial approaches to family involvement and commitment as outlined above may be necessary. However, much more active structural and psychodynamic work will have to be done in most cases. In these families, educative and behavioral methods may provide some initial relief, but will probably not impact on the enmeshed neurotic relationships. Here explicit family psychotherapy is usually required. Often, multiple generations and kinship systems are interlocked with the nuclear family dynamics, and the involvement of the larger social systems, where possible, is likely to be helpful. In contrast to the functional family system, where work with the nuclear family is usually sufficient, work with just the nuclear family in the neurotic enmeshed system may often be insufficient. Further, mechanisms for disengagement of the enmeshed nuclear family members are required. Here concomitant involvement with A.A. or Al-Anon may be very helpful, along with involvement of family members in more significant kinship, friendship, and community relationships.

In the *disintegrated family system,* the use of family interventions might seem irrelevant. However, many of these marriages and families have fallen apart only after severe alcoholic behavior. Further, there is often only "pseudo-individuation" of the alcoholic from marital, family, and kinship ties. These families usually cannot and will not reconstitute during the early phases of alcoholism rehabilitation. Thus, the initial and early stages of treatment should focus primarily on the individual alcoholic. However, potential ties to spouse, family, kin, and friends should be explored early in treatment, and some contact should be initiated. There should be neither explicit nor implicit assumptions that such familial ties will be fully reconstituted. When sobriety and personal stability have been achieved over several months, more substantive family explorations can be initiated to reestablish parental roles and family and kinship relationships—still without reconstitution. These family "definitional" sessions can then serve as the springboard either for appropriate redefinition of separated roles or for structuring the reconciled family. In either case, it is important for both the alcoholic and the family system to renegotiate new roles and relationships on the basis of the person's identity as a rehabilitated alcoholic. Some families may not wish reunion but can achieve healthy separation. Other families which do desire reunion must establish a new base for family relationships.

The *absent family system* prevents rather different problems. Here the issue is not *reconstitution,* but rather *development* of new social networks, new social systems, and new life-styles. Often alcoholics in such circumstances have little ability to form effective social relationships and do best in partially institutionalized social support systems. However, some of these alcoholics do learn to participate in effective social systems over time, in graduated fashion, and may even build new functional families.

Modification of Family Therapy for Alcoholism

In adapting the techniques of family therapy to alcoholism, a synthesis of structural, systems, behavioral, and psychodynamic approaches is utilized. The therapy begins with early joining maneuvers in which the therapist functions as a host and relates to the family and each member using the family's style, language, affect, and rules. Families commonly present with a teenager who uses drugs minimally as the identified patient (IP), but with a hidden parental alcoholic whose problems readily become apparent to the therapist. Joining this family consists of accepting the family's presentation of the teenager as the IP. To initially challenge the alcoholic in such a family is to not join them but perhaps drive them out of treatment. Ultimately the therapist joins the family by understanding them and helping them change. Joining with the total family provides the therapeutic leverage necessary to change the family. Joining with individual family members or subsystems may be a powerful restructuring tool. Joining with the drinking alcoholic is difficult for the nonalcoholic therapist. However, therapists who are recovering alcoholics are able to use their past experiences with alcoholism to join with such patients.

The genogram (Bowen, 1976) is helpful as an information-gathering and synthesizing device. However, family therapists also use a structural map (Minuchin, 1974) as a fluid diagnostic tool which helps to focus the therapy. The map of family structures changes as the therapy progresses. All therapy is diagnostic, since the family's response to interventions reveals their adaptability. The therapeutic techniques which family therapists have adapted to the family treatment of alcoholics include the therapeutic contract, assigning tasks, paradox, interpretation, reenactment, marking boundaries, education and teaching, and the use of the total family network. Many of these principles may be involved in a single therapeutic intervention. Restructuring psychotherapy is used mainly for neurotic enmeshed families. It may also be used with disintegrated families after several months of sobriety have been achieved, as previously described.

The Therapeutic Contract

This deals with establishing the terms, duration, and cost of therapy as well as which members of the family and network should attend. With the alcoholic family, the issue of drinking and how it will be dealt with should be made a part of the contract. The way a family should deal with drinking may vary according to the type of family and extent of drinking. A rule of thumb is to diminish emotional reactivity to drinking behavior.

The therapist may also assign a certain type of task, have the family choose the specifics, and then reinforce their choice. A child in the nuclear family can be asked to chose a peer-related activity that he or she has always wanted to do, and when one is chosen the family is asked to facilitate it. A father who neglects his personal health because of worry about his wife's drinking can be asked to make an appointment with a doctor or a dentist. If tasks are not successfully completed, then the difficulties in achieving them can be the subject of further therapeutic work. A wife who is overinvolved with the amounts of alcohol her husband is consuming on a daily basis could be given the task of estimating how many drinks he has every day and writing it down without telling him. The husband can be asked to write down the actual amounts, so that they can be compared in a subsequent session. The discrepancies will demonstrate the futility of the wife's efforts and diminish her overinvolvement in the husband's drinking. This task is also a paradoxical one, the nature of which will be described below.

The Paradox

The paradox is a universal determinant of human behavior in which individuals do the opposite of what they feel they are being pushed to do (Watzlawick, Weakland, and Fisch, 1974). In recognition of the power of the paradox, paradoxical directives can be used to achieve change. Such tasks may appear absurd because they require families to do what they have been doing, rather than to change, as everyone else has been demanding. If the family follows the advice of the therapist and continues what they have been doing, then the therapist assumes power over the symptom. If the family continues to oppose the therapist, then they will reverse the symptom. If the family complies with the therapist, they can acknowledge their power over the symptom and have the power to change it. The paradox uses the principle of the double bind to change the symptom. It is an overt message which urges the family to obey the opposite covert message. A symptom may be paradoxically exaggerated in order to emphasize the family's needs to extrude it. Examples of this are encouraging a family to continue the "glories" of overindulging and infantilizing the alcoholic. A symptom which is an externalized acting-out of family conflicts (e.g., adolescent stealing, secret drinking) can be prescribed to be performed within the family so that the family can deal with it. Skillfully asking the family to not change or to not change too fast and identifying the reasons they are not ready to change is another paradoxical maneuver which can lead to change (Haley, 1977). When properly delivered, the paradox leaves the family chafing at the bit to make desired changes.

Relabeling or reframing the symptom may also be very helpful, as when adolescent drinking is termed an attempt to bring disengaged or divorced parents together. Then the therapy can more easily shift to the parents' problems as a couple. Frequently, reframing has a paradoxical aspect, as when individuals are praised for maintaining a family system.

Paradoxical techniques work best with neurotic enmeshed families and reconstituted families who were formerly disintegrated, because of their defiance and tendency to interact in rigid, self-defeating cycles. They are unnecessary and perhaps antitherapeutic in compliant families, particularly functional ones.

Interpretation

Interpretations can be extremely helpful if they are utilized without blaming, guilt induction, or dwelling on the hopelessness of longstanding, fixed patterns. The repetitive patterns and their derivatives are pointed out to the patient and family. Their maladaptive aspects are likewise pointed out, and the patient and family are given tasks to help them change these patterns in the here-and-now.

In using a psychodynamic approach, the role of the passive listener, which is ineffective with alcoholics as well as their families, is to be avoided (Forrest, 1984). Rather, the therapist is involved with the family as a genuine human being who deals with the immediate moment of experience between him/herself and the family. Nevertheless, the family history of each family member is helpful in understanding the repetition of patterns from one generation to the next; and pointing out these recurring themes is a way of changing them (Bowen, 1976).

Reenactment (Actualization)

The principle behind this technique is that family interactions are much more revealing than individual descriptions. Patients usually direct their communications to the therapist. They should be required to talk to each other. They should be asked to enact transactional patterns rather than describe them. The entire family should be brought into the interaction so that everyone's roles are experienced. Role playing and family sculpture are helpful ways to facilitate actualization of patterns (as well as change them). Manipulating space (by changing seating or placing one member behind a one-way mirror) is a powerful tool for observing what the family is like when basic structures are changed. Working with the family when the alcoholic is inebriated creates a powerful reenactment of family interactions. One excellent way to utilize this material is for the alcoholic to view it on videotape when he or she is sober. The family should resolve still-unresolved conflicts in the session rather than talk about old disagreements. When a therapist becomes bored with a session, it is frequently because actualization (or change) is not occurring.

Marking Boundaries

Boundaries are delineated around individuals as well as subsystems. Individuals should not answer for or feel for others, should be talked to and not about, and should listen to and acknowledge the communication of others. Reacting to anticipated or assumed reactions (mind reading) is also discouraged, giving individuals room to grow and change. Nonverbal checking and blocking of communications should also be observed, and, when appropriate, pointed out and halted.

Boundaries may be established temporarily by the therapist's placing him/herself or furniture between subsystems. In general the boundary which surrounds the nondrinking spouse and that spouse's children should be replaced by one which surrounds the parental subsystem, protecting it from intrusion by children as well as other adults in and outside the family. Frequently, in order to strengthen the executive, parental system, sessions which exclude everyone else should be held. When individuals are deprived of a key role by a new boundary which does not generally exist in the family, they should be provided with a substitute role. If an adult or older sibling is placed behind a one-way mirror, that person may be given the role of expert observer and permitted to comment later. These artificial boundaries in the session may be so reinforcing to the family that they will be continued or may be supported by tasks to be performed at home. Al-Anon and Alateen are excellent reinforcers of individual boundaries.

Education and Teaching

Giving the family knowledge about alcohol and alcoholism is almost always helpful, as described previously. The support and nurturance that a family can appropriately offer its members should be taught, understood, and encouraged. The therapist may have to assume executive functions as a model and then step back so the family can assume them. Families may be taught how to handle schools or social agencies, parents taught how to confirm each other or react differently to their children. Children may be taught how to deal with their peers, including the use of peers as co-therapists. Helpless family members can be taught to tap their potential in social and vocational areas.

Use of the Total Family Network

Other significant family members and social network members, including employers, housekeepers, siblings, aunts and uncles, neighbors, and friends, may be involved. Families who present as only two persons are very difficult to change. Couples groups or multiple family groups can provide some leverage by supplying other parental figures to such systems. Invariably there is another person such as a boyfriend, sibling, aunt, or grandparent who can be extremely helpful in changing family systems; e.g., the unit of the triangle which led to the problem is reversed in order to achieve otherwise impossible structural changes. In the same manner, significant others can indeed become significant change agents in family systems.

Countertransference

Alcoholics and their families provoke specific types of emotional reactions in therapists. The alcoholic's dependency, relationship suction and repulsion, manipulativeness, denial, impulsivity, and role abandonment will provoke countertransference reactions in the therapist depending on his or her own emotional makeup. However, as family therapists we view our emotional reactions to families in a systems framework rather than a countertransference context. Thus, we must tune into how these families replay their problems with the therapist, and how they detour or triangulate their problems to the therapist. In these families, the therapist must be particularly sensitive about becoming a co-alcoholic who tries to overprotect or is provoked to reject the alcoholic. The relationship between the therapist and the family with alcoholism replicates what happens within the family at home. One example of this is the therapist who alternates between saving and persecution, by first allowing the alcoholic to do almost anything, even coming drunk to sessions, and then switching to a punitive position such as demanding sobriety as a precondition of therapy (Berenson, 1979). In addition, the problem of countertransference must be distinguished from a more generalized negativism or hostility toward alcoholism. Both are antitherapeutic.

Summary

In this chapter the intimate relationship of the problem of alcoholism to family systems has been outlined. This relationship may be rather singular, as in the case of focal individual alcoholism in a stable and healthy family system; or it may be quite generalized, involving several generations or groups of kin. Four descriptive types of family systems of alcoholism, based on research by Pattison (Pattison, Coe, and Rhodes, 1969; Pattison, Coe, and Doerr, 1973), have been presented. These are not definitive types, however, but only illustrative of a broad spectrum of family involvements in alcoholism. Because this spectrum is so broad, the need for the differential utilization of different types of family treatment interventions has been emphasized. Finally, the view of alcoholism as a family systems problem, with therapeutic interventions framed as systems interventions, has been presented.

References

Ablon, J. Al-Anon family groups. *American Journal of Psychotherapy,* 1974, *28,* 30–45.

———. Family structure and behavior in alcoholism: a review of the literature. In B. Kissin and H. Begleiter (eds.), *The Biology of Alcoholism.* Vol. 4, *Social Pathology.* New York: Plenum Press, 1976.

Bailey, M. Alcoholism in marriage: A review of research and professional literature. *Quarterly Journal of Studies on Alcohol,* 1961, *22,* 81–97.

———. Al-Anon family groups as an aid to wives of alcoholics. *Social Work,* 1965, *10,* 68–79.

Ballard, R. G. The interaction between marital conflict and alcoholism as seen through MMPI's of marriage partners. *American Journal of Orthopsychiatry,* 1959, *29,* 528–546.

Becker, J. V., and Miller, P. M. Verbal and nonverbal marital interaction patterns of alcoholics and nonalcoholics. *Quarterly Journal of Studies on Alcohol,* 1976, *37,* 1616–1624.

Berenson, D. The therapist's relationship with couples with an alcoholic member. In E. Kaufman and P. Kaufman (eds.), *Family Therapy of Drug and Alcohol Abuse.* New York: Gardner Press, 1979.

Billings, A. G., Kessler, M., Gomberg, C. A., and Weiner, S. Marital conflict resolution of alcoholic and nonalcoholic couples during drinking and nondrinking sessions. *Quarterly Journal of Studies on Alcohol,* 1979, *40,* 183–195.

Boggs, M. H. The role of social work in the treatment of inebriates. *Quarterly Journal of Studies on Alcohol,* 1944, *4,* 557–567.

Bowen, M. Alcoholism as viewed through family systems therapy and family psychotherapy. *Annals of the New York Academy of Sciences,* 1974, *233,* 115–122.

———. Theory in the practice of psychotherapy. In P. Guerin (ed.), *Family Therapy.* New York: Gardner Press, 1976, 42–90.

Bromet, E. and Moos, R. Environmental resources and the post-treatment functioning of alcoholic patients. *Journal of Health and Social Behavior,* 1977, *18,* 326–338.

Bullock, S. C., and Mudd, E. H. The interaction of alcoholic husbands and their nonalcoholic wives during counseling. *American Journal of Orthopsychiatry,* 1959, *29,* 519–527.

Busch, H., Kormendy, E., and Feverlein, W. Partners of female alcoholics. *British Journal of Addictions,* 1973, *68,* 179–184.

Cadogan, D. A. Marital group therapy in the treatment of alcoholism. *Quarterly Journal of Studies on Alcohol,* 1973, *34,* 1187–1194.

Catanzaro, R. J., Pisani, U. D., Fox, R., and Kennedy, E. R. Familization therapy. *Diseases of the Nervous System,* 1973, *34,* 212–218.

Chafetz, M. E., Blane, H. T., and Hill, M. J. Children of alcoholics: observations in a child guidance clinic. *Quarterly Journal of Studies on Alcohol,* 1971, *32,* 687–698.

Chassell, J. Family constellation in the etiology of essential alcoholism. *Psychiatry,* 1938, *1,* 473–482.

Cohen, P. C., and Krause, M. S. *Casework with Wives of Alcoholics.* New York: Family Service Association of America, 1971.

Cork, R. M. *The Forgotten Children.* Toronto, Canada: Addiction Research Foundation, 1969.

Corder, B. F., Corder, R. F., and Laidlaw, N. L. An intensive treatment program for alcoholics and their wives. *Quarterly Journal of Studies on Alcohol,* 1972, *33,* 1144–1146.

Davis, D., Berenson, D., Steinglass, P., and Davis, S. The adaptive consequences of drinking. *Psychiatry,* 1974, *37,* 209–215.

Davis, P., Stern, D. R., and Van Deusen, J. M. Enmeshment–disengagement in the alcoholic family. In F. A. Seixas (ed.), *Currents in Alcoholism,* Vol. 4. New York: Grune and Stratton, 1978.

Drewery, J., and Rae, J. R. A group comparison of alcoholic and nonalcoholic marriages using the interpersonal perception technique. *British Journal of Psychiatry,* 1969, *115,* 287–300.

El-Guebly, N., and Offord, D. R. The offspring of alcoholics: a critical review. *American Journal of Psychiatry,* 1977, *134,* 357–365.

Edwards, P., Harvey, C., and Whitehead, P. C. Wives of alcoholics: a critical review and analysis. *Quarterly Journal of Studies on Alcohol,* 1973, *34,* 112–132.

Esser, P. H. Conjoint family therapy for alcoholics. *British Journal of Addiction,* 1968, *63,* 177–182.

———. Evaluation of family therapy with alcoholics. *British Journal of Addiction,* 1971, *66,* 251–255.

Ewing, J. A., Long, V., and Wenzel, G. G. Concurrent group psychotherapy of alcoholic patients and their wives. *International Journal of Group Psychotherapy,* 1961, *11,* 329–340.

Ewing, J. A., and Fox, R. Family therapy of alcoholism. In J. Masserman (ed.), *Current Psychiatric Therapies,* Vol. 8. New York: Grune and Stratton, 1968.

Feldman, D. J., Pattison, E. M., Sobell, L. C., Graham, T., and Sobell, M. B. Outpatient alcohol detoxification: initial findings on 564 patients. *American Journal of Psychiatry,* 1975, *132,* 407–412.

Fox, R. Children in the alcoholic family. In W. C. Bier (ed.), *Problems in Addiction: Alcohol and Drug Addition.* New York: Fordham University Press, 1962.

Gliedman, L. H. Concurrent and combined group treatment of chronic alcoholics and their wives. *International Journal of Group Psychotherapy,* 1957, *7,* 414–424.

Gorad, S. L. Communicational styles and interaction of alcoholics and their wives. *Family Process,* 1971, *10,* 475–589.

Haberman, P. W. Psychological test score changes for wives of alcoholics during periods of drinking and sobriety. *Journal of Clinical Psychology,* 1969, *20,* 230–232.

Haley, J. *Problem Solving Therapy.* San Francisco: Jossey-Bass, 1977.

Hanson, K. J., and Estes, N. J. Dynamics of alcoholic families. In N. J. Estes and M. E. Heinemann (eds.), *Alcoholism: Development, Consequences, and Intervention.* St. Louis: C. V. Mosby, 1977.

Hanson, P. G., Sands, P. M., and Sheldon, R. B. Patterns of communication in alcoholic marital couples. *Psychiatric Quarterly,* 1968, *42,* 538–547.

Hersen, M., Miller, P., and Eisler, R. Interaction between alcoholics and their wives: a descriptive analysis of verbal and nonverbal behavior. *Quarterly Journal of Studies on Alcohol,* 1973, *34,* 516–520.

Howard, D. P., and Howard, N. T. Treatment of the significant other. In S. Zimberg, *et al.* (eds.), *Practical Approaches to Alcoholism Psychotherapy.* New York: Plenum Press, 1978.

Janzen, C. Families in the treatment of alcoholism. *Quarterly Journal of Studies on Alcohol,* 1976, *38,* 114–130.

Karlen, H. Alcoholism in conflicted marriages. *American Journal of Orthopsychiatry,* 1965, *35,* 325–326.

Kern, J. C., Tippman, J., Fortgang, J., and Paul, S. R. A treatment approach for children of alcoholics. *Journal of Drug Education,* 1978, *7,* 207–218.

Kogan, K. L., and Jackson, J. K. Alcoholism: the fable of the noxious wife. *Mental Hygiene,* 1965, *49,* 428–453.

Krimmel, H. E. The alcoholic and his family. In P. G. Bourne and R. Fox (eds.), *Alcoholism: Progress in Research and Treatment.* New York: Academic Press, 1973.

Mayer, J., Black, R., and MacDonald, J. Child care in families with an alcohol addicted parent. In F. A. Seixas (ed.), *Currents in Alcoholism,* Vol. 4. New York: Grune and Stratton, 1978.

MacDonald, D. E. Group psychotherapy with wives of alcoholics. *Quarterly Journal of Studies on Alcohol,* 1958, *19,* 125–130.

McElfresh, O. Supportive groups for teenagers of the alcoholic parent: a preliminary report. *Journal of Medical Ecology and Clinical Research,* 1970, *3,* 26–29.

McKany, L. R. Multiple family therapy on an alcoholism treatment unit. *Family Therapy,* 1976, *3,* 197–210.

Meeks, D. E., and Kelly, C. Family therapy with the families of recovered alcoholics. *Quarterly Journal of Studies on Alcohol,* 1970, *31,* 339–413.

Minuchin, S. *Families and Family Therapy.* Cambridge, Mass.: Harvard University Press, 1974.

Mitchell, H. E. The inter-relatedness of alcoholism and family conflict. *American Journal of Orthopsychiatry,* 1968, *24,* 547–559.

Moos, R. H., Bromet, E., Tsu, V., and Moos, B. Family characteristics and the outcome of treatment for alcoholics. *Quarterly Journal of Studies on Alcohol,* 1979, *40,* 78–88.

Orford, J. Alcoholism and marriage: The argument against specialism. *Quarterly Journal of Studies on Alcohol,* 1975, *36,* 1537–1563.

———, Opperneimer, E., Egert, S., Hensman, C., and Guthrie, S. The cohesiveness of alcoholism-complicated marriages and its influence on treatment outcome. *British Journal of Psychiatry,* 1976, *128,* 318–339.

Paolino, T. J., Jr., McCrady, B. S., Diamond, S., and Longaburgh, R. Psychological disturbances in spouses of alcoholics. *Quarterly Journal of Studies on Alcohol,* 1976, *37,* 1600–1608.

Paolino, T. J., Jr., and McCrady, B. S. Joint admission as a treatment modality for problem drinkers: a case report. *American Journal of Psychiatry,* 1976, *137,* 222–224.

———. *The Alcoholic Marriage: Alternative Perspectives.* New York: Grune and Stratton, 1979.

Pattison, E. M., Coe, R., and Rhodes, R. A. Evaluation of alcoholism treatment: comparison of three facilities. *Archives of General Psychiatry,* 1969, *20,* 278–288.

Pattison, E. M., Coe, R., and Doerr, H. O. Population variation among alcoholism treatment facilities. *International Journal of the Addictions,* 1973, *8,* 199–229.

Pattison, E. M., DeFrancisco, D., Wood, P., Frazier, H., and Crowder, J. A psychosocial kinship model for family therapy. *American Journal of Psychiatry,* 1975, *132,* 1246–1251.

Pattison, E. M. A conceptual approach to alcoholism treatment goals. *Addictive Behaviors, An International Journal,* 1976, *1,* 177–192.

———. Ten years of change in alcoholism treatment and delivery systems. *American Journal of Psychiatry,* 1977, *134,* 261–266.

Pattison, E. M., Sobell, M. B., and Sobell, L. C. *Emerging Concepts of Alcohol Dependence.* New York: Springer, 1977.

Pattison, E. M. The Jack Donovan Memorial Lecture 1978: differential approaches to multiple problems associated with alcoholism. *Contemporary Drug Problems,* 1978, *9,* 265–309.

———, and Kaufman, E. Alcohol and drug dependence. In G. Usdin and J. M. Lewis (eds.), *Psychiatry in General Practice.* New York: McGraw-Hill, 1979.

Rae, J. B. The influence of wives on the treatment outcome of alcoholics: a follow-up study at two years. *British Journal of Psychiatry,* 1972, *120,* 601–613.

———, and Drewery, J. Interpersonal patterns in alcoholic marriages. *British Journal of Psychiatry,* 1972, *120,* 615–621.

Rimmer, J. Psychiatric illness in husbands of alcoholics. *Quarterly Journal of Studies on Alcohol,* 1974, *35,* 281–283.

Sands, P. M., and Hanson, P. G. Psychotherapeutic groups for alcoholics and relatives in an outpatient setting. *International Journal of Group Psychotherapy,* 1971, *21,* 23–33.

Scott, E. M. *Struggles in an Alcoholic Family.* Springfield, Ill.: C. C. Thomas, 1970.

Smith, C. J. Alcoholics: their treatment and their wives. *British Journal of Psychiatry,* 1969, *115,* 1039–1042.

Steinglass, P., Weiner, S., and Mendelson, J. H. A systems approach to alcoholism: a model and its clinical application. *Archives of General Psychiatry,* 1971, *24,* 401–408.

Steinglass, P. Experimenting with family treatment approaches to alcoholism, 1950–1975: a review. *Family Process,* 1976, *15,* 97–123.

———, Davis, D. I., and Berenson, D. Observations on conjointly hospitalized alcoholic couples during sobriety and intoxication: implications for theory and therapy. *Family Process,* 1977, *16,* 146–170.

Steinglass, P. An experimental treatment program for alcoholic couples. *Quarterly Journal of Studies on Alcohol,* 1979, *40,* 159–182.

Tarter, R. Personality of wives of alcoholics. *Journal of Clinical Psychology,* 1976, *32,* 741–743.

Ward, R. F., and Faillace, L. A. The alcoholic and his helpers. *Quarterly Journal of Studies on Alcohol,* 1970, *31,* 684–691.

Watzlawick, P., Weakland, J. H., and Fisch, R. *Change: Principles of Problem Formulation and Problem Resolution.* New York: Norton Press, 1974.

Webb, N. L., Pratt, T. C., Linn, M. W., and Carmichael, J. S. Focus on the family as a factor in differential treatment outcomes. *International Journal of the Addictions,* 1978, *13,* 783–786.

Wilson, C., and Orford, J. Children of alcoholics: report of a preliminary study and comments on the literature. *Quarterly Journal of Studies on Alochol,* 1978, *39,* 121–142.

Wright, K. D., and Scott, T. B. The relationship of wives' treatment to the drinking status of alcoholics. *Quarterly Journal of Studies on Alcohol,* 1978, *39,* 1577–1581.

14

The Family and Drug Abuse

Concepts and Rationale

M. Duncan Stanton

Nearly everyone grows up in a family. Even persons who were raised in institutions can usually identify one or more people who were important to their development and whom they therefore consider to be "family."

Families can differ in their composition. Some families have two parents living in the home; others have one parent. Some have one or more grandparents at home, while others have aunts or uncles. Some people were raised by relatives other than their biological parents, while others were raised by adoptive parents. The point is that each person has what he or she defines as a family—people who were important in his or her early and, usually, later years—although the delineation of who is included in that family may differ from person to person.

The bond between family members is unique, distinguishing the family from groups established in work settings or even in therapeutic communities. Family ties manifest their strength perhaps most clearly in people who reject their families yet cannot eliminate the influence of these "significant others" (Bowen, 1978). Accordingly, viewing the individual apart from his or her family can give only an incomplete picture of the person's daily functioning. When we recognize this, we may find it more useful to entertain notions of the family as being more than a simple aggregation of individuals united by blood or living arrangements. The family begins to emerge as a *system*. Its members are *interdependent*, and actions by one or more of them affect the others.

People do not behave apart from the systems within which they are embedded. For example, the illness or sudden success of one member resounds throughout the system and affects the others. These others in turn react or act upon the sick or successful member in ways which may modify his or her behavior. He or she responds again, and so on; an ongoing process is occurring. Thus, a particular behavior by a member (such as a symptom) must be regarded in the light of how the other members of the family are contributing to it or making it possible, and also how the behavior is, in turn, affecting these other members. This is a system at work. Moreover, the system cannot be considered without taking into account both the members involved *and* their interactions. Put another way, the family system is greater than the sum of its parts (Olson, 1970).

A system is often made up of *subsystems*. In a family, a given member might be seen as a type of subsystem. Usually, however, we think of family subsystems as being composed of one or more people. Examples might be the parental (versus the child) subsystem, or the male (versus the female) subsystem.

In most families, the interactions between subsystems will be changing regularly, depending on particular circumstances. For instance, a disagreement over whether to watch a football game or a tennis match on TV might crystallize a male-versus-female subsystem conflict within a family. Another topic could result in a realignment between other subsystems, such as those of father-daughter versus mother-son. A more flexible family system will be more likely to experience a shift in its subsystem composition with differing external requirements or different contexts. A more rigid system does not show this adaptability and tends to stay fixed in its subsystem composition—no matter what outside changes impinge on it.

The above formulations—and those that follow—are generally discontinuous with conventional views of patients, their families, and how symptoms develop within families. For the most part, the views of families and symptoms which have predominated within the drug abuse and mental health fields have been simplistic and naive. Except for consideration of the early developmental years, the family has been viewed as having a more or less inert influence, which, at worst, can bring additional "stress" on the symptomatic member. However, the family's importance in symptom *maintenance* has generally gone unrecognized. In instances where the family *is* mentioned, discussion has usually been couched in terms of, for example, mother-addict or father-addict dyads, or the characteristics of these people as individuals; the idea of an ongoing, continually operating system has been overlooked. In other words, individually and dyadically oriented concepts are not really in tune with what we have learned about families over the past twenty-five to thirty years.

One reason for the aforementioned lag is the view of *causality* which has prevailed throughout the field—i.e., what "causes" what. Generally people have thought in terms of *linear,* or straight-line, causality; e.g., A causes B, or A and B cause C. Examples of this kind of thinking might be expressed as: "He is an addict because of the kind of parents he has," or, "With a son like that, who could blame the parents for being the way they are?" Both of these examples are linear: in the first case, the parents are the cause; and in the second, the son. However, if we reframe a situation in *nonlinear,* or cyclic, terms, we would embrace a paradigm such that A leads to B, B leads to C, and C leads back again to A.

In our example, the parents act toward the son, the son acts toward the parents, the parents react again, etc. It is a repetitive sequence, and we arbitrarily choose the point at which we enter in order to start our observations—our point of "punctuation" (Bateson, 1972; Watzlawick, Beavin, and Jackson, 1967). If we first look at the parents' behavior, then at the son's behavior, but go no further, we would probably end up with a linear explanation. A similar causal notion would emerge if we had started with the son's behavior but went no further than to observe the parents' response. A nonlinear, or "meta," view, however, would dictate that we observe the total sequence within its context.

Further, in looking at a repetitive sequence of people interacting, a simple notion of A-to-B causality becomes inappropriate and constraining. Nonlinear causality requires both a different approach to the ways in which we think about symptoms such as drug abuse and an adjustment in the way we approach the variables involved. It may also hold considerable potential for explaining the addiction process, as will be discussed below.

Family Concepts and Theory

Before dealing directly with family factors in drug abuse, it seems appropriate to acquaint the reader with an overview of some aspects

---

The subsection "Family Concepts and Theory" was adapted from an earlier report by the author entitled *Drug Misuse and the Family,* prepared for the White House Office of Drug Abuse Policy, Washington, D. C., October 1977.

of family theory, particularly regarding the family as a system. Having a basic familiarity with this material is necessary to understand the role of drugs in the family and can also contribute to the formulation of a more sophisticated treatment plan.

The concepts given below have been developed by people working in the family field over the last two or three decades. Although a comprehensive, universally accepted theory of family functioning has not yet emerged, the core concepts are deserving of and have gained widespread attention (Steinglass, 1976).

Family Boundaries

Family boundaries are the rules which both divide family subsystems and separate the family from outside influences. They connote a kind of proximity or distance between members and between subsystems, and they define a family "structure." At the extremes, they can be too rigid or too permeable. For instance, a parent-child (two-person) subsystem which is overly close and interdependent may have a permeable boundary within itself, and a rigid boundary between it and other family subsystems. Such overinvolvement between parent and child—in which the two of them are constantly "into each other's business" and seemingly inseparable—has been called "enmeshment." Subsystems which are extremely separate and perhaps uninvolved have been termed "disengaged" (Minuchin, 1974).

It is also possible to view family boundaries in terms of their relationship to the outside world. Some families have very open boundaries, and are greatly influenced and buffeted by the events and social systems which surround them. Other families are overly encapsulated, so that they become cut off from natural outside support systems and even the subsystems within their own extended family system.

Intergenerational Coalitions

When problems occur with a family member, such as a child, one should first look for struggles between family coalitions which cut across generational lines. An example would be when one parent and a child are overtly or covertly pitted against the other parent and a different child. Since the usual family coalitions in our society divide across generations—parents forming one coalition and children another—overly strong intergenerational coalitions are usually problematic. Sometimes they take the form of parents not talking directly to each other, but instead communicating through a child. This puts the child in the awkward position of attempting to resolve split loyalties. The child is used as a tool in the conflict. It also can give him undue power within the system, which he may exploit to get his own way, or he may become unruly. Most parents prevent this by uniting to form their own generational coalition, but if they cannot do this, the child may "play them off" against each other. Different explanations have been given as to why this occurs; e.g., perhaps one parent is not given permission by his or her own parents to maintain a satisfactory marital relationship. But whatever the explanation, the process is well-recognized in families with one or more "problem" members.

Triads

Related to the above is the notion of triads; i.e., the concept that at least three people are involved in generating and maintaining a psychogenic symptom. It is possible to view the symptomatic person as being caught between the competing requirements of two people or subsystems that are important to him or her. The person's loyalties or involvement with both dictate that he or she find some way to at least partially address their conflicting agendas.

The school-phobic child may get the message from one parent to stay at home because he is needed there, while the school, his peers, the other parent, or a combination of these put pressure on him to go to school. The issue may be partly resolved by going to school in deference to the second group, but leaving school early, or as soon as he arrives, as a way of honoring the parent who needs him at home. As another example, an adult may become a heavy drinker when his job and family escalate their respective demands on him to the point where he can no longer acceptably satisfy both; the drinking serves as a withdrawal from an impossible situation, and also as a way of getting both systems to relax their demands.

The concept of triads or triangles being involved in people's interpersonal problems and symptoms has been a cornerstone of the family therapy field for many years. The assumption that a triad is involved in the problem is almost invariably correct. It usually involves two adults and the "identified" patient. For example, if the symptomatic person is a young adult male who abuses drugs, it can commonly be observed that his mother lavishes affection on him because she is not getting enough time and attention from her husband. Conversely, the husband may retreat because his wife undercuts him—as, for example, when he tries appropriately to discipline the son.

Further, the abuser may serve a function for the parents, either as a channel for their communication or as a disrupter whose distracting behavior keeps the parents' fights from crystallizing; he may seek a "sick" state in order to position himself, childlike, as the focus of his parents' attentions. This kind of thinking is much more attuned than conventional linear thinking to the whole family system, and points to the way in which all members can become caught together in a repetitive, dysfunctional pattern.

In some drug abuser families of origin, one parent (often the father) is absent. In such cases, one would think that a triadic model (like the one described above) would not apply, and that a dyadic framework (e.g., one encompassing mother and son) would be more fitting. It would also appear to be a more parsimonious and less complicated model.

Nonetheless, Stanton et al. (1978) have found that when the matter is pursued closely, a third important member generally emerges as an active participant in the interaction. Usually the triadic system takes a less obvious form, involving, for example, a covert disagreement between mother and grandmother, or mother and ex-husband. This is consonant with a point made emphatically by Haley (1976) that at least two adults are usually involved in an offspring's problem, and that clinicians should look for a triangle consisting of an overinvolved parent-child dyad and a more peripheral parent, grandparent, or parent surrogate. Thus, in addition to the (male) addict and his mother, the triad may include the mother's boyfriend, an estranged parent, a grandparent, or some other relative. These alternative systems appear to exhibit patterns and cycles similar to those in which both parents are present, and they often revolve around an interruption, on the part of the abuser, of conflicts between adult members. However, achieving separation and independence is even more of an issue in single-parent families, since the single parent may be left alone with few interpersonal supports if the drug abuser departs.

Family Homeostasis

The family has a sense of balance and stability. When disruptions occur in the balance, such as with the death of a member, built-in mechanisms take hold in order to compensate and foster a return to stability. In the case of a death, other family members may assume the duties and roles of the deceased. For example, the oldest son, or the last son living in the home, may assume male head-of-household roles upon the death of the father.

Another kind of imbalance could occur when a child starts school and the family has to readjust to a new situation in which this child will not be home all day with one parent, probably the mother. However, if the need for the original homeostatic condition is too great, pressure will bear on the child to stay at home, perhaps leading to a school-phobia symptom. Thus, homeostasis can have either adaptive or maladaptive consequences.

The "feedback loop" is one aspect of homeostasis. This refers to the kind of regulatory, usually repetitive, patterns of behavior which families manifest. An example might be when parents (A and B) and a child (C) are driving in a car together. Spouse A is driving, and spouse B is in a hurry to get to their destination (and conveys this before the trip). Spouse A accelerates through the yellow light, and B grabs a dashboard handle and criticizes A, who retorts and steps on the gas. B protests more loudly, A shouts back, and the child, C, starts crying. At this point the argument stops while B attends to C and A slows down. Thus C's behavior becomes one element in a feedback process which serves to restore homeostasis. Chances are that such a pattern has occurred before and will recur again in the future. All families show patterns—albeit in positive ways, too, such as in rounds of joking or showing affection.

Behavioral Context

It may be apparent, from the discussion thus far, that considerable importance is attached to observing a symptom within its behavioral context. It can be extremely helpful for the clinician to know the conditions leading up to and surrounding a particular behavior. In the case of the car-driving example given above, for instance, the context of the child's crying included not only the three family members but also the car, the pressure to get somewhere on time, and the tardiness in getting started. In addition, it might be important to know where they were going, and if undue pressure to be punctual came from that end. In any case, simply noting that the child cries without clarification of context leaves us with an incomplete understanding of the event.

The "Identified Patient" or "Scapegoat"

From a family viewpoint, difficulties or symptoms which occur in a family member are part of a total family process in which that one member is labeled as the problem. In the car-driving case, the child might be seen as the problem for "crying too much." The child is then scapegoated, and he becomes the "identified patient" if he is brought to a facility for treatment. However, a more realistic assessment might portray the identified patient as the individual expressing, through his behavior, the fact that a disturbance exists in the whole family. He may be protecting or stabilizing the family.

Nonetheless, this should not be misconstrued as being a "poor, mistreated child" syndrome, since the child contributes to the process. If this pattern had occurred many times before, the child might have erupted into crying as soon as the family entered the car, even though no feelings of animosity had existed between the parents at the outset of this particular trip.

The symptomatic member in a family can in many ways be viewed as a sacrificial person. He gives up his reputation and well-being in the service of the family (Boszormenyi-Nagy and Spark, 1973). He may protect other members from the intrusion of outside "helpers" by drawing attention to himself and his problem. Trying to cope with his troubles may be a rallying point which brings the family together; in some families, in fact, he is almost the only person who can unite the system, and, if his problem disappears, the family becomes fragmented. Of course, he also perpetuates the problem, sometimes even in the face of growth or improvement in other members; he may try to get them to "hark back" to the old homeostatic condition.

This view of the symptomatic member is radically new to most people, and is sometimes hard to believe. Perhaps one has to observe it occurring in a family to become convinced of its validity. One may have to see, for example, how a son can temper his success and not realize his potential in order to prevent his uneducated father from appearing as the least competent member of the family. Perhaps one has to observe an "identified patient" who is a child burst out with symptoms at the point where his parents begin to move toward divorce—thus reuniting them in the cause of helping him and effecting a postponement of the separation. Whatever the case, this is a process which does occur in many families, and acknowledging it can indeed help in the understanding of why symptoms occur as they do.

Family Role Selection

Family members are assigned particular roles within their families, often before they are born. These roles (Wegscheider, 1981; Forrest, 1983) depend on multiple variables such as birth order, sex, energy levels, and what is transpiring in the family at the time of the birth.

A child born during a period of parental bereavement will have different experiences than one born at a time of joy or financial success. In the extreme cases, a child may be "assigned" to one parent as belonging to him or her, while the other parent may "adopt" a later child. Sometimes parents "buy" freedom from their own parents by giving away a child to this older couple to raise. The role of "black sheep" is often assigned to one member in each generation of a family, as is the role of the "responsible" or "parentified" child. Reilly (1976) notes that the naming process is important, as children are sometimes raised in the role of the person (usually a relative) after whom they are named; he has also observed that drug abusers are sometimes named after relatives who had an addiction problem.

To believe, then, that the environment is the same for all children in a family is to make a grave miscalculation. Family members are *not* treated identically, although less dysfunctional or less disturbed families will allow offspring more role flexibility. This point is important in the drug and alcohol area because it speaks to the issue of why all siblings do not take drugs with equal frequency, especially if all of them have an equal opportunity to observe the drug-taking patterns of their parents. "Modeling" parents' behavior is only a partial explanation for drug-taking behavior (Stanton, 1979a).

The Family Life Cycle

Most families encounter similar stages as they progress through life. Some of these stages are more child-related than others—for example, the birth of a first child, a child first attending school, the onset of adolescence in a child, or children leaving home. Other stages pertain more to events directly affecting parents, such as the loss of a job, getting a promotion, the death of a grandparent, menopause, or retirement. All such events are part of the family life cycle, and denote changes in the family structure, frequently in terms of *loss* or *increased distance* among members.

For example, the birth of a child constitutes an increase in the number of family members, but it also may mean that the parents can devote less time to each other. A promotion for the family breadwinner may result in that person's having greater demands placed upon him or her by the employer, leaving less time for spouse and children. These, then, are crisis points, which, although sometimes difficult to get through, are usually weathered by most families without inordinate difficulty.

On the other hand, symptomatic families may develop problems because they are unable to adjust to such transitions. The flexibility and requisite adaptability do not emerge. Instead, the family becomes "stuck" at a given point or stage, and is unable to transcend it. A dysfunctional cycle can develop so that, like a broken record, the family repetitively goes through the same process without advancing beyond it. Such repetitive (homeostatic) processes can be rather easily identified, if there is time to observe one or more rounds of the cycle. The family life cycle paradigm is a very useful device and can provide the template for setting the direction for treatment.

Systems, Symptoms, and Change

From the foregoing discussion, the role of the symptom per se within the family system may be apparent. A symptom can be seen as a particular kind of behavior that functions as a homeostatic mechanism regulating family transactions (Jackson, 1965); i.e., it maintains the dynamic equilibrium among the members. It is a communicative act that serves as a sort of contract between two or more members and often occurs when a person is "in an impossible situation and is trying to break out of it" (Haley, 1973). The individual is locked in a sequence or pattern with the rest of his family or significant others, and he cannot see a way to alter it through nonsymptomatic means (Stanton, 1981b).

More specifically, the symptom may help, for example, in the labeling of a member as helpless and incompetent, and therefore unable to leave home. It might serve as a problem that unifies the family and keeps it intact, much as a catastrophe unites people who experience it together. Similarly, the symptom might have diversionary qualities, drawing the attention of other family members to the symptom bearer and away from their own difficulties. These are just a few of the functions which a symptom can serve within a family's homeostatic system.

Lennard and Allen (1973) have emphasized how, in order for drug abuse treatment to "take hold," the social context of the abuser must be changed. Applying this to the family, one could assert, as have Bowen (1966), Haley (1962), and others, that in order for the symptom to change, the *family system* must change. Conversely, treatment that changes an individual will also have effects on his or her interpersonal system. However, if broader system change (rather than change primarily in the individual) does not occur, the chances for prolonged cure are reduced, for there can be considerable pressure on the "improved" symptomatic member to revert to the old ways. This idea has important implications for the way in which drug abuse treatment is approached.

We are dealing here with events and behaviors that often lie outside the purview and experience of most drug abuse treatment providers and researchers; the actions of family members other than the symptom bearer are rarely or only occasionally observed within the context of most conventional programs. When the larger system actually is encompassed, we must make a conceptual leap into new ways of thinking about symptoms such as substance abuse. Such a view is radically different from traditional cause-and-effect explanations. It is a new orientation to human problems. Einstein stated that the theory to which we subscribe determines what we see, and it is hoped that through application of this different perspective, the reader will be better able to understand the material to follow.

Drug Abusers' Family Patterns and Structures

It is beyond the scope of this section to discuss the extensive body of demographic, psychosocial, and interactional literature that has accumulated on the families of drug abusers. At least 370 publications exist (Stanton, 1978a), and the field has been covered by Seldin (1972), Harbin and Maziar (1975), Salmon and Salmon (1977), Klagsbrun and Davis (1977), and, most recently, by Stanton (1979a). Instead, a brief overview will be given of the predominant patterns and structures that have emerged from the body of existent research. Their relevance for treatment will also be noted. Emphasis here and throughout this report will be on findings about families in which a member shows heavy, compulsive drug use rather than occasional or experimental use.

The Family of Origin

In the prototypic drug-abuser family—as described in most of the literature—one parent is intensely involved with the abuser, while the other is more punitive, distant, or absent. Usually, the overinvolved, indulgent, overprotective parent is of the opposite sex. However, Alexander and Dibb (1975) posit that a same-sex parent may assume this role in some middle-class families, and Kaufman and Kaufmann (1979b) note that father–son enmeshment occurs in 40 to 60 percent of Italian and Jewish addicts' families (socioeconomic and cultural factors may play a part here). Sometimes this overinvolvement reaches the point of incest (Cuskey, Richardson, and Berger, 1979; Ellinwood, Smith, and Vaillant, 1966; Wellisch, Gay, and McEntee, 1970), with estimates running as high as 90 percent among female heroin addicts (Kaufman and Kaufmann, 1979b).

Further, the abusing offspring may serve a function for the parents, either as a channel for their communication or as a disrupter whose distracting behavior keeps their own fights from crystallizing. Parents of heavy abusers usually have very dysfunctional marital relationships; they apparently cannot relate to each other satisfactorily and detour their struggles through offspring. The child can even serve as a spouse surrogate for one parent, thus allowing the other parent, if he or she is present, to maintain some sort of distance. Often the child's problem becomes the only "cause" around which the parents can unite, so in a sense he or she keeps them together (Haley, 1973; Stanton et al., 1978).

Among families of youthful drug abusers, problems appear to be unduly common at two particular life-cycle stages. The first of these is when the potential identified patient reaches adolescence. This is a time when the young person is going through the normal but often troublesome process of growing up, experimenting with new behaviors, becoming self-assertive, and developing close (usually heterosexual) relationships outside the family. Drug experimentation is now more a part of the process than it was in the past (Forrest, 1983).

Kandel et al. (1976) propose, from their data, that there are three stages in adolescent drug use, and that each has different concomitants. The first is the use of legal drugs, such as alcohol; this is mainly a social phenomenon. The second stage involves use of marijuana, and it is also primarily peer-influenced. The third stage, frequent or compulsive use of other illegal drugs, appears contingent more on the quality of the parent-adolescent relationship than on other factors. Thus, these authors conclude, more serious drug misuse is predominantly a family phenomenon.

Not infrequently, the young abuser was a "favorite child" or the "easiest to raise" during his/her earlier years, but now he is a problem. This seems to be tied, again, to the family's inability to adjust to his/her growing independence, and, especially, to initial heterosexual involvement with peers, such as occurs when dating begins. Adolescents are becoming less available and less attached to the family, and they cannot tolerate the competition and threatened loss.

The second important life-cycle stage for families of youthful drug abusers is the point at which it is appropriate for the young person to leave home. Since s/he seems to be badly needed by the family, his/her threatened departure heralds parental panic. The family then becomes stuck, falling into a chronic, repetitive process related to his leaving home (Haley, 1980). Sometimes this occurs quite overtly through a number of cycles in which the young person moves out of the home and then back in again. The pressure not to leave can be so powerful that the family will endure (and even encourage) terrible indignities such as lying, stealing, and public shame, rather than take a firm position in relation to the youthful troublemaker. They may also protect him from outside agencies, relatives, and other social systems. Rather than accept responsibility themselves, they blame external systems, such as peers or the neighborhood, for the drug problem. When the parents take effective action—such as evicting their addicted offspring—they often undo their actions by encouraging his return. They seem to be saying, "We will suffer almost anything, but please don't leave us." Thus, it becomes nearly impossible for an addict to negotiate his way out of the family, and he slips into greater abuse as a means of resolving the bind within which he is caught.

A number of writers have described how the family system works to keep the drug abuser in a dependent, incompetent role—undermining his self-esteem and thus helping to maintain family stability and homeostasis (e.g., Alexander and Dibb, 1975, 1977; Huberty, 1975; Noone and Reddig, 1976; Reilly, 1976; Schwartzman, 1975).

Stanton et al. (1978) note that drugs can provide a paradoxical resolution to the dilemma of staying or leaving, for they allow a certain level of competence (e.g., hustling) within a framework of incompetence. The drugs serve the dual function of letting the addict be distant, independent, and individuated while at the same time making him or her dependent, in need of money and substance, and loyal to the family. Stanton et al. have termed this *pseudo-individuation.* Again, the use of drugs by a member can be seen as an example of a family getting "hung up" at a developmental point in its life cycle and not being able to move beyond it.

Until recent years, the extent to which drug abusers are involved with their families of origin (parents) has tended to be overlooked within the drug abuse field. To be sure, it has not necessarily been obvious that, for example, male addicts in their late twenties and early thirties would still be involved with their parents. Their age, submersion in the drug subculture, frequent changes in residence, and, perhaps, military service all seem to imply that they are cut off, or at least distanced, from one or both parents. Thus, they have been predominantly viewed as "drifters" or "loners" with few or no primary ties. However, emerging research is challenging this notion.

While the pattern is less common for female addicts, reviews by the author (Stanton, 1981a, 1980; Stanton et al., 1978) of fourteen studies and reports examining patterns of parent-addict contact have found increasing evidence that despite their (frequent) protestations of independence, and their efforts to protect their parents, the majority of male addicts maintain close family ties. Even if they do not reside with their parents, they may live nearby, and the frequency of contact is high. The general findings are that two-thirds live with their parents or see their mothers daily, while 80 to 90 percent see one or both parents weekly. A study by Perzel and Lamon (1979) indicated that 42 to 48 percent of male and female polydrug abusers live with their parents, compared to 21 percent of patients with other psychiatric diagnoses, and 7 percent of a group of comparable "normals."

Further, this phenomenon does not seem to be limited to North America, as 80 percent of the addicts in Italy and Thailand, 67 percent of those in Puerto Rico, and 62 percent of the addicts in England have been reported to be living with their parents.

These multiple findings document the loose boundaries (enmeshment) that seem to exist between a great many addicts and their parents or parent surrogates, and hint at the possible importance of the family of origin in the addiction process.

Additional evidence on how subsequent family life cycle changes can relate to addictive patterns comes from Noone (1979). He examined patterns of this type among a group of 21 heroin and barbiturate addicts (mean age = 25.5). He interviewed each subject and at least one family member to see if the addition, loss, threatened loss (e.g., heart attack, diagnosis of cancer, etc.), or retirement of a family member coincided with drug-related behavior by the addict. It was found that in 18 of 21 cases (86 percent), at least one such event occurred in the family at about the same time that the primary subject was described as first developing a drug abuse problem. Nodal family events also occurred around most overdoses (7 of 9 cases = 78 percent), arrests (8 of 10 = 80 percent), and points when the addict entered treatment (14 of 21 = 67 percent). These data underscore the utility of viewing drug-related events vis-à-vis changes in the family life cycle.

In line with the theoretical notions presented earlier on repetitive family sequences and homeostasis, Stanton et al. (1978) note that drug taking is often part of a cyclical process involving three or more individuals—commonly the addict and two parents or parental figures (e.g., a grandparent or a parent's paramour). These persons form an intimate, interdependent, interpersonal system.

At times, the equilibrium of this interpersonal system is threatened, such as when discord between the parental figures is amplified to the point of impending separation. When this happens, addicts becomes activated, their behavior changes, and they create a situation that dramatically *focuses attention upon themselves*. This behavior can take a number of forms. For example, they may lose their temper, come home high, commit a serious crime, or overdose on drugs. Whatever its form, however, this action allows the parents to shift focus from their marital or other conflict to a parental overinvolvement with the offspring. In effect, the movement is from an unstable dyadic interaction (e.g., patents alone) to a more stable triadic interaction (parents and addict). By focusing on the problems of the addict, no matter how severe or life-threatening, the parents choose a course that is apparently safer than dealing with their own longstanding conflicts. Consequently—after the intraparental crisis has been successfully avoided—the addict shifts to a less provocative stance and begins to behave more competently. This is a new step in the sequence. As the addict demonstrates increased competence, indicating the ability to function independently of the family—for example, by getting a job, getting married, enrolling in a drug treatment program, or getting detoxified—the parents are left to deal with their still-unresolved conflicts. At this point in the cycle, tensions between them increase and the threat of separation arises. The addict then behaves in an attention-getting or self-destructive way, and the dysfunctional triadic cycle is again completed. Within this framework, then, the drug taking is part of a *family* addiction cycle.

This cycle can vary in its intensity. It may occur in subdued form during treatment sessions or during day-to-day interactions and conversations around the home. For example, a parent hinting at vacationing without the spouse may trigger a spurt of loud talking by the addict. If the stakes are increased, the cycle becomes more explosive, and the actions of all participants grow more serious and more dramatic; e.g., the parents' threatening divorce might well be followed by the addict's overdosing. Whatever the intensity level, however, such patterns have been observed regularly by many clinicians and researchers. Thus, when viewed from this perspective, the behavior of the addict serves an important *protective* function and helps to maintain the homeostatic balance of the family system.

The Family of Procreation

Concerning marriage and the family of procreation, it has generally been concluded that the (usually heterosexual) dyadic relationships that addicts become involved in are a repetition of the nuclear family of origin, with roles and interaction patterns similar to those seen with the opposite-sex parent (Harbin and Maziar, 1975; Seldin, 1972; Taylor, Wilbur, and Osnos, 1966; Wolk and Diskind, 1961; Wegscheider, 1981).

In a certain number of these marriages, both spouses are addicted, although it is more common for one or neither of them to be drug-dependent at the beginning of the relationship (Fram and Hoffman, 1973; Wellisch, Gay, and McEntee, 1970). If the marital union is formed during addiction, it is more likely to dissolve after methadone treatment than if initiated at some other time (Africano, Fortunato, and Padow, 1973). Also, nonaddicted wives tend to find their husbands' methadone program to be more satisfactory than do addicted wives (Clark et al., 1972). Equally important, the rate of marriage for male addicts is half that which would be expected, while the rate for multiple marriages is above average for both sexes (O'Donnell, 1969). Chein et al. (1964), Scher (1966), and Stanton et al. (1978) have noted how parental permission for the addict to have a viable marital relationship is often quite tentative. Although they attempt flight into marriage, there is often a certain pull or encouragement for them to go back. Consequently, they usually return home, defeated, to their parents.

Comparisons with Other Symptoms or Disorders

Since a number of disorders, in addition to drug abuse, show a pattern of overinvolvement by one parent and distance and/or absence by the other, the question arises as to how drug abusers' families differ from other dysfunctional families. The author and associates (Stanton et al., 1978; Stanton, 1981a) have tried to clarify this issue, drawing both from the literature and from their own studies.

In brief, the cluster of distinguishing factors for addict families appears to include the following:

- There is a higher frequency of multigenerational chemical dependency—particularly on alcohol among males—plus a propensity for other addiction-like behaviors such as gambling and watching television. (Such practices provide modeling for children and also can develop into family "traditions.")
- There appears to be more primitive and direct expression of conflict, with quite explicit (versus covert) alliances, for example, between the addict and the overinvolved parent.
- Addictive parents' behavior is "conspicuously unschizophrenic."
- Addicts may have a peer group or subculture to which they (briefly) retreat following family conflict—the illusion of independence is greater.
- Mothers of addicts display "symbiotic" child-rearing practices further into the life of the child, and show greater symbiotic needs, than mothers of schizophrenics and normals.
- There is a preponderance of death themes and premature, unexpected, or untimely deaths within the family.
- The symptom of addiction provides a form of "pseudo-individuation" (false independence) at several levels, extending from the individual-pharmacological level to that of the drug subculture.
- The rate of addiction among offspring of immigrants is greater than might be expected, suggesting the importance of acculturation and parent-child cultural disparity in addiction.

Factors in Family Treatment

Family Factors That Neutralize Treatment for Drug Abuse

From the early papers (e.g., Berliner, 1966–67; Hirsch, 1961; Mason, 1958; Wolk and Diskind, 1961) to the present, many writers have attested to the importance of the family in the maintenance of addiction. Not only is the drug taking of one member often overlooked by relatives, it is frequently either openly or covertly encouraged (Harbin and Maziar, 1975; Klagsbrun and Davis, 1977; Seldin, 1972; Stanton, 1979a; Thompson, 1973; Wellisch and Kaufman, 1975). Further, in addition to supporting the drug-taking pattern, the family may actually work to sabotage those treatment efforts which begin to succeed in reducing or eliminating it. Examples of this have been commonly reported in the literature, such as the wife of the recovering alcoholic who buys him a bottle of liquor for his birthday, or the parent of the heroin addict who gives him money to purchase drugs. Thus, the family is crucial in determining whether or not someone *remains* addicted.

Addicts who are married or are living with a spouse-type partner are involved in at least two intimate interpersonal systems—that of the "marriage" and that of the family of origin. Since more time is spent in the marital context, this system would appear to be more influential in maintaining the drug pattern. A number of writers (e.g., Gasta and Schut, 1977; Wellisch, Gay, and McEntee, 1970) have emphasized the importance of drugs in such relationships, and Hejinian and Pittel (1978) give data indicating that while addicts' spouse-type partners generally voice strong support for the abuser's abstinence, there is also evidence for an unconscious collusion to remain addicted.

However, the author's own studies (Stanton and Todd, 1979; Stanton et al., 1978; Stanton et al., 1981) have underscored the interdependence between the marital couple and one or both of their respective families of origin. In line with the observations (noted earlier) of Chein et al. (1964) and Scher (1966), it has been observed that a "rebound" effect often occurs from marital quarrels, resulting in the addict returning to his or her parents. It has been found that couples therapy often brings stress on the marriage and triggers another rebound, so that treatment has to begin by including both systems; the key is to start with the parental-addict triad and move more toward the

---

The subsection "Factors in Family Treatment" was adapted from a chapter by the author entitled "Some Overlooked Aspects of the Family and Drug Abuse," in B. Ellis (ed.), *Drug Abuse from the Family Perspective: Coping is a Family Affair.* Publication of the Office of Program Development and Analysis, National Institute on Drug Abuse. Washington, D. C., U. S. Government Printing Office, 1980.

family of procreation in accordance with parents' readiness to "release" the addict (Stanton and Todd, 1979; Stanton et al., 1978).

Several investigators have looked at family effects on posttreatment adjustment. Vaillant (1966), in a followup of thirty abstinent versus thirty "worst" outcomes among sixty Lexington addicts, found that of those who become abstinent, "virtually all were living independently from their parents at the time that they achieved abstinence." Zahn and Ball (1972) looked at relapse rates for 108 Puerto Rican heroin addicts discharged from Lexington. They found that 20 percent had been abstinent for three years ("cured"), and also that cure was associated with living with one's spouse after discharge, while noncure was associated with living with one's parents and relatives.

In a comparison of outcomes for four different treatment conditions (N = 118), Stanton et al. (1979) examined correlations between (1) sixteen demographic and family-of-origin variables and (2) posttreatment use of nine different drug variables (illegal opiates, nonopiate illegal drugs, etc.). Seven of the variables produced at least one significant correlation with a drug-use variable. However, the one variable which showed by far the most widespread and significant relationship was whether or not the addict's parents or parent-surrogates (e.g., stepfather, mother's boyfriend, etc.) were living together; this variable produced significant correlations ranging from .22 to .33 on six of the nine drug-use variables. The implication is that if the (male) addict's mother lived alone, prognosis was worse. Further, these investigators found significant correlations between extent of use of illegal drugs (.20) and of marijuana (.23), when measured against regularity of contact with a parent; the correlations between these two drug-use variables and whether the addict actually lived with his parents were, respectively, .21 and .22.

Finally, in their clinical work, Stanton et al. (1978, 1981) observed that prognosis was better for addict families in which the parents were most easily able to release the addict to outsiders during the course of treatment. These findings underscore the importance of the adult addict's family of origin in treatment success and may help dictate the direction of therapy.

Of course, living with parents or seeing them regularly are not, in and of themselves, indications of dysfunction. Depending on the cultural and ethnic milieu, such arrangements can be quite natural, and certainly many young adults who maintain regular family involvement do not become drug addicts. What may be more important is the quality and operational/functional structure within families that develop drug-abusing offspring, with consideration also given to their stage in the family life cycle. Overinvolvement, then, can only be considered an indirect measure of family dysfunction. However, the studies cited above imply that being closely involved with the family of origin is not necessarily "healthy," especially among young men aged twenty-two to thirty-five.

Positive Family Influence

While the above discussion deals with ways in which the family can neutralize the treatment effort, family involvement can also prove beneficial (Dell Orto, 1974; Forrest, 1983). The inherent leverage of significant others can be used to help the drug-abusing member *overcome* the problem, rather than serving as a force that *maintains* it. To this point, Eldred and Washington (1976) found in interviews with 158 male and female heroin addicts that the people the patients thought would be most helpful to them in their attempts to give up drugs were the members of their families of origin or their in-laws; second and third choices were an opposite-sex partner and the patient himself or herself. Macro Systems (1975) researchers found, in interviews with 462 heroin addicts, that the family was second only to treatment (70.9 percent versus 79.6 percent) as the influence they perceived as being most important in changing their lives. Finally, Levy (1972) indicated in a five-year follow-up of narcotic addicts that patients who successfully overcame drug abuse most often had family support.

Family Treatment

Concerning non–drug related disorders, the field of family therapy appears to have come of age. Dozens of books, hundreds of articles, and at least five journals exist in the area. In a review of the literature, Gurman and Kniskern (1978) located over 200 studies of family or marital treatment which presented outcome data. Of those in which family therapy was directly compared with other modes of treatment, it emerged with superior results in two-thirds of the studies and with equal results in the remainder. Gurman and Kniskern also noted that among the various "schools" of family therapy, the most impressive findings have been obtained with a "structural" approach (Minuchin, 1974), corresponding, in general, with results which have emerged with family therapy in the drug abuse field (Stanton, 1979b).

As mentioned above, family treatment is a relative newcomer to the field of drug abuse. However, it has found rapid acceptance. Data from a survey of 2,012 drug treatment facilities by Coleman and Davis (1978) indicate that the majority of our nation's drug abuse treatment programs provide some kind of family services—in many cases family or marital therapy—as part of their therapeutic armamentarium. In at least forty of these programs, involvement of the family is mandatory (Coleman and Stanton, 1978a).

Recently, the author (1979b) reviewed the literature on family treatment for drug problems. Seventy-four papers were located, pertaining to sixty-eight different studies or programs. Many different approaches have been used, including marital treatment, group treatment for parents, concurrent parent and identified-patient treatment, treatment with individual families (both inpatient and outpatient), sibling-oriented treatment, multiple family therapy, and social network therapy.* The most common approach was conjoint family therapy: i.e., treatment of individual families.

Most of the papers held that such approaches are beneficial and effective. Eight of the sixty-eight mentioned the efficacy of their techniques without providing data, twenty presented case studies with outcomes, and fourteen quantified their outcomes. Six of the fourteen involved comparisons with other forms of treatment or control groups. Four of the six (Hendricks, 1971; Scopetta et al., 1980; Stanton, 1978b, and Stanton et al., 1979; Wunderlich, Lozes, and Lewis, 1974) showed family treatment to be superior to other modes, while the remaining two (Winer, Lorio, and Scrafford, 1974; Ziegler-Driscoll, 1977, 1978) obtained equivalent, or equivocal, results. The author concludes that family treatment—especially outpatient-conjoint, multiple family therapy, and group treatment for parents—shows considerable promise for effectively dealing with problems of drug abuse.

Implications

The most basic implication from the foregoing discussion pertains to the conceptual framework applied to drug taking and the people who engage in it. Treatment from a family or interpersonal systems viewpoint rests on certain assumptions about relationships and behavioral patterns which, again, are in some ways discontinuous with most other conceptual schemata. They sit at a different level of theoretical integration.

* The reader is referred to this review for a more complete discussion of the various techniques used.

The subsection "Implications" was adapted from two similar presentations by the author in a chapter entitled "Family Treatment of Drug Problems: A Review," in R. I. Dupont, A. Goldstein, and J. O'Donnell (eds.), *Handbook on Drug Abuse,* Washington, D. C., U. S. Government Printing Office, 1979; and a paper, "Family treatment approaches to drug abuse problems: a review," *Family Process,* 1979, *18,* 251–280.

For example, we tend to apply sociological, political, and legal frameworks, rather than biological ones, in explaining national trends in substance abuse. Conversely, we would be more liable to look at either physiological/biochemical or conditioning factors in explicating the detoxification process. An interpersonal/familial interpretation uses a different basic unit for explanation, and it is neither individualistically nor sociologically anchored. In a way, it falls into an intermediate position within the spectrum of integrational theories. The essential question is whether it "makes sense" of the data upon which it is based, and consequently whether it can lead to (1) legitimate, predictive explanations of drug-taking behavior, and (2) theories and methods which can help bring about efficient, durable change.

While present evidence is indicative and promising, the question, in all its ramifications, is at best only partially answered. However, much as Einsteinian physics requires a different frame of mind from the Newtonian variety, a different thinking cap must be donned to answer questions of import within the interpersonal/familial systems area. It might be helpful to keep such points in mind when considering the discussion of further implications.

Implications for Treatment Activities

Clarification of Technique. While most base their work on certain basic principles, the diversity of family treatment approaches described in the literature is striking. Much of this can be ascribed to attempts to mold familial approaches to fit within existent programs, since funds and other support are not readily forthcoming for new or "radical" modes of treatment. This diversity is probably healthy, since no one can expect to have "the answer" at this stage in the game. What may be most unfortunate, however, is the notable lack of attention given to the efficacy of the treatment employed.

There is also a (related) paucity of information on specifically what can be done, clinically, to bring about change in certain situations with certain clients. Authors have not consistently provided their readers with guidelines or "how to do it" information. This, again, is partly because most of them were exploring, and they hesitated to make conclusive statements. Then, too, most of the existent theories in the drug field were not developed with this kind of treatment in mind, and were, therefore, of little help in ascertaining therapy strategy.

However, we now appear to be at the point where some principles can be offered and their parameters defined. At least two recent volumes in the field should provide structure and impetus for this endeavor (Kaufman and Kaufmann, 1979a; Stanton, Todd, and Associates, 1982).

Family Recruitment. One of the problems that has been identified with this approach is the difficulty involved in getting family members into treatment—particularly fathers. They frequently appear threatened or defensive, wishing to avoid the blame they fear the therapist will place on them. Involving them in treatment seems to require different techniques than have conventionally been applied in family treatment with other kinds of disorders. More energy may have to be devoted to outreach efforts. When this is done, the results can improve considerably. Coleman (1976), Davis (1977–78), and Vaglum (1973) have described various strategies which can help, and Stanton, Todd, VanDeusen, and associates (Stanton and Todd, 1981a, 1981b; VanDeusen et al., 1981) have developed a number of principles for maximizing the effort. In the latter work, successful recruitment of whole families, including *both* parents or parent-surrogates, was achieved 77 percent of the time when the therapist also served as drug counselor—a "hit" rate which is much higher than that noted in other published reports. This may be an area of future investigation in which innovation will be most readily embraced.

Direction and Effectiveness of Treatment. The reader should not be misled into thinking that bringing a family in and discussing problems, per se, constitutes effective therapy. This is no more a precondition for change than is the resolve to be "well-intentioned." Most therapists and therapies are well-intentioned, so the key issue is whether or not their methods work, or at least whether they work better than other modes.

Families of drug abusers (Wegscheider, 1981; Forrest, 1983) can be very difficult to treat, and also quite draining. A certain amount of skills is involved, including the ability to avoid getting triangulated to the point of incapacitation. Having observed the family treatment techniques of a number of drug treatment facilities around the country—either directly or through videotapes—the author is particularly concerned with the "fuzzy" thinking and unsystematic approaches that some of them have applied. Too often, treatment providers have had vague goals, or goals counter to those of the people they were treating. Others have become so enamored of the family dynamics they see, that the means for effecting change escape them. While it is not the intent here to squelch exploration and innovation, more is involved in family therapy than sitting and "grooving" with families. Treatment of this sort benefits neither the clients nor the field of drug abuse as a whole.

Several other points deserve emphasis. First, as Kovacs (1975) and others have asserted, the practice of treating the drug abuser and members of his or her family separately or concurrently does not appear to be as promising or efficacious as treating them *together;* i.e., in a situation where their interactions and relationships can be directly observed and altered.

Second, in the author's opinion, it is doubtful that any family treatment mode for "hard" drug addiction can be effective which does not address the addictive cycle per se. In this cycle, when the addict improves, or tries to "clean up," the family enters into a crisis; frequently the parents begin to split up or talk about divorce. When the individual becomes readdicted, such talk subsides, and the family unites around its "troubled member." So it is really a *family* addictive cycle (whether acknowledged as such by the addict or not). The point is, if treatment is not constructed to *directly intervene in and change the family process surrounding detoxification and readdiction,* such treatment is much less likely to succeed. (See Stanton et al., 1978, for a more complete account of the family system behaviors involved in the addiction cycle.)

Confidentiality. If drug misuse, especially of the heavy or compulsive variety, is seen as a family phenomenon, or as symptomatic of a larger family problem, many of the existent regulations concerning confidentiality—shielding abusers from family members—do not make much sense. While there may be exceptions, such as in acute emergencies, or in situations where an experimenting adolescent has an adverse reaction, some of the standing regulations may serve, in the long run, to perpetuate rather than alleviate the difficulty.

To shield a person's drug problem from his or her family may even be an exercise in self-delusion—they often already know about it—but, at the very least, it results in a "buying into" and rigidification of the existent family system. Drug abusers are frequently protective of their families and often protest that the problem is theirs rather than the whole family's. Confidentiality provisions can give license to this denial by officially sanctioning the identified patient as the problem and denying the importance of the family system and the significant others within it. This can be especially problematic with adolescents and minors who are still the wards of their parents. The author has known of cases where youthful abusers have been sequestered for months and their families not informed of their whereabouts in order to conform to confidentiality constraints.

There is, then, a need to delineate more clearly the boundaries between confidentiality, as it applies to family members, and the safeguards such confidentiality ensures in relation to nonfamily individuals and agencies. While it is recognized that these regulations often were wrested from legislatures and government agencies at considerable cost in time, effort, and lobbying activity, consideration of the family basis to drug problems dictates that many of them be called into question.

Treatment Delivery Systems. A number of implications for drug programs and treatment systems can be identified, based on the material presented thus far. For example, one of the criticisms of traditional therapeutic communities (Rubel, Bratter, Smirnoff, Hartwig-Thompson and Baker, 1982) is that their patients must be discharged back to the "real world" and to the family. If these pretreatment influences remain unchanged, pressure is exerted on the patient to return to his or her old patterns. Including the family in treatment helps to counter this problem, since it amounts in many ways to bringing the real world into the clinic. This also applies to learning and conditioning paradigms, given that the family is a major source of stimuli and reinforcement for many patterns of behavior. Consequently, treating all of the members together allows more control over these prepotent variables (Berliner, 1966–67; Olson, 1974).

If families are to be treated, there appears to be a need for better dissemination of information about available facilities, especially at the local level. Chambers (1977) has data indicating that half the families for whom treatment is indicated either are unaware of existent resources or find them unacceptable.

Another area that needs attention has to do with the administrative handling of family treatment. Many procedures are geared to individually oriented therapies and are not responsive to family approaches (Framo, 1976; Haley, 1975). One problem identified by Coleman and Davis (1978) in their visits to drug programs was that counselors and therapists were not always allowed census credit for seeing family members. In some cases they were directly penalized, because sessions held without the identified patient—e.g., if the parents or spouse were seen alone—were disallowed on their timesheets; they were also not given credit for the additional time required for contacting and coordinating with family members.

Another problem encountered by the author in one particular institution concerned billing procedures. Each family member was registered separately as a patient and billed accordingly. Thus, if one member was present for a session, the fee was, for example, $15. If five members attended, the family was billed five times as much, i.e., $75, for the same one-hour session.

Finally, difficulties can arise even from policies and regulations established at the national level. Kleber (1977) notes that current federal funding mechanisms, by supporting individual "slot" costs (as opposed to treatment unit costs), not only do not provide incentives for attendant therapies, but may induce a disincentive for provision of family therapy and treatments. He notes that the end result is a tendency "to penalize programs that attempt to do effective therapy with the patient and his family."

As mentioned earlier, conceptualizing drug taking within an interpersonal systems or family framework is not always consonant with some of the other ways in which treatment has been administered in the drug abuse field. This can become particularly apparent within actual clinical settings. Schwartzman and Kroll (1977) note how many programs feed into and re-create the family system of the abuser—i.e., "unspoken conflicts between staff members frequently are acted out through individual patients and result in requests for more medication and more frequent illicit drug use." In a sense, such situations can reinforce the family's idea that the identified patient is "sick," incompetent, and unable to stop taking drugs (Schwartzman, 1977; Stanton et al., 1978).

Schwartzman and Bokos (1979) also note how different drug programs compete with and denigrate each other in relation to patients, thus re-creating conflicts similar to those which addicts encounter in their families. These are very real issues, and recognizing them prompts close attention to the ways in which our drug programs may be unwittingly fostering the very behaviors they are mandated to extinguish.

A final note on treatment implications has to do with acceptance by others within the field. New methods and ways of thinking are rarely greeted with open arms in any field of endeavor. The interpersonal/family systems approach has garnered its share of resistance (Haley, 1975). In many ways it is in a position analogous to that of behaviorally oriented treatments several years ago: i.e., proposing new perspectives and methods to groups which were invested in the old ones.

In contrast to its brethren in other mental health areas, however, the drug abuse field has, in the author's estimation, been markedly open to new and different approaches. Perhaps because of (1) the difficulty in treating its patient population; (2) the objectivity acquired in assessing its target symptoms, e.g., urine tests, which permit more accurate assessment of outcome; (3) its shared emphasis with many family treatments on the "here and now"; or (4) its general newness as a field (Dupont, 1978), it has allowed a thousand flowers to bloom. Thus, the "surprising" way in which family treatment modes have gained at least partial acceptance in so many drug programs across the country may not be so surprising after all.

Implications for Training

Perhaps the most notable implication for training in family treatment pertains to the widely expressed need for it that emerged from the findings of the Coleman and Davis survey (1978). Of the programs queried, the majority wanted more training—particularly in the use of videotapes for family therapy training and supervision. The greatest need was by methadone clinics, which also were the least likely to have actually been providing treatment to families. (If they did provide it, however, it tended to be given by less experienced therapists, according to Coleman and Kaplan, 1978.) The overall level of experience and sophistication in family treatment was not considered high—as measured by a progress index (Coleman and Stanton, 1978a)—but the interest in improving this situation was great.

There is one implicit danger in this whole area that must be considered. As family systems methods become more widespread, a "fad" could develop. This might lead to inadequate training of many personnel who then proceed to do ineffective therapy. Family therapy cannot be learned overnight. Although efficient training models have been developed (e.g., Flomenhaft and Carter, 1977), and it appears to take less time to reach competence than is required for most individual modes, the direction, content, and length of future training curricula deserve careful consideration.

Implications for Prevention

Of the various approaches to psychotherapy, family treatment has perhaps the clearest implications for prevention. This is because (1) more people are involved when one sees a family; (2) the therapy engages people (e.g., parents) who may not otherwise have gotten into treatment themselves, but who engender problems in others; and (3) if treatment is effective, a system is changed that previously had the potential to produce problems in other offspring.

For instance, if parents are helped to improve the ways in which they handle a son or daughter with a problem, they are becoming more competent parents. Their experience will hopefully provide them with ways of dealing with younger children as they grow older; i.e., the lessons learned with one offspring can be transferred to others.

In fact, the work of Klein, Alexander, and Parsons (1977) with delinquents indicates that family therapy can result in clear-cut prevention of future problems among siblings. Further, if the family situation is changed so that an addicted member is set free of the needs of his parents and therefore, in part, his need for drugs, he is on the road to becoming a more competent person, and, in the long run, becoming a more competent spouse and parent himself. This, then, is primary prevention.

Some specific target groups for which family treatment appears particularly appropriate as a preventative mode are: children of addicts; siblings of drug abusers; parents of junior and senior high school students; parents threatened with the "empty nest" syndrome; families in crisis; and families in which parents have immigrated from other countries or regions.

Implications for Future Research

While many possibilities exist for research on the families of drug abusers, only a few which pertain directly to treatment will be presented here.

Outcome. It is unfortunate that the same level of scientific activity has not prevailed among programs providing family treatment specifically for drug problems as it has in the family therapy field as a whole. Although the few existent drug abuse studies with outcome data show considerable promise, it is too early to consider them as being conclusive. Rather, there is a glaring need for well-designed research in this area that compares two or more treatments and employs random assignment.

Technique. More precise methods need to be defined and developed for dealing with particular subpopulations. Investigators need to carve out an area and explore it, rather than falling into the trap of a shotgun approach. For instance, one might ask whether approaches should differ in working with single-parent families, marital couples, or intact families. Is the same approach to be taken with families from all ethnic groups, and if not, how should it be adapted? Klagsbrun and Davis (1977) pose the question of whether substance-abusing families are a homogeneous group or whether a meaningful typology can be established which is attended by differences in treatment approach.

Finally, there is evidence that the high rate of death and suicide seen among drug addicts derives from family factors (Stanton, 1977). The means for dealing with this serious problem from a family systems standpoint need further exploration (Coleman and Stanton, 1978b; Reilly, 1976; Stanton and Coleman, 1980).

Responsibility. Families of drug abusers have all too often been able to foist their addicted members on the treatment system, thereby abdicating responsibility. Treatment staff have too willingly accepted this yoke, and then ended up feeling responsible, to boot, when families directly undercut them and treatment failed. We need research on how to turn this situation around. We must develop methods which help families to feel more competent to change their patterns and to care for their own. If, as Blum and Associates (1972) have stated, "the family is a force that helps resist or exaggerate the stress of other environmental factors," the need becomes clear for finding ways to strengthen the resistances and minimize the exaggerations.

References

Africano, A., Fortunato, M., and Padow, E. The impact of program treatment on marital unions in a methadone-maintained patient population. In R. L. DuPont and R. S. Freeman (eds.), *Proceedings of the Fifth National Conference on Methadone Treatment.* Washington, D. C.: NAPAN, 1973.

Alexander, B. K., and Dibb, G. S. Interpersonal perception in addict families. *Family Process,* 1977, *16,* 17–28.

———. Opiate addicts and their parents. *Family Process,* 1975, *14,* 499–514.

Bateson, G. *Steps to an Ecology of Mind.* New York: Ballantine Books, 1972.

Berliner, A. K. Narcotic addiction, the institution and the community. *International Journal of the Addictions,* 1966–67, *1*(2), 74–85.

Blum, R., and Associates. *Horatio Alger's Children: The Role of the Family in the Origin and Prevention of Drug Risk.* San Francisco: Jossey-Bass, 1972.

Boszormenyi-Nagy, I., and Spark, G. *Invisible Loyalties.* New York: Harper & Row, 1973.

Bowen, M. *Family Therapy in Clinical Practice.* New York: Jason Aronson, 1978.

———. The use of family therapy in clinical practice. *Comprehensive psychiatry,* 1966, *7,* 345–374.

Chambers, E. Trends and projections. In *The Epidemiology of Drug Abuse: Current Issues.* National Institute on Drug Abuse Research Monograph no. 10. Washington, D. C.: U. S. Government Printing Office, 1977.

Chein, I., Gerard, D., Lee, R., and Rosenfeld, E. *The Road to H.* New York: Basic Books, 1964.

Clark, J. S., Capel, W. C., Goldsmith, B. M., and Stewart, G. T. Marriage and methadone: spouse behavior patterns in heroin addicts maintained on methadone. *Journal of Marriage and the Family,* 1972, *34,* 496–501.

Coleman, A. F. How to enlist the family as an ally. *American Journal of Drug and Alcohol Abuse,* 1976, *3,* 167–173.

Coleman, S. B., and Davis, D. I. Family therapy and drug abuse: a national survey. *Family Process,* 1978, *17,* 21–29.

Coleman, S. B., and Kaplan, J. D. A profile of family therapists in the drug abuse field. *American Journal of Drug and Alcohol Abuse,* 1978, *5,* 171–178.

Coleman, S. B., and Stanton, M. D. An index for measuring agency involvement in family therapy. *Family Process,* 1978(a), *17,* 479–483.

———. The role of death in the addict family. *Journal of Marriage and Family Counseling,* 1978(b), *4,* 79–91.

Cuskey, W. R., Richardson, A. H., and Berger, L. H. *Specialized Therapeutic Community Program for Female Addicts.* National Institute on Drug Abuse Services Research Report, Department of Health, Education, and Welfare Pub. no. ADM 79–880. Washington, D. C.: U. S. Government Printing Office, 1979.

Davis, D. I. Forum—family therapy for the drug abuser: conceptual and practical considerations. *Drug Forum,* 1977–78, *6,* 197–199.

Dell Orto, A. E. The role and resources of the family during the drug rehabilitation process. *Journal of Psychedelic Drugs,* 1974, *6,* 435–445.

Dupont, R. I. The drug abuse decade. *Journal of Drug Issues,* 1978, *11,* 77–84.

Eldred, C. A., and Washington, M. N. Interpersonal relationships in heroin use by men and women and their role in treatment outcome. *International Journal of the Addictions,* 1976, *11,* 117–130.

Ellinwood, E. H., Smith, W. G., and Vaillant, G. E. Narcotic addiction in males and females: a comparison. *International Journal of the Addictions,* 1966, *1,* 33–45.

Flomenhaft, K., and Carter, R. Family therapy training: program and outcome. *Family Process,* 1977, *16,* 211–218.

Fram, D. H., and Hoffman, H. A. Family therapy in the treatment of the heroin addict. In R. L. DuPont and R. S. Freeman (eds.), *Proceedings of the Fifth National Conference on Methadone Treatment.* Washington, D. C.: NAPAN, 1973.

Framo, J. Chronicle of a struggle to establish a family unit within a community mental health center. In P. J. Guerin (ed.), *Family Therapy: Theory and Practice.* New York: Gardner Press, 1976.

Gasta, C., and Schut, J. Planned detoxification of addict marital pairs: diagnosis and treatment strategies. Paper presented at the National Drug Abuse Conference, San Francisco, May 1977.

Gurman, A. S., and Kniskern, D. P. Research on marital and family therapy: progress, perspective, and prospect. In *Handbook of Psychotherapy and Behavior Change: An Empirical Analysis,* 2nd ed. New York: John Wiley & Sons, 1978.

Haley, J. Whither family therapy? *Family Process,* 1962, *1,* 69–100.

———. *Uncommon Therapy.* New York: W. W. Norton & Co., 1973.

———. Why a mental health clinic should avoid family therapy. *Journal of Marriage and Family Counseling,* 1975, *1,* 3–13.

———. *Problem-Solving Therapy.* San Francisco: Jossey-Bass, 1976.

———. *Leaving Home: The Therapy of Disturbed Young People.* New York: McGraw-Hill Book Co., 1980.

Harbin, H. T., and Maziar, H. M. The families of drug abusers: a literature review. *Family Process,* 1975, *14,* 411–431.

Hejinian, C. L., and Pittel, S. M. Can marriage survive addiction and treatment? Paper presented at the National Drug Abuse Conference, Seattle, April 1978.

Hendricks, W. J. Use of multifamily counseling groups in treatment of male narcotic addicts. *International Journal of Group Psychotherapy,* 1971, *21,* 84–90.

Hirsch, R. Group therapy with parents of adolescent drug addicts. *Psychiatric Quarterly,* 1961, *34,* 702–710.

Huberty, D. J. Treating the adolescent drug abuser: a family affair. *Contemporary Drug Problems,* 1975, *4,* 179–194.

Jackson, D. D. The study of the family. *Family Process,* 1965, *4,* 1–20.

Kandel, D. B., Treiman, D., Faust, R., and Single, E. Adolescent involvement in legal and illegal drug use: a multiple classification analysis. *Social Forces,* 1976, *54,* 438–458.

Kaufman, E., and Kaufmann, P. (eds.). *Family Therapy of Drug and Alcohol Abuse.* New York: Gardner Press, 1979(a).

Kaufman, E., and Kaufmann, P. From a psychodynamic orientation to a structural family therapy approach in the treatment of drug dependency. In E. Kaufman and P. Kaufmann (eds.), *Family Therapy of Drug and Alcohol Abuse.* New York: Gardner Press, 1979(b).

Klagsbrun, M., and Davis, D. I. Substance abuse and family interaction. *Family Process,* 1977, *16,* 149–173.

Kleber, H. D. Methadone maintenance treatment—a reply. *American Journal of Drug and Alcohol Abuse,* 1977, *4,* 267–272.

Klein, N. C., Alexander, J. F., and Parsons, B. V. Impact of family systems intervention on recidivism and sibling delinquency: a model of primary prevention and program evaluation. *Journal of Consulting and Clinical Psychology,* 1977, *45,* 469–474.

Kovacs, J. An approach to treating adolescent drug abusers. In E. Senay, V. Shorty, and H. Alkshe (eds.), *Developments in the Field of Drug Abuse.* Cambridge, Mass.: Schenkman, 1975.

Lennard, H. L., and Allen, S. D. The treatment of drug addiction: toward new models. *International Journal of the Addictions,* 1973, *8,* 521–535.

Levy, B. Five years after: a follow-up of 50 narcotic addicts. *American Journal of Psychiatry,* 1972, *7,* 102–106.

Macro Systems. *Three-Year Follow-Up Study of Clients Enrolled in Treatment Programs in New York City: Phase III—Final Report.* Submitted to National Institute on Drug Abuse by Macro Systems, June 1975.

Mason, P. The mother of the addict. *Psychiatric Quarterly Supplement,* 1958, *32(part 2),* 189–199.

Minuchin, S. *Families and Family Therapy.* Cambridge, Mass.: Harvard University Press, 1974.

Noone, R. J. Drug abuse behavior in relation to change in family structure. Paper presented at the Third Pittsburgh Family Systems Symposium, Western Psychiatric Institute and Clinic, University of Pittsburgh, April 1979.

———, and Reddig, R. L. Case studies in the family treatment of drug abuse. *Family Process,* 1976, *15,* 325–332.

O'Donnell, J. A. *Narcotic Addicts in Kentucky.* Washington, D. C.: U. S. Government Printing Office, 1969.

Olson, D. H. Marital and family therapy: integrative review and critique. *Journal of Marriage and the Family,* 1970, *32,* 501–538.

———. Therapy for addicts: a family affair. In H. Brown and T. J. Cahill (eds.), *Drug Perspectives: A Handbook of Readings in Drug Abuse.* Washington, D. C.: National Institute on Drug Abuse, 1974.

Perzel, J. F., and Lamon, S. Enmeshment within families of polydrug abusers. Paper presented at the National Drug Abuse Conference, New Orleans, August 1979.

Reilly, D. M. Family factors in the etiology and treatment of youthful drug abuse. *Family Therapy,* 1976, *2,* 149–171.

Salmon, R., and Salmon, S. The causes of heroin addiction—a review of the literature, part 2. *International Journal of the Addictions,* 1977, *12,* 937–951.

Scher, J. Patterns and profiles of addiction and drug abuse. *Archives of General Psychiatry,* 1966, *15,* 539–551.

Schwartzman, J. The addict, abstinence, and the family. *American Journal of Psychiatry,* 1975, *132,* 154–157.

———. Systemic aspects of abstinence and addiction. *British Journal of Medical Psychology,* 1977, *50,* 181–186.

———, and Bokos, P. Methadone maintenance: the addict's family recreated. *International Journal of Family Therapy,* 1979, *1,* 338–355.

Schwartzman, J., and Kroll, L. Methadone maintenance and addict abstinence. *International Journal of the Addictions,* 1977, *12,* 497–507.

Scopetta, M. A., King, O. E., and Szapocznik, J. *Relationship of Acculuration, Incidence of Drug Abuse and Effective Treatment of Cuban-Americans: Final Report.* Washington, D. C.: Superintendent of Documents, 1977.

Seldin, N. E. The family of the addict: a review of the literature. *International Journal of the Addictions,* 1972, *7,* 97–107.

Stanton, M. D. The addict as savior: heroin, death, and the family. *Family Process,* 1977, *16,* 191–197.

———. Drugs and the family: a review of the recent literature. *Marriage and Family Review,* 1979(a), *2(1),* 1–10.

———. The family and drug misuse: a bibliography. *American Journal of Drug and Alcohol Abuse,* 1978(a), *5*(2), 151–170.

———. Family therapy: systems approaches. In G. P. Sholevar, R. M. Benson, and B. J. Blinder (eds.), *Handbook of Emotional Disorders in Children and Adolescents: Medical and Psychological Approaches to Treatment.* Jamaica, N. Y.: S. P. Medical and Scientific Books, 1980(b).

———. Family treatment approaches to drug abuse problems: a review. *Family Process,* 1979(b), *18,* 251–280.

———. A family theory of drug abuse. In D. Lettieri, M. Sayers, and H. Pearson (eds.), *Theories on Drug Abuse: Selected Contemporary Perspectives.* National Institute on Drug Abuse Research Monograph Series no. 30. Washington, D. C.: U. S. Government Printing Office, 1980(a).

———. Some outcome results and aspects of structural family therapy with drug addicts. In D. Smith, S. Anderson, M. Buxton, T. Chung, N. Gottlieb, and W. Harvey (eds.), *A Multicultural View of Drug Abuse: The Selected Proceedings of the National Drug Abuse Conference, 1977.* Cambridge, Mass.: Schenkman, 1978(b).

———. Some overlooked aspects of the family and drug abuse. In B. Ellis (ed.), *Drug Abuse from the Family Perspective: Coping is a Family Affair.* Publication of the National Institute on Drug Abuse, Office of Program Development and Analysis. Washington, D. C.: U. S. Government Printing Office, 1980.

———, and Coleman, S. B. The participatory aspects of indirect self-destructive behavior: the addict family as a model. In N. Farberow (ed.), *The Many Faces of Suicide.* New York: McGraw–Hill Book Co., 1980.

Stanton, M. D., and Todd, T. C. Engaging "resistant" families in treatment. Part 2: Principles and techniques in recruitment. *Family Process,* 1981(a), *20,* 261–280.

———. Engaging "resistant" families in treatment. Part 3: Factors in success and cost effectiveness. *Family Process,* 1981(b), *20,* 280–293.

———. Structural family therapy with drug addicts. In *Family Therapy of Drug and Alcohol Abuse* (E. Kaufman and P. Kaufmann, eds.). New York: Gardner Press, 1979.

Stanton, M. D., Todd, T. C., and Associates. *The Family Therapy of Drug Abuse and Addiction.* New York: Guilford Press, 1982.

Stanton, M. D., Todd, T. C., Heard, D. B., Kirschner, S., Kleiman, J. I., Mowatt, D. T., Riley, P., Scott, S. M., and VanDeusen, J. M. Heroin addiction as a family phenomenon: a new conceptual model. *American Journal of Drug and Alcohol Abuse,* 1978, *5*(2), 125–150.

Stanton, M. D., Todd, T. C., Steier, F., VanDeusen, J. M., Marder, L. R., Rosoff, R. J., Seaman, S. F., and Skibinski, E. *Family Characteristics and Family Therapy of Heroin Addicts: Final Report, 1974–1978.* National Institute on Drug Abuse Grant no. RO2–DA–01119, 1979.

Steinglass, P. Family therapy in alcoholism. In *The Biology of Alcoholism,* vol. 5. New York: Plenum Press, 1976.

Taylor, S. D., Wilbur, M., and Osnos, R. The wives of drug addicts. *American Journal of Psychiatry,* 1966, *123,* 585–591.

Thompson, P. Family of the addict explored. *The Journal of the Addiction Research Foundation,* 1973, *2,* 8.

Vaglum, P. The patient-centered family working group—a medium for collaboration with "unmotivated" family members: a model and an example. *Scandinavian Journal of Social Medicine,* 1973, *1,* 69–75.

Vaillant, G. E. A 12-year follow-up of New York narcotic addicts. Part 3: Some social and psychiatric characteristics. *Archives of General Psychiatry,* 1966, *15,* 599–609.

VanDeusen, J. M., Stanton, M. D., Scott, S. M., and Todd, T. C. Engaging "resistant" families in treatment. Part 1: Getting the drug addict to recruit his family members. *International Journal of the Addictions,* 1981, *16*(2).

Watzlawick, P., Beavin, J. H., and Jackson, D. D. *Pragmatics of Human Communication.* New York: W. W. Norton & Co., 1967.

Wellisch, D. K., Gay, G. R., and McEntee, R. The easy rider syndrome: a pattern of hetero- and homosexual relationships in a heroin addict population. *Family Process,* 1970, *9.* 425–530.

Wellisch, D. K., and Kaufman, E. Family therapy. In E. Senay, V. Shorty, and H. Alkshe (eds.), *Developments in the Field of Drug Abuse.* Cambridge, Mass.: Schenkman, 1975.

Winer, L. R., Lorio, J. P., and Scrafford, I. *Effects of Treatment on Drug Abuser and Family.* Report prepared for the Special Action Office for Drug Abuse Prevention, Executive Office of the President, Washington, D. C. (Grant no. DA–4–RG–003), 1974.

Wolk, R. L., and Diskind, M. H. Personality dynamics of mothers and wives of drug addicts. *Crime and Delinquency,* 1961, *7,* 148–152.

Wunderlich, R. A., Lozes, J., and Lewis, J. Recidivism rates of group therapy participants and other adolescents processed by a juvenile court. *Psychotherapy: Theory, Research and Practice,* 1974, *11,* 243–245.

Zahn, M., and Ball, J. Factors related to the cure of opiate addiction among Puerto Rican addicts. *International Journal of the Addictions,* 1972, *7,* 237–245.

Ziegler-Driscoll, G. Family research study at Eagleville Hospital and Rehabilitation Center. *Family Process,* 1977, *16,* 175–189.

———. Family treatment with parent addict families. In D. Smith, S. Anderson, M. Buxton, T. Chung, N. Gottlieb, and W. Harvey (eds.), *A Multicultural View of Drug Abuse: The Selected Proceedings of the National Drug Conference, 1977.* Cambridge, Mass.: Schenkman, 1978.

15

The Differential Therapy of Alcoholism

A Systems Approach

Frederick B. Glaser / Helen M. Annis / Shelly Pearlman / Ruth L. Segal / Harvey A. Skinner

The history of this field contains examples of problems that were originally grouped together but were subsequently found to be separate entities, as well as examples of apparently disparate problems that were at length found to have a common basis.

This phenomenon characterizes the classification of alcohol-related problems. The traditional view treats these as diverse manifestations of a single disease, labeled "alcoholism," with a specific etiology. As a result of the widespread acceptance of this notion, therapeutic approaches to alcoholism have tended to be dominated by single treatment methods which purport to be effective in all cases. More recent research has questioned a unitary view of alcohol-related problems, and suggests that the populations involved are vastly heterogeneous; therefore, differential treatment may be required in order to achieve optimal therapeutic results (e.g., Glaser, 1977a, 1977b; Jacobson, 1976; Pattison et al., 1977; Khantzian, 1983).

It would be tedious to rehearse the many lines of evidence which have been (and continue to be) explored in attempts to understand the nature of alcoholism. The debate regularly rages through the pro-

The authors wish to acknowledge the assistance of Dr. John B. MacDonald, president of the Addiction Research Foundation, in the preparation of this manuscript.

fessional literature. Conclusive scientific evidence on one side or the other is at present unavailable. In order to reach a suitable basis for action one must exercise one's best judgment. That such a judgment is required is due to the major implications of the issue for treatment. Basically, one must decide whether to provide uniform or differential treatment for clients seeking assistance. Such decisions in actual practice tend more to evolve unwittingly over time rather than to be consciously framed and deliberately resolved, but the end results are the same.

In most instances, alcoholism treatment programs offer only a single treatment approach to all clients seeking assistance. This approach implies that there is a single etiology for alcoholism with which the particular treatment selected for implementation deals effectively. A small number of programs offer a multiplicity of treatment approaches to clients, which indicates the acceptance of diverse etiologies (at least as a working hypothesis) and a need for the deployment and evaluation of differential treatment. In a study of eighty programs providing treatment for alcoholism throughout an entire state, only 5 percent of the programs provided more than a single therapeutic option for clients (Glaser, 1978, pp. 68–69). Because of the relative rarity of differential treatment programs, we will describe in detail one of them, located in the Clinical Institute of the Addiction Research Foundation of Ontario in Toronto.

The Background

Since its founding in 1949, Ontario's Addiction Research Foundation has investigated many aspects of drug and alcohol dependence. Major contributions have been made to such areas as the epidemiology of alcoholism, the biochemistry and physiology of tolerance and dependence, the management of medical sequelae of abuse, and the efficacy of public policy measures as preventive devices. But an equivalent interest in treatment research is a comparatively recent development. A landmark was the establishment in 1970 of the Clinical Institute, an 88-bed hospital facility, as the treatment arm of the Foundation. By 1975 an external evaluation of the Foundation's overall research effort clearly underscored the necessity for conducting "treatment research of high calibre with an emphasis on vigorous testing by controlled trials, which can reach firm conclusions on the value of major present treatment modalities, and rigorously test new modalities" (Jaffe et al., 1975, p. 30). With this goal explicitly enunciated, a major step had been taken.

Another factor providing impetus toward treatment research was a controlled study carried out by Dr. Griffith Edwards and his colleagues at the Addiction Research Unit of the Maudsley Hospital in London, England. A population of clients was randomly assigned either to a treatment group, which received an "average package of care" highly congruent with standard treatment for alcoholism in the Western world, or to an advice group, which was provided with no intervention following assessment other than a single session of very general instructions. Follow-up after one year revealed no significant differences between the two groups in terms of outcome (Edwards et al., 1977). This study occassioned considerable comment (Kissin et al., 1977); while various methodological features imposed limitations on the interpretation and generalizability of the data (scrupulously pointed out by the authors themselves), it was nevertheless viewed as a convincing indication that the application of a uniform therapeutic approach across a large population of clients was likely to be a futile exercise. From a formal standpoint the study suggested that critical treatment research questions, hitherto largely obfuscated by well-intentioned but uncontrolled studies, might eventually yield to controlled experimentation.

Finally, there had been a persistent and escalating (though hardly unanimous) call from researchers in the field to abandon unitary concepts of "alcoholism" and its treatment, and to look for more specific interactions between client characteristics and interventions (the "matching hypothesis"). This development replicated a similar thrust in the field of psychotherapy research, exemplified by a classic statement now more than a decade old:

> The . . . question posed, "Does psychotherapy work?", is virtually meaningless. . . . The range of individual differences within standard diagnostic categories remains so diversified as to render meaningless any questions or statement about individuals who become so labeled. . . . the question toward which all outcome research should ultimately be directed is the following: *What* treatment, by *whom,* is most effective for *this* individual with *that* specific problem, and under *which* set of circumstances: (Paul, 1967, p. 18)

Many investigators in the field of alcohol and drug dependence concurred. Though movement toward differential treatment clearly did not please everyone, enough encouragement existed to provide some measure of consensual validation. For example:

> Rather than blindly apply treatments wholesale to hospital and outpatient populations (which is more administratively convenient) it is time that the issue of the patient-treatment fit be investigated using some of these variables. Clinicians intuitively recognize the importance of this issue. . . . Perhaps [their recognition] is based on little more than the operation of erroneous treatment stereotypes. On the other hand, it may indicate

> the clinician's intuitive recognition that different kinds of patients find certain kinds of treatment more acceptable and do better in them than others. Definitive answers to such questions can come only from further rigorously designed treatment research. (Baekelaud et al., 1975, pp. 304–305).

> I am moved to urge a moratorium on all studies . . . which evaluate treatment for heterogeneous groups of alcoholics. I believe funding may more profitably support other types of investigations, such as those evaluating procedures for getting alcoholics to decide to stop drinking and for matching patients with specific treatments. (Glaser, 1977a, p. 62).

> The population of persons with alcohol problems is multivariant. Correspondingly, treatment services should be diverse, emphasizing the development of a variety of services, with determination of which treatments, delivered in which contexts, are more effective for which persons and which types of problems. (Pattison et al., 1967, p. 5)

The Differential Treatment Model: Structure

Given (*inter alia*) a mandate to move decisively into treatment research, the results of the Edwards study, and the persuasive opinions of a segment of the research community, the Clinical Institute opted for implementing an evaluation of differential treatment. To achieve this end, it cast about for a suitable model. The model would not only have to facilitate both differential treatment and treatment research, but be capable of dealing with large numbers of clients. Approximately 2,400 new clients per year enter the Clinical Institute. Ideally, not only would all be differentially treated, but all should potentially be research subjects so that the large samples required for decisive testing of hypotheses could readily be generated. For such a task, a system embodying the principle of division of labor was clearly required.

A particular model was selected for study which had developed out of intensive surveys of treatment programs (Glaser et al., 1978); the so-called Core-Shell Treatment System. After its basic concepts had been further developed, a series of pilot studies were undertaken. They provided results which were highly encouraging. The systems approach proved to be not only quite feasible but enthusiastically accepted by clients and staff. For example, though the elapsed time between initial client contact and eventual assignment to treatment was greatly increased, more than half again as many clients coming through the pilot system appeared for treatment as did clients coming through the standard intake procedure. Given this and other favorable preliminary results, a reorganization was effected which incorporated the model into the Clinical Institute as its basic framework for treatment and treatment research.

The model now in place posits that four essential components are required for treatment and treatment research: primary care, assessment, intervention, and research. These components can further be categorized into those which are required by *all* clients seeking treatment and those which are required by *some* clients. Each client needs to have his case managed by an individual who assumes overall responsibility for his care and assures the continuity of his experience with the treatment system (primary care). If clients constitute a heterogeneous population, each client's strengths, needs, contexts, life-style, and other characteristics need to be individually specified (assessment). And each client's record should be sufficiently well documented for him to be an eligible subject for outcome research, though practical considerations may dictate that only a representative sample will actually be followed up (research). On the other hand, some, but not all, clients will require specialized treatment programs (intervention). Thus primary care, assessment, and research are essential services for all clients, while secondary care (intervention) is required for some, but not all, clients.

These considerations are reflected in the structure of the Core-Shell Treatment System (Figure 15–1). In the center of the diagram the three universally required components are grouped together and constitute the core program; this in turn is surrounded by a shell of intervention programs. Because core services are always required but shell services are not always required, admission to the treatment system is through the core, rather than through the shell. While this seems a matter of simple logic, it nevertheless constitutes a radical departure from the standard practice of admitting directly to a specific treatment program. But such a standard practice creates many difficulties. Clients may be screened with respect to their suitability for that particular program, usually in an impressionistic manner, but are virtually never systematically assessed for the suitability of alternative programs and cross-referred. Consequently, they often begin a specific course of treatment which may be quite inappropriate to their individual needs. The results are high attrition for the clients, poor success for the programs, and early "burnout" for the staff. Nor do treatment programs regularly provide for continuity of care or outcome evaluation. Admission to the core, on the other hand, permits the ready attachment of a primary care worker to each client; enables a comprehensive and meticulous assessment to be completed prior to treatment; and assures that whatever treatment may be utilized will be selected on the basis of that assessment. The availability of comprehensive pre-treatment assessment data also makes every client

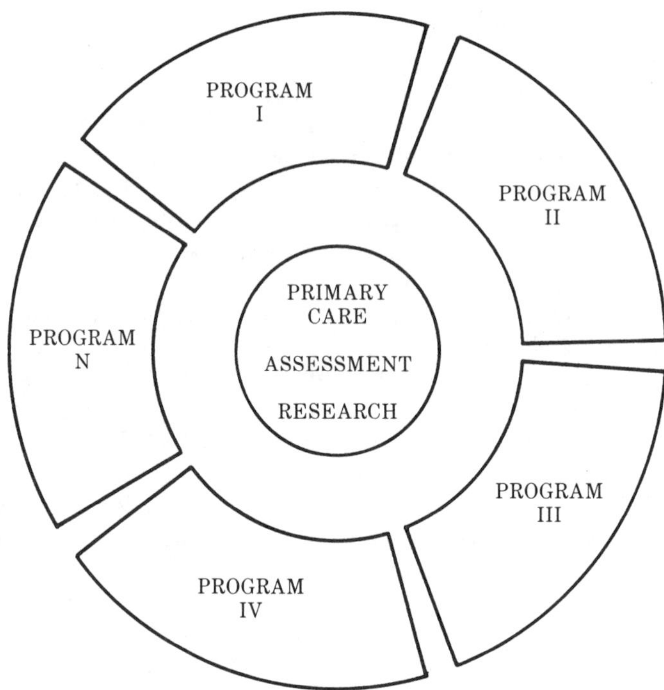

Figure 15–1. Structural relationships in the Core-Shell Treatment System

an excellent candidate for outcome evaluation, which can be performed by a central cadre of follow-up workers unattached to any particular treatment program and hence relatively objective.

A critical structural feature of the system is the *separation* between the core and the shell. It provides great flexibility. While practical guidelines for the differential referral of clients to treatments can readily be constructed, and while making these guidelines explicit is an enormous advantage over the usual practice of deciding intuitively on a referral, validated methods of matching clients to treatment are virtually nonexistent. However, follow-up studies can specify which clients tend to achieve best results in which programs. This data can then be fed back into the system, altering the decision rules regarding assignment to programs. Because of the separation of core and shell, altering referral patterns is a simple administrative act. As time passes and serial cohorts of clients are successively examined, further changes can be instituted and, in general, the stream of clients can be continually redirected toward programs in which (based upon the known outcomes of previous clients with similar characteristics) they are increasingly likely to obtain good results. This feedback is a critical element of the system, allowing it to self-correct for changes which will inevitably occur in such parameters as the characteristics of clients seeking treatment and the treatment programs themselves. But it represents little more than a systematization of standard medical practice, in which the response of clients to treatment is closely observed and their treatment altered accordingly. It also means that the results of treatment interventions, both for the system as a whole and for its individual programs, should improve steadily over time.

The Differential Treatment Model: Function

Functional relationships between the structural components of the system may be appreciated with the assistance of a flow diagram (Figure 15–2), permitting one to trace the path of a client through the system. The diagram is comprehensive, specifying the entire system from initial contact through treatment to follow-up in the community, including whatever reassessment and/or additional treatment may be necessary. It reflects the extensive planning required for a systematic approach to treatment and treatment research.

When a client first contacts the treatment system (A), the initial question to be resolved is whether he or she is in need of immediate care (B). Examples would include such medical problems as acute intoxication, severe withdrawal, or other related emergency medical sequelae of drug or alcohol dependence (e.g., narcotic overdose); or such psychiatric problems as toxic or functional psychosis. Naturally, if these problems exist, they must be dealt with on a priority basis. As a fully-equipped hospital, the Clinical Institute can deal with most such problems itself. Systems operating in other settings might utilize external specialty facilities.

If no emergency exists, or when an existing emergency is resolved, an initial interview is held with a primary care worker (D). One purpose of this interview is to determine whether the prospective client has a problem at least grossly congruent with the aims of the treatment system, and to screen out (E) those who would be exceptionally inappropriate. In practice very few problems are judged inappropriate at this point. Primary care workers are instructed to err on the side of overinclusiveness, since a better-informed decision on suitability can be made subsequently. In addition to this decision, a beginning is made toward the formation of an ongoing relationship with the primary care worker, who will provide continuity of care for the client throughout his or her contact with the treatment system. Another purpose of the initial interview is to determine whether the prospective client is willing to undergo assessment (F). Most clients (more than 85 percent) who are offered assessment accept it. They are sent on to the Assessment

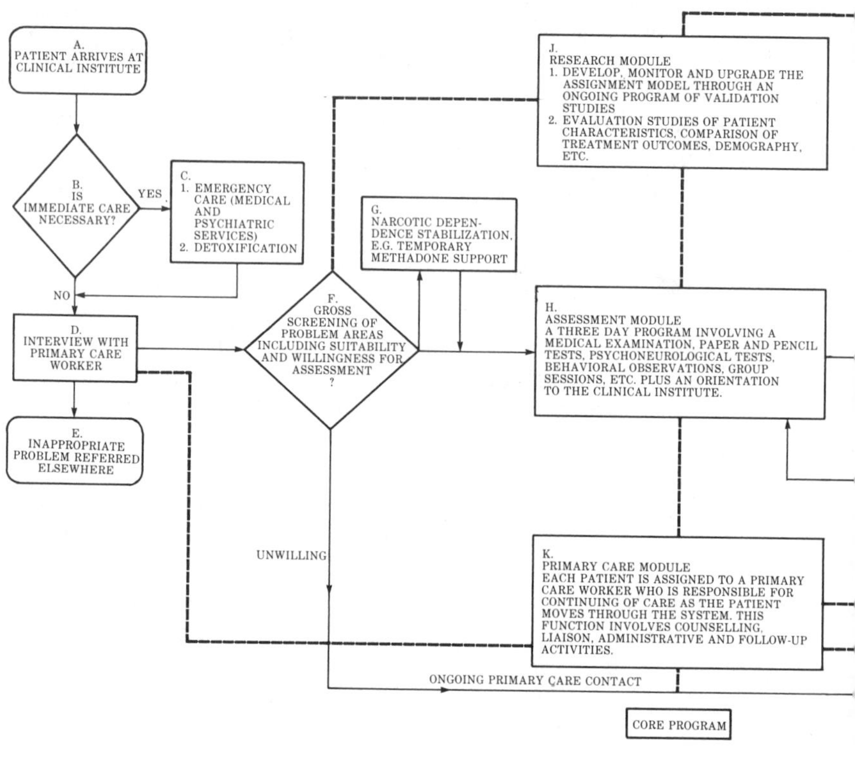

Figure 15–2. Functional relationships in the Core-Shell Treatment System

Unit for a comprehensive evaluation designed to document their general status and to specify their problem areas and strengths.

However, if a client is unwilling to be assessed, the system (under a ruling of the Ethics Committee of the Foundation) cannot offer the client any of the more complex and powerful treatments which are available. To do so would be analogous to treating a patient without making a diagnosis. An obligation to provide all persons who ask for assistance with basic care is recognized, and persons who refuse assessment may continue in ongoing primary care contact, as shown in the diagram. At some subsequent time, such clients may agree to be assessed. But they will be ineligible for definitive treatment until they do. By analogy with findings in psychotherapy research (Bergin, 1971), it is assumed that any intervention sufficiently powerful to help can

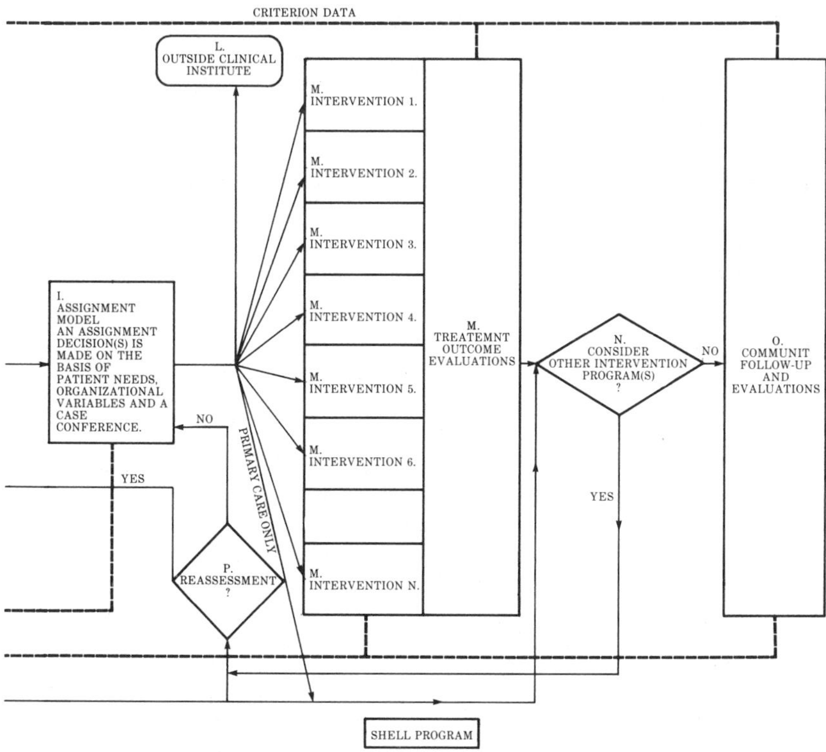

also harm if it is applied to the wrong person. Without an assessment it is not possible to determine whether a given individual is the wrong person. In sum, primary care is available on contact, but secondary care is contingent upon assessment.

Narcotic addicts with active habits may require temporary narcotic maintenance during the assessment period (G) until a determination is made whether long-term maintenance is the optimal treatment alternative. Other clients will enter the Assessment Unit directly (H), and, upon completing the process, will be assigned to treatment programs according to the results obtained (I). Explicit selection criteria keyed to each of the available treatment programs, whether within the Foundation (M) or outside of it (L), have been preestablished, and are all investigated during the assessment. Therefore the assignment conference participated in by the client, his or her primary care worker and assessment worker, and an assessment supervisor, and charged with reaching mutual agreement on a suitable course of action, usually takes only half an hour.

Upon completion of treatment, an initial determination of outcome is made; if necessary, clients are then referred to additional treatments (N), or perhaps to reassessment (P). Eventually all clients will return to the community (O), having completed their secondary interventions. There they remain in contact with their primary care workers for as long as necessary. Should they be selected as part of the follow-up sample, they will be contacted at an appropriate time by a follow-up worker from the Research Unit (J). A determination of long-term outcome will be made, in the light of such criteria as the level of substance currently being used and the status of those problems detected at initial assessment. These data are fed back into the system, and particularly into the assessment and assignment processes. Changes in the system can then be effected.

Aspects of Treatment

The degree to which differential treatment may be said to be available is proportional to the number of distinct treatment options offered. Clients entering the Clinical Institute treatment system have been considered potentially eligible for, and hence have regularly and carefully been screened for, eighteen possible interventions. This number excludes primary care, which is provided to all clients and becomes the principal intervention for some, as well as medical and psychiatric care. Treatment options which have been available will be briefly described below, with a more detailed description of the operations of the differential treatment assignment process and the resultant pattern of service delivery to date. It should be noted, however, that at the present time the inclusion or exclusion of a specific treatment option is not based upon proven efficacy. Such proof is largely the task of the future.

Four inpatient services have been offered to clients, three directed principally at persons with alcohol-related problems and one principally at persons with drug-related problems (approximately 60 percent of the client population states their major problem is with alcohol; 20 percent with drugs; and 20 percent, with both). One relatively traditional inpatient service is utilized largely by older individuals with chronic alcohol problems, providing a respite both from alcohol use and external problems in a supportive setting which features frequent therapeutic group sessions. A halfway-house program is designed principally for those clients who are working or about to begin working. It provides some group interaction, but is used largely for residential support during a transitional period between hospitalization and the community. Another program is conducted on a farm at some distance from the city, which houses a small factory manufacturing antique furniture reproductions of high quality. Its clients tend to be severe alcoholics of the "Skid Row" variety, who work in the factory, and who, it is hoped, would become both sober and employable. The inpatient program for drug abusers accepts a young clientele which characteristically uses many drugs in varying combinations. Opiates are often among the drugs used, but rarely the principal drug; alcohol, on the other hand, is often of major importance. This program is based upon a careful analysis of substance abuse behavior as a learned pattern of response, and utilizes both individual and group contingency management techniques to reinforce desired non-drug-related behavioral patterns. Many privileges that are extended to the group as a whole have to be earned anew each day through the efforts of the individual clients, and are not forthcoming if not earned. The hope is to bring positive peer pressure systematically to bear upon individuals. These programs are approximately one month to six weeks in length except for the farm program, which often lasts several months.

Among the seven outpatient programs offered have been the relatively traditional modes of psychotherapy, such as individual, group, family, and marital therapy. Therapists providing these services have come from a variety of disciplines and training settings and have had different degrees of experience; consequently the therapy given has been eclectic. Relaxation training and assertiveness training, rather less complex techniques provided by fewer therapists, have tended to be relatively consistent in application. Of particular interest has been a cognitive reappraisal program provided on an outpatient basis to clients with relatively intact social circumstances who nevertheless have a significant problem with alcohol. Such clients may have developed maladaptive patterns of construing and dealing with life events, involving them in attempts to cope through alcohol use. These patterns are thoroughly explored. Alternative patterns of a more adaptive kind are developed, rehearsed, and finally employed in the real world. This program is offered with an alcohol consumption goal of either abstinence or controlled drinking. Each client is seen for an initial phase of approximately eight 90-minute individual counseling sessions on a weekly basis, and an active follow-up phase of two years' duration.

Pharmacotherapy has also been regularly employed. While the full panoply of drugs utilized for medical and psychiatric purposes is prescribed as needed, specific drugs which may have a more direct impact upon drug and alcohol consumption are of particular relevance. Of these, Antabuse has been to date the most important. Because of its adverse interaction with alcohol in the human body it serves a protective function for many individuals otherwise prone to impulsive drinking. Another drug which depends upon the same protective mechanism but has rather different pharmacokinetic properties, Temposil, will receive further attention in future.* Both methadone maintenance and methadone withdrawal programs are available for the small proportion of clients who are principally opiate-dependent. Studies of the clinical use of narcotic antagonists (e.g., naltrexone), the protective drugs for opiate abuse, are planned for the future as well.

A number of highly practical and more didactic programs dealing with particular aspects of daily living, such as leisure skill counseling, health and fitness training, and vocational rehabilitation, have been offered to specific clients directly following assessment. This departs from the more traditional use of these modalities subsequent to other, allegedly more critical interventions, as is implied in the commonly used term "aftercare." Experience has suggested that these interventions, in particular cases, are best considered equivalent ways of dealing with the problems of individuals and are not of secondary importance. Finally, an Alcoholics Anonymous group meets regularly at the Foundation and has received referrals from the Assessment Unit.

Since validated methods of matching particular clients to specific treatment programs are virtually nonexistent, reliance has been placed upon a combination of (1) simple and objective eligibility criteria, developed collaboratively and on a *prima facie* basis by system personnel and the leaders of treatment programs, and (2) client preference. The eligibility criteria, while only a first approximation and subject to continuing alteration, have the enormous advantage of being explicit. Both what the criteria are for admission to a given intervention, and how the determination is to be made that a given client meets those criteria, are matters of record. Should future outcome research demonstrate that the criteria fail to predict a positive outcome for most cases, they can readily be changed. This is in contrast to the ordinary state of affairs, in which neither the criteria nor the methods of assessment are fully and completely specified, and in which either the evaluation of the selection criteria or their alteration is consequently very difficult.

Client self-selection of treatments has been advocated by other (e.g., Ewing, 1977), is often quite perceptive (Obitz, 1975), and may enhance compliance (our data suggest this is particularly the case for inpatient

* Temposil is not available for clinical use in the United States.

programs). As it cannot be assumed that clients entering the treatment system are eminently knowledgeable regarding all therapeutic options, an educational program outlining the salient aspects of each intervention in straightforward terms is regularly provided as part of assessment. In addition, all clients are administered a checklist of goal statements. This contains three such statements for each intervention offered. In simple language, they express goals enunciated by program personnel as central to the potential capabilities of their particular program. Thus, for N programs, the list would consist of 3N statements. Clients are first asked to rate all goals on a five-point scale of importance for themselves, and are then asked to rank-order all the important goals. Those goals ranked among the first five are considered to reflect their principal treatment choices.

Two examples of criteria and goals, utilized in the system's Phase II pilot test, may be cited. With respect to individual psychotherapy, it was felt that eligibles should be of at least moderate social stability, in view of the usual time course of the intervention, and therefore that they should score at the level of 6 or above on a fourteen-point scale of social stability. This index is based upon multiple demographic factors relating to present accommodation, family contact, work record, and legal status. It was also felt that at least average verbal ability and abstract reasoning ability should be required, as indicated by a standard score of at least 8 on a version of the WAIS vocabulary scale (Wechsler, 1955), and of at least 40 on Raven's Progressive Matrices (Raven, 1960); these latter two measures are highly correlated with, and may be considered indicative of, general intelligence. In addition, one of the following goals should be selected: "I want a therapist to help me understand why I drink or take drugs." "I want to talk to a therapist about my doubts and fears." "I want a therapist to help me sort out my problems." For relaxation training, in addition to similar requirements on measures of verbal and abstract reasoning ability, it was felt that eligibles should score either above 10 on the Basic Personality Inventory anxiety scale (Jackson, 1976), above 58 on Endler's State Anxiety Scale (Endler and Okada, 1975), or above 20 on Morgan's Social Fear Scale (Morgan, 1974). The goal statements included, "I want to be tense less often." "I want to be able to sleep without pills." "I want to learn how to relax in social situations."

Although these decision rules primarily reflect common sense, they have been quite useful in the selection of clients for specific programs from the Clinical Institute's general client population. For example, although 48.5 percent of Phase II clients were interested in individual psychotherapy (in terms of their ranking one of the relevant goal statements in the top five), only 24.2 percent were eligible; and although 47.5 percent were interested in relaxation therapy, only 31.3

percent were eligible. It is certainly the case that such criteria may not stand the test of time and may be discarded, particularly if follow-up studies indicate they are unrelated to positive outcome. But other, more precise criteria will then be substituted on the basis of these same studies, and there is little doubt that the net effect will be that even fewer clients (albeit much more appropriate ones) will be eligible for a given intervention. Treatment resources are scarce and must be shielded from overuse by individuals unlikely to benefit from them, so that those who are more likely to benefit may be assured of their availability. Consideration will continually be given to the addition of further modalities of intervention to the group of shell programs, especially if they appear to meet the needs of clients not otherwise receiving specific care. Conversely, programs which are found upon prolonged experience not to be relevant to the needs of the particular client population served by the treatment system can be considered for termination.

In terms of actual assignment to programs, eight of the options offered proved to be most frequently utilized (see Figure 15–3, based on 210 representative clients seen during 1977). Of the greatest interest is the fact that the largest single group of clients either wished to have only primary care (goal statements for primary care were included in the checklist) or were eligible for no other interventions. This is consistent with the findings of Edwards et al. (1977), in which such minimal care was found on balance to be equivalent in its effect with standard treatment (see also Edwards, Griffith, and Offord, 1977). For the most part, this sort of care is not widely available. Yet, in terms of both effectiveness and cost, it would appear to be highly promising.

The percentages in Figure 15–3 add up to more than 100 percent, reflecting the fact that a number of clients were assigned to more than a single intervention. For example, clients given Antabuse were *always* assigned to at least one additional intervention, out of a conviction that medications per se can rarely be expected to be a sufficient response to so complex a problem. Nevertheless, despite the advocacy by some workers of treatment "packages" consisting of large numbers of interventions applied simultaneously, combinations of treatments have not been encouraged up to the present time. According to the eligibility criteria utilized, fewer than 28 percent of clients were eligible for more than two interventions. Given the paucity of treatment resources available, the use by a client of more than one intervention seriously limits the choices of other clients. Research on the efficacy of interventions is greatly complicated when multiple interventions are used (Nathan and Lansky, 1978). More importantly, there is reason to suppose that such combinations in some instances may adversely

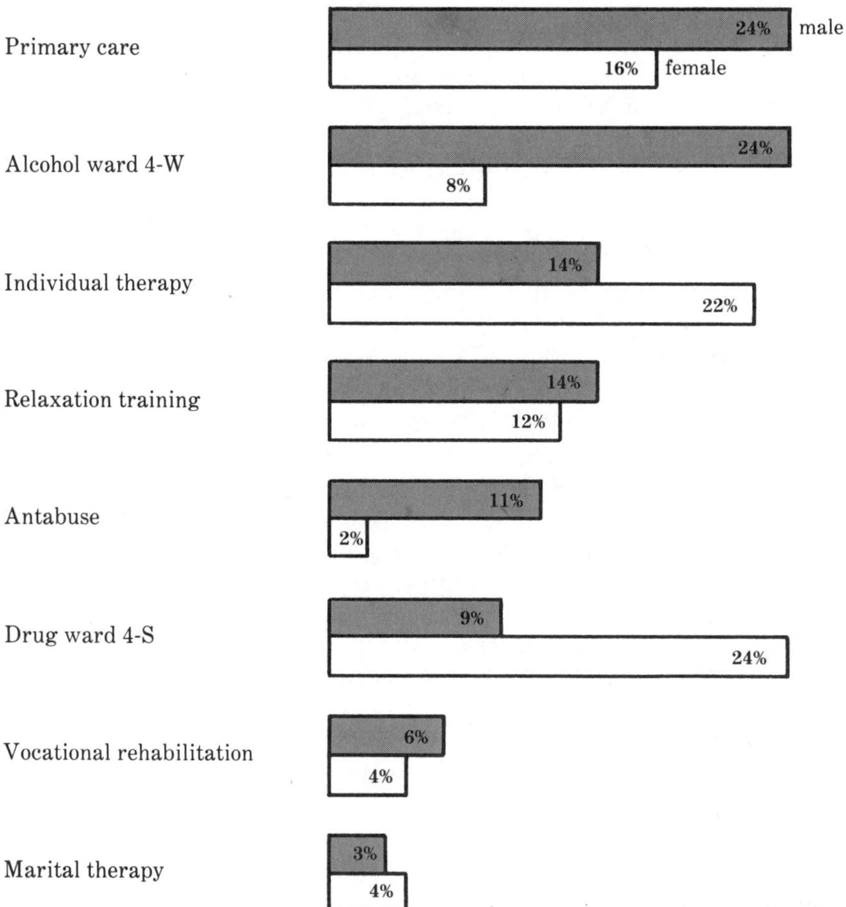

Figure 15–3. Assignments to treatment of 210 representative clients in 1977

effect outcome. It is known, for example, that the use of Antabuse interferes with the metabolism of commonly prescribed benzodiazepines (MacLeod et al., 1978). There is at least presumptive evidence that psychoactive drugs may vitiate the effects of certain sociobehavioral therapies (e.g., Kazarian, 1978). And it seems reasonable, even on a *prima facie* basis, that particular sociobehavioral therapies may interfere with each other if used simultaneously with the same client (e.g., relaxation training and assertiveness training). In brief, it does not seem prudent to utilize combinations of treatments on a large scale until specific treatments are available to more clients, and until careful scientific scrutiny determines that the effects of particular treatment combinations are at least additive.

That simple objective criteria and client preferences, rather than the judgments of highly trained clinicians, are relied upon in so important a matter as the assignment of clients to treatment may appear to some to be an unwelcome development. But the judgments and expertise of clinicians were utilized both in the overall design of the system and in the selection of criteria for assignment to treatment. Clinical judgment is also operative in the primary care, assessment, assignment, and intervention processes. Nevertheless, it must be emphasized that there exists no body of evidence proving that either the deployment of trained clinicians, or any other method utilized to date, results in highly effective treatment assignment. The criteria and goal statements of the system are capable of empirical validation and refinement. With the use of feedback data from outcome studies in the determination of future assignments, there is every likelihood that the system will increasingly direct its clients to those services they uniquely require. No method of dealing with clients could promise more. Nor have concerns that clients would be put off by dealing with a highly structured and presumptively impersonal "system" proven to be valid. The significantly higher proportion of clients appearing in treatment programs and the strongly positive comments which they regularly provide attest to the warmth and human understanding which system personnel have consistently brought to their work.

The Continuing Problems: Practical and Theoretical

In the foregoing discussion many issues are necessarily left unspecified. For example, how are primary care workers selected and trained, and what are the guidelines under which they operate? What is the content of assessment? How is it administered to a large population of clients, and by whom is this done? How may treatments be specified and held relatively constant over time so that their effects upon large numbers of clients can be determined? What outcome criteria are to be used?

These practical issues are not insuperable. Experience to date indicates that answers can be found which will serve in the short run, and which will provide a basis for a more enduring long-run solution. That is to say, the construction and utilization of a comprehensive treatment and treatment-research system is quite feasible. What the answers to such practical issues have been in Toronto may be instructive, but may also be of little absolute importance. Our answers today may not be our answers tomorrow. Others who will attempt to achieve similar goals may well need to find alternative answers, depending upon the exigencies of their particular situation. What in the end will prove to be the commonalities among different treatment systems may well be the questions asked, rather than the answers given.

If there are practical unknowns, there are also theoretical unknowns. At the most basic level, the very nature of the generic problem with which the system purports to deal is unknown. What is alcoholism? Is it, like syphilis, a single disease entity with a single (if undiscovered) etiology? Or is it, like depression, a final common pathway upon which multiple, highly disparate etiologic factors converge? Supposing that the original cause or causes were known, would their resulution eliminate excessive alcohol consumption? Or does that consumption, if it is a feature of an individual's life over a long period of time, develop such momentum that it will continue autonomously, despite the resolution of the etiologic nexus? Even if one assumes that the multiple problems with which clients characteristically present are not causally related to drinking, but are simply associated with it, a similar question arises. For example, if a client who drinks has marital problems, will the successful resolution of the marital problems regularly be accompanied by a reduction to consumption levels? Or will the client then simply resemble others who do not have marital problems but nevertheless drink to excess? Beyond such particular treatment problems, is differential treatment (in the sense of individualized treatment scrupulously matched to comprehensively assessed client needs and abilities) superior in outcome to the uniform treatment of all clients? If superior, is it more cost-effective?

The fact that one can construct a feasible treatment system does not answer these questions. But it does provide a means by which many or most of them can be addressed and eventually answered. By placing all treatment efforts potentially within the compass of research, the system greatly facilitates research. In the long run, it may find its greatest justification in permitting these difficult questions to be answered in a more efficient and less troublesome manner than was hitherto possible.

It will not have gone unnoticed that many of the same types of questions which need to be answered in the field of drug and alcohol dependence also need to be answered in psychiatry. Indeed, the construction of similar systems has been called for in psychiatry (e.g., Hayes-Roth, Longabaugh, and Ryback, 1973), and in some instances they have actually been implemented (e.g., Williams, Johnson, and Bliss, 1975; Johnson, Gianetti, and Williams, 1976; Paitich, 1973). Fortunately much of what is learned in one area about the development of treatment and treatment-research systems can be applied to work in other areas. Therefore the future may hold a productive collaboration between systems operating in different social problem areas (Bratter and Kooyman, 1981). In learning to deal effectively with the manifold and complex phenomena of human behavior, we may one day truly become connoisseurs of chaos.

References

Adler, F., Moffett, A. D., Glaser, F. B., Ball, J. C., and Horvitz, D. *A Systems Approach to Drug Treatment.* Philadelphia; Dorrance & Co., 1974.

Baekeland, F., Lundwall, L., and Kissin, B. Methods for the treatment of chronic alcoholism: a critical approach. In *Research Advances in Alcohol and Drug Problems,* ed. R. J. Gibbins, Y. Israel, H. Kalant, R. E. Popham, W. Schmidt, and R. Smart. Toronto: John Wiley & Sons, 1975.

Bergin, A. E. The evaluation of therapeutic outcomes. In E. Bergin and S. L. Garfield (eds.), *Handbood of Psychotherapy and Behavioral Change: An Empirical Analysis.* New York: John Wiley & Sons, 1971.

Bratter, T. E., and Koogman, M. A structured environment for heroin addicts: The experiences of a community-based American methadone clinic and a residential Dutch therapeutic community. *International Journal of Social Psychiatry,* 1981, *27* (*3*), 189–203.

Edwards, G., and Offord, J. A plain treatment for alcoholism. *Proceedings of the Royal Society of Medicine,* 1977, *70,* 344–348.

———, Egert, S., Guthrie, S., Hawker, A., Hensman, C., Mitcheson, M., Oppenheimer, E., and Taylor, C. Alcoholism: a controlled trial of "treatment" and "advice." *Journal of Studies on Alcohol,* 1977, *38,* 1004–1031.

Endler, N. S., and Okada, M. A multidimensional measure of trait anxiety: the S-R Inventory of General Trait Anxiousness. *Journal of Consulting Psychology,* 1975, *43,* 319–329.

Emrick, C. D. Book review (*The RAND Report*). *Journal of Studies on Alcohol,* 1976, *37,* 1902–1907.

Ewing, J. A. Matching therapy and patients: the cafeteria plan. *British Journal of Addiction,* 1977, *72,* 13–18.

Glaser, F. B. Treatment of individuals dependent on psychoactive drugs. In *Proceedings: Health Research Ontario, 1977.* Toronto: Ministry of Health, 1977(a).

———. The "average package of help" versus the matching hypothesis: a doggerel dialogue. Substudy no. 891, 1977. Addiction Research Foundation, Toronto. Also published in *Journal of Studies on Alcohol,* 1977(b), *38,* 1819–1827.

———, Greenberg, S. W., and Barrett, M., *A Systems Approach to Alcohol Treatment.* Toronto: ARF Books, 1978.

Hayes-Roth, F., Longabaugh, R., and Ryback, R. Mental health: systems and non-systems. *British Journal of Medical Psychology,* 1973, *46,* 317–336.

Jackson, D. N. *Basic Personality Inventory.* London, Ontario: Research Psychologist Press, 1983.

Jacobson: G. R. *The Alcoholisms: Detection, Diagnosis and Assessment.* New York: Human Sciences Press, 1976.

Jaffe, J., Edwards, G., Epstein, N., LeDain, G., Anderson, J., and Nathan, P. Report of the External Evaluation Committee of the Addiction Research Foundation, Aug. 30, 1975. Unpublished ms.

Johnson, J. H., Gianetti, R. A., and Williams, T. A. Computers in mental health care delivery: a review of the evolution toward interventionally relevant on-line processing. *Behavior Research Methods and Instrumentation,* 1976, *8,* 83–91.

Kazarian, S. S., Tekatch, G. M., Ifabumuyi, O. I., Deinum, E. J., and Merskey, H. Effects of antianxiety agents on relaxation therapy: a preliminary investigation. *Canadian Psychiatric Association Journal,* 1978, *23,* 389–394.

Khantzian, E. J. Psychopathological causes and consequences of drug dependence. In E. Gottheil, K. A. Druley, T. E. Skoloda, and H. M. Waxman (eds.), *Etiologic Aspects of Alcohol and Drug Abuse.* Springfield, Ill.: Charles C. Thomas, 1983.

Kissin, B., Tuchfield, B. S., Schuckit, M. S., Rosenberg, C. M., Glaser, F. B., and Matkom, A. J. Comments on "Alcoholism: a controlled trial of 'treatment' and 'advice'." *Journal of Studies on Alcohol,* 1977, *38,* 1804–1829.

MacLeod, S. M., Sellers, E. M., Giles, H. G., Billings, B. J., Martin, P. R., Greenblatt, D. J., and Marshman, J. A. Interaction of disulfiram with benzodiazepines. *Clinical Pharmacology and Therapeutics,* 1978, *24,* 583–589.

Morgan, W. G. The relationship between expressed social fears and assertiveness and its treatment implications. *Behaviour Research and Therapy,* 1974, *11,* 57–65.

Nathan, P. E., and Lansky, D. Common methodological problems in research on the addictions. *Journal of Consulting and Clinical Psychology,* 1978, *46,* 713–726.

Obitz, F. W. Alcoholics' perceptions of selected counseling techniques. *British Journal of Addiction,* 1975, *70,* 187–191.

Overall, J. E., Hollister, L. E., Johnson, M., and Pennington, V. Nosology of depression and differential response to drugs. *Journal of the American Medical Association,* 1966, *195,* 946–948.

Paitich, D. A comprehensive automated psychological examination and report (CAPER). *Behavioral Science,* 1973, *18,* 131–136.

Pattison, E. M., Sobell, M. B., and Sobell, L. C. *Emerging Concepts of Alcohol Dependence.* New York: Springer Publishing Co., 1977.

Paul, G. L. Strategy of outcome research in psychotherapy. *Journal Consulting Psychology,* 1967, *31,* 109–18.

Paykel, E. S. Depressive typologies and response to amitriptyline. *British Journal of Psychiatry,* 1972, *120,* 147–156.

Raven, J. C. *Guide to the Standard Progressive Matrices.* London: H. K. Lewis, 1960.

Watson, S. J., Berger, P. A., Akil, H., Mills, M. J., and Barchas, J. D. Effects of naloxone on schizophrenia: reduction in hallucinations in a subpopulation of subjects. *Science* 1978, *201,* 73–76.

Wechsler, D. *Wechsler Adult Intelligence Scale Manual.* New York: Psychological Corp., 1955.

Williams, T. A., Johnson, J. H., and Bliss, E. L. A computer-assisted psychiatric assessment unit. *American Journal of Psychiatry,* 1975, *132,* 1074–1076.

16

Antatbuse Treatment

Gary G. Forrest

Antabuse (disulfiram) treatment, initially introduced in 1948, is an effective alcohol-antagonizing treatment modality for alcoholism. This chemical substance has little effect on clients unless they ingest alcohol. Antabuse causes the accumulation of a toxin in the body which makes a person who has ingested alcohol extremely sick. Organic sulfur precursors of disulfiram have been used since the 1800s for a variety of indications (Kwentus and Major, 1979).

Pharmacology and General Clinical Considerations

Once disulfiram (Antabuse) is absorbed from the intestine, it is broken down within a matter of minutes to an active metabolite (diethyldithiocarbamate, or DDC) (Cobby, Mayersohn, and Sellink, 1977). Antabuse and its metabolites are excreted through the urine and feces.

The specific mechanism of action of Antabuse is not known (Schuckit, 1981). According to Kwentus and Major (1979), disulfiram and DDC probably work by "chelating metals (primarily copper) essential for the action of acetaldehyde-metabolizing enzymes or through competitive inhibition of enzymatic action on one of the important carbons in acetaldehyde." Various important enzymes are effected by disulfiram, including aldehyde dehydrogenase (ALDH), aniline hydroxylase, WADPH Oxidase, and cythochrome P450 (Haley, 1979). Enzyme inhibition is irreversible; therefore, new enzymes must be produced by means of protein synthesis. The essential clinical result (Schuckit, 1981) "is the accumulation of acetaldehyde." Disulfiram also affects other body systems (such as brain transmitters, especially the catecholamines).

Researchers (Sauter, Boss, and Von Wartburg, 1977; Schuckit, 1981) generally agree that the "Antabuse reaction" occurs as a result of the accumulation of acetaldehyde as the first breakdown product of ethanol. Some of the effects of the Antabuse reaction are hard to explain (e.g., a fall in blood pressure). The Antabuse reaction is a complex phenomenon. It may require more than the accumulation of acetaldehyde and may occur in the presence of mild alkalosis. Serotonin or glucuronic acid conjugation may be associated with the Antabuse reaction.

The ingestion of alcohol while taking Antabuse produces extreme nausea, vomiting, a fall in blood pressure, extreme headache, blurred vision, and breathing difficulties (Forrest, 1978; Knauert, 1979). Antabuse reactions are potentially lethal. Approximately twenty Antabuse-related deaths have been reported in the medical literature (Kwentus and Major, 1979). Hundreds of thousands of alcoholics throughout the world have taken Antabuse. Indeed, there seem to be no medically determined time constraints on Antabuse therapy. Many alcoholics have been on Antabuse maintenance for over twenty-five years without any physical or psychological complications.

The alcoholic patient should complete a medical examination prior to beginning an Antabuse maintenance program. Persons with cardiac and other serious medical problems are not appropriate candidates for Antabuse treatment (Cahill, 1972). Likewise, the brain-impaired alcoholic (Knauert, 1979) is not a suitable candidate for Antabuse maintenance. These patients sometimes cannot remember that they have taken Antabuse. Psychotic patients also tend to be inappropriate candidates for Antabuse. In sum, alcoholic patients who manifest serious heart, kidney, respiratory, liver, diabetes mellitus, neurologic, psychiatric, and other health problems should not be placed on Antabuse maintenance.

Antabuse is retained in the body and will remain in the body system for as long as fourteen days after the patient has discontinued treatment (Ayerst Laboratories, 1981). Clinically, the accumulation of Antabuse in the body presents a strong physiologic deterrent to drinking for four to six days for most alcoholics. The patient must ingest Antabuse daily for several consecutive days during the initial stage of treatment. There are several relatively standard Antabuse dosage schedules. The patient can take 500 to 750 mg. daily for the first five to seven days and then 250 mg. daily. Many clinicians and alcoholic treatment centers suggest that patients remain on an Antabuse maintenance dose of 250 to 500 mg. two or three times per week.

Antabuse treatment is poorly understood by many health promoters and the general public. Indeed, the uses and abuses of Antabuse (Caster, 1978) are best recognized among health providers who are actively involved in treating alcoholics and alcohol abusers. The remainder of this chapter will discuss (1) the "myths" surrounding Antabuse; and (2) sources of treatment gain associated with the use of Antabuse and practical considerations associated with placing alcoholic patients on Antabuse maintenance.

Myths About Antabuse

It is imperative that the physician and/or psychotherapist fully explain and discuss how Antabuse works with the alcoholic patient. Patients need to understand that they must take Antabuse consistently in order for their treatment modality to be effective. The physician needs to explain to the patient that drinking alcohol while involved in an Antabuse maintenance program will precipitate serious medical complications.

Many alcoholics ask their family physician or therapist to give them Antabuse. Some of these patients believe that Antabuse will "cure" them or "take away the urge to drink." These are myths! The health provider needs to openly explain that Antabuse is not a cure for alcoholism. Likewise, the patient should be made aware of the fact that Antabuse does not extinguish the compulsion to drink. Many alcoholics have been told by other drinking alcoholics that Antabuse is a cure for alcoholism and that this cure works by taking away the desire for alcohol.

At present, there are no magical cures for alcoholism. The therapist needs to make this reality known to the alcoholic who requests Antabuse. Antabuse is not a magical solution for alcohol addiction!

A few alcoholic persons who request Antabuse believe or have been told that they can resume drinking "a day or two" after terminating their Antabuse ingestion. This myth can be dangerous or even life-threatening. As touched upon earlier, Antabuse remains in the human body for several days. The therapist needs to actively stress this fact with the patient. It is far more rational for the patient to discontinue Antabuse for two or three weeks and consciously decide to resume drinking than it is to terminate Antabuse for two or three days, impulsively resume drinking, and end up in a hospital emergency room!

Chronic alcoholic patients who have been in several alcoholism treatment programs sometimes report that they have known other alcoholics who were capable of "drinking on Antabuse" without facilitating an Antabuse reaction or even minimal side effects. This is also a potentially dangerous myth—dangerous for the person who verbalizes it as well as for other patients who simply listen and believe. When Antabuse is prescribed and taken according to the basic guidelines delineated earlier, a serious and potentially lethal reaction occurs as a consequence of ingesting an alcoholic beverage. Alcoholic patients sometimes hide Antabuse under their tongues, induce vomiting shortly after taking their Antabuse, or, in other "creative" ways, fail to actually ingest this medication. Such individuals may appear to be able to drink alcohol while taking Antabuse. In reality, they have not established a bodily maintenance level of Antabuse that will precipitate an Antabuse reaction as a result of drinking.

A related Antabuse myth suggests that taking this medication on a very irregular basis is an effective deterrent to drinking. For example, the patient may decide to "pop" an Antabuse tablet prior to a stressful evening involving socializing at a cocktail party. The patient may not have taken Antabuse for several weeks or months. This procedure might prove to be a psychological deterrent to drinking but it will not result in a physiological Antabuse reaction. Antabuse is only effective when taken on a regular and consistent basis. If the patient thinks or assumes that irregular ingestion of Antabuse will result in an Antabuse reaction following drinking and then "discovers" that this is not the case, drinking may actually be reinforced.

Many alcoholics are afraid to take Antabuse because they have been told that this medication is a "drug," and therefore addictive. This is another myth. Antabuse is not a mood-altering substance, nor is it an addictive substance. It is important for the clinician to explain to the alcoholic patient that he or she will *not* develop a physical tolerance and/or physical and psychological craving for Antabuse. The patient will not experience euphoria or "get high" as a result of taking Antabuse. Some alcoholics confuse Antabuse with such minor tranquilizers as Valium and Librium. Antabuse is not a tranquilizer or psychotropic medication. Older members of the Alcoholics Anonymous community sometimes tell new members that they "should not" take Antabuse because of its addictive properties. The clinician needs to actively dispel all of these myths and irrational beliefs.

Another myth associated with Antabuse is that the individual who chooses to take this medication must also be placed on a "special" diet. The patient who takes Antabuse does not have to be on a high-protein, high-carbohydrate, or other special diet. However, it is very important for patients on Antabuse (Ayerst Laboratories, 1981) to avoid consuming foods and substances that contain "hidden" alcohol.

Hidden alcohol can sometimes cause an unpleasant reaction in a person who is taking Antabuse. There are three primary sources of hidden alcohol: foods, medicines, and skin preparations. In general, it is wise to suggest that the patient who is taking Antabuse refrain from inhaling paints, varnishes, and other substances that contain alcohol. The patient should also avoid using vinegars, cough mixtures, mouthwashes, aftershave lotions, and some cosmetics. He or she should be encouraged to read the label of all products and to actively avoid using all substances that contain alcohol.

Various sexual myths are associated with Antabuse, and as a result, alcoholic patients may be reluctant or afraid to take it. A few patients will verbalize to their physician or therapist that they have been told that they should not or will not be able to have sexual relations after they begin Antabuse maintenance. The patient may believe that Antabuse will stimulate his or her sexual desires. A few male alcoholics refuse to take Antabuse because they have been told that this medication causes impotence, arousal and desire dysfunctions (Forrest, 1983a), or other forms of sexual dysfunction.

Alcoholics usually learn these sexual myths from other alcoholics. In reality, Antabuse is not an aphrodisiac! Nor does Antabuse cause myriad sexual dysfunctions. However, Antabuse has been reported to cause erectile difficulties among a very small percentage of alcoholic males. In my experience (Forrest, 1978; Forrest, 1983a), the sexually dysfunctional alcoholic has experienced sexual problems many months or years prior to initiating Antabuse maintenance. It is important for the therapist to reassure some alcoholics that Antabuse will not cause frigidity, impotence, sexual abstinence, or other varieties of gross sexual dysfunction. Many alcoholics experience sexual problems during the initial weeks and months of abstinence and recovery. In fact, some alcoholics appear to be unable to initiate or sustain sexual activities in the absence of drinking! The clinician must be aware of all of these realities associated with alcohol addiction and human sexuality. Indeed, there are many very important sexual psychodynamic issues associated with the use of Antabuse in the treatment of alcoholism.

Alcoholics tend to perceive Antabuse as a "crutch." Unfortunately, many alcoholics believe that it is imperative "to do it on your own." This means that the alcoholic feels that recovery and abstinence must be accomplished by the individual through self-reliance. This is another myth. Recovery from alcoholism usually entails the development and utilization of one or several healthy "crutches." It is nearly impossible to recover from alcohol addiction without the help of others and the use of healthy alternatives to drinking.

Antabuse can be a healthy alternative to alcohol abuse and alcoholism. Thus, Antabuse is an adaptive "crutch." The psychotherapist needs to point out to the alcoholic patient who is considering Antabuse that all people rely upon support and crutches from time to time. A few Alcoholics Anonymous members seem to belittle and berate alcoholics who take Antabuse in order to stop drinking. These individuals criticize Antabuse as a crutch but don't seem to realize that attending Alcoholics Anonymous three or four times a week, seeing a therapist, entering marriage counseling, and even divorcing are all crutches! If an alcoholic patient is an appropriate candidate for Antabuse maintenance and is motivated to take this medication, the therapist should actively support and reinforce the patient's decision to take Antabuse.

Some alcoholics think that they must take Antabuse "forever." This is also a myth. While it is most appropriate for the patient to take Antabuse consistently for several months, it is not required that he or she take this medication regularly for a lifetime. Clinicians (Forrest, 1978; Forrest, 1983b) often recommend that the alcoholic take Antabuse during the initial 90–120 days of psychotherapeutic treatment. In the context, Antabuse is viewed as a treatment adjunct. It is also important for clinicians to realize that thousands of recovered alcoholics have taken Antabuse regularly for well over twenty years.

A few people think that Antabuse is an effective treatment for other drug addictions. This is a myth. Antabuse is not a treatment for narcotic addiction, marijuana abuse, or dependency upon psychotropic medications. Antabuse is a treatment modality that is specific only to alcoholism.

Treatment and Practical Considerations

It is generally believed (Forrest, 1978; Schuckit, 1979; Forrest, 1984) that Antabuse treatment is most efficacious in combination with other treatment modalities. Alcoholics who simply take Antabuse as a deterrent to drinking may or may not attempt to resolve life-style, familial, vocational, sexual, and internal problems which have supported and reinforced their addictive adjustments. It is very difficult for the recovering alcoholic to remain abstinent in the absence of healthy life-style changes and personal growth subsequent to achieving abstinence.

Antabuse can be an integral part of the alcoholic patient's program of recovery, and indeed it is a very important treatment adjunct for many alcoholics. However, the indiscriminate use of Antabuse in the treatment of alcoholism is clinically inappropriate. Mendelson and Mello (1979, pp. 162–163) suggest that the person who will positively respond to Antabuse administration is one who

(1) has a positive stated desire to abstain from alcohol, (2) tends to be obsessive-compulsive and not prone to severe depression, (3) is socially stable and socially competent, (4) is usually not highly introspective, (5) has a propensity to form dependent relationships with trusted figures, and (6) tends to drink sporadically rather than continually and compulsively.

Antabuse can help the patient maintain his or her motivation to stop drinking. This medication can also facilitate the development of a working and productive therapist-patient alliance (Forrest, 1984). There are several significant psychodynamic factors associated with taking Antabuse that foster treatment gains. Taking Antabuse daily, or two or three times a week, "reminds" the patient of his or her commitment to sobriety. Choosing to take Antabuse reflects the capacity to actualize a rational and healthy choice. Antabuse reinforces the choice not to drink and also fosters the actualization of new behaviors and cognitions in the face of everyday life stressors which previously were associated with choosing to drink. The experience of sobriety generalizes and reinforces self-motivation for growth and change. Early in the recovery process, the alcoholic can decide to remain abstinent on a daily or weekly basis simply by taking "the pill." In sum, Antabuse helps the alcoholic learn in myriad ways that he or she does not have to drink. This process facilitates many other potential sources of positive behavioral, cognitive, affective, familial, and life-style change.

The global efficacy of Antabuse treatment remains questionable (Schuckit, 1981). Uncontrolled investigations do not adequately resolve the question of Antabuse effectiveness (Schuckit and Cahalan, 1976). However, short-term follow-up studies (Fuller and Williford, 1980) indicate that Antabuse results in a 77 percent abstinence rate. Milt (1969) suggests that Antabuse treatment has a success rate of approximately 50 percent over a prolonged period of time. In the clinical experience of the author, less than 20 percent of alcoholics who simply take Antabuse can be expected to remain abstinent for twelve to eighteen months. When used in combination with individual therapy, group therapy, family therapy, and Alcoholics Anonymous, Antabuse can help facilitate recovery rates of 60 to 80 percent.

When the alcoholic patient is no longer sufficiently motivated to remain sober, he or she will quickly return to drinking. This reality includes patients who are taking Antabuse. Some alcoholic patients who are legally or in other ways forced to take Antabuse hold pills under their tongues or induce vomiting in order to drink without experiencing the consequences of an Antabuse reaction. Indeed, the alcoholic may develop a rather elaborate behavioral repertoire that is designed to extinguish the effects of Antabuse maintenance. Psychotherapists and rehabilitation personnel need to be cognizant of the many sources of resistance that some alcoholics manifest with regard to taking Antabuse.

Patients should be made aware of the effects of an Antabuse reaction prior to beginning this treatment, and they should be instructed to contact their physician immediately if such a reaction occurs. It is also appropriate for a patient to carry an Antabuse identification card while taking this medication. The card suggests emergency measures for an Antabuse reaction. Medic-Alert necklaces and bracelets are also available to alert health care personnel that the patient might be experiencing an Antabuse reaction. Emergency measures to help counteract an Antabuse-alcohol reaction include "the usual supportive measures to restore blood pressure and to treat shock; inhalation of oxygen, intravenous antihistamine, or intravenous ephedrine sulfate" (Ayerst Laboratories, 1981).

Summary

Alcohol-antagonizing treatments for alcoholism have been available since the 1800s. Antabuse (disulfiram) has been used in the treatment of alcoholism for over thirty years.

The specific mechanism of action of Antabuse is not known. However, it is generally believed (Schuckit, 1981; Knauert, 1983) that the "Antabuse reaction" occurs as a result of the accumulation of acetaldehyde as the first breakdown product of ethanol. The Antabuse reaction is a complex process. The various symptoms of this reaction were discussed. Alcoholics should complete a physical examination prior to initiating Antabuse maintenance. Serious physical, neurological, and psychiatric complications contraindicate the use of Antabuse. Prescription and dosage formats were discussed.

The clinician needs to openly discuss the various aspects of Antabuse with each alcoholic patient that he or she places on the medication. This discussion should also include Antabuse myths. Antabuse is not a cure for alcoholism. Antabuse does not extinguish the "urge," or compulsion, to drink. This medication is not addictive. It is not an aphrodisiac or cause of gross sexual dysfunction or deviation. Several other destructive and potentially dangerous myths about Antabuse were elucidated.

Antabuse can be a rational and healthy treatment alternative to chronic alcoholism and alcohol abuse. Antabuse treatment is most efficacious when utilized in conjunction with other treatment modalities. The indiscriminate use of Antabuse in the treatment of alcoholism is clinically inappropriate. Antabuse appears to be used effectively with alcoholics who are (1) motivated to stop drinking; (2) obsessive-compulsive and not severely depressed; (3) socially stable; (4) not highly introspective; (5) dependent; and (6) prone to binge drinking rather than obsessive-sustained drinking. Antabuse can help the therapist-patient team develop a working and productive therapeutic alliance (Forrest, 1984). Taking Antabuse on a regular basis reminds the alcoholic patient of his or her commitment to sobriety.

The global efficacy of Antabuse treatment is questionable. However, investigations (Milt, 1969; Fuller and Williford, 1980) have indicated that Antabuse treatment results in a 50–77 percent abstinence rate.

Emergency measures to help counteract an Antabuse-alcohol reaction were also discussed.

References

Ayerst Laboratories. *Guidelines for Antabuse (Disulfiram) Users*. New York, 1981.

Cahill, C. A. Safety of disulfiram. *New England Journal of Medicine,* 1972, *287,* 935–936.

Caster, D. U. Tailoring treatment modalities to brain function in sobering alcoholics. Lecture, Psychotherapy Associates, Fourth Annual Advanced Winter Workshop, "Treatment and Rehabilitation of the Alcoholic," Colorado Springs, Colo., Feb. 2, 1978.

Cobby, J., Mayersohn, M., and Sellink, S. The rapid reduction of disulfiram in blood and plasma. *Journal of Pharmacology,* 1977, *202,* 724–731.

Forrest, G. G. *The Diagnosis and Treatment of Alcoholism.* Springfield, Ill.: Charles C. Thomas, 1978.

———. *Alcoholism and Human Sexuality.* Springfield, Ill.: Charles C. Thomas, 1983(a).

———. *Alcoholism, Narcissism and Psychopathology.* Springfield, Ill.: Charles C. Thomas, 1983(b).

Forrest, G. G. *Intensive Psychotherapy of Alcoholism.* Springfield, Ill.: Charles C. Thomas, 1984.

Fuller, R. K., and Williford, W. O. Life-table analysis of abstinence in a study evaluating the efficacy of disulfiram. *Alcoholism: Clinical and Experimental Research,* 1980, *4,* 298–301.

Haley, T. J. Disulfiram (tetraethylthioperoxydi-carbonic diamide): a reappraisal of its toxicity and therapeutic application. *Drugs Metabolism Reviews,* 1979, *9,* 319–335.

Knauert, A. P. The treatment of alcoholism in a community setting. *Family and Community Health,* 1979, *2(1),* 91–102.

———. Using Antabuse Wisely. Lecture, Psychotherapy Associates, Ninth Annual Advanced Winter Workshop, "Treatment and Rehabilitation of the Alcoholic," Colorado Springs, Colo., Feb. 4, 1983.

Kwentus, J., and Major, L. F. Disulfiram in the treatment of alcoholism, *Journal of Studies on Alcohol,* 1979, *40,* 428–445.

Mendelson, J. H., and Mello, N. K. *The Diagnosis and Treatment of Alcoholism.* New York: McGraw-Hill, 1979.

Milt, H. *Basic Handbook of Alcoholism.* Brunswick, N. J.: Scientific Aids Publications, 1969.

Sauter, A. M., Boss, D., and Von Wartburg, J. P. Reevaluation of the disulfiram-alcohol reaction in man. *Journal of Studies on Alcohol,* 1977, *38,* 1680–1695.

Schuckit, M. A. Disulfiram (antabuse) and the treatment of alcoholic men. In Raleigh Hills Foundation, *Advances in Alcoholism,* 1981, *2*(*4*), 1–5.

———. *Drug and Alcohol Abuse: A Clinical Guide to Diagnosis and Treatment.* New York: Plenum Press, 1979.

———, and Cahalan, D. Evaluation of alcoholism treatment programs. In W. J. Filstead et al. (eds.), *Alcohol and Alcohol Problems: New Thinking and New Directions.* Cambridge: Mass.: Ballinger Publishing Co., 1976.

17

The American Self-Help Residential Therapeutic Community

A Pragmatic Treatment Approach for Addicted Character-Disordered Individuals

THOMAS E. BRATTER / ERNEST A. COLLABOLLETTA / ALLEN J. FOSSBENDER / MATTHEW C. PENNACCHIA / JOHN R. RUBEL

The Evolution of the Therapeutic Community: From the Dead Sea Scrolls to the Twentieth Century

F. B. Glaser (1977) traces the philosophical origins of the therapeutic community to the Dead Sea Scrolls, written more than two thousand years ago, which were discovered in 1947 and subsequently translated. He suggests that Vermes's (1966) translation of the Dead Sea Scrolls could serve as the first definition of the therapeutic community:

> And this is the Rule for the men of the Community who have freely pledged themselves to be converted from all evil and to cling to all his commandments according to his will. They shall separate themselves from the congregation of the men of falsehood to become a community in respect to the law and property under the authority of the Sons of Zadok, the Priests who keep the Covenant, and of the multitude of men of the Community who hold fast to the Covenant. Every decision concerning doctrine, property and justice shall be determined by them. (p. 59)

While there seem to be twenty centuries of precedent for the therapeutic community, the fact that the Dead Sea Scrolls were not translated until the 1960s precludes them from being influential in the therapeutic community movement. Although the establishment of mutual trust and cooperation among groups of people living together has been the goal of all social institutions, which Veysey (1973) describes, the use of a communal concept to help people resolve a variety of personal problems has been a relatively new idea which has been refined by the therapeutic community.

The therapeutic community, perhaps, is a reaction (delayed by four decades) to Beers's (1939) 1907 report of his mistreatment while he was a patient in a number of mental institutions. Lief (1948) reports that Beers, with the assistance of Meyer and James (1923), created the National Committee for Mental Hygiene, which sponsored reform in asylum management and treatment innovations. Caplan (1969, p. 10) chronicles the turn of the century as a

> period when physicians other than psychiatrists and citizens attempted to improve mental hospitals, to break the monopoly of asylum staff in managing the insane, and to promote innovative research and treatment. . . . The impetus for reform came first from outside psychiatry, from crusades of indignant laymen, often spurred by the shocking stories of former patients. . . . Psychiatrists became associated in the public mind with conservative and injurious patient management; with political corruption; with failure to evolve scientific insights and treatments at the same rate as other branches of medicine; and with stiff-necked self-importance.

Few realize that in 1911 Bleuler concluded that mental institutions were ineffective for deteriorated schizophrenics. He advocated that the mental hospital should help patients develop self-control and adjust to freedom. Bleuler (1950, p. 328) has written: "The institution will attempt to educate the patient to act in a more acceptable manner. . . . The only and often practical criterion for hospital release is the patient's capacity to react in a positive manner to changes in the environment and treatment. . . . The general task of treatment then consists in educating the patient in reestablishing his contact with reality."

Sullivan (1937) was more explicit and idealistic when he conceptualized the mental institution to be a place where patients could learn to live in society: "The mental hospital . . . can become a school for personality growth rather than a custodian of personality failures. The situation is one of education, broadly conceived, not by verbal teaching but by communal experience—good tutoring." Despite the realistic idealism of Bleuler and Sullivan, mental institutions remained intransigently opposed to positive change. Goffman has compared mental hospitals with prisons and concentration camps, where patients were segregated and shielded from society. In 1961 (p. 361) he protested that

> the patient's life is regulated and ordered according to a disciplinarian system developed for management by a small staff of a large number of involuntary inmates. In this system the attendant is likely to be the key staff person, informing the patient of the punishments and rewards that are to regulate his life and arranging for medical authorization for such privileges and punishments. Quiet, obedient behavior leads to the patient's promotion in the ward system; obstreperous, untidy behavior to demotion.

The sociologist suggests that the primary determinants of behavior of hospitalized mental patients lie in the situation of being incarcerated, not in the alleged mental illness. Bratter (1981) and others have protested the "no win" situation of patients in mental institutions and attribute iatrogenic disturbances to oppression and regression within such institutions. Convicted criminals no longer wish to get transferred from prisons to mental institutions. Kesey's (1962) surrealistic portrayal of McMurphy, who as a consequence of his disruptive behavior receives a lobotomy, becomes a frightening reality. Noting the need to label some incarcerated individuals as mentally deficient, Szasz (1970) has written sardonically that "Institutional Psychiatry fulfills a basic human need—to validate the Self as good (normal) by invalidating the Other as evil (mentally ill)." Ozarin (1954) are concerned with the negative consequences of custodial care in hospital settings which can be characterized by an atmosphere of passivity and dependency.

Within the last quarter of a century in Europe and the United States, there have been two divergent therapeutic community movements which essentially have been a revolt against the punitive "care, custody, and control" mentality of mental institutions. These movements developed simultaneously and independently. The egalitarian, professional model had its origins in hospital settings. Rubel, et. al (1982) p. 222. The attitudes, behavior, status, responsibilities, and rights of the professional staff and patients have been modified so there is increased equality and accountability.

> Briefly, the doctor relinquishes his monopoly on expertise and power. He becomes a member of the team whose job it is to promote the development of the community and the people in it so that the person in direct contact with the patient acts toward him in a manner that is helpful and therapeutic. The nurse assumes more responsibility for treatment in this sense and must develop new interpersonal skills appropriate to the task. The patient also takes on a new role. He cannot wait passively for treatment to be administered to him; he must be active in his own treatment, using the resources of the community to explore his problems, to try out new attitudes and behavior, and to rebuild his personality. In addition, he must assume his share of responsibility for the functioning of the community and the treatment and welfare of his fellow patients.

After the termination of World War II, a group of American psychiatrists toured England to learn about innovative and humanistic techniques which the British had developed during the war. The new approach emphasized the significance of environmental and social factors which positively affected treatment outcomes. As a result of this visit, Main was the first to utilize the term "therapeutic community" to describe the Northfield Military Hospital program. He portrayed the Northfield experiment (1946, p. 69) as "an attempt to use a hospital not as an organization run by doctors in the interest of now greater technical efficiency but as a community with the immediate aim of full participation of all its members in its daily life and the eventual aim of resocialization of the neurotic individual for life in an ordinary society."

In Europe, most therapeutic communities can trace their origins to the democratic and egalitarian principles devised by Jones (1952, 1953). In attempting to differentiate between the therapeutic community and the more traditional mental institution, Wilmar (1958, pp. 824–825) focuses on the "emphasis that it places upon socio-environmental factors in the patient's hospital experience, . . . The hospital is conceptualized literally as a form of community with its special culture and subculture, similar both to the outside world from which the patients have come and to which, it is hoped, they will again be able to return. . . . The basic therapy of therapeutic communities is milieu therapy." Wilmar's conceptualization of the therapeutic community stresses the importance of the professional staff's interaction with the patient and the sharing of decision making, which tends to blur, but does not obscure, the distinct lines of demarcation between the two. Jones attempted to humanize the relationship between the providers of treatment and the receivers. Patients were to be released from the hospital with the same status they had when they entered. Jones wanted to reduce the traditional treatment barrier, the "we–they" dichotomy, which existed between patients and the professional staff. This was a significant and radical departure from traditional institutional policy, in which the physician's status was supreme. In an autobiographical account of his stay in an asylum, where he was treated for acute alcoholism, Seabrook recounts his experiences as a patient. When describing ward conditions Seabrook (1935), illuminates the "we–they" dichotomy which he experienced as a patient:

> And one of its permanent, dominant overtones was this back-to-childhood, back-to-the kindergarten element. We were handled as children—not as delinquent or bad children, necessarily, but rather, as potentially decent, irresponsible children who didn't know what was good for us, and therefore frequently had to be told. It was a "mama knows best" or "teacher knows best" atmosphere, protective and generally kindly, but backed up with

> "mama will spank" when children became unmanageable and just had to be dragged kicking to bed without their suppers. . . . What gave it sometimes a crazy-dream quality—quite apart from the fact that some of us were crazy—was the fact that all of us were grown men, many of us middle-aged or elderly men of the type which generally bosses and orders other people around in the outside world.

Jones (1959, p. 200) provides a comprehensive definition of the therapeutic community, which, he thinks,

> is distinctive among other comparable treatment centers in the way the institution's total resources, both staff and patients, are self-consciously pooled in furthering treatment. This implies above all a change in the usual status of patients. In collaboration with the staff, they now become active participants in the therapy of other patients, and in other aspects of overall hospital work—in contrast to their relatively more passive recipient role in conventional treatment regimes.

In the professional model, which Jones developed, physicians and patients share equally in determining daily operational policy. Jones (1976) believes that "responsibility and authority within the system rests not in one director or administrator, but is shared by a large number of individuals representing significant parts of the system." Filstead and Rossi (1973, pp. 10–11) list five components which constitute Jones's (1968a, 1968b) model:

First: The patient's role is transformed from the traditional one of passivity and obedience which Seabrook described to a more active one.

Second: The traditional "we–they" dichotomy . . . which segregates patients from the credentialed staff is neutralized. The formal authoritarian role of the professional, thus, has been rejected.

Third: The role and power of the credentialed staff is reduced greatly since decision-making becomes a community responsibility. There is a concerted attempt to democratize the ward to elicit equal input by both the staff and patients. Self-government by the patients becomes a treatment goal.

Fourth: Open and direct communication among all members of the therapeutic community becomes essential to the growth of the program and all the individuals within it.

Fifth: The program attempts to approximate the "outside" world in order to facilitate social learning . . . inside the therapeutic community.

As a member of the prestigious and powerful psychiatric-medical establishment, Jones was the first to recognize the ability of patients, when given the opportunity, to govern themselves. Jones's and Wilmar's work represents a courageous attempt not only to humanize professionals but also to provide an alternative democratic method of working with hospitalized individuals. Despite Jones's (1979a) wish to document a linkage between the professional model which he developed with the self-help concept that will be examined below, there are irreconcilable differences. Jones (1980) p. 135 acknowledges the fundamental difference when he writes: "The 'new' therapeutic communities derive from the more recent developments in the treatment of substance abuse. Central to this movement is Synanon and its many modifications which use the clients' peer group to solve their own problems, largely eliminating mental health professionals." Kooyman and Bratter (1980) and Bratter and Kooyman (1981), who appreciate the revolutionary contribution of Jones, contend that the psychopathology of addicted, manipulative, and dishonest individuals precludes initially the implementation of the professional model.

The Ex-Addict, Self-Help, Residential Therapeutic Community: From the Washington and Oxford Movements to Alcoholics Anonymous

In a comprehensive review of the literature, Killilea (1976) discovers that self-help organizations have been categorized as support systems, social/spiritual/religious movements, alternative, care-providing systems, intentional communities/communes, subcultural groups which provide a philosophy of life, and organizations for deviants. The ex-addict–administered residential therapeutic community is representative of what Lieberman and Borman (1979) have described as providing "intensive support systems that uphold the importance of the members' change in behavior. . . . Such groups often specify clear and concrete guidelines through which to obtain desired change . . . [which] focuses much more on adaptation and coping through internal behavioral, attitudinal, or affective changes." The American self-help residential therapeutic community, in contrast to Jones's professional model, is part of the self-help movement. "Therapeutic community" refers to a residential program which not only utilizes recovered persons as the primary agents of change but also subscribes to a specific philosophy that applies learning principles to the treatment process. During the 1960s and 1970s there was a proliferation of self-help therapeutic communities which can trace their origins to Synanon, incorporated in 1958. Since there was so much confusion and competition, the largest American therapeutic communities decided to convene so they could agree upon terminology and methods of evaluation, as well as make recommendations. DeLeon and Beschner (1976, p. 8), who attended this conference, suggest that

> the therapeutic community (TC) is a generic term, describing a wide spectrum of residential approaches and clients served. . . . Fundamental to the TC concept is the necessity for a 24-hour, total influence to render stable changes in life-long self and socially destructive patterns of behavior. . . . Its basic goal is to offer a complete change in life-style which includes drug abstinence, elimination of anti-social (criminal) behavior, development of employment skills, and the acquisition of positive attitudes, values and behaviors which reflect honesty, responsibility, non-violence and self-reliance.

Shankman (1978, p. 156) provides a comprehensive descriptive definition of the self-help therapeutic community:

> The therapeutic community is a highly structured setting which serves as a pragmatic system of social learning, a modality providing suitable intervention into a resident's previously irresponsible life-style. Previous instances of the individual's conflicts with society usually resulted in punishments which neither affected nor educated him. In the residential house, peer group pressure, censure, and support are operating as a consistent twenty-four-hour-a-day process. The therapeutic community has been described as a "university" for self-awareness, self-realization, and resultant behavior change. To make choices and to accept the consequences of those choices is primary to the development of responsibility in each resident. . . . The therapeutic community might best be described as a school which educates people who never have learned how to live or feel worthy without hurting themselves and others. The therapeutic community helps people who have tried again and again to get what they wanted from life and have continually defeated themselves. The principle combines the basic and universal human values of knowledge, love, honesty, and work with the dynamic instrument of intense group pressure in order to recognize and help correct the personality defects which prevent people from living by these values. The results lie in rehabilitation so that the individual may reenter his or her community as an independent and productive person.

The treatment of heroin addiction has been influenced by the enactment in 1913 of the Harrison Act (See U.S. House of Representatives, 1913). Harrison was successful, according to Eldridge (1962), in convincing Congress that opium was "a significant domestic problem which, if not dealt with effectively and immediately, would precipitate widespread destruction." The Harrison Act, in brief, permitted physicians to continue to import, manufacture, produce, and dispense narcotic drugs but required that the medication not only be registered but also taxed. The act did not make it a criminal offense to be a heroin addict, nor did the legislation regulate physicians to prescribe narcotics only to addicts. Neverthelss, regulations became increasingly restrictive and prohibited physicians from prescribing narcotics to sustain addiction without physical cause.

During the next decade, the Supreme Court recognized narcotics addiction to be a legitimate disease (Linder *v.* United States, 1925), but drastically limited outpatient treatment (Webb *v.* United States, 1919, and Jin Fuey Moy *v.* United States, 1925). Rather than jeopardize a medical practice and challenge the Supreme Court, the majority of physicians decided to discontinue treating heroin addicts. Roffman (1973) contends that the subsequent regulations after the Harrison Act "together with a series of Supreme Court decisions . . . effectively changed the course of this country's response to drug addiction, for it transferred the management of the addict population from physicians to law enforcement personnel." The impact of the Harrison Act and the subsequent Supreme Court decisions during the 1920s on social policy has been to reinforce the notions that addiction not only is wrong and evil but also that addicted persons should be isolated from the community.

It has been documented by both Prescor (1943) and Lambert et al. (1930) that before the creation of the therapeutic community, the recidivism rate for heroin addicts was so high in traditional institutional settings that many hospitals and prisons discontinued their attempts as treatment. During the 1940s and 1950s, not surprisingly, no program and no person wanted to work with heroin addicts. In 1956 Alcoholics Anonymous was confronted by a dilemma when Charles Dederich, the future founder of Synanon, who was attending A.A. (and creating problems with his unorthodox style of confrontation and continuous talking), insisted that A.A. permit heroin addicts to attend meetings. In response, a policy of exclusion was determined by A.A. A member of Alcoholics Anonymous at the time, Burns (1975, pp. 210–211), recalls:

> A policy opposing entry of addicts into the Fellowship was laid down in an article by the late Bill Wilson, AA's senior co-founder, in the February 1958 issue of the AA "Grapevine," the Fellowship's monthly magazine. This was six months before the Synanon split. . . . At first reading Bill's article might seem a very simple statement of something AA's had assumed. . . . AA is for alcoholics. . . . It was the first time that an official of AA formally stated that the welfare of the organization should come ahead of the recovery of individuals. . . . The net effect of Bill's article is that AA decided to turn away from drug addicts, not because AA cannot help them—there is the implicit recognition that the AA program is precisely what they need—but because the addicts represented a threat to AA's organization.

Consequently, Dederich and his coterie of addicts elected to leave Alcoholics Anonymous to share an apartment in California in 1957. From this inauspicious start, which has been described by Yablonsky

(1962, 1965), Casriel (1963), Mueller (1964), Cherkas (1965), Holzinger (1965), Sabath (1967), Endore (1968), Markoff (1969), and Enright (1970), Synanon was created. In less than a quarter of a century, the American self-help residential therapeutic community has come to span the globe. Dederich, an exile from A.A., is credited with being the genius behind the TC movement.

Mowrer (1977) and Glaser (1974) have traced the evolution of the therapeutic community from the Washington Movement in the 1840s, which Burns (1975) mentions, and the Oxford Movement in the 1930s, which Barry (1932) and Cunningham (1935) portray. The Oxford Group, independent from any Church, was God-oriented. Its members were taught to surrender totally to Christ and practiced a four-step program which resembled the four absolutes of Alcoholics Anonymous. The Oxford program demanded: (1) absolute honesty; (2) absolute purity, which included sexual abstinence; (3) absolute unselfishness; and (4) absolute love. Buchman (1966) was the catalyst which Howard (1961) has mentioned to the formation of the four absolutes of A.A. The link between the Oxford Movement and A.A. is obvious because listed in an anonymous (1957) account of significant dates in the history of Alcoholics Anonymous are the following dates: August 1934, "Oxford Groups sober up Ebby T., a friend of Bill's" (Bill W. is listed as the co-founder of A.A.); summer 1939, "Midwest A.A.'s withdrew from Oxford Groups." Dederich, the founder of Synanon, was, as mentioned earlier, a member of A.A. The legacy of A.A. to Synanon has been detailed by Anglin, Nugent, and Ng (1976). Synanon rightfully has achieved preeminence because many other therapeutic communities is adopted the philosophy and technology. Within the last decade, however, Synanon has moved away from the treatment of character-disordered individuals who abuse psychoactive substances. More recently Synanon has viewed itself as a religious commune whose members are expected to make a commitment to remain there indefinitely. In view of the problems which beset Synanon, which have been portrayed by Anson (1978), this chapter will focus on the methodology utilized by Daytop Village, one of Synanon's progeny. It is important to stress that the contributions Synanon has made to the therapeutic movement cannot be eradicated by the recent developments which have besmirched the program. Interestingly, a "failure" of Synanon, who elected to leave prematurely without the consent of the staff, David Deitch, inherited an ineffectual Daytop Lodge program which not only was funded federally but was also sponsored by the Supreme Court Probation Department of New York. Shelly and Bassin (1964 and 1965), who wrote the original proposal, describe the modifications of the Synanon program which Deitch made.

The History of the Psychology of Addiction: From the Psychoanalytic Explanation of the "Unconscious" to the Therapeutic Community's "Choice"

Until the emergence of Synanon in 1958, the treatment of heroin addiction had been dominated by the psychoanalytic approach. Psychoanalysis not only proved ineffectual with addicts but also adversely affected the initial credibility of the therapeutic community. Rosenfeld (1966), Glover (1956), Isbell (1955), and Winkler and Rasor (1953) contend that the analytic approach to the problem of drug addiction cannot be considered apart from issues of premorbid psychodynamic influences. Rosenberg (1969), Vaillant (1966), Bender (1963), Ausubel (1961), Osberg and Lewis (1958), Chein (1956), Fort (1954), and Zimmering (1952) suggest that an analytic review often reveals a rather chaotic early experiential background, an uncertain and insecure childhood, and an inconsistent parental approach toward supporting individuation strivings from early adolescence onward.

The psychoanalytic stereotyped views offer the concerned clinician few viable treatment options for helping drug-dependent individuals to experience a positive response from the world. All such global analytic views, which remain imprecise and generated after the fact, are predicated upon unconscious needs and obsessions, and therefore appear to be reductionistic. Indeed, Jurjevich (1974, p. 468), in a scholarly but scathing attack of analysis, concludes:

> We have seen that Freudian claims are built on pretenses and specious reasoning and they end in a process that greatly resembles brainwashing in its essential features. Freudism has usurped psychological and psychotherapeutic authority, without furnishing scientific proofs of its assertions. It has denigrated its critics and accorded unbounded praise to its adherents, even idolizing its founder. It denies suggestion, but uses it as its chief tool to manipulate the patient into accepting the broad beliefs and preconceptions of the analyst. . . . Misusing its medical auspices, Freudism has established a virtual dictatorship in American psychiatry, and, to a large extent, in clinical psychology. With its speculative scientifically unreliable methods, it has impeded progress toward verification of the abundant hypotheses of the mental health field. . . . In view of its unscientific foundations, its misrepresentations and its manifold ill effects, Freudism can be considered as basically a gigantic hoax.

To attempt to document the harmful effects of psychoanalysis upon the lives of heroin addicts and its overall reinforcement of irresponsibility falls beyond the purview of this chapter. Psychoanalysis obfuscates the real issues and further protracts the myths which rarely have been questioned. What the essential nature of addiction is, and how it can be most effectively treated, need to be reevaluated. Psychoanalytic research, thus far, has not produced anything decisive beyond the "discovery" that addiction is due to a psychopathogenic fixation at the oral stage and/or to the disturbances of early object relations.

The therapeutic community has rejected the psychoanalytic formulation which suggests that the entire developmental experience of heroin addiction can be understood as a continuing series of sequentially programmed and naturally unfolding predictable, after-the-fact, emotional traumas. Hurvitz (1973, p. 233) discards the psychodynamic explanation that "people are 'inherently' or 'instinctively' aggressive and hostile, that 'unconscious' biological or instinctual forces are the causes of individual behavior and determine interpersonal relations, social interaction, and social norms. This ideology regards inappropriate behavior or emotional disorder as the 'acting out' of putative 'unconscious conflicts' associated with concepts such as the 'Oedipus complex,' 'infantile sexuality,' 'death instinct,' and others." The analytic model subscribes to the myth of unchangeability because behavior has been blocked by subconscious forces. In this sense, patients subtly are relieved of any responsibility for their acts and behavior. Freud (1966 [1925], p. 131) has provided an operational definition of responsibility when he discusses dream interpretation:

> Obviously, one must hold himself responsible for the evil impulses of one's dreams. What else is one to do with them? Unless the content of the dream is inspired by alien spirits, it is a part of my own being. If I seek to classify the impulses that are present in me according to social standards into good and bad, I must assume responsibility for both sorts; and if in defense I say that what is unknown, unconscious and repressed in me is not my "ego," then I shall not be basing my position upon psychoanalysis.

One of the first to reject the psychodynamic model, Mowrer (1959), believes that behavior should be considered a manifestation of irresponsibility rather than disease and concludes that psychodynamic psychotherapy is "nontherapeutic." Horney (1945, p. 241) has defined the goal of psychotherapy to help the individual "assume responsibility for himself, in the sense of feeling himself the active, responsible force in his life, capable of making decisions and of taking the consequences. With this goes an acceptance of responsibility toward others, a readiness to recognize obligations in those values he holds whether they relate to his children, parents, friends, employees, colleagues, community or country." Dreikurs (1950) suggests that dysfunctional people are not mentally ill, but that the disturbance has been caused by a "cleverly concealed hostility to fellow human beings arising out of their special need for significance." Ansbacher (1956) conceptualizes neurotics as being discouraged by their attempts to solve their problems without cooperating or showing social interest. Their desire to escape personal responsibility is self-deception and the refusal to recognize their choice of antisocial behavior is self-destructive. In 1927 Freud (1947) defined therapy as an attempt "to give the patient's ego freedom to choose one way or the other." Maslow (1962) labeled it a "third force in psychology" which places the individual with freedom and responsibility into its center. Schnee (1972), a psychoanalyst, muses that "the question whether or not a human being is capable of freedom of choice is an exceedingly complex one."

The primary goal of treatment for individuals who are addicted to psychoactive substances, according to Bratter and Hammerschlag (1975), "is to assist them to be aware of the impact of their behavior, to understand the consequences of their acts, and to become more responsible to themselves, others, and to society."

Before discussing the concept of responsibility, it is necessary to understand the explicit connotations of the terms "addiction" and "responsibility" because they appear mutually exclusive. The term "addiction" originates from the Latin *ad dicere,* which suggests surrender. Van Kaam (1968) assumes that "this emphasis on surrender, on giving up, contains a first clue to the understanding of addiction[;] it seems to be related more to the passive than to the active dimension of man's life." Surrender is antithethical to responsibility. Responsibility becomes the crucial concept. The English word "response" appears to be less active than the French term *répondre,* or the German *antworten,* which means to reply or answer. The German term *Verantwortung* appears more comprehensive in that it refers to a person's answering for his or her actions. "Ability" connotes being able to accomplish a task, and this coincides with the therapeutic community's overall definition of "responsibility."

When discussing the concept of responsibility in psychotherapy, Halleck (1982, 300–301) provides some hypothetical but realistic guidelines stressing individual responsibility which the therapist might mention to the patient:

> You will progress more comfortably and effectively in psychotherapy and in life in general to the extent that you assume responsibility for your behavior. Try to assume that you are accountable for everything you think or do and try to be willing to accept praise or blame for your actions. . . . I will constantly emphasize your capacities for autonomy and choice. . . . My major demands for you to be responsible will relate to the present and the future. . . . I will acknowledge that certain conditions or circumstances can limit your capacity to choose and I will constantly try to be aware of those. . . . As therapy progresses and as we come to understand your problems better, it may be easier to define the limits of your capacities. . . . You will never achieve your full potentiality unless you are willing to make demands of yourself. You may choose not

> to push yourself to your limits, but that is your decision. What you cannot do in psychotherapy is to "write off" any failure to maximize your capacities as a product of illness or mental disorder.

It is therapeutically imperative for addicted persons to accept the responsibility for their irresponsible, illicit, stupid, impulsive, and self-destructive behavior. The therapeutic community believes that responsibility is part of a mutually dependent relationship between the individual and society. When individuals are responsible they are aware of their potential contribution, aware of what efforts such action may demand, and aware of the potential payoffs and consequences. Perhaps, the most simplistic operational definition of responsible behavior would be for individuals to fulfill their needs without interfering with anyone else's pursuits.

Before entering into a treatment alliance, Mendel (1966, p. 95) observes, the patient feels "victimized by unconscious needs in himself which seem consistently to lead to self-defeat. He comes into therapy with a completely passive position. He is not responsible and he does not understand. He is the victim. As the patient begins to talk about his behavior, the therapist is able to help him to see how he constructs the world and himself in such a way that consequences are determined by him." Bonime (1966) corroborates Mendel's observation when he delineates the irresponsible nature of compulsive behavior in neurotic depression, which is an absolute refusal to be held accountable as well as feeling victimized. Bonime views the typical obsessive-compulsive symptoms not as a means of gaining control but as a way of avoiding responsibility. Gelfman (1970), when he discusses the clinical role of irresponsibility, concludes that patients, "if put to the test of living up to what may in reality be expected of them, become symptomatic to avoid the genuine responsibility that is called for by their self-imposed positions." Morgenstern (1966), furthermore, has declared that diagnosing a person as "mentally ill" and involuntarily committing that person to an institution "frequently reinforces the immature wish to avoid responsibility, by blaming the illness for failure to achieve desired goals." Szasz (1970) has argued that the diagnosis of "mentally ill" attributes to the person so labeled a specific, socially defined role. The person assumes a "sick" posture of being helpless, hopeless, and debilitated. Davis (1972), Schur (1971), and Szasz (1961a, 1961b) reject this pejorative label as countertherapeutic.

Rather than accept the psychoanalytic orientation which attributes the causes of heroin addiction to early-life deprivations and unconscious factors, the therapeutic community assumes that drug-related behavior is a function of choice. People who elect to use psychoactive substances attempt to escape from pain, feelings of loneliness and inadequacy, and a sense of meaninglessness. Many use drugs to escape from the tensions and anxieties of life. Thomas (1967), Brown (1966), and Burroughs (1953) have contributed autobiographical accounts. Donnellan (1978), Wilson and Mandelbrote (1978), Stephens and Slatin (1974), Klein (1972), Laskowitz (1961, 1972), and Chein et al. (1964) have portrayed addicts as being immature, impulsive, insecure, and irresponsible. Silver (1977), Burke and Eichberg (1972), Gilbert and Lombardi (1967), Hill (1957), Hill, Haertzen, and Glaser (1960), and Winkler and Rasor (1953) view addicts as being psychopathic. The attributes of a psychopath, according to Cleckley (1941, 1959), are an apparent absence of anxiety, an apparent lack of motivation for change, and an apparent inability to feel depression.

Ramirez (1973), the architect of Phoenix House, has identified five characteristics of chronic substance abuse:

1. Emotional response patterns are learned rather than instinctual and can be unlearned and relearned.
2. The learning of concepts, and therefore of at least some insight into the behavioral causes and effects of emotional response patterns, is a necessary adjunct of altering behavior.
3. The learning of concepts follows, rather than precedes, experience and the learning of behaviors.
4. Learning (or relearning) any behavior is based on specific, direct and personal experience.
5. The learning of any behavior from experience must be closely connected to the experience in time and importance as demonstrated by cause and effect; that is, the learning must have a "here and now" quality directly related to realities in the learner's life, to his behavior, and to the behavior in his immediate environment.

Steinfield, Rice, and Mabli (1974, p. 393) suggest that "whatever the physical or biochemical factors leading to addiction, it is undeniable that psychological factors are of great import. If we can help addicts overcome the physical pull back to drugs through some belief system having to do with the nature of their personal responsibility for their lives without the use of foreign elements to deal with human problems in living, then we have clearly developed a productive rehabilitation program." The therapeutic community explicitly assumes that persons can control their behavior in that they retain the elements of freedom of choice as well as the capacity to grow and develop. Singer (1965) emphasizes that the belief in the ability of people not only to control but also to change behavior "underlies all forms of psychotherapy: the proposition that man is capable of change and capable of bringing this change about himself." Bratter (1973) has written that any viable psychotherapeutic approach must stress individuals' abilities to control their behavior, which implies a capacity to transcend what they have done before. While persons cannot control external conditions by which they will be challenged, they can control their responses to those conditions.

Learning presupposes some unlearning. Sartre (1957) summarizes the concepts of freedom and responsibility when he writes: "Man is nothing else but what he makes of himself. Such is the first principle of existentialism." People essentially are neither "good" nor "bad." They cannot be defined either by their thoughts or feelings, because they cannot control them. Behavior, however, becomes the ultimate indicator of the person's quality—i.e., "goodness" or "badness." If individuals, for example, perform "good" acts, then they are "good"; conversely, if they do "bad" things, then they are "bad." This existential approach contends that individuals have the resilience to transcend their past and to profit from their previous mistakes. Rather than analyze the past, the subconscious, and/or feelings, in the TC any failures or mistakes are attributed either to irresponsible choices or to personal weakness.

Psychologically, individuals can regulate their behavior, which implies freedom, so that they have the capacity for new experiences. No growth and development can occur unless the current homeostatic condition is disturbed so that an ephemeral disequilibrium can produce a new differentiation. Individuals have the capacity to improve their behavior. Through this dialectic, more behavior options become available. Agreeing with the TC's conceptualization, Glasser (1965) views "therapy as a special kind of teaching or training which attempts to accomplish in a relatively short, intense period what should have been accomplished during normal growing up. The more irresponsible the person, the more he has to learn about realistic behavior in order to fulfill his needs."

From Encounter to Confrontation: The Evolution of the Therapeutic Community's Primary Psychotherapeutic Process

The Dead Sea Scrolls, as Glaser (1977) has documented, provide the first operational description of encounter/confrontation. "The Qumran community is believed to have been operated by a Jewish sect called the Essenes; Philo was describing a group of one sub-sect of the Essenes, called the Therapeutae, which flourished in the same period . . . near Alexandria, Egypt." Vermes (1966, pp. 59, 61) translates from the Scrolls: "They shall rebuke one another in truth, humility, and charity. Let no man address his companion in anger, or ill-temper, or obduracy, or any prompted by the spirit of wickedness. Let him not hate him (because of the wickedness of his uncircumcised heart), but let him rebuke him on the very same day lest he incur guilt because of him. Furthermore, let no man accuse his companion before the Congregation without having first admonished him in the presence of witnesses."

Antze (1979), who traces Synanon to the Essenes, believes that intimacy can be created by a group confessional which becomes a catalyst for mutual loyalty.

> The Synanon Game has harnessed the most basic need of the addict—his need to discharge stress—in a way that strengthens his relationships with others. The process that relieves his tensions also deepens his emotional investments. Viewed in this light, the Game is a perfect antidote to heroin and its long-range effects. Like heroin, the Game combats stress. But whereas heroin does so at the cost of emotional detachment and social isolation, the Game does so in a way that promotes a deeper engagement in the group and its values. This engagement in turn provides a strong bulwark against the temptation to "split" and return to the world of drugs.

The primary psychotherapeutic tool which the residential self-help therapeutic community utilizes to *force* addicted individuals to assume responsibility for their behavior has been confrontation. Literally thousands of years after the Dead Sea Scrolls, Moreno (1914) defined "encounter." In a more recent work, Moreno (1969, pp. 8–9) has traced the derivation of the concept:

> Encounter, which derives from the French *rencontre,* is the nearest translation of *Begegnung.* The German *zwichenmenschlich* and the English *interpersonal* or *interactional* are anemic notions compared to the living concept of encounter. *Begegnung* conveys that two or more persons meet not only to face one another, but to live and experience one another. . . . It is a meeting on the most intensive level of communication. . . . *Begegnung* is the sum total of interaction, a meeting of two or more persons, not in the dead past or imagined future, but in the here and now, *hic et nunc,* in the fullness of time—the real, the concrete and complete situation.

Confrontation, which insists upon honesty, is a specific treatment aspect of encounter.

The therapeutic community, more than a decade before the human potential movement, recognized the psychotherapeutic potency of confrontation and began applying it in a treatment milieu. Shelly (1966, p. 240) has described Daytop Lodge's group therapy sessions:

> Of the "gut-level" variety, free of phony attempts at self-defense, self-deception, self-pity and extended biographical self-study. The participants are obliged to accept responsibility for their behavior, not to blame their misdeeds on society, poverty, an unloving mother or a punitive father. Honesty, even of the most painful kind, integrity, concentration on the "here and now" are the marks of group therapy experiences. Reality ther-

apy, rather than orthodox psychoanalytical concepts, is the procedure which prevails during the sessions.

One of the first to recognize the profound impact of Synanon, Yablonsky (1965) discovered that Synanon was "a new kind of group therapy . . . a new method of attack therapy; an unusual kind of communication." Carkhuff and Berenson (1967, p. 11–12) view confrontation as an act that has been initiated by the therapist which brings the addict

> "into more direct contact with himself, his strengths and resources. . . . It is a challenge to the client to become integrated. . . . It is directed at discrepancies within the client . . . between illusion and reality. . . . The therapeutic goal is non-destructive and emerging unity within the client. It implies a constructive attack upon an unhealthy confederation of miscellaneous illusions, fantasies, and life avoidance techniques in order to create a reintegration at a higher level of health."

Blank (1971) believes that "frank confrontation and interpersonal feedback provide the stimuli for personal growth." The basic notion is that confrontation provides addicted individuals with a clearer idea of how their behavior adversely affects others. Goodstein (1970, p. 53) suggests that in order to be helpful, "feedback should begin with a description of the behavior in question, as perceived by the person offering feedback. . . . Following the behavior description, the person [who made the description] gives his emotional reaction to having observed, or participated in, the behavior under discussion. . . . The basic notion underlying such feedback is that it gives the person receiving the feedback a clearer idea of how his behavior affects others." Powell (1975, p. 759) states that "through an affiliation with a group the person can share an experience with others who find themselves in a similar struggle and yet [are] able to maintain a measure of respect for themselves as they pursue the task of finding more satisfying solutions to their problems."

The rationale for a confrontational form of psychotherapy can trace its treatment antecedent to James, who has been credited with being the first American psychologist to identify the importance of inner consistency. James (1929) differentiates between the healthy individual, whose inner constitution is "harmonious and well balanced from the outset," and "sick souls," whose "spirit wars with their flesh. They wish for incompatibles, wayward impulses interrupt their most deliberate plans, and their lives are one long drama of repentance and of effort to repair misdemeanors and mistakes." James suggested that for these "divided selves" their primary hope of achieving salvation would be "straightening out and unifying the inner self." Lecky (1945, p. 135), who examines consistency as the attainment of "normalcy," suggests:

> Behavior expresses the effort to maintain integrity and unity of the organization. . . . In order to be immediately assimilated, the idea formed as the result of a new experience must be felt to be consistent with the ideas already present in the system. On the other hand, ideas whose inconsistency is recognized as the personality develops must be expelled from the system. There is thus a constant assimilation of new ideas and the expulsion of old ideas throughout life.

Allport (1961) and Glasser (1981, p. 53) have suggested that the concept of self includes answers to the following existential concerns: "Who am I?" "What am I?" "What would I like to be?" "What should I become?" Confrontation is a psychotherapeutic attempt to assist the individual to resolve the inconsistencies and self-destructive aspects of the personality to achieve an inner consistency. The inner consistency approach challenges the in-vogue psychoanalytic model, as does Salter (1952) and Jurjevich (1974), because insight produces introspection but not necessarily behavioral change. Egan (1970, pp. 299, 326) has stated: "Insight gives the client an out, not to deal with his behavior. Insight . . . deals principally with cognitive systems and relationships between cognitive systems. . . . The focus of interpretation has been on the dynamics underlying behavior, the hypothetical sources of behavior, rather than with behavior itself." Douds et al. (1967, p. 172) recognize that insight can produce a psychological paralysis:

> Insight may, seemingly, reduce confusion by subsuming conceptualizations [the individual] has about himself in a neater package, allowing him the illusionary belief of being "on top of his problems"—he can now explain his anxiousness on high level terms. Victimized by a wishful need for a magic solution, he accumulates insight based on his reactions to different people and situations, hoping for THE ULTIMATE INSIGHT which will be an answer to everything. Still paralyzed to act, he remains dependent and passive, noticeably lacking action and directionality in his existence.

Confrontation in psychotherapy which has been developed by the therapeutic community attempts to achieve a congruence between awareness and constructive behavioral modification. London (1964, p. 133) suggests:

> A comprehensive psychotherapy would be one that uses both insight and action to attack complex psychological problems. But insight within this system would no longer focus so much on motives as those on behaviors, present and historical, that produced the disorder by violating one's relationship with the functional context that lends meaning to one's life. And its primary purpose, once achieved, would be to steer the development of a new action system, one which channels the individual's behavior in ways intended to restore his functioning within that context.

One of the psychiatric pioneer architects of the self-help therapeutic community, Ramirez (1972, p. 61), provides the philosophical rationale for the implementation of confrontation.

> Challenge is very central. . . . Challenge is everywhere; in all forms of illness and disease, in the climate, in the standard structure of civilization, government, institutions, family relations, in the artificial divisions of in-humanity, racial discrimination, social differences, economic inequalities, in every single event that surrounds every single individual regardless of his background or present condition in life. At the same time there is in each one of us a very great capacity to avoid, to ignore and to dismiss challenge. When an individual chooses to overcome the resistance to confront challenge he becomes a better human being. He becomes more human. Becoming more human is not an easy process; it requires challenge on the one hand and the practical possibility to perceive and respond to challenge on the other.

Levin (1973), a psychoanalyst, believes that confrontation can be a treatment technique which the therapist uses to exert pressure "on the patient to give up certain neurotic patterns of behavior." Myerson (1973, p. 24), in the same monograph, writes that confrontation "intervention suggests a contrast with an approach that aims at enhancing the patient's capacity to observe one or another aspect of himself that he has been reluctant to recognize." Myerson defends confrontation as being legitimate when the psychotherapist diagnoses the treatment situation to justify "forceful, persistent, insistent interventions." Another psychoanalyst, who has treated alcoholics, Silber (1970, p. 423), discusses the therapeutic goal, which is to assist the addicted individual "to live and function more comfortably and with greater awareness of himself and his surroundings. . . . The treatment is aimed at making the patient more familiar with his fears, differentiating his wishes from reality, and stressing the differences between impulse, thought, and action." Forrest (1982, p. 35) concludes that "confrontation strategies are a basic ingredient in all systems of effective counseling and psychotherapy. . . . Confrontation is defined as a method by which the psychotherapist attempts to focus or direct the patient's attention upon a particular aspect of his or her self-system." Van Stone and Gilbert (1972, p. 585) describe a psychiatric inpatient program which utilizes the principles and methods of peer confrontation groups for addicts, alcoholics, and ex-convicts. The authors describe the group confrontation sessions as a type of group psychotherapy in which:

> each member in turn is presented with candid, personal facts regarding every observable behavior or attitude recognized by the group as being self-defeating or dishonest. If the member under scrutiny attempts to ex-

> plain or deny any observation, he is ridiculed, browbeaten, shouted down, and insulted as his fellow members hammer away at the distorted ideas that he offers in support of his damaging behavior patterns. Intellectual insight or genetic self-interpretations are derided as an escape from responsibility for current behavior. Honesty, trust in the group, realistic self-assessment, appropriate emotional release, and changed behavior, in particular, are rewarded by sympathetic counsel and encouragement from fellow members.

The group exerts positive peer pressure during this psychotherapeutic inquisition, as Bratter (1972, 1973) depicts; and such pressure helps members to accept responsibility for their behavior and not to rationalize the cuases to external factors. The concept of responsibility remains central to the confrontation group psychotherapeutic orientation. It is therapeutically imperative for addicted persons to accept the responsibility for their irresponsible behavior and not to blame either family or societal conditions which are beyond their control. Addicted individuals, for example, need to recognize that they, in fact, decided to stick the needle in their arm. They learn, furthermore, that they can control their behavior because they retain freedom of choice. Lowinson and Zwerling (1971) explain that participants in confrontation group psychotherapy are expected to make a commitment to change their behavior. Glasser (1965, p. 41) writes that when individuals are confronted with reality by the therapist or group, they are "forced again and again to decide whether or not they wish to take the responsible path. Reality may be painful, it may be harsh, it may be dangerous. This process involves assessing with individuals their continued growth and development in all areas: social, sexual, educational, vocational, and physical." Garner (1970, p. 43) suggests that "confrontation statements tend to encourage the expansion of the discriminatory, reflective, reality testing and socially oriented thought processes and behavioral tendencies of the individual. They also make the patient aware of the obligatory, insatiable, stereotyped nature of his thoughts and behavior." Forrest (1978, pp. 99–100) offers an operational definition of effective confrontation with an alcoholic subpopulation which has relevance for the therapeutic community. Confrontation

> must be a constructive endeavor geared at enabling the patient to more realistically evaluate his own behavior. An essential ingredient of the process of confrontation must be the message that fellow group members have engaged in the same parataxic behaviors, that these behaviors were part of their alcoholism and that the rationale for pointing out these distortions has to do with the fact that the group members are concerned and care about the individual they are confronting.

Discussing group confrontation from a psychoanalytic perspective, Adams (1978) suggests that the group must "move the addict to confront his own pathological defenses . . . when the analyst aligns himself with the pathology. In so doing in a group treatment milieu, the analyst can create an atmosphere within which the patients could test out their powers of perception and judgment and strengthen their reality-testing abilities. Casriel and Amen (1971, p. 136) have documented the necessity for confrontation: "The problem in treatment becomes obvious. One must first remove the encapsulating shell, and thereafter prevent the individual from withdrawing into detachment by acquiring any other kind of encapsulating shell. Then, once exposed to the light of reality, powerless to isolate himself without his fortress-prison-stockade of encapsulation, he is in a position to be taught how to grow up."

Writing about his clinical experiences in a therapeutic community, Hollidge (1980, p. 61) reports that confrontation has proven to be an effective therapeutic technique:

> In the treatment of drug-addicted personalities, the therapeutic community has proven to be a much more effective modality than traditional forms of therapy. Many therapeutic communities claim success in breaking through the pharmacological addictions, disrupting the deviant life-style and significantly reducing personality disturbances. . . . The therapeutic community affords a dynamic treatment approach which meets the specific needs of addicted personalities with severe disturbances. In establishing this modality it is important to recognize that the addict's personality disturbances are created due to poor environmental conditions; therefore, the addicts's ego adapts to the environment and displays symptom formations which make it difficult to adapt and manipulate the world in a productive fashion. . . . The curative factors in the therapeutic community are designed specifically to meet early development defects and then promote healthier ego functioning.

The goals of confrontation are identical with those of psychotherapy, which, Marmor (1966) writes, are "how best to enable or cause a patient to give up certain acquired patterns of thought, feeling or behavior in favor of others which are considered more 'mature,' 'adaptive,' 'productive,' or 'self-realizing.'" Meyer and Chesser (1970) contend that "the aim of treatment is to allow the patient to resolve his own difficulties by the use of the healthy part of his personality. . . . The focus therefore is on the present life situation."

While some criticism about the potential for abuse is justified, those who condemn the therapeutic community do not understand the treatment procedures for working with immature, unconvinced and deceitful individuals. Wurmser (1978, p. 468), a psychoanalyst with extensive experience treating addicts, has written: "Although they are the most devious, manipulative, controlling, lying, unreliable group of patients I know . . . they have to suffer first from the consequences of their illness before they are motivated for treatment. Often they have to reach despair . . . a kind of sociolegal Thermopylae, before they become treatable." These critics decry the intensity of the therapeutic confrontational intervention necessary to penetrate the barriers erected by addicts to insulate themselves from "reality" and change; and this criticism is the basis for much of the controversy about the supposedly dehumanized methods utilized by the therapeutic community. Therapeutic control, which Brill and Lieberman (1969) have discussed, becomes critical because it prevents continued self-deception and self-destructive behavior. The fight–flee dichotomy, which has been described by Rado (1957, 1969), is prominent with these individuals.

Bratter (1975, 1977a, 1977b) has identified seven guiding principles in confrontation psychotherapy which are humanistic, learning-based, and educationally oriented:

1. Confrontation attacks the malignant and dysfunctional aspects of behavior.
2. Confrontation penetrates the facade of justification of behavior.
3. Confrontation forces individuals to accept total responsibility for their behavior.
4. Confrontation helps persons evaluate their behavior.
5. Confrontation assists individuals to be aware and to anticipate the consequences and payoffs of their behavior.
6. Confrontation challenges persons to mobilize their resources.
7. Confrontation defines a directionality so that persons can continue their growth and development.

Hampden-Turner (1976), who describes the Delancey Street Foundation, a third-generation therapeutic community, provides six theoretical aspects of the confrontation process:

1. The use of negative evaluation and highly critical language is essential to trimming back inflated behaviors and pretentious exaggerations. . . .
2. Highly negative judgments and denunciations can only take place within a community that cares for its members and assumes responsibility for them. . . .
3. All effective moral judgments are at least two-dimensional in the full range of their import, not one-dimensional. The second dimension is required to prevent the subject of censure swinging to the other polar position. . . .
4. Persons cannot combine and synthesize moral axioms until they have the full range of these axioms at their command. They must first learn to exercise and to accept the polarities they have repressed. . . .

5. Delancey's contribution to social progress is that it returns us to radical synthesis and turns us away from radical polarity. . . .
6. Value synthesis is not a science but the art and act of creation itself.

Most of the confrontation techniques used in the therapeutic community were developed by Synanon in the form of the "Game." Deitch and Zweben (1979, p. 60) suggest that the basic philosophy behind the Game is the same as "AA's fourth step: to take a fearless and searching look at oneself. Self-examination is fostered by considering all feedback, no matter how seemingly farfetched; hence, all members are encouraged to project freely onto the one on the hotseat. This license to project also allows the members to externalize the negative in themselves and thereby reinforce their own redeemed behavior." Simon (1978, p. 18), who lived at Synanon upon the advice of Maslow while he wrote his dissertation, offers an idealistic and subjective view of the Game, which has become a most effective and unique form of confrontation:

> In Maslow's terms, a gaming organization tends to the metaneeds of its members. The Synanon game meets metaneeds in a generation of metapathologies (meaninglessness, less anomie, alienation, cynicism, nihilism, disintegration, robotizing, depression, despair, loss of zest in life, spiritual illness and crises, futility, aimless destruction and indifference). The game is a reaffirmation of B-values. B-values are for their own sake, for the sake of being, not as means to other ends. For Synanon residents who have gratified their basic needs of security, safety, affiliation, love, and self-esteem, the game, unlike other group processes such as therapy or task oriented discussion groups, also offers an opportunity for becoming a virtuoso performer in the art of playing the game. It thus meets the metaneeds to pursue truth, to dispel dishonesties, to pursue goodness, to attack evil, to root out selfishness, to create beauty in the faces and lives of other people, to sense unity and wholeness, to transcend dichotomies and live by higher principles, to be alive and zestful, filled with energy, and so on with the other B-values of uniqueness, perfection, necessity, completion, justice, order, simplicity, richness, totality, effortlessness, playfulness, and meaningfulness.

The therapeutic community believes the addict to be both immature and somewhat psychopathic. Consequently, the intensity of the therapeutic intervention to penetrate the barriers errected by the addict is what creates controversy. Critics do not understand that the sine qua non of treatment with immature individuals who exhibit psychopathic tendencies is constant confrontation and attempted therapeutic control of their behavior. Control becomes critical because it prevents continued self-destructive behavior and it stimulates intimate interpersonal relationships. Confrontation shatters the barriers which addicts have erected to insulate themselves from being hurt or helped.

While confrontation can be painful personally, as Raubolt and Bratter (1974) contend, it also remains a nurturing, supportive, and caring act. Maslow (1967), pp. 28–29 one of the most respected pioneers in humanistic psychology, has described his reaction to participating in a confrontation group at Daytop Village:

> The assumption in your groups seems to be . . . that people are very tough, and not brittle. they can take an awful lot. The best thing to do is get right at them, and not to sneak up on them, or be delicate with them, or try to surround them from the rear. Get right smack into the middle of things right away. I've suggested that a name for this might be "no-crap therapy." It serves to clean out the defenses, the rationalizations, the veils, the evasions and politeness of the world. . . . IT SEEMS POSSIBLE THAT THIS BRUTAL HONESTY, RATHER THAN BEING AN INSULT, IMPLIES A KIND OF RESPECT. YOU CAN TAKE IT AS YOU FIND IT, AS IT REALLY IS. AND THIS CAN BE THE BASIS FOR RESPECT AND FRIENDSHIP.

Confrontation is the primary therapeutic tool which pierces all attempts to circumvent reality. Residents acquire the courage to confront not only themselves but also others. Residents, furthermore, learn to relate to themselves as vulnerable. Shostrum (1967, p. 41) provides a significant perspective when he writes: "We seem to assume that the more perfect we appear—the more flawless—the more we will be loved. Actually, the reverse is more apt to be true. The more willing we are to admit our weaknesses as human beings, the more lovable we are."

There are two phases of confrontation, i.e., the painful unlearning process and the supportive relearning phase. Initially, the group aggressively demands that all dysfunctional and malignant behavior be terminated without further delay. During the second phase, the group helps recovering individuals establish a unique identity and discover a directionality which assists them to use, rather than continue to abuse, their potential. This part of the learning process has been labeled the "act as if" phase. Casriel (1963, p. 169) has described the results of the act-as-if process:

> At Synanon, the addict learns first how to live in a mature paternalistic, family-type environment. It is an honest, tolerant but critical, anti-criminal, anti-addiction society. The techniques (neurotic and psychopathic defenses), attitudes, behavior and methods of communication the addict previously used in his personal social and antisocial environment are now, at Synanon, unsuited to his functioning. He even feels embarrassed by them. At first, for three to six months, he acts as if he understood what was happening, after that he begins to feel it. His character and personality traits begin to change. Within two years the change is so complete that

> apparently a different personality has emerged. His previous antisocial and addictive defenses seem to have dropped off from disuse and having been "synanized." He may still be neurotic to a greater or lesser degree, but he is no longer an inadequate psychopath, or an addictive personality.

Ramirez (1927b, p. 61) offers five principles which confrontation attempts to help addicted individuals recognize:

1. that they have defective characters
2. that they want to be straight if they only knew how
3. that they need help but have to earn it
4. that addiction is curable until they prove otherwise
5. that no one wants them to be a square, but rather the purpose of rehabilitation is to become creative, self-sufficient agents of social change

Feather (1972) describes two therapeutic tasks which must be achieved in psychotherapy: "to teach the patient new habit patterns . . . and new cognitive insights." Confrontation certainly achieves these tasks. Meyer and Chesser (1970) viewed the learning process of psychotherapy as strengthening the health of the individual and allowing the modification of maladaptive responses instead of engineering a radical reconstruction of the personality. Meyer and Chesser (1970, p. 22) conclude that "the aim of treatment is to allow the patient to resolve his own difficulties by the use of the healthy part of his personality. . . . The focus therefore is on the present life situation. There is no interpretation of transference and free association is not employed." In its most basic form, confrontation can be considered to be one of the several behavioral derivatives. Bratter (1972) conceptualizes confrontation to be a teaching-interpretative-reasoning approach which utilizes the reinforcement model in learning theory, where "emphasis is placed on the *Eigenwelt* (the relation to one's self)—i.e., the immediate experience." The standard definition of behavior therapy, predicated on learning theory, Wolpe (1968) writes, "denotes the use of experimentally established principles of learning for the purpose of changing unadaptive behavior." Wolberg (1967) p. 116 suggests that "it is better to ascribe the effects of behavior therapy to the disciplined use of learning principles than to the dubious application of learning theory." Discussing the professional, democratic concept, Clark and Yeomans (1969, p. 31) believe that "in terms of learning theory, treatment bridges the gap between stimulus-response theory and cognitive theory. The patient's needs, emotions, perceptions, and thoughts are actively engaged in raising hypotheses about himself and his social network and in testing them." Mowrer (1961) specifies that the primary goal of psychotherapy is to help individuals to identify for themselves how they should act.

The Self-Help Concept: Recovered Persons Acting as Responsible Role Models and Treatment Agents

Sack (1974) notes that with the emergence of Synanon as a viable treatment modality, there was an acceptance of the validity of the recovered person as a catalytic treatment agent, which necessitated the rejection of the credentialed mental health professional. Earlier, Ruiteenbeek (1970) had suggested that "perhaps the most controversial element of the Synanon groups is their profound belief that people can help themselves" rather than resorting to professional assistance. The peer self-help concept is anchored in the early work of Alcoholics Anonymous (see Anonymous, 1939, 1952), where, according to Hurvitz (1970, p. 44), "peers are totally involved in a fellowship and each experience is part of therapy which is participation in a way of life. Peers establish a community of relationships which . . . support each other's everyday problems, and [they] help each other function more effectively in their daily lives."

The detached, benign, objective, analytic stance is an anathema to the self-help movement when it comes to treating the character-disordered, addicted individual. Credentialed professionals have been trained to analyze and treat symptoms, but not to identify with patients. Szasz (1965), while defining the analytic contract between the psychotherapist and patient, advised the analyst: "You need not show that you are humane, that you care for him. . . . Your sole responsibility to the patient is to analyze him." The analyst needs to "abstain from making therapeutic decisions about hospitalizing the patient or preventing him from committing suicide." The analyst, Szasz contended, "cannot make vague promises to the patient, such as 'I will take care of you,' 'I will protect you.' " Indeed, Eysenck (1952, 1960, 1965) rejected the benign, detached, and objective mantle of psychotherapists when he compared the outcomes of those who were treated with those who were on the waiting list. The likelihood of remission did not decrease due to a psychotherapeutic relationship. Bratter (1972, 1973, 1977a) has questioned the effectiveness of the analytic model, as described by Brill (1912) and Menninger (1958), while working with alienated, character-disordered, angry, addicted persons.

Raubolt and Bratter (1976) and Bratter (1979) have recognized the need for psychotherapists to become personally involved with addicted individuals whom they try to help to help themselves. Without such involvement, as Glasser (1965) contends, there can be no basis for any therapeutic relationship.

Carkhuff and Berenson (1967, pp. 4–12) condemn mental health practitioners for not providing sufficient nourishment for individuals to effect constructive change:

> If . . . psychotherapists functioned in real life the way most of them do in the therapeutic hour, they would be patients. The professional helpers to whom we turn because human sustenance is not available in the general environment are themselves functioning at ineffectual levels of those dimensions related to constructive change or gain. Beyond their counseling and psychotherapy, their distorted perceptions and communications lead to the deterioration of their own significant human relationships. They find the same lack of personal fulfillment in their daily living that their clients do. Perhaps most important, they cannot allow the clients to find more in life than they themselves have found.

This view becomes more pejorative and passionate when mental health specialists who themselves are recovered persons view credentialed professionals. Devlin (1975) offers such a critique of the credentialed professional, whom he views "as a mercenary or entrepreneur who lacks dedication and has no understanding whatsoever. The professional is viewed as an intellectual giant but an emotional dwarf, who will expect to freely explore the depths of the ex-addict's psyche but who will not permit a reciprocal probe by the ex-addict of his own hang-ups." Vamos and Devlin (1975, p. 25) report that "the majority of psychotherapists are impotent role models." When they identify the value of using recovered persons as therapists, Rosenthal and Biase (1972, p. 127) write:

> Within the therapeutic community framework, these who are role models demonstrate alternative, positive ways of coping with stresses. They do so not in the neutral, didactic fashion of the Freudian therapist but in self-revealing, involved, and involving transactions. . . . Everything is out in the open; the members know practically everything there is to know about one another, contrasting with the typical "staff-patient" disparity of personal knowledge.

The intensely human ingredient has been captured by Sales (1976, p. 152), who has written the biography of John Maher, the founder of the Delancey Street Foundation: "The reason why John gets so much respect is that everyone knows he is not asking you to do anything he doesn't do himself. I got so much trust in the man that he can ask me to do anything, I wouldn't question it, and I never felt that way about anyone. John can relate to you, put you through changes, because he's been there himself, it's not something he's read in a book."

The staff of such a therapeutic community function as responsible role models who are irrefutable proof that creative and positive personal change is possible. In addition, the staff is prepared to share significant experiences in an effort to identify with and relate to the resident. The staff become involved with residents. Weppner (1973,

p. 103) provides the clinical retionale for utilizing recovered persons as helpers:

> The ex-addict knows the belief and value system of the addict, and he is conversant with the street code of addicts. The ex-addict counselor intuitively knows the reasons for using drugs such as the enjoyable effects, peer pressure, status seeking, or escape from a meaningless life-style, and can understand the addict's self-reported motivations. In this respect, he does not communicate the negative attitude of those who may see addiction only as deviant, illegal, wrong, or psychopathological. . . . Since the ex-addict knows about addiction first-hand, he knows many of the cons and hustles which addicts use to manipulate others. He is able to prevent or stop these hustles. An example of this is the prevention of phoney "insights" in therapy groups which can be used to gain advantages such as increased stature in the group or perhaps an early release from the treatment program.

Freud (1927, 1961) has provided the theory of introjection, which explains how the special quality of the treatment relationship can either facilitate or retard the individual's ability to learn through the mechanism of imitation. Persons tend to emulate qualities of those people whom they either admire or fear. Bandura (1971) has modified introjection theory by modeling desirable and appropriate behavior. Kohut (1971) describes the identification process for narcissistic persons. Jourard (1964), Rachman (1975), and Weiner (1971) have discussed the importance of therapist self-disclosure and its relationship to improved patient functioning. Deitch (1973) and Bassin (1973) have identified some of the problems and limitations which can occur when recovered persons are utilized as primary treatment agents. Both, however, recognize the ex-addicts' efficacy.

Milieu Therapy or Social Learning? Positive Peer Pressure to Become More Responsible and Productive

Jones (1976) has stressed the social forces in the treatment environment of patients which combine to produce positive behavior and attitudinal changes. Jacobs' and Spradlin's (1974) monograph, which describes the power of the group to help people change, neglects to mention Jones and the therapeutic community.

Addicts who are newly admitted to such a community (after convincing the program that they are sufficiently motivated to seek change) initially have all freedom and privileges revoked, regardless of their status. They are restricted from making or receiving phone calls. They are denied the right to write or receive letters. The therapeutic community does not want any of the newly admitted residents to be "contaminated" by former family or friends who inadvertently may have condoned the self-destructive and irresponsible behavior. Censorship helps expedite positive behavior change. Bratter (1978b) has described the rationale:

> It is assumed that previously all who find their way to the therapeutic community have abused their status and privileges. The sanctions "you cannot" or "no" dramatically confront residents not only to recognize but also to appreciate all benefits which were abused. By forcing all residents to regress to the status of dependent children, the therapeutic community views an integral part of the residents' problems is that they lack the ability, the discipline, the maturity, to postpone gratification. Their lives can be characterized by the pleasure principle, i.e., demanding immediate gratification for every wish without any concern for future consequences. They cannot tolerate any present discomfort in order to gain greater pleasure at a later time.

Within the therapeutic community, as Levy, Faltico, and Bratter (1977) describe, there exists a rigid system of reward and punishment which facilitates the reeducation and socialization of the resident. Both the staff and residents have explicit job functions in a therapeutic community. Upon admission, as Bassin (1968) writes, new members are viewed by both staff and residents as being irresponsible and immature persons who cannot make productive decisions. Newcomers are given the most menial jobs such as cleaning toilets, washing dishes, or dusting. These unskilled positions are not ridiculed, because they are an integral part of the daily work routine. After residents prove a degree of competence, they are promoted to a more responsible position which entails additional privileges. The social structure of the therapeutic community remains mobile, which permits the individual to progress at his or her own rate of growth and development.

Responsibility and competence are rewarded. Every staff member and resident assumes responsibility for enforcing the rules of the therapeutic community. When someone has been detected engaging in irresponsible behavior or expressing a negative attitude, the person will be confronted by his or her peers. Unlike the business world, where employees generally have little access to their employers, in a therapeutic community the resident can demand accountability from a staff member. The resident (and often the staff) are taught how to be more responsible by the continual candid feedback of the group. Any confrontation which exposes maladjustive behavior is considered to be the ultimate expression of caring. Both the residents and staff share in this confrontation, which demands the best from everyone. In this atmosphere of bondedness, of mutuality, of responsible concern, the surrogate family has been created. Laskowitz (1972) describes the premise justifying the surrogate family environment when he writes:

"The resident's delinquent and addictive behavior is learned in association with others, according to the frequency, intensity, priority, and duration of contacts. Hence, the logic of presenting a family-extended environment in which the street code is 'out' and square behavior is 'in.' " Regarding the social learning environment as it relates to the extended family, Waldorf (1971, p. 55–56) discusses the therapeutic issue of social control. The concepts of responsibility and concern cement social control and create the surrogate family atmosphere.

> The resident is made to feel it is his responsibility to observe and criticize, or comment on, every other resident's behavior and attitudes. Only when a resident does this is he expressing "responsible concern" for other persons in the community, and a principal value in the community is to demonstrate concern for others. In application, the concept of "responsibility and concern" is a conscious attempt by the community to overcome the code of the streets—the code that is epitomized by the Mafia code of *omertà,* where the members of the family or community of the Mafia will not disclose to police or any officials the activity of another Mafioso even when such a person has threatened the life of the first. . . . According to program ideology, real concern for others is shown when one observes the other and confronts him with behavior or attitudes that are objectionable. The responsible person is one who takes concern for others as an individual responsibility. Persons who do not disclose to the community behavior or rule breaking that is a threat to the community are punished as well as the rule breaker.

The staff is not permitted to become complacent or stagnant. The threat of either continuing one's growth and development or being requested to leave is more explicit than implicit. The group not only nurtures but also monitors the dynamic of personal change and growth. Residents learn how to respond and relate to insure a maximum probability of success. Some individuals term this process "brain washing" but the opposite is true; it is a massive rehabilitative effort which helps individuals to receive positive reinforcement from the environment and to become, at the conclusion of their residence, autonomous. This concept of relearning can be understood in the context of Erikson's (1963) theory of social learning. Erikson regards maturation as a series of crises leading to disorganization followed by reintegration of the ego at a higher level, after the crisis situation has been mastered. Ottenberg (1976, p. 158) discusses the significance of positive reinforcement in the therapeutic community treatment process:

> Succeeding at something, knowing the satisfaction of achieving an objective, even a very simple task, receiving earned approval and gratitude reinforces awakening self-esteem. This kind of positive feedback and support differs from the automatic acceptance given by the group and community initially. The resident becomes more aware of assets and strengths

> as the group acknowledges unacceptable attitudes and behavior with criticism. To be useful, both approval and disapproval must be offered at an appropriate stage in recovery: coming too early, both praise and criticism tend to be blocked, and they remain unincorporated and not useful for internal reparative processes.

Devlin (1978, pp. 462–463) recognizes that "self-help cannot exist without self-respect, and the only way one achieves self-respect is by doing, not by having someone do for you." Accordingly, he writes, Daytop Village insists that residents "act as if," which is defined as constituting "positive behavior and attitudes, and more important, performance. You act as if you are an adult. Children want what they want when they want it. They have poor impulse control and often go into rages and tantrums when they are under pressure or denied immediate gratification. The addict is typically an emotional infant encased in an adult body."

In addition to psychotherapeutic confrontation, the therapeutic community attempts to reeducate residents. Piperopoulous (1978, p. 69) offers a pragmatic definition of resocialization:

> The original assumption that the individual has adopted an irresponsible style of life defines his social status position within this miniature system. Irresponsible human beings, notably children, are not charged by society with tasks requiring high levels of commitment and adequate degree of sense of responsible conduct. Thus, the initial tasks afforded the individual resident immediately after his "critical interview" are menial, mechanical, and carry little if any social prestige, e.g., grounds maintenance, kitchen work, laundry, etc. It is performing such menial tasks that the individual begins to perceive the low status he holds in this society of addicts and ex-addicts. Free of "drugs" with which to escape his current reality, the resident will follow one of two possible courses of action: first, he will accept his predicament stoically and attempt to show improvement of his attitudes by being cooperative and zealous in the performance of his role, or second, he will attempt to escape from this reality, usually by "splitting" from the program.

Conclusion: The Need for an Interface of the Therapeutic Community with More Traditional Mental Health Services

Some Europeans, who have been victimized by political oppression, view the American self-help therapeutic community model as fascist (Bratter, 1980). These European critics unfortunately confuse admittedly intense psychotherapeutic interventions whose ultimate goal is to liberate the individual from chemical bondage and dependence with systematic attempts to change the resident's political beliefs and values. There is no "brainwashing" other than to convince addicts they no longer need to continue their drug dependency. The therapeutic community is concerned only with helping individuals reclaim their lives from chemical slavery and in so doing become responsible and productive members of society. Aside from encouraging the most talented graduates of their respective programs to seek staff positions, the American self-help therapeutic community retains no vested interest or conflict of interest regarding the graduate's intermediate to long-term educational/vocational/political choices and goals. The claim of fascism can be repudiated, furthermore, because unless individuals not only verbalize a request to go to a therapeutic community but also convince the staff of their sincerity and motivation, they will not be accepted. All residents recognize that there is an open door policy which permits them to leave whenever they so choose. In the case of some residents, who have had conflicts with the legal system, if they decide to leave prematurely without the consent of the program, the therapeutic community reports their departure to the authorities, which, in turn, retain the option to prosecute.

Many critics of the self-help therapeutic community confuse the fundamental difference between the "authoritarian management" of people and "authoritative treatment." Politically, authoritarian management would describe a totalitarian system of rule that people are forced by oppressive and repressive methods to obey. Authoritative treatment implies a hierarchical structure of leadership. Fromm has labeled authoritative treatment "rational authority" which utilizes a logical system of rewards and punishments, and he has delineated several conditions for such authority (1947, p. 19–20).

> Rational authority has its source in competence. The person whose authority is respected functions competently in the task with which he is entrusted by those who conferred it upon him. He need not intimidate them or arouse their admiration by magic qualities. . . . Rational authority not only permits but requires constant scrutiny and criticism of those subjected to it. . . . The source of irrational authority . . . is always power over people. . . . Power on the one hand, fear on the other, are always buttresses on which irrational authority is built. Criticism of the authority is . . . forbidden. Rational authority is based upon the quality of both authority and subject, which differ only with respect to degree of knowledge or skill in a particular field.

Earlier Fromm (1941) defined rational authority as the "condition for helping . . . the person subjected to authority. . . . In the rational kind of authority, it will tend to decrease in direct proportion to the degree in which the person subjected to the authority becomes stronger and thereby more similar to the authority."

The prevalent misunderstanding of the type of authority exercised by the therapeutic community is ironic. The TC is often viewed as cooperating in a massive effort to punish and humiliate the heroin addict, when in fact it is a reaction to the cruel, dehumanizing trends which have victimized the addict. Bratter (1975a) has discussed some of the reasons why the heroin addict has emerged as a political enemy in the United States. Dumont (1972), quite understandably, is concerned about the frightening trend to portray the addict as the enemy, and he worries about the violations of "due process" under the guise of treatment and social control. Dumont concludes:

> People are incarcerated in prisons, but civilly committed to treatment programs. When treatment programs are concerned with issues of custody and security, they function like prisons but maintain the rhetoric and righteousness of hospitals. They develop an institutional press, which calls the individual sick but treats him like he is a criminal. The confusion of the patient role with its connotations of helplessness and dependency and the criminal role with its implications of deviancy and willfulness has profoundly destructive mental health implications.

The self-help American therapeutic community is an integral part of the revolution against the punitive trend. The therapeutic community, as Bratter (1977c) has described, has developed an innovative treatment technology. Unquestionably, in its efforts to motivate, to rehabilitate a most difficult to work with subpopulation, there have been abuses and errors. Bratter *et al.* (1985a & b) Deitch and Zweben, (1983), and Rachman and Heller (1974) have reported some of the abuses, which at times have been countertherapeutic and counterproductive. Horn (1978) discusses some practices which have brutalized and humiliated individuals rather than providing a therapeutic climate in which they could grow and develop. There can be no excuse or justification when residents have been stripped of their dignity. Yet, in comparison to some of the irrevocable and insidious treatment tactics adopted by the prestigious and powerful psychiatric-medical establishment in both the United States and Europe, the therapeutic community's practices and policy appear benign. Chemotherapeutic practices such as prescribing 1,500 milligrams of Thorazine to nonconforming, unmotivated patients need to be questioned. Methadone maintenance programs, which are predicated on an unsubstantiated and esoteric assumption of a metabolic deficiency, can be viewed as a "no exit" and "no win" conspiracy against addicts, which Bratter (1974, 1975b), Casriel and Bratter (1974), and Bratter and Pennacchia (1978) have discussed. Electroshock treatment, which generally is administered punitively or as a warning to the potentially disruptive patient, needs to be subjected to more dispassionate control. Psychosurgery can be eliminated except for meticulously documented cases of sadistic criminal violence.

Inasmuch as the staff of the therapeutic community are former residents, there are necessary checks and balances. All residents know that their mentors are "recovered persons" who have successfully completed the program. Theoretically, any resident who enters the therapeutic community system can become part of the staff. If viewed from this perspective, the American self-help therapeutic community model becomes the ultimate democratic system of self-rule where the eventual rulers are trained by virtue of their participation, their involvement, their commitment to the system. In no other correctional or treatment system, in contrast, can a former participant become the director. In a hospital, the patient becomes the ex-patient. In a prison, the inmate becomes the ex-con(vict). Indeed, with the exception of the self-help therapeutic community, where the former resident becomes the director, there is no such guarantee.

Unfortunately, the nurturing aspects of confrontation have been misunderstood by the psychiatric-psychological-medical community, which views the treatment technique as being brutal and hostile. This simply is not the case. Confrontation stimulates an intense and intimate relationship which is the quintessence of the therapeutic process. French and Raven (1960), who discuss coercive power, which undeniably is a component of confrontation, contend that "the more legitimate the coercion the less it will produce reistance and decreased attraction." Egan (1970) writes: "The hypothesis is that contractual legitimation of confrontation will increase its frequency, responsibility, acceptability, and effectiveness. Such legitimation will also allow stronger degrees of confrontation to be used." Before being admitted by the TC, the addict knows precisely what will be expected and, in fact, retains the opinion to refuse to go. Unless the addict agrees to abide by the rules of the therapeutic community, (s)he will not be accepted.

Although written more than a decade ago, Rasor's (1972, pp. 19–20) conclusion still is an appropriate end for this chapter:

> There is need for imagination, innovation, experimentation, and flexibility involving behavioral-social scientists working together with mental health professionals in a research atmosphere, seeking new approaches and constantly re-evaluating the old. All patients who received treatment should be followed and evaluated for any change that can be recognized, and an attempt should be made to understand the nature of, and reasons for the change. This is the hope for rehabilitation programs for the future and will be a challenge to the scientists who will work in this important, exciting, but difficult field.

The challenge is for recovered persons to cooperate with credentialed mental health practitioners and scientists to facilitate an understanding of the dynamics of the self-help residential therapeutic community and to make whatever modifications are necessary to keep it a viable treatment modality for addicted, character-disordered individuals.

References

Adams, J. W. *Psychoanalysis of Drug Dependence: The Understanding and Treatment of a Particular Form of Pathological Narcissism.* New York: Grune & Stratton, 1978.

Allport, G. W. *Pattern and Growth in Personality.* New York: Holt, Rinehart, & Winston, 1961.

Anglin, S. W., Nugent, J. F., and Nq, K. Y. Synanon and Alcoholics Anonymous—is there really a difference? *The Addiction Therapist,* 1976, *1,* 6–9.

Anonymous. *Alcoholics Anonymous.* New York: Alcoholics Anonymous World Services, 1939.

Anonymous. *Twelve Steps and Twelve Traditons.* New York: Alcoholics Anonymous World Services, 1952.

Anonymous. *Alcoholics Anonymous Comes of Age.* New York: Alcoholics Anonymous World Services, 1957.

Ansbacher, H. L., and Ansbacher, R. Introduction. In A. Adler (ed.), *The Individual Psychology of Alfred Adler.* New York: Basic Books, 1956.

Anson, R. S. The Synanon horrors. *New Times,* 1978, *11,* 28–50.

Antze, P. Role of ideologies in peer psychotherapy groups. In M. A. Lieberman and L. D. Borman (eds.), *Self-Help Groups for Coping with Crisis.* San Francisco: Jossey-Bass, 1979.

Ausubel, D. P. Causes and types of narcotic addiction: a psychosocial view. *Psychiatric Quarterly,* 1961, *35,* 523–531.

Bandura, A. Psychotherapy based on modeling principles. In A. E. Bergin and S. L. Garfield (eds.), *Handbook of Psychotherapy and Behavioral Change.* New York: John Wiley & Sons, 1971.

Barry, F. R. The Oxford Movement. *The Spectator,* 1932, *149,* 147–148.

Bassin, A. Daytop Villages: stopover or cure? *Psychology Today,* 1968, *7,* 48–51.

———. Taming the wild paraprofessional. *Journal of Drug Issues,* 1973, *3,* 333–340.

Beers, C. W. *A Mind That Found Itself.* New York: Doubleday, Doran, & Co., 1939.

Bender, L. Drug addiction in adolescence. *Comprehensive Psychiatry,* 1963, *4,* 131–134.

Blank, L. The uses and abuses of encounter groups. *Group Process,* 1971, *4,* 106.

Bleuler, E. *Dementia Praecox or the Group of Schizophrenias.* New York: International Universities Press, 1950.

Bonime, W. The psychodynamics of neurotic depression. In S. Arieti (ed.), *American Handbook of Psychiatry,* Vol. 3. New York: Basic Books, 1966.

Bratter, T. E. Group therapy with affluent, alienated, adolescent drug abusers: a reality therapy and confrontation approach. *Psychotherapy: Theory, Research and Practice,* 1972, *9,* 308–313.

———. Treating alienated, unmotivated, drug abusing adolescents. *American Journal of Psychotherapy,* 1973, *27,* 585–598.

———. The crime of methadone maintenance treatment programs: a conspiracy against the heroin addict. In L. Miller (ed.), *Abstracts of the Third International Symposium on Drug Abuse.* Jerusalem: Graphress, 1974.

———. Dynamics of group psychotherapy for heroin addicts: a confrontation orientation. In A. Uchtenhagen (ed.), *Group Therapy and Social Environment.* Berne, Switzerland: Hans Huber, 1975(a).

———. Methadone: try it, you'll hate it! *The Addiction Therapist,* 1975(b). *1*(*1*), 48–49.

———, and Hammerschlag, C. A. Advocate, activist, agitator: the drug abuse program administrator as a revolutionary-reformer. In R. L. Rachin and E. H. Czajowski (eds.), *Drug Abuse Control: Administration and Politics.* Lexington, Massachusetts: 1975(c).

Bratter, T. E. Confrontation groups: the therapeutic community's gift to psychotherapy. In P. Vamos and J. J. Devlin (eds.), *The First World Conference on Therapeutic Communities.* Montreal: Portage Press, 1977(a).

———. Konfrontationsterapi. *Socionom Forbundets,* 1977(b), *14,* 6.

———. The positive self-fulfilling prophecy of reality therapy. *Together: Journal of the Association for Specialists in Group Work,* 1977(c), *2,* 60–77.

———. Motivating the unmotivated: the self-help therapeutic community's biggest challenge. In P. Vamos and J. E. Brown (eds.), *Proceedings of the Second World Conference on Therapeutic Communities.* Montreal: Portage Press, 1978.

———. Rebirth, responsibility, reality, and respect: the four "R's" of the American self-help therapeutic community. *The Addiction Therapist,* 1978(a), *4,* 51–66.

———. The four "R's" of the American self-help therapeutic community: rebirth, responsibility, reality, and respect. In J. Corelli, I. Bonfiglio, T. Pediconi, and M. Collomb (eds.), *Proceedings of the Third World Conference on Therapeutic Communities.* Rome: International Council of Alcohol and Addictions Press, 1978(b).

———, and Pennacchia, M. C. Methadone maintenance: a negative self-fulfilling prophecy. In J. H. Lowinson, B. J. Primm, and S. D. Coletti (eds.), *Critical Concerns in the Field of Drug Abuse.* New York: Marcel Deeker, 1978.

Bratter, T. E. The psychotherapist as a twelfth-step worker in the treatment of alcoholism. *Family and Community Health: The Journal of Health Promotion and Maintenance,* 1979, *2,* 31–58.

———. Les Communautés thérapeutiques aux U. S. A.: une approche nouvelle et humaniste de la toxicomanie." *Transitions: Revue de l'Innovation Psychiatrique et Sociale,* 1980, *3,* 86–98.

———. Some pre-treatment group psychotherapy considerations with alcoholic and drug-addicted individuals. *Psychotherapy: Theory, Research and Practice,* 1981, *18,* 508–515.

———, and Kooyman, M. A structured environment for heroin addicts: the experiences of a community-based American methadone clinic and a residential Dutch therapeutic community. *International Journal of Social Psychiatry,* 1981, *27,* 189–203.

Bratter, T. E. Games mental institutions play: iatrogenic disturbances caused by oppression and repression. *International Journal of Therapeutic Communities,* 1983, *4,* 57–66.

———, Bratter, E. P., Fossbender, A. J., and Heimberg, J. F. Uses and abuses of power and authority within the American self-help therapeutic community: A perversion or a necessity? In G. DeLeon and J. Ziegenfuss (eds.), *Therapeutic Communities for the Addictions.* Springfield, Ill.: Charles C. Thomas, 1985(a) (in press).

Bratter, T. M., Collabolletta, E. A., Fossbender, A. J., Gauya, D. A., Pennacchia, M., and Radda, H. T. The American self-help residential therapeutic community: a structured confrontative treatment milieu for character-disordered addicted individuals. In G. DeLeon and J. Ziegenfuss (eds.), *Therapeutic Communities for the Addictions.* Springfield, Ill.: Charles C. Thomas, 1985(b) (in press).

Brill, A. A. *Psychoanalysis: Its Theory and Practical Application.* Philadelphia: W. B. Saunders Co., 1912.

Brill, L., and Lieberman, L. *Authority and Addiction,* pp. 49–80. Boston: Little, Brown & Co., 1969.

Brown, C. *Manchild in the Promised Land.* New York: New American Library, 1966.

Buchman, F. N. D. *Remaking the World: The Speeches of Frank N. D. Buchman,* A. Thornhill (ed.). London: Blandford Press, 1966.

Burke, B. L., and Eichberg, R. H. Personality characteristics of adolescent users of dangerous drugs as indicated by the Minnesota Multiphasic Personality Inventory. *Journal of Nervous and Mental Diseases,* 1972, *154,* 291–298.

Burns, J. *The Answer to Addiction.* New York: Harper & Row, 1975.

Burroughs, W. *Junkie.* New York: Ace Books, 1953.

Caplan, R. B. *Psychiatry and the Community in Nineteenth-Century America: The Recurring Concern with Environment in the Prevention and Treatment of Mental Disorder.* New York: Basic Books, 1969.

Carkhuff, R. R., and Berenson, B. G. Man and his nourishment. In R. R. Carkhuff and B. G. Berenson (eds.), *Beyond Counseling and Therapy.* New York: Holt, Rinehart, & Winston, 1967.

Casriel, D. *So Fair a House: The Story of Synanon.* Englewood Cliffs, N. J.: Prentice-Hall, 1963.

———, and Amen, G. *Daytop Village: Three Addicts and Their Cure.* New York: Hill & Wang, 1971.

Casriel, D., and Bratter, T. E. Methadone maintenance treatment: a questionable procedure. *Journal of Drug Issues,* 1974, *10,* 359–375.

Chein, I. Narcotics use among juveniles. *Social Work,* 1956, *4,* 56–60.

———, Gerard, D., Lee, R., and Rosenfeld, E. *The Road to H.* New York: Basic Books, 1964.

Cherkas, M. S. Synanon Foundation: a radical approach to the problem of addiction. *American Journal of Psychiatry,* 1965, *121,* 1065–1068.

Clark, A. W., and Yeomans, N. T. *Fraser House: Theory, Practice and Evaluation of a Therapeutic Community.* New York: Springer Publishing Co., 1969.

Cleckley, H. M. Psychopathic states. In S. Arieti (ed.), *American Handbook of Psychiatry.* New York: Basic Books, 1959.

———. *Mask of Sanity.* St. Louis: C. V. Mosby Co., 1941.

Cunningham, E. The group movement: a valuation: Part 2. *The Spectator,* 1935, *144,* 601–602.

Davis, N. J. Labelling theory in deviance research: a critique and reconsideration. *The Sociological Quarterly,* 1972, *13(4),* 447–474.

Deitch, D. Treatment of drug abuse in the therapeutic community: historical influences, current considerations and future outlook. In National Commission on Marijuana and Drug Abuse (ed.), *Drug Use in America: Problem in Perspective. Vol. 4, Treatment and Rehabilitation.* Washington: U. S. Government Printing Office, 1973.

———, and Zweben, J. E. Synanon: a pioneering response to drug abuse treatment and a signal for caution. In S. Halpern and B. Levine (eds.), *Proceedings of the Fourth International Conference on Therapeutic Communities.* New York: Daytop Village Press, 1979.

———. Coercion in the therapeutic community. *Journal of Psychoactive Drugs,* 1984, *16,* 35–41.

DeLeon, G., and Beschner, G. M. (eds.) *The Therapeutic Community: Proceedings of Therapeutic Communities of America Planning Conference.* Washington: D. C.: National Institute on Drug Abuse, 1976.

Devlin, C. Daytop Village: an overview of philosophy, treatment techniques and scope. In J. Corelli, I. Bonfiglio, T. Pediconi, and M. Collomb (eds.), *Proceedings of the Third World Conference on Therapeutic Communities.* Rome: Centro Italiano di Solidarietà, 1978.

Devlin, J. J. Treatment of the addictions: a territorial imperative? *The Addiction Therapist,* 1975, *1,* 25.

Donnellan, B. The lay community: a therapeutic community for drug abusers. *Oxford Medical School Gazette,* 1978, *1,* 16–18.

Douds, J., Berenson, B. G., Carkhuff, R. R., and Pierce, R. In search of an honest experience: confrontation in counseling and life. In R. R. Carkhuff and B. G. Berenson (eds.), *Beyond Counseling and Therapy.* New York: Holt, Rinehart, & Winston, 1967.

Dreikurs, R. *Fundamentals of Adlerian Psychology.* New York: Greenberg, 1950.

Dumont, M. P. The junkie as political enemy. *American Journal of Orthopsychiatry,* 1972, *43,* 538–539.

Egan, G. *Encounter: Group Processes for Interpersonal Growth.* Belmont, Calif.: Brooks/Cole Publishing Co., 1970.

Eldridge, W. B. *Narcotics and the Law: A Critique of the American Experiment in Narcotic Drug Control.* Chicago: Chicago University Press, 1962.

Endore, G. *Synanon.* New York: Doubleday & Co., 1968.

Erikson, E. H. *Childhood and Society.* New York: W. W. Norton & Co., 1963.

Enright, J. B. Synanon: a challenge to middle-class views of mental health. In D. Adelson and B. Kalis (eds.), *Community Psychology and Mental Health: Perspectives and Challenges.* Scranton, Pa.: Chandler Publishing Co., 1970.

Eysenck, H. J. The effects of psychotherapy: an evaluation. *Journal of Consulting Psychology,* 1952, *16,* 319–324.

———. The effects of psychotherapy. In H. J. Eysenck (ed.), *The Handbook of Abnormal Psychology.* New York: Basic Books, 1960, 1962.

———. The effects of psychotherapy. *International Journal of Psychotherapy,* 1965, *1,* 99–178.

Feather, B. W. Psychodynamic behavior therapy: theory and rationale. *Archives of General Psychiatry,* 1972, *26,* 499.

Filstead, W. J., and Rossi, J. J. Therapeutic milieu, therapeutic community, and milieu therapy: some conceptual and definitional distinctions. In J. J. Rossi and W. J. Filstead (eds.), *The Therapeutic Community.* New York: Behavioral Publications, 1973.

Forrest, G. G. *The Diagnosis and Treatment of Alcoholism.* Springfield, Ill.: Charles C. Thomas, 1978.

———. *Confrontation in Psychotherapy with the Alcoholic.* Holmes Beach, Fla.: Learning Publications, 1982.

Fort, J. Heroin addiction among young men. *Psychiatry,* 1954, *17,* 251–259.

French, J. R. P., and Raven, B. The bases of social power. In D. Cartwright and A. Zander (eds.), *Group Dynamics Research and Theory.* New York: Harper & Row, 1960.

Freud, S. *The Ego and the Id,* translated by J. H. Riviere. London: Hogarth Press and Institute of Psychoanalysis, 1947.

———. *The Ego and the Id,* translated by J. Strachey. New York: W. W. Norton & Co., 1961.

———. Moral responsibility for the content of dreams. In S. Freud (ed.), *The Standard Edition of the Complete Psychological Works of Sigmund Freud,* vol. 19. London: Hogarth Press and Institute of Psychoanalysis, 1966 (1925).

Freudenberger, H. J. How we can right what's wrong with our therapeutic communities. *Journal of Drug Issues,* 1974, *4(4),* 381–392.

Fromm, E. *Escape from Freedom,* New York: Holt, Rinehart, & Winston, 1941.

———. *Man for Himself: An Inquiry into the Psychology of Ethics.* New York: Holt, Rinehart, & Winston, 1947.

Garner, H. *Psychotherapy: Confrontation Problem-Solving Technique.* St. Louis: Warren H. Green, 1970.

Gelfman, M. The role of irresponsibility in obsessive-compulsive neurosis. *Contemporary Psychoanalysis,* 1970, *7,* 36–47.

Gilbert, J. G., and Lombardi, D. N. Personality characteristics of young male narcotic addicts. *Journal of Consulting Psychology,* 1967, *12,* 127–139.

Glaser, F. B. The first therapeutic community. *The Addiction Therapist,* 1971, *2,* 8–15.

———. Some historical and theoretical background of a self-help addiction treatment program. *American Journal of Drug and Alcohol Abuse,* 1974, *1,* 37–52.

———. The origins of the drug-free therapeutic community: a retrospective history. In P. Vamos and J. E. Brown (eds.), *Proceedings of the Second World Conference on Therapeutic Communities.* Montreal: Portage Press, 1977.

Glasser, W., *The Identity Society.* New York: Harper & Row, 1972.

Glasser, W. *Reality Therapy: A New Approach to Psychiatry.* New York: Harper & Row, 1965.

Glover, E. On the etiology of drug addiction. In *On the Early Development of Mind.* New York: International Universities Press, 1956.

Goffman, E. *Asylums: Essays on the Social Situation of Mental Patients and Other Inmates.* Chicago: Aldine Publishing Co., 1961.

Goodstein, L. D. Some issues involved in intensive group experiences. *Counseling Psychologist,* 1970, *2*(2), 53.

Halleck, S. The concept of responsibility in psychotherapy. *American Journal of Psychotherapy,* 1982, *36,* 300–301.

Hampden-Turner, C. *Sane Asylum: Inside the Delancey Street Foundation.* San Francisco: San Francisco Book Co., 1976.

Hill, H. E., Haertzen, D. A., and Glaser, R. Personality characteristics of narcotic addicts as indicated by the MMPI. *The Journal of General Psychology,* 1960, *62,* 127–139.

Hill, H. E. How to help the addict. *Contemporary Psychology,* 1957, *2,* 113–114.

Hollidge, C. Psycho-dynamic aspects of the addicted personality and their treatment in the therapeutic community. In G. Schakel and M. Sikkens (eds.), *Readings of the Fifth World Conference on Therapeutic Communities.* The Hague: Samsom Sijthoff, Publishers, 1980.

Holzinger, R. Synanon through the eyes of a visiting psychologist. *Quarterly Journal of Studies on Alcohol,* 1965, *26,* 304–309.

Horn, F. Encounter group therapy in a T.C.: leaders and casualties. In P. Vamos and J. E. Brown (eds.), *Proceedings of the 2nd World Conference on Therapeutic Communities.* Montreal: Portage Press, 1978.

Horney, K. *Our Inner Conflicts: A Constructive Theory of Neurosis.* New York: W. W. Norton & Co., 1945.

House of Representatives, No. 23, 63rd Congress, 1st Session 2 (1913).

Howard, P. *Frank Buchman's Secret.* New York: Doubleday & Co., 1961.

Hurvitz, N. Peer self-help psychotherapy groups and their implications for psychotherapy. *Psychotherapy: Theory, Research and Practice,* 1973, *7,* 44.

———. Psychotherapy as a means of social control. *Journal of Consulting and Clinical Psychology,* 1973, *40,* 233.

Isbell, H. Medical aspects of opiate addictions. *Bulletin of the New York Academy of Medicine,* 1955, *31,* 886–901.

Jacobs, A., and Spradlin, W. (eds.)., *The Group as an Agent of Change.* New York: Behavioral Publications, 1974.

James, W. *Principles of Psychiatry.* New York: Henry Holt & Co., 1923.

———. *The Varieties of Religious Experiences,* pp. 77–162. New York: The Modern Library, 1929.

Jin Fuey Moy *v.* United States, 254 U. S. 189 (1920).

Jones, M. *Social Psychiatry: The Therapeutic Community.* London: Tavistock Publications, 1952.

———. *The Therapeutic Community—A New Treatment Method in Psychiatry.* New York: Basic Books, 1953.

———. Toward a clarification of the therapeutic community concept. *British Journal of Medical Psychology,* 1959, *32,* 200.

———. *Beyond the Therapeutic Community—Social Learning and Social Psychiatry.* New Haven: Yale University Press, 1968(a).

———. *Social Psychiatry in Practice.* London: Penguin Books, 1968(b).

———. Groups and social learning. In A. Uchtenhagen, R. Battegay, and A. Friedmann (eds.), *Group Therapy and Social Environment.* Berne, Switzerland: Verlag Hans Huber, 1975.

———. *Maturation of the Therapeutic Community.* New York: Human Sciences Press, 1976.

———. Therapeutic communities: old and new. *The Addiction Therapist,* 1979(a), *3,* 2–9.

———. Therapeutic communities, old and new. *American Journal of Drug and Alcohol Abuse,* 1979(b), *6,* 137–149.

———. Therapeutic communities in perspective. In G. Schakel and M. Sikkens (eds.), *Readings of the Fifth World Conference on Therapeutic Communities.* The Hague: Samsom Sijthoff, Publishers, 1980, p. 135.

Jourard, S. M. *The Transparent Self.* New York: D. Van Nostrand Co., 1964.

Jurjevich, R. M. *The Hoax of Freudism: A Study in Brainwashing the American Professionals and Laymen.* Philadelphia: Dorrance & Co., 1974.

Kesey, K. *One Flew Over the Cuckoo's Nest.* New York: Viking Press, 1962.

Killilea, M. Mutual-help organizations: interpretations in the literature. In G. Caplan and M. Killilea (eds.), *Support Systems and Mutual Help: Multidisciplinary Explorations.* New York: Grune & Stratton, 1976.

Kincheloe, M. Democratization in the therapeutic community. *Perspectives in Psychiatric Care,* 1973, *11,* 75–79.

Klein, D. F. Youthful rebels—diagnosis and treatment. *Adolescence,* 1972, *7,* 351–369.

Kohut, H. *The Analysis of the Self.* New York: International Universities Press, 1971.

Kooyman, M. The history of the therapeutic community movement in Europe. In P. Vamos and J. E. Brown (eds.), *Proceedings of the World Conference on Therapeutic Communities.* Montreal: Portage Press, 1978.

———, Bratter, T. E. De Noodzaak Van Confrontatie En Structuur Bij De Behandeling Van Drugverslaafden. *Tijdschrift Voor Alcohol, Drugs En Andere Psychotrope Stoffen,* 1980, *6,* 27–33.

Lambert, A., et al. Report of the Mayor's Committee on Drug Addiction to the Honorable Richard C. Patterson, Commissioner of Corrections, New York City. *American Journal of Psychiatry,* 1930, *10,* 433–438.

Laskowitz, D. The adolescent drug addict: an Adlerian view. *Journal of Individual Psychology,* 1961, *17,* 68–79.

———. Psychological characteristics of the adolescent addict. In E. Harms (ed.), *Drug Addiction in Youth.* Oxford: Pergamon Press, 1968.

———. Treatment models for opiate abusers. *Drug Forum,* 1972, *2,* 79.

Lecky, P. *Self-Consistency: A Theory of Personality.* New York: Island Press, 1945.

Levin, S. Confrontation as a demand for change. In G. Adler and P. G. Myerson (eds.), *Confrontation in Psychotherapy.* New York: Science House, 1973.

Levy, E. S., Faltico, C. J., and Bratter, T. E. The development and structure of the drug-free therapeutic community. *The Addiction Therapist,* 1977, *2,* 40–52.

Lieberman, M. A., and Borman, L. D. Overview: the nature of self-help groups. In M. A. Lieberman and L. D. Borman (eds.), *Self-Help Groups for Coping with Crisis.* San Francisco: Jossey-Bass, 1979.

Lief, A. (ed.). *The Common Sense Psychiatry of Dr. Adolf Meyer.* New York: McGraw-Hill Book Co., 1948.

Linder *v.* United States, 268 U. S. 5 (1925).

London, P. *The Modes and Morals of Psychotherapy.* New York: Holt, Rinehart, & Winston, 1964.

Lowinson, J., and Zwerling, I. Group therapy with narcotic addicts. In H. I. Kaplan and B. J. Sadock (eds.), *Comprehensive Group Psychotherapy.* Baltimore: The Williams & Wilkins Co., 1971.

McEneaney, K. What is therapeutic in a therapeutic community? In G. Schakel and M. Sikkens (eds.), *Readings of the Fifth World Conference on Therapeutic Communities.* The Hague: Samson Sijthoff, Publishers, 1980.

Main, T. F. The hospital as a therapeutic institution. *Bulletin of the Menninger Clinic,* 1946, *10,* 69.

Margolis, P. M. *Patient Power: The Development of a Therapeutic Community in a Psychiatric Unit of a General Hospital.* Springfield, Ill.: Charles C. Thomas, 1973.

Markoff, E. L. Synanon in drug addiction. *Current Psychiatric Therapies,* 1969, *9,* 261–272.

Marmor, J. Theories of learning and the psychotherapeutic process. *British Journal of Psychiatry,* 1966, *112,* 364.

Maslow, A. H. *Toward a Psychology of Being.* Princeton: D. Van Nostrand Co., 1962.

———. Synanon and Eupsychia. *Journal of Humanistic Psychology,* 1967, *7,* 28–29.

May, R. *Existential Psychology.* New York: Random House, 1961.

Mendel, W. M. Psychotherapy and responsibility. *The American Journal of Psychoanalysis,* 1966, *26,* 95.

Menninger, K. *Theory of Psychoanalytic Technique.* New York: Basic Books, 1958.

Meyer, V., and Chesser, E. S. *Behavior Therapy in Clinical Psychiatry.* Harmondsworth, England: Penguin Books, 1970.

Moreno, J. L. *Einladung zu Einer Begegnung (Invitation to an Encounter).* Vienna: Anzengruber Verlag, 1914.

———. Behavior therapy. *American Journal of Psychiatry,* 1963, *120,* 195.

———. The Viennese origins of the encounter movement, paving the way for existentialism, group psychotherapy and psychodrama. *Group Psychotherapy,* 1969, *22,* 8–9.

Morgenstern, F. V. Letter to the editor, *New York Times Magazine,* July 3, 1966, p. 4.

Mowrer, O. H. *The Crisis in Psychiatry and Religion.* Princeton: D. Van Nostrand Co., 1959.

———. Therapeutic groups and communities in retrospect and prospect. In P. Vamos and J. J. Devlin (eds.), *Proceedings of the First World Conference on Therapeutic Communities.* Montreal: Portage Press, 1976.

Mueller, E. E. Rebels—with a cause: a report on Synanon. *American Journal of Psychotherapy,* 1964, *18,* 272–284.

Myerson, P. G. The meanings of confrontation. In G. Adler and P. G. Myerson (eds.), *Confrontation in Psychotherapy.* New York: Science House, 1973.

O'Donnell, J. A. A follow-up study of treated narcotic addicts: mortality, relapse, and abstinence. *Journal of Orthopsychiatry,* 1964, *34,* 948–954.

Osberg, J. W., and Lewis, J. M. Treatment of narcotic addicts: observations on institutional treatment of character disorder. *American Journal of Orthopsychiatry,* 1958, *28,* 730–749.

Ottenberg, D. J. The process of recovery in the therapeutic community. In P. Vamos and J. J. Devlin (eds.), *Proceedings of the First World Conference on Therapeutic Communities.* Montreal: Portage Press, 1976.

Ozarin, L. D. Moral treatment and the mental hospital. *American Journal of Psychiatry,* 1954, *111,* 371–378.

———. Moral treatment and the mental hospital. In J. J. Rossi and W. J. Filstead (eds.), *The Therapeutic Community: Sourcebook of Readings.* New York: Behavioral Publications, 1973.

Page, R. C. Social change in a therapeutic community. *International Journal of the Addictions,* 1983, *18,* 769–776.

Patterson, C. H. *Theories of Counseling and Psychotherapy.* New York: Harper & Row, 1966.

Piperopoulous, G. The blueprint for the establishment of a "model re-entry facility" as a cooperative effort between a therapeutic community and any department of corrections. In J. Corelli, I. Bonfiglio, T. Pediconi, and M. Collomb (eds.), *Proceedings of the Third World Conference on Therapeutic Communities.* Rome: Centro Italiano di Solidarietà, 1978.

Powell, T. J. The use of self-help groups as supportive reference communities. *American Journal of Orthopsychiatry,* 1975, *45,* 759.

Prescor, J. J. Follow-up of treated narcotic addicts. *Public Health Reports Supplement,* 1943, *170,* 1–18.

Rachman, A. W., and Heller, M. E. Anti-therapeutic factors in therapeutic communities for drug rehabilitation. *Journal of Drug Issues,* 1974, *4,* 393–403.

Rachman, A. W. *Identity Group Psychotherapy with Adolescents,* pp. 197–214. Springfield, Ill.: Charles C. Thomas, 1975.

Rado, S. Narcotic bondage: a general theory of dependence on narcotic drugs. *American Journal of Psychiatry,* 1957, *114,* 165–170.

———. *Adaptational Psychodynamics: Motivation and Control.* New York: Science House, 1969.

Ramirez, E. The Addiction Services Agency of the City of New York. In L. Brill and L. Lieberman (eds.), *Major Modalities in the Treatment of Drug Abuse.* New York: Behavioral Publications, 1972(a).

———. The dome model in the management of addiction. In L. Brill and L. Lieberman (eds.), *Major Modalities in the Treatment of Drug Abuse.* New York: Behavioral Publications, 1972(b).

———. Phoenix House: a therapeutic community program for the treatment of drug abusers and drug addicts. In L. Brill and E. Harms (eds.), *Yearbook of Drug Abuse.* New York: Behavioral Publications, 1973.

Rasor, R. W. The United States Public Health Service and institutional treatment program for narcotic addicts at Lexington, Kentucky. In L. Brill and L. Lieberman (eds.), *Major Modalities in the Treatment of Drug Abuse.* New York: Behavioral Publications, 1972.

Raubolt, R. R., and Bratter, T. E. Beyond group psychotherapy: the caring community. *The Addiction Therapist,* 1976, *1,* 10–16.

———. Games addicts play: implications for group treatment. *Corrective and Social Psychiatry,* 1974, *20,* 7.

Roffman, R. A. Heroin and social welfare policy. *Social Work,* 1973, *18,* 26.

Rosenberg, C. M. Young drug addicts: background and personality. *Journal of Nervous and Mental Disease,* 1969, *148,* 65–73.

Rosenfeld, H. A. The psychopathology of drug addiction and alcoholism: a critical review of the psychoanalytical literature. In *Psychotic States.* New York: International Universities Press, 1966.

Rosenthal, M., and Biase, D. V. Phoenix Houses: therapeutic communities for drug addicts. In H. I. Kaplan and B. J. Sadock (eds.), *Groups and Drugs.* New York: Jason Aronson, 1972.

Rubel, J. G., Bratter, T. E., Sminoff, A. M., Hartwig-Thompson, L., and Baker, K. G. The role of structure in the professional model and the self-help concept of the therapeutic community: different strokes for different folks? *International Journal of Therapeutic Communities,* 1982, *3,* 222.

Ruiteenbeek, H. *The New Group Therapies.* New York: Avon Books, 1970.

Sabath, G. Some trends in the treatment and edpidemiology of drug addiction: psychotherapy and synanon. *Psychotherapy: Theory, Research and Practice,* 1967, *4,* 92–96.

Sack, M. Therapeutic community movement. *Journal of Psychedelic Drugs,* 1974, *6,* 169.

Sales, G. *John Maher of Delancey Street: A Guide to Peaceful Revolution in America.* New York: W. W. Norton & Co., 1976.

Salter, A. *The Case Against Psychoanalysis.* New York: Holt, 1952.

Sartre, J. P. *Existentialism and Human Emotions.* New York: Wisdom Library, 1957.

Schaap, G. E. Democratic and concept-based therapeutic communities. In G. Schakel and M. Sikkens (eds.), *Readings of the Fifth World Conference on Therapeutic Communities.* The Hague: Samsom Sijthoff, Publishers, 1980.

Schnee, J. Freedom of choice. *The American Journal of Psychoanalysis,* 1972, *30,* 206.

Schur, E. M. *Labeling Deviant Behavior: Its Implications.* New York: Harper & Row, 1971.

Seabrook, W. *Asylum.* New York: Harcourt, Brace & Co., 1935.

Shankman, S. Criteria and factors affecting admission into and completion of the therapeutic community program. In J. Corelli, I. Bonfiglio, T. Pediconi, and M. Collomb (eds.), *Proceedings of the Third World Conference on Therapeutic Communities.* Rome: Centro Italiano di Solidarietà, 1978.

Shelly, J. A. and Bassin, A. Daytop Lodge: halfway house for drug addicts. *Federal Probation,* 1964, *28(4),* 46–54.

———. Daytop Lodge—a new treatment approach for drug addicts. *Corrective Psychiatry,* 1965, *11,* 186–195.

Shelly, J. Daytop Lodge—a two-year report. In S. B. Sells (ed.), *Rehabilitating the Narcotic Addict.* Washington, D. C.: U. S. Government Printing Office, 1966.

Shostrum, E. L. *Man, the Manipulator: The Inner Journey from Manipulation to Actualization.* Nashville: Abingdon Press, 1967.

Silber, A. An addendum to the technique of psychotherapy with alcoholics. *Journal of Nervous and Mental Disorders,* 1970, *150,* 423.

Silver, A. M. Some personality characteristics of groups of young drug misusers and delinquents. *British Journal of the Addiction,* 1977, *72,* 143–150.

Simon, S. Synanon: toward building a humanistic organization. *Journal of Humanistic Psychology,* 1978, *18,* 18.

Singer, E. *Key Concepts in Psychotherapy.* New York: Random House, 1965.

Steinfeld, G., Rice, A. H., and Mabli, J. Once a junkie, always a junkie: an evaluation of a therapeutic community for drug addicts, using attitude questionnaire data. *Drug Forum,* 1974, *3,* 393.

Stephens, R. C., and Slatin, G. T. The street addict role: toward the definition of a type. *Drug Forum,* 1974, *3,* 375–389.

Sugarman, B. *Daytop Village, a Therapeutic Community.* New York: Holt, Rinehart, & Winston, 1974.

Sullivan, H. S. Socio-psychiatric research. *American Journal of Psychiatry,* 1937, *87,* 989.

Szasz, T. S. *The Myth of Mental Illness.* New York: Harper & Row, 1961(a).

———. The uses of naming and the origin of the myth of mental illness. *American Psychologist,* 1961(b), *16,* 59–65.

———. *The Ethics of Psychoanalysis: The Theory and Method of Tutonomous Psychotherapy.* New York: Basic Books, 1965.

———. *The Manufacture of Madness: A Comparative Study of the Inquisition and the Mental Health Movement.* New York: Harper & Row, 1970.

———. The ethics of addiction. *American Journal of Psychiatry,* 1971, *128,* 541–546.

———. *Ceremonial Chemistry.* New York: Anchor Books, 1974.

Thomas, P. *Down These Mean Streets.* New York: New American Library, 1967.

U. S. House of Representatives. *Congressional Record.* Washington, D. C. (June 26, 1913), p. 2205.

Vaillant, G. E. A twelve-year follow-up of New York narcotic addicts: some social and psychiatric characteristics. *Archives of General Psychiatry,* 1966, *15,* 599–609.

Vamos, P., and Devlin, J. J. The evolution of the addiction therapist: a training imperative. *The Addiction Therapist,* 1975, *1,* 27.

Van Kaam, A. Addiction and existence. *Review of Existential Psychology and Psychiatry,* 1968, *8,* 54–64.

Van Stone, W. W., and Gilbert, R. Peer confrontation groups: what, why and whether. *American Journal of Psychiatry,* 1972, *129(5),* 585.

Vermes, G. (ed.). *The Dead Sea Scrolls.* Westerham, England: The Limited Editions Club, 1966.

Veysey, L. *The Communal Experience.* New York: Harper & Row, 1973.

Wachtel, P. L. *Psychoanalysis and Behavior Therapy: Toward an Integration.* New York: Basic Books, 1973.

Waldorf, D. Social control in therapeutic communities for the treatment of drug addicts. *International Journal of the Addictions,* 1971, *6,* 55–56.

Webb *v.* United States, 249 U. S. 96 (1919).

Weiner, M. F. *Therapist Disclosure: The Use of Self in Psychotherapy.* Boston: Buttenworth Publishers, 1971.

Weppner, R. S. The role of the ex-addict. *Drug Forum,* 1973, *2,* 103.

Wilmar, H. Toward a definition of the therapeutic community. *American Journal of Psychiatry,* 1958, *114,* 824–825.

Wilson, S., and Mandelbrote, B. The relationship between duration of treatment in a therapeutic community for drug abusers and subsequent criminality. *British Journal of Psychiatry,* 1978, *132,* 487–491.

Winkler, A., and Rasor, R. W. Psychiatric aspects of drug addiction. *American Journal of Medicine,* 1953, *14,* 566–570.

Wolberg, L. R., *The Technique of Psychotherapy.* New York: Grune & Stratton, 1967.

Wolpe, J. Learning therapies. In J. G. Howells (ed.), *Modern Perspective in World Psychiatry.* Edinburgh, Scotland: Oliver & Boyd, 1968.

Wurmser, L. *The Hidden Dimension: Psychodynamics in Compulsive Drug Use.* New York: Jason Aronson, 1978.

Yablonsky, L., and Dederich, C. E. Synanon: an analysis of some dimensions of the social structure of an antiaddiction society. In D. M. Wilmer and G. G. Kassebaum (eds.), *Narcotics.* New York: McGraw-Hill Book Co., 1965.

Yablonsky, L. The anticriminal society: Synanon. *Federal Probation,* 1962, *26,* 50–57.

———. *The Tunnel Back: Synanon.* New York: The Macmillan Co., 1965.

Zimmerling, P., Drug addiction in relation to the problems of adolescence. *American Journal of Psychiatry,* 1972, *109,* 272–278.

Zimmerman, R. S. The (mis)use of ex-addicts in drug abuse treatment programs. *Drug Forum,* 1972, *1,* 367–372.

18

Behavioral Contracting in Psychotherapy with Alcoholics

GARY G. FORREST

A VALUABLE THERAPEUTIC TOOL in the treatment of alcoholic and problem-drinking patients is that of behavioral contracting. Behavioral contracting is not new to the clinical literature (Forrest, 1978; Forrest, 1984a). However, as a treatment concept it has come to encompass a potpourri of procedures and methods. There is a very obvious lack of continuity of meaning expressed between various professional and paraprofessional alcoholism treatment personnel with reference to the concept of "behavioral contracting." It clearly means different things to different therapists and change agents.

In this article, I have provided a basic definition and description of behavioral contracting in psychotherapy with alcoholic persons. Following this is an in-depth discussion of the sources of therapeutic gain afforded by the use of this treatment technique. The present article encompasses behavioral contracting within the explicit realm of psychotherapy and rehabilitation work with alcoholic and problem-drinking patients. In this sense the article is limited.

Construction and Content of the Behavioral Contract

Behavioral contracting simply involves the development upon the part of both therapist and patient of an explicit treatment plan or treatment contract. This treatment plan, jointly developed and agreed upon, becomes a comprehensive tool for facilitating the patient's behavioral growth and change; and it also, among other things, is an instrument for the assessment of therapeutic outcome by the psychotherapist or counselor. Perhaps the key word or essential phrase in this definition of behavioral contracting is "explicit" or "jointly developed, explicit treatment contract." Effective behavioral contracting is first and foremost a function of the therapist-patient dyad jointly deciding upon and agreeing as to what exactly will constitute the actual program of treatment or rehabilitation for the patient (Forrest, 1978; 1982; Bratter, 1979).

It is extremely advantageous, at a more basic level, to determine if in fact the patient feels that he or she has an alcohol-related "problem." Once the therapist and patient concur on this basic issue, assuming that the patient perceives significant difficulty related to the addiction process, further joint decisions are made relative to the exact behaviors, thoughts, and/or feelings that the patient wishes to change. The rationale for attempting to ascertain whether or not the patient feels that he or she has a "problem" not only involves focusing upon particular areas of desired change, but in large part has to do with the matter of pathological denial genetic to the character structure of alcoholic and problem-drinking individuals (Blane, 1968; Forrest, 1978, 1980, 1983).

The vast majority of individuals referred to community-oriented alcohol and drug rehabilitation centers or private alcoholism therapists do in fact manifest marked interpersonal and intrapersonal difficulties as a result of their alcohol abuse or alcohol addiction (Knauert, 1979). Many individuals who are referred to such agencies as a direct result of their alcoholism or substance abuse behaviors do not feel that a significant problem exists in these areas of their life. Such individuals deny a plethora of problems associated with their drinking behavior. In these situations, therapists and rehabilitation staff members are confronted with two basic treatment alternatives: (1) attempt to initiate treatment and rehabilitation of the individual, realizing that the issue of denial is at this point of paramount importance to the treatment and rehabilitation process, or (2) simply refuse to treat the patient at this time. Within community alcohol and drug treatment agencies it is not at all atypical for the counselor or therapist to be frequently confronted with angry, hostile individuals, who have been directly referred to the agency as a result of their alcohol and drug–facilitated "craziness" and grossly inappropriate social behaviors. In many cases, this global pattern of denial may be such that worthwhile and effective treatment measures are at this particular time a virtual impossibility.

In cases such as this it is efficacious to schedule a series of perhaps four to six individual therapy sessions during which the individual's denial, anger, hostility, and resentments are the sole focus of consideration. If these resistances, as they relate to the current interpersonal style and intrapersonal adjustment of the individual, cannot be significantly resolved or worked through in the course of a few initial individual therapy sessions, then attempts at subsequent psychotherapy and rehabilitation may be a waste of the therapist's time (Forrest, 1982). Frequently, individuals who manifest this negative stance toward the therapist and treatment "show up" at the therapist's office or treatment agency a few months later desirous of entering treatment. During this time interval many of these individuals have experienced further medical, legal, or interpersonal difficulties as a result of their drinking behaviors. At this point incarceration or other drastic consequences may have become a reality with which the individual is faced. Effective treatment and rehabilitation, to include behavioral contracting, may be quite feasible at this juncture.

Defining and identifying the patient's problematic areas, major concerns, complaints, and sources of dissonance, as a function of effective behavioral contracting, must incorporate a primary and ever-present emphasis upon the role of alcoholism and drinking behavior in the patient's present, as well as historic interpersonal and intrapersonal difficulties (Forrest, 1984a). As such, the behavioral contract must include the patient's agreement to refrain from all alcohol use while in treatment. While many counselors and psychotherapists (Armor, Polich, and Stambul, 1978) might perhaps feel uncomfortable with the patient's being required to agree upon total abstinence from alcohol (and other mood-altering drugs) during the treatment period, it has been my experience that anything less stringent, in the case of alcoholics and problem drinkers, results in eventual resistance and a therapeutic impasse completely antithetical to the successful completion of treatment (Forrest, 1978, 1979a). This becomes a matter of joint agreement between the therapist and the patient within the context of the behavioral-contracting process.

Secondary to the inclusion in the behavioral contract of the patient's agreement to terminate the use of all mood-altering substances while in therapy, the patient and therapist can choose to work on any possible number of the patient's other conflicts. Frequently, the behavioral contract will include dealing with the patient's overwhelming feelings of anxiety, depression, depersonalization, and other incapacitating negative affective states. Marital discord, vocational difficulties, parenting problems, and general communication and social skills are consistently grist for inclusion in the behavioral contract.

The behavioral contract simply loses the essence of its therapeutic potency in the absence of the patient's commitment to a chemically free life-style while in treatment. If the individual is unable to relinquish drinking behaviors while in treatment, it is reality-oriented to expect that very little, if any, therapeutic gain will be evidenced by attempting to deal with the more secondary constituents of the behavioral contract.

The behavioral contract should represent a rather comprehensive and mutually well understood document. It is the responsibility of the therapist to make every effort to assure that the patient clearly understands the total range of specifics incorporated within the contract. Depending upon the patient's intellectual abilities, educational background, and degree of emotional disturbance and treatment motivation and resistance, the therapist must be able to organize the contract document in such a fashion that the patient has a meaningful grasp of what he or she is *behaviorally* expected to do. With a number of patients this may well boil down to an exercise for the therapist in articulating the concrete. At the other end of the continuum we frequently deal with very bright, articulate patients who readily comprehend even the more psychodynamically oriented dimensions of the behavioral contract.

The behavioral contract should address the following issues: (1) treatment modalities (individual therapy, group therapy, Antabuse maintenance program, marital couples group therapy, etc.); (2) frequency of treatment (individual therapy one hour weekly, group therapy two hours weekly, 250 mg. of Antabuse daily, etc.); and (3) duration of treatment (weekly individual therapy for a period of six months, weekly group therapy for a period of eight months, daily Antabuse maintenance for a period of one year, etc.). It is apparent from these specifics that the patient in a very real sense potentially becomes locked into a highly structured program of rehabilitation or treatment once he or she actively participates in the development of the behavioral requirements of the treatment contract. Again, it must be remembered that the specific content of the behavioral contract is decided upon and constructed by both therapist and patient. Furthermore, a good deal of intercontractual variance is to be expected between different therapists and even from patient to patient with the same therapist. Additionally, all behavioral contracts should include a statement or clause allowing for renegotiation of the initial contents of the contract at a given later date, or perhaps a more global renegotiation procedure at the time of expiration of the original contract. Frequently, I have had patients in treatment on a contractual basis who felt very good about the growth and progress they were able to actualize within the course of ninety-day treatment contract. At the point of contractual expiration these patients requested another identical three-month contract. Thus, the opportunity for renegotiation of the contractual procedure should be built into the original treatment agreement.

Once the specific contents of the initial behavioral contract have been constructed and agreed upon by both the patient and therapist, or rehabilitation team, the primary contractual parties (therapist and patient) both sign the contractual document. (The therapeutic or psychodynamic rationale for this procedure will be discussed later.) Furthermore, in many instances it is efficacious to require the patient's spouse, employer, or immediate job supervisor to sign the contract. In fact, there may well be clinical justification to actually include the employer, immediate job supervisor, or perhaps even the spouse in the initial development of the behavioral contract. Such a procedure is contingent upon a multiplicity of patient-oriented variables, the treatment and philosophical orientation of the counselor or therapist, and the nature of the treatment milieu. Treatment modalities encompassing the inclusion of the employer or spouse in the actual construction of the behavioral contract (Forrest, 1984b) are perhaps most appropriate within the confines of institutional psychotherapy and rehabilitation programs. This method of behavioral contracting with alcoholic patients works very well within military alcohol and drug rehabilitation centers. Any individual who has been directly referred or "forced" into treatment by his or her agency of employment as a result of alcoholism or problem-drinking behaviors, regardless of the specific type of employing agency, should be strongly "nudged" in the direction of including the employer and the spouse in the development of the behavioral contract. In essence, the employer or immediate job supervisor and spouse thus become potentially significant reinforcers of behavioral change and positive growth from within the patient's immediate environment. It can be therapeutically beneficial to include other significant individuals from within the patient's immediate life space in the development of the behavioral contract.

Pragmatic considerations and the creactivity of the psychotherapist ultimately dictate the scope and value of the behavioral contract. In this regard, it can be stated that the purpose and rationale for behavioral contracting in psychothreapy is that of providing for more viable and total contingencies of reinforcement conducive to the modification and elimination of the patient's alcoholism and alcohol-facilitated maladaptive behaviors. With alcoholic and problem-drinking patients, "maladaptive behavior" begins in a nuclear fashion with the addiction process. As such, psychotherapeutic efforts, including the behavioral contract, must initially and continually focus on this particular psychodynamic aspect of the patient's self-system (Forrest, 1983).

Therapeutic Gains from Behavioral Contracting

Behavioral contracting is a particularly appropriate and effective therapeutic technique in the treatment of alcoholic and chemically dependent individuals (Forrest, 1978, 1982; Bratter, 1980). While this procedure has been found to be of significant clinical worth with other treatment populations—i.e., the various so-called neurotic disorders, sociopathic states, and depressive reactions—behavioral contracting as a singular, adjunctive treatment modality is clearly most useful and effective with alcoholic patients, for whom it provides numerous sources of therapeutic gain. It should also be remembered that this particular strategy, like all other treatment techniques or modalities, is subject to inherent weaknesses and flaws (Paolino and McCrady, 1977; Fann, Karacan, Pokorny, and Williams, 1980). Behavioral contracting by no means represents a therapeutic or rehabilitation panacea, regardless of treatment population.

As already alluded to, effective behavioral contracting is but one dynamic strategy of treatment. It must be strongly emphasized that behavioral contracting per se is of limited therapeutic or rehabilitative benefit. As a part of the total ongoing treatment process, behavioral contracting potentially becomes one of the most significant or potent singular facilitators of patient behavioral change and growth, including the fundamental matter of initiating and maintaining a chemically free life-style. It is necessary to reinforce the position that behavioral contracting represents but one dimension, and a clinically significant dimension, of the overall rehabilitation process. Unfortunately, it has been characteristic of the behavioral science professions to veiw new or relatively innovative treatment models or strategies as cure-alls or panaceas (Forrest, 1983). As we increasingly come to understand the procrustean nature of this aspect of the behavioral science professions, we must correspondingly initiate conscious, perhaps evaluation and research–oriented, methodologies designed for the explicit purpose of assessing the actual merit and clinical worth of "new," innovative, or perhaps radical treatment approaches and techniques. This is a recondite task.

The behavioral contract is an excellent tool with which to therapeutically manage a multiplicity of issues relating to the matter of patient responsibility. Responsibility is a key concept, relating to both the process and outcome of virtually all systems of counseling and psychotherapy (Glasser, 1965; Corsini, 1979; Forrest, 1978; Bratter, 1979). A basic characteristic of many individuals seeking and becoming involved in psychological and psychiatrically oriented therapies or "treatment" is that of simply being irresponsible. Indeed, a sizeable segment of any population of individuals engaged in programs of rehabilitation or psychotherapy have led rather grossly irresponsible lives. The irresponsible life-style becomes a matter of chronic adjustment difficulty. The alcoholic patient, as well as the problem drinker (Forrest, 1980), is an individual who has never successfully come to grips with the matter of behaving and living responsibly. The vast majority of alcoholics have chronically experienced difficulty paying bills on time, if at all, in the absence of external pressure. They have neglected many of the various responsibilities of their parental and marital roles. On-the-job performance or behaviors reflect this same lack of responsibility. Indeed, the global interpersonal adjustment style of the alcoholic is characterized by an inability to behave responsibly.

The behavioral contract is a document, employed within the psychotherapy relationship or the rehabilitation program, that requires a very circumscribed degree of responsible behavior upon the part of the patient. Agreeing to attend weekly group therapy, to attend Alcoholics Anonymous, and to take Antabuse daily for a period of three to six months (within the context of the behavioral contract) may not impress the neophyte alcoholism counselor as a tremendously potent or significant event upon the part of the patient. However, this circumscribed acceptance of responsibility, and the ability developed through the medium of the treatment process to actually be successful in following through with the explicit terms of the contract, constitutes a very significant first step in the process of learning responsible patterns of behavior. Learning more responsible patterns of interpersonal behavior means becoming more effective in the process of daily living. Quite simply, as the alcoholic individual acquires the capacity to be more globally responsible, he or she in a congruous fashion becomes emotionally stronger and better integrated. As change agents we must appreciate the clinical significance of the responsibility issue as it relates to the pathology of alcoholism and addiction. Likewise, we msut consistently focus our therapeutic efforts in this particular area.

As we positively reinforce the patient for his or her growing ability to live more responsibly, we as well as the patient begin to expect (Frank, 1961) an ongoing and growing capacity upon the part of the patient to be increasingly more successful at behaving responsibly. The behavioral contract, in a structured manner, provides the patient with an excellent program for learning responsible behaviors. It also provides rather direct feedback relative to the progress of the patient in this process of learning more responsible patterns of interpersonal behavior. In an ongoing fashion the treatment progress of the patient, as defined and delineated within the context of the behavioral contract, is continually monitored by both therapist and patient. This becomes a viable methodology for dealing with patient denial, rationalization, resistance, and indeed the basic character structure of the alcoholic in a therapeutic fashion.

Another source of gain offered by the method of behavioral contracting has to do with the matter of commitment. While commitment very directly relates to behavioral responsibility, it encompasses perhaps a more elementary and fundamental parameter of the alcoholic individual's character structure. Alcoholic patients, as a group, tend to have life-styles devoid of long-term commitments (Forrest, 1980, 1983). The relationship-oriented commitments of the alcoholic tend to be clearly neurotic. Self reports as well as direct feedback from parents and significant others indicate that alcoholic individuals have not been capable of "stick-to-it-ness" during childhood; they "never finished anything they started" during adolescence; and in adulthood the number of occupational changes, divorces, and so on supports this same pattern of generalized noncommitment. Obviously, responsibility problems are central to this form of adjustment style. Active participation in the construction of the behavioral contract, signing the document, and actually following through with its specifics constitutes a potentially significant learning experience in the commitment realm.

Many alcoholic patients spontaneously report very positive feelings about having been able to carry through and complete the requirements of the contract. Verbal statements such as "This is the first time in my life that I've ever really been able to stick to something and actually see it through" are typical expressions of this type of feeling. Genetic to this process is also a feeling of success, of having accomplished something. As most alcoholic individuals have been plagued with failure throughout their lives, it is extremely important that they undergo and learn to effect more successful life experiences on a day-to-day basis. The experience of making and successfully fulfilling an extended commitment, one that is interpersonally oriented, provides a rewarding behavioral sequence for the alcoholic individual. When these success-oriented experiences are generalized, learned, and repeated, they soon inhibit the addiction process and the warped or parataxic behaviors genetic to this adjustment style. The behavioral contract is a tool for teaching the addicted patient more healthy commitment-oriented behaviors. Failure or partial failure upon the part of the patient to carry out the various commitments of the behavioral contract provides the therapist with a wealth of reality-oriented feedback which must be resolved within the therapy relationship. Indeed, the therapeutic management of partial commitments or a lack of commitment upon the part of the patient, as directly evidenced by the patient's ongoing responses to the behavioral contract, often facilitates the successful resolution of the addiction process and contributes to the development of more effective interpersonal behaviors.

Alcoholic patients entering a rehabilitation program or becoming involved in psychotherapy feel rejected and unwanted. Such individuals have reached the point at which parents, relatives, friends, and significant others have quite frankly "given up" on them (Forrest, 1979b). Likewise, these alcoholics have given up on themselves. At the point of entering treatment many of their close friends and acquaintances have initiated movement away from them. Perhaps these patients have been "disowned" by spouse, children, or parents at this juncture. Such a rupture in the interpersonal realm, in spite of an alcoholic patient's denial system and other defensive maneuvers, is a major trauma. The psychotherapy relationship often represents for alcoholic patients a renewal of hope, a significant interpersonal reengagement, and a potential source of meaningful involvement with self and significant others (Forrest, 1979a). The behavioral contract, as a concrete and symbolic representation of these various sources of therapeutic gain, often means to the patient that "someone still cares." Similarly, the belief "I can care about myself" evolves from this same source. Becoming involved in a psychotherapy relationship explicitly and implicitly means to the alcoholic patient that the therapist cares, that the therapist somehow feels capable of "helping" the patient, and that positive growth and behavioral change can occur. The behavioral contract, as a part of the therapy relationship, in a concrete and observable manner conveys these same basic messages to the alcoholic patient. It also rather explicitly lets the patient know to what extent the therapist is willing to become involved in the treatment process. Limit setting, as a therapeutic issue, thus becomes very much a part of the behavioral contract.

Behavioral contracting in the psychotherapeutic treatment of alcoholic individuals is simply another method of conveying to the hurt, rejected, and frequently overwhelmed patient that things can be changed for the better and that the therapist has in no way "given up" on the patient. Furthermore, the behavioral contract constitutes a program which has helped initiate "recovery" by many other similar patients the therapist has treated. Also, the contract is a concrete method by which the patient can begin to effectively help himself or herself. Individuals experiencing intrapersonal and interpersonal difficulties other than the addictions may not "need" the behavioral contract for the therapeutic purposes thus far delineated. However, the therapeutic sources of gain associated with the contract prove extremely beneficial in the overall rehabilitation management of the chemically dependent patient. The behavioral contract frequently synergizes the effective treatment process.

As indicated earlier, the ongoing response of the alcoholic patient to the content of the behavioral contract often constitutes a major psychodynamic consideration in the therapist-patient relationship. This is particularly true in long-term treatment cases. Clearly, all of the ramifications of the transference-countertransference phenomena come into play here. It is appropriate for the nuclear core of the psychotherapeutic process to periodically encompass the explicit domain of the patient's response to the content of the behavioral contract. Basic therapeutic consideration of the patient's management of the contract's specifics constitutes a reasonable measure of progress or regression during treatment. Indeed, at certain points in the therapy relationship the matter of patient response to the behavioral contract may well be likened to a barometer of treatment progress and effectiveness (Forrest, 1984b). Infrequently, psychotherapy or rehabilitation becomes a matter of solely dealing with the behavioral contract per se.

The assessment of both the psychotherapeutic process and outcome can, in part, be equated with the alcoholic patient's global management of the behavioral contract. The actual process of rehabilitation or psychotherapy can be evaluated from the patient's response to the behavioral contract perspective. Patients who terminate therapy or rehabilitation prematurely, or in other blatant ways eventually qualify for the evaluation of rehabilitative or therapeutic "failure," most obviously are not capable of successfully dealing with the content of the behavioral contract, and thus reflect this reality in a treatment outcome–oriented perspective. At the opposite end of the continuum are patients who respond remarkably well to the rehabilitation program. Almost without exception such patients manage the content of behavioral contract in an eqully effective and therapeutic fashion. In both of these situations the behavioral contract provides another source of valid and meaningful outcome data. At least 50 percent of alcoholic persons becoming involved in a comprehensive rehabilitation program or psychotherapy relationship (Forrest, 1978; Emrick, 1980) are eventually evaluated as treatment "successes." The behavioral contract, as a measure of treatment outcome, is perhaps less useful and meaningful with the remaining percentage of patients involved in psychotherapy or rehabilitation. However, even in these more nebulous cases of outcome assessment this document can provide worthwhile clinical data. The patient who, by virtue of a psychotherapy relationship or rehabilitation experience, terminates alcohol addiction, yet intermittently abuses or uses another mood-altering substance, poses a more difficult problem with regard to outcome evaluation (Armor, Polich, and Stambul, 1978). The matter of how this patient has managed the content of the behavioral contract can potentially be quite relevant with regard to meaningful outcome assessment (Forrest, 1984b).

This discussion of potential sources of therapeutic gain afforded by the method of behavioral contracting is in no way final or complete. The major sources of therapeutic gain associated with the utilization of this treatment strategy have been touched upon. Behavioral contracting, as a treatment technique, is for the most part a product of the last decade. This general procedure is much akin to the pervasive marketing character of Western culture, also a recently acknowledged phenomenon. As such, one could speculate upon the possible sources of gain, or perhaps psychologically noxious effects, of this treatment methodology as a cultural byproduct. Hopefully, the reader will be able to incorporate into the article other avenues of therapeutic gain offered by the method of behavioral contracting. Direct experience with this adjunctive treatment strategy will certainly enhance the reader's ability to contribute in this manner.

It must again be emphasized that behavioral contracting is a particular adjunctive treatment strategy. Effective psychotherapy and rehabilitation efforts with addicted patients must encompass a multiplicity of individually designed treatment strategies (Forrest, 1983, 1984a). Behavioral contracting is not a panacea. As a treatment methodology, it is subject to numerous flaws and weaknesses. While this article has not focused upon the specific weaknesses of this treatment strategy, a number of the more global deficits of the procedure have been pointed out.

Legal Considerations

Invariably in the discussion of the procedure of behavioral contracting in psychotherapy or rehabilitation work, the question of the legality of the contractual document arises (Bratter, 1977). For the most part this question is of little, if any, clinical or legal relevance. Essentially, the behavioral contract is an agreement between a therapist or counselor and a patient (Bratter, 1979). Should the specific contents of the contract be violated, this becomes a clinical matter pertaining to both parties, within the explicit confines of the treatment relationship. This matter must be resolved, in a therapeutic fashion, by the limited parties within a very limited context. This situation may become more complicated when the behavioral contract includes the patient's employer or spouse, or perhaps the treatment agency, rather than simply a therapist or counselor. Again, however, legality in the strict sense of the word is of little relevance in this matter.

A potentially complex exception to this general situation pertains to patients directly and mandatorily referred to the therapist or rehabilitation agency by the courts or a similar legal source. This apparently sticky issue need not become the feared specter that it is often made out to be by many therapists and treatment personnel. In cases directly referred to the therapist by a legal agency, in which the behavioral contract is employed as a specific tool in the rehabilitation process, the decision to include or not to include the referring party in the actual treatment contract must be made in the initial one or two therapy sessions. This decision rests with the therapist and patient. Should the referring party be included in the actual development of the behavioral contract, this particular person or agency must both make known the direct consequences of the patient's failure to meet the behavioral requirements of the contract and have the legal power or authority to carry out these specified consequences. Should the referral source lack either of these capabilities, it is of little clinical importance to the therapist, assuming that he or she has not constructed treatment around these consequences.

If the legal source of referral is not capable of clearly spelling out the direct behavioral (legal) consequences of the patient's failure to manage the specifics of the behavioral contract, and if the legal source also lacks the power or authority to carry out these consequences, the therapist or treatment agency simply is placed in the singular position of deciding: (1) whether or not in fact to treat the patient, and/or (2) what exactly "treatment" or "rehabilitation" will encompass for this particular patient. The therapist is rarely responsible for developing or initiating legal consequences specific to a patient's failure to comply with the contents of his or her behavioral contract. In some cases an employer or legal agency is involved in the direct referral of a patient for treatment or rehabilitation. If the behavioral contract is employed in the treatment process of this patient, only to be behaviorally invalidated by the patient, the therapist should provide direct feedback on this matter to *both* the patient and the referring agency. Subsequent treatment or rehabilitation–oriented decisions rest primarily with the therapist and patient, while the various legal ramifications of the patient's behavior must be managed by the patient and the legal source of referral.

The referring person or agency will, it is hoped, consult with the therapist regarding professional treatment-oriented recommendations. When the therapist decides to treat a legally referred patient it is his or her responsibility to directly inform the patient that behavioral feedback relative to the patient and the specifics of the behavioral contract will be provided to the referral source. Psychotherapy and rehabilitation work with alcoholic patients demands this basic format. In the absence of this type of treatment format, the therapist (or agency) and the patient quite frequently become involved in a rather crazy, clandestine transactional game of "cops and robbers." Such transactions can be extremely iatrogenic.

This discussion of the legality of the behavioral contract is admittedly truncated. Three points should be stressed: (1) the legality of this document is seldom a primary concern of the patient and therapist; (2) cases in which the behavioral contract does carry explicit legal consequences for the patient should be open-ended; in other words, feedback is provided by the therapist to all parties participating in the behavioral contract and treatment program; and (3) treatment or rehabilitation efforts should not be constructed solely around the legal or behavioral consequences of the patient's failure to manage the specific content of the behavioral contract. A somewhat tangential point to be noted is that counselors and psychotherapists, as well as the other rehabilitation staff members, are responsible for treatment and rehabilitation per se. For the most part, this means that becoming involved in the politics and legality of treatment is not a primary matter of concern for the psychotherapist. Rehabilitation centers as well as psychotherapists sometimes victimize themselves to the extent of allowing political and legal figures to dictate the policy and practice of therapy and treatment (Bratter, 1980). This is at the expense of the expertise and potential for facilitating positive change specific to both professions.

Conclusion

The behavioral contract is a comprehensive treatment plan, jointly constructed by the therapist (perhaps rehabilitation agency) and the alcoholic patient. In certain cases, the spouse, employer, and significant others may be involved in the actual construction of the contract. In addition to defining the behavioral specifics of the treatment or rehabilitation process, the behavioral contract is signed by all parties involved in its construction. The patient and therapist work out the exact treatment format (treatment goals, objectives, duration, etc.) of the contract and jointly agree upon this specific program of recovery. The primary sources of therapeutic gain afforded by this treatment strategy include: (1) teaching the patient to deal more effectively with the matter of personal responsibility, (2) helping the patient make commitments, (3) setting limits, (4) conveying the therapist's concern, (5) helping the patient realize that he or she can change, grow and "recover," and (6) allowing both patient and therapist to evaluate the treatment process and outcome.

The behavioral contract is a method for concretely assessing the specific behaviors of the alcoholic patient. The concrete, treatment-related, reality-oriented aspects of the behavioral contract help the therapist-patient dyad resolve patient conflicts associated with the avoidance defense system (Forrest, 1982, 1983) and faulty self-perceptions.

The legal aspects of the behavioral contract are of little importance in most actual therapy situations. However, guidelines have been presented for utilization of the behavioral contract in therapist-patient relationships which involve the legal referral process.

Behavioral contracting is a therapeutically efficacious treatment adjunct. However, it must be emphasized that it is but one strategic component of effective psychotherapy and rehabilitation with the alcoholic patient.

References

Armor, D. J., Polich, J. M., and Stambul, H. B. *Alcoholism and Treatment.* New York: John Wiley & Sons, 1978.

Blane, H. T. *The Personality of the Alcoholic: Guises of Dependency.* New York: Harper & Row, 1968.

Bratter, T. E. The psychotherapist as advocate: extending the therapeutic alliance with adolescents. *Journal of Contemporary Psychotherapy,* 1977, *8*(*2*), 199–126.

———. The psychotherapist as a twelfth-step worker in the treatment of alcoholism. *Family and Community Health,* 1979, *2*(*2*), 31–58.

———. Advanced reality therapy techniques in the treatment of alcoholism and substance abuse. Lecture presented at Psychotherapy Associates, P.C. Sixth Annual Advanced Winter Workshop, "Treatment and Rehabilitation of the Alcoholic," Colorado Springs, Colo., Feb. 5, 1980.

Corsini, R. J. *Current Psychotherapies,* 2nd ed. Itasca, Ill.: F. E. Peacock, 1979.

Emrick, C. D. Perspectives in clinical research: relative effectiveness of alcohol abuse treatment. In S. V. Davidson, *Alcoholism and Health.* Germantown, Md.: Aspen Systems Corp., 1980.

Fann, W. E., Karacan, I., Pokorny, A. D., and Williams, R. L. *Phenomenology and Treatment of Alcoholism.* New York: SP Medical and Scientific Books, 1980.

Forrest, G. G. *The Diagnosis and Treatment of Alcoholism,* rev. 2nd ed. Springfield, Ill.: Charles C. Thomas, 1978.

———. Alcoholism, object relations, and narcissistic theory. Lecture presented at Psychotherapy Associates, P.C. Fifth Annual Advanced Winter Workshop, "Treatment and Rehabilitation of the Alcoholic," Colorado Springs, Colo., Jan. 29, 1979(a).

———. Negative and positive addictions. *Family and Community Health,* 1979(b), *2*(*2*), 103–112.

———. Alcoholism, identity, and sexuality. Lecture presented at Psychotherapy Associates, P.C. Sixth Annual Advanced Winter Workshop, "Treatment and Rehabilitation of the Alcoholic," Colorado Springs, Colo., Feb. 3, 1980.

———. *Confrontation in Psychotherapy with the Alcoholic.* Holmes Beach, Fla.: Learning Publications, 1982.

———. *Alcoholism, Narcissism, and Psychopathology.* Springfield, Ill.: Charles C. Thomas, 1983.

———. *Intensive Psychotherapy of Alcoholism.* Springfield, Ill.: Charles C. Thomas, 1984(a).

———. Psychotherapy of alcoholics and substance abusers: outcome assessment revisited. *Family and Community Health: The Journal of Health Promotion and Maintenance,* 1984(b), *7*(*2*), 40–50.

Frank, J. D. *Persuasion and Healing.* Baltimore: John Hopkins University Press, 1961.

Glasser, W. *Reality Therapy: A New Approach to Psychotherapy.* New York: Harper & Row, 1965.

Knauert, A. P. The treatment of alcoholism in a community setting. *Family and Community Health,* 1979, *2*(*1*), 91–102.

Paolino, T. J., and McCrady, P. S. *The Alcoholic Marriage: Alternative Perspectives.* New York: Grune & Stratton, 1977.

19

Special Clinical Psychotherapeutic Concerns for Alcoholic and Drug-addicted Individuals

THOMAS E. BRATTER

An Introduction: The Failure of Traditional Psychotherapy and Psychoanalysis to Meet the Clinical Challenges of Addicted Individuals

It is not coincidental that Pattison (1982), Canter (1969), and Hill and Blane (1967) suggest that the more traditional approaches of psychoanalysis and psychotherapy are relatively ineffective for addicted individuals. Responding to a volume devoted to adolescent addiction, Tyson (1982) cogently provides reasons why few psychoanalyst are willing to work with this treatment subpopulation: "Drug-dependent adolescents typically have been viewed as double pariahs, thought to be neither suitable in terms of the requirements to come, to pay, and to associate freely, nor analyzable in terms of suffering from an inner conflict from which help is sought." Gitlow (1973), p. 235), however, explicitly condemns the psychoanalytic orientation when he writes:

> A return to the psychoanalytic approach to alcoholism as a symptom dependent on some deeper psychiatric defect . . . is a therapeutically bankrupt concept abandoned by all but the most naive or unexperienced. Addicted individuals have discovered the undeniable fundamental truth that when

they elect either to inject or ingest any psychoactive substance for a brief period of time, they will feel temporary relief.

Krystal and Raskin (1970, p. 15) present the psychoanalytic view:

> The drug-dependent person invariably is seeking relief, modification or avoidance of a painful state. In his drug he has found something that he knows will put an end to unbearable tensions, pain. His own ego resources, organization, and functions suffer from impairments and defects which produce an insidious, an inexorable helplessness to deal with pain and tension without his drug.

Addicted individuals feel that their reality is too painful and unavoidable to confront without drugs, so they elect to withdraw "into a state which might best be called narcissistic tranquility," as Ostrow (1962) has described. Addicts and alcoholics feel they need drugs to sustain them. Consequently they become alienated from themselves and from non–drug users, whom they perceive, in perjorative terms, as being significantly different. Chein et al. (1964) have portrayed addicts as becoming increasingly isolated from abstinent individuals while concurrently electing to associate with those who have similar-life styles. They reject and are rejected by relatives and friends who do not subscribe to their chemical-dependent life-styles. A "we–they" dichotomy is formed. Addicts become encapsulated by their irresponsible, deceitful, and self-destructive behavior.

Glover (1932) and Rado (1933), who have influenced psychoanalytic thought, view the addict as suffering from a narcissistic disorder. Fenichel (1945), p. 385) provides the rationale for a psychoanalytic treatment orientation:

> There is still much contention over the psychoanalytic therapy of persons with . . . addictions. An understanding of the mechanisms involved makes it plain that in principle such patients are amenable to psychoanalytic treatment, but that from a practical point of view there are particular problems to be overcome. Not only is the symptom itself pleasurable . . . but besides, the pregenital narcissistic constitution of the patients makes it necessary to work back to the deepest layers, and intolerance of tension necessitates modification of technique.

Fenichel proposes a "modification of technique" but never specifies the innovations. Adams (1978) ignores Fenichel's suggestion and uses the traditional approach of "an in-depth exploration of the etiological constructs of drug dependency," which has proven ineffective with a character-disordered addicted subpopulation. Chrzanowski (1980, p. 34) suggests that "the standard approach based on a traditional psychodynamic model has limited general therapeutic applicability and usually does not work with problem patients. Neither does the transferential reactivation of past events contribute a great deal in that respect."

Traditional psychotherapy and psychoanalysis have failed to help drug and alcoholically addicted persons extricate themselves from "narcissistic tranquility" because the practitioners try to remain neutral so that patients will avoid repeating their infantile conflicts without resolving their feelings. Many psychotherapists fail to recognize that two assumptions which apply to other individuals are irrelevant for addicts: they neither wish to consider options other than getting intoxicated nor do they respect or trust the practitioner. All the erudite interpretations which produce insight persuade few to discontinue their drug-related behavior. Psychotherapists who elect to dogmatically cling to the orthodox principles of psychoanalysis rarely will achieve sufficient personal credibility and therapeutic leverage to "motivate" individuals to become abstinent. It is important to recall that Freud (1955 [1904], p. 70) believed that psychoanalysis was contraindicated for "those patients who do not possess a reasonable degree of education and a fairly reliable character. . . . Now analytic psychotherapy is not a process suited to the treatment of neuropathic degeneration; on the contrary, degeneracy acts as a hindrance to its effectiveness."

Currently psychotherapy has been modified to be relevant for people who are suffering from psychic pain and who feel dissatisfied with their lives. Therapists presumably help individuals reduce the incongruities in their lives and resolve conflicts which create pain. Addicted persons, in contrast, do not require the services of mental health practitioners to rid themselves of discomfort. They already have discovered a potent pharmacological solution. Brill (1918), p. 362) applied the Freudian construct of the pursuit of pleasure to alcoholics when he wrote: "Men are untiring pleasure seekers, and find it extremely difficult to renounce pleasure once experienced. . . . These feelings are especially enhanced by alcoholic indulgence, under which influence the grown-up again becomes a child. He derives pleasure from a free disposal of his mental stream which is now unencumbered by the restraint of logic." Addicts rationalize, furthermore, that since most psychotherapists lack personal experience regarding alcohol and drug addiction, their advice is suspect.

There can be no absolutes in the practice of psychotherapy because personalities, circumstances, environments, and potential outcomes continually change. Working with adolescents and adults who use and abuse psychoactive substances, furthermore, creates additional philosophical issues which complicate both the helping relationship and the practice of psychotherapy. After a consideration of clinical material, what behavior is appropriate and ethical for psychotherapists when they deduce that either a continuation or an escalation of drug-related behavior can culminate in permanent psychological decompensation (impairment) or result in death? What moral and legal obligations, if any, do psychotherapists have to society to protect the innocent against future crimes or to try to extinguish antisocial acts of substance abusers? Predictably, in all aspects of psychotherapy, consensus is rarely achieved; more frequently there is contradiction, confusion, and controversy. Unless psychotherapists will consider modifying their therapeutic techniques, their ways of relating and responding to addicted individuals who need to be convinced there are non-drug-related ways to achieve happiness, the recovery rate will continue to remain low. Psychotherapists who elect to abide by current professional ethical guidelines rarely will achieve the personal credibility and therapeutic leverage necessary to convince alcoholically and drug-addicted people that they can become abstinent and responsible, and in so doing, begin to justify their existence. If, in fact, psychotherapists and psychoanalysts choose not to become more humanistic, active-directive, and pragmatic, they would be advised to avoid working with an addicted subpopulation. An explanation by Googins (1984), p. 163) of some of the reasons why social workers are reluctant to work with alcoholics is pertinent to these professionals as well:

> The successful treatment of alcoholism often requires confrontation to break down the strong denial and alibi system that operates in the disease. It is unfortunate that many social workers have not incorporated this strategy . . . and thus become overwhelmed with the protracted and convoluted series of excuses, denials, and confabulations that alcoholics weave. . . . The social worker's fear of and discomfort about confronting alcoholics leave the alcoholic unchallenged and free to continue deviant drinking; the social worker is left to deal with the problem without having the appropriate tools to achieve the treatment goal.

This chapter will suggest that there needs to be a reconceptualization of the treatment relationship in view of the special psychological needs and behavior problems of an addicted subpopulation. The impact of therapeutic limit setting, violation of confidentiality, and judicious self-disclosure by the psychotherapist will be examined.

Psychotherapeutic Limit Setting: Dealing with Potentially Death-defying Drug-related Behavior

The most controversial aspcet of the treatment relationship, and rightfully so, is when psychotherapists impose themselves as the rational, restraining forces who define and enforce therapeutic limits. The three goals of limit-setting crisis intervention, according to Schulberg and

Sheldon (1968), are: (1) the elimination or modification of the potential life-threatening or dangerous behavior; (2) the reduction of the individual's participation in the dangerous situation; and (3) the external control of the person's vulnerability by a concurrent increase in coping capacity. Behavior control is a specific form of psychotherapeutic strategy for behavioral change which is justified in potential crisis situations.* Invariably, during short-term psychotherapy, the treatment goal is to induce change. Haley (1961) believes that the issue of control needs to be examined because it will be the primary determinant of outcome. "No form of therapy can avoid this problem. If the patient gains that control, he will perpetuate his difficulty, particularly if he gains it by his usual symptomatic means."

Halleck (1974) identifies three therapeutic conditions when limit setting, or, as he terms it, "coercive treatment," can be justified: (1) the person in psychotherapy has been diagnosed to be potentially self-annihilative and/or dangerous to others; (2) there exists a reasonable probability that the treatment intervention will benefit primarily the individual and secondarily significant others; (3) the person may not be competent to either recognize the necessity for therapeutic limit setting or understand the future effects of treatment. In some cases, when two of these three criteria exist, Halleck contends it may be warranted to set therapeutic limits. Central to this treatment concern would be the question of who determines the diagnosis according to what criteria. Should a dangerously incompetent individual be treated involuntarily when questions exist as to whether therapy may prove to be ineffectual? Whose interests should prevail—those of the individual or the protection of society? Should individuals whose treatment prognoses are positive be subjected to personality and behavior change when there is little concern about potential harm to themselves or danger to others? What about self-destructive or potentially dangerous individuals, who are competent to refuse treatment and have not committed any crimes? Should they be treated against their will?

Before determining whether limit setting and behavior control are necessary to the survival of the individual, the concerned clinician who elects to provide intensive psychotherapeutic services to alcoholically and drug addicted individuals and their families needs to exercise much diligence in formulating a four-dimensional diagnosis:

First: The assessment of imminent behavior that threatens the life of the patient or other people must be completed immediately by the psychotherapist. The criteria utilized in this crucial diagnosis

* Electric shock treatment, lobotomies, and drug and adversive therapy fall outside the purview of this inquiry because these are not psychotherapeutic options for drug dependence and addiction.

are similar to those employed when the individual in psychotherapy discusses a possible suicide. Khantzian (1980, p. 13) writes:

> In the initial phases of treatment, the prime concern is neither etiologies and diagnosis nor whether psychotherapy or psychotropic drugs are indicated. Rather, priority must be given to addressing the drinking behavior, understanding quickly and emphatically its present determinants, and immediately engaging the patient's cooperation to the greatest extent possible to establish control over the drinking. . . . Once I have ascertained the patient's drinking is out of control, I emphatically and empathically point out that fact and warn the patient that he is endangering himself. . . . I acknowledge how difficult it will be to stop drinking, but then share with the patient my conviction about the urgency for establishing control at the outset and how this will remain the primary focus of concern until such control is achieved.

Masterson, who agrees with Khantzian about the urgency of establishing control, believes (1972, p. 238) that when individuals may be too impulsive to control their behavior, the psychotherapist must set limits:

> Customarily, it has been thought that one must establish a relationship before one can set limits with an outpatient. In other words, one must deal quite gingerly with the issue of patient behavior, avoiding direct confrontation until enough time has elapsed for the patient to develop a positive transference. For borderline adolescents, the converse is true. Not only is it impossible to wait for a relationship to be established before starting to set limits to their acting out, but the setting of limits as early as possible is the unique means of establishing the therapeutic alliance and, indeed . . . is the very gesture of caring that the patient hungers for.

Second: The diagnostician needs to predict whether there will be any significant and permanent personality decompensation or irreversible pathology as a result of continued or escalated ingestion or injection of psychoactive substances. Wise (1970, p. 265) provides guidelines when she suggests determining

> how frequently must these drugs be used and what is the degree of pathology assigned to this? Is this rebellious behavior based on healthy self-assertiveness and self-realization in certain spheres, or is it pathologically pervasive in all relationships? . . . Can attempts at self-realization and self-identity be discerned in the esoteric interests of youth, as well as in their sometimes provocative strivings for ideals?

Obviously, the clinician must decide whether or not the individual has sufficient motivation and strength to control and contain substance abuse so that it does not result in a drug overdose. In Chapter 4,

Kauffman, Shaffer, and Burglass provided a summary of the psychological and physiological consequences of addiction.)

Third: If the patient has been selling illegal substances, the mental health practitioner needs to compute the probability of him or her being incarcerated and the probable length of incarceration. Lengths of sentences vary based on the specific substance sold, the quantity, the location, and the political climate. If a lengthy sentence appears likely, the psychotherapist may wish to devise a strategy to minimize the legal consequences. Most legal incarcerations, furthermore, no matter how brief, automatically will result in a permanent record which will deleteriously affect the individual's future vocational and educationsl options.

Fourth: An estimate regarding the individual's intactness, reality-testing ability, understanding of possible consequences of behavior, and tolerance to endure frustration and pain needs to be completed as soon as is pragmatically possible. Often it is difficult to formulate an accurate initial-tentative diagnosis because addicts and alcoholics initially remain suspicious, fearful, and dishonest. The act of self-medication, furthermore, can obfuscate crucial psychological and physical symptoms, which have been labeled by Wurmser (1978, p. XXIII) as the "hidden dimension":

> the severe inner problems underlying the compulsive use of mind-altering drugs, the use of drugs to prop up defective defenses, the interplay between individual psychopathology, severe family disorders, and socio-cultural conflicts ("collective pathology"). Drugs are not the problem. Even drug abuse is not really the core but solely the symptom hiding what it proclaims to reveal.

Not until the practitioner can understand the substance abuser's clinical dynamics and potential and probable consequences of continued drug dependence, will a relatively realistic tentative diagnosis and prognosis be formed and a judicious treatment plan be created. Modlin (1962) cautions the practitioner not to hesitate to intervene in emergency situations, which he defines as "threats of suicide, hunger strikes, ardent protestations of love, persistent self-destructive behavior." In these situations, the psychotherapist may need to respond by setting limits in an effort to preserve not only the life of the individual but also the treatment relationship.

Intervention and Limit Setting: Political and Psychotherapeutic Antecedents

With the possible exception of psychoanalysis, which provides insight—i.e., making conscious the unconscious—all forms of psychotherapy attempt to create a climate which will nurture the personal growth and development of the individual who seeks assistance. Writing from a psychoanalytic orientation, Salzman (1962), an analyst who disagrees with the more traditional conceptualization of his discipline, defines psychotherapy as a "benevolent influence" on the individual and adds: "Consequently, intervention might be considered to be the essence of the therapeutic process." Such intervention, and limit-setting techniques, may have a salutary impact on the individual who feels out of control, because the psychotherapist can be the external catalyst to create internal restraint.

The psychotherapeutic literature is replete with diverse goals of therapy: the acquisition of insight, adjustment, personal change, autonomy, problem solving, increased self-confidence, elimination of specific behavior patterns, self-actualization, increased assertiveness, and so on. While in its most simplistic form psychotherapy is a systematic intervention or intrusion into the individual's life, most persons do not require therapeutic limit setting because they can make relatively reasonable, rational, realistic, and responsible decisions.

In general, psychotherapy is based on the premise that individuals have the capacity to coexist and respect the rights of each other. In 1690 Locke concluded that government could assume people will not interfere with their neighbors' inalienable rights, which he defined as life, health, liberty, and possession (see Locke, 1894). Agreeing with Locke, Biestek (1957) suggests that clinicially speaking, freedom incorporates the premise that "the right of the individual is accompanied by the duty to respect the right of others." Hofstein (1968, p. 64) concludes that at certain times, in order to attain their potential, people must surrender their individual rights to those of society by recognizing the existence of laws and norms: "When social reality sets no limits to choice, when there are no introjected values as guidelines, the scope of alternatives for choice becomes so broad that they leave the individual confused and unable to make any choice." Locke proposed that government needs adequate power not only to control extreme abuses of people's inalienable rights but also to prohibit specific acts which can conflict with the common good. Since individuals basically are rational, reasonable, decent, and responsible, according to Locke, the government does not need great or unlimited power. Locke (1894) writes: "But though this be a state of liberty, yet it is not a state of license; though man in that state has an uncontrollable liberty to dispose of his person or possessions, yet he has not liberty to destroy himself, or so much as any creature in his possession, but where some nobler use than its bare preservation calls for it."

Locke makes a distinction between freedom and license which has profound implications for the practice of psychotherapy with individuals who temporarily have lost the capacity to control themselves. Josselyn (1952, p. 27) clarifies the distinction between freedom and license for psychotherapists:

> Although in principle our culture places value on the individual's right to choose his own pattern of self-development, in practice it penalizes those who do not recognize the difference between license and liberty. Certain controls of the behavior of individuals are essential for the maintenance of society. Such standards, however, are difficult to formulate and do not have the rigidity of the taboos of a primitive society. Because of the difficulty in formulating standards, and the complexity of translating them into the realities of social living, together with the difficulty of integrating them within the framework of individual rights, the concept of acceptable behavior is a confused one.

As long as individuals elect to recognize the validity of the rationality and constraints of society, its fundamental principles, and be responsible for themselves and to others, there is no need for external control. Individuals choose to coexist within some sort of organized order. There exists a social contract which imposes obligations and responsibilities that infringe upon the individual's freedom. Pragmatically, society's survival is dependent upon the establishment of basic goals and values. The individual is granted the freedom to select a life-style which is consistent with fundamental democratic values. When an individual disrupts the legitimate institutionalized social authority necessary for a harmonious existence, Locke contends that society has the right either to restrain or punish the offender—and this provides the concerned clinician with the moral basis for the application of therapeutic, nonpolitical limit setting. Locke (1894) stresses that "all men may be restrained from invading others' rights and from doing hurt to one another . . . whereby everyone has the right to punish the transgressors of [the law of Nature] to such a degree as may hinder its violation."

Much of Locke's appeal to psychotherapists and politicians is his portrayal of individuals as being reasonable, rational, and responsible—a portrayal which contrasts with Freud's essentially pessimistic view of people. Jones (1952) concludes that "the spirit of our Declaration, of our Constitution, and our Bill of Rights was thoroughly Lockian; indeed, our political ideal today is still the Lockian state." America has fought wars to preserve the Lockian democratic concepts of self-determinism, freedom of choice, and individuality. Psychotherapists, who are members of this society, recognize that citizens retain the right to determine a life-style predicated on choice. Implicit in this political and psychotherapeutic recognition is the assumption that, when given the freedom to select, people will make appropriate decisions which will harm neither themselves nor others.

Reflecting this essentially optimistic self-actualization view of human beings, Rogers (1946) maintains that "the individual has the capacity and the strength to devise, quite unaided, the steps which will lead him to a more mature and more comfortable relationship to his reality." Consistent with this Lockian democratic view, Rogers (1958, p. 13), when describing the characteristics of a helping relationship, asks: "Am I secure enough within myself to permit him [the individual in psychotherapy] his separateness? Can I permit him to be what he is—honest or deceitful, infantile or adult, despairing or over-confident? Can I give him the freedom to be? Or do I feel he should follow my advice, or remain somewhat dependent on me, or mold himself after me?" Rogers (1942, p. 128), however, cautions that this approach "applies to the overwhelming majority of clients, who have the capacity to achieve reasonable adequate solutions for their problems. Counseling from this viewpoint cannot be the only method for dealing with that small group—the psychotic, the defective . . . who have not the capacity to solve their own difficulties." Rogers hints at the need for additional therapeutic crisis intervention for those who cannot control their lives but never specifies what types of assistance may be necessary.

Potter and Austin (1938) identify a professional concern which Rogers elects not to confront that still remains unresolved for all mental health professionals and practitioners: "Social workers as a group and as individuals fear—as a Puritan feared witchcraft—the use of the word 'authoritative' in speaking of their own approach or technique." More recently, Szasz has protested against the abrogation of individual rights and freedom by the state. When society prevents an individual from exercising personal choice, then the person's rights (which have some political, psychotherapeutic, and philosophical validity) are violated. In observing that police departments arrest significantly more colored (black, brown, red, and yellow) addicts and pushers than white, Pierce (1973), who condemns the repressive drug laws of the Nixon administration, angrily contends: "If anyone in society lives in a police state, then society is a police state, even if some pretend that unfair and repressive measures can affect only disenfranchised minority folk." Pierce perhaps exaggerates to illustrate his thesis, yet the underlying issue is important. When a conflict of interest occurs between the state and the individual, at what point can personal freedom be restricted and can the state intervene? Under existing legal statutes, all individuals who elect to use drugs without a physician's supervision and approval are violating the intent of societal laws. More significant than the consideration of whether society should be granted the power to legislate morality is the realistic issue that many individuals commit crimes involving innocent third parties in order to finance their purchase of drugs. Many psychotherapists share Szasz's (1971) concern that the state threatens the individual's right to self-determination by attempting to legislate morality. Tragically, many psychotherapists confuse Szasz's political contention and become reluctant to intervene when individuals engage in potentially life-threatening behavior. Some psychotherapists believe that in order to respect self-determination, they need to maintain a neutral, analytic, objective posture which entails neither values nor standards. By remaining uninvolved, these psychotherapists may be denying the concept of personal choice. Those who refuse to intervene and define limits suggest that any action, no matter how well-intentioned, is an attempt to control and to rule another. Kubie (1964) raises the clinical consideration that "we must ask whether we want to prevent every suicide if such an effort will render us therapeutically impotent." Szasz (1973) objects to medical paternalism which regulates drug usage. Since the essence of a democratic society is free choice, the political activist psychiatrist believes all adults retain the right to medicate themselves. Szasz, therefore, rejects the traditional notion that only physicians have the right to prescribe medication. Since adults have the right to "buy, possess, and consume alcoholic beverages," Szasz believes they should retain the prerogative to purchase psychoactive drugs. Szasz (1973, p. 7) argues that the same conditions can prevail for psychoactive drugs as for alcohol:

> Regardless of how offensive drunkenness might be to a person, he cannot interfere with another person's right to become inebriated so long as that person drinks in the privacy of his own house or at some other appropriate location, and so long as the drinker conducts himself in an otherwise law-abiding manner. In short, we have a right to become intoxicated—in private. Public intoxication is considered an offense against others and is therefore a violation of the criminal law. . . . Acts that may injure others—such as driving a car—should, when carried out in a drug-intoxicated state, be punished especially strictly and severely.

Psychologists, psychiatrists, and social workers have apparently confused the concepts of authoritarianism with authority, as has Szasz (see Bratter et al., 1985). Authoritarianism is the domination of one person by another who has an ulterior motive. There is an element of self-gain which characterizes authoritarianism; conformity, subordination, dependence, and material gain are involved. Authoritarianism is a noxious relationship in which the powerful profit at the expense of the impotent. Generally, there is no attempt by the powerful to neutralize the power relationship and replace it by one of equality. The aim of authoritarianism is control. Perhaps the best examples of authoritarianism would be those of prison administration or an oligarchy, in which the goals are care, custody, conformity, and control of individuals. In contrast, Hollis (1964) suggests that the primary ingredients of the application of authority in a social work context are derived from a "clinical understanding of the nature of superego defects (delinquency and character disorders)[;] the definition, when necessary of limits within treatments . . . [and] a relationship which is fundamentally a giving one on the part of the worker." Studt (1959) conceptualizes authority as a unique interpersonal relationship in which the social worker attempts to influence the behavior of the client. Sheriffs (1953), who adds another dimension to therapeutic authority, believes its application helps "to open up the possibility for an improved life in the future," motivating individuals to begin to use, rather than to continue to abuse, their talents and assets.

The reluctance or refusal by psychotherapists to set treatment limits appears to be a misunderstanding of the humanistic values of self-actualization and freedom of choice. In emphasizing only the rights of the individual, there is no recognition of the rights of others. To free the individual from all restraint while attempting to provide absolute freedom would be unrealistic. Absolute freedom is synonymous with anarchy. Even in totalitarian societies, there is some freedom which negates the concept of absolute control.

Chwast (1957, p. 817) addresses the controversy regarding therapeutic limit setting—which some view as behavior and thought control—when he writes that while he "fully appreciates the values of . . . the therapist's democratic acceptance of the right to self-determination of the client, some adaptation of this principle which emphasizes the helpful role of control and authority with antisocial clients . . . requires consideration."

The Legislation of Morality by Society or the Protection of Individual Rights?—a Psychotherapeutic Treatment Issue

Szasz addresses an important philosophical issue when he asks whether a democratic society can legislate morality. Does the government have the obligation to protect individuals against potential psychological and physical harm by prohibiting individual freedom? The Supreme Court determined that society can infringe upon individual choice for the promotion and protection of public health. The state has the right, as *Jacobson* v. *Massachusetts* (1904) illustrates, to require an individual to be vaccinated against his wishes. Currently, the Supreme Court is considering whether involuntarily hospitalized mental patients have the constitutional right to refuse medication. Applebaum (1982, p. 58) portrays the philosophical dilemma which the Supreme Court must resolve:

> Although the desire to affirm the autonomy of involuntarily committed psychiatric patients is certainly admirable, the most nagging question is whether granting them a right to refuse treatment is an appropriate means to that end. That such a move would subvert society's interest in seeing these people restored to the highest level of functioning is undisputed. . . . Does it make sense to protect individual autonomy by allowing someone to remain severely mentally ill, when the illness itself may be at least as destructive of autonomy as forced treatment and, if left untreated, of much longer duration?

Robitscher (1969, p. 305) affirms the state's right to protect its citizens by utilizing legislation as it applies to the issue of self-medication which Szasz discussed:

> Without going into such questions as the relationship between drug use and escalation to more addicting drugs, to crime, to driving accidents; without consideration of how pathological drug users may be and whether they use drugs as defenses against depression, acting out, loss of identity and whether this use of drugs compounds instead of cures their problems, or to what extent drug-taking and efforts to destructure represent urges to destruction aimed against the self and society as well, we can ask if drug use is compatible with the continuation of such structured institutions as family and government which provide the framework in which individual liberties can be protected by the law.

The Threat of Suicide: To Intervene Therapeutically or Not to Intervene?

It would appear incomprehensible without examining the underlying philosophical assumptions, but a significant number of eminent psychotherapists contend that individuals retain the right to commit suicide without any intervention by the mental health professional—which implies sub rosa approval. There exists a countertherapeutic confusion between the political-philosophical proposition of self-determination and freedom of choice, on one hand, and the self-actualization goal of psychotherapy, on the other. Central to the political-philosophical orientation are the democratic personal liberties guaranteed by the Constitution regarding individuality and freedom of choice. Rather than debate this multifaceted issue, the majority of psychotherapists, when confronted by the threat of a patient's suicide, immediately would refer the individual to an inpatient setting and in so doing circumvent the profound professional issue which involves the selection of dangerous drug–related, death-defying behavior versus the decision to survive and live. Szasz (1973) argues: "I don't see how anyone can take seriously the ideal of personal self-determination and responsibility and not insist on his right to take anything he wants to take. . . . But a person must, if he is to be free, have the right to poison and kill himself." Szasz creates a curious paradox for psychotherapists like Litman (1965), who naively exacerbates the issue when he indicates a reluctance to respond decisively to the urgency and emergency of an impending suicidal act. Indeed, earlier Litman (1959) articulates his indifference to the fact that the patient might attempt suicide. He compounds the problem by stating that the psychotherapist can reject any responsibility for the patient's death by suicide!

In cases of a life-or-death struggle, there can be no confusion by the psychotherapist between the act of attempting to prolong the person's life and the possible longer-term adverse reactions. Lesse (1975) defines the treatment goal when working with suicidal individuals as being "to save a patient's life, nothing more; nothing less." The management and treatment of potentially suicidal persons will force the psychotherapist not only to take therapeutic risks but also to recognize that it is impossible to prevent all suicides. By virtue of an active-directive crisis intervention approach for individuals who are potentially suicidal, psychotherapists can reaffirm their positive regard for the value and dignity of life. Bratter (1975, p. 98) had criticized those psychotherapists who by their inaction and apathy elect not to intervene and extinguish life-threatening behavior when he rhetorically asks:

> Can we be therapeutically immobilized to the democratic ideal of freedom when we believe the client/patient may die of an overdose? If viewed from this perspective, the benign neglect by the psychotherapist appears to be the ultimate irresponsible and non-caring act. When clients/patients are encouraged explicitly by a lack of crisis intervention by the psychotherapist to indulge their feelings when they feel like killing themselves, it must be considered more than a misguided act; it is accessory to murder.

Ironically, perhaps, the most significant philosophical examination of the controversial issue of life-saving therapeutic limit setting has been made in a play, *Whose Life Is It Anyway?* The play describes an intellectually sensitive and alert paraplegic (Ken) who decides he no longer wishes to live in a continual state of dependency on hospital personnel. The attending physician (Dr. Emerson) refuses to prostitute his professional ethics and permit the patient to die by deliberate and systematic starvation. Here lies the conflict which has profound relevance for psychotherapists. The playwright, Clark (1980), cogently capsulizes the physician's philosophical opposition to permitting the patient to die. Dr. Emerson states: "It is my duty as a doctor to preserve life!" Emerson usurps the patient's right to make the decision because he believes Ken is depressed and therefore remains incapable "of making a rational choice about his life." A psychiatrist, who has been retained by the patient, challenges the physician's conclusion by diagnosing the depression to be reactive rather than endogenous. The psychiatrist concludes that the patient is "reacting in a perfectly rational way to a very bad situation." The moral-legal dilemma is appropriately defined when Ken protests that he lacks the right to decide: "If I choose to live, it would be appalling if society killed me. If I choose to die, it is equally appalling if society keeps me alive." Whose value system should prevail? Does the patient retain the right to elect to commit suicide or can the physician intercede and decide for the individual? In real life, a patient has a number of options which were not explored in the play. He could discharge his physician and find one who will honor his death desire. He could refuse to eat. The physician could withdraw from the case. The play ends before the patient, who wins the right to make the determination, dies, so the reader never knows the conclusion.

Halleck (1971, pp. 159–178) addresses the issue of the psychiatrist's role when an individual either discloses a potential suicide attempt or threatens to kill someone. The physician-psychiatrist is obligated to intervene to preserve life, even if it entails some sort of coercive strategy, because

> the value of saving a person's life should still, in most instances, take precedence over the value of his freedom to take his own life. Suicide is a form of violence that diminishes respect for life throughout an entire society; it is self-murder. . . . It can increase the possibility of subsequent suicide attempts among the surviving members of the victim's family. . . . Suicide is irreversible. It destroys the possibility of discovering alternative means for solving one's difficulties. [pp. 163–164]

If psychotherapy and medicine can be reduced to their lowest common denominator, the primary concern would be with survival—i.e., life, living, and health. With the introduction of sophisticated life-saving support systems and apparatus, hospital personnel are confronted by the issue of when "to pull the plug" if a person's normal existence no longer is possible—lest someone with a more optimistic prognosis die by being deprived of the machine. Hospitals during the ninth decade of the twentieth century have retained philosophers to debate the specifics. Recently, psychotherapy has included death and dying within its discipline. Psychotherapy can assist terminal patients and their families to prepare for the inevitability of death and to plan how to die with dignity. Currently there is a debate regarding the validity of the concept of euthanasia and the legal definition of death which tangentially will affect the practice of psychotherapy. Do therapists have the right to restrain those who may be committing self-destructive acts which will kill them or will affect them deleteriously in the future? What about the youthful LSD or PCP user? What about the alcoholic? Psychotherapy with substance abusers must resolve the issue of therapeutic intervention and produce guidelines for ethical and professional behavior.

Therapeutic for Justification Limit Setting: A Brief Review of the Psychotherapeutic Literature on Acting-out Delinquent Adolescents

Many psychotherapeutic orientations have offered explanations regarding impulsive, self-destructive behavior. To change and control potentially self-annihilative behavior may require that the psychotherapist intervene, defining and enforcing behavior limits so that the life-threatening behavior can be contained and ameliorated. Vaillant (1969, p. 310) provides the justification for the therapeutic constraint of the addicted individual:

> To alter self-destructive behavior may require controlled intervention. . . . But to suggest that such intervention should occur raises the specter of thought control. . . . Probably, the authoritarian treatment of addiction . . . is effective not because it punishes, but because it enforces. By providing external support, such treatment meaningfully cares about the addict's needs. Perhaps, the management of drug abusers should resemble the management of ignorance or immaturity.

Most of the psychotherapeutic literature which discusses the issues of intervention and limit setting pertains to juvenile and adolescent delinquents. Bromberg and Rodgers (1946), who write about their treatment experiences with older adolescent delinquents, emphasize that those with inadequate superego formation require an authoritative treatment approach. Symonds (1974, p. 365) recounts a humorous, but clinically valid, example of an authoritative treatment approach when immediate limit setting enhanced the formation of a helping relationship between an "action-oriented twelve-year-old who exhibited reflexive behavior" and a worker:

> A new worker was placed in charge of the cottage where Charles lived. He met her and asked, "Did they tell you about me?" She said, "No." And he repeated, "Didn't they tell you about me?" She again said, "No." Charles then asked, "Didn't they tell you that I throw chairs at workers when I don't get my way?" She said, "No," and continued, "Did they tell you about me?" Charles said, "No." She then said, "Didn't they tell you about me?" Charles said, "No." The worker then said, "Didn't they tell you I would break your motherfucking head if you threw a chair at me?"

Symonds reports that Charles confided to him that the worker "is the only one I can trust and talk to. She tells me true. She don't let me get away with nothing." This controlled crisis provoking confrontation by the psychotherapist can reassure the adolescent that his potentially self-destructive or sadistic behavior can be curtailed. The more traditional passive or permissive orientation often can be mistaken by adolescent delinquents as being similar to the confused or disinterested parental responses to them. When the therapist can assume an active-directive approach, in contrast, which includes the ability to define and set limits for maladjustive behavior, a treatment structure can be provided in which superego development can occur. Adler and Shapiro (1973, p. 551) concur with a limit-setting approach, based on their experience with aggressive, acting-out patients, when they conclude:

> Any limit-setting intervention does ultimately extract a price the therapist has to pay later, for example, arousing omnipotent fantasies about the therapist after such an intervention that have to be resolved in future treatment. But, without the intervention, therapy may be impossible, for the patient frequently does not have the choices ascribed to him. Instead, he often can only repeat earlier patterns; to flee instead of acting impulsively, or to put an aggressive, destructive fantasy into action. If the therapist chooses not to intervene, he risks losing the patient, who may have no choice but to view the therapist as the same as his non-caring, non-protective parents.

Grossbard (1962, p. 3) attributes uncontrolled, self-destructive acting-out by adolescent delinquents to defective ego development rather than superego deficiencies. Adolescents tend to act out their conflicts rather than to resolve them by rational means or symptom formation. Consequently, the therapist

> must first create a situation that will stimulate the delinquent's capacity to form object relationships and to internalize images. The delinquent must be provided with an experience in the present through which he can master the learning problems of the early developmental years. He needs a living rather than a reliving experience. The therapist does not represent to the delinquent, as he does to the neurotic, a maternal or paternal figure. Instead, the therapist functions as a surrogate parent to the delinquent.

Leventhal and Sills (1963) and Cohen and Grinspoon (1963) suggest that these impulsive adolescents require external controls. Based on their experiences with delinquent adolescent males, Jacobs and Christ (1967) advocate that the group psychotherapist "must provide the model for what is right; he is the ego ideal for the boys and must stand up and be counted in this regard. He must be able to state explicitly what can and what cannot be done and must be prepared to back up his words with actions." This position had been described by Redl and Wineman (1957) as the "technique of authoritative *verboten*. . . . We simply say No, and we say it in such a way that it is clear that we mean it and don't soften it up by arguing, explaining."

The judicious and therapeutic application of rational authority can curtail life-threatening behavior by imposing a series of coercions and controls. Brill and Lieberman (1969, p. 15) articulate the treatment rationale:

> In the sense of providing a firm structuring of the treatment relationship, setting limits, and providing controls through the use of a graduated series of sanctions, it was conjectured that rational authority might minimize the addict's acting-out behavior, help him grow within the structure and internalize the controls he lacks, and, hopefully, help him give up his destructive way of life.

Utilizing more humanistic language but agreeing with his predecessors, Samorajczyk (1971) poetically assumes that alienated, acting-out adolescents "want to know where the limits are—and that someone 'gives a damn' enough to guide [them] in [their] search of what's expected of [them]."

Limit Setting with Individuals Involuntarily in Psychotherapy

At the earliest appropriate time, as Bratter (1980) notes, the psychotherapist needs to ascertain if the individual has voluntarily decided to begin a treatment relationship or is responding to external pressures from either significant others or the environment. Frequently, family members might have learned that drug-related behavior has escalated beyond casual or recreational use. A relative may have discovered pills, a hypodermic syringe, prescriptions, empty bottles. An adverse drug reaction could have necessitated a visit to the hospital or a physician. Sometimes the patient fears retribution from drug associates or detection by the police. Bratter (1980) has discussed the specifics of negotiating with individuals who feel pressured to attend psychotherapy.

Under optimal treatment conditions, individuals in psychotherapy formulate goals, assume responsibility for their behavior, and play an active part in the recovery process. Often addicted individuals do not wish to achieve abstinence; they wish to decrease the degree of their drug dependence. Beier (1952) has defined a reluctant individual as one whose resistance toward terminating symptoms is more intense than the desire for help. Redl (1966) suggests that resistance occurs when there is a vested interest in protecting pathology and thereby maintaining a homeostatic condition. Few mental health practitioners would argue that candidates for psychotherapy, whenever possible, be given a choice regarding what treatment services will be offered, how these services will be delivered, and by whom. When the court has stipulated that psychotherapy will be a requirement for remaining in the community, there needs to be an explicit understanding by all concerned parties regarding reporting procedures and accountability. The ultimate decision that will affect the substance-abusing individual will be made by the correctional agency which retains legal jurisdiction. The psychotherapist needs to negotiate specifically, before agreeing to become involved, as to how influential the information shared will be in determining the decision-making process. There may be times when continued or escalated substance abuse could therapeutically warrant inpatient treatment, and other situations when no action would be required. Issues of intervention and reporting must be acceptable to the individual seeking psychotherapy before any meaningful helping relationship can be formed. Kittrie (1971), analyzing the ramifications of enforced therapy, has suggested the need for legal guidelines and limitations which psychotherapists and institutions must recognize and respect for those who wish "to be different." When a correctional agency has a supervisory role and commensurate power to insist that unless behavioral changes are initiated, incarceration can result, this can provide the psychotherapist with much leverage. However, there needs to be a dispassionate examination of the potential for abuse of power by the therapist as well as the individual's legitimate right to refuse not only to undergo treatment but also to change. Psychotherapy can be considered in its most benign state as a form of social control whereby the individual is encouraged to alter behavior patterns so as to become more acceptable to society.

Dumont (1973, p. 538) warns about potential dangers of involuntary incarceration:

> People are incarcerated in prisons, but civilly committed to treatment programs. When treatment programs are concerned with issues of custody and security, they function like prisons but maintain the rhetoric and righteousness of hospitals. They develop an institutional press, which calls the individual sick but treats him like a criminal. The confusion of the patient role with its connotations of helplessness and dependency and the criminal role with its implications of deviancy and willfulness has profoundly destructive mental health implications.

Lindblom (1965) discusses the strategic utilization of authority, which becomes a type of persuasion. Thorne (1968, p. 285) writes: "Usually persuasion and advice involve dominance-submission ratios in which an attempt is made to 'convert' the client to the advisor's conceptions of a more adequate style of living. This dominance-submission ratio implies a degree of influence which may or may not be healthy for the client, since it removes responsibility from him for the regulation of his own conduct."

Murdach (1980) recognizes that the individual and the psychotherapist may possess divergent views regarding both the presenting problem and the solution. The probability for a conflict of interest between the referral source, the individual in psychotherapy, and the therapist is omnipresent. Before a meaningful treatment relationship can be established, a mutually acceptable compromise must be achieved. Often the psychotherapist is placed in a treatment situation where a choice needs to be made. If an adolescent, who currently is on probation, for example, confides to the psychotherapist that he plans to use the family car to secure illicit drugs, there are a number of possibilities. The psychotherapist elects to honor confidentiality and, aside from attempting to discourage the adolescent, do nothing. Obviously, either the probation department or the parents could be notified. Aside from obvious ethical and humanistic considerations, will the psychotherapist be subjected to future legal action should the adolescent have an accident, hurting or killing himself or the other occupants of the car and/or innocent bystanders? To whom does the psychotherapist owe loyalty: the adolescent, his family, the court?

Rational Authority: The Rationale for Therapeutic Limit Setting

Despite all diligent efforts to prove the contrary, the psychotherapist who works with addicts and alcoholics personifies authority which potentially can force the cessation of drug use. Rather than waste time denying the reality of authority, the psychotherapist needs to discuss the issue of limit setting with addicted individuals. Krasner (1962, pp. 4–5) writes:

> Most therapists are uncomfortable in a role labeled as a "controller" or "manipulator" of behavior. The evidence . . . is . . . this is an accurate description of what the therapist's role actually is. . . . The therapist . . . has the power to influence and control the behavior and values of other human beings. For the therapist not accept this situation and to be continually unaware of influencing effects of his behavior on his patients would in itself be unethical.

No matter what the setting, initially the addicted individual views the psychotherapist as being a powerful representative of society. Often there are significant age and status differences between the psychotherapist and the drug-dependent person, which also creates the aura of authority. There are some exceptions, when the addicted person has achieved more power and status than the psychotherapist, and such a situation needs to be resolved before a treatment relationship can be established.

Unless the psychotherapist becomes active and assertive, in all probability drug-dependent persons will not terminate their addictive life-styles. When the psychotherapist represents rational authority, addicted individuals will remain in treatment against their wishes until they can tolerate tension, will become less self-destructive, will understand the realistic demands of society, and will begin to assume responsibility for their behavior. The application of rational authority by the psychotherapist helps substance abusers begin resolving their resistances to treatment, begin creating a therapeutic alliance, and begin controlling their self-annihilative actions. By insisting that addicts continue their treatment while concurrently setting limits, the psychotherapist can help them to reorient their attitudes and restructure their relationships so as to maximize their chances to exist within the social system. Soden (1961) has termed this process, which utilizes compulsion, rational authority, and limit setting, "constructive coercion."

Kelman (1952, p. 58) has defined a person's feeling of rational authority as being something that is

> open to and encourages rational discerning evaluations by that person and others. It [rational authority] therefore is not concerned with its perpetuation for its own sake but with its affirmation or negation on rational grounds. Such a rational feeling is based on rational cooperation, participation, conflict. It allows for, derives from, and encourages rational change and rational growth. It is extended and expanded through a number of sequences of the giving-receiving process.

Tiebout stresses the importance of confronting the malignant aspects of drinking immediately. Until alcoholics agree to limit their drinking, there can be no therapy. More than twenty years ago, discuss the specifics of therapeutic intervention, limit setting, and rational authority, Tiebout (1962, pp. 78–79):

> Intervention has a stopping, curbing, controlling action. It is an essential step when the individual loses his capacity to restrain himself. . . . The effect of hitting bottom . . . [puts] the alcoholic through an experience of crisis during which he [feels] extreme anguish and despair, making him unable to continue to be indifferent toward his drinking problem. . . . Intervention thus functions in two directions: It takes over when the individual needs to be checked, and it acquaints him with the fact that a world exists outside himself. . . . Intervening was found to be effective in conditions other than alcoholism, leading to the conclusion that the therapeutic role of necessity contains elements which seem in conflict

and probably are to some extent. This fact every therapist must accept. He cannot simplify his role because he does have a dual responsibility. He must be firm without being overbearing and he must be kind without being soft. He must teach his patient that intervention is not a manifestation of hostility but a message from reality. When that position is taken, the therapist can operate with maximum effectiveness.

Confidentiality: Historical Precedents

Purrington (1906, p. 391) reports that "during the 1820's and 1830's, a person sedulously wanted to conceal from the community the fact that he was the victim of some 'dreadful disease.' . . . With confidence protected by the law, people were encouraged to have a checkup." New York State in 1828 enacted legislation which prohibited physicians and surgeons from disclosing any personal information which was acquired professionally. There were provisions protecting the confidentiality of the patient. The intent of the New York State law was to create the necessary climate for the patient to discuss any information that would help the physician not only make the appropriate diagnosis but also form an effective treatment plan while concurrently protecting the patient from being ostracized.

In 1959, Georgia became the first state to grant privileged communication protection to psychiatrists. Before the twentieth century, the law had neglected to provide any legal guidelines affirming the right to privacy. Warren and Brandeis (1890) were the first to petition the Court to demand that Warren had the right to be protected from public scrutiny by the newspapers regarding his family's personal affairs when his daughter decided to marry. Significantly, aside from Westin's (1967) seminal work, there have been relatively few scholarly and legal attempts to discuss the issues of the right to privacy and the parameters of confidentiality. Currently, there exists much confusion about and conflict between professional ethics and various state and federal statutes.

Patients, clients, and parishioners have been guaranteed confidentiality by physicians, attorneys, the clergy, psychiatrists, psychologists, and social workers. Although religion and psychiatry have divergent orientations, Ewalt and Farnsworth (1963, p. 299) note several similarities:

> Both disciplines begin with the desire to help people. . . . The relationship of psychiatrists and clergymen to those they help is based on concern, sensible involvement, sympathy, and a respect for the dignity of the individual. This latter element is expressed in part in the tradition of privileged communication, a tradition long upheld by custom, although seldom by

> law. The patient or parishioner is encouraged to place full confidence in the psychiatrist or clergyman—in fact, this confidence is almost absolutely necessary to effective treatment—and he may rest assured that what he discloses in the course of consultation will remain completely confidential.

The helping professions assume individuals will be reluctant to seek assistance unless they are reassured their disclosures will be confidential. The law has attempted to provide individuals with some protection. In *Taylor* v. *United States* (1955), the court concluded that "a psychiatrist must have his patient's confidence or he cannot help him." The Group for the Advancement of Psychiatry (1960) concurs with the *Taylor* decision, because even if courts are deprived of some relevant information by a psychiatrist's refusal to divulge confidential data, "the social value which effective psychiatric treatment has for the community far outweighs the potential loss of evidence." Ironically, Frank (1945), an attorney, provides a legal perspective which parallels the Group for the Advancement of Psychiatry's mandate: "The lawyer aims at victory, at winning the fight, not at aiding the court to discover the facts."

The proponents of absolute confidentiality claim that many will refuse psychotherapy rather than risk detection, exposure, and embarrassment. Slawson (1969) recommends that "the psychotherapist-patient relationship be absolute . . . free of exception and not subject to waiver by the patient." Hollander (1965) and Siegel (1976) elaborate on the rationale of absolute confidentiality. Langs (1976a) proposes that the exclusive one-to-one relationship with total confidentiality remain the nucleus of the treatment alliance, because any deviation would impact negatively upon the analyst's objectivity. Perr (1971), wanting to protect the anonymity of patients, views the potential for abuse by the release of privileged data to constitute a breach of the right to privacy. Slovenko (1960) emphasizes that psychotherapy is a special relationship which discusses "confidential personal revelations about matters which the patient is and should be normally reluctant to discuss. Frequently, a patient in analysis will make statements to his psychiatrist which he would not make even to the closest members of his family." The inviolability of confidentiality is essential, Slovenko and Usdin (1966) contends, because "psychotherapy affords a corrective emotional experience—it would be grave indeed if the therapist also turned out to be a traitor. It is of the utmost importance for the therapist to be honest with the patient. The therapist must be trustworthy." In *People* v. *Newman* (1973), the director of a methadone clinic refused to permit the authorities to view photographs of patients although an eyewitness thought she had seen the murderer attend the clinic. Many states have enacted laws pertaining to confidentiality and privileged communication which prevent psychotherapists from divulging information without patients' previous consent. Jagim, Wittman, and Noll (1978) warn, however:

> Absolute confidentiality refers to the ethical position which demands that the therapist not break confidentiality under any circumstances. In many states, a position of absolute confidentiality would conflict with legal statutes requiring disclosure of information in certain circumstances in which the welfare of others is endangered. Thus, it is possible that a therapist who adheres to absolute confidentiality would be in violation of the law.

More recently, Weinstein and Berger (1981, p. 506) have concluded that the patient possesses

> a privilege to refuse to disclose and to prevent any other person from disclosing confidential communications made for the purpose of diagnosis or treatment of his [physical], mental or emotional condition including alcohol or drug addiction, among himself, his [physician or] psychotherapist, and persons who are participating in the diagnosis or treatment under the direction of the [physician or] psychotherapist, including members of the patient's family.

Recognizing the person's right to expect confidentiality, furthermore, professional societies actively have pressured the courts to hold sacrosanct the conversations and confessions of therapeutic relationships. Fromm-Reichmann (1950), Greenacre (1954), and Menninger (1958)—all prominent psychoanalysts—never have suggested total confidentiality because each has described conditions under which some contact with relatives can be justified to obtain crucial background information. This type of deviation, authorized by the patient, implies that confidentiality is not an absolute. Roth and Meisel (1982) discuss therapeutic strategies which involve social and environmental manipulations. The psychotherapist can request or demand that the individual in treatment cease and desist from any potentially self-destructive or violent act(s) and make it a condition for continued therapy. The psychotherapist also retains the right to discuss the possibility of breaching confidence should the act(s) either continue or escalate. Ideally, the mental health practitioner initially should attempt to obtain the individual's consent and then make the call during a session in the presence of the individual. The Constitution protects persons against incriminating themselves by giving them the prerogative to "plead the Fifth Amendment" and remain silent in the face of any charge, no matter how heinous, without exception. This section does not wish to challenge the sanctity of confidentiality as an important ingredient in medicine, law, psychotherapy, and religion, but instead desires to suggest that some modifications can be in the best interest of the individual.

The Psychotherapist as a Double Agent: The Rights of Society versus the Rights of the Individual

The courts already has legislated exceptions to maintaining confidentiality when the physician is required to divulge the identity of a patient who has contracted a communicable disease. The psychiatrist and physician are protected by law and indemnified when they protect the welfare of the community. In *A. B.* v. *C. D.* (1905), for example, a physician alerted the patient's wife to the fact that her husband had contracted a venereal disease which was thought to be contagious. In another case, *Simonsen* v. *Swenson* (1920), after diagnosing syphilis, the physician suggested that the patient vacate the hotel in which he was residing to avoid infecting others. When the patient refused, the physician notified the hotel manager to disinfect the room. The physician consequently was sued. The courts ruled in favor of the physician on the basis of public policy—i.e., *salus populi suprema lex.* A contemporary legal dilemma which still has not been resolved is whether a physician can report a bus driver or pilot who may have a history of alcohol or drug addiction. Britton (1975, p. 31) asks:

> What may physicians reveal from medical records and to whom? To what extent will courts protect patients when revealing information to their physicians? Case law is sparse; guidance must come from the logic in the few extant decisions and in analogous areas of the law. Several theories of law might be employed, including conversion of property, equality, breach of contract, and negligence, as well as invasion of privacy.

Sidel (1961, p. 1133) recognizes the validity of confidentiality but nevertheless realizes that there will be specific situations when disclosure will be warranted: When the patient communicates to the psychotherapist, "Please protect me from my urge. This is usually true also of the patient who tells the doctor that he plans to commit suicide. The doctor will not hesitate to make appropriate revelations to prevent violence, either self-inflicted or inflicted on others, because in so doing, he is furthering his professional goals for his patient and his community."

Menninger (1952, p. 176) in a sense, refutes confidentiality when he presents another perspective regarding the responsibilities of the psychiatrist-physician:

> It is true that the physician has a loyalty to his patient and a responsibility for treating the professional relationship with respect and honor. But the doctor also has other responsibilities . . . to society, to the hospital, to the rest of the medical profession, and to science. No patient has a right to exploit the confidential relationship offered by the physician *a particeps*

> *criminis.* The physician cannot condone moral and legal irresponsibility on the part of the patient and to do so may be actually harmful to the patient. For example, a patient comes to a VA hospital with certain psychiatric symptoms and in the course of his history, he confesses that he has been receiving compensation for self-inflicted gunshot wounds, which he had claimed were received in combat. The psychiatrist who receives this information has no right to withhold from the hospital clinical record the fact that the patient has been defrauding the government, even though this confession was made in confidence.

Szasz (1967), in describing the potential conflict of interest the psychotherapist may have to resolve, refers to the therapist's "double agent" role. To whom does the psychotherapist have a primary obligation—the individual or society? Noll (1974, p. 4) discusses the need for selective confidentiality (to which Menninger probably would agree) when he uses the example "If a patient tells a doctor in confidence that he has brought a time bomb into the hospital and hidden it under the bed of one of the other patients, it is the strange doctor indeed who would feel this professional confidence should not be violated."

Recently, there appears to be a modification regarding the justification for absolute confidentiality. In 1974 (*Tarasoff* v. *Regents of the University of California*) a psychologist who worked in a university outpatient clinic was notified by a patient of his intention to murder a woman when she returned from vacation. Immediately the psychologist discussed the situation with the supervising psychiatrist, who alerted the campus police about the threat. Subsequently, the campus police interviewed the individual but released him when he promised not to molest the victim. Two months later, the murder was committed. The court found that "the public policy favoring protection of the confidential character of patient-psychotherapist communication must yield in instances in which disclosure is essential to avert danger to others. The protective privilege ends where the public peril begins." Bersoff (1976) wonders whether psychotherapists, as a result of the *Tarasoff* decision, will expand their roles to be protectors and policemen. Bersoff advises psychotherapists to notify clients that there may be times when confidentiality will not be legally binding. Failure to alert a client "can result in both loss of liberty and privacy to the client as well as loss to the clinician of reputation and money damages to unwarned victims."

The appeal of *Tarasoff* v. *Regents of the University of California* (1976) did not resolve the primary issue regarding the therapist's "duty to warn" because there was no litigation, so the court never determined whether the therapist had been negligent. Dix (1981) concludes that the failure to warn can be circumvented by alternative action. Siegel (1979, p. 253) presents the more traditional viewpoint:

> If the psychologist had accepted the view of absolute, inviolate confidentiality, he might have been able to have kept Poddar in treatment, saved the life of Tatania Tarasoff, and avoided what was to become the *Tarasoff* decision. Indeed, if the psychologist in this case rejected the judgmental role of considering Poddar "dangerous," there would probably have been no liability on his part. The only potential protection for Ms. Tarasoff was for the psychologist to keep Poddar in treatment, and this was eliminated when he contacted the police.

It is, indeed, curious that Siegel believes that the psychologist was judgmental. It would seem that to diagnose Poddar as "not dangerous" would have been equally judgmental. Had the campus police stipulated to Poddar that unless he continued psychotherapy with either the same clinic or found another therapist, he would have been subjected to inpatient treatment, perhaps the eventual murderer could have been persuaded to seek additional assistance. Denkowski and Denkowski (1982, p. 374) state that "until a *Tarasoff*-like case is actually litigated, it remains questionable whether warning endangered third parties is the only reasonable action in any situation. The fact that suits similar to *Tarasoff* have not been reported over the past four years implies a legal opinion that counselors are not bound by a 'duty to warn.' " Moore-Kirkland and Irey (1981, p. 319) suggest that

> to define confidentiality only in relation to the one-on-one psychotherapeutic process between worker and client places unnecessary limits on social workers. The definition of confidentiality must deal with people in their social environments—the very relationship that social work claims as its unique focus. Social workers cannot view individuals—including individuals in their relationship to workers—apart from the social context.

In a development related to the *Tarasoff* case, the court refused to require credentialed mental health workers to violate confidentiality regarding suicides. In *Bellah* v. *Greenson* (1977), the court refused to hold Dr. Greenson liable for the suicide of Bellah because there was no duty to protect—which implies that there was no duty to warn. Yet the California court found that Greenson statutorily was permitted to alert the family, though he could not be found guilty of failure to do so. Liability can result only when the need of confidentiality can be demonstrated to be less necessary than protection of public interest. Knapp and Vandecreek (1982, p. 516) provide an update of the impact of the *Tarasoff* case. They conclude:

> Although a [California] court refused to extend the duty to protect to suicidal persons, courts have differed as to the liability when patients have harmed persons who were not specifically threatened. Finally, most courts have found *Tarasoff* applicable to their jurisdiction. Psychotherapists are reminded that good clinical judgment can circumvent many potential *Tarasoff*-like situations.

Involving and Notifying the Family of the Addicted Person: A Violation of Confidentiality or the Expression of Concern by the Psychotherapist?

The most important ingredient in the treatment relationship for addicted individuals is trust. Perhaps the more contemporary connotation of trust is action by the psychotherapist rather than passivity. When addicted individuals demonstrate they no longer can control their self-destructive behavior, the psychotherapist may wish to consult family members or friends to ascertain what can be done in the way of limit-setting therapeutic action. Psychotherapists need to recognize that generally, no matter how heroic their rescue efforts, no matter how committed they are to the ultimate welfare and survival of addicted individuals, no matter how creative and energetic their treatment plans, they cannot help substance abusers curtail their life-threatening drug-related behavior by themselves. This stance contradicts Freud's condemnation (1920, p. 398) of the family's culpability regarding the patient's illness:

> Psychoanalytic treatment may be compared to a surgical operation, and has the right to be undertaken under circumstances favorable to its success. You know what precautions the surgeon is accustomed to take: a suitable room, good light, assistance, exclusion of relatives, etc. How many operations would be successful . . . if they had to be performed in the presence of all the members of the family, who would put their fingers into the field of operation and cry aloud at every cut of the knife? The interference of relatives in psychoanalytic treatment is a very great danger, a danger one does not know how to meet. It is important to approach the relatives of the patient with any sort of explanation, one cannot influence them to hold aloof from the whole affair, and one cannot get into league with them because we run the danger of losing the confidence of the patient, who rightly demands that we in whom he confides take his part. Besides, those who know the rifts that are often formed in family life will not be surprised as analysts when they discover that the patient's nearest relatives are less interested in seeing him cured than in having him remain as he is.

Any contact initiated by family members or friends needs to be welcomed, because this information may enable the psychotherapist not only to gain a more realistic assessment of what actually is occurring but also to simultaneously form a treatment team. Assuming the immediate family would not notify others, the only way for relatives and friends to know about the treatment relationship would be when the drug-dependent person discussed it. Rather than becoming the collateral "treatment agent," the psychotherapist can function as a consultant by providing constructive and creative suggestions for relatives and friends to help the addicted individual. Even though Freud discouraged this type of contact with relatives, significantly he neglected to specify any guidelines for maintaining confidentiality. At times Freud (1905) disregarded confidentiality—most notably in the case of Dora, when he advised the child's father how to interact to help her. Roberts (1984, p. 67) apparently agrees with Freud's treatment of Dora, because he writes that "the therapist should also attempt to convey [to the family] whatever opinions he or she has on the possible origins of the problem including . . . a discussion of the role of organic and environmental factors. . . . The therapist may also provide some initial recommendations." In contrast, Langs (1976b) has criticized Freud for having a misalliance, because he insisted upon continuing a relationship with Dora's father which may have prompted her to seek a premature termination of psychoanalysis. Everstein et al. (1980), Messenger and McGuire (1981), and Plotkin (1981) have discussed the issue of confidentiality with children. Sobel (1984, p. 116) suggests that

> adolescent patients are usually more concerned with confidentiality than children. The limits of confidentiality need to be clearly defined for them including what and how information if any will be released to their parents and other parties, if necessary. . . . The issues of dangerousness and duty to warn are sensitive ones in any psychotherapeutic practice.

Mariner (1967, p. 69) discusses the dual roles of credentialed professionals, which may cause some sort of conflict of interest, and explains: "If a therapist is guiding other agencies in their dealing with the patient, and in turn, is being guided by them . . . through the exchange of information and opinion, then he no longer has a therapeutic relationship with the patient in the usual sense. "Indeed, it may be warranted for the psychotherapist to extend the treatment limits further. Awad (1983, pp. 193–194) assumes that it may be necessary to modify psychoanalytic techniques for antisocial adolescents and provides another justification for communication with an agency:

> Antisocial adolescents have the penchant to get into trouble and not talk about it. In addition, many parents, teachers, probation officers and group-home workers are troubled by the behavior of the adolescents and would like to discuss it with the therapist. Some therapists elect to have no contacts with these people in order to protect the confidentiality and the transference. However, this attitude may provoke termination of therapy when these people get frustrated by the unavailability of the therapist. Instead, what seems to be more useful is to allow the important figures in the adolescent's life to have access to the therapist but on conditions that are clear to them and to the patient. Thus, it might be decided that the parents and/or significant adults could call the therapist if they are concerned. However, these calls are not confidential and every call will

> be discussed with the patient, even though sessions cannot be discussed with the parents. . . . Such contacts rarely affect the therapeutic relationship. In addition, they give the patient the message that every aspect of his life is a focus of therapy.

This assumes a one-way kind of communication which does not compel the psychotherapist to divulge any material. Confidentiality may need to be sacrificed, however, when the psychotherapist assumes the role of protector. Currently, there simply do not exist any specific guidelines. Precedent for therapeutic contact with others, however, has been established by Speck and Attneave in their work with family networks. Adhering to the more traditional definition of absolute confidentiality would limit therapeutic intervention, since, by definition, the psychotherapist would be forced to work with the individual in isolation. Speck and Attneave (1973, pp. 153–154) write:

> Part of the effectiveness of social network intervention involves opening up communication channels within the network so that members experience some relief from their private burdens and develop trust in one another. The fear of exposing secrets that some subsystems of the network may have been holding onto tenaciously and often self-destructively—in spite of their good intentions—is often one of the major barriers to giving and receiving help. A good deal of energy is bound up in preserving these distorted half-truths, as any psychotherapist knows. When secrets are disclosed in the presence of the network, the attendant relief frees the group to do its work. This not only generates excitement, it provides the opportunity for the total system to develop new options on a realistic basis.

When family members have been excluded from the treatment process, reports Bratter (1975a, 1974), they have been known to sabotage the individual's progress. Family members are most cooperative during the malignant acting-out and testing of limits phase, but when the person stabilizes and decides to discontinue drug-related behavior patterns and become abstinent, families often nurture regressive activities. When the psychotherapist has proven to be credible, then it may be possible to help families become a cohesive, constructive, and creative force rather than conspiring against the individual. Concurrently, while attempting to include family members and friends as an integral part of the treatment team, which can facilitate recovery, the psychotherapist can gain a serendipitous reward if ongoing communication has been encouraged—i.e., the acquisition of independent data (Weinberg, 1973). There is no reason why a psychotherapist cannot listen without being compelled either to confirm or deny what the outside source is reporting. Addicts and alcoholics, at times, distort or can be dishonest regarding their activities. The psychotherapist can obtain realistic reports which are invaluable assets for determining treatment plans. Weinberg also writes that psychotherapists who feel uncomfortable receiving data from sources other than those involved directly in the recovery process "may be more successful with nonalcoholics."

Beyond Confidentiality: Therapeutic Trust

When individuals engage in potentially self-destructive and dangerous drug-related behavior (which becomes so blatant that the psychotherapist learns about it), clinicians should anticipate limit-setting therapeutic attempts which could involve a violation of confidentiality. There is no conflict ethically if the psychotherapist explicitly has defined the parameters of therapeutic intervention regarding limit setting and conversations with significant others. In *Lora* v. *Board of Education of New York* (1981), the court ruled that when a patient has been advised that any communication may be disclosed, there is no privilege. There is a "waiver" of confidentiality. Bratter (1980) suggests that the therapist discuss this issue candidly and concretely as soon as possible with the patient, so that there can be no misunderstanding. The individual needs to be apprised by the psychotherapist and he or she can be seen as desperate, as needing to be restrained from using more drugs, committing more crimes, jeopardizing lives, etc. The intent of treatment is to perpetuate life and the therapist's motivation is a sincere concern for ultimate welfare. Any discussion about the degree of drug involvement which is destructive can be interpreted by the psychotherapist as a desperate plea for help. When there is any reasonable evidence of drug-related, death-defying behavior, conditions exist which may justify the violation of confidentiality. Adherence to the more traditional model of maintaining confidentiality by joining the conspiracy of silence will more than likely be experienced by the drug-dependent person as connotating the psychotherapist's approval of the current behavior. By notifying others and, in extreme cases, even the authorities, therapists let addicted individuals know that someone cares sufficiently to become involved with them in a responsible, limit-setting way. Often families and friends have not intervened with sufficient intensity previously, so that the addictive cycle has never been disrupted and hence has been permitted to proliferate malignantly. The pragmatic and humanistic solution may be for psychotherapists to inform substance-abusing individuals who seek their services, prior to initiating a formal treatment alliance, that when there is an imminent danger either to a patient or to others, the therapist reserves the right to determine to what extent intervention is appropriate. Drane (1984) discusses the concept of "informed consent," which in the specific situation of drug-dependent persons may provide the psychotherapist with adequate leverage to insist that they decrease their dangerous drug-related behavior or risk the threat of notification, which can be justified in extreme life-or-death cases. Precipitating this sort of therapeutic crisis, furthermore, may create the conditions whereby the psychotherapist may be able to coalesce relatives and friends to provide the external restraint which the addicted individual lacks.

Most dramatically, the message communicated to the addict is that the psychotherapist has no ambivalent feelings about the gravity of the situation but is committed to a heroic rescue no matter what the future consequences may be. Corwin (1972) contends that the individual in distress might recognize that the psychotherapist "cared enough to interact in a vital way with him, in a manner which indicated that the love of the therapist was available—but it was conditional." In an effort to avoid the issue of violation of confidentiality which inevitably, and rightfully so, arises when information will be divulged, sometimes the psychotherapist can convince the individual who is experiencing a life-or-death crisis to notify significant others. Should the addict feel some reluctance, the psychotherapist can recommend that a three-way phone conversation or a conference can be arranged so the information can be transmitted. Sometimes significant others can offer direct assistance to help the individual regain stability. They can suggest, in addition, other therapeutic strategies.

Addicted individuals do not discuss their drug-related activities for catharsis. They do so with the desperate, though unverbalized, hope that someone will try to restrain them from hurting themselves or others. There is no other plausible explanation why addicts would communicate the degree of their drug dependence with the therapist, whom they perceive to be an extension of rational authority. Prout (1962) has conceptualized intervention "as a therapeutic action which tends to direct or influence the client's (patient's) behavior, during therapy sessions or in general." According to Bijou (1966, p. 44), who traces the evolution of the psychotherapist's roles and goals, the therapist has usually been considered "a reflector of feelings, or an explorer of resources, or a habit changer, or a remediator of self-concepts and values, or a releaser of repressions," but "we might come to think of him as a behavior engineer."

There needs to be a distinction between unauthorized disclosure of embarrassing personal material, the reporting of data for epidemiological purposes, the transfer of information for placements, and the legitimate therapeutic concern for potentially destructive/dangerous behavior. The *Tarasoff* decision did not resolve the issue of warning potential victims. The role of the credentialed psychotherapist in court, while important, creates more confusion than clarity. Psychotherapy is a special relationship in which the therapist becomes a prescribed healing and catalytic agent. Implicit in such a role is the commitment to act, to intervene, to violate confidentiality for the benefit of the patient. The issue of the psychotherapist assuming a *parens patriae* role is valid when clinical circumstances indicate that there is imminent danger either to the individual in treatment or to others. When the individual's life or that of others is endangered, the caring psychotherapist will need to consider which is more important—the ethical principle of absolute confidentiality or the concept of life.

Self-Disclosure: Therapeutic or Countertherapeutic?

In an orthodox psychoanalytic relationship, the analyst has been trained not to divulge any information regarding his or her own personality or values. When a patient asks a specific question, instead of answering, the analyst is supposed to attempt to explore the intent of the question. The analyst's interpretations are supposed to concern the patient's resistance or transference. Any deviation by the analyst from a neutral, objective posture is said to contaminate the traditional analysis. Freud (1964 [1912]) compared the analyst to a "surgeon who puts aside all his feelings."

Psychoanalysts traditionally have been reluctant to disclose to patients any personal information no matter how seemingly innocent or objective. Freud (1964 & 1912), suggests that "the doctor should be opaque to his patients and, like a mirror, should show them nothing but what is shown to him." Since Freud, Kernberg (1975), Kubie (1975), Kohut (1971), Greenson (1967), Szasz (1965), and other orthodox psychoanalysts have subscribed to Freud's original position of neutrality.

During the twentieth century, as with every other societal institution, the process of psychotherapy has changed radically. During the Victorian era, Freud and his coterie were influenced by the relatively rigid and repressive mores and values of their time. Psychoanalysis was designed for individuals whose life-styles could be characterized as lacking pathology. The primary goal of psychoanalysis was the acquisition of insight in a value-free setting, not the modification of behavior. During Freud's time, both analysts and analysands identified with upper-middle-class mentality and morality, which created a homogeneous situation.

Because of rapidly changing values and life-styles, today, perhaps more than in any other period in history, it is necessary for the mental health practitioner and the consumer to achieve an agreement *before* any treatment relationship can be formed. Working with alcoholically addicted and drug-dependent persons whose life-styles and values differ from those of the psychotherapist can create many areas of possible conflict. The majority of academically trained psychotherapists do not believe their individuality and freedom are threatened by the realistic constraints of a democratic society. By virtue of the fact that they have attained academic credentials, psychotherapists can be viewed as sufficiently compliant to reap the rewards in a capitalistic and competitive society. Addicted individuals, in contrast, have become disenfranchised from the system, which they perceive to be inimical.

With suspicious, alienated, hostile persons, if the psychotherapist avoids answering a legitimate question, the formation of a meaningful treatment alliance may be jeopardized. In all probability, the person who currently is drug-dependent will conclude that since the psychotherapist is less than honest, there is no reason to be trusting and candid. There seems legitimate reason for the psychotherapist to become a responsible role model and judiciously share personal experiences in an effort to minimize the barriers which, the addicted individual feels, preclude trust.

There will be times when judicious self-disclosure, which Bratter (1985) discusses, can facilitate a treatment relationship. Glazer, in contrast, describes a patient who feared that his psychologist was a homosexual because he did not deny the accusation and state categorically that he, in fact, was heterosexual and planned to marry. Instead, the patient's fears and fantasies were analyzed. Only when the patient by chance opened a box in the psychologist's office and read a love note from his fiancee was he reassured that the therapist was not homosexual. Glazer (1981, p. 152) provides six conditions when adherence to the traditional psychoanalytic stance of anonymity can be countertherapeutic:

> (1) the personality and working conditions of the therapist; (2) the capacity for an existence of a therapeutic alliance; (3) whether the patient's defenses are allo-or autoplastic; (4) whether the transference is object-related or narcissistic; (5) the specific dynamics under analysis; and (6) whether the self-disclosure pertains to experiences within or outside of the therapeutic interaction.

Rachman (1982, 1979, 1977, 1975), Weiner (1975), and Jourard (1964) mention conditions when judicious self-disclosure by the psychotherapist can be a positive therapeutic experience for the individual.

The variable of identifying with the individual and remaining a responsible role model rather than an anonymous agent who treats symptoms has much significance for an addicted subpopulation. Whitehorn and Betz (1954) studied the retrospective improvement of schizophrenics and discovered that effective therapists were warm and attempted to understand the patient in a personal way. The improvement rate was 75 percent for the empathetic therapist as compared with 27 percent for the more uninvolved one. This study has confirmed the correlation between high levels of liking, nonpossessive warmth, and empathy, on one hand, and behavior change, on the other. Rogers (1957) and Truax and Carkhuff (1967) focused on the combination of warmth and empathy. According to Glasser (1965, pp. 21–22):

> Usually the most difficult phase of therapy is the first, the gaining of the involvement that the patient so desperately needs but which he has been unsuccessful in attaining or maintaining up to the time he comes for treatment. Unless the requisite involvement exists between the necessarily responsible therapist and the irresponsible patient, there can be no therapy. The guiding principles of Reality Therapy are directed toward achieving the proper involvement, a completely honest, human relationship in which the patient, for perhaps the first time in his life, realizes that someone cares enough about him not only to accept him but to help him fulfill his needs in the real world. . . . The ability of the therapist to get involved is the major skill of doing Reality Therapy.

Swensen (1971, p. 34) confirms Rogers's and Truax's hypothesis when he concludes (based on a twenty-year analysis of the literature): "The successful psychotherapist is the one who genuinely cares about and is committed to his client. . . . The really crucial element in the therapist's contribution to therapeutic success is the therapist's commitment to the client."

The Psychotherapist's Personal Experience Regarding Psychoactive Substances: The Individual's Right to Know

A therapeutic crisis can occur when the consumer asks the psychotherapist about the latter's previous personal drug use, abuse, and/or addiction. The extent to which (if at all) the therapist has used mood-altering drugs becomes crucial because it will affect treatment goals and techniques. Invariably, drug-dependent persons will inquire whether or not the psychotherapist has indulged, and, if so, to what extent and when. By acknowledging past or current use/abuse of psychoactive substances, the therapist is confessing to engaging in illicit behavior. Legally, all citizens are permitted by the Constitution to remain silent and thereby not incriminate themselves in court. However, when the psychotherapist deliberately avoids legitimate self-disclosure to a patient, therapeutic trust will be adversely affected. Any attempt by the therapist to circumvent the truth will exacerbate suspicion and mistrust. There is a difference between a legitimate inquiry which will affect treatment orientation and outcome and one which is a violation of personal privacy. When the psychotherapist refuses to respond to questions about personal use, substance-abusing individuals, who are adept at discovering inconsistencies and hypocrisies in others, will assume there is current drug-related activity.

Despite publications by Bissell (1973, 1976, 1980), Gitlow (1977), Larson (1981), and Nathan (1982) which discuss substance-abusing mental health practitioners who are impaired, the psychology, psychiatry, and social work professions have been reluctant to protect the unsuspecting public, who are vulnerable to the deleterious effects of poor advice. It is important to examine the rhetoric of Thoreson et al. (1983, p. 672) because it accurately reflects professional sentiment regarding this specific problem:

> Undisputedly, psychologists drink, many drink heavily, and a sizable percentage of such heavy drinkers exhibit alcohol dependency symptoms—physical dependency (such as repeated withdrawal or hangover symptoms), increased tolerance for alcohol, increased obsession with alcohol (preoccupation, scheduling of life events around drinking and preoccupation with control . . .). However, most heavy drinking professionals (including psychologists) do not suffer obvious adverse social, personal, and economic difficulties. . . . Although a sizable minority of psychologists who use alcohol on a daily basis may develop alcohol dependency and may feel an intense sense of squalor and despair, many probably do so without obvious social, vocational, and economic consequences.

Why psychologists apparently are exempt from experiencing the same debilitation as the general public never is mentioned. Curiously, no sanctions or remedies are described, essentially because later Thoreson et al. (1983, p. 674) make the unsubstantiated assumption, which certainly cannot be proven that, "work performance for alcoholic psychologists tends to be as good as it ever was, only in a narrower domain."

What is the solution for the former or currently drug-dependent psychotherapist? Keith-Spiegel (1977), chairman of the Committee of Scientific and Professional Ethics of the American Psychological Association, avoids discussing "the sick doctor" phenomenon—which no other professional organization officially has recognized: "It is beyond the scope of our committee to adequately diagnose people who are complained against as being irrational, beastly, or irresponsible." At the very least, every drug-impaired psychotherapist should be required to inform individuals in treatment regarding the specifics of his or her drug-related disability. Any refusal to comply should be grounds for a professional reprimand of unethical behavior, and, in more severe situations, even the charge of incompetence. Whether these impaired mental health practitioners should be restricted from providing psychotherapeutic services certainly needs to be discussed and debated by professional societies. Clearly, there is a mandate for all surgeons and airplane pilots not to continue their respective professions while they are impaired. Consumers of psychotherapy are likewise entitled to be protected.

Since, thus far, professional organizations have abdicated their responsibility to define the parameters of ethical behavior, inevitably the issue will be decided by the courts. Clearly, questions arise regarding the psychotherapist's competence to be a treatment agent if there is current substance use or abuse. If the therapist currently is intoxicated, this admission would destroy the treatment relationship. The credibility of the therapist would be destroyed with the admission of current substance dependence and use. The drug-dependent individual would rationalize that if the psychotherapist can use psychoactive substances, there is explicit approval to do so. Aside from legal consequences, current illicit use of any psychoactive substance by any psychotherapist who works, in particular, with an addicted subpopulation should be considered prima facie evidence of malpractice. Five years of responsible and productive sobriety would be the minimum period of time for those academically trained psychotherapists before they could continue to work with addicted individuals in unsupervised settings. Professional organizations, at the very least, should recommend to recovering psychotherapists that they need to discuss the specifics of their recovery/rehabilitation because it will influence their future treatment orientation and outcome, the direction and duration of therapy, and their personal and professional biases.

Ironically, should the psychotherapist initially acknowledge some previous experience with drugs and alcohol abuse, the individual in treatment may feel more comfortable relating to him or her. There undeniably is some immediate gain for the treatment alliance when psychotherapists discuss their relevant personal experiences judiciously. Recovered addicts and alcoholics who can identify with those whom they wish to help retain a fundamental advantage during the early phases of treatment when compared with academically trained psychotherapists. More recently, furthermore, there is evidence to suggest that recovered persons, who not only share their experiences but also identify with addicted individuals, have more impact than their academically trained counterparts. Alcoholics Anonymous, a self-help organization, which was described by Ogborne and Glaser in Chapter 6, has a documented record of successful recoveries that no other treatment program can approach. Those treatment programs which have proven to be most effective for addicts employ former addicts. Once academically trained psychotherapists reveal their prior experimentation and involvement with mood-altering drugs, their treatment integrity may be jeopardized because an ambivalence about drug dependence will be communicated to persons who are trying to achieve abstinence and sobriety unless they emphasize the self-defeating aspects.

The Goal of Treatment: Abstinence or Controlled Drinking?

Should clinicians stress abstinence as the only treatment goal or can some clients learn how to moderate their control of alcohol?

Clinically, there is sufficient evidence to suggest that certain types of alcoholics should be discouraged from drinking. Jellinek (1960) identified two varieties of alcoholism—the gamma type, which can be characterized by a loss of control, and the delta type, which is the inability to stop drinking—in which abstinence must be attained to prevent any relapse. A sufficient number of alcoholics encounter difficulty regulating their consumption after the first drink to warrant the treatment objective of abstinence. Dodes (1984) writes: "For alcoholic patients in long-term psychotherapy, abstinence from alcohol is a useful and important goal, whether [or not] it can be achieved initially." Chafetz, the founding director of the National Institute on Alcohol Abuse and Alcoholism, also has represented the interests of the powerful alcohol lobby, and his ambivalence suggests a potential conflict of interest. In his book, *Why Drinking Can Be Good for You,* Chafetz (1976, p. 25) attempts to issue a universal statement which will be acceptable to all kinds of groups:

> In the best of all possible worlds, who can argue with that statement [A recovered alcoholic should never drink again]? And if you are a recovered alcoholic person and have a choice, I guess a guarantee that you'll never drink again means—in the classic sense—that you'll never have an alcohol problem. That was the logic underlying prohibition: Remove alcohol by law, and poof! No more alcohol problems. . . . We know what that logic cost us.
>
> I am not suggesting that alcoholic people try to drink. I've always told my patients, "After the misery you've gone through, why take the risk of finding out whether or not you can drink again? Alcohol is not a necessity of life."

Chafetz curiously avoids stating categorically that abstinence is the preferred treatment goals for alcoholics. Ewing and Rouse (1976) reject the concept of controlled drinking and consequently stress abstinence. This is essentially the treatment posture of Alcoholics Anonymous, which is viewed as the most effective program for alcoholics. Compulsive eaters illustrate the problem of the futility of moderation when periodically, sometimes without provocation, they consume prodigious amounts of food. Working with obese individuals who are compulsive eaters, however, becomes a different psychotherapeutic proposition, because without food people will perish. Obviously, for compulsive eaters, moderation is the only realistic goal. Alcoholically and drug-addicted persons, in contrast, despite their contentions, simply do not need any psychoactive substance(s) to survive. Those studies which contend that moderate—i.e., social or occasional—use is permissible ignore the reality presented by Jellinek and Alcoholics Anonymous. Rather than placing addictive individuals in potentially "no win" and "no exit" positions, unquestionably it is prudent for the psychotherapist to adopt the Alcoholics Anonymous (1952, 1939) requirement of refraining from drinking twenty-four hours at a time.

While perhaps an oversimplification, if it were hypothetically possible for the credentialed mental health practitioner to create a twenty-four-hour-a-day, seven-days-a-week environment of surveillance, in which all the drug-dependent individual's behavior was monitored and the penalty for indulgence was either prolonged incarceration or death, it would be possible to guarantee a cessation of drug-related behavior. Abstinence and sobriety are realistically achievable goals and are prerequisite to meaningful recovery, remission, and/or rehabilitation. Clinically, there is no harm when the psychotherapist maintains this as a primary treatment goal which can be revised should conditions change.

Davies (1962) probably was the first physician-researcher to propose that controlled drinking could be a realistic treatment goal for some former alcoholics. In so doing, Davies challenged the traditional sacrosanct treatment tenet of total abstinence. Armor, Polich, and Stambul (1976) created a furor by doing a study of controlled drinking, financed by the Rand Corporation, which indicated that some recovered alcoholics apparently could drink moderately. Armor, Polich, and Stambul (1978, p. 294) write:

> The majority of improved clients are either drinking moderate amounts of alcohol—but at levels far below what could be described as alcoholic drinking—or engaging in alternating periods of drinking abstention . . . this finding suggests the possibility that for some alcoholics moderate drinking is not necessarily a prelude to full relapse and that some alcoholics can return to moderate drinking with no greater chance of relapse than if they abstained.

A follow-up study disclosed that only 28 percent of the treatment population in 45 alcoholism centers remained abstinent for at least six months. A minuscule 4 percent refrained from ingesting any alcoholic beverage. Polich, Armor, and Braiker (1981, p. 214) conclude: "When we examined longer time periods and multiple points in time, we found a great deal of change in individual status, with some persons continuing to improve, some persons deteriorating, and most moving back and forth between relatively improved and unimproved."

Coinciding with the Rand report was the Sobell and Sobell (1978, 1976) study, which claimed significant success in a two-year follow-up of those who had received controlled-drinking training. The subjects learned how to problem-solve, resolve stress, and use other techniques to permit them to drink in moderation. Pendery, Maltzman, and West (1982) attacked the Sobells by questioning the validity of the study, claiming: "Most subjects trained to do controlled drinking failed from the outset to drink safely. The majority were rehospitalized for alcoholism within a year after their discharge from the research project." Marlatt (1983) defends the work of the Sobells. Adding to the confusion and controversy generated by the advocates of the controlled-drinking approach, Vogler and Bartz (1982) have written a book, *The Better Way to Drink: The Alternative That Works,* which describes with forceful endorsement a social-learning orientation for excessive drinkers. Emrick (1982) sincerely believes that former alcoholics can be helped to resolve their developmental deficits so that they "can choose whether or not to drink at all and in what manner if they choose to drink." Brown et al. (1983) conclude succinctly: "The issue of controlled drinking versus abstinence is hardly resolved." Miller (1983) affirms: "Moderation approaches are here to stay, and will make important contributions not only to treatment but to the prevention of problem drinking." The responsible and caring clinician has no option but to urge former alcoholics not to drink until this critical treatment issue has been researched further and has been resolved.

Conclusion: A Plea for Recognition of the Special Clinical Problems of Drug-dependent Persons and the Formulation of Humanistic Guidelines

When an emergency occurs which threatens life, rather than puzzling over transference-countertransference issues or what constitutes optimal treatment, the concerned clinician who works with addicted individuals needs to be prepared to respond decisively to neutralize the death-defying, drug-related, desperate situation. The primary psychotherapeutic concern is for the ultimate survival of the individual. De la Torre and Smith (1978) state: "There is no question that it is better to transfer a patient to another colleague than not to have a patient to transfer at all." Wachtel (1977) has criticized the psychoanalytic legacy of the benign, detached, analytic orientation which negates any therapeutic intervention. There is a profound difference between heroic psychotherapeutic intervention (which attempts not only to minimize self-destruction but also to prolong life) and intrusion to modify a person's political beliefs.

This chapter does not presume to be the definitive work regarding prescriptive psychotherapeutic changes for professionals who work with addicted persons. The justification for this chapter is more modest and realistic: to document some of the significant psychological and clinical concerns which are unique to an addicted subpopulation; to suggest why more traditional psychotherapeutic practices have proven to be relatively ineffective with addicts; and to propose that the psychotherapeutic process can become more effective in producing behavioral and attitudinal changes with addicted individuals. Complicating the formulation of guidelines for precise psychotherapeutic parameters and the specifics of ethical therapeutic behavior for addicted individuals are the divergent and different circumstances for each situation. At times, the setting and enforcement of behavior limits can produce a salutary therapeutic outcome. In contrast, not every alcoholic or drug-addicted individual needs to be monitored so restrictively. The circumstances and conditions for what constitutes effective psychotherapy for persons whose impulsive behavior can produce a life-or-death confrontation continually change. Since clinical discretion remains an integral part of the treatment decision–making process, it is difficult to define in advance what constraints and therapeutic principles must be followed. This author has found it necessary, at times, to "extend the treatment alliance" when life-or-death crises arise. Optimally, any creative treatment plans can be discussed and agreed upon by the individual in psychotherapy and the therapist before being implemented. In extreme cases, however, to preserve life, any therapeutic intervention can be justified. The ends, indeed, do justify the means.

Unless psychotherapists are willing to consider more recent creative and constructive innovations, they will remain impotent to combat the vicious cycle of pharmacogenic adaptation which addicts desperately employ to regain their psychological equilibrium. The decision by the individual to use or abuse psychoactive substances is a personal choice. Psychotherapists retain the same right to choose whether they wish to work with or exclude addicted individuals from their caseloads. Not every professional has the concern, commitment, and competence to provide psychotherapeutic services for addicted individuals.

There are two reasons why professional organizations and societies no longer can ignore the special clinical concerns of drug-dependent and drug-addicted persons:

First: The number of individuals who have become trapped in the "no win"–"no exit" labyrinth of drug dependence and addiction continues to proliferate. The estimate of alcoholics already exceeds 15 percent of the population. Those who can be classified as drug-dependent or drug-addicted are probably another 5 percent. The number of children who are becoming addicted to alcohol and drugs continues to escalate. When statistics estimate that more than 50 percent of all traffic accidents, homicides, and suicides are either drug- or alcohol-related, the number of unaffected individuals and families decreases significantly. It is not possible, for example, to calculate how many people have been injured or killed due to faulty automobile repairs by individuals whose abilities have been impaired by their addiction.

Second: Potent psychotherapeutic techniques are being devised which can cure psychological disorders and control individuals. Society must attempt to achieve and maintain the delicate balance between the preservation of civil liberties and the protection of citizens from criminal acts. Rogers and Skinner (1956, p. 1057) discuss the problem of the moral responsibility of behavioral scientists who are in the process of perfecting behavior control technology:

> The dangers inherent in the control of human behavior are very real. The possibility of misuse of scientific knowledge must always be faced. We cannot escape by denying the power of a science of behavior or arresting its development. It is no help to cling to familiar philosophies of human behavior simply because they are more reassuring. . . . the new techniques emerging from a science of behavior must be subject to the explicit counter-control which has already been applied to earlier and cruder forms.

There are legitimate clinical reasons for therapeutic limit setting and for the violation of confidentiality in specific situations. When evidence predicts that lives are threatened by self-destructive and/or sadistic acts, when individual rights and liberties are being violated, an explicit articulation of the specific goals and parameters of control is required. Individual constitutional rights need to be protected so that treatment concepts do not become confused with authoritarian social control. Shapiro (1972, p. 55) poses a number of relevant considerations for concerned clinicians regarding the potential abuses of psychotherapy:

> These arguments require a clear statement of the nature and limits of the technologies; an explicit articulation of the specific goals of such behavior control; and a sensitive consideration of the very difficult legal and moral issues at stake. These requirements necessitate a careful review of the major concepts that have historically informed both penal/correctional practices and the treatments of the mentally ill; "rehabilitation"; "treatment"; "conditioning"; "freedom to—"; "freedom from—"; "privacy." The paramount questions—Who controls/treats/conditions/demolishes? Who, Why, How, and Under What Considerations?—require thoroughgoing analysis, not a mere observation that [these questions are] troublesome.

This chapter, then, is a plea that professional organizations and societies begin to consider and debate the special clinical concerns of an addicted subpopulation which require special therapeutic action. London (1969, p. 17) warns:

> Behavioral scientists had better start thinking about this now because few people are in equally good positions to do so. Physicists did not devote themselves much to the implications of atomic physics until after they had found the means to blow up the world—and their worried deliberations since then have not been terribly productive or useful to the politicians who must implement these things. Behavior science is still on the verge of powerful control technology. It has not yet accomplished it so thoroughly that it must be taken out of scientific hands, though it is too important to be left entirely in them. Suppose there is no atomic holocaust: What kind of a world must we make, knowing we must make one?

If psychotherapeutic societies abdicate their responsibility to determine appropriate ethical guidelines regarding therapeutic practice, then inevitably these issues will be determined in courts by persons who will be less qualified to make such determinations, since they will have limited experience with precedents and practice.

References

A. B. v. *C. D.* 7F (Scott) 72 (1905).

Adams, J. W. *Psychoanalysis of Drug Dependence: The Understanding and Treatment of a Particular Form of Psychological Narcissism.* New York: Grune & Stratton, 1978.

Adler, G., and Shapiro, L. N. Some difficulties in the treatment of the aggressive acting-out patient. *American Journal of Psychotherapy,* 1973, *27*(*4*), 551.

Anonymous. *Twelve Steps and Twelve Traditions.* New York: Alcoholics Anonymous World Services, 1952.

Anonymous. *Alcoholics Anonymous.* New York: Alcoholics Anonymous World Services, 1939.

Applebaum, P. S. Can mental patients say no to drugs? *New York Times,* section VI, March 21, 1982, p. 58.

Armor, D. J., Polich, J. M., and Stambul, H. B. *Alcoholism and Treatment.* New York: John Wiley & Sons, 1978.

———. *Alcoholism and Treatment.* Santa Monica: Rand Corp., 1976.

Awad, G. A. The middle phase of psychotherapy with antisocial adolescents. *American Journal of Psychotherapy,* 1983, *37*(*2*), 193–194.

Beier, E. C. Client-centered therapy and the involuntary client. *Journal of Consulting Psychology,* 1952, *16,* 332.

Bellah v. *Greenson,* Cal. App. 3d, 141 Cal. Rptr. 92 (1977).

Bersoff, D. N. Therapists as protectors and policemen: new roles as a result of Tarasoff? *Professional Psychology,* 1976, *7(3)*, 272.

Biestek, F. *The Casework Relationship.* Chicago: Loyola University Press, 1957.

Bijou, S. W. Implications of behavioral science for counseling and guidance. In J. D. Krumboltz (ed.), *Revolution in Counseling.* Boston: Houghton Mifflin Company, 1966.

Bissell, L., Fewell, C. H., and Jones, R. W. The alcoholic social worker: a survey. *Social Work in Health Care,* 1980, *5,* 431–432.

Bissell, L., and Jones, R. W. The alcoholic physician: a survey. *American Journal of Psychiatry,* 1976, *133,* 1142–1146.

Bissell, L., Lambrecht, K., and Von Wiegant, R. A. The alcoholic hospital employee. *Nursing Outlook,* 1973, *21,* 708–711.

Borriello, J. Group psychotherapy with acting-out patients: specific problems and techniques. *American Journal of Psychotherapy,* 1979, *33(4)*, 535.

Bratter, T. E. Group psychotherapy with alcoholically and drug addicted adolescents: special clinical concerns and challenges. In F. Azima and L. Richmond (eds.), *Group Psychotherapy.* New York: International Universities Press, 1985 (in press).

———, Bratter, E. P., Fossbender, A. J., and Heimberg, J. F. Uses and abuse of power and authority with the American self-help residential therapeutic community: a perversion or a necessity? In G. DeLeon and J. Ziegenfuss (eds.), *The American Self-Help Therapeutic Community.* Springfield, Ill.: Charles C. Thomas, 1985 (in press).

Bratter, T. E. Some pre-treatment group psychotherapy considerations with alcoholic and drug-addicted individuals. *Psychotherapy: Theory, Research and Practice,* 1981, *18(4)*, 508–515.

———. Negotiating the therapeutic alliance with unmotivated, self-destructive adolescent substance abusers in independent practice: some pre-treatment issues. In R. Faukinberry (ed.), *Drugs: Problems of the 70's. Solutions for the 80's.* Lafayette, Louisiana: Endac Enterprises, 1980.

———. The psychotherapist as a twelfth-step worker in the treatment of alcoholism. *Family and Community Health: The Journal of Health Promotion and Maintenance,* 1979, *2(2)*, 31–58.

———. The psychotherapist as advocate: extending the therapeutic alliance with adolescents. Journal of Contemporary Psychotherapy, 1977, *8(2)*, 119–127.

———. Responsible therapeutic eros: the psychotherapist who cares enough to define and enforce behavior limits with potentially suicidal adolescents. *The Counseling Psychologist,* 1975, *5(4)*, 98.

———. Wealthy families and their drug-abusing adolescents. *Journal of Family Counseling,* 1975a, *3(1)*, 62–76.

———. The methadone addict and his disintegrating family: a psychotherapeutic failure. *The Counseling Psychologist,* 1975b, *5(3)*, 110–125.

———. Helping affluent families help their acting-out, alienated, drug-abusing adolescents. *Journal of Family Counseling,* 1974, *2*(*1*), 22–31.

———. Treating alienated, unmotivated, drug-abusing adolescents. *American Journal of Psychotherapy,* 1972, *27*(*4*), 585–598.

———. Group therapy with affluent, alienated, adolescent drug abusers: a reality therapy and confrontation approach. *Psychotherapy: Theory, Research and Practice,* 1972, *9*(*4*), 308–313.

Brill, A. A. *Psychoanalysis: Its Theories and Practical Application.* Philadelphia: W. B. Saunders Co., 1918.

Brill, L., and Lieberman, L. *Authority and Addiction.* Boston: Little, Brown & Co., 1969.

Britton, A. H. Rights to privacy in medical records. *The Journal of Legal Medicine,* 1975, *6,* 31.

Bromberg, W., and Rodgers, T. C. Authority in the treatment of delinquents. *American Journal of Orthopsychiatry,* 1946, *16,* 672–685.

Brown, R. T., Jackson, L. A., and Galizio, M. Controlled drinking versus abstinence: where do we go from here? *Bulletin of the Society of Psychologists in Addictive Behavior,* 1983, *2*(*3*), 191.

Canter, R. M. The future of psychotherapy with alcoholics. In C. J. Fredrick (ed.), *The Future of Psychotherapy.* Boston: Little, Brown & Co., 1969.

Chafetz, M. *Why Drinking Can Be Good for You.* New York: Stein & Day, 1967.

Chein, I., Gerard, D. C., Lee, R. S., and Rosenfeld, E. *The Road to H: Narcotics, Delinquency, and Social Policy.* New York: Basic Books, 1964.

Chrzanowski, G. Problem patients or trouble makers? Dynamic and therapeutic considerations. *American Journal of Psychotherapy,* 1980, *34*(*1*), 34.

Chwast, J. The significance of control in the treatment of the anti-social person. *Archives of Criminal Psychodynamics,* 1957, *2,* 817.

Clark, B. *Whose Life Is It Anyway?* New York: Avon Books, 1980.

Cohen, R., and Grinspoon, L. Limit setting as a corrective ego experience. *Archives of General Psychiatry,* 1963, *8*(*1*), 74–79.

Corwin, H. A. The scope of therapeutic confrontation from routine to heroic. *International Journal of Psychoanalytic Psychotherapy,* 1972, *1*(*3*), 80.

Davies, D. L. Normal Drinking in recovered alcoholic addicts. *Quarterly Journal of Studies on Alcoholism,* 1962, *23*(*2*), 94–104.

de la Torre, J., and Smith, W. Neutrality or negligence: interpret or act? *American Journal of Psychotherapy,* 1978, *32*(*3*), 444, 447.

Denkowski, K. M., and Denkowski, G. C. Client-counselor confidentiality: an update of rationale, legal status, and implication. *Personnel and Guidance Journal,* 1982, *60*(*6*), 374.

Dix, G. E. Tarasoff and the duty to warn potential victims. In C. K. Hofling (ed.), *Law and Ethics in the Practice of Psychiatry.* New York: Brunner/Mazel, 1981.

Dodes, L. M. Abstinence from alcohol in long-term psychotherapy with alcoholics. *American Journal of Psychotherapy,* 1984, *38,* 254.

Drane, J. Annotations on informed consent for psychiatry. *Bulletin of the Menninger Clinic,* 1984, *48*(2), 111–124.

Dumont, M. P. The junkie as political enemy. *American Journal of Orthopsychiatry,* 1973, *43*(*4*), 538.

Emrick, C. D. Psychologists offer alcohol abusers a chance for self-growth. *Bulletin of the Society of Psychologists in Substance Abuse,* 1982, *1*(*2*), 38.

Everstein, L., D. Sullivan, G. M. Heyman, R. H. True, D. H., Frey, H. G. Johnson, and Seiden, R. H. Privacy and confidentiality in psychotherapy. *American Psychologist,* 1980, *35,* 828–840.

Ewalt, J., and Farnsworth, D. *Textbook of Psychiatry.* New York: W. W. Norton, 1963.

Ewing, J. A., and Rouser, B. A. Failure of an experimental treatment program to inculcate controlled drinking in alcoholics. *British Journal of Addiction,* 1976, *71,* 123–134.

Fenichel, O. *The Psychoanalytic Theory of Neurosis.* New York: W. W. Norton, 1945.

Frank, J. *Courts on Trial.* Princeton: Princeton University Press, 1945.

Freud, S. *A General Introduction to Psychoanalysis.* New York: Boni & Liveright, 1920.

———. *The Dynamics of Transference.* Standard edition, vol. 12. New York: International Universities Press, 1964 (originally published 1912).

———. A fragment of an analysis of a case of hysteria. In *The Standard Edition of the Complete Psychological Works of Sigmund Freud,* vol. 7. London: Hogarth Press, 1905.

———. On psychotherapy. In E. Jones (ed.), *Sigmund Freud: Collected Papers,* vol. 1. New York: Basic Books, 1955 (originally published 1904).

Fromm-Reichmann, F. *Principles of Intensive Psychotherapy.* Chicago: University of Chicago Press, 1950.

Gitlow, S. E. The disabled physician: his care in New York State. *Alcoholism, Clinical Experience and Research,* 1977, *1,* 131–134.

———. Alcoholism: a disease. In P. G. Bourne and R. Fox (eds.), *Alcoholism: Progress in Research and Treatment.* New York: Academic Press, 1973.

Glasser, W. *Reality Therapy: A New Approach to Psychiatry.* New York: Harper & Row, 1965.

Glazer, M. Anonymity reconsidered. *Journal of Contemporary Psychotherapy,* 1981, *12*(2), 147–148.

Glover, E. On the aetiology of drug addiction. *International Journal of Psychoanalysis,* 1932, *13*(*3*), 298–328.

Googins, B. Avoidance of the alcoholic client. *Social Work,* 1984, *29*(*2*), 163.

Greenacre, P. The role of transference: practical considerations in relation to psychoanalytic therapy. *Journal of the American Psychoanalytic Association,* 1954, *4,* 681.

Greenson, R. *The Technique and Practice of Psychoanalysis.* New York: International Universities Press, 1967.

Grossbard, H. Ego-deficiency in delinquents. In *New Approaches to the Treatment of Delinquency.* New York: Family Association of America, 1962.

Group for the Advancement of Psychiatry. *Confidentiality and Privileged Communication in the Practice of Psychiatry,* Report no. 45. New York: Group for the Advancement of Psychiatry, 1960.

Haley, J. Control in brief psychotherapy. *Archives of General Psychiatry,* 1961, *4*(2), 139–140.

Halleck, S. L. Legal and ethical aspects of behavior control. *American Journal of Psychiatry,* 1974, *131*(*4*), 585.

———. *The Politics of Therapy.* New York: Science House, 1971.

Hill, M. and Blane, H. T. Evaluation of psychotherapy with alcoholics: a critical review. *Journal of Studies on Alcoholism,* 1967, *28*(*1*), 76–103.

Hofstein, S. Inner choice and outer reality. *Journal of the Otto Rank Association,* 1968, *3,* 64.

Hollander, M. H. Privileged communication and confidentiality. *Diseases of the Nervous System,* 1965, *26,* 169–175.

Hollis, F. *Casework: A Psychosocial Therapy,* pp. 80–89. New York: Random House, 1964.

Jacobs, M. A., and Christ, J. Structuring and limit setting as techniques in the group treatment of adolescent delinquents. *Community Mental Health Journal,* 1967, *3*(*3*), 244.

Jacobson v. *Massachusetts,* 197 US 11, 1904.

Jagim, R. D., Wittman, W. D., and Noll, J. O. Mental health professionals' attitudes toward confidentiality privilege and third-party disclosure. *Professional Psychology,* 1978, *9*(*3*), 459.

Jellinek, E. M. *The Disease Concept of Alcoholism.* New Brunswick, N. J.: Hillhouse Press, 1960.

Jones, W. T. *A History of Western Philosophy.* New York: Harcourt, Brace & Co., 1952.

Josselyn, I. M. *The Adolescent and His World.* New York: Family Service of America, 1952.

Jourard, S. *The Transparent Self.* New York: Van Nostrand, 1964.

Keith-Spiegel, P. Violation of ethical principles due to ignorance or poor professional judgment versus willful disregard. *Professional Psychology,* 1977, *8*(*3*), 290.

Kelman, H. Rational and irrational authority: a holistic viewpoint. *American Journal of Psychoanalysis,* 1952, *12*(*1*), 58.

Kernberg, O. *Borderline Condition and Pathological Narcissism.* New York: Jason Aronson, 1975.

Khantzian, E. J. The alcoholic patient: an overview and perspective. *American Journal of Psychotherapy,* 1980, *34(1),* 13.

Kittrie, N. N. *The Right To Be Different: Deviance and Enforced Therapy.* Baltimore: Penguin Books, 1971.

Knapp, S., and Vandecreek, L. Tarasoff: five years later. *Professional Psychology,* 1982, *13(4),* 516.

Kohut, H. *The Analysis of the Self.* New York: International Universities Press, 1971.

Kransner, C. The therapist as a social reinforcement machine. In H. H. Strupp and L. Luborsky (ed.), *Research in Psychotherapy,* vol. 2. Washington, D. C.: American Psychological Association, 1962.

Krystal, H., and Raskin, H. *Drug Dependence: Aspects of the Ego Function.* Detroit: Wayne State University Press, 1970.

Kubie, L. S. *Practical and Theoretical Aspects of Psychoanalysis.* New York: International Universities Press, 1975.

———. Multiple determinants of suicidal attempts. *Journal of Nervous Mental Disorders,* 1964, *3(2),* 138.

Langs, R. *The Bipersonal Field.* New York: Jason Aronson, 1976(a).

———. The misalliance in Freud's case histories: the case of dora. *International Journal of Psychoanalytic Psychotherapy,* 1976(b) *5,* 301–317.

Larson, C. Psychologists ponder ways to help troubled colleagues. *American Psychological Association Monitor* (September 1981), pp. 16, 50.

Lesse, S. The range of therapies in the treatment of severely depressed suicidal patients. *American Journal of Psychotherapy,* 1975, *29,* 3.

Leventhal, T., and Sills, M. The issue of control in therapy with character-problem adolescents. *Psychiatry,* 1963, *26(2),* 149–167.

Lindblom, C. E. *The Intelligence of Democracy,* pp. 76–78. New York: Free Press, 1965.

Litman, R. E. When patients commit suicide. *American Journal of Psychotherapy,* 1965, *19(4),* 570.

———. Immobilization response to suicidal behavior. *Archives of General Psychiatry,* 1959, *81(8),* 360.

Locke, J. *An Essay Concerning Human Understanding,* I, II. Oxford, 1894.

London, P. *Behavior Control.* New York: Harper & Row, 1969.

Lora v. *Board of Education of the City of New York,* 74 F.R.D., 565 37 NYD 3rd. 534.

Mariner, A. The problem of therapeutic privacy. *Psychiatry,* 1967, *30,* 66–72.

Marlatt, G. A. The controlled-drinking controversy. *American Psychologist,* 1983, *38,* 1109.

Masterson, J. F. *Treatment of the Borderline Adolescent: A Developmental Approach.* New York: Wiley-Interscience, 1972.

Menninger, K. *Theory of Psychoanalytic Technique.* New York: Basic Books, 1958.

———. *A Manual for Psychiatric Case Study.* New York: Grune & Stratton, 1952.

Messenger, C. B., and McGuire, J. M. The child's conception of confidentiality in the therapeutic relationship. *Psychotherapy: Theory, Research and Practice,* 1981, *18,* 123–130.

Miller, W. R. Controlled drinking: a history and a critical review. *Journal of Studies on Alcohol,* 1983, *44(1),* 79.

Modlin, H. D. Varieties of intervention in psychotherapy. *American Journal of Psychoanalysis,* 1962, *22(1),* 61.

Moore-Kirkland, J., and Irey, K. An appraisal of confidentiality. *Social Work,* 1981, *26(4),* 319.

Murdach, A. D. Bargaining and persuasion with involuntary clients. *Social Work,* 1980, *25(3),* 458.

Nathan, P. E. Psychologists in distress—who will help? *American Psychological Association Monitor* (Dec. 1982), p. 5.

Noll, J. O. Needed: a Bill of Rights for clients. *Professional Psychology,* 1974, *5(1),* 4.

Ostrow, M. *Drugs in Psychoanalysis and Psychotherapy.* New York: Basic Books, 1962.

Pattison, E. M., and Kaufman, E. (eds.). *Encyclopedic Handbook of Alcoholism.* New York: Gardner Press, Inc. 1982.

Pattison, E. M. Rehabilitation of the chronic alcoholic. In B. Kessin and H. Begleiter (eds.), *The Biology of Alcoholism.* New York: Plenum Press, 1982.

Pendery, M. L., Maltzman, I. M., and West, L. J. Controlled drinking by alcoholics? New findings and a reevaluation of a major affirmative study. *Science,* 1982, *217,* 169–174.

People v. *Newman,* 32 NY 2nd 379, 345 NYS 2nd 502 298 N.E. 651 (1973).

Perr, I. N. Problems of confidentiality and privileged communication. In C. Wecht (ed.), *Legal Medicine Annual,* 1971, *8,* 73.

Pierce, C. M. Pushing us towards a police state. *American Journal of Orthopsychiatry,* 1973, *43(4),* 528–529.

Plotkin, R. When rights collide: parents, children and consent to treatment. *Journal of Pediatric Psychology,* 1981, *6,* 121–130.

Polich, J. M., Armor, D. J., and Braiker, H. B. *The Course of Alcoholism: Four Years After Treatment.* New York: John Wiley & Sons, 1981.

Potter, C. M., and Austin, L. The use of the authoritative approach in social casework. *The Family,* 1938, *19,* 19.

Pray, K. L. M. The place of social casework in the treatment of delinquency. In S. Glueck (ed.), *The Problem of Delinquency.* Boston: Houghton Mifflin Co., 1959.

Prout, C. T. Intervention in psychiatry. *American Journal of Psychoanalysis,* 1962, *22(1),* 66.

Purrington, W. A. An abused privilege. *Columbia Law Review,* 1906, *6,* 391.

Rachman, A. W. Humanistic analysis in groups. *Psychotherapy: Theory, Research and Practice,* 1981, *18(4),* 457–477.

———. Active psychoanalysis and the group encounter. In L. and R. Wolberg (eds.), *Group Therapy 1979: An Overview.* New York: Stratton Intercontinental Medical Book Corp., 1979.

———. Self-disclosure, self-analysis, and self-actualization for the group therapist. In L. and R. Wolberg (eds.), *Group Therapy 1977: An Overview.* New York: Stratton Intercontinental Medical Book Corp., 1977.

———. *Identity Group Psychotherapy with Adolescents.* Springfield, Ill.: Charles C. Thomas, 1975.

Rado, S. The psychoanalysis of pharmacothymia (drug addiction). *The Psychoanalytic Quarterly,* 1933, *2(1),* 1–23.

Redl, F. *When We Deal with Children.* Chicago: Free Press, 1966.

———, and Wineman, D. *The Aggressive Child.* Chicago: Free Press of Glencoe, 1957.

Roberts, R. Psychoeducational consultations with parents of conduct-disordered older adolescents. *Psychotherapy: Theory, Research, Practice and Training,* 1984, *21(1),* 67.

Robitscher, J. The right of society to protect its members. In J. R. Wittenborn, H. Brill, J. P. Smith, and S. A. Wittenborn (eds.), *Drugs and Youth: Proceedings of the Rutgers Symposium on Drug Abuse.* Springfield, Ill.: Charles C. Thomas, 1969.

Rogers, C. R. The characteristics of a helping relationship. *Personnel and Guidance,* 1958, *37(1),* 13.

———. The necessary and sufficient conditions of personality change. *Journal of Consulting Psychology,* 1957, *21,* 95–103.

———, and B. F. Skinner. Some issues concerning the control of human behavior. *Science,* 1956, *124,* 1057.

Rogers, C. R. Significant aspects of client-centered therapy. *American Psychologist,* 1946, *1,* 419.

———. *Counseling and Psychotherapy.* Boston: Houghton Mifflin Co., 1942.

Roth, L., and Meisel, A. Dangerousness, confidentiality, and the duty to warn. *American Journal of Psychiatry,* 1982, *134,* 508–511.

Salzman, L. Psychotherapy as intervention. *American Journal of Psychoanalysis,* 1962, *22(1),* 43.

Samorajczyk, J. The psychotherapist as a meaningful parental figure. *American Journal of Psychotherapy,* 1971, *25(1),* 115.

Schaar, J. H. *Escape from Authority.* New York: Basic Books, 1961.

Schulberg, H. C. and Sheldon, A. The probability of crisis and strategies for preventive intervention. *Archives of General Psychiatry,* 1968, *18(5),* 556.

Shapiro, M. H. The uses of behavior control technologies: a response. *Issues in Criminology,* 1972, *7(2),* 55.

Sheriffs, A. D. Authority in the client-worker relationship: asset or liability? *Federal Probation,* 1953, *17,* 24.

Sidel, M. Confidential information and the physician. *New England Journal of Medicine,* 1961, *264,* 1133.

Siegel, M. Privacy, ethics, and confidentiality. *Professional Psychology,* 1979, *10*(*2*), 253.

———. Confidentiality. *The Clinical Psychologist,* 1976, *1,* 1.

Simonsen v. *Swenson,* 104 Neb. 244, 177 N.W. 831 (1920) 20.

Siporin, M. Social treatment: a new-old helping method. *Social Work,* 1970, *15*(*3*), 21.

Slawson, P. F. Patient-litigant exception: a hazard to psychotherapy. *Archives of General Psychiatry,* 1969, *21,* 347–352.

Slovenko, R., and Usdin, G. L. *Psychotherapy, Confidentiality and Privileged Communication.* Springfield, Ill.: Charles C. Thomas, 1966.

———. Psychiatry and a second look at the medical privilege. *Wayne State Law Review,* 1960, *175,* 184–185.

Sobel, S. B. Independent practice in child and adolescent psychotherapy in small communities: personal, professional and ethical issues. *Psychotherapy: Theory, Research, Practice and Training,* 1984, *21*(*1*), 116.

Sobell, M. B., and Sobell, L. C. *Behavioral Treatment of Alcohol Problems.* New York: Plenum Press, 1978.

———. Second-year treatment outcomes of alcoholics treated by individualized behavior therapy results. *Behavior Research and Therapy,* 1976, *14,* 195–215.

Soden, E. W. Constructive coercion and group counselling in the rehabilitation of alcoholics. *Federal Probation,* 1966, *30,* 55–60.

Speck, R. V., and Attneave, C. L. *Family Networks.* New York: Pantheon Books, 1973.

Studt, E. Worker-client authority relationships in social work. *Social Work,* 1959, *IV*(*1*), 18.

Swensen, C. H. Commitment and the personality of the successful therapist. *Psychotherapy: Theory, Research and Practice,* 1971, *8*(*1*), 34.

Symonds, M. Therapeutic approaches to acting out. *American Journal of Psychotherapy,* 1974, *18*(*3*), 365.

Szasz, T. S. Medicine and the state: the First Amendment violated. *The Humanist,* 1973, *33*(2), 7.

———. The ethics of addiction. *American Journal of Psychiatry,* 1971, *128*(*5*), 541–546.

———. The psychiatrist as double agent. *Trans-Action,* 1967, *4,* 16–24.

———. *The Ethics of Psychoanalysis: The Theory and Method of Autonomous Psychotherapy,* pp. 178–190. New York: Basic Books, 1965.

Tarasoff v. *Regents of University of California,* 17 Cal. 3d 425, 551 P. 2d 334, 131 Cal. Rptr 14 (1976).

Tarasoff v. *Regents of University of California,* 13 Cal. 3d 177, 529 P. 2d 533, 18 Cal. Rptr 129 (1974).

Taylor v. *United States,* 222 F 2nd 398, 401 D.C. Cir. (1955).

Thoreson, R. W., Nathan, P. E., Skorina, J. K., and Kilburg. R. R. The alcoholic psychologist: issues, problems, and implications for the profession. *Professional Psychology: Research and Practice,* 1983, *14*(5), 672, 674.

Thorne, F. C. *Psychological Case Handling: Establishing Conditions Necessary for Counseling and Psychotherapy,* vol. 1. Brandon, Vt.: Clinical Psychology Publishing Co., 1968.

Tiebout, H. M. Intervention in psychotherapy. *American Journal of Psychoanalysis,* 1962, *22*(*1*), 78–79.

Truax, C. B., and Carkhuff, R. R. *Toward Effective Counseling and Psychotherapy: Training, and Practice.* Chicago: Aldine Publishing Co., 1967.

Tyson, R. L. Discussion [Adolescent addiction: varieties and vicissitudes], *Psychoanalytic Inquiry,* 1982, *2*(*4*), 677–678.

Vaillant, G. E. If the drug abuser is a danger to himself, who should intervene? In J. R. Wittenborn, H. Brill, J. P. Smith, and S. A. Wittenborn (eds.), *Drugs and Youth: Proceedings of the Rutgers Symposium on Drug Abuse.* Springfield, Ill.: Charles C. Thomas, 1969.

Vogler, R. E., and Bartz, W. B. *The Better Way to Drink: The Alternative that Works.* New York: Simon & Schuster, 1982.

Wachtel, P. L. *Psychoanalysis and Behavior Therapy.* New York: Basic Books, 1977.

Warren, S. D., and Brandeis, L. D. The right to privacy. *Harvard Law Review,* 1890, *4,* 193–220.

Weinberg, J. Counseling recovering alcoholics. *Social Work,* 1973, *18*(*4*), 85.

Weiner, M. F. *Therapist Disclosure: The Use of Self in Psychotherapy.* Boston: Butterworth, 1978.

Weinstein, J. B., and Berger, M. A. *Weinstein's Evidence: Commentary on Rules for the United States Courts and for State Courts,* vol. 2, pp. 504–508. New York: Matthew Bender, 1981.

Westin, A. F. *Privacy and Freedom.* New York: Atheneum Press, 1967.

Whitehorn, J. G., and Betz, B. A study of psychotherapeutic relationships between physicians and schizophrenic patients. *American Journal of Psychiatry,* 1954, *3,* 321–331.

Wise, L. J. Alienation of present-day adolescents. *Journal of the American Academy of Child Psychiatry,* 1970, *9,* 265.

Wurmser, L. *The Hidden Dimension: Psychodynamics in Compulsive Drug Abuse.* New York: Jason Aronson, 1978.

Part Four

SPECIAL CLINICAL ISSUES

THE FIRST CHAPTER in this part (Chapter 20) addresses various ethical and legal issues in the treatment of alcoholics and substance abusers. Florence W. Kaslow and Thomas Mountz point out that local, state, and federal laws which have been enacted to help the substance abuser are often unclear or inconsistent and can actually be harmful. Issues of confidentiality, the scope of the alcohol problem in the United States, legal statutes and regulations governing confidentiality of patient records, and professional ethical standards are considered in this chapter. Finally, the authors discuss the problem of defining "who is the client."

The second chapter in this part (Chapter 21) discusses the clinical management of sexual problems in substance abusers. The author, Robert C. Kolodny, indicates that most drugs are pharmacologically likely to be disruptive to sexual functioning. As substance abuse escalates, the probability of sexual difficulties also escalates. The impact of acute alcohol intoxication on sexual performance, sexual problems of alcoholics, sex and narcotics, sex and stimulants, marijuana and sex, and various strategies of sexual therapy with alcoholics and substance abusers are considered in this chapter. Dr. Kolodny presents a step-by-step approach to the clinical management of alcohol- and drug-related sexual problems.

The final chapter in this part (Chapter 22) explores the many social and clinical realities associated with women and alcohol. Social perceptions and stereotypes of the woman drinker tend to be negative. Sheila B. Blume reports that in ancient Rome, drinking of wine by women was an offense punishable by death. The author explores physiological and psychological research pertaining to women and alcohol. Fetal alcohol syndrome, blood alcohol levels, alcohol and the menstrual cycle, problems of feminine identity, and patterns of consumption are elucidated. Finally, treatment and intervention strategies for alcoholic women are developed, along with guidelines for helping society deal with women who drink.

20

Ethical and Legal Issues in the Treatment of Alcoholics and Substance Abusers

Florence W. Kaslow / Thomas Mountz

Since the advent of treatment of individuals for alcoholism, drug addiction, and substance abuse–related problems, a host of ethical issues about confidentiality have come to the fore that have perplexed members of the legal and mental health communities. The first issue is: Why does confidentiality constitute such a difficult and special problem with this patient population? Second, there are a group of corollary concerns, including the magnitude of addiction in this country, the numbers of persons affected in the families of alcoholics and drug addicts, the strong impact on their friends and on those involved in the same treatment program, and finally, what the guidelines are and should be for privacy and disclosure in relation to the patient's significant others. The third problem emanates from the complexity implicit in the often unclear or contradictory web of local, state, and federal laws which supposedly have been enacted to help the substance abuser, yet which may in actuality prove harmful. In deciding which law and which interpretation one will follow, the therapist or agency director can face a serious moral dilemma. The fourth issue also concerns the therapist directly, as there are occasions when legal and ethical dilemmas surface in regard to his or her actual practice. What the therapist deems to be professionally ethical behavior may mean being in violation of the law and vice versa. The fifth area of concern lies in the determination of who has the ultimate responsibility for maintaining confidentiality and who is the primary client in the treatment situation. What happens when there are multiple clients? What are therapists' concurrent obligations to the institution in which they work, to their profession, and to the community that supports their license to practice? Professionals must clearly understand to whom they are responsible and the specific consequences that may eventuate from their behavior (Monahan, 1980; APA, 1981).

In this chapter we will explore each of these issues separately, with the hope that a broader synthesis and fuller interpretation of the integrated data may begin to point the way toward a better moral and ethical resolution. Similarly, it is our intention to encourage readers toward self-evaluation of the personal ethical principles which guide them in the course of treating an addict patient. Finally, it is hoped that this material will stimulate further research into the issues discussed here and will lead to the pragmatic application of humanistic values to the complex dilemmas and dynamic issues being addressed.

Problems Regarding Confidentiality

Issue One. Professionals offering services to addict patients cannot be impervious to the multifaceted nature of the problems of confidentiality. As in most health care arenas, there is a widespread acceptance of the obligation to keep records and information confidential. But just what does this mean, and how is it translated into the exigencies of daily practice?

The professional of today is being seriously challenged in efforts to maintain confidentiality by computerized record-keeping systems and growing third-party inquiries and requirements. Local, state, and federal legislative bodies are constantly revising and extending the scope and extent of their jurisdiction, and it is incumbent upon the practitioner to remain abreast of changing laws and regulations. The courts increasingly are involved in litigation from both the public and private sector pressing to resolve who may "own" information. The holdings from judicial decisions often are confusing to individual therapists, since they may appear to be contradictory. This furthers the ethical-legal dilemma (see Exhibit I, pp. 590–591).

Insurance companies as well as legal and court officials have increased their demand for information from therapists and institutions regarding the scope and nature of addiction-related problems and also the individual abuser. Historically, health care professionals have been able to maintain confidentiality of records and protection for the individual. This has been viewed as comparable to the confidentiality accorded the traditional doctor–patient relationship. However, since 1975 the aforementioned insurance and court bodies have been gaining the right to legal acquisition of data for a multitude of purposes, including research, decisions on payment or reimbursements of fees, prosecution of drug abuse cases, and epidemiological data collection. Often, although the professionals involved exercise great care to protect confidentiality, information is released through auxiliary medical staff, family members of the patient, or even the patient. From this it becomes evident that the problem of safeguarding the data is monumental, and the question of who the records belong to is an extremely complex one to answer (Rinella, 1980).

When providing services, the professional must determine what data or information is to be kept in the record. This is imperative whether it be a private or agency file. Other questions to be resolved are: Is the record to be used as a storehouse for data upon which to predicate treatment decisions because it provides critical information about the nature, extent, and possible etiology of the patient's complaint? Might such a repository for information later be subpoenaed? It is assumed that records are an accurate reflection of the person's history and are current enough to provide both baseline and treatment data. Whether records are open or closed is a salient issue. If they are open to other treatment staff, who will have access (Halleck, 1980, pp. 179–191)? One must consider how such a decision is likely to influence the patient's level of trust and freedom of expression. Simultaneously, one must assess how best to protect both a patient's right to treatment and right to privacy—when there may be an inherent conflict in these if too much historic, dynamic data is recorded (*Health Records and Law and Practice,* 1978; APA, 1981; AHA, 1972; NASW, 1979).

Possible confusion about and abuse of the doctrine of confidentiality within an agency, institution, or private practice represents yet another level of concern. The need for nonprofessional staff to transcribe and handle records is obvious. Professionals must train staff regarding the critical emphasis on privacy of records and make certain that all proper safeguards are built in, including locked files. It is urgent that all staff personnel maintain a continuing awareness of statutes and limits for handling privileged information (Schuchman, 1980).

The matter of what data can and should be shared with a third party outside the primary care setting is a delicate one. Recorded information should be detailed, accurate, current, and appropriate to the case at hand. However, clear guidelines for levels and amounts of data to be disclosed are (to our knowledge) nonexistent. Thus, agencies or individual service providers must exercise great care in examining requests for information to determine what, how much, and why such specific information is required and to what extent they will comply with the request (Exhibit I).

A patient often compounds the dilemma by querying, "May I have access to my own records?" Again, as in third-party situations, the question of need, extent, and level of information must be evaluated thoroughly. Several states have made legal provisions for the consumer to obtain his or her own complete record. The trend is toward more liberal access laws, and these are constantly undergoing revision. Consumers have the right to know what is in the record and to ascertain that it is accurate, relevant, and justified in their particular cases (Houghkirk, 1977). There are cases in which total access to information by the consumer is not warranted because of the sensitivity of the material or because its acquisition may be deemed harmful to the person at the time. When this occurs, the clinician must address the reasons underlying nondisclosure, not only in his or her written reports but also in informal notes and comments (Schuchman, 1980).

Consumers should have the right to some control over their records and the contents of these records. (Brodsky, 1972). They must be aware of the kinds of questions raised by third parties and the responses given by the primary provider. However, for this to be feasible it is essential that consumers have maximum access to their records and interpretation of the information the records contain. This is virtually mandatory before a consumer can grant knowledgeable consent for the release of information. The patient should be told what is to be transmitted and to whom, and must be apprised of the time limits on the material, both historically and for the future. All of this presupposes that the patient is in sufficient contact with reality to be capable of giving informed consent. If not, and if the individual is suffering from severely impaired or diminished mental capacity, or is in a state of virtual "psychological unconsciousness" (Tepper and Kaslow, 1981), then a significant other should be asked to sign the informed-consent form for the release of information.

A similar multifaceted problem is posed in regard to the records of minors. Judicial rulings tend to be predicated upon the patient's age and the nature of the condition being treated. However, states vary greatly on such rulings, and even vary in designating at what age someone is no longer a minor. The situation is further complicated because of variations in, and a lack of coordination of, designation of guardianship. The determination of who is responsible for the minor is often cloudy. When the minor is living in a family setting with his/her own biological family or a court-assigned family, the questions of who the information belongs to and how it is to be disseminated must be considered by the professionals involved (J. N. Perr, 1976).

Federal laws provide guidelines for restriction of access and sharing of health records on the pact of agencies sponsored or supported by federal funds. However, the question of the extent of these guidelines and their applicability to individual private providers remains in litigation (I. Perr, 1971; Ney, 1980).

In most states, "privilege" belongs to the primary patient. It is assumed that the health care provider is responsible for what goes into the record, but where the record can go is to be determined by the patient. Yet state and local statutes, as well as federal law, have numerous loopholes surrounding privilege and its waiver that place both the patient and provider at risk. Court-ordered examinations in relation to an involuntary commitment, or in criminal cases in which there is an incompetency or insanity plea as a legal defense, do not necessarily carry a guarantee of privileged status. It is, therefore, the responsibility of the professional to inform the patient of the limits of the privilege (Popiel, 1980; Cleary, 1972; Lanman, 1980; Privacy Protection Study Commission, 1977, 1979).

Often incidents arise that seem to necessitate sharing information in cases of particular mental health and physical disorders. The number of situations requiring disclosure is increasing and being supported by courts at all levels. Serious questions of privacy versus protection of a person's physical well-being are often contested in litigation and in the minds of therapists (*Zurcher et al.* v. *Stanford Daily, et al.*, 1978). Where there seems to be a strong likelihood of potential danger to another person from a patient, some states have promulgated the principle that a therapist has a "duty to warn" (*Tarasoff* v. *Regents . . .* , 1976; Wise, 1976; *McIntosh* v. *Milano,* 1979). In the case of clear and present danger, the California and New Jersey state supreme courts, in the *Tarasoff* and *McIntosh* cases, implied that protection of life is a higher value than protection of confidentiality. More specifically, the New Jersey Superior Court (*McIntosh* v. *Milano,* 1979) held that the statutory physician–patient privilege is not absolute; it is subject to extrajudicial disclosures where there is a supervening societal interest. Further, and of interest here, the court stated that psychiatrists cannot avoid liability by taking the position that it is impossible to predict dangerousness.

Magnitude of the Substance Abuse Problem

Issue Two. The scope of the *alcohol problem* alone in the United States is monumental. The number of persons involved, even remotely, is staggering. It is estimated that alcoholism afflicts some 10 million persons in the U.S. annually, and that for every identified patient there are at least two to four others (e.g., members of the immediate or extended family) who are directly involved, plus unknown numbers of friends and co-workers whose lives are seriously influenced. The annual statistics on mortality due to alcohol are staggering: an estimated 20,000 deaths from cirrhosis and other related diseases, 25,000 alcohol-related traffic deaths, and 15,000 homicides or suicides. Crime reports reveal about 2,500,000 arrests per year which involve intoxication.

The dollar costs of treatment and incidental physical damage are estimated in Berry's study (1976) at near $31 billion. This figure does not take into account the untold damage in emotional and psychosocial adjustment, nor the lost days of productivity in the labor market. It is further estimated that perhaps 40 percent of all hospitalized patients are in some way involved with abuse of alcohol. With a disease that is so costly in all aspects, that affects so many people directly, and that has such widespread familial, social, and economic ramifications, it is no simple task to determine where our responsibility lies or how to interpret the labyrinth of regulations and directives on the confidentiality of material contained in the abusers' records.

The determination of the extent of the *drug abuse problem* in the U.S. is even more complex than computing statistics for alcoholism. It is complicated by the illicit nature of the substances abused, by fear of prosecution for disclosure, and by the fact that most information available must be laboriously derived from clinical, medical, police, court, or military records. In a 1979 National Survey on drug usage by a civilian population, marijuana/hashish was used within the preceding 30 days by 42 percent of those surveyed aged 18–25, and within the past year by 54 percent of that age-group surveyed. Cocaine-abuse figures were 10 percent in the prior 30 days and 23 percent within the past year. Amphetamines, barbiturates, hallucinogens, tranquilizers, and heroin were individually abused by less than 5 percent of the population within the previous 30 days and nearly 12 percent during the preceding year. (Alcohol was by far the most frequent substance used, with 82 percent imbibing during the prior 30 days and 90 percent over the past year. The national survey clearly indicates that in 1979 alcohol was the substance of choice for use/abuse by persons aged 18 to 25.) (Smith 1980)

The survey also reflected close similarities between military personnel and civilians in patterns and frequency of substance abuse. The National Survey on drug usage report (1979) indicated that the most vulnerable population was the single male with less education than his cohorts. The survey revealed that about 27 percent of the population sampled had impaired work/school functioning during the preceding year because of their substance abuse.

In 1980, Burt and Associates of Bethesda, Maryland, surveyed more than 15,000 U.S. service members. Their survey results (Smith 1980) indicated that usage patterns and frequency were strikingly similar to those reported by the *National Survey on Drug Abuse* (1979). The fact that military personnel serve in remote areas of the world separated from family and home may account for some of the minor statistical differences. Consideration is also given to the availability of drugs to service members on duty throughout the world. The drastic change in life-style may be another contributing factor, and certainly high stress levels are probable, with an accompanying desire for escape from feelings of tension and anxiety. On the other hand, the military does provide structure and stability to its personnel, and this may in some cases offset the need for reliance on alcohol or drugs.

Alcohol appears to be the substance used most frequently in the military, with reports of indulgence by 75 percent or more of the members in all the services. The only notable disparity between civilian and military substance abuse is the slightly greater use of heroin in the military. This may be explained by greater and easier availability of heroin in many areas around the world where bases are located. Army Brigadier General Willaim C. Louisell, Deputy Assistant Defense Secretary for Drug and Alcohol Abuse, has reported that in most studies of substance abuse, civilian and military population have been essentially the same (Smith, 1980).

Legal Statutes and Regulations Governing Confidentiality of Patient Records

Issue Three. Protection of the confidentiality of the records of drug- and alcohol-abuse patients is provided for in Federal Law HR5935 (1975). Further, the March 19, 1980, Report of the U.S. House of Representatives Committee on Government Operations (HR Report #96–832) recommended the enactment of legislation that would guarantee privilege and protection of confidentiality. The report, *Confidentiality of Alcohol and Drug Abuse Patient Records* (42 Code of Federal Regulations [CFR], Part 2), and the specific legislatively enacted laws (21 U.S. Code [USC] 1175, on drug abuse, and 42 U.S. Code [USC] 4582, on alcohol abuse: see Exhibit I), offer guidelines that have been incorporated into Department of Health and Human Resources (HHR)–funded treatment programs dealing with drug and alcohol abuse. These statutes offer a broader range of protection for the confidentiality of records on diagnosis and treatment of alcohol abusers than are incorporated in other laws, probably because of the possible criminal nature of the patients' behavior and the implications of the disclosure.

That the stigma attached to drug and alcohol abuse was clearly recognized in congressional efforts to develop these guidelines is evident in the following statement:

> The conferees wish to stress their conviction that the strictest adherence to the provisions of this section is absolutely essential to the success of all drug abuse prevention programs. *Every patient and former patient must be assured that his right to privacy will be protected.* Without this assurance, fear of public disclosure of drug abuse records or of records that will attach for life will discourage thousands from seeking the treatment they must have if this tragic national problem is to be overcome. (HR Rep. #92–920, 92nd Congress, 2nd Session, 22, 1972)

Specific identifying information to be contained in health records is defined in § 2.11 (o), 2.13 (c) and (f), and 2.11 (p. 3) of the regulation cited above (1972). The congressional guidelines recommend that stigmatic information that would identify the patient as a drug or alcohol abuser not be included. It appears that the intent is to insure that no data is recorded in the patient's record that would reveal his or her involvement in substance abuse (Ney, 1980; Lanman, 1980; Schuchman, 1980. However, inclusion of data on the record that the person received treatment does not appear to be restricted. It seems that if an individual seeks treatment, he or she may expect to be asked to permit release of information of a medical nature to other involved practitioners. Permission for written or oral disclosure may be necessary if the treatment program is to be effective. This necessitates that all those involved have their efforts coordinated.

Recommendations for alternatives in the disclosure of information have been presented by the Privacy Protection Study Commission (1977, p. 14). These state:

> No medical care provider should disclose . . . any information about any individual who is the subject of a medical record it maintains without the individual's explicit authorization, unless the disclosure would be limited to location and status information (such as room number, dates of hospitalization and general condition).

Due to the potential negative implication of a patient's history if there has been drug or alcohol abuse, the difficulty for the professional lies in determining which data is appropriate to release. Lanman (1980) suggests that the dilemma can be eliminated by protecting all information.

The federal regulations (21 USC 1175, drug abuse, and 42 USC 4582, alcohol abuse) specifically prohibit disclosure of information that either initiates or substantiates any criminal charge against the patient or authorizes the legal system to conduct drug- or alcohol-related investigations against the patient. There are several exceptions to this regulation. As Lanman (1980, pp. 106–107) states, the court can authorize an investigation into a case:

> The regulations implement and broaden this authority by: (1) setting forth (at 42 CFR SS 2165) specific criteria for entry of court orders permitting disclosure of patient records for the purpose of conducting an investigation or prosecution of an individual who is or who is believed to be a present or former patient in a program; and (2) providing (§ 2.19) that undercover agents and informants may not be placed in a treatment program by law enforcement authorities except to the extent specifically permitted by court order entered in accordance with § 2167 of the regulations. These provisions respectively have had the effect of absolutely protecting (1) the use of a patient record to investigate or prosecute a patient for a crime that is not extremely serious or believed to have been committed on the premises of the program or against personnel of the program, and (2) the placement of an undercover agent as an informant in a treatment program for the purpose of investigating patients.

Nonetheless, the regulations, in Section 2.11 (p. 3), allow certain communication of drug and alcohol records. To be specific: (1) There is no restriction on communication between professionals within an agency who need to share essential information with other members of the treatment team; nor is there restricted communication between the agency and other "qualified" service organizations that render collaborating necessary services to the agency and its patients. (2) The qualified service agency is bound by the same regulations and restrictions on information-sharing as the initiating agency. (3) There is no restriction on making known any data that does not provide patient-identifying information (Lanman, 1980).

The regulations provide for disclosure of information with written consent. The manner, content, and circumstances are well defined in § 231, 2.33–2.40 of the federal regulations. A "blanket" form or consent is not applicable and would not be adequate for the release of information about patients who are substance abusers.

Since there may be circumstances that necessitate disclosure without consent, the law provides for limited exceptions to, and interpretation of, application of rules that offer further guidelines to the professional. Regulations covering such exigencies are found in § 2.51–2.67. All such disclosures are clearly circumscribed and are only permissible as a legal measure when "just cause" for the release of information is evident.

There are emergencies that may demand the release of information either with or without the consent of the patient. Part 2.51 provides a means for professionals to both disclose and document their release of information in emergency situations. A compelling circumstance that would constitute a medical emergency is when the physician or other therapist in charge, in his or her best professional judgment, decides that the health and safety of other persons would be in jeopardy in the event of nondisclosure of information. For example, an employer in a law enforcement agency might be notified that a candidate for police officer is actively involved in substance abuse. The "good of the citizen" would take precedence over the entitlement of the candidate to confidentiality, since the potential social and psychological harm to the applicant would be adjudged to be less than the potential damage to the community's citizenry (Lanman, 1980). This proviso is also consistent with Supreme Court decisions regarding the duty to warn, such as *Tarasoff* (1976), discussed earlier.

The question of research also is well-defined in the regulations under Part 2.52. In a research format, no identifying data may be used, but nonidentifying data may be ethically and legally disclosed. Although a researcher's obligation to obtain an individual's informed consent to participate in any study which may expose the person to physical or psychological harm is widely recognized, the researcher's duty to obtain patients' permission to use information compiled in records about them has always seemed less compelling. For one thing, the practical difficulties are considerable. Insistence on patient authorization would make many important studies impossible to conduct (Privacy Protection Study Commission, 1977) and slow up progress toward improved treatment. Nonetheless, great care should be expended in how records are used in research, with the patient being assured that no identifying data is revealed and that information is only made available to ethical, qualified researchers.

The law now clearly defines enforcement procedures and penalties for failure to adhere to the regulations. Violations of confidentiality regarding those involved with drugs and alcohol are considered noncriminal offenses, with a $500 maximum fine for a first offense and a $5,000 maximum fine for each subsequent offense. Enforcement of these laws may put a tremendous burden on law enforcement agencies. Their dilemma, as well as that of the courts, is in the determination of criminal intent and the actual nature of the offense when the data in these records are to be kept so highly confidential that this will be difficult to ascertain. To date, it appears there has been no litigation regarding violation of confidentiality, and no civil actions have been cited. In any event, the professional does have guidelines that are reasonably protective for all parties concerned, if they are properly applied (Lanman, 1980).

Since the enactment of the federal law, several states have drawn up their own statutes. In particular, Illinois has developed a law that has great promise as a model for other states or for local communities (Shlensky, 1977). Finding one's way through the maze of statutes in order to effectively treat patients, protect their right to confidentiality, and adhere to requirements for disclosure in emergency situations is indeed a complex task.

The Potential Conflict Between Legal Guidelines and Ethical Standards of One's Profession

Issue Four. In the previous discussion, specific laws and their implications were explored. But more consideration needs to be given to the moral and ethical issues confronting the professional dealing with the substance-abusing patient. Often questions of what, when or how much to disclose are moot to the question of why disclose at all. Is the involvement of family, friends, and agencies important enough to justify violation of confidentiality? One's moral principles and values are critical. Here questions regarding the stage of moral development of the patient and his/her therapist(s) come into the foreground. All too often the stage of moral/value development of the patient is overlooked or deemed inconsequential in determining a plan of treatment and consequently in deciding what information to share.

We believe that the stages of moral development elaborated by Kohlberg (1969) offer illumination which can lead toward the resolution of this particular dilemma. Kohlberg sees values and morals as ideals of justice that mature in keeping with one's level of cognitive development (Piaget, 1966) and life experiences. A person's own ethical standards constitute part of the primary foundation that undergirds the therapeutic alliance, treatment plan, goals, and ultimate resolution of problems (Van Hoose and Kottler, 1980). The following six stages of moral development (Abroms, 1978) should be useful in ascertaining (1) at what level of development both the therapist and patient are functioning, and therefore at what level the treatment can proceed; (2) whether the cognitive stage reached can permit further moral development; and (3) whether the gulf between the therapist's and patient's levels of moral development it too great to permit a viable, fruitful therapist–patient match. If therapist and patient are at vastly different stages in their relationship development they will hold widely divergent views of the world and of acceptable, appropriate attitudes and behaviors, and will find it difficult to comprehend each other. In such instances a different therapist might be assigned.

Abroms's overview, (1978, pp. 11–13), with accompanying goals and treatment modalities appropriate to each stage, seems particularly informative and applicable here.

> Stage 1. *Punishment and Obedience Orientation.* Morality serves to avoid punishment. Parental and social authority is deferred to primarily out of fear. The relevant health goal is the fostering of physical and material well-being: physical vigor and health, intellectual alertness, appropriate territoriality, adequate nutrition and exercise, productive work, living wage—in short, progressive physical and material achievement commensurate with biological endowment. . . .
>
> Stage 2. *Instrumental Relativistic Orientation.* Moral behavior is conceived primarily to satisfy the requirements of egoistic hedonism. The needs of others are considered only out of enlightened self-interest. In terms of health goals, the business of survival-and-status must be tempered by pleasure-seeking. . . .
>
> Stage 3. *Interpersonal Concordance Orientation.* Morality is primarily approval-seeking and is directed towards family and friends. The recognition here is that survival-and-status tactics and hedonistic satisfactions must be socialized. . . .
>
> Stage 4. *The "Law and Order" Orientation.* Moral behavior is judged in terms of dutiful observance of fixed rules necessary to the maintenance of the social order. The recognition here is that tribal togetherness, as an end in itself, is an insufficient basis for social stability. . . .
>
> Stage 5. *The Social Contract, Legalistic Orientation with Utilitarian Overtones.* Duty to law and order, once achieved, must be transcended if novel circumstances are to be created and managed. The emphasis moves from duty to rigid law and vested authority to the contractual procedures for the orderly generation of new structures. . . .

Stage 6. *The Universal Ethical Principle Orientation.* Morality here is based on universal principles of justice, like Kant's categorical imperative (1949). The relativity implied in adaptive flexibility must be subordinated to a set of universal values. Mental health depends of the formation of inspiring ideals, and treatment is therefore directed towards developing an embracing belief-system incompatible with disillusionment. . . .

It appears that most substance abusers have only achieved stage 1 or 2 in Abroms's schema and chose not to function at a level of law-abiding or principled behavior.

Hoffman (1970), a developmental theorist, typifies satisfactory moral development as exhibiting four characteristics. He indicates that the well-adjusted, healthy, moral individual conforms within "sensible" limits, views most authority as rational and fair, can inhibit inappropriate impulses, and is usually considerate of others. He cites four indicators of moral identification in human development, implying that if a person's actions are ethical, they are indicative of the following:

1. An internalized moral code—the ability to resist temptation and not engage in unethical practices even though there is little likelihood of being detected.
2. A sense of guilt—feeling badly when having done something wrong; an internalized conscience.
3. Personal standards—an internal belief and value system.
4. Responsibility for one's own actions and the consequences of one's behavior.

Hoffman's schema, although much less sophisticated than Abroms's is consonant with the latter and describes the kind of thinking and action one sees in people functioning at stage 5 and stage 6—principled behavior.

In gaining an understanding of the nature of the ethical and value system of the substance abuser, the therapist becomes able to consider more options in treatment. This also facilitates the therapist's ability to resolve some of the dilemmas inherent in the treatment, as it enables knowing the patient at his or her particular stage of moral development. It seems logical to apply such a holistic developmental perspective rather than limit one's conceptualization to assessing the patient's physical, emotional, and cognitive areas.

Who Is Supposed to Protect Whom

Issue 5: Where does the responsibility rest in protecting the confidentiality of patient records and information in the alcohol and drug treatment setting? And exactly who (or what) is the responsible agent supposed to protect? In respect to the first part of this question, reference is once again made to federal law, rules, and regulations, and to the literature of the field (Rinella, 1980). No one seems to deal concretely with the question of who the records belong to or who has the ultimate responsibility for maintaining confidentiality. Rather, the therapist must work from vague statements such as the following, (Health Records and Law Practice 1978 Sec 333A):

> Records of the identity, diagnosis, prognosis, or treatment of any patient which are maintained in connection with the performance of any program or activity relating to alcoholism or alcohol abuse education, training, treatment, rehabilitation, or research, which is conducted, regulated, or directly or indirectly assisted by any department or agency of the United States shall, except as provided in subsection (e), be confidential and be disclosed only for the purposes and under the circumstances expressly authorized under subsection (b) of this section.

The position taken here is that the treating therapist is the pivotal responsible individual and that his or her obligation to maintain confidentiality extends to interpreting this ethical and professional doctrine to support staff as well as other collaborating members of the treatment team. In private practice, the charge falls solely on the independent clinician, who must insure that all office staff respect this dictum. In agency or institutional practice, the executive director has the final responsibility regarding protection of the confidentiality of all records and the ultimate authority to determine when disclosures are warranted or imperative. When in doubt, legal counsel should be sought.

Even if the designation of responsibility is clear, a most perplexing question remains: Who is the client? Initially the answer seems straightforward. It is the person one is evaluating or treating. As one ponders further, one may conclude that the identified patient is the *primary* client but that there are also one or more *secondary* "clients" in the broadest sense of the concept. Therapists also have an obligation to (1) the agency in which they practice—they should follow its policies and procedures; (2) the patient's significant others, in terms of a systems-oriented understanding of the influence of the family (or staff) members' behavior on others, how changes in that behavior are likely to impact on others, and when it is advisable to involve them directly in treatment—when this occurs there are multiple patients; (3) their profession—to act in accordance with its code of ethics (see, for example, APA, 1981; NASW, 1979); and (4) society, as respresented in the state and its body of laws and statutes, particularly since the state gives the agency its charter and the clinician his or her license/certification to practice. The greatest dilemma occurs when commitment to one is in contradiction with duty to another. This, then, is the pervasive theme of this chapter—that confidentiality is a complex issue, that responsibility to maintain it and protect the client may conflict with the legal "duty to warn," that there are no a priori infallible answers, and that, in the final analysis, each therapist must handle each situation on a case-by-case basis in order to make the best possible knowledgeable, informed choice within the law and consonant with his/her own level of moral development.

We think that the six "Considerations in Confidentiality Dilemmas" discussed by Monahan (1980, p. 147) in his book about psychological intervention in the criminal justice system are pertinent, with minor adaptations (inserted by us in brackets), in the treatment of substance abusers and may provide some of the key questions to ask oneself when confronted with such dilemmas.

EXHIBIT I: CONSIDERATIONS IN CONFIDENTIALITY DILEMMAS

1. Assessment of Seriousness of Past or Planned Crimes [substance abuse]
   a. Where does crime fall on "seriousness" continuum?
   b. How much harm to society?

2. Assessment of Risk to Society if Unreported
   a. What is previous history of criminal [addictive] behavior?
   b. What is best "prediction of dangerousness?"
3. Assessment of Probable Consequences for Client if Reported
   a. What individual liberties will be lost?
   b. What is effect on therapeutic relationship?
4. Prognosis of Client Given Current or Potential Treatment Programs
   a. What is probability of eventual return to society?
   b. What is probability of community adjustment given continuation of current treatment?
   c. What is estimated efficacy of existing treatment programs?
5. Extent of "Informed Consent"
   a. Prior to initiation of therapy relationship, to what extent did the client recognize the limits of confidentiality imposed on the psychologist?
6. Consequences for Psychologist and for Therapy Relationship with Subject and with Others
   a. What is the probability of various negative "personal consequences" associated with a confidentiality breach?
   b. What is the probability of various negative "personal consequences" associated with not breaching confidentiality?

References

Abroms, G. The place of values in psychotherapy. *Journal of Marriage and Family Counseling,* 1978, *4,* (*4*), 3–17.

AHA (American Hospital Association). *Hospital Medical Records: Guidelines for Their Use and the Release of Medical Information.* Chicago: American Hospital Association, 1972.

APA (American Psychological Association). *Ethical Principles of Psychologists.* Washington, D.C.: American Psychological Association, 1981 revision.

Berry, R. E., Jr. Estimating the economic costs of alcohol abuse. *New England Journal of Medicine,* 1976, *295,* 620.

Brodsky, S. Shared results and open files with the client: professional irresponsibility or effective involvement? *Professional Psychology,* 1972, *4,* 554–561.

Cleary, E. *McCormick's Handbook of the Law of Evidence,* 2nd ed. St. Paul: West Publishing Co., 1972.

Halleck, S. L. *Law in the Practice of Psychiatry.* New York: Plenum Medical Book Co., 1980.

Health Records and Law and Practice. Washington, D.C.: National Commission on Confidentiality of Health Records, 1978.

Hoffman, M. Moral development. In P. H. Mussen (ed.), *Carmichael's Manual of Child Psychology.* New York: John Wiley & Sons, 1970.

Houghkirk, E. Everything you've always wanted your clients to know but have been afraid to tell them. *Journal of Marriage and Family Counseling,* 1977, *3,* (2), 27–34.

Kant, I. *Critique of Practical Reason.* Chicago: University of Chicago Press, 1949.

Kohlberg, L. Stage and sequence: the cognitive development approach to socialization. In D. A. Goslen (ed.), *Handbook of Socialization Theory and Research.* New York: Rand-McNally Corp., 1969.

Lanman, R. B. The federal confidentiality protection for alcohol and drug abuse patient records: a model for mental health and other medical records. *American Journal of Orthopsychiatry,* 1980, 50, (*4*), 666–667.

McIntosh v. *Milano,* 168 N.J. Super. 466, 402 A 2d, 500 (1979).

Monahan, J. *Who Is the Client?* Washington, D.C.: American Psychological Association, 1980.

NASW (National Association of Social Workers). *Code of Ethics.* Washington, D.C.: National Association of Social Workers, 1979.

National Survey on Drug Abuse. Washington, D.C.: Government Printing Office, 1979.

Ney, S. G. Patient confidentiality and privacy: the federal initiative. *American Journal of Orthopsychiatry,* 1980, *50* (*4*), 649–658.

Nye, S. Commentary on model law on confidentiality of health and social service records. *American Journal of Psychiatry,* 1979, *136,* 145–147.

Perr, I. Problems of confidentiality and privileged communication in psychiatry. *Annals of Legal Medicine,* 1971, *327,* 77–81.

Perr, J. N. Confidentiality and consent in psychiatric treatment of minors. *Journal of Legal Medicine,* 1976, *4,* 9–12.

Piaget, J. *Psychology of Intelligence* (M. Piercy and D. E. Berlyne, translators). Totowa, N.J.: Littlefield, Adams & Co., 1966 (originally published, 1947).

Popiel, D. J. Confidentiality in the context of court referrals to mental health professionals. *American Journal of Orthopsychiatry,* 1980, *50* (*4*), 678–685.

Principles of Medical Ethics with Annotations Especially Applied to Psychiatry. Washington, D. C.: American Psychiatric Association, 1978.

Privacy Protection Study Commission. *Personal Privacy in an Information Society.* Washington, D.C.: U.S. Government Printing Office, 1977.

———. *Personal Privacy in an Information Society.* Washington, D. C.: U.S. Government Printing Office, 1979.

Rinella, V. J., and Goldstein, M. R. Family therapy with substance abusers: legal considerations regarding confidentiality. *Journal of Marital and Family Therapy,* 1980, *6,* (*3*), 319–325.

Schuchman, H. On confidentiality of health records. *American Journal of Orthopsychiatry,* 1975, *45,* 732–733.

———. Confidentiality: practice issues in new legislation. *American Journal of Orthopsychiatry,* 1980, *50,* (*4*), 641–648.

Shlensky, R. Informed consent and confidentiality: proposed new approaches in Illinois. *American Journal of Psychiatry,* 1977, *134,* 1416–1418.

Smith, P. Survery shows extent of drug and alcohol use. *Navy Times,* Dec. 1980.

Tarasoff v. *Regents of U. of California, et al.,* 551 P. 2d 334 (1976).

Tepper, A. M. and Kaslow, F. W. Informed decision-making capacity as it relates to patient's ability to participate in treatment determinations. *Alabama Law and Psychology Review,* 1981, 31–45.

Von Hoose, W. H., and Kottler, J. A. *Ethical and Legal Issues in Counseling and Psychotherapy.* San Francisco: Jossey-Bass, 1980.

Wise, T. Where the public peril begins: a survey of psychotherapists to determine the effects of *Tarasoff. Stanford Law Review,* 1976, *31,* 165–190.

Zurcher, et al. v. *Stanford Daily, et al.,* 98A SC, 436 U.S. 547, 98 S. Ct. 1970. (1978).

21

The Clinical Management of Sexual Problems in Substance Abusers

Robert C. Kolodny

Considerable data has been gathered in the last decade documenting the high prevalence of sexual dysfunction and other sexual difficulties in populations of alcoholics and drug abusers. However, very little of what has been written deals directly with the treatment issues that confront clinicians working with these populations. In this chapter, after a brief review of the types of sexual problems caused by substance abuse, attention will be focused on treatment strategies for the sexual rehabilitation of such clients.

Sexual Problems Resulting from Drug Abuse: An Overview

Human sexual behavior and human sexual functioning are complex processes that remain only incompletely understood despite the best efforts of a variety of researchers. As a conceptual generalization, however, it can accurately be said that most aspects of human sexuality depend on a delicate interplay between biological and psychosocial forces. For example, sexual desire (libido), although undeniably primed by neuroendocrine stimuli, seems to be more forcefully governed by cognitive and affective processes; as a result, human sexual behavior is far less dependent on hormonal status than the sexual behavior of other animal species (Hutchison, 1978; Beyer, 1979; Masters, Johnson, and Kolodny, 1982). As another example, although a reasonably intact endocrine system, vascular system, and neurologic system are generally requisite for "normal"—i.e., unimpeded—sexual functioning in humans, anxiety, guilt, anger, embarrassment, and other similar feelings can effectively inhibit or disrupt natural sexual reflexes so that a temporarily dysfunctional state occurs (Masters and Johnson, 1970; Kaplan, 1974). Conversely, in the most idyllic, relaxed, and undistracted erotic encounter, a man with a testosterone deficiency or a woman with a neurological problem may find it difficult, if not impossible, to function sexually in a satisfactory way.

Despite the fact that many drugs of abuse are touted as aphrodisiacs—stimulants to a person's sexual interest and/or performance—the reality is that most of these agents are pharmacologically far more likely to be disruptive to sexual functioning than to enhance it. However, there is a powerful expectancy among many drug users that "substance X" will lead them to quicker turn-ons or more intense sexual experiences, and the power of the placebo (user expectation) effect is such that, at least a portion of the time in the early stages of their drug use, this expectancy produces a self-fulfilling prophecy. (Whether this represents a truly "better" sexual experience or whether the person's judgment of the experience is simply altered is, for the purposes of this discussion, irrelevant. In either event, the person's *perceived* experience reinforces the preexisting motivation for drug use and thus is likely to contribute to repeated use of drugs before sex. In the event the sexual enhancement effect is *not* obtained, drug users may repeat the experiment on one or more occasions in an attempt to "prove" their sexual normality.)

As substance abuse escalates in frequency, the probability of sexual difficulties escalates too. This occurs for one or more of a number of different reasons, including: (1) the sexual side-effects of most drugs are dose-dependent, and as the frequency of drug abuse increases, there is often a concomitant increase in quantities used; (2) the biological effects of many drugs of abuse are in part cumulative, so that with frequent use, tissue levels build to the point where toxic effects occur; (3) as substance abuse becomes more frequent, a variety of health problems may surface, including increased susceptibility to infection and poor nutritional status, which themselves may predispose toward or precipitate sexual difficulties; (4) as drug-seeking behavior and drug use rituals become more and more central to the user's life, sexual opportunities are likely to be reduced and sexual energies may actually be sublimated into the drug use pattern; and (5) the substance abuser's attractiveness as a sexual partner is likely to be diminished as his or her frequency of use escalates—this is true both in terms of physical attractiveness and in terms of the attractiveness of interpersonal behavior that typically serves as a prelude to sexual intimacy or even finding a willing sexual partner.

In addition to these general factors, the inherent pharmacologic properties of the substance being abused may express themselves in terms of sexual problems. Thus, alcohol, narcotics, sedatives, and most tranquilizers act as depressants to the central nervous system, which ultimately integrates all afferent and efferent sexual impulses (including the cognitive); central nervous system stimulants, including such drugs as amphetamines and cocaine, may induce a hyperexcitability that either neurologically or, via a torrential endocrine discharge, can also lead to sexual dysfunction.

Finally, it should be observed that some substance abusers have sexual difficulties that temporally precede their drug use problem. Frequently, in fact, one finds that the initial motivation for drug experimentation was to find a means to cope with this sense of sexual inadequacy. For instance, many young adult males troubled by premature ejaculation find that a few drinks of an alcoholic beverage help to control their unwanted ejaculatory swiftness. Adolescents who feel sexually inhibited and "uptight"—whether from religious teachings about sex, parental edict, or other sources—may discover that smoking marijuana or using alcohol helps them relax and overcome their sexual inhibitions. Needless to say, these preexisting sexual difficulties, which are often intertwined with a poor sense of self-esteem, body image problems, and deficiencies in interpersonal skills, are not usually helped by a pattern of drug abuse except in the most perfunctory, illusory way.

With these general observations in mind, we will now turn to a discussion of the sexual problems found in association with various drugs of abuse. No attempt will be made to be encyclopedic in terms of either a literature review or the discussion of the physiological and psychological mechanisms producing drug-related sexual problems; rather, information is presented in a fashion aimed at providing readers with sufficient facts to intelligently integrate this material into clinical management strategies, as discussed in the latter portion of this chapter.

Sex and Alcohol

Acute Alcohol Intoxication

Although alcohol is thought of by many people as a sexual stimulant, in recent years research has generally succeeded in documenting

Shakespeare's observation that alcohol "provokes the desire but . . . takes away the performance" (*Macbeth,* Act II, Scene 3). In 1970, Masters and Johnson described excessive alcohol consumption as the leading cause of secondary impotence in their extensive clinical population. Soon thereafter, using penile plethysmography to measure changes in penile tumescence as an objective sign of sexual arousal, Farkas and Rosen (1976), Briddell and Wilson (1976), and Rubin and Henson (1976) independently documented a significant negative linear effect of increasing blood alcohol levels on sexual arousal in healthy male college students who were social drinkers. More recently, Malatesta et al. (1979) showed that increasing levels of blood alcohol lead to a significant deterioration in male masturbatory effectiveness, including a systematic increase in ejaculation latency, decreased sexual arousal, decreased pleasure and intensity of the orgasmic experience, and greater difficulty in reaching orgasm.

Studies of the acute effects of alcohol on measures of female sexual arousal generally have shown findings that parallel the studies in males just mentioned. Thus, Wilson and Lawson (1976) also found a negative linear effect of blood alcohol levels on physiological sexual arousal as measured by vaginal photoplethysmography in female social drinkers. However, the subjective reports of the women in their study indicated that the more intoxicated the women were, the more they predicted they would experience sexual arousal while viewing an erotic movie and the more their self-reports indicated heightened sexual arousal during the actual viewing. This general finding—a discrepancy between women's cognitive responses to sexual arousal during alcohol use and the objective physiological evidence of sexual arousal during alcohol use—was recently confirmed (Malatesta et al., 1982). In this study, involving 18 university women who were social drinkers, tested at four different blood alcohol concentrations (0, 25, 50, and 75 mg. %) in counterbalanced order, using a repeated measures design with monthly experimental sessions, it was shown that increasing blood alcohol levels significantly reduced the intensity of orgasm, significantly increased the difficulty of reaching orgasm, and "exerted a progressively greater physiological depressant effect upon female orgasmic response measured by latency to orgasm." However, subjective sexual arousal and orgasmic pleasuribility *increased* with greater blood alcohol concentrations, raising the intriguing possibility that a woman who is actually impaired in her physiological sexual responsiveness by acute alcohol use may view her experience as one of increased sexual pleasure.

From a clinical perspective, chronic female sexual difficulties rarely appear to be caused by isolated episodes of alcohol intoxication. However, it is quite common to find that long-term secondary impotence results from a single episode of erectile failure attributable to excessive alcohol use, since the initial episode of erectile dysfunction may trigger an overwhelming sense of performance anxiety and fear of failure that maintains the dysfunction even with the pharmacologic depressant removed (Masters and Johnson, 1966, 1970; Kaplan, 1974; Munjack and Oziel, 1980; Forrest, 1983). In fact, chronic impotence can also result from anxiety over the failure to ejaculate caused by a single episode of alcohol intoxication, although this outcome is a relatively infrequent occurrence.

There has been considerable speculation in the past about the "disinhibition" effect of alcohol on sexual feelings and sexual behavior. Basically, the disinhibition effect is said to occur at low doses of alcohol ingestion, as ordinary social constraints regarding sexuality are lowered and a person feels freer to express sexual feelings or participate in sexual acts that would be avoided when completely sober. Wilson (1977) has reviewed the evidence in support of this theory in detail and concludes that it is an oversimplified and generally erroneous concept. He points out that people may *act* less sexually and socially inhibited when they believe they are "under the influence" of alcohol, but that this effect is a misattribution since it is likely to occur whether or not alochol has actually been consumed. Once again, we see that people's expectancies about a particular substance and how it will influence their sexual status play an important role in determining their ensuing behavior.

These expectancies are fostered by myths, jokes, and alert Madison Avenue executives attuned to the public pulse. Alcohol is widely thought of by adolescents as a facilitator of relaxation and tension-release, just as it is also perceived by them as an instrument of seduction. Realizing that alcohol use can be symbolic of "growing up" (or acting grown up), realizing that alcohol use confers this status most explicitly in social situations, and realizing that being able to use alcohol without getting physically ill is a sign of a "real" man, teenagers also use alcohol as a means of creating sexual opportunity. The teenage male has probably been told by friends that getting a girl drunk (or at least "loosened up") will facilitate his sexual advances by either "turning her on" or reducing her objections to his intimacies. Many teenage girls are also quick to recognize that drinking allows them to have a perfect "excuse" to engage in sex without having to feel personally responsible for their actions, thus simultaneously satisfying their desire to experiment and their moral sensibility. This early conditioning is reinforced by advertisements that stress the social niceties of alcohol consumption, the physical attractiveness of those who imbibe, and the not-so-hidden undercurrent of sexual energy that is linked to alcohol use, whether at parties or at a private tête-à-tête.

It's not by accident that the reputation of alcohol as a sexual enhancer is so prevalent despite overwhelming evidence to the contrary.

Sexual Problems of Alcoholics

Accurate prevalance figures for rates of sexual dysfunction in alcoholics are not presently available, but most reports support the likelihood of substantial sexual problems in this population. For example, Jensen (1981) found that 33 percent of alcoholic men were impotent, while 35 percent had reduced libido and 12 percent had retarded ejaculation, for an overall rate of 59 percent of his population experiencing sexual dysfunction. Kolodny, Masters, and Johnson (1979) estimated that one-half of alcoholic men and one-quarter of alcoholic women had significant sexual disturbances; while in alcoholic men with end-stage cirrhosis, 78 percent were found to have impaired potency and libido (Van Thiel, Sherins, and Lester, 1973). However, the lack of reliable generalizable data in this area is illustrated by the fact that Lemere and Smith (1973), in a methodologically poorly conceived study, found only an 8 percent rate of impotence in approximately 17,000 male alcoholics, and Murphy et al. (1980) found little statistical evidence for sexual dysfunction in female alcoholics, although the authors stated: "We have some reasons to believe that the percentage of problems reported by our sample was not consistent with the actual extent of problems in this population." When earlier reports of a 57 percent rate of inadequate sexual response among female alcoholics (Browne-Mayers, Seelye, and Sillman, 1976) and a 72 percent rate of not experiencing orgasms by female alcoholics (Kinsey, 1966) are examined, the confusion that pervades this area is easily apparent.

There are many organic factors contributing to the sexual disorders commonly encountered in alcoholic men. Since these have been extensively discussed elsewhere (see, for example, Kolodny, Masters, and Johnson, 1979; Van Thiel and Lester, 1979; Valimaki and Ylikahri, 1981), they will be outlined only briefly here. Endocrinologically, chronic alcohol abuse commonly lowers circulating levels of testosterone both by decreasing the endogenous production rate and by increasing breakdown of this hormone in the liver. Simultaneously, the normally delicate balance of the hypothalamic-pituitary-testicular axis is disrupted, causing a further reduction in gonadal testosterone synthesis. The usual increase in sex hormone binding globulin in the blood found in alcoholic men produces a situation in which the reduced amounts of circulating testosterone are more tightly bound, thus leaving less free testosterone available for action at the target tissue level. Additional endocrine problems include: (1) testicular atrophy (shrinkage) and damage to sperm production, and (2) elevated levels of estrogen, which antagonizes the action of testosterone and also leads to gynecomastia (abnormal male breast enlargement).

An even broader array of nonendocrine problems contributes substantially to the sexual difficulties of male and female alcoholics. Although both clinical impressions and animal experimental data support the probability that disruption of ovarian function and alteration of the hypothalamic-pituitary-ovarian axis in female alcoholics are commonplace, there is no supporting research in humans as of this writing. Peripheral neuropathy, anemia, cirrhosis and other forms of alcoholic liver disease, increased susceptibility to infection, poor nutritional status, and changes in physical appearance secondary to ascites (accumulation of fluid in the abdomen) are all pertinent here but beyond the scope of this discussion. Furthermore, a persistently high concentration of blood alcohol is likely to superimpose onto the picture the suppression of sexual reflexes that occurs via central nervous system depression resulting from acute intoxication.

These organic processes are only one part of the problem, however, Psychosocial elements of a diverse nature conspire to produce and perpetuate the organic contributions to sexual distress, as shown by the fact that sexual problems persist in about half of all alcoholics who had such problems while they were abusing alcohol even after they have abstained from alcohol use for a year or longer. (The treatment implications of this statement will be considered later in this chapter.)

As is true for most substance abusers who have preexisting sexual difficulties which they seek to help or even "cure" by pharmacologic means, the persistence or, frequently, worsening of the underlying conditions that created the sexual problem to begin with is common during the period of chronic substance abuse (but is frequently unrecognized by the person involved, who mistakenly thinks it has "gone away"). Thus, a man with poor self-esteem and a general feeling of sexual inadequacy may find that the tranquilizing properties of alcohol help reduce his anxiety in sexual situations, or may find that he simply doesn't care about sex as much if his libido shrinks substantially, yet has made no meaningful progress in coping with his basic sexual uncertainties. Following the cessation of abusive drinking, he may be faced with more severe sexual problems than he had before his alcohol abuse began, since his original problems may be compounded by a further reduction in self-esteem ("My inability to control my drinking proves how worthless I am") and by a heightened sense of guilt.

Alcoholics (Forrest, 1984) are frequently deficient in their capacity to develop and maintain intimacy with a partner, a problem which necessarily has considerable impact on their sexual relations. The alcoholic is apt to misjudge ways in which intimacy is initiated and maintained; is likely to be manipulative, inflexible, and often hostile when things aren't going "just right"; and, in sexual terms, may show little regard for his or her partner's feelings or preferences. High rates of marital discord further complicate the picture when one spouse is an alocholic; typically, as part of this pattern, the denying, blaming, and avoiding of responsibility that the alcoholic displays are apt to create anger and retaliatory measures from the spouse.

The female alcoholic may attempt to atone for her misbehavior by sexual compliance to her husband's needs; in fact, she may behave in a deliberately seductive fashion to attempt to circumvent his anger or to get him to overlook her irresponsibilities. While this may prove temporarily to be an effective coping mechanism of sorts, it typically produces a situation in which the woman feels little, if any, sexual arousal because of her own noninvolvement (essentially, she is engaging in a form of prostitution), which may eventually lead to conditioned response in which sexual interaction is distasteful and unrewarding to her. In addition, her husband or partner is likely to lose interest in this type of manipulative sex for at least three different reasons: (1) he gradually comes to recognize her lack of involvement (which tends to increase his hostility); (2) he tires of "letting her off the hook" in return for sexual favors; and (3) he is likely to find his partner less physically attractive as the ravages of alcohol mount along with the inattention to personal hygiene and grooming that is typical of chronic alcoholics.

In contrast, the woman married to or living with a male alcoholic is apt to withdraw from sexual activity as a means of demonstrating her resentment of his drinking, punishing him for his defiance, and protecting herself from the physical abuse and lack of tenderness that is apt to be inherent in such a sexual relationship (Kolodny, Masters, and Johnson, 1979). That he may not perceive such withdrawal as punishment as his own sexual interest wanes is apt to further infuriate her or reinforce her sense of helplessness in dealing with the alcoholism.

Additional aspects of the many psychosocial factors involved with the sexual problems of alcoholics will be discussed in the latter portion of this chapter.

Sex and Narcotics

Narcotic addiction is associated with a high rate of sexual problems in both sexes. For example, Cushman (1973) reported that 12 of 19 male heroin addicts had impaired libido, while 10 were impotent and 15 had delayed ejaculation. Similarly, Cicero et al. (1975) found that libido was suppressed in 100 percent of the male heroin addicts they studied and in 96.5 percent of male methadone users; both groups showed a high frequency of potency problems and ejaculatory impairment, as well. Bai et al. (1974) described decreased libido in 60 percent of the female addicts they studied; more recently, orgasmic dysfunction was noted in 27 percent of 85 female addicts, and decreased libido in 57 percent of this sample (Kolodny, 1982), while the same study found that among 162 male addicts, 48 percent were impotent, 59 percent had retarded ejaculation, and 66 percent had depressed libido.

The mechanism underlying the high rate of sexual disturbances in narcotic addiction seems to be in large part an endocrine problem. Decreased serum testosterone levels have been reported in male heroin and methadone addicts (Azizi et al., 1973; Mendelson, Mendelson, and Patch, 1975; Mendelson and Mello, 1975; Kolodny, 1982), although other studies, probably due to methodological heterogeneity, have shown less consistent endocrine alterations (Cushman, 1973; Cicero et al., 1975). It now appears that the opiate drugs act on the hypothalamic-pituitary-gonadal axis by producing an acute suppression of luteinizing hormone release from the pituitary, which in turn leads to a secondary drop in circulating testosterone concentrations by inhibiting testicular output of testosterone (Mirin et al., 1980). This is consistent with the high incidence of amenorrhea found in female narcotic addicts (Bai et al., 1974; Santen et al., 1975), which presumably occurs because of disruption of the normal hypothalamic-pituitary mechanisms controlling the cyclicity of gonadotropin release in women which regulates the menstrual cycle. Fortunately, these endocrine-suppressive events are relatively short-lived and generally disappear within one to three months after drug withdrawal (Mendelsohn and Mello, 1975; Kolodny, 1982).

Other biological mechanisms are likely to play a role in the frequent occurrence of sexual disturbances among narcotic addicts. These include the characteristically poor nutritional status of these individuals, their increased general susceptibility to infections, and the common problems of hepatitis resulting from contaminated needles. In addition, since many addicts are polydrug users (including the use of alcohol), the combined pharmacological effects of several types of drugs may also cause major sexual disruptions.

To these biological processes must be added a lengthy list of disturbances in the psychosocial sphere that effectively undermine sexual interest and sexual functioning in narcotic addicts. Chessick (1960) suggested that the intensive, euphoric "rush" of mainlining, followed by feelings of tension-release, provides a "pharmacogenic orgasm" to the addict which gives a sense of ego mastery while concomitantly reducing libidinal needs, Mirin et al. (1980) relate this hypothesis to the time-course of neuroendocrine events with opiate use, speculating that the "rush" of mainlining is due to "a massive release of catecholamines at both central and peripheral sites," and that the subsequent tension-release phase is actually "a drive reduction model of opiate reinforcement, in which the drug acts as an antianxiety agent and reduces sexual drive and tension."

As a more practical level, the addict typically becomes preoccupied with drug procurement and then "nods off" while under the acute influence of the drug, so that time for sexual relationships becomes increasingly crowded out even if the capacity for sexual performance is maintained. Rosenbaum (1981) has noted the typical sequence in an eloquently titled paper, "When Drugs Come into the Picture, Love Flies out the Window: Women Addicts' Love Relationships." According to this author, the addictive experience "begins with excitement and an expansion of options" but then works in highly destructive ways: female addicts typically have mates who are also addicts; the males are generally uninterested in sex and unable to perform; many of the women find that the "hit" of heroin is far more powerful, pleasurable, and easy to attain than having an orgasm by sexual interaction (one woman remarked, "it wasn't worth the energy you had to put out"); and, significantly, for many women the "sensuality and sharing aspects of doing heroin together (with their mate) are another replacement for sexual intercourse." When this is coupled with the facts that (1) neither partner misses their sexual interaction, since each of them is likely to experience reduced libido; (2) the female is often forced to turn to prostitution in order to earn money to support the drug habit, which is likely to have an impact on how she thinks about sex and men; and (3) the other problems produced by the addiction, including nearly constant bickering over money, entry into illegal activities, and a sense of reduced self-esteem, undermine the affectional side of the relationship, it is no wonder that "love flies out the window."

The addict who is not involved in a love relationship is likely to be socially withdrawn, somewhat secretive and defensive, and suspicious of the motives of others who may indicate some social/sexual interest. The male addict, in particular, often knows from past experience that he is impotent, which leads him to avoid attempts at new sexual relationships in order to avoid embarrassment and to protect his "macho" image. In some cases, the male addict will participate in sexual activity with a partner to a limited extent (that is, he may perform cunnilingus while claiming to be uninterested in intercourse)—either for the purpose of "ripping off" his newfound lover (e.g., asking her for a "loan," stealing her money, getting a key to her apartment which he later uses for thievery) or to save face by avoiding the issue of sexual dysfunction. More frequently, however, the male who is heavily addicted simply loses his interest in sex and rarely thinks about it, as the following comment from a twenty-eight-year-old client shows: "When I was hooked on heroin, sex was about the farthest thing from my mind. My body had no sexual urges, my brain didn't work the way it did before—or now—and the excitement of sex was completely dwarfed by the high from smack. I just didn't care about sex at all . . . it was like I'd been temporarily castrated."

Even among nonaddicts who are occasional narcotic users, the self-reported ratings of heroin as an enhancer of sexual behavior or sexual function are remarkably low, well below the ratings for alcohol, amphetamines, the psychedelic agents, and other drugs (Gay et al., 1975).

Sex and Stimulant Drugs

Much less reliable research data are available documenting the effects of pharmacologic stimulants on sexual feelings and behavior. Both the amphetamines and cocaine are central nervous system stimulants or sympathomimetic drugs that increase the pulse rate, raise the blood pressure, and cause increased blood flow to the genitals, thus inducing a state that is physiologically similar to the excitement phase of the human sexual arousal cycle. Since both types of drugs also induce euphoria and a sense of heightened energy and alertness, it is easy to understand why stimulants have been widely touted as "aphrodisiacs" that will improve sexual performance, prolong sexual endurance, and heighten sexual sensations.

Although the relatively sparse literature on the sexual effects of stimulant drugs suggests, on the one hand, that these agents are likely to increase sexual desire and the capacity for prolonged sexual performance (Angrist and Gershon, 1976; Friesen, 1976; Jones and Jones, 1977; Bush, 1980), there is also documentation of the occurrence of a variety of disturbances of sexual function in stimulant users (Bell and Trethowan, 1961; Greaves, 1972; Gay et al., 1975; Smith, 1979; Kolodny, 1982). For example, more than one-third of 39 experienced drug users reported loss of erection during cocaine use in one study (Gay et al., 1975), while 17 percent of 168 men surveyed more recently reported such an effect. Priapism, a persistent, painful erection lasting for hours or longer, has also been occasionally noted in male cocaine users (Gay et al., 1975; Jones and Jones, 1977; Kolodny, 1982).

As mentioned previously in this chapter, deleterious sexual effects of drugs are generally dose-related and also depend, at least in part, on the route of administration, the frequency of use, and other factors including underlying health status and the existence of pre–drug use sexual difficulties. In this regard, it can be said that persons injecting amphetamines or "free-basing" cocaine on a regular basis (i.e., at least several times a week) are far more likely to experience sexual problems than are those using other routes of administration. It appears that more than half of the men in this category have erectile problems in at least 50 percent of their erotic encounters and that nearly two-thirds describe difficulty reaching orgasm, while close to a third of women showing this high a frequency of intravenous stimulant use do not usually have orgasms. Fortunately, these sexual problems generally disappear promptly on cessation of drug use.

It should also be noted that cocaine acts as a sexual facilitator in several different ways socially. Because cocaine is very expensive and highly regarded as a sexual enhancer, when a man offers to share his cocaine with a woman, there is often an implicit sexual invitation understood by both parties; as one user noted, "Cocaine is too expensive to waste by myself" (Bush, 1980). Widely available at singles bars and in the economically advantaged "just-got-a-divorce" crowd, cocaine literally opens the doors of sexual access for many males and provides a convenient excuse for females who otherwise might pass on having "instant" sex with a partner they hardly know. Here, it is not a matter of the drug lowering sexual or social inhibitions; rather, there is a pattern of sexual and social expectations. If one wishes to indulge in the excitement/risk/pleasure of coke, one must play the game "by the rules," and the etiquette of cocaine use clearly includes a high premium on sexual mutuality. Interestingly, while some women enjoy the increased stamina and endurance that their partners temporarily acquire with cocaine, other women report that their prolonged bouts of sexual activity become more like work than play, and post-coital soreness when the drug effect wears off is fairly common.

Marijuana and Sex

Considerable controversy surrounds the question of the sexual effects of *Cannabis sativa,* with a remarkable lack of well-controlled studies to shed light on this issue. Only a brief summary of the pertinent facts will be discussed here.

There is general agreement that sporadic use of marijuana is unlikely to have significant negative effects on sexual functioning in most users. Occasionally, female users describe vaginal dryness as a side effect of marijuana use (mimicking the dry mouth which most users report), which may lead to pain during intercourse or attempts at penile insertion, but most marijuana users agree that this substance enhances their sexual experiences (Kolodny, Masters, and Johnson, 1979; Bush, 1980). Although more than three-quarters of experienced marijuana users claimed that marijuana increased their sexual pleasure, most denied that this occurred because of a greater intensity to their sexual response (e.g., "bigger" or "firmer" erections, more intense ejaculations in males; more intense orgasms or more frequent multiple orgasms in females). Instead, users consistently claim that marijuana exerts its erotic enhancement by: (1) slowing their sensation of the passage of time; (2) putting them in closer rapport with their partners; and (3) providing greater tactile sensitivity all over the body (not simply enhancing genital sensitivity). The subjectivity of each of these "mechanisms" is paramount; for instance, when one partner is high on marijuana and the other is not, sex generally seems dysynchronous and unpleasant; and when tactile acuity is studied in marijuana users when they are high versus not high, actual tactile perception is either no different or actually diminished while under the influence of marijuana. Thus, it appears that the "sexual enhancement" effects of marijuana are typically *perceived* effects rather than actual effects—which doesn't necessarily render them illusory (since enjoyment is often in perception rather than measured fact), but at least raises a question as to whether this is a true drug effect.

Among those using marijuana on a chronic, frequent basis, additional considerations are of interest. Heavy use of marijuana may lead to suppressed serum testosterone levels (Kolodny et al., 1974, 1979) and suppressed sperm production (Kolodny et al., 1974; Hembree et al., 1976). In addition, 19.2 percent of men using marijuana on a daily basis for a minimum of six months have been found to be impotent, compared to an impotence rate of 8.4 percent among an age-matched control group of men who never used marijuana and rates of under 8.5 percent in men using marijuana only sporadically (Kolodny, 1982). While there does not appear to be an increased rate of sexual dysfunction among women who are heavy marijuana users, one study indicates that changes in ovarian function may occur as a result of chronic, frequent use of this drug (Bauman et al., 1979).

Miscellaneous Drugs of Abuse and Sexuality

Although there are no good data available describing the sexual impact of other drugs of abuse such as LSD, PCP, and amyl nitrite, it is clear that clinicians frequently encounter sexual disturbances in those abusing these agents. It is also safe to say that rates of sexual dysfunction exceed 50 percent in men and women who are barbiturate addicts, and that persons using large amounts of Quaaludes, Valium, and similar drugs are highly susceptible to sexual difficulties as well. Again, it is important to recognize that among the sexual problems encountered in this group are those directly related to the effects of the drugs as well as problems that antedated the substance-abusing behavior. However, a better understanding of the mechanisms by which these drugs exert their deleterious sexual effects awaits further research.

Clinical Management Strategies: An Overview

Some general observations about dealing with the sexual problems of substance abusers can be considered as almost universally applicable to this population. Without question, the most important point is that attempts at reversing the sexual distress produced by drugs will invariably fail unless the person first succeeds in overcoming his or her chemical dependency. Although intensive therapeutic attention may succeed temporarily—and in a limited fashion—in improving sexual function among those continuing their substance abuse behavior, it is fair to say that this approach is both a waste of time and a Band-Aid operation with little merit to recommend it. A period of at least three to six months of drug abstinence allows time for physiological reequilibration (to the extent possible in an individual case, cirrhosis will not disappear, of course, and other types of medical problems may or may not resolve themselves) and will also permit a reasonable proportion of "problem" cases to revert spontaneously to relatively normal sexual function. In some cases, this spontaneous-reversion phenomenon is due to restoration of normal hormonal status; in other cases, it represents a return from a perpetual state of central nervous system depression; and in still other cases, it appears to be principally related to a return toward psychosocial stability and improved interpersonal behaviors.

A second general observation is that treating the sexual problems of substance abusers is next to impossible unless they have a partner available to participate in treatment with them. While the exact reason for this is unclear—and sex therapy for individuals without partners is certainly possible in other circumstances (see, for example, Kaplan, 1974; Annon, 1976; Leiblum and Pervin, 1980)—it seems that the presence of a cooperative, caring partner is a key variable in determining the potential outcome of such cases.

Additional factors to be considered include the following:

1. *It is important to convey to clients that there are few quick and easy cures.* Unrealistic expectations for an instant improvement in

sexual problems is particularly likely among substance abusers and correspondingly likely to backfire on them when things prove more difficult than expected. To prevent them from prematurely dropping out of therapy or giving up while remaining in therapy, it is useful (and honest) to be circumspect in initial prognostic statements and discussions of what therapy can achieve.

2. *Sexual problems among substance abusers are usually complexly determined and intertwined with a wide variety of personality issues.* Avoid leaping to instant judgments about the etiology of the problem and the most desirable treatment plan. It is advisable to recognize that difficulties in impulse control, poor assertiveness, deficient social skills, high guilt, and depression may be present, and to deal with these problems concurrently with specific sexual issues, since they are all apt to be interacting components of the situation.

3. *Don't ignore the importance of the biomedical side of assessment and treatment.* In many cases, appropriate medical evaluation can point the way to certain treatment modalities that will improve the chances of sexual rehabilitation materially. For example, the alcoholic male who has abstained from drinking for a year may still continue to have a low testosterone level; dealing with his problem of impotence may be considerably easier once he is given appropriate hormone replacement therapy.

4. *Be certain to focus on relationship issues and dynamics as well as individual problems, because often the relationship holds the most important keys to unlocking the sexual problems of the individual.*

Clinical Management Strategies: A Step-by-step Approach

It is not the purpose of this chapter to provide a detailed review of the concepts and techniques of sex therapy. Readers interested in obtaining a reasonably comprehensive review of these matters can consult Masters and Johnson (1970), Kaplan (1974) LoPiccolo and LoPiccolo (1978), Leiblum and Pervin (1980) for detailed information on the principles of sex therapy. Here, we will present a working outline useful in the step-by-step management of substance abusers with sexual problems.

Phase 1: Intake and Assessment

As previously mentioned, attempts at definitive sex therapy should be delayed until at least three to six months of abstinence from the abused substance have passed. However, this is not to say that sexual issues should be ignored prior to this time; indeed, it is highly beneficial to make inquiries about the sexual function and satisfaction of patients at as early a point as possible and to follow up on this information with some fundamental sex education, which can also provide an opportunity for patients to ventilate—an important step in setting the stage for further progress, and in fact a step not devoid of therapeutic power on its own. It is not unheard of for the individual who has previusly had a chemical dependency to snap out of his or her sexual distress when given a brief amount of information that includes a permission-giving (and reassuring) component. It sometimes seems that this early attention to sexual issues acts to overcome the libidinal inertia that often characterizes substance abuse; in effect, the client is reminded of sex as a potential source of gratification, is encouraged to risk the interpersonal intimacy that most sexual behavior requires, and is steered toward the ordinarily obvious option of taking control of his or her life again by a nondestructive, inexpensive, yet enticing form of behavior.

Those individuals who are able to reestablish fairly normal sexual functioning with only these minimal interventions may still require subsequent counseling to help them deal with residual sexual difficulties (for example, being able to function physically but not enjoying it much), but in some cases no further assistance is required. However, these are the fortunate few; many substance abusers dealing with sexual problems will find that they persist, to a greater or lesser degree, until further professional help is obtained.

It is at this point that a definitive assessment of the sexual problem should be undertaken. At a minimum, this should include a careful physical examination and appropriate laboratory tests (e.g., measurement of serum testosterone in impotent men; see Kolodny, Masters, and Johnson, 1979, for more information), assessment of current physiological status (both by interviewing and by standardized tests such as the MMPI and appropriate depression questionnaires), and assessment of the current relationship, if any. In addition, a careful and detailed sex history should be taken, documenting patterns of sexual behavior and also sexual functioning, as well as searching for possible past sexual traumas (e.g., incestuous victimization, rape, episodes of sexually transmitted diseases) and ascertaining information about sexual attitudes and knowledge. Although it is not always possible to determine the exact etiology of a sexual problem from these approaches, the information obtained will be useful in formulating further plans for therapy.

At the practical level, the next considerations are matters of format. Assuming that the assessment information does not point toward the likelihood of a primarily organic problem, which is unlikely to be amenable to sex therapy, a decision must then be made about the type of treatment likely to be beneficial. The available options include: (1) standard Masters and Johnson therapy, which involves a dual-sex co-therapy team working with a couple on a day-to-day basis for an intensive two-week period (see Masters and Johnson, 1970, and Kolodny, Masters, and Johnson, 1979); (2) various modifications of the original Masters and Johnson model, including treatment by a single therapist rather than a co-therapy team, weekly rather than daily visits (lasting, on average, four to six months), or integration with psychoanalytic approaches (see Kaplan, 1974, for example); or (3) use of group sex therapy formats, as described by a variety of authors (e.g., Barbach, 1980; Perelman, 1980; Kaplan et al., 1978; McGovern, Kirkpatrick, and LoPiccolo, 1978). Each of these options has certain advantages and disadvantages; since at present there does not seem to be a clearcut superiority of one format over the others, the choice depends partly on the preferences and experience of the therapist and partly on the wishes of the client. Whichever format is chosen, it is important to formulate a clear therapeutic contract that spells out the expectations and goals of therapy from everyone's perspective before going any farther. This may prove to be particularly useful in minimizing the manipulative and often irresponsible behaviors typically found among substance abusers: for example, explaining at the outset that missing two therapy sessions will be grounds for ending treatment may help prevent later battles over just such an issue.

Phase 2: The Early Stages of Therapy

The initial objectives of the therapist working with a client with sexual problems related to a past pattern of substance abuse are simply summarized as follows: (1) establish a sense of empathy and rapport; (2) discuss etiology and prognosis in a straightforward but nonthreatening way; and (3) enlist the client's willingness to invest him/herself in the work of therapy with a reasonable degree of commitment. The client must understand that the therapist has no magic wand to wave or incantation to invoke—whatever progress that is possible will depend in part on the client's efforts. The first and most critical expression of this fact, as previously emphasized, is the almost absolute necessity to have the client maintain drug abstinence during the course of sex therapy. Of almost parallel importance is agreement on the part of the client to carry out, with a high degree of regularity, assigned behavioral tasks outside the therapy setting ("homework" is not a good phrase to use in sex therapy to describe these tasks, since the word connotes an attitude of "sex as work" rather than the more productive, less anxiety-producing notion of "sex as play" most therapists strive for). The third aspect of initial departure is asking the client and his or her partner to deliberately refrain from direct sexual interaction via physical stimulation until the therapist directs them to begin such activities. This is, for some couples, more of a relief than a burden, but many couples initially voice skepticism or dismay at having sexual contact "banned" by the therapist and may express initial incredulity or resistance to the idea.

The primary reason for the ban on sexual stimulation is to reduce anxiety surrounding the client's perceived need to "perform" sexually in particular situations. Although substance abusers may have less awareness of their performance anxieties than other people with sexual problems—perhaps due to their drug use as an anti-anxiety maneuver, which at least partly succeeded in blocking or blurring their anxiety—the ubiquity of this problem is such that anxiety-reducing measures constitute one of the cornerstones of effective sex therapy.

The early focus of therapy will depend in part on the nature of the sexual dysfunction that presents and in part on the nature of the relationship in treatment. For obvious reasons, if a couple entering therapy has a major degree of hostility or other severe problematic dyadic dynamics, these elements require therapeutic attention and moderation before much meaningful progress can be made dealing with the sexual side of the relationship. Standard marriage counseling techniques are typically employed in the early phase of sex therapy; however, it is a mistake to do this to the exclusion of working concurrently on sexual issues, since the two sets of problems are often intertwined.

Even in cases where no serious dyadic problems exist, it is usually imperative to focus on enhancing communication skills in the early stages of therapy, since verbal communication processes in many ways mirror the types of interactions that occur in sexual interaction. In fact, it is helpful to point out to clients that sex *is* a form of communication—perhaps the most intimate level of communication there is—and that learning how to communicate more effectively in nonsexual situations is likely to have positive benefits in sexual situations as well. Emphasis is placed on both sending and receiving/interpreting messages as part of the communicating package, with one obvious aspect often requiring attention being the need to train at least one member of the dyad in assertiveness skills. Broadly conceptualized, this communications enhancement helps a couple to get more closely in touch with their feelings; convey more information about feelings, need, concerns, or fears to each other with less time-lag than they had probably done before; develop an enhanced sense of intimacy and trust; and develop effective problem-solving skills. Each of these aspects of communications training has a very direct relevance to dealing with sexual problems.

The early therapy sessions are also generally a time to gently introduce some sex education to the couple. The exact nature of the material covered may vary from a fundamental discussion of male and female sexual anatomy and the nature of the human sexual response cycle to more sophisticated discussions dealing with sex roles, sex fantasies, the nature of sexual arousal, and so forth. Typically, it is useful to explain the naturalness of sexual functioning to couples, and to indicate how, in their circumstances, the natural aspects of sexual function were disrupted. The advantage of this approach is that it permits the clients to see that they will not be "taught" how to function sexually, but rather that the therapist will work with them to help them remove the impediments to their natural functioning.

However, with all of this as background, it is important to recognize that the key element of the early stages of sex therapy is the introduction of sensate focus assignments: structured behavioral tasks done by the clients in the privacy of their own home, which serve as the primary catalyst and means of assessment of the sex therapy process.

Sensate focus methods, first devised by Masters and Johnson (1970), consist of a series of touching exercises that are structured so as to foster anxiety reduction while enhancing sensory awareness and intimacy. The purpose of the sensate focus procedures, especially in the early stages, is *not* to produce sexual arousal or even sexual pleasure, but rather to develop an attunement to physical feelings and a concomitant diminishing of cognitive distractions. Thus, the first sensate focus assignment involves each partner taking turns exploring the other's body by touch, with the breasts and genital regions deliberately excluded from the process, with the sole emphasis on "What am I feeling (physically)?" and with no attempt to assess "success" or "failure" by any response criteria at all. Once this is accomplished smoothly and without major anxiety, the couple is assigned the next level of sensate focus: general body touching that includes exploration of the breasts and genitals. Again, it is stressed to clients that sexual excitation is *not* expected (although it may occur); that giving one's partner pleasure is *not* the purpose (although, again, there's nothing wrong if it happens); and that the emphasis should be on the tactile, physical sensations experienced, sometimes described to clients as "living in your fingertips." At this level of the sensate focus assignments, couples are explicitly reminded that even if they find themselves becoming sexually aroused they should not attempt to go on to intercourse, nor should they feel that they must do something with their arousal.

Against this backdrop of sensate focus exercises, an incredibly rich and complex array of therapeutic issues can emerge. The depths of performance anxieties are likely to manifest more clearly than is usually apparent from the history alone; problematic interactions and ingrained maladaptive habits of the couple will usually show up in stark relief as well. Thus, the therapist begins to gain a better view of the reasons sexual problems continue to exist, so that in this sense the sensate focus exercises serve as an important *in vivo* diagnostic tool. Furthermore, the structure of the sensate focus assignments provides an opportunity for therapeutic resistances to emerge and be confronted: it is particularly common in once-a-week therapy to find that a couple tells the therapist, "We just didn't have time to get around to trying the sensate focus this week." Exploring the meanings of this type of pattern has obvious relevance to the couple's eventual insight into their difficulties. In addition, the sensate focus opportunities provide a means of restructuring expectations and reducing anxiety while simultaneously implementing a "relearning" component so that couples can find a comfortable, nondestructive means of interacting together sensually and sexually.

Phase 3: The Middle Stage of Therapy

In the early phases of sex therapy, almost all couples experience a sense of relief at being told that no specific sexual responses are expected and that even if they become aroused they should not attempt to pursue the arousal. By the middle stage of therapy, this initial relief may change in several different ways. For many couples, the lowered anxiety that resulted from the preceding phase of therapy allowed sexual responses to emerge to a surprisingly strong degree. For instance, an alcoholic male having potency and desire problems might find that much to his surprise, during the first sensate focus experience he had a firm, long-lasting erection (perhaps for the first time in years). This results in: (1) improved sexual confidence; (2) improved trust in the therapist's wisdom; and (3) a greater willingness to invest himself in the therapy process (those who worry that therapy won't work are likely to hold back so that they can later claim, "Well, I didn't really try hard at it"). However, early "success" in therapy can also breed a false sense of security or even cockiness, with the client(s) not recognizing that one or two erections does not a cure make. Thus, the therapist must guard against undue optimism (and its resurgent expectations for automatic, instantaneous sexual response every time) on the client's part and must also be careful to distinguish carefully between reinforcing adaptive behaviors and inadvertently setting up performance paradoxes.

Other clients will not have shown significant improvement in their sexual functioning during the early stages of therapy. These cases can be divided generally into several different groups: (1) clients who are cooperative and appear committed to therapy, but in whom no major progress is evident; (2) clients who are either resistant or "slow learners"; (3) clients who have an underlying problem "blocking" the emergence of their sexual feelings (e.g., depression, phobias about sex); and (4) clients whose partners are uncooperative or even deliberately destructive and thus impede progress. The management of each of these types of cases will obviously be quite different.

The cooperative/committed group of clients who show little or no progress is likely to require specific attention to dealing with a phenomenon called "spectatoring" that is closely allied to fears of performance and that is very likely to interfere with sexual function. In the spectator role, one or both partners closely observe and evaluate their own or their partner's sexual response as a means of relieving their performance anxieties ("If I've got an erection, everything must be okay"). As an almost preordained effect, spectatoring reduces a dysfunctional person's involvement in sexual activity via the cognitive distraction that occurs as well as by reducing the spontaneity of the situation. Furthermore, even the slightest sign of decreasing sexual arousal is seen by the spectator as cause for alarm ("My God, I'm *losing* it!"), which necessarily dampens sexual response to a significant degree. Specific techniques for dealing with the spectator role have been discussed elsewhere (Kolodny, Masters, and Johnson, 1979; Leiblum and Pervin, 1980). In addition to the spectatoring phenomenon, therapists should be alert to the existence of self-esteem problems, high levels of sexual guilt, sexual orientation problems or ambivalence, and the possibility of an underlying organic cause for the sexual problem in this group of clients.

Dealing with client resistance has been extensively covered by a number of other authors and will not be discussed here. Similarly, clients with particular problems blocking their success in sex therapy must be dealt with on a highly individualized basis which is mainly beyond the scope of this discussion. Those clients whose problem is primarily a sexual phobia can typically be dealt with successfully by systemic desensitization techniques that are integrated into the sex therapy model. In most cases, imaginal (*in vitro*) desensitization is not particularly efficacious and direct movement to an *in vivo* model is called for. For cases where an antecedent sexual trauma such as incest or rape is the principal blocking factor, long-term individual therapy may be needed before sex therapy can be effective, but it is often difficult to determine this after just a few therapy sessions.

In cases where the spouse or partner seems to be deliberately undermining the progress of therapy, direct confrontation is usually called for but will not always succeed. It may be warranted to continue therapy for a while longer to attempt to maximize the gains made by the cooperative client, but there are risks involved in doing this that must be assessed separately in each case. The destructive behavior of the partner may, of course, be a way of gaining revenge for years of substance abuse, and individual therapy may be useful in some cases in helping to attain insight into this dynamic that ultimately can free the individual of the need to seek retribution by exacting a sexual pound of flesh.

Many people undergoing rehabilitation from a substance abuse problem have difficulties awakening their levels of sexual desire. While this is typically seen as a more serious problem for men, since men are generally expected to be the sexual aggressors or initiators in our society, many women are distressed by their lack of sexual interest and their partners may have a particularly difficult time dealing with this problem, too. The middle phase of sex therapy is an important time for dealing substantively with inhibited sexual desire if it is present. Most often, however, much the original genesis of the loss of sexual desire was pharmacologically induced, it is now perpetuated as a learned emotional "set." The affected individual has grossly altered expectations about sex (for instance, "My sexual pleasure depends on my being interested from the very beginning; if I'm not interested, I won't enjoy it") and also fails to recognize early physical "cues" of sexual arousal. Furthermore, such individuals are quite likely to have turned off their use of sexual fantasies, thus avoiding "priming the pump" or using fantasies to facilitate arousal during sexual activity, and often preferring to "think about other things" during sex, which of course makes it more mechanical and less enjoyable for both partners. While the principles of treating inhibited sexual desire are complex (see, for example, Kolodny, Masters, and Johnson, 1979; Kaplan, 1979; and LoPiccolo, 1980), it can be stated that anxiety reduction alone is not typically sufficient to overcome this type of sexual difficulty. Restructuring unrealistic expectations, fostering creative use of sexual imagery, and dealing with dyadic intimacy issues are typically pursued in the middle phase of therapy in order to make progress in this area.

Different approaches are used for dealing with various types of sexual dysfunctions: for example, the squeeze technique (Masters and Johnson, 1970) or the stop-start technique (Kaplan, 1974) is used to treat premature ejaculation; the insertion of graduated vaginal dilators is combined with behavioral approaches in treating vaginismus; anorgasmic women may be taught techniques of sexual self-pleasuring (Barbach, 1980). Although specific discussion of these methods is impossible here, proper selection and implementation of these strategies, combined with other aspects of the psychotherapy process, is highly germane to the outcome of each case.

Late in the middle stage of therapy most couples will exhibit sufficient sexual arousal during sensate focus opportunities that they are instructed to proceed with sexual intercourse. It is important that this is not given as an assignment that induces a high level of performance anxiety, but that it is presented as an extension of the sensate focus touching to simply a form of genital-to-genital touch. In fact, it is best to not use the term "intercourse" at all in discussing this assignment. Furthermore, it is also important to remind the couple that (1) the emphasis is to be on awareness of physical sensations, not "making something happen" or trying to turn on the partner; (2) genital-to-genital touch is possible even in the unaroused state, so that they shouldn't panic if penile insertion isn't done; and (3) this is not a "test" or a "do-or-die" situation—in fact, making it seem like a final exam will only create pressures that will detract from the experience. Obviously, juggling the potentially conflicting issues at this juncture is no easy task and requires good judgment, smooth presentation, and careful preparatory work creating a proper attitudinal climate preceding the actual time intercourse is suggested.

The middle stage of therapy is also a time that clients are apt to experience major "crisis days" in which all therapeutic progress seems to have been lost as they regress to their old, ingrained, maladaptive ways of reacting. The precise precipitating factors may be sexual or nonsexual, and may revolve around a central, dominant issue or arise from some seemingly trivial detail of everyday life such as an argument over which television show to watch. Whatever the exact nature of the crisis, its successful resolution can be a valuable learning opportunity for the client couple and can help prepare them to face subsequent conflicts and problems with intact coping strategies rather than a "give up in the face of adversity" attitude. Thus, it is particularly important to stress to the couple that experiencing difficulties is not a sign of failure or a sign of impending doom, but rather an opportunity for creatively seeking ways to reestablish their desired type of interaction.

Phase 4: The Latter Stages of Therapy

By this point in the therapy process, cases seem to divide into three relatively distinct categories: the obvious successes, the obvious failures, and those with equivocal progress. Working with the obvious successes is generally a straightforward task where the therapist aims to (1) work through any remaining individual or relationship issues, which are usually of minor moment at this point; (2) reinforce the therapeutic gains made previously; (3) complete the transmission of relevant sex education material, including discussions of the effects of aging on sex; (4) attend to issues of potential separation anxiety; and (5) guard against premature termination of the case under circumstances of a dramatic "success" but before the success has truly been consolidated.

Those cases that are obvious failures entering the latter stages of therapy are highly unlikely to show an abrupt turnaround at the last minute. In fact, careful consideration should be given to the possibility of terminating therapy in order to send the couple to another therapist utilizing a different psychotherapeutic viewpoint; in addition, other treatment alternatives should be considered. For example, in some cases it may be that therapy has been undertaken too close to the period of substance abuse, and an additional six months' wait before resuming therapy—during which the couple continues to apply the principles they were exposed to in therapy—may be highly beneficial. In cases of secondary impotence where an organic component seems prominent, and where sex therapy was undertaken on a trial basis, if reasonable erectile function has not been restored, consultation with a urologist may be advisable in order to consider the possibility of surgically implanting a penile prosthesis.

The "equivocal progress" category is undoubtedly the most difficult group with which to work. Here, attempting to understand the dynamics impeding progress and confronting these successfully is the key task for the therapist. In cases involving previous substance abuse, the therapist should be particularly alert for the existence of masked hostility within the relationship that lurks below the surface but interferes with intimacy and trust. The therapist should also search carefully for dependency problems, fear of success, boredom as a limiting factor, and persistent unresolved anxiety. Although only a portion of these cases will turn out to be successfully resolved, improvement in the sexual status of other clients in this category will be significant enough, while not resulting in a true "cure," to provide some hope for further progress if the couple continues to apply the basic principles they have learned to their posttherapy relationship.

A Concluding Note

The substance abuse behaviors all involve some forms of indulgence to attain short-term pleasure at the profound risk of long-term negative consequences (Miller, 1980). One of the paradoxes of this is that typically, the short-term chemical pleasure attained is at the cost of sexual pleasure, which is ordinarily one of the most intense, least expensive, most ego-supportive forms of experience that humans attain. This paradox may be better understood by realizing that the substance abuser often believes initially that the chemical agent he or she is using will enhance sexual experiences—by making them more relaxed, by augmenting their sensory perception, by "turning on" their reflex responses, or by giving them better control—but this is an illusion that has little basis in fact.

In many cases, the substance abuser is also a person who fears intimacy and seeks a more profound private existence in part to avoid the trials and tribulations of coping with the vulnerable underside of close relationships. These individuals may use alcohol or drugs as agents of seduction to buffer the intimacy requirements of ordinary sexual interactions and to also instill a false sexual self-confidence. Only too late do they discover the sexual damage that is occurring, and at that point their dependency or addiction is usually so firmly established that they simply don't care about the sexual consequences.

Once the substance abuser has decided to become chemically abstinent and has gone through a detoxification period, he or she is confronted by a series of immense challenges. Since alcohol comes to (maladaptively) define the identity of the alcoholic, and heroin serves the same purpose for the heroin addict, there is suddenly a need for the detoxified individual to either resume an old, familiar (and probably unhappy) identify or seek to construct a new sense of self, which is a difficult task at best. The immensity of this endeavor is compounded by the need to attend to disrupted or ignored love relationships—a task which is apt to be further compounded by the guilt the individual feels for his or her neglect (or worse) of spouse or partner during the period of substance-abusing behavior. Furthermore, added to the difficulties with sexual functioning that are quite likely to exist at this point, one must also consider the fact that substance-abusing behavior is often pursued by men to augment their sense of masculinity and by women to support their sense of feeling feminine: stripped of their chemical "support," there may be a significant degree of sex role confusion further compounding these individuals' sexual difficulties.

Attempting sex therapy in this quagmire of problems is a difficult task but one that has a reasonable chance of success with a skilled therapist. A key point to grasp is that sex therapy techniques must be employed on a highly individualized basis, integrated with a sophisticated psychotherapeutic approach that attends simultaneously to existent personal and interpersonal issues that interact with the sexual domain. It is likely that 50 to 60 percent of individuals with substance abuse problems can be successfully treated with such an approach, but there are few easy cases in this population and in a good many instances therapy will be relatively unsuccessful in resolving the sexual difficulties that present themselves. Although this is not an optimistic appraisal of the current state-of-the-art, it is a realistic one; optimism will have to wait for new approaches.

References

Angrist, B., and Gershon, S. Clinical effects of amphetamine and L-dopa on sexuality and aggression. *Comprehensive Psychiatry,* 1976, *17,* 715–722.

Annon, J. S. *Behavioral Treatment of Sexual Problems.* New York: Harper & Row, 1976.

Azizi, F., Vagenakis, A. G., Longcope, C., Ingbar, S. H., and Braverman, L. E. Decreased serum testosterone concentration in male heroin and methadone addicts. *Steroids, 22,* 467–472.

Bai, J., Greenwald, E., Caterini, H., and Kaminetzky, H. A. Drug-related menstrual aberrations. *Obstetrics and Gynecology,* 1974, *44,* 713–719.

Barbach, L. *Women Discover Orgasm.* New York: Free Press, 1980.

Bauman, J., Kolodny, R. C., Dornbush, R., and Webster, S. Effectos endocrinos del uso cronico de la mariguana en mujeres. In *Simposio Internacional Sobre Acutalization en Mariguana, Cuadenos Cientifico Cemesam 10,* July 1979, pp. 85–97.

Bell, D. S., and Trethowan, W. H. Amphetamine addiction and disturbed sexuality. *Archives of General Psychiatry,* 1981, *4,* 74–78.

Beyer, C. (ed.), *Endocrine Control of Sexual Behavior.* New York: Raven Press, 1979.

Briddell, D. W., and Wilson, G. T. The effects of alcohol and expectancy on male sexual arousal. *Journal of Abnormal Psychology,* 1976, *85,* 225–234.

Browne-Mayers, A. N., Seelye, E. E., and Sillman, L. Psychosocial study of hospitalized middle-class alcoholic women. *Annals of New York Academy of Sciences,* 1976, *273,* 593–604.

Bush, P. J. *Drugs, Alcohol, and Sex.* New York: Richard Marek, 1980.

Chessick, R. D. The "pharamacogenic orgasm" in the drug addict. *Archives of General Psychiatry,* 1960, *3,* 545–556.

Cicero, T. J., Bell, R. D., Wiest, W. G., Allison, J. H., Polakoski, K., and Robins, E. Function of the male sex organs in heroin and methadone users. *New England Journal of Medicine,* 1975, *292,* 882–887.

Cushman, R., Jr. Plasma testosterone in narcotic addiction. *American Journal of Medicine,* 1973, *55,* 452–458.

Farkas, G. M., and Rosen, R. C. Effect of alcohol on elicited male sexual response. *Journal of Studies on Alcohol,* 1976, *37,* 265–272.

Forrest, G. G. *Intensive Psychotherapy of Alcoholism.* Springfield, Ill.: Charles C Thomas, 1984.

Friesen, L. V. C. Aphrodisia with mazindol (letter). *Lancet,* 1974, *2,* 974.

Gay, G. R., Newmeyer, J. A., Elion, R. A., and Wieder, S. Drug-sex practice in the Haight-Ashbury District or "the sensuous hippie." In M. Sandler and G. L. Gessa (eds.), *Sexual Behavior: Pharmacology and Biochemistry.* New York: Raven Press, 1975.

Greaves, G. Sexual disturbances among chronic amphetamine users. *Journal of Nervous and Mental Disease,* 1972, *155,* 363–365.

Hembree, W. C., Zeidenberg, P., and Nahas, G. G. Marijuana effects upon human gonadal function. In G. G. Nahas (ed.), *Marijuana: Chemistry, Biochemistry and Cellular Effects.* New York: Springer Publishing Co., 1976.

Hutchison, J. B. (ed.). *Biological Determinants of Sexual Behavior.* New York: John Wiley & Sons, 1978.

Jensen, S. B. Sexual dysfunction in male diabetics and alcoholics: a comparative study. *Sexuality and Disability,* 1981, *4,* 215–219.

Jones, Hardin, and Jones, Helen. *Sensual Drugs.* Cambridge, England: Cambridge University Press, 1977.

Kaplan, H. *The New Sex Therapy.* New York: Brunner/Mazel, 1974.

———. *Disorders of Sexual Desire.* New York: Brunner/Mazel, 1979.

———, Kohl, R. N., Pomeroy, W. B., Offit, A. K., and Hogan, B. Group treatment of premature ejaculation. In J. LoPiccolo and L. LoPiccolo (eds.), *Handbook of Sex Therapy.* New York: Plenum Press, 1978.

Kinsey, B. A. *The Female Alcoholic.* Springfield, Ill.: Charles C. Thomas, 1966.

Kolodny, R. C. Drugs and sex. Paper presented at the Masters and Johnson Institute Seminar on Sexual Medicine, Sept. 10–11, 1982, Washington, D.C.

———, Masters, W. H., Kolodner, R. M., and Toro, G. Depression of plasma testosterone levels after chronic intensive marihuana use. *New England Journal of Medicine,* 1974, *290,* 872–874.

Kolodny, R. C., Masters, W. H., and Johnson, V. E. *Textbook of Sexual Medicine.* Boston: Little, Brown & Co., 1979.

Leiblum, S. R., and Pervin, L. A. *Principles and Practice of Sex Therapy.* New York: The Guilford Press, 1980.

Lemere, F., and Smith, J. W. Alcohol-induced sexual impotence. *American Journal of Psychiatry,* 1973, *130,* 212–213.

LoPiccolo, J., and LoPiccolo, L. (eds.). *Handbook of Sex Therapy.* New York: Plenum Press, 1978.

LoPiccolo, L. Low sexual desire. In S. Leiblum and L. Pervin (eds.), *Principles and Practice of Sex Therapy.* New York: The Guilford Press, 1980.

McGovern, K., Kirkpatrick, C., and LoPiccolo, J. A behavioral group treatment program for sexually dysfunctional couples. In J. LoPiccolo, and L. LoPiccolo (eds.), *Handbook of Sex Therapy.* New York: Plenum Press, 1978.

Malatesta, V. J., Pollack, R. H., Crotty, T. D., and Peacock, L. J. Acute alcohol intoxication and female orgasmic response. *Journal of Sex Research,* 1982, *18,* 1–17.

Malatesta, V. J., Pollack, R. H., Wilbanks, W. A., and Adams, H. E. Alcohol effects on the orgasmic-ejaculatory response in human males. *Journal of Sex Research,* 1979, *15,* 101–107.

Masters, W. H., and Johnson, V. E. *Human Sexual Response.* Boston: Little, Brown & Co., 1966.

———. *Human Sexual Inadequacy.* Boston: Little, Brown & Co., 1970.

———, and Kolodny, R. C. *Human Sexuality.* Boston: Little, Brown & Co., 1982.

Mendelson, J. H., and Mello, N. K. Plasma testosterone levels during chronic heroin use and protracted abstinence: a study of Hong Kong addicts. *Clinical Pharmacology and Therapeutics,* 1975, *17,* 529–533.

———, Mendelson, J. E., and Patch, V. D. Plasma testosterone levels in heroin addiction and during methadone maintenance. *Journal of Pharmacology and Experimental Therapeutics,* 1975, *192,* 211–217.

Miller, W. R. (ed.). *The Addictive Behaviors.* New York: Pergamon Press, 1980.

Mirin, S. M., Meyer, R. E., Mendelson, J. H., and Ellingboe, J. Opiate use and sexual function. *American Journal of Psychiatry,* 1980, *137,* 909–915.

Munjack, D. J., and Oziel, L. J. *Sexual Medicine and Counseling in Office Practice.* Boston: Little, Brown & Co., 1980.

Murphy, W. D., Coleman, E., Hoon, E., and Scott, C. Sexual dysfunction and treatment in alcoholic women. *Sexuality and Disability,* 1980, *3,* 240–255.

Perelman, M. A. Treatment of premature ejaculation. In S. Leiblum and L. Pervin (eds.), *Principles and Practice of Sex Therapy.* New York: The Guilford Press, 1980.

Rosenbaum, M. When drugs come into the picture, love flies out the windows: women addicts' love relationships. *The International Journal of the Addictions,* 1981, *16,* 1197–1206.

Rubin, H. B., and Henson, D. E. Effects of alcohol on male sexual responding. *Psychopharmacology,* 1976, *47,* 123–134.

Santen, R. J., Sofsky, J., Bilic, N., and Lippert, R. Mechanism of action of narcotics in the production of menstrual dysfunction in women. *Fertility and Sterility,* 1975, *26,* 538–548.

Smith, D. E. Amphetamine abuse and sexual dysfunctions: clinical and research considerations. In D. E. Smith, (ed.), *Amphetamine Use, Misuse and Abuse.* Cambridge, England: G. K. Hall, 1979.

Valimaki, M., and Ylikahri, R. Alcohol and sex hormones. *Scandinavian Journal of Clinical Laboratory Investigation,* 1981, *41,* 99–105.

Van Thiel, D. H., and Lester, R. The effect of chronic alcohol abuse on sexual function. *Clinics in Endocrinology and Metabolism,* 1979, *8,* 499–510.

Van Thiel, D. H., Sherins, R. J., and Lester, R. Mechanisms of hypogonadism in alcoholic liver disease (abstract). *Gastroenterology,* 1973, *65,* A50/574.

Wilson, G. T. Alcohol and human sexual behavior. *Behaviour Research and Therapy,* 1977, *15,* 239–252.

———, and Lawson, D. M. Effects of alcohol on sexual arousal in women. *Journal of Abnormal Psychology,* 1976, *85,* 489–497.

22

Women and Alcohol

SHEILA B. BLUME

WOMEN AND ALCOHOL have been associated in human tradition throughout history and in many parts of the world. Youcha (1978) tells us the 4,000-year-old Persian legend of the discovery of wine. A mythical Persian king, Jamshid, loved grapes and stored them in large vats in his cellar. When some of the vats collected a sour liquid at the bottom, he stored it in jars marked POISON, and saved this liquid for future use. According to the legend, a lady of his court, suffering from sick headaches, had decided to end her life. She came upon the jar marked POISON and drank some of the liquid. Instead of death she found joy and relief, and began to sneak into the storeroom to consume the magic liquid until the supply was exhausted. Perhaps she was the first alcoholic woman. The lady, who is nameless in the legend, then confessed to the king, who ordered that grapes be fermented and wine be made available to all.

Hathor, the ancient Egyptian goddess of wine, whose worship was associated with drunkenness, is associated with an early myth of destruction by flood (McKinlay, 1959a). The chief god, Re, had become angry and decided to punish humans for their wickedness. He sent Hathor to earth for this purpose and she became so carried away with killing that she waded in human blood. Fearing that all of mankind might be destroyed, Re magically turned the blood into red beer.

Hathor drank the beer, became drunk, and thus spared some of the people. Through the drunkenness of a woman, mankind was saved.

Western society has also linked women and alcohol, chiefly in a disapproving way. In the early days of ancient Rome, drinking of wine by women was an offense punishable by death. Cases are recorded in which women were starved or stoned to death for this crime (McKinlay, 1959b). Even more revealing of the Romans' attitude toward women's drinking was the fact that the law which prohibited alcohol use was linked to the prohibition against adultery by women. Thus the idea that drinking was associated with lascivious behavior in women was established early in Western tradition. In this vein, it is also interesting that the Old Testament links drunkenness with both family discord, in the case of Noah, and incest, in the story of Lot and his daughters. In Genesis 9:16–25 Noah lays a curse upon the one of his three sons, who looked upon Noah's naked body as he lay drunk in his tent. In Genesis 19:30–38 the two daughters of Lot purposely make him drunk with wine and commit incest so that they may carry on the family line, no other men being available. In both these cases, however, it is the male who becomes intoxicated. In the story of the birth of Samson (Judges 13:1–15), his mother is told by an angel that she will conceive and bear a son, and is counseled against drinking any wine or liquor.

In 1798 the philosopher Immanuel Kant wrote about women and alcohol (as reported by Jellinek, 1941, pp. 777–778). He compared women and Jews, two groups thought to have low alcoholism rates, stating that both avoid getting drunk because their community status rests upon the fact that others believe them pious and chaste. He wrote: "All separatists, that is, those who subject themselves not only to the general laws of the country but also to a special sectarian law, are exposed through their eccentricity and alleged chosenness to the attention and criticism of the community, and thus cannot relax in their self-control, for intoxication, which deprives one of . . . cautiousness, would be a scandal for them." A similar comparison has led to the belief that both Jewish and female alcoholics are "sicker" than non-Jewish alcoholic males, since they are more deviant from normal standards of behavior for their respective groups. This hypothesis has been questioned for both groups (Blume, Dropkin, and Sokolow, 1980; Blume, 1980). According to the same hypothesis, alcoholic women also are harder to treat and have poorer treatment outcomes.

The above mentioned illustrations show only a few of the many sources which have produced the intense social stigma attached to the alcoholic woman in contemporary American society. The woman who drinks to excess is triply stigmatized. First, she is included in society's negative attitude toward all alcoholics. Secondly, she is subject to a special disgust focused on the intoxicated woman.* Lastly, the idea that drunkenness and sexual promiscuity are linked add to the burden of disapproval. Is it surprising, then, that solitary drinking is a more common pattern in alcoholic women than in men, and that the female is often referred to as the "hidden alcoholic"?

The intense negative attitude of society in general influences not only the behavior of the alcoholic woman herself, her family, and her friends, but also unfortunately affects the attitudes and expectations of those in the helping professions: physicians, nurses, psychologists, social workers, clergymen, and counselors. Alcoholism often remains undetected in a woman, especially a respectable middle- or upper-class woman, in spite of considerable clinical evidence. Sensitivity, acceptance, and a high "index of suspicion" will uncover many cases in earlier and more treatable stages than are recognized today.

The woman suffering from alcoholism also shares with her nonalcoholic sisters a number of sociocultural influences which may be important factors in the development and treatment of her problem. For example, it is believed that low self-esteem is an important feature of all alcoholism, but particularly of female alcoholism (Beckman, 1978a). How a woman feels about herself will depend on many genetic, familial, developmental, and psychological factors, but the views of woman's appropriate social role held by the individual's culture and subculture will interact with these personal factors in the development of a sense of identity and self-esteem.

An important component of identity for both sexes is occupation. It is this basic fact of American culture which is largely responsible for the outstanding success of employee alcoholism programs. Thus the lesser value assigned to tasks normally identified as "women's work," and the lower salaries earned by women, are important considerations in their self-esteem. Housekeeping and childcare are assigned little or no economic value when performed as part of a marriage ("Does your wife work?" "No, she's a housewife"), and command very low wages when performed as regular employment. Women are often paid less than men for the same jobs. Most married women in the workforce carry the major responsibility for the family cleaning, shopping, cooking, laundry, and childcare in addition to their outside employment (Schultz, 1980; Shainess, 1980). Thus many women in American society are undervalued, underpaid, and overstressed. Both as a factor in her illness and in her recovery, the importance of occupation should be explored individually with every alcoholic woman. Vocational rehabilitation, more adequate childcare, and changes in family

* To illustrate: consider the expression "drunk as a lord," a common, amused, and approving description of intoxication. Now try "drunk as a lady"!

attitudes and behavior will be critical in many cases. The highest rates of both problem drinking and heavier drinking are found among women who are both married and employed (Johnson et al., 1978).

Because responsibility for the care of children is part of the female role in American society, and because alcoholic women are frequently separated or divorced, the female alcoholic entering treatment is far more often the head of a single-parent family than is the alcoholic male. Provision for adequate childcare will often be necessary before effective treatment can begin.

Women alcoholics (Forrest, 1983a) are often married to men who suffer from the same illness. A woman who marries a heavy drinker will usually be expected by family and friends to be a "good influence" on him. If she cannot arrest the progression of his drinking problem, she will often consider herself a failure and may hide the family's problem out of shame. Because of her emotional distress and heavy exposure to alcohol, she is also at risk for developing alcohol dependence. A woman who is already alcohol-dependent will often marry a man with a similar drinking pattern, especially as a second partner. An excellent discussion of the marriages of alcoholic women may be found in Corrigan's study of women in treatment (Corrigan, 1980).

Another important aspect of female identity is that a woman is often defined through her relationship to others. She is somebody's daughter, somebody's wife, or somebody's mother—sometimes even somebody's ex-wife or widow. Helping the alcoholic woman confront her feelings about herself as an independent individual is an important part of rehabilitation.

Other aspects of female identity are also important in alcoholism, particularly those related to sexuality. The physiological aspects of alcohol's effects on women have received little research attention, in spite of (or perhaps because of) the societal stereotypes mentioned earlier. Although much time and effort have been devoted to studying the influence of alcohol on male sex hormones and performance, one pair of researchers remarked: "Most experts comment on human sexual behavior and alcohol as though only males drink and have sexual interests" (Carpenter and Armenti, 1972). The repeated observation by clinicians that alcoholic women in treatment have a high incidence of obstetric and gynecological problems would suggest this as an important area for future study (Beckman, 1975; Gomberg, 1979).

Finally, a woman's sense of identity and self-esteem will be greatly influenced by the socioeconomic and cultural subgroup to which she belongs. Economic dependence will often keep a woman in a destructive marriage from which she would otherwise seek a divorce. Minority-group membership will influence social status and self-esteem in a variety of ways. Sensitivity to such factors is most important in attracting women to treatment and in designing effective treatment plans. Constructive use of the extended family network becomes possible in certain subcultures, if education about alcoholism and the disease concept are provided to all members of the group. Treatment by female therapists or in all-female groups may be more acceptable in subcultures in which men and women do not ordinarily communicate about personal problems.

What Do We Know About Women Who Drink?

Most of the early research which established our basic knowledge about the physiology and pharmacology of ethyl alcohol in the human being was performed on male subjects. It was always assumed that these findings could safely be extrapolated to the female of the species. Only recently has it been discovered that when normal men and women are given equivalent single doses of alcohol (in grams of alcohol per kilogram of body weight) under standard conditions, women will reach peak blood alcohol levels that are both higher and far more variable than those of men, and these levels will show some correlation with the menstrual cycle (B. M. Jones and M. K. Jones, 1976). Exogenous female hormones such as those taken for birth control or postmenopausal replacement tend to slow the rate of fall of the blood alcohol level. These factors make the average daily quantity of alcohol consumed an even less reliable indication of the presence of alcoholism in the female than it is in the male. Relatively little is known about these differences, and further research into the effects of alcohol on female physiology is very much needed.

The discovery that alcohol can act as a teratogen in both humans and animals has greatly stimulated research interest in alcohol and pregnancy, and both public and professional interest in identifying female problem drinkers of childbearing age. The fetal alcohol syndrome (FAS) consists of a combination of birth defects including both prenatal and postnatal growth retardation, small head circumference, mild to moderate mental retardation, small eyes (often with strabismus and/or ptosis), hypoplasia of the maxilla, a long upper lip with a flattened philtrum and thinned vermillion, and a small upturned nose. In addition, there may be skeletal, joint, genital, renal, skin, and cardiac defects (Clarren and Smith, 1978; Streissguth et al., 1980). Although the full fetal alcohol syndrome has been seen to date only in women who were very heavy drinkers during pregnancy, safe levels of alcohol intake both in terms of timing during pregnancy and pattern of drinking are as yet unknown. There is evidence, however, that interruption of excessive drinking during pregnancy leads to a lower incidence of birth defects (Rossett et al., 1978). FAS is now considered the third most common cause of mental retardation due to birth defects in the United States (after Down's syndrome and spina bifida). Of these, only FAS is entirely preventable.

In addition to the full fetal alcohol syndrome, researchers have identified a wide range of alcohol-related birth defects in both human and animal studies. Average daily quantities as low as two drinks per day have been shown to be associated with statistically significant differences in birth weight and neonatal behavior in humans, although the significance of these differences for later life is not yet clear (Streissguth et al., 1980). For this reason many agencies concerned with public health recommend that women abstain from all alcoholic beverages immediately before and throughout both pregnancy and lactation, just as the angel recommended to Samson's mother (Blume, 1981). There is evidence that some normal women experience a spontaneous decrease in alcohol use during pregnancy, probably due to hormonal changes (Little, Schultz, and Mandell, 1976).

Just as there are great differences in male and female psychology, probably determined in part by physiology and even more strongly by differential socialization, there are also differences between men and women in cognitive, emotional, and behavioral effects resulting from acute and chronic alcohol use. Wilsnack (1976, 1973) found that women who drank became more feminine in outlook as measured on the thematic apperception test (TAT). This contrasted with the male, who tended to become more power-oriented. Based on this finding as well as other evidence, a theory of sex-role conflict to explain alcoholism in women was developed. The theory postulates that the alcoholic woman has a strongly feminine identity at the conscious level (as noted, for example, on the M–F scale of the Minnesota Multiphasic Personality Inventory) but a masculine identification at an unconscious level. Alcohol, by enhancing feelings of femininity, relieves this conflict, thus increasing the risk for alcohol dependency. Beckman (1978b) recently reviewed this theory and presented her findings on a series of 120 alcoholic women, matched with two control groups: nonalcoholic women in treatment for emotional problems, and nonalcoholic "normals." She found the predicted pattern in one-quarter of the alcoholic women, a higher percentage than in the controls. When sex-role conflict was defined to include both conscious femininity and unconscious masculinity, and also the reverse, there was no significant difference between the incidence of sex-role conflict in the alcoholic women and the normal controls. Sixty-six percent of the alcoholic women, 72 percent of the treatment controls, and 71 percent of the normal controls scored feminine on both conscious and unconscious measures. Those alcoholic women who manifested sex-role conflict differed from the remainder of alcoholic women in showing lower self-esteem and a higher incidence of having had an absent parent during childhood. Beckman also assessed "androgyny" (flexible utilization of traits considered stereotypically "masculine" and "feminine" by one's culture), and found the alcoholic women significantly less androgynous than the normal controls but not different in this measurement from the women in treatment.

Longitudinal studies of groups of women studied at first during their teens and then later as adults have offered suggestive evidence that girls who have general feelings of low self-esteem may be predisposed to problem drinking in adulthood (M. C. Jones, 1971). This predisposition was different from that found in a comparable group of boys (M. C. Jones, 1968). In a 28-year follow-up of a study of drinking among American college students, Fillmore, Bacon, and Hyman (1979) found that factors predictive of problem drinking in later life differed considerably between males and females. Analysis of the data made it necessary to construct different definitions of "alcohol involvement" at the college level and of "problem drinking" at follow-up for males and females. The best predictor of later problems for college women was a high score on the "feeling adjustment" scale, composed of such items as drinking to relieve shyness, drinking to get high, drinking to be cheerful, and drinking to get along better on dates. Among men, those with "incipient problems" in college were most likely to show up in the problem-drinker group at follow-up. In addition, both men and women with overt alcohol problems in college were more likely to be problem drinkers later in life when compared with abstainers or non–problem drinkers.

Reference has already been made to the effect of sociocultural factors on women's drinking. Periodic studies of drinking by adolescents have shown a gradual change in the drinking patterns displayed by young girls (Wechsler, 1980; Forrest, 1983b). Wechsler (1976) has studied this change and refers to sex differences in adolescent alcohol and drug use as "a disappearing phenomenon." Nevertheless, according to the 1981 National Institute of Alcoholism and Alcohol Abuse (NIAAA) report, *Alcohol and Health,* adolescent girls are still less likely to be heavy drinkers and to have alcohol-related problems when compared with boys of the same age.

What Do We Know About the Alcoholic Woman?

Wide variations in the use of the term "alcoholism" have led to a preference for the term "alcohol dependence syndrome" by both the World Health Association (*International Classification of Diseases,*

1979) and the American Psychiatric Association (*DSM* III, 1980). The definition of this term includes both physical and psychological dependence, interference with the individual's ability to function, and pathological drinking patterns. It is roughly equivalent to Jellinek's (1960) "gamma" and "delta" alcoholism, and to the disease described by the National Council on Alcoholism Criteria (1972). These diagnostic criteria apply to men and women alike. However, there are differences in family and personal history, as well as symptoms and subtypes of alcoholism, between men and women which are of considerable importance in identifying and treating the women suffering from this illness.

In taking a drinking history, additional questions specifically appropriate for a woman include: Do you ever carry an alcoholic beverage in your purse? Does your drinking vary with your menstrual cycle? Has your drinking had any effect on regularity or quantity of your menstrual periods? How has your drinking changed during pregnancies? What effect do you feel your drinking has had on your children? How would you feel if one of your children were drinking the way you are drinking now? Has there been physical violence in your home? Alcoholic women are often the target of spouse abuse. They may also be responsible for child abuse or neglect in respect to their own children. In addition to these specific questions for women, the so-called "CAGE" questions developed by Ewing (1981) are particularly useful in identifying alcoholism in both sexes. The four questions are as follows:

1. Have you felt the need to *C*ut down your drinking?
2. Have you ever felt *A*nnoyed by criticism of your drinking?
3. Have you had *G*uilt feelings about drinking?
4. Do you ever take a morning *E*ye-opener? [Note the mnemonic "C–A–G–E."]

The most useful clinical categorization of alcoholism into subtypes (Schuckit and Morrissey, 1976) is the distinction between primary alcoholism (which develops in a person who has no preexisting diagnosable emotional disorder) and secondary alcoholism (which develops in a person with a preexisting diagnosable emotional disorder, or in a person who develops such a disorder during a prolonged period of abstinence). When categorized in this way, most alcoholic patients appearing for treatment are of the primary type (Forrest, 1984). Among men the most common secondary alcoholism is that associated with sociopathy. In women the most common type is so-called "affective alcoholism," usually associated with unipolar depression. This latter pattern may be seen in one-fifth to one-quarter of a typical female treatment population. Diagnosis must be based on a careful life history, since the presence of depressive symptoms at the time of treatment will not differentiate between primary and affective alcoholism. Once a woman is diagnosed as a secondary alcoholic suffering from affective alcoholism, an appropriate long-term treatment plan would include, in addition to full-scale treatment for her alcoholism, continuing long-term therapeutic contact during sobriety, with attention to possible recurrence of depression. Early treatment of such recurrence can help the patient maintain her sobriety and well-being.

Clinical characteristics of alcoholic women differ in some respects from the characteristics of their male counterparts. Alcoholic women drink less, on the average, than alcoholic men. In one large-scale study, for example, non–problem drinking women averaged 0.44 ounces of absolute alcohol daily compared to the male average of 0.91. Women accepted for treatment in the NIAAA-sponsored alcoholism programs surveyed in the report averaged 4.5 ounces of absolute alcohol per day compared to the male average of 8.2 ounces (Armor, Polich, and Stambul, 1978). As the alcoholic woman ages, her tolerance falls and she will drink even less than before, while still experiencing adverse health and social consequences from her drinking.

Women start drinking and begin their pattern of alcohol abuse at later ages but appear for treatment at about the same age as male alcoholics. This points to a more rapid development, or "telescoping," of the course of the illness in women (Corrigan, 1980). They are also more likely to relate their alcoholic drinking pattern to a stressful life event such as divorce or illness in the family. Such a report should not be looked upon as a rationalization, but rather as an indication of the psychological underpinnings of the patient's alcohol dependence and an important clue for the direction to be taken in psychotherapy.

There is a high incidence of both alcoholism and depression in the family histories of alcoholic women (Lawson, Ellis, and Rivers, 1984). Female alcoholics also report a history of suicide attempts and of depression more often than males. As indicated earlier, all alcoholic women should be evaluated carefully for possible subtyping as "affective alcoholics." Alcoholic women are more likely to be motivated into treatment by problems related to health and family, whereas the male alcoholic most often complains of problems on the job or with the law. Women are seldom identified through drinking driver rehabilitation programs or special programs for public inebriates, probationers, or parolees (Blume, 1980b). A number of studies have shown that women are more likely to enter treatment with a history of using and abusing non-narcotic drugs along with alcohol. These drugs, particularly the minor tranquilizers, sedatives, and amphetamines, are usually prescribed by physicians (Lyons et al., 1979). Female alcoholics are also more likely to report psychiatric symptoms such as anxiety and depression, and have lower self-esteem than comparable groups of alcoholic men (Beckman, 1978a).

Many of the other characteristics of alcoholism are similar in men and women. For example, recent evidence demonstrates a similar pattern of impaired perceptual and cognitive functioning in males and females suffering from alcoholism (Fabian, Parsons, and Selberstein, 1981).

An excellent analysis of the histories, symptoms, course of illness, and outcome of 150 women treated for alcoholism was performed by Eileen M. Corrigan (1980). Among her very interesting findings were the following: not all alcoholic women consume "heavy" quantities of alcohol. Although 83 percent of the women usually drank five or more drinks at a time, 17 percent drank less than five drinks at a time in the preiod before treatment. The average age of onset of drinking problems was thirty-three years, and treatment began in the women's late thirties. There was thus a relatively short interval between recognition of drinking problems and the attempt to get help. Most of the alcoholic women drank alone, and this tendency was correlated with higher socioeconomic status. As many as 42 percent of Corrigan's group took tranquilizers and 24 percent took sleeping pills while drinking. This tendency was more pronounced in younger women and those who drank the most, and was not correlated with socioeconomic group. Sixty-one percent of the study group had one or more relatives with a drinking problem, including the approximately two-fifths of the group who had an alcoholic parent. Twenty-seven percent of the group had attempted suicide and the number reporting psychiatric symptoms was high. Automobile accidents, falls, burns, and other injuries were also common. When treatment was successful these symptoms tended to disappear.

Studies of the outcome of treatment for alcoholic women compared to men have produced mixed results. The data seem to indicate that, on the whole, comparable groups of male and female alcoholics do equally well in treatment (Blume, 1980a). In the study by Corrigan quoted above, a one-year follow-up was completed for 116 women of the study group. Of these, 41 percent had been abstinent throughout the entire period and an additional 12 percent had taken only an occasional drink. Seventy-one percent of the women had been abstinent in the month prior to follow-up, and for more than half of this group the period of abstinence was at least six months. Among those women who continued to drink at rates higher than the "rare-occasion" rate, there was a nonsignificant increase in the amount consumed. Socioeconomic status correlated with outcome.

What Can We Do to Help Women Who Drink?

Helpful intervention should not be reserved for women already in trouble with their drinking. A great deal can be done to prevent the emergence of alcohol problems in dealing with young people and with women of any age undergoing stressful situations. As the long-term follow-up of the college drinking study showed, young women who used alcohol to feel better about themselves and to improve their behavior on dates were the ones most prone to later problems. A combination of educating youth to the dangers of psychological dependence on alcohol, and helping them find other answers to their very real personal problems, will prevent alcohol dependence. Fetal alcohol syndrome and alcohol-related birth defects may be prevented by public education concerning the effects of alcohol on the fetus. Women who are normal drinkers should be counseled to give up drinking for the duration of the pregnancy and lactation. It should be made clear, however, that having an occasional drink, consumed along with food, either during the pregnancy or taken before pregnancy was recognized, will not harm the fetus. The harm done seems to be directly proportional to the quantity consumed, and there is clear evidence that heavy drinkers who are able to stop drinking during pregnancy greatly increase their chance of producing a normal infant. For women who are problem drinkers, the wish to give birth to a normal child is an excellent motivation for entrance into treatment.

Appropriate treatment for the alcoholic woman will depend, as for men, on the stage of the illness, the patient's physical condition, associated or preexisting emotional illness, and the types of social, economic, and family support available (Blume, 1983).

During the period of detoxification, either in an inpatient setting or on an outpatient basis, special attention must be given to the female alcoholic in obtaining a clear and accurate history of psychotropic drug use. Since women are more likely to be users and abusers of minor tranquilizers, sedatives, and stimulants, prolonged and/or unusual detoxification symptoms may be noted. Symptoms of benzodiazepine withdrawal are likely to begin between two and ten days after the abrupt discontinuation of alcohol and drug use. The symptoms include grand mal seizures, insomnia, tremor, anorexia, disorientation, and hallucinations (Benzer and Cushman, 1980). Substance abuse should always be considered in the differential diagnosis of delayed convulsions during alcohol withdrawal along with head trauma and other causes of seizures.

During the rehabilitation phase, education on alcoholism for the patient and family are important for both sexes. In dealing with women, however, stress on the effects of alcohol on the fetus and the need for evaluation of the patient's children should be stressed. The dangers of secondary psychotropic drug abuse as a special risk for alcoholic women should also be included. Another effort made early in treatment is connecting the alcoholic patient and his or her family with the appropriate self-help groups. In the case of the alcoholic woman being referred to A.A., a female sponsor should be sought. There are all-female A.A. groups in some areas, and afternoon groups with associated babysitting for mothers of young children. An all-female self-help group, Women for Sobriety (Kirkpatrick, 1978), is also available in many areas of the United States. Such groups help the alcoholic woman identify with other women who have overcome their illness, instilling hope and allaying guilt and shame. This is particularly important in view of the social stigma discussed earlier in this chapter.

Psychotherapy during this initial treatment period may be performed individually or in groups. Mixed-sex groups, all-female groups, family groups, and couples' groups may all be used to good effect in treating the alcoholic woman. The treatment goals during this early phase include the establishment of abstinence (Forrest, 1984) and a beginning exploration of the previous role of alcohol in the life of the patient. With the relief of initial anxiety and depression, a great deal of buried anger may surface. This anger must be evaluated in terms of the patient's own psychological, interpersonal, and social reality, bearing in mind the societal roles assigned to women and the special problems in self-esteem and identity discussed earlier in the chapter. As treatment continues, a reevaluation of the patient's feelings about herself, her role, and the role of alcohol in her life becomes the major focus of treatment. Additional help may be needed through vocational rehabilitation, spiritual counseling, assertiveness training, or a wide variety of other services, depending on the needs of the individual. It is believed that alcohol problems are frequent among lesbian women and that special attention must be paid to the therapeutic needs of this group, but research in this area has been scarce (Blume, 1980b). Increased staff sensitivity, the implementation of specialized groups (all-lesbian if possible; if not, all-female; or gay groups of both women and men), and role modeling by recovering lesbian alcoholic women are helpful (Weathers, 1980).

In individual psychotherapy, special problems may arise when the female alcoholic is treated by a therapist accustomed to treating males. If the therapist measures success only in terms of adjustment to the societal stereotype of the female role, he may avoid helping the patient to confront her feelings about individuality and independence, and thereby miss the best possible opportunity to enlarge her range of conscious choices about her life. This narrow "adjustment" goal may also fail to raise self-esteem and may reinforce dependent, childlike, or seductive behavior toward the therapist, rather than encouraging straightforward, aboveboard communication. Since the responsibility for her sobriety must continue to rest squarely on the shoulders of the alcoholic woman in treatment, dependence in the therapeutic interaction becomes a threat to that sobriety. Should the patient return to drinking during therapy, care must be taken not to reinforce this behavior by oversolicitousness or a level of interest not accorded her in the sober state. The therapist should always make sure that, while not rejecting the patient who relapses, he makes clear the expectation that she will return to the sober state and helps her make realistic plans to do so. (Forrest, 1984).

The use of psychoactive drugs should be kept to a minimum because of the dangers of drug dependence. Most women recover from the depressive symptoms present during and immediately after detoxification without antidepressant drugs, in response to psychotherapy and group support, as their sobriety becomes established. In cases in which depression is unusually severe or in which suicidal thoughts are prominant, antidepressants and hospitalization are necessary. In dealing with the affective alcoholic woman discussed above, antidepressants may play an important role in the treatment of recurrent depression at later stages of treatment.

Disulfiram (Antabuse) may be of considerable value as an adjunct to therapy for the first year or two in the nonpregnant alcoholic woman. It should never be used as a treatment in and of itself, nor should test doses of alcohol be given in order to demonstrate the alcohol Antabuse reaction. Disulfiram selectively interferes with the conversion of acetaldehyde, the first breakdown product of ethyl alcohol, to acetate. Acetaldehyde builds up in the blood and body fluids, causing intense dysphoria in the patient. A regular daily dose of disulfiram allows the patient to make his or her decision to remain abstinent once a day, avoiding a minute-by-minute struggle during a temporary period of frustration, depression, or anxiety. A full explanation of the dangers of disulfiram is essential, and the use of a written agreement is most desirable. In addition to information about the drug, such a statement should specify that the patient agrees she will *not* increase her disulfiram dose for "extra protection" during times of stress, and will not discontinue the drug "because I don't need it any more" without prior discussion. Since the effectiveness of the drug depends largely on the patient's motivation, small doses (for example, 125 mgs. per day), are sufficient and should decrease the likelihood of adverse side-effects. If a patient refuses disulfiram initially, it should be held in reserve. In case of a relapse, the physician and patient will reevaluate the treatment and will often choose to add the drug at that time.

A number of special treatment methods have been developed for the alcoholic woman, but none has yet undergone statistical evaluation. Common themes in these methods are special sensitivity to the needs of women, provision for appropriate childcare, assertiveness training and preparation for more straightforward communication, and the provision of appropriate female role models.

In addition to prevention, treatment, and rehabilitation measures aimed at the individual who drinks, the interested professional has an ongoing responsibility to influence social change. This may be done, first of all, by example, in one's own attitudes and behaviors. It also involves education of the public to dispel misconceptions about alcoholism and remove stigma, particularly that applied to alcoholic women. Finally, those societal changes which lead to true equality between the sexes will be of ultimate benefit in both the prevention of alcoholism and the treatment of the alcoholic woman.

References

Armor, D. J., Polich, J. M., and Stambul, H. B. *Alcoholism and Treatment.* New York: John Wiley & Sons, 1978.

Beckman, L. Self-esteem of women alcoholics. *Journal of Studies on Alcohol,* 1978(a), *39,* 491–498.

———. Sex-role conflict in alcoholic women: myth or reality? *Journal of Abnormal Psychology,* 1978(b), *84,* 408–417.

———. Women alcoholics: a review of social and psychological studies. *Journal of Studies on Alcohol,* 1975, *36* (7), 797–824.

Benzer, D., and Cushman, P. Alcohol and benzodiazepines: withdrawal syndromes. *Alcoholism: Clinical and Experimental Research,* 1980, *4,* 243–247.

Blume, S. Alcoholism. In H. Conn (ed.), *Current Therapies.* Philadelphia. W. B. Saunders, 1983.

———. Drinking and pregnancy: preventing fetal alcohol syndrome. *New York State Journal of Medicine,* 1981, *81,* 95–98.

———. Women with alcoholism: the impact of treatment. *Journal of Psychiatric Treatment and Evaluation,* 1980(a), *2,* 225–229.

———. Researches on women and alcohol. In NIAAA Research Monograph 1, *Alcohol and Women,* U. S. Department of Health, Education, and Welfare publication no (ADM) 80–835, pp. 121–151, 1980(b).

———, Dropkin, D., and Sokolow, L. The Jewish alcoholic: a descriptive study. Alcohol, Health and Research World, NIAAA, 1980, *4* (*4*), 601–617.

Carpenter, J. A., and Armenti, N. P. Some effects of ethanol on human sexual and aggressive behavior. In B. Kissin and H. Begleiter (eds.), *The Biology of Alcoholism,* vol. 2. New York: Plenum Press, 1972.

Clarren, S., and Smith, D. The fetal alcohol syndrome. *New England Journal of Medicine,* 1978, *298* (*19*), 1063–1067.

Corrigan, E. M. *Alcoholic Women in Treatment.* New York: Oxford University Press, 1980.

Diagnostic and Statistical Manual of Mental Disorders (*DSM* III). Washington, D.C.: American Psychiatric Association, 1980.

Ewing, J. *Drinking to Your Health.* Reston, Va.: Reston Publishing Co., 1981.

Fabian, M. S., Parsons, O. A., and Selberstein, J. A. Impaired perceptual-cognitive functioning in women alcoholics. *Journal of Studies on Alcohol,* 1981, *42,* 217–229.

Fillmore, K. M., Bacon, S. D., and Hyman, M. Final Report, 1979, to NIAAA contract (ADM) 281–76–0015. *The 27-Year Longitudinal Panel Study of Drinking by Students in College.* National Institute of Alcoholism and Alcohol Abuse, 1979.

Forrest, G. G. *Alcoholism, Narcissism and Psychopathology.* Springfield, Ill.: Charles C Thomas, 1983(a).

Forrest, G. G. *How to Cope with a Teenage Drinker: New Alternatives and Hope for Parents and Families.* New York: Atheneum, 1983(b).

Forrest, G. G. *Intensive Psychotherapy of Alcoholism.* Springfield, Ill.: Charles C Thomas, 1984.

Gomberg, E. S. Problems with alcohol and other drugs. In E. S. Gomberg and V. Franks (eds.), *Gender and Disordered Behavior: Sex Differences in Psychopathology.* New York: Brunner/Mazel, 1979.

International Classification of Diseases, 9 (ICD–9). Ann Arbor, Mich.: Commission on Professional and Hospital Activities, 1979.

Jellinek, E. M. *The Disease Concept of Alcoholism.* New Haven: College and University Press, 1960.

———. Immanuel Kant on drinking. *Quarterly Journal of Studies on Alcohol,* 1941, *1,* 777–778.

Johnson, P., Armor, D. J., Polich, S., and Stambul, H. *U.S. Adult Drinking Practices: Social Correlates and Sex Roles.* Santa Monica, Calif.: Rand Corporation, 1978.

Jones, B. M., and Jones, M. K. Women and alcohol: intoxication, metabolism, and the menstrual cycle. In M. Greenblatt and M. A. Schuckit (eds.), *Alcoholism Problems in Women and Children.* New York: Grune and Stratton, 1976.

Jones, M. C. Personality antecedents and correlates of drinking patterns in women. *Journal of Consulting and Clinical Psychology,* 1971, *36,* 61–69.

———. Personality correlates and antecedents of drinking patterns in adult males. *Journal of Consulting and Clinical Psychology,* 1968, *32,* 2–12.

Kirkpatrick, J. *Turnabout: Help for a New Life.* Garden City, N. Y.: Doubleday & Co., 1978.

Lawson, G. W., Ellis, P. C., and Rivers, P. C. *Essentials of Chemical Dependency Counseling.* Rockville, Md.: Aspen, 1984.

Little, R. E., Schultz, F. A., and Mandell, W. Drinking during pregnancy. *Journal of Studies on Alcohol,* 1976, *37,* 375–379.

Lyons, J., Welte, J., Hines, G., et al. *Outcome Study of Alcoholism Rehabilitation Units.* New York State Division of Alcoholism and Alcohol Abuse, Nov. 1979.

McKinlay, Arthur P. Non-classical peoples. In R. G. McCarthy (ed), *Drinking and Intoxication.* New Haven: College and University Press, 1959(a).

———. The Roman attitude toward women's drinking. In R. G. McCarthy (ed.), *Drinking and Intoxication.* Glencoe, Ill.: Free Press, 1959(b).

National Council on Alcoholism Criteria Committee. Criteria for the diagnosis of alcoholism. *Annals of Internal Medicine,* 1972, *77,* 127–135.

NIAAA. *Alcohol and Health,* 4th Special Report to the U. S. Congress, 1981.

Rossett, H. L., Ouellette, E. M., Werner, L., et al. Therapy of heavy drinking during pregnancy. *Obstetrics and Gynecology,* 1978, *51,* 41–46.

Schuckit, M., and Morrissey, E. R. Alcoholism in women: some clinical and social perspectives with an emphasis on possible subtypes. In M. Greenblatt and M. A. Schuckit (eds.), *Alcoholism Problems in Women and Children.* New York: Grune & Stratton, 1976.

Schultz, T. Does marriage give today's women what they really want? 30,000 *Journal* readers share their intimate lives. *Ladies Home Journal,* June 1980, pp. 89–155.

Shainess, N. The working wife and mother—a "new" woman? *American Journal of Psychotherapy,* 1980, *34,* 374–386.

Streissguth, A. P., Landesman-Dwyer, S., Martin, J. C., et al. Teratogenic effects of alcohol in humans and laboratory animals. *Science,* 1980, *209,* 353.

Weathers, B. Alcoholism and the lesbian community. In C. C. Eddy and J. L., Ford, *Alcoholism in Women.* Dubuque, Iowa: Kendall/Hunt, 1980.

Wechsler, H. Epidemiology of male/female drinking over the last half century. In NIAAA Research Monograph 1, *Alcohol and Women.* U. S. Department of Health, Education and Welfare publication no. (ADM) 80–835, pp. 3–31, 1980.

———, and McFadden M. Sex differences in adolescent alcohol and drug use: a disappearing phenomenon. *Journal of Studies on Alcohol,* 1976, *37,* 1291–1301.

Wilsnack, S. C. The impact of sex roles on women's alcohol use and abuse. In M. Greenblatt and M. A. Schuckit (eds.), *Alcoholism Problems in Women and Children.* New York: Grune and Stratton, 1976.

———. Sex role identity in female alcoholism. *Journal of Abnormal Psychology,* 1973, *82* (2), 652–664.

Youcha, G. *A Dangerous Pleasure.* New York: Hawthorn Books, 1978.

INDEX

Index